THE SECOND SKIN

AN INTERDISCIPLINARY STUDY OF CLOTHING

THIRD EDITION

Marilyn J. Horn
University of Nevada

Lois M. Gurel
Virginia Polytechnic Institute
and State University

HOUGHTON MIFFLIN COMPANY   Boston
Dallas   Geneva, Ill.   Hopewell, N.J.
Palo Alto   London

Cover photograph by
Ann McQueen

Printed in the U.S.A.
Library of Congress Catalog Card Number: 80-81918
ISBN: 0-395-28974-2

CONTENTS

PREFACE

Audience for this Book

This book was written for the person who is approaching an interdisciplinary study of clothing for the first time. This beginner may be at any academic level, from undergraduate to graduate, may be from any curriculum, may have had no exposure to clothing as an applied discipline, or may have had several unrelated clothing and textile courses at the college level—perhaps construction, textile science, and fashion merchandising. In most textile and clothing programs, a student would normally encounter the book early in the freshman or sophomore years. However, the graduate student from another discipline, or an undergraduate in a textiles and clothing program in which isolated courses are taken first and integration comes only after several years of prerequisite study, might first encounter the book at the upper-division undergraduate or even beginning graduate level. Primary use for the book is in the course concerned with the socio-psychological aspects of clothing, at whatever academic level it falls.

One book cannot serve all needs and be directed to all levels of scholarly achievement. Some teachers would like to see more of a research orientation in Part Two. I remind them that this book is designed to serve the needs of beginners to whom the word *research* is at best unknown and at worst a turn-off. Most current research in areas related to the social and psychological aspects of clothing is being done at colleges and universities that have graduate degree programs. Current research information from these institutions is not widely disseminated, but, with perseverance, the advanced student can track it down. The *American Home Economics Research Abstracts* and the Association of College Professors of Textiles and Clothing *Newsletter* are readily available sources. Directions on how to obtain these publications are included in the Instructor's Manual, with references to other sources of information.

Prior knowledge of sociology, psychology, economics, history, and art will make material in this book easier to comprehend and therefore more meaningful to the individual. However, the book was devised specifically to eliminate those subjects as prerequisites. I have used this book for many years in an introductory freshman core course required for all home economics majors. In a few places, supplementary materials are helpful for some additional information and explanation. Many students who reread the book in later years have commented on subtleties missed the first time. I have also assigned sections of the book to graduate students and found that even at this level, the book provides a particularly good refresher for these older students, since it does not talk down to the reader.

Purpose

The purpose of this book, as was so well stated by its original author, is to blend many aspects of clothing, often studied from different books and in different courses, into one homogeneous but multifaceted whole. Individuals do not live in isolation but in societal groups. The moral and ethical values of these groups, their norms and expectations, levels of technological development, aesthetic tastes and judgments, and economic systems blend into a composite that overtly, subtly, or invisibly directs a set of standards governing dress. Only by studying these group influences can clothing satisfy the many wants, needs, and desires people seek to gain from it.

A textbook author is forced to write about the present, hedging all bets against what is likely to be, not just when the book is first released but for the several years in which it will be used. This fact is particularly significant for subject matter that deals with such ever-changing components as fashion, clothing, and textile technology. To complicate the situation, this book was revised at the time of a census. Therefore, much of the demographic material, particularly in Part Five, is based on past figures or is projected for the future. Percentages, CPIs, and GNPs recede into the past just as quickly as clothing does.

A textbook can provide factual information and a great deal of material for thinking, but it cannot take the place of an awareness of current happenings. The teacher is responsible for directing students to other sources of information, such as the fashion press, style sections in large Sunday newspapers, and the latest professional journals. Students should be encouraged to use their eyes and ears. All this supplementary material should be incorporated into an interdisciplinary approach to the study of clothing.

The Instructor's Manual will help in some cases by providing more current numerical data, but more importantly by helping the users of this book find materials themselves. The wealth of material provided by the federal government from Washington-based agencies should be used to supplement the information in Part Five.

Changes in the New Edition

Material on the origins and original functions of clothing is included in a new Chapter One. The reader can begin with theoretical answers to the questions, When did people first wear clothes? and Why did they first wear them? The rationale for this addition stems from my belief that it is easier and more logical to begin at the beginning. And, since much of this information is indeed theoretical, it is often controversial and thought provoking. I have found it an effective way to gain student interest.

Another major change was to move Chapter 5 in the second edition from Part One to Part Two. Although values and beliefs are culturally induced they are behaviorally manifested. Clothing attitudes, values, beliefs, and interests are part of human behavior and are placed after chapters dealing with other social and psychological aspects of dress. Chapter 21 and the appendixes of the earlier editions have been omitted. Some parts of the chapter were redundant and others were placed elsewhere in the book. Inclusion of the appendixes seemed to be an unnecessary use of space. This material is incorporated into the more flexible format of the Instructor's Manual.

Minor changes, primarily additions, were made in several chapters in Part Two. Social science theories explaining clothing behavior are discussed and research pertinent to the theory included. I believe that students at this level can be introduced to the use of a theoretical framework for analyzing clothing behavior. It will help them relate clothing to their studies in the root disciplines of sociology and psychology.

One further addition of importance is the inclusion of the Prang color system in Chapter 12. Most students are already acquainted with this system of color notation, even if not by name, from their elementary and secondary school experiences. Starting with the Prang system will make it easier for them to understand the more complex system of notation used by Munsell.

Special Features

As in the earlier editions, the in-text summaries at the ends of the main chapter sections are included to help the student grasp the import of chapter contents. Boldface type is used for significant terms or phrases, and the Glossary at the end of the book includes almost all such entries. "For Further Reading" lists at the ends of the chapters provide additional source and reading material for student use.

Accompanying Instructor's Manual

This manual has been greatly revised and expanded. In addition to the objectives, lists of key terms, and suggested approaches given in the earlier edition, each manual chapter is followed by a list of references and audio-visual materials that may be used to clarify or expand text chapter content. A number of "Complete Assignments" also are provided in the manual, for use as presented or for alteration to suit particular class need.

Acknowledgments

An undertaking like the revision of this book obviously depends on the assistance, understanding, and encouragement of many people. By far the most important contributor and guide in this revision has been the unseen but always present Marilyn Horn. I would never have been able to complete the revision had it not been for the original material I had to work with. Further, I probably would not have undertaken the work in the first place. I have used Dr. Horn's book continuously since the first edition came out in 1968. I have based a good part of my teaching on the two editions. The more intimately I worked with the second edition, the more impressed I became with her thoroughness, scholarship, and breadth of vision. Many parts of the book, written over a decade ago, are as current as if written yesterday. The book is what it is because of Marilyn Horn. My changes have been made only to update and broaden material of extremely high quality.

The revisor and the publisher are grateful for the assistance of those who made professional reviews of the manuscript. These reviewers were Nancy Ann Rudd, The Ohio State University, and Grovalynn Sisler, Oklahoma State University.

I would like to acknowledge my co-workers, Jeanette Bowker and Robert Merkel, for their answers to an endless stream of questions and for their continuing support and encouragement. In particular, I would like to thank my office mate, Kitty Dickerson, for her assistance and critique of Part Five, and my friend and colleague, Marianne Beeson, for taking responsibility for the chapter bibliographies and the Instructor's Manual.

My sister, Paula Kozol, helped from the beginning stages of "cut and paste" to the final proofing and assembly of the index. Primarily she introduced me to the editorial process, helped me understand what was to come, made it easier and more palatable when it did come, and assured me always that not only could "it" be done, but that I could do "it." I can see her love and faith in me on every page.

Most of all, I would like to thank Lance, Larry, and Lane. To them, all that I have done seemed possible. Without their encouragement, it is indeed doubtful that I would ever have come this far.

Lois M. Gurel

Introduction

Throughout recorded time and probably even before, clothing, along with food and shelter, has been recognized as one of the primary needs of all peoples in all parts of the world. In recent years other basic necessities have been added—health care, transportation, and sufficient economic assets to obtain an adequate level of living. Whatever the priorities, clothing remains an essential element necessary for human well-being. And contrary to past beliefs, we now recognize that the utilitarian functions of clothing—these purposes that can be defined purely in physical terms—are not the only ones of importance. Protection against the elements, against cold and heat, and against insects and other physical hazards are not the only needs that clothing fulfills. Every individual has a variety of social, psychological, emotional, and aesthetic needs that also must be met in some way; clothing can and does fulfill some of them.

From the past we also inherited a set of beliefs that held that traditionally a concern for clothes was a feminine preoccupation. Men took pride in the facts that they were completely free of clothes constraints and lacked clothes consciousness. Clothing did not mean a thing to them—they said. This stereotype has changed, not only in American culture but in most parts of the world. Masculine attire is varied and colorful and men care as much about how they look as do women. Norms change over time and with them clothing norms as well. The typical office worker may wear a white *or* a blue shirt, the boss a pair of blue jeans, the executive woman a gray flannel suit. Whatever the prevailing mode, time, and place the importance of dress has not changed. It is significant in the lives of individuals at all ages, of both sexes, and in different social and economic status groups.

In looking at the nonutilitarian or nonphysical aspects of dress, courses and textbooks traditionally consider the topic in terms of clothing's relationship to personality. Although psychologists do not always agree on an adequate definition of personality, they do believe that in general it means the sum total of an individual's behavior patterns. The commonly accepted view is that many aspects of personality are not fixed and static throughout life, but undergo change through growth, development, and experiences in the social situation. The general assumption is that clothes are used to reflect, express, or enhance one's personality. They are so used whether a person goes about it consciously or not. Dress is discussed in this context to help the individual achieve some consistency between the tangible aspects of the self and intangible aspects of the clothing worn. Both communicate impressions of the self to others in the social environment.

By using psychology as a framework for study, clothing can be seen as an intimate part of the personality or self. Hurlock described this relationship as follows:

We are apt to think of clothes as we do of our bodies, and so to appropriate them that they become perhaps more than any of our other possessions, a part of ourselves . . . in spite of the constant changes in clothing, it is still impossible to disassociate ourselves from this intimate part of our material possessions. We appropriate the admiration our clothes call forth, and this tends to enhance our own self-esteem. Indeed the Bohemian immigrant girl who, it is related, expressed her life philosophy in the short sentence: "After all, life is mostly what you wear," expressed the life philosophy of the majority of people who have inhabited this world, either in the past ages or in our modern twentieth century.[1]

On the basis of social psychological research, as well as on the points of agreement found in some early writings concerning the interpretation of clothing behavior, we see that clothing is a symbol

---

[1]Elizabeth Hurlock, *The Psychology of Dress* (New York: Ronald Press Company, 1929), p. 44.

of crucial importance to the individual. As a nonverbal language it communicates to others an impression of social status, occupation, role, self-confidence, intelligence, conformity, individuality, and other personality characteristics. In most cases clothing behavior is influenced by the very same forces—social, psychological, and economic—that affect other aspects of human activity. This fact can best be seen by examining the ways in which individuals and families have fulfilled their clothing needs over the years. Ample evidence shows that the patterns of clothing production, distribution, and consumption make up a large part of a country's economic development. We will see, in fact, that the textile industry is the first to develop in emerging nations and that it is soon followed by the apparel industry. The general economic growth of underdeveloped countries tends to parallel their investment in the manufacture of textile and apparel goods.

When clothing behavior is expressed in fashion, the behavior is still regular and predictable. Fashions in any area of life, especially fashions in clothing, are not random and purposeless. They reflect the cultural patterns of the times. Fashions follow a progressive and irreversible path from inception through acceptance to culmination and eventual decline, and they also tend to parallel to some extent the larger events of history.

In a detailed study of dress styles from 1788 to 1936, anthropologist Kroeber noted that the first forty-five years were marked by rather agitated fluctuations in design forms, and the modes in dress from 1835 to 1905 were relatively steady and tranquil. This was followed by another thirty years of comparative instability. He attributed the first period of agitation to the sociopolitical tensions that accompanied the French Revolution and the Napoleonic wars that followed. The seventy years of tranquillity coincided exactly with the peaceful reign of Queen Victoria and the industrial development. The second period of instability was accounted for by the mounting unrest that preceded and followed World War I.[2]

In an earlier analysis, Kroeber presented the following observations in the comparison of long-term fashion swings and the growth in art styles:

In painting, neoclassicism, romanticism, impressionism, expressionism, cubism, have each lasted no longer than some trends in Western dress; and the degree of change effected by them is no greater. The total form and effect of Occidental clothing in 1815, 1865, and 1915 seem about as different as canvases painted in the classic manner in 1790 are different from the romantic ones of 1840 and these from the impressionisms of 1890 and surrealisms of 1940. The main difference is that we like to think of picture-painting and art exhibitions as serious and dignified, and of clothes and fashion shows as frivolous. But the behavior manifestations of the two sets of phenomena are much alike, so that we are justified in assuming that the processes at work are similar. One might even suspect the genuineness of the greater formal or avowed respect accorded the painter's activity. Presumably for every ten people in our civilization really exercised about a change in the manner of paintings there are a thousand who participate personally in changes of dress style, and who would be intensely perturbed if poverty or a sumptuary law prohibited them from conforming.[3]

Clothing is one of the most personal components of daily life, and at the same time it is an expression of social activities deeply embedded in the cultural patterns of an era.

AN INTERDISCIPLINARY APPROACH

Behavior related to clothing can be interpreted from many viewpoints. Physical scientists were the first to be aware of the clothing needs of people. By the end of the nineteenth century, however, behavioral scientists were beginning to write about dress. In the last fifty years there has been an exciting growth in the subject matter that constitutes this field of study. The theories advanced by early writers are now tested by anthropologists, historians, home economists, psychologists, and sociologists, many of whom work together on problems of common interest. By its very nature, the study of clothing involves a number of root disciplines in the natural and social sciences.

An understanding of many of the reasons for dress comes to us from **anthropologists,** who make cross-cultural comparisons of primitive societies. Anthropological studies enable us to conclude, for example, that using clothing to express modesty is a function that is determined by the culture, learned by the individual, and not very likely instinctive in nature. People

[2]A. L. Kroeber, *Style and Civilization* (Ithaca, N.Y.: Cornell University Press, 1957), pp. 10–18.

[3]A. L. Kroeber, *Anthropology* (New York: Harcourt, Brace and Company, 1948), p. 392.

cover or decorate their bodies for a variety of reasons and modesty is only one. Other reasons include protection, the desire to be sexually attractive, and adornment.

Historians' methods make it possible to interpret current clothing phenomena against the perspective of time. By noting repeated regularities or fluctuation in dress over extended periods, we are better able to explain and predict the probable effects of social change on patterns of dress. Contemporary styles are not the unique, spontaneous creations of the era in which we now live. They come from the past, and what they will be in the future depends to a great extent on the conditions and influences on them today.

Psychologists are concerned with how the individual organism responds to specific stimuli. Their interests center around the basic concepts of motivation, learning, and perception. Much clothing behavior is psychological in nature. In psychological terms, clothing is both a stimulus and a response. People perceive a clothing stimulus in different ways, and they interpret its meaning according to the associations they have learned to make with it over a long period of time. In addition, clothing is a tangible and observable phenomenon that is important to the concept of self and the development of personality. It often indicates suppressed needs and desires, and the analysis of dress can lend insight to a number of hidden psychic processes.

Sociologists are also concerned with human behavior, but in a collective sense. They study the results of human action that stem from society rather than that which is peculiar to the individual. For example, the normative aspects of dress as seen through the rise and decline of fashions demonstrate a basic social tendency—the sharing of habits and ideals and conformity to a set of group expectations. The link between the individual and society as a whole is provided by the concepts of role and status. In this respect, clothing is a symbol of the individual's role and status in society, and it provides rewards of recognition, approval, and identification for the wearer.

Psychology is the study of individual behavior and **sociology** is the study of group behavior. Subject matter that falls within the overlapping areas between these two disciplines constitutes a third field of study, **social psychology**. Social psychologists combine theories and concepts from both psychology and sociology and study the behavior of individuals in groups and the effects of groups on the individual. Most of the behavioral research concerning clothing falls within the realm of social psychology.

Although classified as a humanity rather than as a science, **art** also contributes significantly to a study of clothing. The universal search for beauty and adornment is a most remarkable human characteristic. The standard for what is considered "beautiful" is subject to rather powerful cultural changes, but any aspect of dress that provides perceptual pleasure can be considered a part of the aesthetic experience. The ornamental potential of clothing is an important outlet for artistic drives and self-expression, as well as a source of tremendous sensuous satisfaction. Clothing also can be seen as human creations that capture and reflect the whole spirit of an art movement resulting from a particular set of social conditions.

The urge to beautify through dress and adornment is perhaps second only to the basic drives linked to biological survival. Clothing acts as a buffer between the environment and the people living in it. Clothing shields them from the harmful elements of climate, infections, and trauma. In order to make the most effective use of clothing in the purely physical sense, one must understand the fundamental principles of heat exchange and have a supplementary knowledge of the physical properties of fibers, fabrics, and apparel.

Additionally, the human organism makes a number of physiological adaptations to the environment that affect body comfort and alter the need for protective clothing. Conversely, a body covering can reduce the need for caloric intake and can influence other physiological processes as well. Need for protection is closely allied with desire for comfort. An understanding of the anatomical structure of the human body and its related movements is essential to the creation of functionally designed clothing that is comfortable, utilitarian, convenient, and attractive.

The economic significance of clothing is readily seen in relation to the individual and the family, yet its greatest impact lies in the contribution of the textile and apparel industries to the American economy as a whole, and in their role in international trade. By studying clothing we can observe the factors of consumer demand, purchasing power, and market supply, and we can relate them to production, distribution, and consumption of textile and clothing products at all levels.

Thus the study of clothing is truly an interdisciplinary one. No single theory, no one field of knowledge, no isolated concept can fully explain the importance of clothing in people's lives. Those who think that a study of clothing from other than a purely physical frame of reference is a frivolous endeavor might try to think of another subject that involves so many diverse disciplines in an attempt to improve lives for individuals and families. An integrated theory, comprised of many component parts, is necessary in order to study clothing needs and practices in an objective and satisfactory way. This book is organized around such an approach. Each section contributes a different viewpoint to an overall understanding of dress as a second skin.

Part One, Clothing and Culture, discusses clothing and its anthropological and historical origins and relates it to the development of technology, folkways, mores, customs, and laws. Part Two deals with the social and psychological aspects of dress, including its relevance to the self-concept and expression of personality, role, social status, and adherence to group expectations and normative social patterns.

The related disciplines of art and philosophy are drawn upon in Part Three, Aesthetics and Dress. Clothing is analyzed as a medium for artistic perception, expression, and experience; as such, it is a parallel to other movements in the arts. Parts Four and Five emphasize the physical and economic aspects of clothing.

Considered all together, the parts of the book will help the reader form a workable value pattern that will be different for each individual. By examining one's personal needs and desires it is possible to organize a system for managing clothing resources that will minimize conflict and still achieve the desired goal. This approach to clothing decisions, from an interdisciplinary point of view, should avoid the distortion of values that may result from a fragmented study of selected aspects of dress.

THE ANALYSIS OF CLOTHING BEHAVIOR

In any field of inquiry, a scientific approach depends on the organization of observation and experiences. In ordering our observations of clothing behavior, we seek to identify the common, regular, and repetitive elements in the action patterns of individuals and groups. We also attempt to account for such patterning by noting the relationships between clothing and other phenomena in the environment. Obviously, the patterns that are followed by the greatest number of individuals, and that are repeated in many successive situations, offer relatively high predictability.

The main characteristic of scientific analysis is objectivity. Developing objectivity toward clothing is far more difficult than in other areas of study. Clothes are so intimately involved with personal feelings that each individual has a set of preconceptions that can lead to biased observations or distorted interpretations. Very often what we "see" in making clothing observations is what we expect to see or what we are looking for. In order to control for such biases, we establish a systematic plan for testing observable behavior, using hypotheses and theories. The resulting body of knowledge is then organized into some type of structure. An understanding of this structuring is necessary in order to put the study of clothing into proper perspective.

The first step toward understanding any field of study is to master certain basic concepts. By *concepts* we mean words or descriptive terms that refer to abstract ideas. The most fundamental concept in the whole book is, of course, *clothing*. It could be the abstract name or title given to anything that serves as a body covering. But much clothing is not intended to cover the body at all, but rather to call attention to it. In the broadest sense, therefore, clothing or *dress* may be defined as any body adornment or appearance modification made to the human form. This definition would include such features as tattooing, cicatrization, use of cosmetics, hair styles and hairiness, and so forth. It is the definition we use in this book.

Additional concepts related to clothing are *fashion, lifestyle, porosity, proportion, taste*, and others that are the building blocks of the field. Once the particular language is understood, concepts can be related to one another in statements that explain how these concepts interact. Such statements may be called *hypotheses, propositions, postulates, principles*, or *laws*.

The final goal, however, is building a body of logically interrelated generalizations known as *theory*. By theory, we mean a general summary of statements that explains the interrelationships among principles or propositions. The purpose of theory is to organize ideas into an integrated scheme. The goal is to move from narrow, specific observations to broader, more abstract applications.

Many chapters in the book are designed to emphasize this kind of a structure. When applicable, a section first presents some of the generally accepted theories related to the topic. This introduction is followed by specific illustrations that support the theory and identify common or uniform elements so the reader can generalize to a more abstract idea. Related research is cited whenever empirical data are available. The generalized statements in boldface type at section ends are intended to pull out the key idea in each unit of the chapter. Rather than memorize such statements from the book, however, readers should try to formulate their own statements of relationships. A summary at the end of each section ties the ideas together in general terms. Essentially, the summary is a restatement of the theory or, in some cases, of the introductory remarks. Every field of study must proceed on the basis of acceptable theories even though many of these theories may not be subjected to scientific investigation for many years to come. The dynamic nature of clothing makes it necessary to reexamine clothing theories constantly in the light of changing social and technological conditions. Theories are essential to the analysis of clothing behavior because they enable us to predict the possible consequences of particular clothing choices, not only in the lives of individuals, but in society as a whole. Thus, given a particular set of circumstances, the enlightened individual can make clothing decisions that will satisfy personal needs, communicate an image to others, and contribute to the best interests of the group, all at the same time.

The idea that clothes may be used to achieve certain goals is often considered distasteful to those who consider "use" synonymous with "manipulate." To them, using clothes is similar to tampering with nature, particularly when clothing is used in its broadest sense to include corporal or body decorations. But to employ no design in the utilization of our resources is to expect that the best will happen through a series of happy accidents. The aim of decision making in regard to clothing choices should be to secure, as Hartmann described it, the optimal value pattern— the choice that produces the maximum good.[4] This statement implies a conscious investigation and assessment of the functions of clothing as well as an ordering of one's clothing values. Those who see the "good" in clothing as the prestige that it affords, or as the comfort it provides, may still take their choice, but in full knowledge of the consequences.

[4]George Hartmann, "Clothing: Personal Problem and Social Issue," *Journal of Home Economics*, 41, No. 6 (June 1949), 295–298.

Part One

INTERRELATIONSHIP
OF CLOTHING AND CULTURE

Chapter 1

ORIGINS AND

FUNCTIONS OF CLOTHES

Culture and society exist in the present but they derive from the past. Clothing, the material objects of society and culture, also began in the past. Some thought about its origins in antiquity will help further our understanding of the clothing behavior of people, past and present. The first question to ask, then, is: *When* did people first begin to wear clothes? So, too, in order to gain even a limited understanding of the meanings of dress and adornment for modern societies, it is important to consider theories that attempt to explain *why* clothes were first worn. Why did people, accustomed to nakedness, begin to cover or decorate their bodies? Only by having some awareness of the possible answers to that question can we talk about why people

wear clothes today. Can these original functions or purposes of clothing still be used to explain the reasons that clothing is worn today? This chapter discusses all these aspects of clothing.

The root disciplines of archaeology and anthropology provide some answers. Archaeologists study the lives and cultures of ancient peoples. Anthropologists compare societies past and present in order to speculate about the original functions of dress.

For thousands of years a great deal of time, money, and energy has been devoted to clothing and decorating the human body. In many ways and in many places attempts have been made to change or improve upon the naked form. Various peoples have used paints, tattooing, and mutilation as well as ornaments, skins, furs, and fabrics. These articles used by people to cover and to decorate themselves can be called by many names, but **clothing** can be used collectively to include them all. To some people the words *dress* or *clothing*, refer only to items used to cover the body, and *adornment* refers to the things used to decorate it. Here the words will be used interchangeably. Therefore, the word *clothing* refers to all items of apparel *and* adornment. By clothing we mean body decorations such as cosmetics, tattoos, hair color, and hair arrangements; ornaments of jewelry; badges and insignia of office or rank; extensions of the body in the form of canes, umbrellas, and handkerchiefs; as well as apparel or garments.

Using this broad definition of clothing, the following flat statement may be made: There are no peoples known, past or present, who do not wear clothing of some type. People may be unclothed, but they are never completely unadorned.

If he wears not so much as a G-string, he certainly sports a nose, ear, or lip plug, or bears his tattoos or scarifications, or paints his face, or curls his hair, or cuts it off, or blackens his teeth, or knocks them out, or perhaps merely files them to a point.[1]

The expression "naked savage" has become conventional, but it is essentially inaccurate. I will not assert that, in the infinite variety of nature, there is no naked savage; but I will assert that the chief distinction between the savage and the beast is that the savage is adorned. As soon as man swung earthward from the tree-tops, he began to wonder how he could improve, or at least employ, the phenomena with which he was surrounded to increase his own power and dignity. The animal accepts things as they are. Man endeavors to mould and modify things.[2]

THE ORIGINS OF CLOTHING

When did clothing originate? We can only speculate as to what people who lived before history was recorded may have worn. Because it was made of organic materials, clothing did not survive (except in very rare situations) as did stone tools, pottery jars, and cave paintings. Scanty though it may be, a review of the available evidence about the origin of clothing allows for some general answers to the question.

The Wanderers and Hunters

Only through indirect evidence and logical thinking can we assume that very early in prehistoric times people wore something to cover and protect themselves. Probably the first use of clothing was for protection from the cold. Archaeological evidence indicates that early hunters and wanderers of 500,-000 to 300,000 years ago moved from the tropics, where they originated, to areas with cooler climates. Although no actual garments remain from these ancient times, when people moved north they needed something to keep them warm. They soon

[1]E. Adamson Hoebel, *Anthropology: The Study of Man* (New York: McGraw-Hill Book Co., 1972), p. 326.
[2]Sisley Huddleston, Introduction to *From Nudity to Raiment*, by Hilaire Hiler (New York: The Educational Press, 1930), p. 1.

discovered, for example, that it was warmer inside caves than it was outside and

so, he smoked the bear out, killed and ate him with relish, then used the hide for the first form of human clothing. He had noticed that the bears did not freeze and, correctly, he attributed this to the fur, the uneatable outer layer of the bear. It was a racial emergency. If man could not connect in one plan of action such simple ideas, as bears, caves and furs, he was doomed.[3]

On a rocky ledge above a sandy beach near what is now Nice, France, archaeologists found evidence of *Homo erectus*, the first people. A cave, called *Terra Amata*, was inhabited about 400,000 years ago. Fossils and sand imprints show that after the meat was scraped away, the hides were used for something. Again, deduction and a reliance on logic led scientists to assume that the hides were used as some form of covering (Figure 1.1).[4]

The Cave Dwellers

The first direct evidence that body decoration as well as body coverings was used comes from the Neanderthal burial sites of the Middle Paleolithic era of the Old Stone Age 100,000 to 60,000 years ago. When the Neanderthal skeletons were discovered in Dusseldorf, Germany, in 1856, people of the enlightened nineteenth century refused to accept these shocking skeletons as the remains of modern people. Despite considerable skepticism in the scientific community and from the general public,

Figure 1.1 Probably the earliest garment was a hip covering made from the uncut skin of an animal.

investigation continued and, with surprisingly little evidence in the form of artifacts, anthropologists learned a great deal about this period of prehistory. The few remains that were found were highly perishable and almost impossible to study once exposed to the air. This was particularly true of organic materials from which clothing probably was made. Both organic and inorganic matter may be dated with a fairly high degree of accuracy using one or more of the several techniques available to archaeologists for this purpose. All methods involve assessing the change and arrangement over time of the atoms in the molecules.[5]

[3]M. D. C. Crawford, *Philosophy in Clothing* (New York: The Brooklyn Museum, 1940), p. 8.

[4]Edmund White, *The First Men* (New York: Time-Life Books, 1973), p. 86.

[5]For a detailed description of some of the methods used to date archaeological finds, see George Constable, *The Neanderthals* (New York: Time-Life Books, 1973), pp. 60–69.

Even when actual garments (Figure 1.2) do not survive in archaeological deposits, indirect evidence is derived from the tools found (Figure 1.3) among the remains. An untreated hide is stiff and boardlike, but if the inside is thoroughly scraped to remove fat and flesh and then softened by beating, it becomes flexible enough to cover the body. We know that the Neanderthals fashioned crude stone-skinning knives and bone scrapers. Therefore, the simplest and probably the first article of clothing was the untreated bear skin wrapped around the body like a cloak.[6] Pigments of red and yellow ochre have been found in caves and burial sites indicating that, even in this prehistoric period, the body was decorated and perhaps the inner surface of the fur coverings as well. The use of these colors provides the first hint of adornment and the very beginnings of decorative art and design. The Neanderthals probably also learned about clothing from *Homo erectus*, who lived at a slightly earlier time and in a colder climate during the beginning of a former ice age.

Fragments of Old Stone Age fur and leather from a similar period have since been found, however, in the northern part of the Soviet Union, preserved by the extreme cold. This direct evidence in the form of actual pieces of clothing verified earlier speculations. The remains of two young boys, aged nine and twelve, were found by Russian archaeologists in the frozen rock layers near Moscow. These remains are believed to be approximately 100,000 years old. The boys wore leather trousers and shirts, beads, and fur-lined boots. Arrows, a spear, and a finely carved needle, all made of ivory from a mammoth, a large elephantlike animal, were found

[6]Crawford, *Philosophy in Clothing*.

Figure 1.2 During the Upper Paleolithic era people wore garments cut from animal skins and laced together.

Figure 1.3 Paleolithic tools: stone implements used to scrape the insides of animal skins to prepare them for cutting and needles made from bone and ivory.

with the bodies. "Dr. Otto Bader, the leader of the expedition, says that the craftmanship of the clothing and tools suggest that these Stone-Age people may not have been very different from present-day inhabitants of the Far North and Arctic."[7]

[7]"Modern Stone-Age Man," *Science News*, XCVI (December 20, 1969), 583.

The Cro-Magnons lived in Europe during the Upper Paleolithic era, from 40,000 to 10,000 years ago. An ochre-sprinkled grave of a Paleolithic mammoth hunter that is at least 33,000 years old was found near Moscow. This male skeleton was dressed in tailored pants and a pullover shirt made of fur. Mammoth ivory was used as beading for the clothing decoration and for bracelets. A necklace fashioned from Arctic fox teeth completed his outfit. Because of the extreme cold, the clothing and decorations were preserved and archaeologists were able to reconstruct the funeral rites from so long ago.[8]

The Cro-Magnons were also cave people, but they were intelligent and artistic. Their tools were more specialized and better made than were those of their ancestors. In addition to weapons, they made scrapers and cutters for dressing hides, burins (pointed tools) for engraving antlers and ivory, and needles from bone. These first bone needles are conclusive evidence that these people knew how to sew (Figure 1.4). In fact, the needles were superior to any found until the Renaissance, forty centuries later. Development of these very thin, sharp needles meant that

the fabrication of carefully sewn, fitted clothing enabled them to conquer the far north and eventually to penetrate the virgin continent of North America. . . . The hide clothing of these people was probably much like that of the Eskimos of recent times. A tunic or pullover, with tightly sewn seams to keep heat from escaping, pants easily tucked into boots, and some sort of sock, perhaps of fur, would have been warm enough in all but the coldest weather. For frigid days, outer clothing consisting of a

[8]"Paleolithic Funeral," *Scientific American*, CCXII, No. 2 (February 1965), 53–54.

Figure 1.4 Near the end of the Paleolithic period, clothing construction became an art. The Magdalenian woman uses a needle to sew and to decorate her garments with geometric patterns.

hooded parka, mittens and high boots would have served to keep a person from freezing. Female figurines from Stone Age Russia seem to be clothed in fur.[9]

The Cro-Magnons strung fish and animal vertebrae or pierced teeth on leather thongs and wore them around their necks. Using burins, they engraved bracelets made from ivory. They also decorated their clothes with colored beads. Personal adornment, according to anthropologist John E. Pfeiffer, "involved a new level of assertiveness, a new degree of individuality."[10] Cave paintings (Figure 1.5) have also been discovered from this period and they show forms that might be human, decorated in ways that suggest body adornments of some type, even if not actually garments. The cave paintings of a slightly later period are much more sophisticated and reveal more about the lives and habits of the people. These paintings of

[9]Tom Prideaux, *Cro-Magnon Man* (New York: Time-Life Books, 1973), p. 35.
[10]Ibid., p. 93.

Figure 1.5 Cave paintings indicate that early peoples decorated their bodies as well as their clothing.

20,000 years ago show decidedly human forms of both sexes. The women wore feathered skirts, the men, ceremonial masks. The paintings on the wall of Lascaux Cave in France were made by an ancient hunter-wanderer people about 15,000 years ago. Since many of the paintings on this cave wall were colored with a variety of pigments, we can speculate as to whether these people used color on their clothing as well.

Although all evidence is scanty, we can assume that very early in the Old Stone Age, probably a half million years ago, people began to wear clothing. We can also state with much more certainty that by the Middle Paleolithic era of the Old Stone Age, 50,000 to 25,000 years ago, not only was clothing worn, it was fairly well developed.

The First City Dwellers

The wanderers of very early times settled down to farming life by 8000 B.C. (10,000 years ago) and, shortly thereafter, the first cities appeared. By the year 6500 B.C. a fairly well established pattern of interacting city-states existed. Ideas were exchanged along with traded goods. We know that by then people wore leather sandals and light, loose-fitting loincloths made of wool. Many excellent wall murals remain depicting everyday life at that time, as well as evidence of tools, cooking utensils, and even furniture. In the murals, men appear in ceremonial leopard-skin garments and harlequin-painted bodies.

The earliest direct evidence that people knew how to weave yarns into fabrics also comes from the Neolithic period starting about 10,000 years ago. In 1854, following a severe drought in Switzerland, the remains of an ancient people were found at the bottom of a lake. These people built their cities over the surface of the water on wooden piles. Fragments of linen cloth were found indicating that the Swiss Lake Dwellers were highly skilled weavers. Since they cultivated the flax from which the linen fabrics were made they were successful farmers as well. So far, these are the oldest extant fragments of woven cloth in the world. **Extant** means the opposite of extinct, that is, something that still exists. Something that is **extinct** no longer exists. The Swiss Lake Dwellers did not cut and sew their fabrics into shaped garments, they draped them loosely around the body.

The oldest extant fragments of clothing found in North America are almost as old. A pair of fiber sandals made from shredded sagebrush bark, found at Fort Rock Cave, Oregon, has been dated by the carbon 14 method as about 9,000 years old.[11] The carbon 14 method of dating archaeological finds utilizes the radioactive properties of elements. These radioactive parts break down at a specific rate for each element. The radioactive part of carbon is called carbon 14 and, in living matter, it is constantly disintegrating and being replaced. However, when living cells die, the carbon 14 continues to disintegrate but is not replaced as are the rest of the carbon atoms. Scientists can measure the proportion of carbon 14 still present compared to the ordinary carbon, which does not change. Although there are more sophisticated methods of measuring the age of substances, this method is important because it subjects investigations of the past to more objective measurement than had been possible before.

Extant small squares of cloth dating from about 6000 B.C. indicate that the people of Catal Hüyük in southern Turkey were also weavers. The cloth found was used to cover the body for burial. Preservation of these bits of fabric is, in itself, somewhat miraculous, yet

the burial process itself helped preserve the fabric remains: the bones and cloth were interred where they were protected from the deteriorating effects of air—in the clay under the sleeping platforms of houses or shrines. A catastrophic fire in 5880 B.C. destroyed the buildings but preserved the fabrics. Since there was little oxygen in the burial places, the flames could not consume the fragile cloth. Instead, the heat converted most parts of the fibers into carbon without altering their shape—just as wood is converted by heat into charcoal. Carbon does not

deteriorate with age, so the carbonized fabrics endured without change through the ensuing eight millennia.

Today these relics of ancient cloth are small, brittle swatches that when scrutinized look like burlap. Yet the experts who have examined them say that the threads were spun well and evenly, and that the fibers were carefully prepared for spinning. The threads are smooth, with none of the "hairs" that denote hasty preparation or lack of skill, and each lies neatly parallel to the next.

Even more impressive is the fineness of the work. Weavers traditionally define their finished products by the number of threads per inch of warp and woof. The woven materials from Catal had thread counts as high as 30 per inch in one direction, 38 in the other. The cloth was thus as finely woven as one of today's lightweight wools.[12]

By the time the Sumarian cities of 3500 B.C. (approximately 3,000 to 5,500 years ago) appeared almost 2,000 years of history was recorded in statuary and wall paintings. These relics indicate that the Sumarians had a rich civilization; their sculpture shows gowned and tasseled figures dressed in woven fabrics (Figure 1.6). Males and females are well defined, at least partially by the hair styles, but also by their clothing. The Sumarians also invented a form of writing, which, when deciphered, revealed a great deal of information about these people.

Extant bits of fabric indicate that by 10,000 years ago people in farming settlements were using woven fabrics made of wool and flax. Wall murals in remains of ancient cities show clothing that is both functional and decorative.

[11]T. R. Henry, "Ice Age Man, the First American," *National Geographic Magazine,* CVIII, No. 6 (December 1933), 787.

[12]Dora Jane Hamblin, *The First Cities* (New York: Time-Life Books, 1973), p. 74.

Figure 1.6 Statuary from the ancient Sumarian cities records the clothing of the people.

SUMMARY

The Origins of Clothing

The evidence that is available concerning the clothing worn by peoples of prehistoric times consists of some fossils and prints on a Mediterranean beach; ochre and scrapers from the tombs of the Neanderthals of about 50,000 years ago; fragments of fur and leather garments from the same period; and a few cave paintings and some bone needles dated between 40,000 and 25,000 years ago. In addition, extant fragments of woven cloth and a pair of sandals have been found from the last part of the Neolithic period, 9,000 to 10,000 years ago. Wall paintings and a few remains from the early cities give some information from a slightly later date. The evidence is not much to go on, it is true, but archaeologists and anthropologists have been able to use it to piece together a story of prehistory that is more than a guess. It is a composite of plausible, possible, and probable theories. The actual history of dress usually starts about 5,000 years ago or in the year 3000 B.C. in the ancient civilizations of Egypt and Mesopotamia.

THE FUNCTIONS OF CLOTHING

Even less definitive answers may be given to the second question raised at the beginning of this chapter. Why did people first begin to wear clothing, that is, what were the original functions of clothing? Next, can these original functions be used to explain the wide variety in clothing observable today? Many writers in the behavioral sciences have considered these points.

Anthropologists often turn for answers to primitive peoples still found in some parts of the world. Because of their relatively simple lifestyles these nonliterate cultures are ready social laboratories in which customs and social systems may be studied away from the complexity of modern society. Problems appear in simpler terms; copying from one group to another is less; psychological and sociological events may be observed in relatively uncomplicated form.

In modern technological societies a study of one group involves other individuals and groups that interact with it. These others have different standards, social aims, home life, traditions, and morality. In an isolated group, events and behavior can be studied without having to consider the effects of other groups on it. In fact, in primitive societies, cultural traditions are often simple enough to be completely described by one individual. Manners and morals follow a well-defined general pattern. Clothing and clothing customs, too, follow a well-defined general pattern and so are easier to study.

Two words that have vastly different meanings have been used almost interchangeably thus far in this book. The word *primitive* is generally used to refer to a society that operates on a lower technological level than the society used for comparison. Since people generally compare another culture to their own, they often tend to think of any group of people operating at a lower level of technology than they do as primitive. This may or may not be true. The word *nonliterate* simply means only the absence of a formal written language; not all primitive societies are nonliterate. Certainly not all nonliterate societies are or were primitive. Primitive implies a value judgment, that the society used for comparison is superior. Eskimos may have made a better adjustment to their environment than we have to ours. In many ways they would not be considered primitive, but they are nonliterate. The high civilizations of Old

Mexico had no written language (that we know of) but they would not be considered primitive. A study of some of the American Indian cultures, most notably the Cherokee Nation in Tennessee and North Carolina, would show that they are neither primitive nor nonliterate and that they have been highly civilized and literate for several generations.

There is a marked difference between these two words and we should not place our own personal values or those of our society on peoples whose mode of operation and lifestyle differ from our own. We need another word or phrase to describe the many different cultures or societies that exist around the world, one that has no value judgment attached to it. The phrase *folk societies* has been suggested. Robert Jaulin, a French anthropologist, said that "even recently, we still talked about 'primitive peoples.' Now we are a little more subtle about it, we say **so-called** primitive peoples. But we should get something straight right away. They are simply **other civilizations**, nothing less than that."[13]

In an attempt to find a universal reason for the original function of clothing, psychologists often study the behavior of young children. The principle is similar to the assumption made by anthropologists; young children are not under some of the strains and influences of modern society. Students of clothing draw on all these several disciplines—archaeology, anthropology, and psychology—to establish some major theories about the original function of clothing.

We do not know for certain why people first began to wear clothing or why they wear clothing today. Many suggestions

[13]Francoise Morin and Jacques Nousseau, "La Paix Blanche," *Psychology Today*, September 1971, 63.

have been made and there is general agreement on four major theories and several interrelated minor ones to explain the reasons clothes were first worn. A theory is a plausible, or possible, or scientifically acceptable principle based on facts that is used to explain something unusual. The four major theories for the original function of clothes are: the **modesty theory**, the **immodesty theory**, the **protection theory**, and the **adornment** or **decoration theory**.

The Modesty Theory

Are clothes really necessary? To those who believe that the modesty theory is the only acceptable one, the answer to this question would be yes. Moralists believe that our innate feelings of guilt and shame resulting from exposure of particular parts of the body date back to Adam and Eve. "And the eyes of both of them were opened, and they knew they were naked; and they sewed fig leaves together and made themselves aprons, unto Adam also and to his wife did the Lord God make coats of skins and clothed them."[14] Since this passage comes from the Old Testament, the book of Genesis, it is often called the Mosaic theory, or the Biblical version for why people wear clothes.

The idea that a sense of modesty underlies all original motives for clothing the body may be a popular belief but it is neither generally accepted by scholars in the field nor borne out by observable fact. The modesty theory has been disputed on three counts. Most people in the world do use dress to conceal parts of the body but the parts it conceals vary from culture to

culture. Modesty, or a sense of shame associated with an unconcealed body part, is not universal. What is covered or left uncovered varies among societies. Even within one particular culture, variations occur depending on age, sex, subcultural groupings, locations, and situational factors. And even if we accept the theory that feelings of natural shame are common, a number of illustrations can be cited to disprove the assumption that such shame is necessarily associated with a lack of clothes.

The women in the Suyá tribe (Figure 1.7) in the Amazon jungle wear large cylindrical wooden plugs in their ear lobes and disks in their lower lips and little else. They are not ashamed of their naked bodies, but they are terribly embarrassed if outsiders see them without their disks in place. Few English people or Americans see anything indecent about the nude in art, but even today some people are horrified at the idea of the sexes bathing together. In Japan, the sexes customarily bathe together, but nude art is considered indecent. The women on the island of Yap

Figure 1.7 Lip disks and earplugs are indispensable to the Suyá Indians of Brazil.

[14]Genesis 3:7.

Figure 1.8 Cultural concepts of modesty differ. In some cases, breasts may be exposed, but never thighs, as is the case for these people in Ecuador.

Figure 1.9 Men of the Tuareg tribe of Mali wear caftans and veils.

in the South Pacific hold to a very strict tradition of modesty, but what must never be exposed are the thighs, not the breasts. This is also true in parts of Central America (Figure 1.8).

Mohammedan women in certain parts of Africa would be shamed to discover that someone watched them as they bathed, but they would quickly cover their faces, not their bodies. One of the most interesting and unusual examples of a different concept of modesty comes from the Tuareg tribe in Southern Algeria and parts of Nigeria. Here the veil is worn, but only by the men (Figure 1.9), and virtually all the time—at home, traveling, eating, sleeping. The veil is raised only far enough to eat, never high enough for the mouth to be seen. It is considered shameful for a man to expose his mouth, particularly to his own people. Even men who have adopted Western dress still wear the veil. In China up until the establishment of the Peoples Republic in 1949 and the Communist philosophy of uniform dress, clothing was customarily worn very high at the neck,

covering the breasts, but it was slit quite high up the leg.

It is also an error to assume that nakedness is found only in primitive societies, past or present, since it was prevalent in several early but highly developed civilizations. The honored bull dancers of ancient Crete performed in the arena wearing only their armrings and necklaces, and the conventional Cretan feminine dress consisted of elaborate skirts in tiers and flounces with a short-sleeved bodice that left the breasts bare (Figure 1.10). Moreover, the tight lacing at the waist encouraged an overly erect posture, giving greater emphasis to the bosom, which Cretan women exhibited with great pride. The royal and upper class Egyptian women of the Old and Middle Kingdoms wore straight sheath dresses extending from below the breasts to the ankles, hung from the shoulder by a strap or two (Figure 1.11). A young man in ancient Greece usually traveled in only a short rectangle of cloth fastened on one shoulder and a broad-brimmed hat.

Figure 1.10 Minoan goddess wears the fashionable costume of highborn Cretan ladies, c. 1600 B.C.

Figure 1.11 The typical costume of Egyptian women of the Middle Kingdom, c. 2000 B.C., was a straight sheath dress with a shoulder strap.

Figure 1.12 Concepts of modesty are not instinctive. They are culturally induced habits. Naked babies are not the least bit modest.

To summarize, the first reason for rejecting the modesty theory as a major explanation for wearing clothes is the wide variety of ideas people have about what constitutes modesty and nakedness.

Another reason for rejecting the theory is that there is now evidence that indicates that modesty is not an instinct, but a culturally induced habit that varies depending on the time and place. A sense of modesty is completely lacking in young children of our own society, who at the age of three may well undress on the front lawn and go to visit the neighbors (Figure 1.12).

Additionally, the concept of modesty changes with age. Pictures of naked babies appear in magazines and in family albums. Not only is photographing naked babies acceptable, it is often encouraged, much to the embarrassment of children looking at their baby pictures in later years. A small child may be undressed in public, for example, at the beach, and a baby's diaper

may be changed there. At some point, at some age, this practice becomes indecent exposure and is strictly punishable by laws in most states, and in many Western countries.

Several investigations have confirmed the idea that modesty is not a very potent force in clothing behavior. In a very early but classic research study, an attempt was made to identify the underlying motives in women's choice of dress. Barr discovered that of all the attitudes associated with clothes, modesty was probably the least important.[15] And at a later date Creekmore analyzed the relationship between clothing behavior and the general values held by college women and concluded that in the eight personality types studied, modesty was significant only to the student who placed great emphasis on religious values, and then only when physiological needs were satisfied.[16]

Even casual observation of dress at the end of the 1970s indicated even less concern with modesty. Bare looks, bare backs, no bra, and see-through clothing seemed to defy the concept of modesty. In fact, predictions now indicate that by the year 2000 we may all be wearing one-piece Plexiglas jumpsuits complete with heating and cooling systems. If we wear anything under these suits it will be flesh-colored body suits and helmets equipped with telephone and radio hook-ups.

Many people in today's society wear clothes for reasons of modesty, but it is probably not of primary importance and it cannot account for the origin of clothes.

[15]Estelle de Young Barr, "A Psychological Analysis of Fashion Motivation," *Archives of Psychology*, No. 171 (1934), 77.
[16]Anna M. Creekmore, "Clothing Behaviors and Their Relation to General Values and Basic Needs". Ph.D. diss., Pennsylvania State University, 1963.

Although a popular belief, the modesty theory as an explanation for the original function of clothing has been discounted by scholars for three reasons: modesty is not the same in all cultures and it is not universal; expressions of modesty are habits set by the society one lives in, they are not instinctual; and concepts of modesty vary with age.

The Immodesty Theory

Some writers contend that clothing is not the result of modesty, but the cause of modesty; children are not embarrassed by lack of clothes until they become accustomed to wearing them. The second theory suggested to explain the original function of dress can be labeled the immodesty theory. Clothing is used not to cover the body but to attract attention to it. The removal of garments is far more erotic than is going without them in the first place. One argument nudists give is that once the sight of the human body becomes common the importance attached to sex differences soon disappears (Figure 1.13). To those who believe in the immodesty theory, the function of clothing is to enhance or attract, and the origin of clothes thus swings from the theory of modesty to the opposite extreme—exhibitionism (Figure 1.14).

According to the immodesty theory, the body was first covered as a sexual lure and clothes were used to call attention to the body parts that were covered. To support this theory we can note many articles of clothing that seem to have as their sole or primary purpose the task of calling attention to parts of the body: short skirts and pants (Figure 1.15); narrow skirts with long slits, front, side, or back; tight clothes

Figure 1.13 Once the sight of the human body becomes commonplace, the importance attached to sexual differentiation soon disappears.

in general, specifically knit tube tops, tight jeans, and tight sweaters; the bare look, bare backs, shoulders, or low necklines; textured stockings and pointed shirt tails. Many items worn in the past had a similar purpose—the codpiece (Figure 1.16), the waist cincher, and the bustle.

Figure 1.14 Body adornment often deliberately calls attention to sensual parts of the body.

Figure 1.16 During the Renaissance, the male codpiece was an essential part of the costume. According to our standards, it seems almost obscene.

Figure 1.15 Clothes that cover the body do not necessarily conceal it.

Through the ages women were restricted to less than direct approaches to heterosexual relationships. They used clothing to display physical attributes in positive and classically feminine maneuvers. This form of attraction was considered part of the customs of most societies. Although not as common or as necessary today, it is still used. Even amid the most ardent feminists and proponents of the women's movement, women still use clothing to cover the body in various degrees, with attraction as the major purpose.[17]

It is true that when skirts were long, the sight of an ankle was more intriguing than is the sight of a whole leg today. However, it is very unlikely that primitive peoples, who had been naked, would realize that parts of the body would be more alluring if covered and would for that reason alone start to cover parts of the body.

The Protection Theory

Few would disagree with the importance of protection, both physical and psychological, as evidenced by the use of clothing generally and by the selection of specific items of clothing in different parts of the world. However, was protection the original reason that people covered and decorated their bodies, or did the need for protection come later in the evolutionary process? Lacking a natural protective coat such as most animals have, humans were forced to make their own. Anyone who has shivered in the cold or blistered in the sun appreciates the physical protection that

clothing provides. The use of clothing for psychological security, as a good luck symbol or for protection from evil, is at least as universal and obvious and, in many places, more important than clothing for purely physical protection.

A plausible assumption concerning the use of dress for protection is that the earliest article of clothing was an animal skin draped around the body for warmth. But since evolution began in areas with warm climates, Langner suggested that the invention of clothes did not necessarily arise from the need for protection against the cold. He said that the need for protective covering derived from the shift to erect posture. Standing upright exposed external organs. In a four-legged animal, those organs are shielded by the back and forepart of the body.[18] Hence, a protective apron or loincloth was devised. Physical protection of the sex organs has always been important. Most G-strings, sheaths, supporters, loincloths, or aprons worn by primitive peoples are for protecting rather than hiding the sex organs (Figure 1.17). People who live in exposed areas need protection from physical hazards such as thorns, underbrush, and the sun. Certainly the conspicuously decorative coverings— gourds, beads, shells, paint, palm leaves—do not divert attention from, but rather direct the attention to these parts. Physical protection, and not only from the climate, is certainly a motivating factor for many clothing items today—hiking boots, chemistry lab coats, face masks, coveralls, space suits, protective goggles, and sunglasses (Figure 1.18).

In many instances, clothing has been used in a minimal way to adapt to the

[17]A Freudian analysis of the use of clothing to attract attention is presented by E. Harms in "The Psychology of Clothes," *American Journal of Sociology*, 44 (1938), p. 243.

[18]Lawrence Langner, *The Importance of Wearing Clothes* (New York: Hastings House, 1959), p. 21.

Figure 1.17 Loin cloths are used to protect the sexual organs, not to hide them.

environment. Numerous people today live in extremely cold sections of the world and require little in the way of clothing. The Patagonians in the southern part of South America use only a small square of animal skin draped over the shoulder. This patch of material is shifted from side to side, depending on wind direction. The Onas

Figure 1.18 Modern protective garments for steel workers.

and Yahgans on the islands of Tierra del Fuego, off the southern tip of South America, wear only a loose fur cape and a smear of grease. When the scientist Charles Darwin visited Tierra del Fuego, he watched the snow melt on the natives' skins and offered a sizable piece of cloth to a Fuegian for protection. Instead of using it to cover his body, the native tore it into strips and gave each of his tribesmen a piece for decoration.[19] In another part of the world, African safari porters wear all the clothes they own during the heat of the day so they have nothing extra to carry. They then sleep naked through the cold desert night.

One might also argue that women's sheer hosiery does little to warm the legs in winter and that the collars of men's shirts contribute little to comfort in summer. Many articles of dress in civilized society not only lack a protective function, but they actually defy it. Even though clothing is used for various kinds of physical protection, people are willing to endure a certain degree of discomfort when fashion demands it. People may have realized belatedly that clothes provide comfort in cold weather and that by covering the body they could remain active when other animals were forced to seek shelter, but it is unlikely that people first dressed for this reason.

Clothing is also used for protection from dangers that are primarily psychological in nature. Many items that fall into this category have become part of the folkways and customs of a society, their origins and meanings often lost in history. The bride who wears something borrowed or something blue at her wedding and even the

[19]Hiler, *From Nudity to Raiment* (W. & G. Foyle, Ltd., London, 1929), p. 64.

woman who wears a hat in church show examples of clothing symbolism associated with magical or spiritual powers. Mystical or magical meaning is often assigned to such ordinary articles as a rabbit's foot, a coin, a seashell, or even a lucky sweater.

Psychological protection of the genital area is as important in primitive societies as is physical protection. The sex organs, the seat of fertility and reproduction, need protection from the evil eye and must be covered. Although we tend to think that the use of clothing to please spirits is practiced only in primitive societies, many people today have a "lucky garment" to which they resort in times of crisis.

Psychological fears may also relate to real or imaginary moral danger. Some psychologists in the past believed that all feminine attire was the result of a man's unconscious fears of a woman's body and the equally hidden fantasies connected with it. Bergler suggested that men tend to cover their fears with moralistic standards of decency and that clothing becomes an outward sign of such fears.[20] Although the latter theory as yet has little evidence to support it, neither can it be disproved. The fear of possible rejection or ridicule if we reveal ourselves as we really are is a potential threat to our psychological security and one from which our clothing may protect us.

The use of clothing for protection has many modifications and varies extremely among the peoples of the world. Protection against the elements and against physical hazards, as well as protection against enemies real and supernatural, are important all over the world and at all levels of

development. However, it is unlikely that protection was either an original or a primary reason for the first use of clothing.

The Adornment or Decoration Theory

The most widely accepted theory used to explain the original purpose of clothing relates to adornment or decoration, the creative urge for an artistic experience. To adorn means to "make attractive" or to "lend beauty" and in the case of clothing, the object of adornment becomes the self. Adornment includes anything worn above and beyond purely physical needs. Those who accept this theory believe that all people have an urge to express themselves creatively and this urge to improve the appearance is universal. It is a fact that there are no peoples known to us, past or present, who do not adorn their bodies in some fashion.

The idea that the need to adorn is an important part of human activity is supported by the observation that even apes attempt to decorate themselves with bits of string or cloth. Experiments at the London Zoo have shown that apes like bright objects and they seem to have some color awareness and color preferences as well. It appears that the color is worn by the male for the female to appreciate.

It is probable that various forms of adornment, such as body painting, tattooing, scarification, mutilation, and deformation, preceded the actual wearing of clothes. Many of these practices are still found in primitive societies, or in modified form in our own, but all such forms of decoration, including clothing, have in common a desire for admiration, a striving

[20] For a psychoanalytic approach to the theories of clothing behavior, see Edmund Bergler, *Fashion and the Unconscious* (New York: Robert Brunner, 1953).

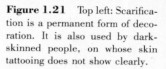

Figure 1.19 Left: Body painting is a form of adornment.

Figure 1.20 Right: The ears of this Masai girl are pierced with wire and sinew rings strung with beads.

Figure 1.21 Top left: Scarification is a permanent form of decoration. It is also used by dark-skinned people, on whose skin tattooing does not show clearly.

Figure 1.22 Top right: Body deformation is an indication of status in many cultures.

Figure 1.23 Right: Shaving is as much a modification of body appearance as many other practices.

to make the body more beautiful than nature made it (as beauty is conceived in a particular cultural setting) (Figures 1.19, 1.20, 1.21, 1.22, 1.23.). There are few people who do not decorate or mold the body in some way in order to appear more beautiful, and many will submit to extreme pain to do so. The use of lipstick and eyeshadow falls in the same category, and the modern American woman may still pierce her ears, pluck her eyebrows, shave her legs, or undergo plastic surgery.

The desire for beauty is consciously recognized by most people; it is accepted so generally that there has been little systematic research that attempts to establish the relative importance assigned by individuals to the aesthetic values in dress. However, in the study by Barr cited earlier, the desire to be beautiful was found to be one of the most common attitudes in individual and group motivation; subjects attached relatively high value to the aesthetic factors in clothing selection. Lapitsky's work also indicates that aesthetic values in clothing are extremely significant among adult women.[21] Consumer prefer-

ence studies give further indication that a nice appearance in dress is often rated higher than such factors as price and durability in making clothing decisions. As long ago as the 1940s appearance was found to be one of the most important criteria considered by men in the selection and purchase of shirts and other articles.[22] As the environment becomes more controlled and our clothing easier to care for, the functional nature of clothing becomes even less important. Men have become fashion conscious and place high value on their appearance. Recent evidence indicates that style and fashion have become important reasons for men's buying motivations.

[21]Mary Lapitsky, "Clothing Values and Their Relation to General Values and to Social Security and Insecurity." Ph.D. diss., Pennsylvania State University, 1961.

[22]*Men's Preferences Among Selected Clothing Items*, Miscellaneous Publication, no. 706, U.S. Department of Agriculture, Washington, D.C., 1949.

At this point it is convenient to divide the discussion of clothing used for adornment or decoration into several categories. These subgroups are sometimes considered as separate theories but here they will be considered subdivisions of the adornment theory since all have decoration or ornamentation of the human body as their primary purpose.

Figure 1.24 The trimming and arranging of hair is one of the most basic status representations in all cultures of the world.

Sexual Attraction

All peoples decorate or alter the human form in some way to attract the attention of the opposite sex. However, what is considered beautiful and what is sexually attractive are not the same for all people. Members of each society have standards that are used mutually to evaluate one another and these standards vary. Every society has its own concepts of physical attractiveness—its own ideals of beauty. In some tribes in Africa, for example, a woman's beauty is evaluated by how fat she is. A girl who wishes to make herself attractive to the young men of the tribe goes to the fattening house and gorges herself for weeks. When she waddles out, she is considered beautiful and a desirable matrimonial "catch." Such a standard of beauty seems strange to us because Americans encourage girls to stay thin and to diet if they put on the least amount of weight. American counterparts to the African fattening houses are exactly the opposite— rest resorts or "milk farms" where the wealthy are massaged and starved into shape and local health spas or exercise clubs for those who cannot afford the exotic resorts. From the viewpoint of this African tribe, however, American women are emaciated; the American concept of dieting is unbelievable. Why should women in the richest country in the world voluntarily starve themselves?

In another African tribe, the ideal wife is shiny. So the women use melted butter. Zulu women use hippopotamus fat to get just the right degree of shine that is considered beautiful and sexually attractive. Fattening and greasing are relatively harmless, even if repulsive to us. But what some other peoples do in the name of beauty may seem not only peculiar but outrageous and unlawful as well—lip-stretching, foot-binding, tattooing, head-shaping, scarification, and nose-piercing. But consider what we do in the name of beauty: bathing, anointing, and coloring the skin; cutting, shaving, plucking, braiding, waving, and coloring the hair; deodorizing and scenting the body; coloring or marking the lips, hands, nails, eyes, and face; and molding various body parts with girdles, corsets, bras, and pointed shoes (Figures 1.23 and 1.24).

Clothes have still another important role in regard to sex and sexual attractiveness, perhaps as sexual attractiveness in reverse. Clothes serve as a regulating mechanism. The ambivalence of clothes, for instance, work clothes versus party-leisure clothes, serves as a way to tell when sex interest should be active or inactive. Because of the type of clothes worn men and women can work side by side without becoming sexually aroused; dress clothes "at their best . . . supply a discrete invitation to indiscretion. At their worst, they represent a vulgar display of her [sic] wares like an overcrowded shop window."[23] According to Langner, clothes and their sexual attractiveness are important in preserving marriage, home, and family. Clothes assist women in their efforts to capture and hold the men of their choice. "A wife must be able to defend herself against the use of attractive clothes by the seductress who wears her finery to aid her in breaking up another's home." Langner tells women never to hesitate to buy new clothes if they feel their homes are being threatened by other women. And furthermore, he says, "make your husband pay for them for you are on the side of the angels."[24]

Trophyism

This form of decoration is used to show off the wearer's strength, courage, or skill. When the hunter kills his prey he often wears the skin, antlers, teeth, or claws in order to demonstrate to his people what a mighty hunter he is. A bear-claw necklace means many kills. And for the Peruvian Indian, the many toucan feathers in his earrings and headband mark him as a good marriage prospect because of his skill as a hunter. We may be tempted to think that trophyism occurs only among primitive peoples, but bearskin rugs and stuffed animal heads attest to the fact that the need to show off is found in all societies. We can also place in this same category the war medals that say, "see how brave I am," or a Phi Beta Kappa or other honor society key

that says "see how smart I am." The path from Cub to Eagle Scout (Figure 1.25) is marked by a succession of trophies in the form of merit badges. These trophies are proudly worn on the Boy Scout uniform until they are too numerous. They then are just as proudly displayed on a sash worn over the uniform.

Trophyism may also be seen in the *Oizuru* jacket worn by Japanese religious pilgrims. At each shrine visited the jacket is carefully stamped with the shrine's seal; the object is to collect as many seals as possible during one's lifetime. A similar display used to be seen on the luggage of world travelers, in the array of stickers pasted on by steamship companies, resorts, customs officers, and so on. In the 1960s and 1970s, trophyism appeared in the form of tailgate window and bumper stickers on cars and on message T-shirts.

Terrorism

As a form of decoration, terrorism refers to wearing an article of clothing or decoration to strike fear into the hearts of one's

Figure 1.25 War medals and merit badges are contemporary examples of trophyism.

[23]Langner, *The Importance of Wearing Clothes*, p. 46.
[24]Ibid., p. 47.

enemies. Many such items are of a religious or a magical nature; war paint, face masks, and religious medals might be included in this category.

Totemism

Closely related to terrorism, this form of decoration uses totems or amulets of a magical or religious nature to ward off evil or bring good luck and protection to the wearer. The difference between a totem and an amulet is slight. The power or mystical qualities of a totem remain with it regardless of ownership. Thus, a totem can be bought and sold, traded, or otherwise passed around without losing its power. An amulet, on the other hand, has magic only for the intended owner. It cannot be given away. If given to someone else or found by someone else, it loses all its force. A stone that is lucky for one person becomes merely a pebble if picked up by someone else. A lucky sweater or a dress that always brings luck when taking an exam would be an amulet, its power reserved only for the wearer.

Many primitive peoples have deep-seated beliefs in totems and amulets. Among the American Indians, most notable are the elaborate totem poles of the Pacific Northwest. The Eskimo people are great believers in amulets. They may wear amulets strung around their necks or wrists, but most commonly they sew them to their clothing, particularly their undergarments. In some cases the symbolism of the amulet is obvious; owl claws ensure that the owner will have strong hands. In other cases, the meaning is more obscure, but to the wearer just as important.[25]

[25]For additional information on such uses of clothing, see Hiler, *From Nudity to Raiment*.

Identification

It is conceivable that clothing could be designed so that it would (1) provide a modest body covering, (2) accentuate and not obscure the body's physical attractions, (3) protect the body against the elements and potential mystical beings, and (4) be aesthetically satisfying to wearer and beholder. And yet this clothing could still not be completely acceptable to the majority of people in the society. Another important decorative function of clothing is that it serves to identify and distinguish people in many ways. The symbolization of clothing can indicate the wearer's status, occupation, religion, and group memberships both formal and informal. We shall consider each of these forms of identification in turn.

Status Clothes are used to identify the economic, social, and prestige layers of a society. Status symbols are used in subtle ways to establish position. The earliest status symbols may be noted in Paleolithic times, when hunters adorned themselves with antlers or skins of animals as badges of achievement. The leader of any sect or tribe usually was accorded some mark of distinction in dress to signify position, and a complex set of status differentiations evolved from these beginnings. Some status symbols are easily seen—the crowns of kings and queens and the robes that distinguish the Pope, cardinals, bishops, and other officials in the religious hierarchy. Other obvious examples are academic gowns that mark one's degree of scholastic attainment; military uniforms; and the uniforms worn by the police officer, the nun, the jurist, the nurse, the pilot, the cook, and the firefighter.

Other forms of clothing status symbols are even more subtle. Thorstein Veblen was one of the first to subscribe to the status theory for explaining dress. He was a sociologist and economist whose most famous work, *The Theory of the Leisure Class*, was published in 1899. His theory of economic consumption was based on the idea that people choose their clothing primarily to indicate their status to others. To Veblen, dress and fashion demonstrated both conspicuously and vicariously that the wearer not only had wealth and could display it, but also that he or she was a member of the leisure class, and did not have to engage in menial labor. Tight-fitting corsets, high-heeled shoes, long, full gowns, bound feet, and hobble skirts were all offered as examples that tell the world that this person did not need to work. Jewels and furs, while not prohibiting work, demonstrated wealth. As Veblen saw it,

our dress, in order to serve its purpose effectually, should not only be expensive, but it should also make plain to all observers that the wearer is not engaged in any kind of productive labour. . . . The pleasing effect of neat and spotless garments is chiefly, if not altogether, due to their carrying the suggestion of leisure—exemption from personal contact with industrial processes of any kind. Much of the charm that invests the patent-leather shoe, the stainless linen, the lustrous cylindrical hat, and the walking stick, which so greatly enhance the native dignity of a gentleman, comes of their pointedly suggesting that the wearer cannot when so attired bear a hand in any employment that is directly and immediately of any human use. Elegant dress serves its purpose of elegance not only in that it is expensive, but also because it is the insignia of leisure.[26]

Although much of what Veblen said is outdated today, he wrote about his world, that of the late nineteenth century. He was one of the first to write about dress and the first to see that motivations are not always what they seem on the surface. He did not agree with the common causes and reasonings of his day and he encouraged people to look deeper for underlying motives to explain clothing behavior. Modern writers have attacked Veblen's ideas on the grounds that our improved standard of living rules out such class distinctions by making leisure and patent-leather shoes available to everyone. Nevertheless, the elements of conspicuous consumption, leisure, and waste are easily seen in contemporary clothing. The practice of displaying one's wealth through clothes is probably as significant today as it was at the dawn of history.

Any article or costume that will gain a feeling of recognition, approval, or belonging for the wearer may be considered an example of the search for status. Evidence in support of status-seeking as a major force in clothing behavior is furnished by a number of research studies. Evans's investigation of motives in the clothing behavior of adolescents revealed that in 50 percent of the cases the desire to wear clothing that would win recognition from others was the most intense desire determining the clothing wearing behavior of both boys and girls.[27] Reasons given most often for the importance of being well dressed in Ryan's study of college women related to the social contribution made by clothing. The responses included statements such as "it creates a better impression on people,"

[26]Thorstein Veblen, *The Theory of the Leisure Class* (1899; reprint ed., New York: Modern Library, 1931), pp. 170–171.

[27]S. E. Evans, "Motivations Underlying Clothing Selection and Wearing," *Journal of Home Economics*, 56 (1964), 743.

"popularity has much to do with one's appearance," "to get anywhere we have to impress others," and "people judge others by what they wear."[28]

Today, mass communication media and mass production have had a leveling effect on clothing and the trend is toward narrowing the gap between how the rich and poor dress still further. Michael Harrington, in his book *The Other America*, says that we have the best-dressed poverty in the world: "It is much easier in the United States to be decently dressed than it is to be decently housed, fed, or doctored."[29] He adds that American cities have people with shoes and even stylish clothing, who are hungry. However, subtle status differences remain for the trained eye to see. Just as the make of car one drives is more important when everyone has a car, so too, the tailoring and fabric of a sport jacket are more important in a society in which everyone has at least one sport jacket. No amount of mass production has completely eliminated the status symbols like a mink coat or Brooks Brothers suit. Status will be discussed further in Chapters 7 and 8, which deal with clothing symbolism, role, and status.

Rank is another form of status that requires clothing for differentiation, as in protective agencies, occupational groups, and the military. Langner asserts that governments would never have been established if it were not for clothing. Complex systems that make governments possible are based on domination of the masses by those in power. Not only is there need for

clothing to indicate the superiority of these leaders, but without clothing in the form of uniforms, there would be no way to demonstrate the authority of the army, the navy, and the police force. This premise can be applied to all forms of government—monarchy, dictatorship, and democracy. Without uniforms to distinguish friend from foe it would also be impossible to wage war. "A disarmament conference which resulted in a general agreement among the nations to prohibit the use of soldiers' uniforms as contrary to international law might possibly bring the world closer to universal peace than any other measure."[30]

Occupation Nurses, police officers, and flight attendants are readily distinguished from the people they serve by the uniforms they wear (Figure 1.26). Sometimes these uniforms are fairly standardized. Even though the details differ, a police officer's uniform is generally recognized throughout the civilized world. So, too, the nurse's apparel may differ minutely, perhaps in the cap, or even in the color, but it remains similar enough to be easily identifiable.

In the last decade a new category of work clothes has appeared: career apparel. Designed to give a corporate fashion look, this type of clothing is supposed to provide a sense of professionalism and company loyalty to the employees as well as identify them to the public (Figure 1.27). Where a uniform is not worn, differences in dress still distinguish many occupations. Some retail stores still require, if not a uniform, dark skirts or pants and white blouses or shirts, or even suits and ties. Teachers are readily distinguishable from their students, in part because of their clothing.

[28]Mary S. Ryan, *Psychological Effects of Clothing, Part I*, Cornell University Agricultural Experiment Station Bulletin 882, 1952, p. 24.

[29]Michael Harrington, *The Other America* (New York: Penguin Books, Inc., 1972), p. 5.

[30]Langner, *The Importance of Wearing Clothes*, pp. 127–131.

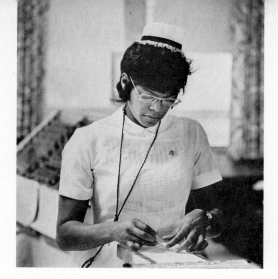

Figure 1.26 Uniforms identify many occupational groups; airline personnel, nurses, police.

Figure 1.27 Career apparel provides a fashionable corporate look.

In several religious groups within the larger American society all the faithful subscribed to minutely detailed styles of dress, strictly enforced by self-imposed sanctions. The Hasidic community, a group of orthodox Jews from Eastern Europe who live in the Williamsburg section of New York City, are set apart from their neighbors by their traditional clothing. Their double-breasted dark suits and long black overcoats button from right to left. Their black, large-brimmed beaver hats are worn over long hair, side locks, and unshaven faces.

The Amish dress in surprisingly similar fashion but their clothing has no buttons at all. Buttons represent the military, which they oppose, so they use hooks and eyes to fasten all their outer garments. Dress is closely prescribed by the laws of the church, a mixture of traditional and Biblical interpretations. Their clothing not only identifies them to others, but contributes to group solidarity and intentional isolation from the rest of the world. To outsiders the clothing may seem monotonous and merely identifies them as Amish. Within their social structure, something as simple as the width and shape of a hat brim may indicate an individual's age, marital status, and position in the community.

Religion Still another form of identification is that used by many religious groups. Clerical collars and Buddhists' robes distinguish the wearers from the general population and also identify them to their followers. By way of example, within the Catholic Church, the clothing worn by many nuns identifies them to all as members of the Church, and specific details of the habit allow further identification of the order by those who know the differences.

Group Membership Clothing is used to identify one's affiliation with formal and informal groups. Uniforms of Boy Scouts, Girl Scouts, Campfire Girls, and Shriners fall into this category. In informal group membership, clothing becomes a part of the identification process. This type of clothing behavior is perhaps most typical of boys and girls of junior high school and early high school age. Much of the fad behavior of these years distinguishes groups within the school community. We will consider this type of behavior in clothing in Chapter 9.

Extension of the Self

Whenever an object is brought into contact with the body, the conscious existence of the self is extended into the extremities of the object, thereby giving the individual an increased sense of size, power, movement, rigidity—whatever the characteristic of the object may be. Thus, in the 1890s the wearer of the corset took on the straight-laced qualities of the garment, and the high-boned collar helped Victorians maintain their stiff-necked pose of reserve and decorum. During the Middle Ages the knight assumed the steel-plated strength of armor. The graceful movement of floating chiffon gives the dancer more mobility. This sense of increased motion and rhythm increases when the garment is trimmed with fluttering ribbons, tassels, or flounces. The individual is taller in a high hat, more forceful in striking colors, less sophisticated in coarse fabric. Theater costumes are often designed to create the feelings of body extension for the performer and to project an image to the audience.

This concept of clothing as an extension of self has often been considered separately from adornment since its purpose is not necessarily to beautify the body. For the sake of simplicity it is included here as part of the adornment theory, since clothing items in this category are most often decorative. The extension of self through the use of clothing reinforces the attitude or the emotion the individual would like us to feel.

Research has shown that individuals vary in the degree to which they extend their self-feelings beyond the boundaries of their bodies.[31] Compton's work was done with psychotic patients, but her findings suggest that clothing does indeed function in strengthening or weakening body-image boundaries.[32] Unlike status, which is derived entirely from the social situation, extension of the self is determined primarily within the individual. This aspect of motivation in dress will be covered more extensively in Chapter 6.

SUMMARY

The Functions of Clothing

Four major theories have been developed in the attempt to determine why people first began to wear clothing. Although a popular belief is that modesty is the fundamental basis for all clothing, many writers believe that modesty is the result of clothing, not the cause of it. A second theory holds that covering the body often serves to call attention to it, thus increasing the element of sexual

[31]S. Fisher and S. Cleveland, "Body-Image Boundaries and Style of Life," *Journal of Abnormal and Social Psychology*, 52 (1956), 373–379.

[32]Norma H. Compton, "Body-Image Boundaries in Relation to Clothing Fabric and Design Preferences of a Group of Hospitalized Psychotic Women," *Journal of Home Economics*, 56 (1964), 40–45.

attraction. A third theory concerns the protection and utility clothing may provide. Here clothing is seen as a buffer between people and their environment, shielding them from harmful elements, both physical and psychological. A fourth theory involves the ornamental values of clothing, which provide aesthetic experiences and sensuous satisfactions in the individual's search for beauty.

This last theory, called the adornment theory, includes all the many aesthetic uses of clothing. In this viewpoint, clothing is used as a sexual lure as well as an indicator of bravery and skill. It indicates one's status in society and obtains for the wearer the rewards of recognition, approval, or identification. By means of clothing, individuals are identified also as members of groups, both formal and informal. And as an extension of the self, clothing provides an expansiveness to the wearer's attitudes and emotions. This theory probably explains the original and the most important function of clothing.

This functional analysis of clothing is not intended to be oversimplified by presenting purposes in order. Dress is a product of a complex set of motives, all of which are interdependent and arise out of varied physical, psychological, and social conditions. The factor of adornment alone may have many modifications. Striving for beauty may be motivated by a desire to be sexually attractive or by a need for status. Sexual attractiveness and status, therefore, become the causative factors and adornment simply the manifestation. It is obvious, then, that even if there is a primary or an original function that may be used to explain the wearing of clothes, other contributory reasons must be included. Seldom is an individual clad and adorned in such a way that all items utilized serve a single purpose. Thus an integration of many theories is necessary in order to explain adequately the function of dress.

FOR FURTHER READING

Flugel, J. C. *The Psychology of Clothes*. 1930. Reprint. London: The Hogarth Press Ltd., 1966. Chapters I–V.

Garland, Madge. *The Changing Form of Fashion*. New York: Praeger Publishers, 1970. Chapter 2.

Gurel, Lois M. "The Origins of Dress" and "The Functions of Dress." In *Dimensions of Dress and Adornment: A Book of Readings*, 3rd ed. edited by L. M. Gurel and M. S. Beeson, pp. 2–3, 3–7. Dubuque: Kendall/Hunt Publishing Co., 1979.

Kemper, Rachel H. *Costume*. New York: Newsweek Books, 1977. Chapter 1.

Langner, Lawrence. *The Importance of Wearing Clothes*. New York: Hastings House Publishers, 1959. Parts I and II.

Laver, James. *Modesty in Dress: An Inquiry into the Fundamentals of Fashion*. Boston: Houghton Mifflin, 1969.

Morris, Desmond. *Manwatching: A Field Guide to Human Behavior*, pp. 213–220, 222–229. New York: Harry N. Abrams, Inc., 1977.

Chapter 2

PATTERNS OF CULTURE

All human behavior stems from three basic sources: first, actions may result from *instinct*, appearing automatically without prior opportunity for learning; second, responses may develop through *trial and error*, a process that varies with individual experiences; and third, behavior may be *learned from other individuals*, either through imitation or direct instruction. The last, by and large, accounts for the distinction between human and animal behavior. This ability to transmit learned and adapted behavior from one generation to another gives humans an overwhelming advantage in the struggle for existence. Such learned behavior constitutes culture, or social heredity. In his now-classic definition of culture Tylor included all the abilities and habits that people acquire throughout their lives. He believed that it was the whole complex of knowledge, beliefs, morals, laws, customs, and folkways that make up society.[1] Without this accumulation and transmission of ideas and skills, the human race would never have progressed beyond the achievements of the Old Stone Age.

CHARACTERISTICS OF CULTURE

In the last chapter the origins and functions of clothing were explored. Even without definitive answers to the questions raised about the early reasons for first donning clothes, the question that logically follows is: Why do people wear certain kinds of clothes? Even more specific: Why do

[1]E. B. Tylor, *Primitive Culture* (London: John Murray Publishers, 1891).

people in different parts of the world dress differently? In this chapter we will consider these topics.

The primary influence on the type of clothing worn is cultural. The societal group to which people belong largely determines the overall clothing practices they follow. Although there is some cultural breakdown and spread due to the influence of the mass communication media and modern transportation, cultural patterns pertaining to dress are still firmly set in much of the world. In the United States, male attire is considered to be shirt and pants, no matter how varied. In the Sahara the *burnoose* is still worn, as is the *shalivar* and *kmeez* in Pakistan and the *sari* in India. Eskimo parkas may no longer be made only from caribou skins, but the parka is still the predominant form of dress for these northern peoples.

What is culture? What are some of its common characteristics? What are some of the reasons for differences between cultures? What are the effects of culture on clothing? First of all, by culture we do not refer to a common use of the word as applied to those skilled in the arts and certain social graces. Culture, as used by social scientists, refers to the beliefs and customs of all people, educated and uneducated. It is the complex whole that includes all we learn from others, the whole body of learned behavior passed from generation to generation, all the traditions that make up the background of a group of people.

The following six characteristics of culture are those commonalities that help to define it. Culture is *transmitable* and *transmutable*. It is *shared, learned, communicated*, and it is *cumulative*.

The elements that make up a particular culture are transmitted, that is, passed down from one generation to the next. Traditional dress of folk societies are examples of the transmission of clothing customs to succeeding generations. The Scottish tartan is another example of a form of dress that is transmitted, intact, from one generation to another. At the same time that culture is transmitted it is often transmuted, that is, changed or altered in the process. Such changes may be as subtle as the style variations of the traditional white wedding dress of Western societies. Or the changes can be more extreme, as shown in the drastic transmutations that have taken place in infants' and children's clothing in recent years. Babies still wear diapers, but the difference between the traditional birdseye and Curity diapers of the predisposable days and the Pampers that keep baby dry today are very great.

Culture is, above all else, learned. It is not biologically inherited. Cultural patterns are learned at first from parents, siblings, and other family members, then from playmates and working companions. People learn about their culture, copying and adapting, from books, newspapers, television, and other communication media. This learning may take place informally through observation and subtle direction or formally and purposefully through direct instruction. In fact, a guiding principle behind a free public school system is to see that each succeeding generation learns the culture, generally the dominant one. Our knowledge of proscribed and prescribed dress as well as of proper clothing for specific occasions and situations is acquired through the learning process.

Culture is communicated by language, written and oral, and by nonverbal and symbolic behavior. Culture is shared. The behaviors that may be personal idiosyncrasies or individual habits do not become part of a culture. The fact that one individual or even several individuals decide independently to tie their hair back in hot weather does not make this type of hair arrangement part of the culture. When it is shared with a wide segment of society it becomes part of the folkways of society and can even be named—the ponytail. Perhaps an even better example of something that probably started as an individual (or small group) action and soon became a cultural norm is the message T-shirt, now a relatively permanent part of at least Western attire.

At the same time that cultural patterns are transmitted and transmuted to future generations, they are constantly being added to. Culture is dynamic, never static, always changing. Although most fads and fashions fade into oblivion after a short life, many remain and are added to the general fund for transmission. The sport shirt and turtleneck, fad items for the man in the 1940s, have become classics and an integral part of the male wardrobe. As such, they can be classified as additions to the traditional cultural patterns of dress.

"A culture is a particular way of life of a people. These 'ways' cannot be seen directly, but they are expressed by behavior and, of course, by the product of some of that behavior, material things."[2] Clothing, one category of these material things that may be observed, is a tool or key used by those attempting to understand other cultures as well as their own. It is useful because it is obvious, all people use it in some form,

and it has been found in tombs, temples, and burial sites of peoples from the past, either as actual remains or shown on walls in paintings and in statuary.

● The primary influence on the type of clothing worn by individuals within a society is cultural. Culture is not biologically inherited. Culture is transmitted, transmuted, shared, learned, communicated, and cumulative.

Our mode or manner of dress is a part of our social inheritance. The clothes we wear are derived partly from the past and partly from new developments that appear in our own lifetimes. The evolution of certain forms of dress as the characteristic style of an era in Western civilization as a whole is the same evolutionary process that establishes the customs of dress for different tribal, geographical, social, and age groups within that civilization. Clothing is an excellent example of the basic forms that occur within the context of particular technical, economic, moral, and aesthetic backgrounds. Although the variety of differences in dress are as numerous as there are cultures to interpret them, some factors appear to be common to all clothing and adornment, both cross-culturally and historically, over the vast span of time in which the arts of dress have developed.

Our purpose here is to examine the patterns of universality and diversity in dress by means of a limited cross-cultural comparison. In cultural terms the word *pattern* is used to describe certain aspects of behavior that are consistent, orderly, or repetitive (as opposed to those that are random). In making such a comparison, we will find some common patterns of response in clothing that evolve in association with a

[2]Rachel Reese Sady, *Perspectives from Anthropology* (New York: Teachers College Press, 1970), p. 10.

given set of social and ecological circumstances. These common patterns are called **universalities.** As each society builds its culture, however, it makes a limited selection of patterns from all those that are available, and it rejects or ignores the others. This unique selection of patterns makes every culture different in some respect from every other culture. A few such variations or **diversities** are described in the second section of this chapter.

Recognizing some of the commonalities or universalities in the uses and meanings of clothing makes it easier to understand at least a part of the orderliness and predictability of human action. At the same time, an analysis of cultural diversity helps us see beyond the confines of our own habits and customs. Because our cultural conventions are so much a part of our own existence, we scarcely ever question their logic or rationality; they are "right" simply because they are familiar to us. If, on the other hand, we know that on entering a

place of worship the Jew puts on a hat, the Christian takes one off, while the Moslem removes shoes, it becomes clear that one ritual of dress is no more "right" than the others, except within its own cultural setting.

This attitude is particularly prevalent in our views of primitive societies or folk cultures. We tend to place value judgments on the behavior of these people, to assess the acts of those who differ from us with an ethnocentric, twentieth-century, Western civilization attitude. **Ethnocentrism** is an emotional response to those who differ; it assumes the superiority of one's own race or culture. We must look at other civilizations, other cultures, other social organizations without prejudice in order to be more accepting of those in the world with whom we need not necessarily agree, not necessarily like, but with whom we must coexist. An acquaintance with other conventions should diminish ethnocentrism and lead toward a more rational understanding of clothing behavior.

SUMMARY

Characteristics of Culture

The society or culture that people live in is the primary determinant of the type of clothes they wear. This culture makes up the social order and is a composite of the beliefs and customs of all peoples in the society. Patterns of culture appear that make each society somewhat different from every other. Still, there are similar patterns common to many peoples living in different parts of the world. These universalities and diversities can be used to study the clothing of a people and its importance to them.

Clothing specialists, teachers, and researchers study other civilizations, past and present, without personal value judgments. An ethnocentric approach to a study of clothing results in bias and prejudiced viewpoints. Such an approach hampers a true understanding of people who may be different.

UNIVERSALITIES IN DRESS

Although the origins of dress and adornment remain obscure, several plausible theories may be used to explain the universal functions of clothing. As we saw in the last chapter, the earliest garments may have developed from the need for protection from intense cold. The protection theory is still obviously important in explaining dress today. However, as soon as physical needs are provided for, any further creation or accumulation of items can serve only to gain greater prestige for the owner. A rich man may be able to wear more jewelry or clothing of finer quality, but the functional aspects of dress are the same for rich and poor alike. Natural acquisitive tendencies can be seen in the inclination to accumulate personal property, and, because clothing is portable, it is highly probable that such items were one of the earliest indexes of wealth. The form clothing takes, however, is influenced by the physical environment, the available resources, and the technical skill in utilizing those resources.

Many diverse ways have been found to fabricate and design clothing, and yet from the technical standpoint only three basic patterns of dress have evolved: the **tailored garment**, the **draped garment**, and a **composite type**, which combines some of the characteristics of the other two.

The Tailored Garment

Concern and interest in personal appearance and comfort can be traced back as far as the Old Stone Age. Since the Neanderthals lived in and survived the years of glacial cold, it is logical to assume that they must have had some form of protective covering. In the earliest stages, the animal skin was probably tied crudely about the waist and neck with sinew thongs, but people soon realized that the warmth and comfort of garments could be improved by shaping the skins to conform more closely to the body. Evidence from the later Paleolithic periods shows that people had learned how to cut the large skins into body-conforming shapes. At first, sewing awls, sharp pointed instruments made of bone or stone, were used to punch holes along the edges of the skins so that they could be laced together with thongs. Later, skins were joined by sewing with needle and thread. The invention of the eyed needle was a product of the Magdalenian people who inhabited Europe from about 14000 to 8000 B.C. This simple yet brilliant device pierced the leather with its point and drew the binding thread through the hole all in one operation. Judging from the fineness of the needles found in the caves, we can assume that they were used for decorative stitching as well as for sewing costume pieces together. In addition to the needles, other bone artifacts, such as buttons and toggles used to fasten the clothing, have been discovered. Thus we see the evolution of the first tailor-made garment, cut from animal skins, shaped to fit the human body, and sewn together with needle and thread.

The best examples of tailored garments, even today, are those of the northern Eskimo tribes (Figure 2.1). Eskimo women are probably the best tailors in the world and their winter garments the warmest and most waterproof of any known. In fact, women who lack the skills necessary to keep their families warm and dry through the long Arctic winter may be discarded,

Figure 2.1   The best example of tailored garments are those of the Eskimo people.

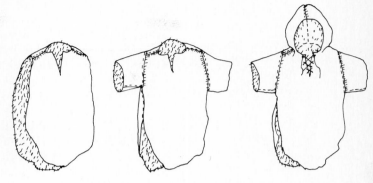

Figure 2.2   The evolution of tailored garments from the two-skinned poncho of South Americans, to the skin shirt of the American Indians, to the Eskimos' parka.

since this alone is sufficient grounds for divorce in many Eskimo tribes. Their main garment, the parka, can be traced to similar primitive garments throughout the world. The South American poncho consists of two skins sewn together only at the shoulder, with an opening for the head and neck. If this two-skinned poncho is sewn up the sides and fitted with sleeves, it becomes the skin shirt of the American Indians; if it is then fitted with a hood, it is the Eskimo parka (Figures 2.2 and 2.3).

Tailored garments have not been highly esteemed throughout most of civilization. Such sophisticated societies as Greece and Rome got along quite well without them. In fact, they considered those who wore sewn and fitted garments barbarians. The insulating value of closely fitted garments was not easily understood and was not necessary in tropical or semitropical climates.

Tailored garments developed first in cold climates. They were cut and sewn to the shape of the body, thus creating clothing with greater insulating abilities. The invention of the sewing awl and the eyed needle was necessary for their development.

Figure 2.3   Tailored garments cut from the skins of animals are highly prized articles of clothing in the modern world.

The Draped Garment

Clothing of the ancient historic Mediterranean civilizations, such as the Egyptian, Greek, and Roman cultures, was not cut and fitted, but rather was draped from a continuous length of woven cloth. The weaving of fabric was an outgrowth of two earlier developments, the cultivation of plants and the domestication of animals, both of which had appeared during Neolithic times, around 7000–6000 B.C. People of the New Stone Age also had needles, but they seem to have used them largely to decorate cloth rather than to construct garments.

It might be interesting at this point to pause and speculate as to why so much time elapsed between the capability to produce woven fabric and the actual appearance of draped clothing, and why both appeared first in this particular part of the world. After all, tailored garments had been used since prehistoric times. Why not continue to cut and sew fabrics together to conform to the human body?

Several theories can be offered. Animal skins had to be sewn together to fit. They were irregular, and, at first, they were the only material available for clothing. When weaving was invented the first primitive looms were very narrow. They did, however, produce fabric with the equivalent of a selvage on all four sides that would not fray out as long as the piece was not cut. These first woven fabrics could be used as is for belts and decorative banding (Figure 2.4), but for clothing, the pieces had to be sewn together. To get fabrics wide enough to drape around the body, or even just to completely cover it, was extremely time-consuming. Also, since bands of fabric pieced together usually do not have the flexibility required for soft, comfortable garments, they have seldom been used for

this purpose. Major exceptions can be found among primitive societies, historically and in the present. Where there is no choice, where narrow looms and raw animal and vegetable fibers are all the technology has provided for fabric construction, fabric is made in narrow strips and sewn together for clothing. The Sherpas, goat herders of Tibet, weave wool cloth on their narrow 12-inch back-strap looms (Figure 2.5). Although many of these looms are still used today for both decorative and utilitarian purposes, in modern societies they have become recreational items, and the products of these looms are considered handcrafted work.

The tool theory has been suggested as an explanation for the shift to draped garments at this time. As we shall see in the next chapter, the invention of a truly functional pair of scissors, capable of cutting fabric, had to wait until the fourteenth century. Fine needles also were not available during this period in history. The tools available to cut and sew skins (knives, scrapers, bone needles) were not suitable for cutting and sewing the exqui-

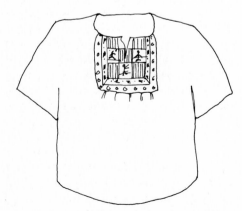

Figure 2.4 Narrow fabrics from early primitive looms were used for decorative bandings and trim, seldom for entire garments.

Figure 2.5 A narrow, 12-inch back strap loom.

sitely fine, sheer fabrics available. There have been other times in textile history when one part of the production process was not able to develop technology as fast as another part and so progress was slowed, at least temporarily.

Perhaps the most widely accepted explanation for development of draped garments in the Mediterranean civilizations refers to the mild climate there. Draped clothing was practical, and, if necessity is the mother of invention, then it may have been need that provided the push for development of wide looms. Contemporary civilizations in other places did wear cut and sewn clothing. The Medes and the Persians wore tailored coats with sleeves and pants. In fact, **bifurcated garments**, having two parts (in clothing, the term refers to pants), were worn by both sexes among the Germanic tribes who lived north of Rome.

The development of the wide, upright looms significantly advanced textile production. The speed with which fabrics could be produced was of primary importance. Not only was the weaving process itself faster, but the tedious task of sewing strips (or animal skins) together was no

longer necessary. Another important advantage of the wide looms was the variety of fabrics that could be produced. Most significant was the softer, more comfortable, and easier to manipulate cloth that was woven in one piece. This fabric made draping possible and practical.

The Egyptians, Romans, and Greeks were the first to produce fabric wide enough to cover the body. In fact, they considered the weaving and the production of a rectangle of fabric so important that they thought it wasted beautiful fabric to cut it into shapes and sew it together again. They were strongly disinclined to cut into loomed cloth, preferring instead to drape a rectangle of fabric around the body and hold it in place either by its own folds or by a band around the waist. In very warm climates, the fabric was often nothing more than a small loincloth, draped around the hips and tied with a cord or girdle. The modern hand-weaver hobbyist can attest to this reluctance to cut into a length of handwoven fabric. Many pieces are "shaped on the loom" or cut into very basic shapes with simple seaming to create an ethnic look reminiscent of the garments made from these early looms.

This preference can also be seen in some fabric designers' preference for simply cut, almost draped garments. Jack Lenor Larsen, noted American weaver and fabric designer, has created leisure-wear clothing (Figure 2.6) with absolute simplicity of design to show off fabrics. He "rejects the concept that a length of cloth must be cut into pieces before being assembled, fitted, and sewn together into a garment."[3] The clothes he designs are simple and require very little cutting and fitting.

[3]"Fashion with the Stress on Fabrics: Jack Lenor Larsen," *American Fabrics Magazine*, 53 (Summer 1961), 53–55.

Essentially, the *schenti* of the Egyptians, the *chiton* of the Greeks, the *toga* of the Romans, the *dhoti* and *sari* of the Indians, the *poncho* of the South Americans, and the *sarong* of the Malayans are all forms of the draped garment. Figures 2.7 and 2.8 show modern versions of the toga and draped, wrapped skirt still worn by males in different parts of the world. Various cultures throughout history have decorated their fabrics by using dyes or prints, embroideries, or intricate weaves. An infinite number of design effects have been achieved by varying the size and shape of the piece of cloth. However, in most draped garments (Figure 2.9), the arrangement of folds is of equal importance to the decorative quality of the fabric.

Draped garments, made from woven cloth that was never cut and seldom sewn, originated in farming cultures where the wide, upright looms had been invented.

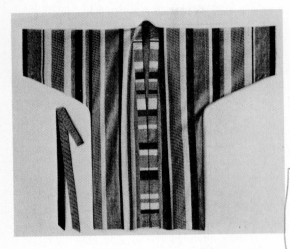

Figure 2.6 Simply cut, almost draped garment designed by Larsen is made of hand woven Mexican cotton.

Figure 2.7 A contemporary version of the draped garment: a decorative toga in Ghana.

Figure 2.8 A simply draped Indian skirt.

Figure 2.9 An Indian woman wears the draped *sari*, a long rectangle woven with decorative borders along each selvage and across the end.

The Composite Garment

Roughly 1,500 years after the dawn of civilization in the Middle East, sometime between 1500 and 1200 B.C.[4] the Shang people in the Orient developed a culture that was almost contemporary with and fully comparable to the great civilizations of Mesopotamia and Egypt. This culture provided the foundation for the civilizations that later evolved in China, Japan, and other Far Eastern regions. The Shang learned to cultivate the silkworm and wove its gossamer filaments into beautiful fabrics. The development of the traditional Oriental costume, the kimono, provided a way to display the intricately woven and patterned fabric. The kimono involves some sewing but very little cutting and no waste of fabric. Sewing was necessary because looms were narrow, 18 to 22 inches wide. This narrow fabric would not adequately cover the body and so the kimono style evolved. Although the kimono can be classified as tailored because it is cut and sewn, it also conveys the effects of a draped garment through its straight-hanging lines and loose sleeves. Although the ancient Chinese were a weaving people, their long contacts with the tailor-making, needle-users resulted in a costume with some of the characteristics of both cultures. The pieces of the garment, rather than conforming to the body shape, were nearly rectangular and usually were seamed on the straight grain of the cloth.

Whereas in many times and places the tailored or draped form of garment has been used exclusively, the composite garment (Figure 2.10) has always coexisted with other forms of dress. One might

Figures 2.10 (Top) Extant Bronze Age garments of the composite type. The material was woven of sheep's wool. (Bottom) The man's costume consisted of an undergarment that was wrapped around the body. The woman's dress was a waist-length, short-sleeved blouse with a slit at the neck for the head and a skirt that was draped around the lower part of the body.

[4]Charles O. Hucker, *China's Imperial Past* (Stanford, Calif.: Stanford University Press, 1975), p. 21.

speculate as to whether, combining both types as it does, the composite is the most effective compromise between efficiency and aesthetics. Light, airy, and free of form, like the draped garment, it is at the same time more economical in fabric use, a characteristic of the tailored dress. Composite clothing can utilize the inherent beauty of a fabric and require less of it.

At any rate, it has been the fashionable item of clothing during many periods of history. The beginning of the composite form of dress, at least in the Western world, occurred during the early medieval period in Europe. Clothing at that time had most of the characteristics of draped garments, but some sewing was done, primarily in the development of sleeves. Following the French Revolution and Napoleon's campaigns in Egypt, Greece, and Italy, a revival of all things classical became the fashion. In clothing, women's gowns were patterned after the Greek chiton. Although the effect was draped, it was not completely so. The needle arts that had developed during the Gothic and Renaissance periods were not forgotten and the "draped look" was achieved with some seaming.

In recent years fad items, such as the tent dress of the 1960s and the wraparound skirt of the 1970s, are modern examples of composite clothing. In other cultures, the *burnoose*, the *caftan*, and the *dashiki* are also created by draping cloth and using a minimum amount of stitching to hold shapes.

Modern clothing in the Western world is predominantly of the composite type, that is, cut from woven cloth and shaped and sewn to conform to the body contours (Figure 2.11). Modified versions of the draped garment can be seen, particularly in formal gowns, although they are rarely designed without seaming and stitching.

Figure 2.11   A modern-day garment of the composite type.

Tailored garments of fur are still worn, not just by Eskimos, but by other people who live in suitably cold climates and have money enough to buy them.

A composite type of clothing, resulting from the early contact of skin sewing and weaving cultures, is the predominant type in use today.

Cultural Diffusion

Although all the characteristics of culture in general can be seen as individual components or requirements necessary to formulate a description of what culture is, they do not operate in a vacuum. Within an isolated community or tribal group, interactions among group members may be only sharing. However, when we consider culture on a global basis this sharing is interrelated among many separate human groups. All societies share and borrow cultural elements and incorporate them into their own system. Thus civilization advances. "This transfer of cultural elements from society to society is known as *diffusion*."[5] Diffusion is a more pervasive idea and really integrates the other cultural characteristics. Therefore, diffusion is the process by which the peoples of the world can share and then improve on individual discoveries, inventions, and ideas. In fact, the more rapidly a society can borrow from other societies, the more rapidly culture is advanced.

Most of the inventions used by those in contact with other civilizations have been borrowed and no more than 10 percent of the items people make and the ideas, ideals, and values of a society are native to a particular cultural group. The following paragraphs illustrate these points. Considering the beginning of an average person's day, the following lists only points of origin and not regions of the world where most of these products are obtained on today's world market.

Our solid American citizen awakens in a bed built on a pattern which originated in the Near East but which was modified in Northern Europe before it was transmitted to America. He throws back covers made from cotton, domesticated in India, or linen, domesticated in the Near East, or wool from sheep, also domesticated in the Near East, or silk, the use of which was discovered in China. All of these materials have been spun and woven by processes invented in the Near East. He slips into his moccasins, invented by the Indians of the Eastern woodlands, and goes to the bathroom, whose fixtures are a mixture of European and American inven-

[5]Ralph Linton, *The Study of Man* (Englewood Cliffs: Prentice-Hall, 1936), p. 324.

tions, both of recent date. He takes off his pajamas, a garment invented in India, and washes with soap invented by the ancient Gauls. He then shaves, a masochistic rite which seems to have been derived from either Sumer or ancient Egypt.

Returning to the bedroom, he removes his clothes from a chair of southern European type and proceeds to dress. He puts on garments whose form originally derived from the skin clothing of the nomads of the Asiatic steppes, puts on shoes made from skins tanned by a process invented in ancient Egypt and cut to a pattern derived from the classical civilizations of the Mediterranean, and ties around his neck a strip of bright-colored cloth which is a vestigial survival of the shoulder shawls worn by the seventeenth-century Croatians. Before going out for breakfast he glances through the window, made of glass invented in Egypt, and if it is raining puts on overshoes made of rubber discovered by the Central American Indians and takes an umbrella, invented in southeastern Asia. Upon his head he puts a hat made of felt, a material invented in the Asiatic steppes.

On his way to breakfast he stops to buy a paper, paying for it with coins, an ancient Lydian invention. At the restaurant a whole new series of borrowed elements confronts him. His plate is made of a form of pottery invented in China. His knife is of steel, an alloy first made in southern India, his fork a medieval Italian invention, and his spoon a derivative of a Roman original. He begins breakfast with an orange, from the eastern Mediterranean, a canteloupe from Persia, or perhaps a piece of African watermelon. With this he has coffee, an Abyssinian plant, with cream and sugar. Both the domestication of cows and the idea of milking them originated in the Near East, while sugar was first made in India. After his fruit and first coffee he goes on to waffles, cakes made by a Scandinavian technique from wheat domesticated in Asia Minor. Over these he pours maple syrup, invented by the Indians of the Eastern woodlands. As a side dish he may have the egg of a species of bird domesticated in Indo-China, or thin strips of the flesh of an animal domesticated in Eastern Asia which have been salted and smoked by a process developed in northern Europe.

When our friend has finished eating he settles back to smoke, an American Indian habit, consuming a plant domesticated in Brazil in either a pipe, derived from the Indians of Virginia, or a cigarette, derived from Mexico. If he is hardy enough he may even attempt a cigar, transmitted to us from the Antilles by way of Spain. While smoking he reads the news of the day, imprinted in characters invented by the ancient Semites upon a material invented in China by a process invented in Germany. As he absorbs the accounts of foreign troubles he will, if he is a good conservative citizen, thank a Hebrew deity in an Indo-European language that he is 100 percent American.[6]

As we study the early beginnings of clothing and trace the diffusion of the three basic patterns from one culture to another, it is the same story. As Crawford put it,

no fundamentally new idea, either in costume or in fabric, in texture, design or color combination, has been evolved in the two hundred years which include the age of the machine. We are still working with the basic ideas evolved by craftsmen in different parts of the world and at different periods in the history of the world, brought together by the commerce of the world at various points of focus.[7]

Western dress predominates in much of the world today, yet many contemporary cultures still preserve the ancient traditions from which their costumes originally derived. These basic patterns of dress are visible expressions of the technical development of the peoples and of their physical environment and their entire way of life.

The disappearance of basic patterns represents changes far more fundamental than a mere passing fashion, for the style of dress is linked to basic patterns of life and culture that are subject to the same forces of social change. The great diversity that now seems characteristic of our own form of dress reflects the intense mixing that occurs in the modern world.

SUMMARY

Universalities in Dress

The learned behavior that is transmitted from generation to generation constitutes the social heredity or culture of a people. The basic patterns of clothing and clothing behavior are part and parcel of the cultural configuration, and they reflect the technical, economic, moral, and aesthetic backgrounds of a given society.

[6]Ralph Linton, THE STUDY OF MAN, © 1936, pp. 326–327. Reprinted by permission of Prentice-Hall, Inc., Englewood Cliffs, New Jersey.
[7]M. D. C. Crawford, Philosophy in Clothing (New York: The Brooklyn Museum, 1940), p. 19.

In spite of the varied patterns that have developed over the centuries, most of our clothing can be classified into three basic types: (1) the tailored garment, which probably originated in the regions of intense cold and was first cut and sewn from animal skins; (2) the draped garment, which developed in farming cultures having the invention of the loom and was neither cut nor sewn; and (3) a composite type that resulted in a cut and sewn costume, made from woven cloth, either fitted or unfitted. The development of each basic pattern was closely linked to the cultural setting of the times.

DIVERSITY IN CLOTHING PATTERNS

As we compare the way clothing is affected by cultural patterns from society to society, we are struck by the infinite number of ways that human beings have found to utilize or fabricate materials and design and wear their clothing. What determines, for example, whether a man arises in the morning and dons a shirt and pair of trousers as he does in America or wraps himself in a decorative toga as he does in Ghana? Several centuries before Christ, a young boy in the Aegean world (Figure 2.12) might have described his attire as follows:

On the feast day I woke at dawn. My old nurse dressed me in my best: my new doeskin drawers with braided borders, my red belt rolled upon rope and clasped with crystal, and my necklace of gold beads.[8]

A few thousand years later near the end of Queen Victoria's reign, a little ragamuffin, about the same age as the boy above, slipped into Windsor Castle only to be discovered by the scullery maid. After a thorough scrubbing by the Grenadier soldiers,

. . . he was thrown a bundle from the housekeeper's charity bin. In this he found a boy's black trousers (patched) and stockings (heavily darned) which pretty well fitted him, a cambric shirt somewhat too large, a pair of shoes, battered but still serviceable and approximately

Figure 2.12 How the Aegean youth may have looked. (Painted stucco relief from the Palace at Knossos: "Prince with Plumed Headdress." Sixteenth century B.C.)

[8]Mary Renault, *The King Must Die* (New York: Pantheon Books, 1958), p. 5.

the right size, a short jacket only slightly too long at the wrists, and an old cap. There was also a novel garment that delighted him. It was made of wool and had long arms and legs, and he had intended to put this on last as a sort of coverall, but the soldiers stopped him and made him put it on first. It felt pleasantly snug and warm, but it irritated his skin and he was not at all satisfied with the arrangement. But . . . he was thrilled with all these new clothes, the finest he had ever had in his life.[9]

The period of time separating these two boys is not as significant as other differences we may note in cultural patterns. Effects of the natural environment can be seen as one factor that influences the diversity of clothing design; a lad dressed only in a pair of leather shorts and a necklace would not be comfortable in the cold dampness of Great Britain, nor would the snugly warm long wool underwear be a desirable garment in the sunny Mediterranean climate. The use of materials varies markedly, but we might suppose that it was due more to a difference in the supply of raw materials than to a wide difference in technical skills. The Aegean culture had highly developed techniques for tanning leather, fashioning braid, and working precious metals and stones. The nineteenth-century British had the same techniques but found it more economical to use a great deal of wool. Perhaps the most striking difference between the two cultures would be recognized in the aesthetic ideals expressed through dress: the jeweled, decorated youth with his bright red belt and gold necklace stands out in strong contrast to the drab little English boy in black suit and off-white shirt. Further, in Victorian society the idea of exposing the chest and

[9]Theodore Bonnet, *The Mudlark* (Garden City, N.Y.: Doubleday, 1940), pp. 151 ff.

legs—even those of a small boy—would have been considered highly improper.

The second passage illustrates two additional culturally determined patterns. The patched trousers and heavily darned stockings, even in the royal household, indicate the extreme frugality so characteristic of Victorian times. But more than that, a strict holding to custom was demanded. Why was it necessary to wear a long wool garment next to the skin if it made the person itch? Would it not have been just as warm and practical worn as a coverall as the boy originally supposed? Despite the logic of alternate patterns, the wearing of *under*wear as a permanent social habit precludes any possibility of wearing it as *outer*wear. Not only is there great variety from one culture to the next in the kind and amount of body covering required, but within the same culture, standards for dress are modified over time.

Variation Between Cultures

At any given moment, diverse patterns in dress serve to identify the cultural and often the geographic affiliation of groups and individuals. Although striking differences still can be found in Far Eastern, Middle Eastern, and Western cultures, less striking but significant variations appear in nearly all cultures. In spite of the fact that the American heritage is so closely related to the British, for example, it is still fairly easy to spot Americans in London, especially if they are over thirty. The American version of the business suit is likely to be lighter in weight and more loosely cut than the Englishman's tailored tweeds. The American's softly finished wash-and-wear shirt also contrasts with the more stiffly starched varieties worn by the British.

Even though the Savile Row tailors were jolted by the Carnaby Street fashions, most of them continue to "speak in the tradition that accepts English tailoring as a symbol of English moral and political rectitude. A gentleman's attire, representing as it does a recognition of fashion but a denial of eccentricity, is an allegory of progress without revolution."[10] For example, the British did not give up the five-button fly and accept the zipper in the name of progress until the middle of the 1960s.

On the other hand, American travelers still are regularly confronted by Britishers with offers to buy their authentic Levis and well-made shirts. While European ready-to-wear may have more flair in terms of fashion appeal, its quality and workmanship is decidedly inferior to what Europeans call "American off-the-peg" clothing. Probably the only uniquely American fashion, Levis have become popular the world over. But even when worn with a Western shirt, subtle cultural differences are often apparent in accessories.

To the French, the style of the true gentleman is still epitomized, however, by the London standard: closely fitted suit with vest, bowler hat, black polished shoes, and a rolled umbrella with wood handle.[11] Even though the London style is worn by few Frenchmen, it represents a cultural distinctiveness that is easily recognized.

Another diversity is that standards for what is considered an acceptable degree of body exposure vary from culture to culture. Many societies expose parts of the body that would be considered highly immoral in

our own culture. An American male is expected to remove his hat in public, but certainly not his trousers—even though in most cases he would still be more adequately covered than he would be at the beach. A Chinese gentleman, on the other hand, may remove the outer layer of clothes without arousing anybody's indignation. Morality in dress is discussed more thoroughly in Chapter 4, but it is important to note here that dress as an expression of modesty is a cultural variation rather than being based on any universal laws.

It cannot be denied, however, that the jet age has rapidly supplanted these cultural variations with an international style of dress. In the large cities of the world—Barcelona, Paris, London, Athens, Tel Aviv, Tokyo—there are more similarities than there are differences, especially among the youth. Does the disappearance of these distinctions in dress foreshadow the elimination of all other cultural differences as well?

The cultural patterns reflected in clothing develop from a social setting characterized by customs, mores, and religion, not just from dress styles.

Variation Within Cultures

Thus far we have discussed the widely diverse patterns of dress as they vary from culture to culture. But culture itself is never completely static or uniform; each age, each generation, each year, brings some modification of custom and accompanying clothing habits.

A good example developed in the early 1970s in London. A large number of boutiques sprang up on that city's Kings Road and, in sharp contrast to the fine

[10]John Canaday, "British Gentlemen's Tailor Advocates Zippers—In the Name of Progress," *New York Times*, December 19, 1966, p. 49.

[11]"Est-il encore intéressant de s'habiller à Londres?" *Paris Match*, October 1972, pp. 32–33.

Leopard-
trimmed
coats

Fringed
vests

Crepe-soled
shoes

Safari
suits

Striped jerseys
and canvas shoes

Figure 2.13 A sampling of men's wear from London's Kings Road.

English tailoring tradition, began to offer a wide variety of fashions that changed from week to week (Figure 2.13). Customers for these boutiques were usually young men from the working class. What they lacked by way of social position was counteracted by a relatively high income typical of young people in industrial societies. The far-out clothing these young men adopted had a global impact on men's fashion in general; the fact that these styles worked up gradually from the lower classes to the higher indicated that Britain had moved toward a less class-oriented society. Observers of the scene at that time noted, "Somewhere in all this is the classic London Pinstripe. There'll always be an England!" Another comment was "If style is a social expression, the jolt that Carnaby Street has given to English tailoring has its parallel in the jolt that the popular vote has given British government."[12]

[12]Canaday, "British Gentlemen's Tailor," p. 49.

Cultural change is always more rapid, and by the same token more obvious, when enforced through political disorganization or social upheaval. Radical changes in Western dress followed the French Revolution, and it is probably for this reason that the costumes of the Directoire and Empire periods are the favorite topics of fashion historians, for the events in France during those years influenced the costume of the entire Western world.

Oriental dress has undergone more radical changes since the beginning of the twentieth century than at any other time during its thousands of years of history (Figure 2.14). Under the Manchus, who ruled China from the seventeenth to the twentieth century, all Chinese males were ordered to wear their hair in Manchu style, that is, shaved in front with the hair from the sides and crown braided into a long queue at the back. The traditional costume, which was native to China, was the accepted form of dress for both ceremonial and everyday wear. Clothing symbols were prescribed rigidly according to rank and were enforced by law. Soon after 1900, the traditional patterns began to show subtle influences of alien designs, but the basic styles remained Manchu until the Revolution of 1911. It is significant, however, that these minor deviations in dress signaled the crumbling of the Manchu dynasty before the actual revolt.

The Revolution abruptly abolished the monarchy and began to tear down the entire structure of the former civilization. Sun Yat-sen introduced the military tunic with the high collar, worn with Western-style trousers. The elaborate costumes of the Imperial court were the first to be discarded, but the pageantry that had inspired all the Chinese decorative arts and dress gradually disappeared as well. An edict was issued for men to cut off their long queues. Although many resisted, a Westernized haircut—formerly regarded as a suspiciously alien influence—suddenly became the symbol of nationalistic pride, and

the founding of the Republic in 1911 heralded deep-seated changes in China's political system and as a consequence her social structure. The everyday life of the people in the cities became subject to the increasing onslaught of outside

Figure 2.14 Transition in Chinese men's dress. A simplified version of the military uniform that symbolized the Communist national spirit is still worn.

Chinese official
c. 1850

Government official
late 19th Century

20th Century

Men's formal dress
1911–1949

Military dress
1936

influences and foreign methods which affected their manner of living, including their dress.[13]

A process of experimentation developed, and an intermingling of Western elements of dress with Eastern styles continued throughout the next few decades. After 1911, the most common Chinese men's costume consisted of the long gown worn with a soft, felt fedora-type hat and Western-style shoes. For formal wear, men retained the Eastern style dress, a long blue gown worn with a short black silk tunic fashioned with wide sleeves and a mandarin collar. This series of changes appears to be a typical phenomenon in men's wear; traditional styles are relegated to formal dress before they completely disappear. In Western culture, the tailcoat, which started out as part of a riding habit, ended up as formal attire and is now virtually extinct.

The increasing influence of Western dress was nourished by the missionary schools and the fact that growing numbers of Chinese students went abroad to study in Europe and the United States. Chinese officials continued to wear their uniforms for most occasions, and this also contributed to the gradual disappearance of traditional dress. Although many men reverted to the gown or the loose tunic and trousers in the privacy of their homes, few wore anything but the typical Western business suit in public.

When the Communists came to power in 1949, they rejected the influence of both tradition and the West, turning instead to the examples set by Russia. Dress reforms were intended to symbolize elimination of

Figure 2.15 In China today, the loose tunic and baggy trousers are the uniform of the common man.

all class distinctions, and the entire nation—men and women alike—was cast into the drab, baggy uniform that marked the liberation of a new national spirit (Figure 2.15).

Yet, when an American president visited China in 1972, the resulting influence on American clothing styles was not on what the Chinese were wearing at the time, but on the former upper-class Oriental dress. What became popular were the elaborate fabrics and ornate garments of China's past history, beautiful silks made into brocades (or imitations), used in traditional mandarin garments.

Still another example of cultural change is the gradual demise of the traditional *fez*, or *tarboosh*, in the Middle East. The dark red, brimless, cone-shaped hat was once the proud symbol of Arab manhood. Except for the servant classes in cities like Cairo and Beirut, the fez has now virtually disappeared from the scene. The first strike against the tarboosh came in Turkey, when Ataturk took over the Ottoman Empire in 1925. At first he tried to keep all govern-

[13]A. C. Scott, *Chinese Costume in Transition* (New York: Theatre Arts Books, 1960), p. 59.

ment officials from wearing the fez by giving them a special allowance to buy new hats. When this failed, he forbid any male citizen to wear the fez. Thus, the glory of the once proud symbol gradually waned in other parts of the Middle East as well, and as young Arab men took up the ways of Western culture, they discarded the fez entirely.

Among women the changes in clothing within a culture have been no less dramatic even if slower to be accepted. The movement for freedom and equality, begun in the United States, has spread around the world and has had considerable impact on traditional clothing. Pants, suits, skirts, and dresses mingle freely with the *sari* and *shalivar* and *kmeez* in the streets of New Delhi and other cosmopolitan cities of India. The younger Indian women are turning to the more functional dresses of the West, which are not only cheaper but more durable. One textile advertisement proclaims, "Three gowns at the cost of one sari."[14] The traditional sari is made of six yards of fabric (generally silk), and wrapped around the body in several symbolic ways. Considered more graceful and sexually alluring by Indian men, the women see change from the sari as a symbol of freedom from the kitchen and from traditional women's roles in a highly role-oriented society. Many young women who still cling to the traditional dress now wrap the sari tighter and move the waist below the navel, and the *choli* (blouselike top) up above the waist to reveal a considerable amount of bare midriff. Variations within a culture can be seen not only by the

coexistence of the traditional and nontraditional but in the cut, drape, and seductiveness of the sari itself.

In few countries can the varieties of dress within a culture be more obvious and dramatic than in modern Spain. While people in the major cities of Madrid and Seville are hardly distinguishable from those in New York, London, or Rome, one need only travel off the major highways and into the back country to observe all varieties of folk dress. The Moorish influence is still evident in the villages. In Mojacar, in southern Spain, married women have been veiled since the Muslims arrived from North Africa more than 1300 years ago. "Last year marked the first time since 711 that the majority of married women in Mojacar were seen on the streets without their faces covered."[15] Probably those most disappointed in the change are the tourists who seek out this tiny town precisely for its Moorish characteristics. Paradoxically, it is probably true that these same tourists were most influential in causing the Mojacarans to abandon the traditional veil. The same kinds of parallel changes in costume and culture occur in all societies although they tend to be less noticeable when accomplished through evolutionary rather than revolutionary processes. Culture constantly is modified by developments in the technical, political, social, and economic spheres of societies, and such changes are reflected visibly in the clothing of the people. The next three chapters deal specifically with the relationships between dress and the various cultural components that make for diversity in patterns of clothing behavior. In all societies, standards of dress are modified by cultural changes that take place during a period of time.

[14]Ram Suresh, "Sari About That," *Washington Post,* December 9, 1973, p. 14.

[15]Carmen Anthony, "Mojacar Women Left Veil," *Christian Science Monitor,* February 14, 1972, p. 15.

SUMMARY

Diversity in Clothing Patterns

There are an infinite number of ways to satisfy clothing needs. In different parts of the world and in different periods of history, people have utilized materials and designed their garments in a multitude of patterns, each of which reflects the unique combination of cultural elements that characterize the society as a whole. Factors that influence the diversity of costume design include the effects of the natural environment, the supply of raw materials, the technical skills of the people, moral standards and religious values, as well as aesthetic and political ideals. As these cultural differences disappear, dress styles also merge into more universal patterns.

FOR FURTHER READING

Chesi, Gert. *The Last Africans*. Austria: Perlinger-Verlags Ges. m.b.H., 1977.

Davis, Marian L. *Visual Design in Dress*, pp. 297–309. Englewood Cliffs, N.J.: Prentice-Hall, Inc., 1980.

Flugel, J. C. *The Psychology of Clothes*. 1930. Reprint., pp. 167–180. London: Hogarth Press Ltd., 1966.

Holderness, Esther R. *Peasant Chic: A Guide to Making Unique Clothing Using Traditional Folk Designs*. New York: Hawthorn Books, Inc., 1977.

Keshishian, John M. "Anatomy of a Burmese Beauty Secret." *National Geographic*, 155 (June 1979), 798–801.

Rudofsky, Bernard. *The Unfashionable Human Body*. New York: Doubleday and Company, Inc., 1971.

Stannard, Una. "Clothing and Sexuality." *Sexual Behavior*, 1 (May 1971), 25–33, 64.

Chapter 3

CLOTHING AND
THE MATERIAL CULTURE

Anthropologists use many systems of classification to describe culture. Among the broadest and most generally agreed on subdivisions of culture are the **artifacts** (articles made by people), the **sociofacts** (divisions and behaviors devised for social organization), and the **mentifacts** (ideas, ideals, and values that people live by). Clothing, classified as artifacts, is only one of many elements that make up the total culture of a group of people, yet it is one of the most visual expressions of the habits, thoughts, techniques, and conditions that characterize a society as a whole. A famous French philosopher, noting this close relationship between dress and culture, commented:

If I were permitted to choose from the rubbish which will be published a hundred years after my death, do you know which I would take? . . . No, it is not a novel which I would pick in this library of the future, nor a work on history—when it offers something of interest it is only another novel. . . . I would take simply a fashion magazine in order to see how women will dress themselves a century after my death. And their fantasies would tell me more about future humanity than all the philosophers, the novelists, the preachers, or the scientists.[1]

[1]The quotation by Anatole France is a translation by J. R. Hopkins, published in *Anatole France Himself*, ed. J. J. Brousson (Philadelphia: J. B. Lippincott Company, 1925).

Through the eyes of the anthropologist we can see how the design of a given costume depends on the raw materials, the tools, and the levels of technology available to the maker of the garment. Also, by comparing clothing with other art forms, we observe that it reflects the typical mode of expression that characterizes the culture. In any given period, the style of painting, the design of a chair, the structure of a building, or the "look" of a woman are essentially the same.

As we shall see later, the development of certain styles in these artifacts of a culture reflects the less tangible mentifacts and sociofacts that are ascendant in that culture. Also, a study of the historical development of styles shows that changes in dress are conditioned by world events. This chapter focuses on the relationships among the availability of raw materials, the technological developments of different societies, and the resulting evolution of typical styles.

TECHNOLOGICAL PATTERNS

There is no unbroken correlation between the amount of clothing worn and the natural habitat of a people, yet in general we can say that tailored garments made from animal skins are usually found among aborigines in the colder regions, whereas draped clothing is characteristic of cultures in warmer areas. Numerous ways have been found to utilize the environmental resources to fashion a body covering, and none of these techniques seems to be shared by all peoples of the world. Materials used for clothing, however, need to be fairly soft and pliable; relatively few are suitable in the natural state without some further processing. Consequently, methods have been devised and the necessary tools invented for fabrication or manufacture of some form of textile.

Raw Materials

Probably the first articles of clothing were made either from the leaves and grasses available in the natural environment or from the uncut skin of a large animal. The two familiar examples are the Neanderthal fur coverings (Figure 3.1) and the Polynesian grass skirts (Figure 3.2).

Sometimes the spongy bark of certain trees, such as the fig or mulberry, was stripped off in layers and pounded together to form a large sheet of cloth. Because of its paperlike qualities, bark cloth (tapa cloth) was not suitable for cutting and sewing and was limited to use as a wrapped skirt or sarong. Tapa cloth made in the same manner is still fabricated into clothing in many parts of the South Pacific. Unprocessed vegetable materials in the form of leaves and grasses have limited durability. Over the years people perfected techniques for improving the serviceability and versatility of plant fibers (Figure 3.3). In the Western world, cotton was and still is the most extensively used vegetable product, although flax (Figure 3.4), hemp, henequen, and pineapple fibers are also made into fabrics. The people who use these fibers to make cloth also cultivate the plant, so use of vegetable materials tends to be characteristic of farming rather than nomadic or hunting cultures.

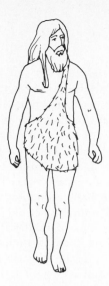

Figure 3.1　An animal skin hung over one shoulder as an early garment.

Figure 3.2　The Polynesians' skirts were made from natural vegetable fibers.

Figure 3.3　The Indians gathered the long bark fibers from sagebrush to make fiber clothing. A Paiute Indian woman twines the sagebrush bark with a hemp cordage into predetermined shapes. The resulting garments look like those in the bottom photos. The pants would be tied around the waist and legs with strips of buckskin.

Figure 3.4 A worker stacks bundles of flax in preparation for retting. The stalks are soaked in warm, soft water to loosen the flax fibers from the outer woody portions.

Animals provide pelts for fur coats and hides for leather, although a more common method for utilizing animal products is to shear the hair or wool and process it as a fiber. Although the wool from certain varieties of sheep is the most satisfactory fiber for cloth making, the hair from camels, rabbits, horses, and numerous other animals has been used to manufacture cloth. The outer covering of birds is used for fabric also. Feathers are particularly valued in making headdresses, but they are used for other articles such as capes and hip coverings. Thus, even in the modern world, animal and vegetable fibers are a major source of supply for the textile industry on a global basis.

According to legend, the use of silk as a textile fiber goes back to 2600 B.C., when the Empress Hsi-ling-shi dropped a cocoon into a bowl of warm water and discovered that the incredibly fine filament could be drawn out in a continuous length to form an unbroken thread. The Chinese managed to keep the secret of the silkworm for over 2,000 years. Several explanations are offered to explain the spread of sericulture (the cultivation of silk) to the rest of the world. One version states that it was smuggled out in A.D. 300 by a Chinese princess who hid the silkworm eggs and the seeds from the mulberry trees in her hair. A less romantic explanation involves two monks who hid the silkworm eggs in their hollow bamboo staffs. Other countries have attempted the tedious cultivation of the silkworm, but none has ever rivaled the Far East. Because the production and manufacture of silk requires not only the worm, but vast quantities of mulberry leaves to nourish it, sericulture is limited to those areas having suitable climatic conditions. Another essential is cheap hand labor. The Japanese are now the principal silk producers of the world.

Reeling, the tedious job of unwinding the silk fiber from the cocoons, traditionally was a household industry largely carried on by women. With the industrialization of Japan, women do not have to do this kind of work to maintain survival for their families; they can make more money in the factories.

Silk may become even more of a luxury fiber than it presently is. Its cost is high and probably always will be. A segment of the fashion world places silk high above other fibers and possibly will continue to do so. But the old-time ambition of every woman to own a good silk dress someday no longer holds. The younger generations, who have had no former experience with silk and its prestige and status, seem to be indifferent to it.

Mention should be made of the materials used for protective clothing, or armor, since they are most conspicuously related to advances in technological developments. From the time of the Bronze Age, which began about 2500 B.C., metal in various forms became a part of the warrior's costume. In the Greco-Roman period, a hinged cuirass of brass or bronze was molded to the shape of the chest and abdomen and held in place with leather straps. Later the breastplate was made of iron, and then of small iron rings sewn closely together. This form gradually evolved into the flexible coat of chain mail that became the typical garb of the knights of the Crusades. By the end of the fifteenth century the knight was encased in shining steel-plated armor, from head to toe. Modern combat has become largely airborne and our attention is focused on flight suits and space suits. For these, we have the ever-expanding group of man-made fibers and synthetic materials, including aluminized fabrics, fiber glass, polyurethanes, and many others.

Man-made fibers also figure largely in civilian clothing consumption and they have rapidly displaced the natural fibers as the predominant material used for clothing throughout the world.

Fabric Processes

Obviously few raw materials can be used in their natural state as wearable textiles without further processing of some kind. Animal skins must be thoroughly scraped and softened before they are suitable for clothing. Eskimos accomplish this by chewing the hides bit by bit until they are pliable (Figure 3.5). In other cultures, the skins are softened by mechanical methods such as alternate beating and wetting and rubbing with oil. A more advanced technique is to treat the hide with tannic acid secured from the bark of certain trees, which keeps the leather soft and pliable even after repeated wettings. The true tanning process is known only in those cultures with a fairly well developed technology. In some areas where no large

animals are available, several smaller skins must be joined together to make a complete garment (Figure 3.6). Skilled craftsmen can produce highly decorative patterns by combining different kinds of fur into one costume. Very often the most luxurious furs come from the smallest mammals. Modern furriers utilize a technique known as the **letting-out process,** in which a small pelt is cut into narrow diagonal strips and sewn back together in such a way that one skin will extend the entire length of a coat (Figure 3.7). This greatly enhances the beauty of the fur and also increases its pliability.

People who live in milder climates often completely remove the hair from the animal and cure or tan only the skin to produce leather. American Indians favored buckskin for much of their clothing, and many early American settlers adopted this durable leather for their own garments. The hair or the wool, minus the skin, can be used in still another way to fabricate a material suitable for clothing. The scaly structure and crimp of the fibers causes them to stick together when agitated in a

Figure 3.5 Eskimos prepare animal skins by chewing the hides until they are soft and pliable.

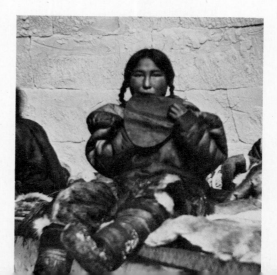

Figure 3.6 In primitive societies, when hides from larger animals are hard to obtain, the skins of smaller creatures are tied into ropes and woven into robes or blankets. After the pelts are stripped from the animals, they are scraped and linked together by tying the end of each skin through its own eyehole. The fur chain is tied to a stick and twisted into a rope. The fur rope is next hung up to dry, and later the brittle ears are snapped off. The rope is then twined together with strings of hemp into the desired shape and size.

Figure 3.7 Modern furriers use a technique known as the *letting-out* process. The pelt is cut into small pieces and then resewn into a long, narrow strip.

moist condition. Again legend attempts to explain this discovery of a fabric we now call felt. An ingenious camel driver, wanting to soften the hard inner soles of his sandals as he trekked across the desert, picked up shedded camels' hairs and put them in his shoes. At the end of the day, the heat, moisture, and friction resulting from the day's walk had produced a soft felt pad inside his sandals. In actuality these properties of the wool fiber were probably first discovered and utilized by an Asiatic people; they spread out the fibers in layers on a mat, moistened them with water, and then rolled the mat tightly back and forth from one end to the other for several hours until the fibers were firmly matted together. The resulting felt was commonly used for tents, saddlebags, boots, and rugs.

Our modern use of wool felt is confined primarily to hats and decorative craft items since the fabric lacks strength and pliability. Although wool and other hairs are the only fibers with natural felting properties, many synthetic fibers with **thermoplastic** qualities (the property of a fiber that allows it to melt or soften at high temperatures) can be felted by applying adhesives and heat. These synthetic nonwoven fabrics are thin, strong, and pliable and are found in consumer products other than those reserved for wool felt. Many are inexpensive to produce and are widely used in a rapidly growing textile market, disposables.

The other principal methods of converting fibers into fabrics all require an intermediate step of spinning short lengths into long continuous yarns. A textile yarn is a continuous strand of fibers grouped or twisted together in a form suitable for use in making fabrics. The simplest method is to draw out the fibers, twist them together between the fingers, and wind the resulting thread onto a spindle. Many cultures used a distaff to hold the fibers and weighted the end of the spindle so that it could be twirled and left hanging to provide a continuous, even tension to the drawn-out strand (Figure 3.8). The transition from distaff and spindle to modern spinning frames spans 10,000 or more years, but the basic operations of spinning fibers are the same now as when people first made yarns. Today's high-speed machinery does basically the same, faster than the eye can see.

Yarn is then made into cloth by weaving, knitting, or other processes such as braiding or knotting. Of all the cloth-making processes, weaving is by far the most common. Interlacing yarns at right angles is essentially the same technique employed to make baskets and grass mats, except that the soft, pliable yarns require some tensioning device at the ends to hold them in place. The prime implement in weaving, of course, is the loom, which consists of

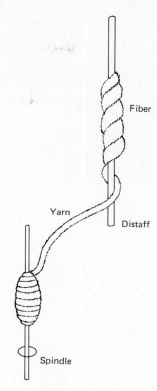

Figure 3.8 A distaff and spindle were used to spin fibers into yarn.

some sort of frame across which the warp (lengthwise) yarns may be stretched and held in place as the filling (crosswise) yarns are inserted.

The second major fabric-making process is knitting. Knitting is a method in which loops of yarns are interlocked in either a lengthwise or a crosswise direction (Figure 3.9). The freedom of movement within these loops accounts for the comfort-stretch quality associated with many knits.

Cloth is usually given some added treatment to improve its aesthetic qualities. Decorative patterns often are formed in the weave or knit in with different colored yarns, or the cloth is dyed, painted, or

Figure 3.9 A knitter places packages of yarn on a creel from which the yarn will be fed directly to a knitting machine like the one behind her.

embroidered. The technical skills and characteristic styles developed by different peoples of the world in the decoration of cloth reveal many insights into their cultural habits. For example, design motifs are often symbolic in nature, and the source of an inspiration is sometimes a clue to cultural beliefs and ideals.

The development of new processes in the construction of clothing promises to change the character of our garments in the future. Tubular fabrics are already being preformed by steam-setting into a variety of seams, pleats, and gathers; the process reduces the necessity for cutting and sewing operations.[2] Shapes can be set permanently into knitted fabrics made from thermoplastic fibers by pulling them over heated metal forms and then cooling them. The tube of fabric is subsequently cut at the neck and sleeves.[3] Other molding and fusing techniques are rapidly replacing the traditional methods of clothing construction. Although the apparel industry waits for completely preformed garments in order to eliminate entirely the need for cutting and sewing, a wide variety of fusible items are already available to both the needle trades and the home sewer. These products eliminate much tedious hand sewing— hems, patches, mending, fastenings.

Color selection, particularly color matching, is now largely done with computers. Since matching color involves the measurement of reflected light, not only is a wider range of color available to the textile producers, but there is less likelihood of human error.[4] From the technical standpoint, once a more efficient way to accomplish a task is found, society seldom goes back to the more primitive method. Slow sharing of every progressive improvement from one culture to another is the process through which modern technology has evolved.

[2]A. Sawhney, "Apparel Weaving—A New Concept," *Textile Industries*, December 1972, 40–56.

[3]"Teijin 'Heat Sets' Dresses," *Women's Wear Daily*, December 22, 1972.

[4]Ralph A. Stanzioloa. "Computer Color Matching in Textile Printing," *Textile Chemist and Colorist*, May 1979, 22–32.

Tools

Advances in technological processing depend on the invention or improvement of

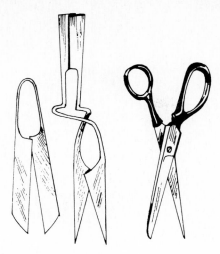

Figure 3.10 On the left are early versions of shears and scissors. On the right, a modern pair of shears.

tools. The invention of shears, for instance, did not come about until people learned to work with metals. The earliest implement, probably devised to clip wool from sheep, was forged from a single bar of metal and then bent until the blades came together. The first cross-bladed shears with a central pivot screw did not appear until centuries later. The art of tempering metals to a hard, sharp cutting edge developed slowly. The first steel scissors were not made until the fourteenth century, and scissors did not come into the reach of those besides the very wealthy until after the famous Bessemer steel process was invented in 1856. This process greatly reduced the cost of metal products (Figure 3.10).

Today, electric cutters with blades mounted vertically in a maneuverable housing can slice with great speed and precision through many layers of cloth at a time. The laser beam is even more precise. The laser light, which is brighter than the sun, is aimed automatically at the cloth by mirrors and lenses. It can cut as close as the width of a single thread, simultaneously sealing the edge of the fabric to prevent fraying. The laser system also includes

programmed cutting instructions, stored in a computer for repeated use. Computers are also used to produce pattern layouts capable of minimizing fabric waste in the cutting operation.

Tools for sewing garments together came long after cutting tools but date back some 30,000 years. As noted in Chapter 1, the first implement was probably the awl, which pierced the animal hide so a sinew thread could be drawn through. Early needles, with the all-important eye, were made from polished bone, mammoth ivory and walrus tusks, wood, and drilled thorns. Later, the Mesopotamian cultures fashioned needles from copper, bronze, silver, and gold. Fine needles did not appear until the Renaissance when, paralleling the development of shears, the first steel needles were produced (Figure 3.11).

Figure 3.11 Tools that were forerunners of the modern sewing machine. Tambour needle and frame show the method of forming the chain stitch, 1763.

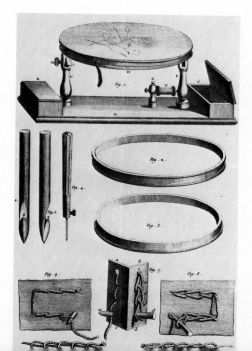

Figure 3.12 Howe's patent model sewing machine, 1846.

Figure 3.13 One of the first commercial sewing machines, Wilcox and Gibbs, 1857.

Figure 3.14 A sewing machine of the 1980s.

Attempts to mechanize the needle came as early as 1790, when an Englishman named Thomas Saint obtained a patent for a sewing machine to stitch leather. Some forty years later, Barthélmy Thimonnier in France produced a chain-stitch machine that used a needle resembling a crochet hook. By 1832, Walter Hunt, a New Yorker, had invented a lock-stitch machine that used two sets of threads and prevented the stitches from pulling out as they did in the older chain-stitch model. The invention of the modern sewing machine (Figure 3.12), however, is usually attributed to Elias Howe, who in 1846 patented a lock-stitch machine with a needle having the eye near the point rather than near the blunt end. A few years later, another machinist named Isaac Merritt Singer devised a machine with other improvements and, after negotiating with Howe, finally paid him $15,000 for the right to use his needle with the eyed point.[5] After

these inventions appeared, the needle trades expanded tremendously (Figure 3.13). Steam, water, and electric power (Figure 3.14) replaced the old treadle, and many industrial machines now operate at speeds of more than 4,000 stitches per minute.

Gradual improvements in yarn spinning over the years also were made possible through the invention of tools and machines (Figure 3.15). In Neolithic times, the distaff and spindle were used to twist wool, cotton, and linen fibers into continuous threads. The earliest spinning wheel was developed in India, but it was not

[5]M. D. C. Crawford, *Philosophy in Clothing* (New York: The Brooklyn Museum, New York, 1940), p. 12.

Figure 3.15 Evolution of spinning processes (a) Distaff and spindle (b) Early spinning wheel (c) Improved spinning wheel (d) Improved spinning wheel (e) Modern spinning frame.

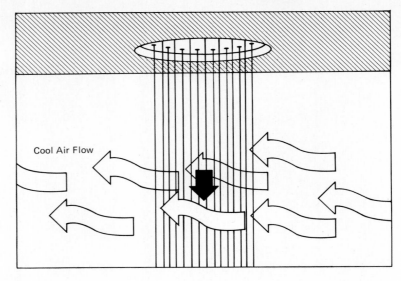

Figure 3.16 Today synthetic fibers are made by pumping chemical solutions through a spinneret.

Cool Air Flow

introduced in England until the sixteenth century. The spindle was attached to a driving belt and wheel, which spun it rapidly. All spinning was done in the home until the latter part of the eighteenth century.

In 1764 James Hargreaves devised a way to mount eight spindles vertically on a board so that one wheel could spin them all at the same time; by 1779, more than 20,000 "spinning jennies" were in operation. Arkwright's spinning machine was an improvement over the spinning jenny, but it was so heavy that it had to be operated by water power. This requirement gave rise to the establishment of a number of small factories that could provide the force necessary to run the large water frames. This period, beginning in the last half of the eighteenth century, has been called the Industrial Revolution; it marked the transition of textile making from home production to the factory system. Mechanical spinning on modern machines can whirl spindles at a rate of 10,000 times per minute. The newer man-made fibers undergo a process called *chemical spinning* in which the liquid is extruded through the tiny holes of a spinneret, a small thimble-

like nozzle, solidified into continuous filaments, and twisted together to form a yarn (Figure 3.16).

Many forms of primitive looms are still used, both functionally as a major source of fabric in some societies and decoratively in the production of art and craft items. Probably the earliest contrivance to weave cloth suspended the warp threads from a pole with the strands hanging free, but weavers soon discovered they could save much time by attaching alternate threads to a rod or stick that could be raised and lowered to form a space or shed for the filling thread to pass through. Also, a firmer cloth could be made by keeping the warp yarns under tension. This was first accomplished by constructing a rectangular frame the size of the finished piece of cloth. This system later was improved by rolling the cloth onto a beam or roller as the weaving progressed (Figure 3.17). Weaving remained a hand process until John Kay devised the flying shuttle in 1738, followed by Cartwright's heavy power loom. In 1801 a Frenchman named Jacquard designed an intricate loom (Figure 3.18) that made it possible to control each individual warp yarn by a series of

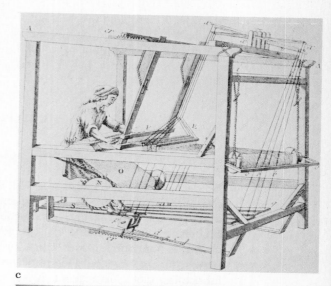

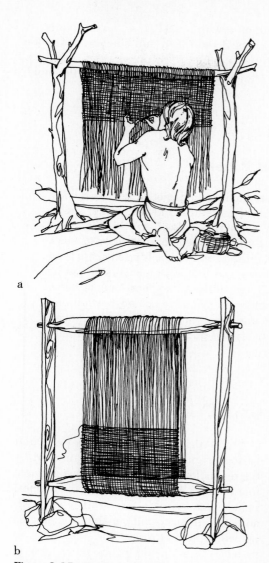

a

b

c

d

Figure 3.17 Evolution of the loom. (a) Earliest weaving apparatus (b) Simple primitive loom (c) Floor loom with pedals (d) Modern power (missile) loom.

Figure 3.18 The Jacquard loom manipulates the warp threads, raising or lowering them according to the punch tape design. Products from these looms include fancy towelling and upholstery fabric.

punched cards; it facilitated the weaving of elaborate floral patterns and figured damasks by a machine rather than by a hand process. Modern automatic power looms and sewing machines have greatly increased the speed and efficiency of producing clothing. Even so, the loom and needle may one day give way to the mold.

SUMMARY

Technological Patterns

From a technical standpoint, it is clear that each method used to fashion a body covering is influenced by the availability of materials and the worker's skill and ingenuity in perfecting construction techniques as well as the refinement and efficiency of available tools. In some cultures, people know how to tailor garments from animal skins; some braid grasses or produce fringed skirts from leaves; others have knowledge of the loom and knitting machines to use in fabricating cloth for apparel. A few cultures utilize more than one of these technical patterns, but it is rare—particularly in primitive societies—that one pattern is not predominant. Even in our own technologically advanced civilization, we still wear mostly woven or knitted garments cut and sewn into body-conforming shapes.

EVOLUTION OF STYLES

It is an error to assume that because our modern scientific knowledge permits us to choose from all the technical patterns that have thus far been employed, our contemporary style of dress is the most advanced order of apparel ever produced. In spite of all our mechanical and chemical progress in the textile field, we have never been able to devise a garment that surpassed the efficiency of the Eskimo's dress in keeping out the cold. Yet, when the temperature drops below zero, we rarely see an American on the way to work in fur parka and mukluks. In all except a few primitive societies, there has always been an element of choice in the selection of one pattern over another.

Styles that are unique to a particular period or culture are of course limited by the technology. We might prefer a garment that is warm in winter and cool in summer, lightweight, wrinkle-free, soil-proof, self-adjusting in size, and capable of changing its color and texture for the sake of variety—if we could figure out a way to make it. On the other hand, numerous techniques reached the pinnacle of perfection in some bygone era, but are now unknown. For example, modern textile machinery has yet to duplicate the sheerness and quality of linen fabrics produced by the ancient Egyptians. Extant mummy wrappings preserved in the dry Egyptian climate are available for us to see today

Figure 3.19   Navajo woman at the loom.

and provide evidence of a magnificent textile technology.

In order to study the relation of clothing to the material aspects of the culture, we can sample from the thousands of years of history, comparing primitive and advanced societies, Oriental and Occidental, as well as ancient and modern styles of dress.

The Navajo

Perhaps more than any other aspect of the culture, costume reflects the historical experience of the Navajo people. If we know nothing else about this tribe of southwestern American Indians, we know at least that they weave rugs, which were made originally as wearing apparel (Figure 3.19). Like many other elements of their culture, however, rug weaving did not originate with the Navajos. Known as great culture borrowers, the Navajos took over traits from nearly every group with which they came in contact. The culture of the modern Navajos, therefore, is quite different from that of their ancestors who migrated into the Southwest from the northern regions of Canada.

Anthropologists believe that several hundred years ago these Indian people wore breechcloths and skirts made from yucca and grass fibers that were twisted and braided into a kind of cloth. Since they made their livelihood by hunting wild game, they probably also used buckskin for some clothing. About 1539, Spaniards began to invade the Southwest, and the Spanish advances caused many Pueblo people to flee into Navajo territory. This contact with the Pueblos resulted in the development of weaving as a part of the local pattern of culture.

The earliest Navajo textiles were made in the natural colors of the wool—white, black, and various shades of brown or gray—and were used as robes by both sexes. They were warm and provided good protection against both wind and water. At first the only colors used with the neutral tones of the wool were a greenish-yellow derived from the flowers of rabbit brush, blue obtained from boiling sumac with blue clay, and a deep dull red from the roots of mountain mahogany. Indigo blue was added when the Navajos came in contact with Mexican traders.

The uniforms of the Spanish soldiers also influenced the designs of these woven blankets and belts when

the bright red of the infantry and the yellow of the cavalry were either bought or taken from the bodies of those killed—and *bayeta*, that rarest and most precious of blanket materials, was obtained by unravelling the fabric. This colored yarn was generally split and retwisted and, spun fine and hard, was used to make Squaw Dresses or other show garments for men or women.[6]

[6]Dane and Mary Roberts Coolidge, "Navajo Rugs," *Enjoy Your Museum* (Pasadena, California: Esto Publishing Company), 1933, unpaged booklet.

The Spanish had still another influence on Navajo clothing habits. Their tight-fitting leather knee-breeches and their leggings worn with hard-soled shoes were adopted by the Indian men. By 1750, most of the men wore buckskin shirts and short breeches and the hard-soled moccasin copied from the Spanish shoe. Occasionally they also wore the loose cotton pants of Spanish design that were slit along the outseam almost to the knee.

Women generally wore a leather moccasin with a wrapped top and a unique type of dress fashioned with red and blue designs on a black background.

The dresses were made by sewing two woolen blankets together along the top edge and sides leaving a hole for the head and one at each side for the arms. . . . A woven sash was also worn. The dress may have been an adaptation of the Pueblo women's dress, or . . . a copy in woven material of the dress of buckskin worn by Plains Indian women. This costume was used by Navajo women until well into the American period.[7]

It is interesting to note how the Navajos took over certain aspects of the European technology and not others. They knew about spinning wheels and probably could have traded for them, but they preferred to use the distaff and spindle to twist their woolen yarns. The Navajo loom also remained primitive, consisting of two cross-poles crudely attached to two uprights, with the warp stretched taut by the weight of rocks. Since the Navajos were essentially a nomadic tribe, they rarely owned more than could be packed onto a horse and moved elsewhere. A spinning wheel and permanently constructed loom were too much to lash to the back of a horse.

[7]Malcolm Farmer, "The Growth of Navaho Culture," *The San Diego Museum Bulletin* 6, no. 1 (1941), p. 15.

The pigments used to dye the yarns came primarily from vegetable sources until about 1880, when aniline dyes were first introduced. The immediate result was such a violent combination of colors that the term "Indian blanket" soon meant any textile of garish design in loud discordant hues. Up until this time, American traders who traveled into Navajo country exchanged horses for blankets, and the blankets were eventually shipped to the East and West Coasts. But as the colors became more and more brilliant, the traders finally refused to buy them, so the weavers gradually went back to their natural colors and vegetable dyes, turning their creative instincts instead to greater variation in weave and pattern.

Navajo rugs are no longer used as items of apparel; their production is primarily for commercial purposes. When they do wear blankets, modern Navajos go to the trader for soft Pendletons made from the fine Oregon wool that is more comfortable against the skin. The dress of the men is now a colorful variation of the cowboy's costume—wide-brimmed hats, colored shirts, blue jeans, and high-heeled boots, although many still wear moccasins at least a part of the time. Sometimes the shirts and the trousers show the early Pueblo and Spanish influences. Many men continue to wear the bowguard, ornamented with silver and set with turquoise. In times past, it was intended as protection against the bow-string, but today is purely ornamental.

For many years the dress styles of the Navajo women reflected the fashions worn by American army officers' wives of the mid-nineteenth century. The long and full, fluted calico skirt, worn with a bright velveteen blouse and intricately woven belt was typical. Today traditional dress is seen only rarely, usually for ceremonial occa-

Figure 3.20   The dress of this woman shows the mixture of styles charactistic of the modern Navajo.

sions. The fluted cotton skirt is more often combined with a ready-to-wear blouse (Figure 3.20). Although they would like to preserve their age-old crafts, few of the women are able to pass their skills on to their children. The young find more lucrative outlets for their labor out in the modern world. Like pottery making and basketry, weaving among the Navajos is becoming a vanishing art.

Navajo clothing, however, clearly revealed their successive contacts with the Plains Indians, the Pueblos, the invading Spaniards, and finally the American traders and officers. In each case, they took over aspects of the material culture, reshaping them to their own needs in such a way that the products that emerged seemed typically Navajo. Their culture today is still characterized by a unique talent for absorbing alien ideas and American culture traits and making them seem consistent with the Navajo way of life.

The Classical World

Much of our knowledge of classical dress in ancient Greece comes to us from numerous vase paintings and pieces of sculpture. Greek artists must have studied anatomy as well as the techniques of weaving, carving, building, metalworking, and ceramics, for their work emphasized the play of garment folds against body contours and points of articulation of the human form. Like the Egyptians, the Greeks became expert weavers, and apparently each garment was woven in proportion to the wearer's size, with a selvage on all sides. This eliminated the necessity for hemming and further enhanced the graceful folds of drapery that were so characteristic of all Greek clothing.

Flax and wool were the two principal fibers used, and the wealthier classes had garments made from extremely fine yarns. The fabric considered most luxurious was a transparent linen that fell into soft narrow folds when draped on the body. A common method of weaving the flax in olive oil produced a silken effect and gave the fabric increased softness and drapability. It may be that the art of weaving a pattern into cloth was unknown to the early Greeks; most of their cloths were plain with decorative borders and surface designs applied by painting or embroidering on the fabric. The spinning and weaving were usually done by the women of the household, and the distaffs and spindles of the ladies of high rank were often made of gold or ivory. Weaving plain fabric was generally the task of the female servants, but the lady and her handmaidens embroidered the material with beautiful decorative designs. Very often lengths of cloth were sent to the goldsmith to be embellished further with fine threads of gold and silver.

Figure 3.21 Two forms of the male chiton.

Figure 3.22 The Greek himation.

The two principal garments of the Greeks were the **chiton** and the **himation**. Both were made from uncut lengths of material, draped and fastened around the body. The man's chiton was a rectangular piece of linen or wool, reaching from the shoulder to just above the knees. It was fastened at the shoulders at points A and B (Figure 3.21), girded about the waist, and worn open down one side. Another form of the chiton was made in the shape of a double square. An opening for the head was left in the center of the piece during weaving, and the selvages were then joined together below the armholes, so the arms emerged from the garment sides instead of from the top edge as they did in the first chiton.

The himation (Figure 3.22) was usually the sole garment of the Greek philosophers, but it was sometimes worn as a voluminous cloak over the chiton. There were several methods of draping the himation, but it was common to fold it over the left arm, around the back of the body, under the right arm, and over the left shoulder again. No fastenings held the drapery in place, and considerable practice and skill were needed to arrange the cloth into graceful folds. The wearer's prestige was judged by the precision of the drapery and only those who had time to devote to its careful arrangement could afford to wear it. Since aristocratic Athenians considered all forms of manual labor degrading, draped garments were a visible symbol of lofty status.

The woman's chiton was based on the same principle as the man's but it was always full-length. One version called the Doric chiton (Figure 3.23) consisted of a length of cloth that exceeded the height of the wearer. The extra length was arranged in an overfold and fastened together on the shoulders at points A and B so the pin went through four thicknesses of fabric. Sometimes the overfold was long enough to be caught into the band at the waist, but since

Shape and folding
of the
Doric chiton

Doric chiton
draped on
the Figure

Greek Doric
5 1/2 Diameters High

Figure 3.23 The Doric order.

the Doric chiton was often made from wool, the upper edge usually hung loose for about 12 or 15 inches over the chest and back without adding to the waistline bulk. The Ionic chiton was much fuller than the Doric and made from a fine transparent linen. The width of the garment was equal to twice the distance from fingertip to fingertip with the arms outstretched (see Figure 3.24) and the front and back edges were fastened together at intervals along the shoulders and arms with a row of pins or buttons. A band that circled the waist and crossed over the back and chest held the fabric to the body in graceful folds and gave the costume an illusion of having sleeves. Women also wore the himation as a cloak or mantle. Sometimes they used a narrower length of cloth draped over the arms like a shawl.

Both Doric and Ionic chitons were clearly designed to resemble their architectural counterparts. The Greek figure was treated in much the same way as a vertical column, and the two styles of dress were examples of the same feeling shown in the corresponding orders of architecture. The Doric column was thick and sturdy with wide flutings, and its capital ended in a flat, square member. In like manner, the Doric chiton with its thick folds of wool drapery gave the feminine form a solid appearance; the overfold gave the same effect as the square capital. The Ionic conception of form, on the other hand, was considerably lighter and more delicate than the Doric. The column was taller and more slender, with narrower fluting, and its capital was a graceful double spiral derived from the curl of the nautilus shell. The

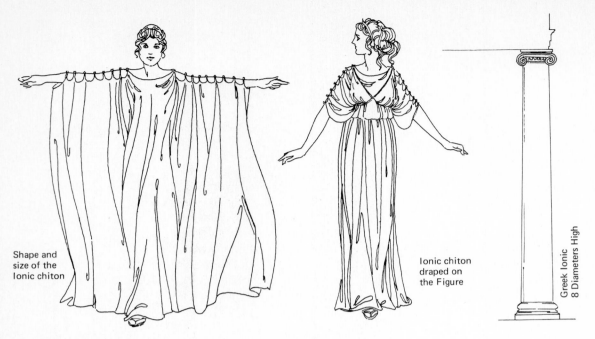

Figure 3.24 The Ionic order.

Shape and size of the Ionic chiton

Ionic chiton draped on the Figure

Greek Ionic 8 Diameters High

folds of the sheer Ionic linen were lighter and more numerous than those in the heavier Doric, and the curve of its false sleeves repeated the curving scroll of the Ionic capital.

Oriental Designs

From about the third century A.D. to the present, the cultivation of the silkworm and the weaving of elaborate silk fabrics has been a very important and highly creative industry in Japan. The remarkable developments in fabric designs were achieved by the Japanese in many ways, but the most important technique was that of weaving the pattern into the cloth itself. Beautiful brocades were made of silk yarns, sometimes mixed with gold or silver threads, in which the pattern was superimposed by an independent weaving of the shuttle. Elaborate damasks, woven in patterns of foliage and flowers, were solid in color, but the long float threads of the design reflected more light than did the groundwork, giving the fabric a sculptured effect (Figure 3.25).

Some of the woven designs were decorated further with artistic embroidery, although many patterns were developed solely through the use of this weaving technique. Decoration also was achieved by covering the design area with a wax that resisted the color when the cloth was dyed, as is done for Javanese batik. Another coloring technique was that of tie-dyeing, in which beautiful effects were obtained by wrapping tiny areas of cloth tightly with a fine thread before the cloth was put in the dye bath. Block prints, hand-painted designs, cut-work, and appliqué also were used. The designs were usually stylized versions of the orchid, chrysanthemum, plum, bamboo, birds, or scenery. The composition of the patterns and the beauty of their spacing on the cloth made these textiles superb works of art.

No wonder then that the Japanese costume developed into a simple form that would display the beautiful fabrics to their best advantage. The cloth is not cut into small pieces and sewn into shapes that emphasize body curves, nor is it draped

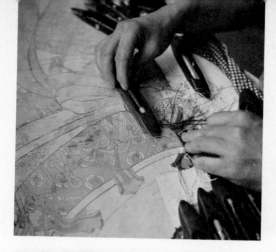

into numerous and intricate folds as it was by the Greeks. The Japanese kimono wraps the body like an artist's canvas, ignoring the breasts and the waistline, drawing full attention to the beauty of the cloth (Figure 3.26). The cut of the kimono is essentially the same for both sexes and all ages except that the **furisode** (with long sleeves) is worn only by young married women. The variation and ornamental qualities are achieved solely through the decorative character of the textile, and the beauty of the garment depends on the wearer's skill in choosing compatible fabrics for the kimono and contrasting *obi*, a broad sash with a wide bow in back.

The Middle Ages

The medieval age covered a period that extended roughly from the eleventh through the fifteenth centuries, reaching its height of brilliant color and pageantry in the later era known as Gothic. It was an age of heroism, chivalry, superstition, and a childlike enthusiasm for glittering stones, precious metals, and lavish ornamentation. The forces of Christianity and the art styles of barbarian Celts and Franks fused into a culture in which art was only decoration for swords, shields, and churches. The richness of the time was reflected nowhere more brilliantly than in the cathedral windows and the dress of the wealthy. The Crusaders were back from the Near East with fabulous tales and souvenirs of Byzantine and Islamic art, which contributed to a revived interest in goldwork, tapestry weaving, stained glass, and enamel work.

Two technical innovations, the pointed arch and the flying buttress, gave rise to the character of Gothic architecture (Figure 3.27). Crusaders had seen the pointed arch first in Mohammedan architecture,

Figure 3.25   A weaver works on an intricate pattern of silk brocade.

Figure 3.26   The simple cut of the kimono directs attention to the decorative quality of the fabric.

Figure 3.27 A Gothic interior showing the rib-vaulted ceiling and the high, pointed arch.

Figure 3.28 Gothic costumes. The ladies wear the towering hennins and their trailing skirts can be seen below the table. The men wear the short doublet, tight hose, and long, pointed shoes.

and the idea was gradually developed into extremes of great height. Stones set into thin, high ribs bore the weight of the entire vaulted ceiling, the ribs in turn being supported by buttresses anchored in the ground outside the building itself. Such construction techniques made possible the building of unbelievably high and narrow rooms in which all horizontal lines seemed to disappear.

This vertical conception of style governed clothing design as well. Pointed, elongated forms were considered the ideal, and Gothic costume went beyond the limits of the body—the crown of the head and the soles of the feet—to give an illusion of slenderness to the figure and an emphasis on vertical lines. For men, this was achieved by wearing tall hats with sugar-loaf crowns and shoes with exaggerated points that extended far beyond the end of the foot. The total effect was accented further by revealing the full length of the leg in long tight hose beneath a shortened doublet. The practice of dividing the body with a vertical line and making the right and left halves of the garment in two different colors was another manifestation of the Gothic preference for the vertical. The

supreme expression of this preoccupation with elongated forms was seen in that towering bit of fanciful eccentricity, the **hennin** (Figure 3.28). It was a conical-shaped headdress that often extended several feet into the air, supporting a floating, transparent veil. The hennin grew to such enormous size that castle doors had to be enlarged to allow ladies to pass through without lowering their heads. Eventually it became necessary to pass laws regulating the height of the hennin in accord with the wearer's rank. At the opposite end, the woman's dress grew into a train that trailed along behind her, and her long tight sleeves added two more vertical forms to her total costume (Figure 3.29).

By the end of the fourteenth century, the art of weaving scenic picture-hangings had reached its highest degree of perfection. These skills developed in tapestry making carried over to production of other luxurious fabrics that were rich in color and elaborate in design (Figure 3.30). Velvets, damasks, and brocades contributed to the lavish ornamentation of garments for both men and women. Because of the cold interiors, multiple layers of clothing were found to be desirable, and many garments

Figure 3.29 A fifteenth-century painting by an unknown German artists that shows medieval lovers, who symbolized their pledge by wearing identical left sleeves. The gentleman's pose is intended to display an elegant, long-limbed figure to the best advantage.

Figure 3.30 Detail from *Hunt of the Unicorn*, a medieval French tapestry.

were lined with fur and trimmed extravagantly with ermine and sable.

Probably at no other time in history did the knight's armor have a greater influence on fashion than it did in the Gothic period. The long, loose surcoat with deep armholes, eventually worn by both sexes, was originally intended to be worn over the chain mail to reduce the sun's glare. Gradually, sections of chain mail were replaced with pieces of solid steel plate. By 1450, metalsmiths had become so skillful that a fighting nobleman was solidly covered in carefully jointed steel (Figure 3.31). The sharp metal edges required thick padding against abrasion and the male's doublet became expertly cut, padded, and quilted, "with sleeves so cleverly designed that the wearer could move his arms freely in a full circle—a highly desirable advantage in time of danger. The cut (was) surprisingly sophisticated."[8] As war weapons became more destructive, knights used heavier and heavier armor, until eventually they were practically immobile. Finally, after several centuries, armor was rendered obsolete by the invention of firearms.

The Gothic period in Europe represents the first emergence in Western culture of widespread use of the composite form of clothing, cut and sewn, but retaining some characteristics of the draped garment. It also marked for the first time a basic difference in styles of dress for men and for women. Previously, draped or tailored garments were essentially the same for both sexes. The Crusades had demonstrated the practicality of trouserlike leg coverings for horseback riding. The development of plate armor, as opposed to chain mail, also

[8]Blanche Payne, *History of Costume* (New York: Harper & Row, 1965), p. 180.

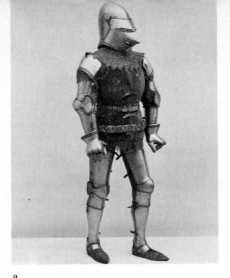

a

b

Figure 3.31 (a) composite armor shows the last stage of the change from chainmail to steel plate. (b) full-plated Gothic-style armor of the fifteenth century.

lent itself to trousers rather than to the skirt. Until then, there had been nothing essentially masculine about pants or essentially feminine about skirts. In other cultures, skirts for men developed as the traditional costume, and bifurcated garments are still traditional for women among the Chinese and Eskimos. Later influences in Western culture led to pants for men and skirts for women, and now pants or skirts for women, but never skirts for men.

James Laver pointed to this period as the beginning of fashion because it was the first time that the seduction principle operated in dress. Women's clothing began to reveal sexual attributes and, unlike previous periods in history, young girls dressed differently from older women. His idea does explain the differences in Gothic dress, with its low necklines, tight waists, and extremes of exaggeration of height and length, from the shapeless dress of the centuries just before. But, it is only one man's theory; we cannot say, for instance, that the transparent, revealing draped garments of the ancient Egyptians did not involve the seduction principle.

Gothic dress was closely related to the architecture of the period, just as dress was in ancient classical times, yet it was the very opposite of the classical conception of style. Greek garments, like Greek buildings, were in perfect harmony with the natural proportions of the human figure. The Gothic preference for exaggerated forms and overornamentation led to showy distortions of body and building. Gothic textiles were every bit as intricate as the Japanese, yet they lacked the restraint that coupled elegant fabric with simplicity of cut. The shaping of Gothic garments to body contour was perhaps the most precise technique ever developed in the history of costume. Although these characteristics seem on the surface to reflect a difference in aesthetic values, their distinctive qualities of style are rooted at least partly in the evolving technical patterns of the age.

Contemporary Dress

Many aspects of our modern technology have contributed to the evolution of styles that are distinctly contemporary. Central heating and closed cars brought the ever-increasing trend toward lighter weight clothing. Air-conditioning in many homes and cars and most public buildings less-

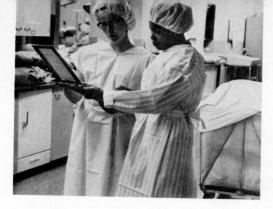

Figure 3.32 The idea of disposable clothing grew out of developments in paper towels and handkerchiefs and hospital gowns. With further technological improvements, inventive fashion applications may one day make some clothing available in handy tear-off rolls.

ened the need for seasonal clothing. Modern laundering equipment and fabric innovations reduced the number of clothing items needed. A shortened work week and greater affluence brought an entirely new concept in clothing—recreational and leisure-time clothing. The trend toward functionalism, again, a conception rooted in architectural form that began in the 1920s, shortened skirts, put the woman into pants, freed her from the corset, and gave her the most practical wardrobe known to date. Men, too, have been freed—from the traditional gray flannel suit. In Western cultures at least, sportswear reflects a whole new concept of freedom in dress for both sexes in colors, comforts, and care.

The biggest story of the twentieth century, however, concerns the development of man-made fibers for clothing. For thousands of years, only natural fibers were available—predominantly cotton, wool, flax, and silk. New materials, like nylon, polyester, acrylic, polyurethane, and spandex, provide unique combinations of properties that have allowed many innovations in garment design. Elasticized and stretch fabrics, for example, permit body-conforming fit with flexibility. Shaping

processes require fewer darts and seams. New fibers that are inherently flame-retardant have been developed, primarily for the space research programs. They are rapidly becoming available for consumer use as well. Other new fibers with amazingly high bulk and loft produce furlike fabrics. Leather also can be simulated with man-made materials so effectively that it is difficult to tell the difference from the natural product. In addition, the man-made fabrics are usually machine washable (Figure 3.32).

New fibers and finishes have eliminated the need to iron much of our clothing. The prospect of garments that are completely disposable eventually may eliminate the need for the washing machine. Nonwoven webs of spun-bonded thermoplastics are used widely for hospital surgical gowns and throw-away underwear. Simple designs with a minimum of construction in easy-to-care-for materials are consistent with our speedy production methods and increased tempo of modern life.

However, new technology has developed at a time when natural resources are seriously threatened. Conservation and preservation were the catchwords of the 1970s and are the watchwords of the 1980s. This is often true. Technology advances at differing speeds. The ability to produce may not coincide with the availability of resources. The important point is that the possibility of innovative approaches to solving the age-old clothing problems of supply and demand are either already available or will be in the near future. How soon such products will be available for consumer purchase will depend on how innovatively science tackles the allocation of dwindling natural supplies or develops means of synthesizing materials as yet unknown.

SUMMARY

Evolution of Styles

Many cultural factors influence the development of characteristic styles that are unique to a particular people or period. A strong relationship between design forms and the material aspects of any given culture may be demonstrated in primitive and advanced, Oriental and Occidental, as well as ancient and modern societies.

To some extent, there has always been an element of choice in the selection of one pattern over another. The Navajo Indian, for example, was aware of improved techniques for spinning but continued to use the distaff and spindle to prepare yarns for weaving. The ancient Greeks were expert weavers, but they preferred to fabricate plain cloths that would accentuate the graceful folds of their garments.

Among the Japanese the weaving of patterned brocades and damasks, painted, printed, and embroidered silks has always been a highly creative industry. Rather than arrange their fabrics in intricate folds, the Japanese use the simply cut, straight-hanging kimono to display their textile skills to best advantage. People of Gothic times had similar skills but combined them with highly developed techniques for cutting and tailoring pieces to conform to the body's shape. This complex Gothic costume was dictated partly by concurrent technical innovations in architecture and armor. Just as the ancient Greek and the Gothic dress styles followed architectural prototypes, so our modern clothing reflects functionalism and streamlined design. Modern styles are further influenced by relatively recent developments in the area of man-made fibers, chemical finishes, and the bonding, molding, and fusing processes.

FOR FURTHER READING

American Craftsmen's Council. *Body Covering*. New York: Museum of Contemporary Crafts of the American Craftsmen's Council, 1968.

Batterberry, Michael and Ariane. *Mirror, Mirror: A Social History of Fashion*. New York: Holt, Rinehart and Winston, 1977.

Buchman, Diane Dincin. "Ancient Health and Beauty Secrets of Egypt," *Harper's Bazaar*, October 1979, pp. 186–87.

Dockstader, Frederick J. *Weaving Arts of the North American Indian*, pp. 13–80. New York: Thomas Y. Crowell, 1978.

Kluckhohn, Clyde, W. W. Hill, and Lucy Wales Kluckhohn. *Navaho Material Culture*, pp. 203–315. Cambridge, Mass.: The Belknap Press of Harvard University Press, 1971.

Tilke, Max. *National Costumes: from East Europe, Africa and Asia*. New York: Hastings House Publishers, Inc., 1978.

Chapter 4

FOLKWAYS, CUSTOMS,
MORES, AND LAWS

As a human organism, every individual is motivated by a certain set of impulses or drives. Among these are the basic biological needs for food, air, elimination, temperature control, and sexual gratification. There are also social needs for prestige, status, and responsiveness from others—secondary drives that gain in importance once the basic needs are satisfied. All societies exert considerable control over the ways in which such needs are met. People who learn to gratify their urges according to the proscriptions of the cultural environment in which they live are generally regarded as normal or well-adjusted individuals.

The selection of customs that govern need gratifications usually are based on deep-seated ideas about the "goodness" or "badness" of things or actions. It is on the basis of such ideas that every culture develops a fairly consistent system in which each custom bears a specific relationship to a total way of life. Thus, in every society there are certain accepted standards of dress that are considered right, proper, or appropriate, whereas other ways of using clothing are regarded as wrong, improper, or inappropriate. Social habits such as the norms that govern the way people dress may be described more specifically as **folkways, customs, convention, etiquette, fashion, mores, taboos,** or **laws.** Each of these terms has a slightly different meaning, although they are often used interchangeably and refer to the whole group of behavior patterns that characterize a particular cultural group.

Most social scientists prefer to use the word *norms* to cover all types of social habits, and they define each of the other terms in a more restricted sense. Although all are considered **social norms**, they differ in the degree of conformity required and the severity of the sanctions by which they are enforced.

Folkways generally are accepted as the conventional ways of doing things, but people do not usually insist on them. The braless woman may be regarded unfavorably by some, but seldom is she excluded from group participation. The rebuff she gets from certain societal segments may be strong, but, within her own group, acceptance is not compromised. So too, "good clothes" are generally worn for special occasions and dining out, although even these folkways have changed. Restaurants that once refused service to men without ties and jackets have relaxed their dress restrictions considerably. And even a quick examination of a high school or a college campus shows that the old category of "school clothes" really no longer exists.

Although the line between folkways and customs is hardly noticeable, custom generally implies a social habit that is more deeply rooted in tradition. Many customs originate in association with magical or religious practices and thereby attain some measure of sanctity. The sanctions imposed against a man for failing to remove his hat in church are far more stringent than those imposed against him for failing to wear a suit, a shirt, and a tie to church.

Social norms that carry the connotation of being morally or ethically right or wrong may be called mores or taboos. Clothing habits that are in some way associated with the control of sexual relationships in society are, by and large, part of a group's mores and taboos. Violation of the standards of decency or modesty in dress usually is regarded as a threat to the welfare of society; therefore, violation of mores may result in more severe penalties than the violation of either customs or folkways. Mores are enforced through strong social sanctions: "Thou shalt wear clothes." Taboos are merely negative mores: "Thou shalt not expose thyself in public." Such prescriptions, however, vary from society to society. What is accepted as decency or modesty in dress by one group may very well be regarded as sexually stimulating by another.

When social rules are enacted by those in political power and enforced through the machinery of the state, they become laws. Although laws pertaining to clothing were quite common in bygone eras, today relatively few rules of dress are prescribed by law. Many states and most cities, however, maintain statutes against indecent exposure. The interpretation of what constitutes indecency in different parts of the country is an enlightening study in itself. Any regulation, however, that is enforced through some designated authority (such as a military uniform or a school dress code) may be considered a law.

All these social habits overlap so much that it is impossible to draw precise lines of distinction among them. Rather than clear categories, there is a continuum of conformity and enforcement that ranges all the way from approved behavior to obligatory behavior, from disapproved to forbidden. Precise definitions are complicated by the fact that some departure from the code is expected. The obligation felt by an individual within the group may vary all the way from complete nonconformity to elaborate overconformity. Nevertheless, people are so inclined to take their own cultural habits for granted that they often assume that their ways of dressing are natural and inherent. ("Of course men wear pants! What else would they wear?") An ethnocentric view of clothing customs in which the practices of one's own group become the standards by which all other patterns are judged merely reinforces and strengthens the norms in a given society. A social habit is normal for no other reason than that it is both learned and shared.

Fashion innovation and acceptance are treated in more detail in other parts of this book, but it should be noted here that fashions are also a part of the normative system of society. Because they are more fleeting, less deeply imbedded in tradition, their changes may be observed more readily. But all social habits are subject to change over a period of time. Fundamental environmental changes often run counter to existing customs, and the custom gradually is modified in the direction of greater harmony with the spirit of the times. Bifurcated garments for women (as outer wear at least) were scandalous in 1850. With the advent of the bicycle near the turn of the century, it became more scandalous for a woman's skirt to billow in the breeze than to accept a modified version of the masculine pants. The factors that influence fashion change are the same forces that modify other folkways, customs, mores, and laws over time. The main difference between fashion and other social norms is time. Fashions come and go more rapidly; customs and mores are more persistent, but they are no more rational, logical, or inevitable simply because they are durable. Nystrom differentiated between custom and fashion by explaining that in fashion, people imitate their contemporaries; in custom they imitate their elders.[1]

FOLKWAYS AND CUSTOMS

Both folkways and customs are manners or practices of dress that are transmitted from one generation to another. They are established through periods of relatively long usage. Folkways of dress are usually very persistent without ever being strongly enforced. On men's clothing, for example, buttons are always placed on the right side of the garment, whereas on women's clothing the buttons are always on the left. The logic of this habit has been explained by reasoning that a man could adjust his buttons with the left hand, leaving the right hand free to continue its work or fight with implement or sword. The woman, who habitually carries a child with the left arm, would have to use her right hand when buttoning or unbuttoning. Another expla- nation for the reversed buttoning is equally interesting. In the thirteenth century buttons were very valuable and thus became status symbols. Many buttons meant high status, and so the French court went button crazy, buttons from neck to toes. Since most people are right-handed and since men customarily dressed themselves, their garments were made to button left over right, the easiest way to do it. Women were dressed by maids, and the majority of maids were also right-handed. From their vantage point, in front of their lady (or behind her) it was more convenient to button from right to left, using the right

---

[1]Paul Nystrom, *Economics of Fashion* (New York: Ronald Press Company, 1928), p. 123.

Figure 4.1 Because of custom, women's garments still button right over left.

Figures 4.2 and 4.3 Many traditional costumes for women include some type of bifurcated garment. Left, Turkish women in wide pants. Right, Indian woman in baggy trousers.

hand (Figure 4.1). Try it yourself and you will see why. Although this reason for a custom may be more fancy than fact, it does make sense.[2] Whatever its origin, the habit persists. But if an inept seamstress made the buttonholes on the wrong side of a blouse, it would probably be noticed only by the person who tried to wear it. Violation of such a norm would hardly concern the group or subject the wearer to any social disapproval. In fact, in some Western subcultures—the Hasidic Jews and the Old Order Amish—closures are reversed, for men right over left. These customs are firmly rooted in tradition based on Biblical interpretations. They serve as a distinguishing clothing feature that helps to set the wearer apart from mainstream culture and enhances group identification and solidarity.

Customs, like folkways, are slow to change, particularly in activities that have rather strong emotional or spiritual con-

tent, such as weddings, funerals, graduations, and other types of religious or civic ceremonies. When such norms are violated, the reaction ranges from mild to strong disapproval. The details of custom are spelled out in etiquette books, although such volumes rarely cover the wide variation that exists among different social classes and ethnic groups even within American society.

Probably more deeply ingrained than any other clothing customs are the habits that serve to distinguish the sexes. For centuries, Western code has decreed pants for men and skirts for women. The growing influences of sports and functionalism have resulted in an increasing relaxation of the code as far as women are concerned, but in American society at least, men have not yet taken to wearing skirts. This distinction, however, is far from universal. Traditional costumes in other parts of the world include some type of bifurcated garment for women (Figures 4.2 and 4.3); and many a vigorous Scot or Greek male is extremely proud of his skirts (Figure 4.4).

[2]*Fashion Hang-Ups* (New York: Monsanto Textiles Company).

Figure 4.4 Many a vigorous male has been serenely proud of his skirt: Scotsman in his kilt.

Figure 4.5 Arabian men also wear skirts.

A visitor from a foreign country wearing a *dhoti* or *kilt* would attract many a curious stare on the streets of Middletown, U.S.A., but because his customs of dress are expected to be different, no further social sanctions would be imposed. A Middletown native, however, who dared to wear a knee-length skirt on Main Street would cause his fellow citizens to laugh or ridicule him, question his sanity, pretend not to know him, and/or report him to the police. In a cosmopolitan or international community the varied customs that come from different cultures result in an atmosphere in which no one is made to feel out of place no matter what is worn. In the smaller homogeneous society, customs tend to be stronger and more persistent because of their widespread use and acceptance (Figure 4.5).

Essentially this pattern describes society's system for rewarding or punishing behavior. A slight infringement of the rules (such as the violation of a folkway) will tend to elicit only mild forms of response—an amused look or chuckle or two. When departure from the norm is more conspicuous, group disapproval is correspondingly stronger (Figure 4.6). Questioning a person's sanity is making the assumption that one is not "normal," and, therefore, not to be trusted somehow. When this suspicion is strong enough, association with these individuals is no longer desired and they are either avoided or barred from group participation. If they are reported to the police, the assumption is made that the infringement is severe enough to be covered by some type of law.

One of the strongest deterrents to the violation of customs, however, is not the external sanction from others. Rather, it is the internalized sanction produced by feelings of guilt, shame, embarrassment, or just being "out of it." The man who fails to wear a tie when everyone else is wearing one may experience only a minor form of discomfort, but a man who forgets his pants suffers considerably more embarrassment.

"Another tradition going by the boards—tennis whites! WHAT hath God wrought?"

Figure 4.6 Changing lifestyles have altered many of our traditions.

Over the years, there probably has been no more universal custom of dress in Western culture than the traditional wedding gown. Although the long white dress and transparent veil are not customary in all societies, special or distinctive garb for the bridal couple is a common characteristic of most cultures. White has been worn for centuries by English and Hebrew brides as a symbol of their innocence and purity. Actually the custom may be traced back to the days of the ancient Greeks, but it has not been in continuous practice since. The Romans added a red veil, and, up until the time of the Renaissance, most European brides wore red. Red, a color that was thought to have the power of repelling demons, is still the traditional color in India.

There were periods in history, even in fairly modern United States history, where practicality won out over traditional attire for bridal wear. The old saying "Wed, bred, and dead" in the same dress often meant a brown wedding dress for the thrift-conscious, careful nineteenth-century woman, a dress that could be worn on future dress-up occasions and not reserved, in all its costly splendor, for a one-time use.[3]

So many stories have been told about the origin of the wedding veil, that almost all must be considered legend. No person knows for sure, even within a particular societal group. One of the most contemporary and appealing stories to Americans has to do with Nellie Curtis's decision to pin a long white scarf in her hair at her marriage to George Washington's aide and favorite nephew. Her decision to wear the scarf resulted from the comments her fiancé made after glimpsing her through a lace curtain at an open window.

Historically, the wedding veil is far more significant than the dress itself. Its origin has been attributed to many sources, but the veil appears in China, Korea, Manchuria, Burma, Persia, Russia, and Bulgaria, as well as in the majority of Western civilizations, both ancient and modern (Figure 4.7). The symbolism of the veil, however, has varied. Primitive peoples believed that it protected the woman from evil spirits; more widespread perhaps was the idea that the veil concealed the bride's face and form from all eyes save those of her husband.

The bridegroom, too, usually dons some special attire, although the male's "Sunday best" is often the common pattern. In many cultures the groom is treated like a kind of "king for a day" and garbed in the raiment of a chief, prince, or knight. Our own customs are really not too different; the common practice of renting formal attire for the groom is fair indication that he does not expect his exalted status to last very long.

[3]*Woman's Day*, September 4, 1979, p. 20.

Figure 4.7 In modern Yugoslavia, the bride's clothing combines traditional costume with modern shoes. Behind her veil, her eyes are downcast and for a full year, she must keep them that way.

It is interesting to note here that there seems to be more universal agreement on what is considered appropriate for brides and grooms than there is on what is suitable for men and women in general! Yet we have never had any written laws (outside the rules of etiquette books) that regulated wedding attire, whereas we have had, and still do have, numerous ordinances against transvestism (wearing the clothes of the opposite sex).

Similarly, the clothes prescribed for other rites of passage, such as christenings, confirmations and bar mitzvahs, funerals, coronations, and ordinations, are also matters of custom. Ceremonial dress connected with religious observances, and the opening of Parliament and other governmental formalities is almost always customary in nature. Academic regalia is a colorful example of a firmly entrenched custom. Although not always worn by academicians for commencement and other official university ceremonies, the cut of

the gown and the colors of the hood are very specifically assigned (Figures 4.8 and 4.9). The academic gown stems from the *gardcoup,* a travel garment worn by both sexes in the thirteenth century,[4] The differences in cut of gowns, especially the shape of the sleeves, immediately indicates to those who know the symbolism the degree that the wearer holds. The bachelor's gown has pointed sleeves; the master's sleeve is oblong in shape and open at the wrist, and it hangs down in the traditional manner. The sleeve on the doctoral robe is very wide and bell-shaped. The color of the velvet bands on the doctor's robe and the trimming on the hood indicate the various fields of learning, while the color of the stripes on the hood are the official colors of the university conferring the degree.

Changing lifestyles more recently have challenged many of our traditions (Figure 4.10). In the early 1970s there was an outbreak of weddings in the most unlikely places—in treetops, on horseback, in cow pastures, and under the sea. Mothers and aunts nearly fainted and fathers proclaimed that the whole social system was falling apart. In many ways it was. The deliberate violation of widely accepted custom is a symptom of basic changes in a society's structure. The new forms of wedding ceremonies were inevitable reflections of the changing role of women, attitudes toward premarital sex, communal living, and rising divorce rates. Although the young adults of the seventies have been influential in the inevitable change in the social order, the dire predictions of their parents did not come to pass. Society, and with it civilization, survived and so did the customs of the culture. By the end of the

[4]Blanche Payne. *History of Costume* (New York: Harper & Row, 1965), p. 169.

Figure 4.8 The traditional master's gown sleeve drapes freely to the wrist, with the back end extending below the knees in a crescent shape.

Figure 4.9 The velvet panels and chevrons of the doctor's gown represent the wearer's area of study.

decade weddings were as large, traditional, and expensive as before. Bridal shops and formal rental stores flourished in shopping malls (Figure 4.11). The colors of the ruffled shirts of the ushers matched the long gowns of the bridesmaids. The attendants were as colorful as peacocks, but the bride wore white. All predictions for the eighties indicate that the customary, traditional wedding attire will remain in vogue

for those of marriageable age as well as for their younger siblings.

The white gown, the religious ceremony, the reception, are all making a comeback in the 1980s. There has been a trend away from such things as marriages in forest preserves with the bride and groom in dungarees, and back to the traditional

Figure 4.11 Although ruffled and colorful, the basic style for male wedding attire is still traditionally formal.

Figure 4.10 Nontraditional wedding attire and wedding ceremonies in nontraditional places reflect a changing social structure.

weddings. Old-fashioned weddings are in, even if the mother of the bride sits in the back row holding the bride's baby. "White no longer stands for purity, it stands for security," said Priscilla Kidder, better known as Priscilla of Boston, noted bridal authority and owner of a retail outlet.[5]

Abrupt change in custom is always more alarming than the gradual modifications that come about over time. Until the 1950s, the accepted form of dress for presidential inaugurations always included formal cutaway coat and high silk hat. President Eisenhower was the first to substitute the less formal Homburg. A decade later, President Kennedy landed another blow to custom when he abolished white tie and tails from the annual White House reception for foreign diplomats. The public reaction to this apparent disregard for tradition was reflected in newspaper editorials such as the following:

The occasion will not be improved by this departure from the formal to the semicasual. A sense of occasion and the ability to dress properly for it are among the refinements of civilization.

"Casual," a word whose meaning is much abused these days, too often means slack and slovenly. In this context it is a short step from a business suit to a sports jacket.[6]

The incident illustrates not only the inevitable change to which custom is subjected, but the resistance with which such change is met. Innovations in the material culture have contributed to the obsolescence of the high silk hat; few men, even those of less-than-average height, can manage a high hat in a low-slung modern car with any semblance of comfort, much less dignity.

These changes gradually paved the way for President Johnson to make his inauguration appearance in an oxford gray business suit and black fedora. A more conservative President Nixon restored a bit of tradition to the ceremony in 1973 by choosing semiformal daytime wear. It was clear by then that the life of the silk hat had expired. Although a president has yet to appear in a sport shirt for traditional ceremonies, President Ford did bring considerable informality in attire to the Oval Office. President Carter's dress is on the conservative side of middle for business and he also chose the semiformal daytime outfit for his inaugural walk from the Capitol to the White House.

Conformity to the folkways of dress is usually not considered essential to society. Violation of clothing customs that are both strong and persistent is likely to incur more severe social sanctions.

DRESS AND MORALS

[5]Shelly Cohen, "Tradition Regaining Standing with Brides," *Roanoke Times and World Report*, September 21, 1976, p. C-10.

[6]"JFK's 'No White Tie' Edict an Unhappy Fashion Note," *Nevada State Journal*, June 10, 1962.

When customs are elevated to a higher level of concern for the welfare of society, they may be described as **cultural mores**. In all the world's societies regulation of sexual activity appears to be hedged by various taboos and restrictions, most of which are considered essential to the orderly functioning of the kinship system. The role clothing plays in stimulating or diminishing sexual interest, therefore, becomes a matter that is symbolic of the moral standards in any given culture. In general, the relationship between clothes and sex centers on the degree of exposure, concealment, or emphasis given to particular parts of the body.

Casual observers are apt to think that the standards of decency and morality of their own culture are the only right ones. They see bizarre aspects of clothing in alien cultures but not their own. Viewed in the historical and anthropological perspectives, however, any one pattern of morality is really only one of many variant configurations—a kind of local, rather than logical, temporary bias.

In any discussion of decency in dress, one must consider the total range of possibilities, from complete nudity on the one hand to complete coverage on the other. One American made first-hand observations of several tribes inhabiting the interior of Africa and followed it with a study of the people of the city of Khartoum, a center of Moslem culture. Among the primitives who habitually go naked, he noted total lack of self-consciousness about the human body and concluded that a guiltless exposure of the anatomy was "the most normal, nonprurient, everyday thing in the world."[7] In contrast, the women of Khartoum were voluminously garbed and wore face veils that covered all of the face except the eyes. When one young girl accidentally unhooked her veil, she looked up in startled embarrassment and quickly fumbled for the corner of her veil to fasten it back into place. One might ask if the Moslem with the misplaced veil felt any more or less naked than the woman whose only body covering was a string of beads.

Even if we accept the theory that feelings of natural shame are universal in human beings, several illustrations can be cited to disprove the assumption that such shame is necessarily associated with lack of clothes. Among the Suyá Indians of Brazil, for example, neither men nor women are the least bit embarrassed by their naked bodies, but they are humiliated if caught without their lip disks. And in another South American tribe, complete nudity for both sexes provokes no shame, provided their painted clothing is "in place." In fact, they were embarrassed by the clothes worn by the first outsiders they met. They still think the fully clothed people who deal with them, in the heat and humidity of the Amazon jungle, are somewhat strange. They have tried, to no avail, to get the traders and missionaries to adopt their version of dress. Chapter 1 mentioned other examples that illustrate the cultural differences in the concept of modesty.

Some authorities claim that nudity makes the sight of a human body commonplace and asexual, and this is why wearing clothes has become such a firmly established social habit. The fact that human beings, unlike other mammals, are not restricted to a mating season has led to development of sexual stimuli intended to maintain the mating instinct the year round. When clothing is the norm, "temporary nudity is the most violent negation possible of the clothed state."[8]

---

[7]Thomas Sterling, "On Being Naked," *Holiday*, August 1964, 8.

[8]Ernest Crawley, *Dress, Drinks, and Drums*, ed. T. Besterman (London: Methuen and Company, 1931), p. 111.

The exposure of almost every part of the human anatomy has been considered indecent or immoral in some period of fashion history. Even an area of the body that is not normally sex-connected (for example, the arm, the ear, the foot, the nape of the neck) will become so if covered long enough.

Following the collapse of the Greco-Roman civilization, Western culture was dominated largely by Christian doctrine, which viewed the body as the source of temptation. In attempting to divert attention from the body, early Christians sought to hide it, and the loose, transparent classical garment was transformed into a heavy, enveloping costume that encased but dared not define the figure.

The church instilled strong feelings of guilt and shame in connection with the body, but it fought a losing battle against the forces of fashion. Many exaggerations in dress originated in a demand for modesty. For example, the tight hose that evolved during the Middle Ages were extremely revealing, to say the least. At the same time, the man's doublet grew shorter and shorter until all of the hosed leg was exposed, all the way to the waist in fact. Without modern zippers, elastic, or other means to make a functional fly-front opening, a problem arose as to how to cover the opening resulting from the separate legs of the hose. The church decreed the wearing of a codpiece to cover the front opening of the breeches. Intended as concealment, the codpiece began as a small pouch. Gradually it developed into such fancy forms that it soon became the focal point of the entire costume. Slashed and padded, it was decorated and exaggerated until it became a large bun or crescent-shaped ornament suggestive of the male organ it covered. Was this perhaps the seductive principal operative in male clothing?

And, probably originally meant as a joke or a very limited fad item, a modern codpiece, the only item of merchandise, was sold in a small boutique owned by co-founder of the Black Panther Society, Eldridge Cleaver. He marketed a version of men's pants with a discreet front pouch reminiscent of the fifteenth-century adornment. In his Beverly Hills, California, establishment, these codpieces conspicuously adorned the front of contemporary jeans and retailed for between twenty and thirty dollars.

For women, décolletage was extremely limited in medieval times, but by the end of the sixteenth century, an exposed female bosom was regarded as a maidenly virtue and necklines were cut low and square. But at the same time, any exposure of the arms or legs would have been openly obscene. Arms were encased from shoulder to wrist, and like the skirts, sleeves were sufficiently widened so as not to reveal even the contour of the form beneath them.

The enormous crinoline that became the symbol of mid-nineteenth-century decorum reached its popularity peak at the same time that Victorians exposed the bosom to such a degree that the look became known as the famous "Victorian valley" (Figure 4.12). As if the crinoline were insufficient to hide that sacred part of a woman, her legs, the proper maiden also wore pantalettes beneath her petticoats and high-topped shoes. Neither women nor pianos had legs; both were well covered. If legs had to be mentioned in polite conversation, they were called "limbs."

Hands, too, have been known to be body areas that must be kept covered at all times, indoors and out. At one time a lady was never to remove her gloves, except at meals when she changed to fingerless mittens. The Mohammedan's mortification

Figure 4.12 Victorian dress may have covered the legs, but decolletage exposed the bosom.

Figure 4.13 The 1920s flapper: a shocking revelation of the legs.

Figure 4.14 The 1930s: all eyes were on women's backs.

at exposing the mouth in public has already been noted. As late as 1930, Moslem women who dared to discard their face coverings were burned alive by outraged mobs for blasphemy.

Even today in many parts of the world, religious bans continue to impose restrictions on dress and appearance. Islamic law, for instance, forbids a woman to show her hair to a stranger, much less to allow a man to touch it. Consequently, females who visit beauty salons are considered sinners who face eternal damnation. Hairdressing is interpreted as "giving women an appearance other than that which God created,"[9] and, along with hair dye and make-up, it is strictly taboo. At one time, a woman could be stoned to death for violating such a taboo; today she is promised a curse by God.

The changing standards of decency and morality may be observed easily within a

[9]"Egyptian Women Defy Religious Hairdo Ban," Cairo UPI News release, August 17, 1970.

ten-year period. If, for example, someone suggested in 1915 that women would expose their knees in public, the idea would have been considered shocking. By 1921, however, the trend began to rear its ugly and obscene head, and a number of states enacted laws that prohibited the wearing of skirts shorter than a specified number of inches from the floor (Figure 4.13). Roaring and racy as the twenties may have been, women showed their legs, but not their backs or their bosoms! The backless evening gowns of the 1930s revealed a part of the anatomy that had not been revealed before (Figure 4.14). Not only was the spinal column exposed to the waist, but for the first time in fashion history the bias-cut skirts suggested that the gluteus maximus consisted of two parts rather than the more modest mono-buttock. But then, people in the 1930s would never have believed that women would ever dare to expose their navels as they did when the bikini bathing suit was introduced, nor would people in 1950 ever have imagined that anything like the topless bathing suit would even be suggested in the 1960s (Figures 4.15–4.18).

Most people were outraged by the topless suit, and females who dared to wear one on the public beaches during the sixties were promptly arrested. By the early 1970s, however, we had been through a decade of see-through blouses, topless bars, and breast-revealing movies. A ban-the-bra movement became part of women's liberation. By 1972, the monokini made its debut on European beaches, and everyone casually ignored the phenomenon. By the summer of 1978, the naked breast was acceptable, at least on European beaches and Southern Pacific islands. When interviewed at these places, seven out of ten people said that they felt no shame on seeing a naked woman on a beach. In fact, the Greek government tourist office stated "Anyone can appear naked so long as they don't disturb other people."[10] In a Corsican resort village often the only people wearing clothes in a restaurant were the waiters. The fashion spread to a few seasides in California and Florida, and although the reaction in the United States was somewhat more hostile, the police chose to "look the other way" rather than make arrests. Clearly the female breast had lost much of its seductive suggestiveness. Nude bathing, though still not found on every public beach, is not a rarity. Occasional groups raise alarmed cries about morality and decency but somewhere along the major coastal beaches, areas have been either formally set aside or informally adopted for nude bathing.

Fashion serves to maintain interest in the body by concealing parts of it long enough to build up its "erotic capital," as fashion historian Laver calls it. "You have to save up for quite a while to get any thrill out of seeing it," he said.[11] The female bosom had not been exposed publicly since the end of the eighteenth century, so it had had ample time to accumulate "capital." The leg had just as much capital in the early 1900s, and counterparts of the modern topless shows were called "leg shows" at the beginning of the twenties.

Does this mean then that there can be no immodesty in dress if practically every kind of a standard has been held as socially acceptable at one time or another in history? Quite the contrary, it means that as long as any state of dress is accepted as a permanent social habit, some costume or some style will always be considered immodest. Fashion is a part of the mores, and like the mores, it constitutes a kind of implied agreement about what is right and what is wrong. Acceptance into the mores can transmute an obscene fashion into innocence, and vice versa. Conflict over the question of decency in the modern world arises when standards are established independently by different cultural or subcultural groups.

During the 1960s, teenagers eagerly adopted shortened hemlines, much to the dismay of school officials. It is a fair assumption to say that within the teenage culture itself, short skirts were no more suggestive of sexual impropriety than short socks. In the adult world, however, they *were* suggestive, and some high school students are more adult than others. If, in

---

[10]"Toplessness—Emancipation vs. Imagination," *Boston Evening Globe*, August 16, 1978.

[11]James Laver. "What Will Fashion Uncover Next?" *Reader's Digest*, September 1965, 142–145.

Figure 4.15 A One-piece knitted wool swimming suit from 1918.

Figure 4.16 In the 1930s knit wool suits featured vibrant colors and a little shaping through the bust area.

Figure 4.17 Gernreich's 1964 topless bathing suit. Many who wore it were arrested for indecent exposure even though it covered more of the body than the monokini of the 1970s.

Figure 4.18 In the late seventies, the move was back to one-piece suits of man-made fibers that provided excellent fit.

fact, "everyone's wearing it" (the teenager's ever-present explanation), then *not* wearing it would be the most attention-getting device possible. When only one girl in a school is sent home because her lack of underclothes is too revealing, it is fairly obvious that everybody has not forsaken underwear. Any girl who inspires a catcall should know she is either doing or wearing something that is just beyond the pale of the accepted mores of the times. If, by chance, every girl in the school wore something suggestive enough to bring on a catcall, one might imagine that the boys would be hoarse by noon. But obviously, this could never happen; by the time a once-suggestive style reaches mass acceptance, the taboo is broken and the style no longer is regarded as immodest.

The phenomenon can be explained simply enough: complete nudity in itself is not erotic. It becomes so only when preceded by or contrasted to a state of dress. In this very limited context, then, all clothes become somewhat immoral, if we define immorality as inciting sexual interest. Habitual nakedness may indeed be capable of elevating man to a higher mental plane; but as one gentleman stated his dilemma, "I don't mind about the exposure, but won't it deaden the senses?"[12]

Although most research has indicated that modesty is a relatively unimportant motivation in clothing behavior (see Barr, 1934; Creekmore, 1963, on page 22), associations have been found between religious orthodoxy and measures of modesty in dress. In general, individuals who express a higher degree of commitment to religious tenets tend to be more conservative in their selection of clothing, particularly in regard to body exposure and tightness of fit, than do those with less commitment.[13]

Aside from the religious issue, however, the relationship between clothing and moral values has been demonstrated in other ways. A survey of a group of college men, for example, revealed that those who expressed lower moral values also held more liberal clothing attitudes. In 1971, these "liberal attitudes" were defined as favoring greater body exposure, going barefoot to class, sunbathing in the nude, men wearing beads, chains, and longer hair, and women wearing slack suits for most occasions.[14] Concern with modesty in clothing, both one's own and others, may also change with age. Drake discovered that while men in the twenty-five- to thirty-five-year-old age group expressed little concern about degree of body exposure or tightness of clothing, men over sixty-five were the most concerned about modesty in clothing.[15]

Not only does modesty seem to be increasingly unimportant in clothing selection, but immodesty does not rank very

[12]Jessica Daves, "Can Fashion be Immoral?" *Ladies' Home Journal*, January 1965, 92g–92h.

[13]See, for example, J. A. Huber, "A Comparison of Men's and Women's Dress and Some Background Factors Relating to Those Attitudes," Master's thesis, Ohio State University, 1962; J. K. Kleinline, "The Relationship of Mennonite Church Branch, Age, and Church Attendance and Participation to Attitudes Toward Conservativeness of Dress," Master's thesis, Ohio State University, 1967; and K. Christiansen and A. Kernaleguen, "Orthodoxy and Conservatism— Modesty in Clothing Selection," *Journal of Home Economics*, 63, no. 4 (April 1971), 251–255.
[14]C. Mahla, "The Relationship of Selected Clothing Attitudes and Specific Moral Values for a Group of Undergraduate College Men," Master's thesis, Stout State University, 1971.
[15]Doris Drake, "Clothing Interests of Young Adult, Middle Aged, and Elderly Men," Master's thesis, Virginia Polytechnic Institute and State University, 1978.

high either as a motivating factor. As we saw in Chapter 1, proponents of the immodesty theory believe that clothing is worn as a sexual lure, to attract attention to parts of the body and not to conceal them. Investigations concerning the use of sensuous clothing—that is, clothing to enhance the wearer's physical appearance to attract the attention of the opposite sex—indicate that, although subjects did wear sensuous clothing for many occasions, they did not do so very often.[16] Thus the morality or immorality of specific clothing practices can be evaluated only in terms of the behavior patterns that we considered normal for a given cultural group.

The wearing of clothing as an expression of modesty is not universal in mankind; it is determined by the culture, learned by the individual, and very likely not fundamental in nature.

CLOTHES AND THE LAW

Restrictions on dress that are enacted into laws and sanctioned through some type of legal enforcement are usually those considered necessary to maintain social, political, or moral order. The issue of effective enforcement is always clouded by the difficulties encountered in drawing clear-cut lines of distinction between mores and law, or between customs and law. There are two basic types of legislation concerning clothing, laws that proscribe or prohibit how individuals may dress and those that prescribe or decree what people must wear. Legislation of proscription is more common. There is more resistance to the idea of a government telling its people how to dress than to the idea of a government telling people how not to dress.

[16]Ann Elizabeth Snyder, "Sensuous Clothing in Relation to Self-Esteem and Body Satisfaction," Master's thesis, University of Tennessee, 1975; Elizabeth Ann McCullough, "Attitudes of Black and White College Females Toward Sensuous Clothing, Selected Body Attributes, and the Use of Sensuous Clothing," Master's thesis, University of Tennessee, 1975.

Laws of Proscription

Laws of proscription are primarily those that attempt to regulate morality by defining what constitutes indecent exposure. Also included are laws that prevent wearing clothes to deceive, as when clothes of the opposite sex, of the military, or the police forces are worn to deceive.

Since dress is such a fundamental social habit, public removal of garments generally comes under the regulation of law. In the United States as well as in most European countries, exposure of the person has for many years been considered a criminal offense. It seems somewhat paradoxical that such laws in Western culture are becoming increasingly lax and permissive at the same time that developing countries—where nakedness was once the norm—are enacting new statutes to regulate dress. Uganda, for example, has an official ban against miniskirts, hotpants, and maxis with a V-shaped slit down the front. The Ugandan president was quoted as saying, "These styles . . . are a disgrace to our culture. African women must

Figures 4.19 Vatican coverup: Visitors to St. Peter's Basilica are required to cover "improper dress" with black cloaks. The rule for women is that dresses must cover the knee. Men may not wear shorts. Visitors who refuse to wear the cloaks are barred from entry.

In Italy, Vatican guards refuse admission to the Eternal City to anyone dressed in what the church regards as improper clothing (Figure 4.19); in Singapore and Saudi Arabia, male visitors with long hair are turned back by airport police.

Although the phenomena of the topless bathing suit and the monokini was discussed as part of the mores of a culture, historically the propriety of the bathing suit has always been a subject for legal action. Early in the twentieth century, women were arrested for appearing on the beaches in bloomers. Such laws were not confined to beachwear, however. In 1895, Chicago passed a law requiring that "all cycle riders must wear baggy continuations. No knicker knee breeches or revealed stockings are permissible, but full and loose nether garments down to the heels." From time to time, lawmakers have attempted to legislate the length of women's skirts. In the early 1900s, two young ladies in Buffalo were arrested for raising their full-length skirts too high while crossing a muddy street. Several years later, women were given jail sentences for appearing in split skirts and, during the twenties, several states attempted to pass laws that prohibited the wearing of any skirts that did not reach at least 4 inches below the knee.

These historical examples may lend some perspective to the widespread controversy over school dress codes that dominated the educational scene in the late 1960s and early 1970s. The usual penalty for violating the school's code of proper dress was being sent home to change, but repeated offenses often drew permanent suspension. Early in the sixties girls were sent home for outsized hairdos and boys for wearing their pants too tight. By the middle sixties, regulations were aimed at controlling the length of boys' hair and the length

wear decent dresses, so that they can get the respect they deserve."[17] The law makes no exceptions: foreign as well as African women are fined for having hemlines too far above the knee.

In similar fashion, the Masai citizens of Tanzania were ordered to replace their loose shoulder cloaks with Western-style trousers, and Tanzanian office women were forced to lower their hemlines in the name of African culture. The move was made to destroy the sartorial indecency that was "alien both to African culture and to the socialist policies of the government."[18] The African republic of Malawi also maintains official restrictions against miniskirts and hotpants and has deported foreign tourists for violating the code.

[17]"East Africa's Hot Mini-Skirt War," *San Francisco Chronicle*, May 29, 1972.

[18]Nicholas Moore, "Sartorial Strictures," *Chronicle Sunday Punch*, March 21, 1971.

Figure 4.20 Some people believe that police are overly suspicious of long-haired males.

of girls' skirts. The long hair issue continued well into the seventies, and numerous court battles were fought over the school's authority to regulate students' appearance. It may well be that society's deeply rooted feelings of morality regarding an appropriate distinction between the sexes accounts, in part, for the open hostility encountered by many young men who adopted shoulder-length hair styles (Figure 4.20).

Several research studies have demonstrated that there is a relationship between students' appropriateness of dress and their behavior in school. One study, however, found that students with records of discipline problems tended to epitomize the dress norms of the peer group, but their clothing differed significantly from the styles that were selected by teachers as appropriate.[19] This finding suggests that clothing does, in fact, single out individuals for disciplinary action.

In spite of the fact that public opinion overwhelmingly supported the school's

[19]Thelma Leigh, "Discipline Problems as Related to School Dress Codes and Clothing Norms," Master's thesis, University of Nevada, 1971.

prerogative to establish and enforce dress regulations, most school boards gradually relaxed their codes to conform to the current fashion. By the mid-seventies the issue of hair lengths had died a natural death. As the older generation copied the youth culture with its hirsute appearance, the young men cut their hair and shaved their beards.

Skirt lengths, on the other hand, were absorbed into the general "do-your-own-thing" attitude toward clothing in general that gradually emerged from the seventies (Figure 4.21). Skirts—mini, maxi, and all lengths in between—coexisted with pants, symbolic of women's liberation from fashion dictates. While men still tended to conform to the accepted norms of their group—changed norms—it was not uncommon to see at a social gathering women dressed in skirts of all lengths or in pants with several variations of fullness and formality, almost, but not quite, jeans to ball gowns. The disaster of the maxi in 1973 indicated that women were not to be dictated to by the fashion press. At that time, hundreds of small apparel manufacturers went out of business when women refused to buy the longuette and wore their pants instead. A brief revival of long skirts occurred in the late seventies but did not last. By the early 1980s skirt lengths were once again on the rise.

Ordinances on the legal limitations of dress (or undress) also apply to performers. In many states, dancing in the nude is still considered "indecent exposure," although a strip artist usually can meet the requirements of the law with a pastie on each breast and a G-string. The exact requirements vary with the state, sometimes the city.

Another category of regulations pertaining to dress involves laws that attempt to

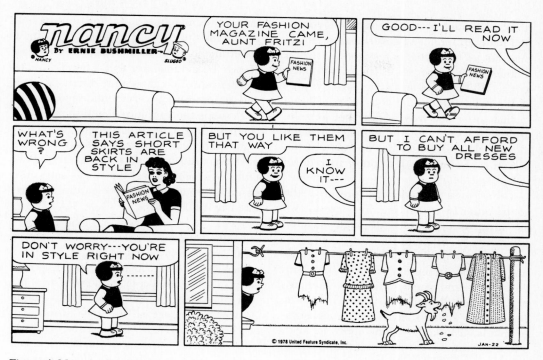

Figure 4.21

protect society from the evils of misrepresentation. Where such laws exist, a person may be imprisoned, for example, for wearing a military or police uniform without the proper authority, and the death penalty is usually given to a wartime spy caught wearing the enemy's uniform. Such laws also prohibit the impersonation of one sex by the other. Langner posed the following question:

The prohibition against men wearing women's clothing in public is far more strictly applied and is based on the belief that this would, if permitted, increase male homosexuality. Since many women are now habitually dressing in men's clothes, it is interesting to speculate whether or not this will also increase female homosexuality.[20]

City ordinances against transvestism are quite common, and any deliberate attempt by a man to pass himself off as a woman (or a woman as a man) is regarded as immoral, improper, and, in some places, illegal. Transvestism is wearing the clothes of the opposite sex. It is not synonymous with homosexuality.

Laws of Prescription

It is harder to think of **laws of prescription** and one is tempted to assume, especially in free and democratic countries, that there are no such regula-

[20]Lawrence Langner, *The Importance of Wearing Clothes* (New York: Hastings House, 1959), p. 171ff.

tions. Although it is true that we do not find many examples of governments dictating what all their people may wear, they do dictate what some of its members must wear. Military uniforms are strictly prescribed. The individual does have a choice in that he or she may or may not join the armed forces, but once the choice is made to join, the individual has no voice in the selection of clothing. It is prescribed down to the last detail.

Other laws intended to preserve the social order by restricting dress are known as **sumptuary laws**. Although enacted primarily to distinguish class, rank, or status, they also attempt to preserve morals and act as protection devices for both consumers and home industries. Sumptuary laws are designed to control the way people may spend their money on consumer goods. Thus, they may apply to food, shelter, furnishings, and entertainment as well as to clothing. Many such laws were first of moral or religious origin, but they are not made or enforced by religious groups. They are laws passed and enforced by governmental agencies, state, local, or national.

The study of sumptuary legislation during any period of history is interesting. They tell much about the life and times of the period, the economic and social conditions, the spiritual concept of government, and the customs and dress of the people. There probably have been sumptuary laws ever since there were governments to pass them. Some Old Testament clothing prohibitions were forerunners of actual laws. Long ago in ancient Egypt laws regulated clothing, particularly the use of wool in garments. Wool was considered unclean and priests or anyone working in the temples could not wear woolen garments. The problem with applying a strict defini-

tion of sumptuary laws to the ancient Egyptians involves the fact that their government and their religion were so closely bound together that it is possible to determine which laws were religious ones and which were governmental concepts.

Perhaps the first formal sumptuary laws occurred in Roman times when church and state were clearly separate and some means of designating rank was extremely important. The colors of the togas and the banding around them were carefully regulated by rank, and

only the emperor could wear the purple toga. . . . Every free-born son of a Roman citizen was entitled to wear, not just the ordinary toga of citizenship, but the toga praetexta of the governing class, a white toga with a purple border. At the age of 16, when such a lad reached maturity, this toga . . . was ceremoniously laid aside and dedicated to the household gods. He then donned the plain white toga which was the badge of all Roman citizens. To wear the toga praetexta again he had to earn the right by becoming a senator or one of the higher magistrates.[21]

Down through history there have been many examples of sumptuary laws. They changed rapidly, often were ignored, and sometimes were only slightly enforced. The great mass of sumptuary laws were passed between 1300 and 1700. In fact, they are often associated only with the Middle Ages, but they are a part of all periods. Although harder to find today, they are still a part of the laws regulating how people may dress.

During the Medieval period "Government was a paternalistic ruling body that sought to regulate the lives of its subjects

[21]Payne, *History of Costume*, p. 103.

not only legally and politically but morally and spiritually as well. Sumptuary legislation was a pronounced expression of this concept of government."[22] Extravagance in dress was considered a social evil if indulged in by the wrong people. Also, prior to this time, only the nobility and the rich, those in the very top layer of society, could afford to have the luxuries of dress, fine cloth, jewels, and dyes. With the rise of a moneyed middle class, many more people could afford to copy the clothing of royalty and nobility. Therefore, laws were enacted, not just as an attempt to regulate extravagances, but to protect the upper classes as well. Laver coined the phrase *Hierarchical Principle* to describe the use of dress to symbolize one's position in society. Dressing to demonstrate the pride of one's wealth, he claimed, is

inevitably viewed with suspicion and distaste by our rulers, both ecclesiastical and civil. . . . Sooner or later the rich, rising man ventures to assume the fine clothes none-the-less, and consternation, not to say panic, ensues among the upper classes. Hastily a sumptuary law is drafted, and hastily passed.[23]

During the reign of Charles IX in France, only ladies of high rank were permitted to wear dresses of silk and carry fur muffs. The width of the farthingale and the amount of ornamentation was also prescribed according to the wearer's rank. Edward III of England restricted the use of ermine and pearls to members of the royal family, and Henry VIII decreed that any-

one below the rank of a countess was not entitled to wear a train. Queen Elizabeth I attempted to regulate the size of her subjects' neck ruffs, the color and lavishness of their gowns, and the length of men's hair and beards! Her stringent clothing edicts caused a good deal of resentment against the crown, and they were eventually repealed to avoid open rebellion.

Today the lower classes still try to copy the rich and with modern technology, mass production, and installment buying they can almost accomplish their goal. Latest fashions from the top design studios are quickly copied. Intricate seaming and fine fabrics are reduced to simplicity of form and fabrics made from man-made fibers. A wide range of clothing is available at all price levels. There are fewer formal restrictions on dress, although codified regulations have not disappeared entirely. You can still tell a corporal from a colonel, and even in academic circles the ceremonial gown distinguishes the doctors from the masters, the masters from the bachelors, and the bachelors from those who have no degree at all.

Although few sumptuary laws exist today to regulate clothing use for maintaining status and prestige, remember the other purposes of these laws. Even in democratic countries, people still look to governments for protection from shoddy, fraudulent, and unsafe consumer goods and from excessive or unfair competition on the international market. A country's wealth hinges on keeping money within the country; in the past, foreign styles and foreign-made clothing were often prohibited entirely. Today, almost all modern countries have some type of import and export restrictions or quotas as well as tariffs to protect home industries. We also accept governmental regulations requiring manufacturers and

[22]Joana W. Phillips and Helen K. Staley, "Sumptuary Legislation in Four Centuries," *Journal of Home Economics,* October 1961, 673–679.

[23]James Laver quoted in "Laver's Law," *Women's Wear Daily,* July 13, 1964, p. 5.

retailers to meet certain standards in the apparel products they sell.

The Permanent Care Labeling Ruling of the Federal Trade Commission can be considered a modern-day example of a sumptuary law designed to protect the consumer by providing adequate care instructions in easily understandable language. These labels must be permanently attached to apparel products and designed to last for the life of the garment. Congressional acts have been passed requiring the content labeling of a wide range of textile products. Under the Flammable Fabric Act several specific textile products now have to pass certain minimum safety standards in order to be sold. All these laws and rulings are sumptuary in nature since they have some effect directly or indirectly on how the average person can spend money on clothing.

Clothing practices considered necessary for preserving moral, political, or social order often are enacted into law and enforced through the machinery of the school or state.

SUMMARY

Folkways, Customs, Mores, and Laws

Habits of dress are a part of the folkways of a society. Like other social norms, they may be differentiated by the degree of conformity required and the severity of the sanctions used to enforce them. Folkways, such as the wearing of a tie, the direction of a garment closing, or the hatband of a hat, represent conventional ways of dressing, but their violation is considered no particular threat to society. Clothing customs, on the other hand, have stronger emotional content and require a stricter adherence to prescribed form. Customs are established through tradition and transmitted from one generation to another. In contrast, fashions are also a part of the normative system of dress, but they have a relatively short duration.

Clothing norms that carry the connotation of being morally right are included in the mores of society; taboos are considered morally wrong. Those aspects of dress that appear to be related to the regulations of sexual activity in society are usually subject to serious enforcement. Clothes might be expected to promote greater sexual morality by covering those parts of the body that stimulate feelings of eroticism, but the fact is that any part of the body may become erotic if it is habitually covered by clothing. When a state of dress is the social norm, temporary nudity is sexually stimulating only because of its sharp contrast with the clothed state. Mores, like customs, change with the times. Fashions serve to maintain interest in the body by shifting the focal point from one area to another, revealing some parts, concealing others. Through this constant shifting, exposure of almost every part of the human anatomy has at some time in fashion history been regarded as indecent or immoral.

Clothing practices enforced through legal measures usually are construed as necessary for maintaining social, political, or moral order. Most societies have laws that regulate the degree of body exposure that is permissible in public. In some areas it is illegal to impersonate an officer or a member of the opposite sex by the unauthorized wearing of their garments.

Governmental regulations that attempt to control the way people may spend their money on consumer goods are called *sumptuary laws.* In the past they were used to maintain the social order and preserve morals by restricting certain items of dress to those in the upper layers of society. Today they include laws that attempt to protect the consumer from unsafe products and home industries from foreign competition.

Cultural habits of dress are usually so taken for granted that people are inclined to believe that they are inevitable and logical; clothing norms are seldom rational, but they are almost always rationalized by the people who conform to them. Viewed within the perspectives of history and anthropology, we can see contemporary patterns of dress as only one of many variations. Just as each age had its clothing themes, so too does the clothing of today follow the general folkways, customs, mores, and laws of contemporary society.

FOR FURTHER READING

"Come to the Prom," *Forbes*, 122 (July 24, 1978), 57.

Johnson, Bettye. "Good-by to Dress Codes—For Now," *Phi Delta Kappan*, 61 (November 1979), 217.

Kirkham, George L., and Edward Sagarin, "Cross-Dressing," *Sexual Behavior*, 2 (April 1972), 53–59.

Langner, Lawrence. *The Importance of Wearing Clothes*, pp. 141–200. New York: Hastings House, 1959.

Phillips, Joana W., and Helen K. Staley, "Sumptuary Legislation in Four Centuries," *Journal of Home Economics*, 53 (October 1961), 673–677.

"Students' Attire Again HEW Target," *U.S. News and World Report*, 87 (December 3, 1979), 14.

Chapter 5

FASHION CHANGE
AND THE SOCIAL ORDER

The term *social order* refers to the entire structure of the society in which a people live—all the organizing forces and organizations, political, social, and economic. It includes the customs and traditions, the values and beliefs of a people. It exists through time and, as social patterns and social organizations change, the social order also changes. The stability and continuity of a culture is directly related to the importance of custom and tradition within it. However, culture is seldom static; change is inevitable. All past social orders have changed. The present social order is currently in the process of changing, and it is safe to assume that changes will continue in the future. The degree and speed of change varies from culture to culture, as does the value placed on change itself. As the sociofacts or institutions society creates to govern behavior inevitably change, so too does the clothing worn in that culture. In simple folk societies, stability rather than change is desirable. Tradition is stressed and change is slow. Patterns of dress may change only slightly from year to year. In complex industrial societies, people have a strong faith in progress through change. Fashion change is often swift, highly desirable, and actively pursued.

Fashion in clothing or other material artifacts does not appear out of thin air. Fashion grows out of the culture and is influenced by its sociofacts and mentifacts. Fashion, like culture itself, is also dynamic, not static. It may be defined, in fact, as the prevailing style or mode accepted by large numbers of people at a given time and place. Such a definition implies change, however slow and subtle it may be. There is a relationship between changes in fashion and changes in the social order, so that each historical period leaves its visual imprint stamped on the fashion of the times. It is for this reason that most items of apparel, by virtue of their style, material, and workmanship, can be dated at least within the decade of their origin.

Consistently wearing old-fashioned dress is a sign that the individual is somehow out of step with the times. Yet this changing aspect of dress is the characteristic most often criticized by observers of the social scene. The need to discard a garment—not because it has outlived its

usefulness but because it has outlived the fashion—implies senseless economic waste. In any age, some forces that tend to restrict or impede fashion change are at work, whereas other forces stimulate or accelerate such change. The rate of change in any given period depends on the balance that exists between these two sets of forces. The factors that promote rapid changes are particularly important in our own society and are responsible for the current increased fashion obsolescence.

RESISTANCE TO CHANGE

If we go back several hundred years, we can observe a time when the rate of fashion change was slow enough to be unnoticeable within the span of an individual's life, when

a land-owner of the fourteenth century, for instance, would dress in clothes very similar to those of a land-owner of the eleventh century. A cowherd of the fourteenth century might have inherited his garment from his great, great . . . grandfather (several times removed) in so far as the style and cut were concerned. Moreover, a cowherd in either century would no more have thought of dressing like a land-owner than a corporal in the army would think of dressing in a colonel's uniform; that is to say, he might well think of it, but would not dare to do it.[1]

The acceleration of changes in fashion began in the Renaissance, when a rising class of wealthy merchants sought not only to copy the knights and their ladies, but to outshine them in the richness of their dress.

Rigid Class Distinctions

A society in which a ruling class can maintain both wealth and power has little need for fashion-racing. The line between the feudal lords of the Middle Ages and the poorer classes was strictly drawn; serfs had no possibility whatever of copying the dress of their lords and masters. When extreme differences in wealth exist and only a few can have a costly wardrobe, fashions tend to remain stationary for a longer time. In earlier days, moreover, clothing was so expensive that even the wealthy could not afford a frequent change of costume. Most finer fabrics had to be imported from the Far East, and the intricate cut of the garments required such tedious and skilled workmanship that the cost of each item was prohibitively high. It is reported, for example, that the shoes Richard II wore were worth $2,000 a pair and his cloak, $90,000.[2] Even as late as 1850, when voluminous gowns were the vogue, the yardage required was so great that even if

[1]James Laver, *Dress* (London: John Murray Publishers, 1950), p. 8.

[2]Elizabeth Hurlock, *The Psychology of Dress* (New York: Ronald Press Company, 1929), p. 78.

made of the cheapest of fabrics, a single dress was unbelievably costly. Few women could afford more than two or three dresses in their entire wardrobes and "Sunday best" had to serve for many years. When the lower classes are thus prevented from copying the clothing of the privileged few, the rich need not change their style of dress in order to preserve their distinctiveness.

A rigidly defined class system, reinforced by an unequal distribution of wealth, retards fashion movement and gives rise to traditional forms of dress.

Figure 5.1   Fifteenth-century *poulaines*.

Sumptuary Laws

In the last chapter, sumptuary laws were discussed in connection with legal restrictions on dress. Such restrictions are often used when a ruling class cannot maintain its position of fashion supremacy by controlling wealth. The ruling class enact sumptuary laws to control consumption by lesser citizens. When the feudal lords, for example, found themselves outdone by the showy extravagance of the newly rich merchant classes, they resorted to legal prohibitions for dress and personal decoration. In the fifteenth century, imitation of the long-toed hose and shoes called *poulaines* (Figure 5.1) led to a regulation on the number of inches that shoes could extend beyond the toe: 24 inches or more for a nobleman; 12 inches for a gentleman; and 6 inches for a commoner.

Although sumptuary laws to maintain status are rare in modern society, they are prevalent in almost every nation in which class distinctions are recognized, and they appear when the social structure reaches a stage of development at which the national wealth is no longer in the hands of the nobility alone.[3] Such laws helped to curb extravagances and in that sense were moralistic, but their primary function related to the preservation of class distinctions.

Sumptuary laws that restrict fashion imitation reduce the necessity for rapid change.

Custom

Customs were also discussed in Chapter 4, but they must be recognized here as important factors in retarding fashion change. Traditions are carried on by symbolic use of clothing and reverence for the past makes people cling to the time-honored forms of dress that signify status, role, or position. National costumes, such as the Japanese kimono, the Indian sari, the colorful provincial costumes of Brittany, Normandy, Yugoslavia, and many others, are fast giving way to the Western style of dress, but most people give up

[3]Hurlock, *The Psychology of Dress*, pp. 64ff.

traditional garb with great reluctance. Bridal gowns, academic attire, judicial robes, church vestments, and various other forms of ceremonial dress remained relatively unchanged through centuries of use. Although recent attempts have been made to uproot many of these traditions, such elements of dress are slow to give way to newer modes of fashion. And even where traditional clothing is abandoned for the more utilitarian Western jeans and T-shirts for everyday wear, national costume is retained for special days and events. In a highly technical and nontraditional social system, nostalgia for the past combined with a psychological desire to discover ancestral roots has caused many ethnic or national groups to organize and to wear complete authentic national dress. The clans gather annually in many places. One of the most popular places is in western North Carolina, where every July thousands of Scottish descendants, complete with kilts, take part in the Highland Games Festival. Faithfully copied medieval Scottish outfits and more modest kilts of clan tartans provide "a kind of mystical connection with Old Scotland."[4]

Traditional forms of dress that are deeply rooted in custom and habit tend to preserve the existing forms of dress.

Isolation

When people are out of touch with the fashion world, their mode of dress falls into conventional patterns that usually come from local custom or tradition. Isolation formed the basis for much of the provincial attire that characterized remote villages and communities. At one time, there were marked differences between urban and rural populations, but today, because of improved communication and transportation, relatively few areas lack access to fashion information. In places like Hawaii, for example, it is far easier to hang onto the muumuus and the poi pounders than it would be if the islands were attached to the mainland. Their geographic isolation imparts—even to the tourist—the tendency to abandon current fashions for the comfortable garb that symbolizes the Hawaiian way of life.

Susceptibility to fashion change is greatly reduced by geographic isolation.

Fear

Fear of the new and unknown is another factor that heightens resistance to fashion change. A certain security is afforded by familiar styles, and most people refrain from buying anything startlingly new or daringly different for fear of being ridiculed. Primitive and uneducated peoples often attach symbolic significance to particular designs or styles, and they feel that discarding the old is risking the possible evils and misfortunes that may accompany the new and unproven. To depart from the sure and the safe way of doing things requires a great deal of courage and an adventurous spirit.

Fear of the new inhibits fashion change.

Government Restrictions

When the source of raw materials is limited, legal regulations are sometimes

[4]*Newsweek*, July 24, 1978, p. 88.

necessary to insure equitable distribution of the available supply. In the United States, the L-85 restrictions during World War II retarded fashion changes by limiting the amount of fabric that could be used for specific articles of dress. Skirts stayed at knee length for four war years. The extreme reaction to these restrictions was the unprecedented change introduced in 1946 by the House of Dior. The "new look" dramatically dropped skirts many inches. Accustomed to gradually changing skirt lengths, women were quick to discard their wartime wardrobes.

In Britain, the wartime designs were known as CC41 styles, and they were rationed to consumers by a coupon system in which each person was issued sixty coupons for a period of fourteen months. A man would exhaust his allowance if he bought one suit (twenty-six coupons), a set of underwear (ten), one shirt (five), a pair of shoes (seven), and four pairs of socks (at three coupons a pair). People "made do" with what they had and repaired old clothes. Even in peacetime importation of goods from other countries may be restricted. Excise taxes imposed on articles that are considered luxury items, such as furs and leather goods, restrict rather than promote their widespread use.

Shortages and/or restrictions imposed on the use of raw materials retard fashion changes.

Form of Government

The many forms of socialistic or totalitarian governments are characterized by their attempts to do away with all class distinctions or inequalities in dress. In their early stages at least, this is accomplished by a uniform type of clothing. The Marxist-Lenin brand of Communism produced the drab jackets, ill-fitting trousers, and crude black boots that were so long a part of the image of the typical Russian citizen.

In previous chapters, we discussed the effects of the Communist revolution in China, when "almost overnight as it seemed, the nation was garbed in a dress whose sexless regimentation of style and shapelessness symbolized the liberation of a new national spirit according to Marxist theory, although to less politically perceptive eyes it appeared, however utilitarian, unnecessarily drab."[5]

In like manner, Castro's regime in Cuba produced the familiar bearded, green-clad *Barbudos;* men and women dressed exactly alike; smart clothes were "unpatriotic" and inconsistent with the spirit of the times. Austerity in dress is like a badge of honor that symbolizes the leveling of classes.

This expression of classlessness through dress is by no means a twentieth-century phenomenon. Costume in England under the Commonwealth of Oliver Cromwell showed the same drabness and uniformity of style, and our own Puritan ancestors went to great extremes to avoid all forms of ornamentation in dress that would distinguish one colonist from another.

It is particularly interesting, however, to note the gradual renewal of interest in fashionable clothes once the major crisis has passed. As the American colonists became more wealthy, new styles were adopted almost as quickly as they were in Europe. By 1957, GUM department store in Moscow held fashion shows that promoted ivy-league suits for men and fashionable

[5]A. C. Scott, *Chinese Costume in Transition* (New York: Theatre Arts Books, 1960), p. 92.

clothes for women. In the late 1950s communist China had its first fashion show in Peking, featuring modern versions of the traditional *ch'i p'ao*, the woman's long sheath gown with side slits.

No population is content for long with drab, uniformlike clothes; a renewal of status incentives and aesthetic drives is the inevitable outcome of an improved standard of living.

Elimination of class distinctions by totalitarian or socialistic regimes by suppressing fashion results in adoption of austere forms of dress. Fashion change, if it occurs at all, is very slow.

SUMMARY

Resistance to Change

The degree of change that occurs in any society in a given period depends on the balance between the forces that promote fashion obsolescence and those that impede progress. Factors that tend to work against fashion change include (1) rigid class distinctions, (2) sumptuary laws, (3) custom, (4) isolation from the fashion world, (5) fear of the new, (6) government restrictions, and (7) form of government.

AGENTS OF CHANGE

The tremendous acceleration of fashion change in contemporary society has been the subject of much social criticism. Those who oppose planned obsolescence treat it as a kind of social disease for which we have not yet discovered an effective cure. In order to weigh the value of such criticism the forces that increase the tempo of change and their possible alternatives must be examined.

An Open Class System

Both rigid class distinction and its opposite, the classless society, function in ways that limit the degree and speed of fashion change. Democracy, on the other hand, provides the ideal climate for fashion-racing. The constant push of the middle classes up the social ladder creates the driving force for an ever-changing shift in the design of clothes worn by the upper classes.

The foundations of fashion-racing were laid in the Renaissance, which gave rise to a wealthy merchant class and at the same time made available luxurious importations from all over the world. The Industrial Revolution then gave considerable momentum to the fashion movement by increasing the ease with which styles could be reproduced and distributed and also by contributing to the elevation of the working class; the number of people who were both willing and able to be fashionable rose greatly.

Fashion changes flourish in the open class system that characterizes a democratic form of government.

Abundance

Two of the most important factors in speeding up fashion movement are a wide diffusion of wealth and an increase in the family income that exceeds the amount required for the bare necessities. The purchasing power of the average consumer in the United States has increased tremendously in the last quarter of a century. At the same time, commercial expansion and intense competition among ready-to-wear manufacturers have greatly increased the range of fashion goods to which such purchasing power may be applied (Figure 5.2). Greater equality in income distribution has been further intensified by the system of taxation and the numerous social services provided at government expense. Many more people today can afford the additional comforts of middle-class life. Thus, an increasingly affluent society indulges in greater spending for luxury items and, as they do, wardrobes change and expand.

It is also significant that at the same time that Parisian couture houses find it difficult to stay in business, the number of designer-owned firms is increasing in the United States. Most of these houses retail garments at prices between $250 and $500. While fewer women can afford to pay $1,500 for a St. Laurent, many will buy a Bill Blass original design at $350.

Diffusion of wealth in the mass society increases consumption and greatly speeds up fashion change.

Figure 5.2   Mass production and an abundance of goods greatly increase the availability of ready-to-wear garments.

Leisure

The natural accompaniment to increasing affluence is a decreasing need for long hours of work, and

in the last century a drastic decline has occurred in the work week. In 1850 it is estimated to have averaged just under seventy hours, the equivalent of seven ten-hour days a week or roughly six at from six in the morning to six at night. A hundred years later the average was 40.0 hours or five eight-hour days.[6]

The spread of leisure to the lower- and middle-class groups has the effect of intensifying the importance of fashion in individual lives. Not only do people have more time to think about fashions, but leisure provides greater social opportunity to wear them. Even though many jobs may require work clothes or a uniform, few people today lack occasion to array themselves in a wide variety of dress for evening or weekend activities. Leisure time can also lead to boredom and a search for amusement and novelty, both of which find direct outlets in fashion change.

[6]J. K. Galbraith, *The Affluent Society* (Boston: Houghton Mifflin Company, 1958), p. 334.

Increased leisure speeds fashion change. People have time to think about clothes, and they also have more social opportunity to wear them.

Sports

Probably the most important single influence on fashion during the last seventy years has been the world of sports. In the early development of fashion, position and wealth were indicated largely by the elaboration of dress; but by the end of the eighteenth century, the English country gentleman's costume began to set the pace for all masculine attire (Figure 5.3). Enormous prestige was attached to the huntsman since the sport implied that he owned a vast acreage. The embroidered coat, the satin breeches, and the white silk stockings were not suitable for riding to the hounds, so the Englishman fashioned a "sports costume" consisting of a plain cutaway coat and riding boots, which soon became so popular that it was worn for hunting and also for regular day dress. Gradually elements of the hunting costume crept into formal wear, and its influence was complete.

Nineteenth-century sports were confined mostly to hunting, archery, and lawn croquet. The costumes for these activities were decidedly nonfunctional from a modern point of view, but they slowly evolved toward greater utility. It is important to realize that prior to the advent of sports, functional utility in clothes implied that they were intended for physical labor; no prestige value could be attached to comfortable garments. But participating in sports meant that one had sufficient leisure to devote time to play activity, and modifications in dress that permitted strenuous

Figure 5.3 The English country gentleman's dress c. 1790.

movement became entirely acceptable as long as everyone knew the physical exertion was all in fun (Figure 5.4).

Although bloomers appeared earlier, bifurcated garments for women became socially acceptable through the sport of cycling. But perhaps the most drastic changes in the female wardrobe originated on the tennis courts and bathing beaches. When Suzanne Lenglen walked onto the courts in 1920 wearing a pleated skirt shortened to midcalf, it may have shocked the spectators, but it paved the way for the gradual rise of skirt lengths in the ensuing five years. Gussie Moran's lace-trimmed bloomers still made news in the mid-twentieth century. The feats of serious swimmers like Annette Kellerman in the early 1900s were facilitated by streamlining the bathing suit. In 1910, the maillot was scandalous, but by 1924 it had been stripped down to essentials and given social approval. And even the maillot of

Figure 5.4 Participation in the world of sports revolutionized women's dress.

1924 was modest compared to the 1979 return version, which did not cover much more than the bikini had. Thus, as people—and women in particular—began to lead more active lives, their clothing gave greater freedom to their limbs. Sports accustomed the eye to body exposure, which in turn had a lasting effect on all other categories of dress.

Sportsmen and sportswomen continue to enjoy widespread popularity and publicity, and their actions are followed as eagerly as those of fashion leaders. The functionalism of sports extends even into areas in which functionalism is not needed. The sale of tennis outfits and jogging "sweats" far outnumber the quantities of rackets and balls sold or the number of runners on the streets. Clothes for active sports are "in," even for those not inclined to physical exertion (Figures 5.5 and 5.6).

Sports and sports apparel have been directly affected by another social change. The widespread concern for health in general, and hypertension and heart disease specifically, has increased public awareness of the role exercise and physical fitness play in longevity. President Kennedy first brought this point to the attention of the American public at a national level. He called on the public schools to emphasize physical education at all levels. And with television providing ringside seats at Olympic contests, soon every young man of junior high school age knew that you could run faster in Addidas and only the lack of Danskins kept teen-aged girls from accomplishing the same gymnastic feats in their own high school gymnasiums.

People of all ages, particularly the "high-risk" group, the American male thirty-five years of age and over, took to the courts and roads. Tennis outfits and jogging clothes, along with special pants and shirts designed for bicycling, are not just fashion items, but utilitarian clothes designed for the special needs of a changing time. Helmets required for motorcyclists have been adopted by bicyclists. Add to these the leotards and swimwear and it is readily apparent that large numbers of people concerned about their health are supplementing their wardrobes accordingly.

Greater utility and functionalism in clothing has been a direct result of partici-pation in active sports, particularly by women.

Education

Widespread education also speeds up fashion changes. It opens the door to new areas of experience, and it increases interest in and desire for a more fashionable appearance. Entrance into what Galbraith has called the New Class of leisure is accomplished overwhelmingly through increased education. Education not only helps increase earning power, but it extends consumer wants especially into areas in which fashion plays a part. Moreover, knowledge lessens fear of the new and the unknown and frees people from inhibitions rooted in custom. People become more aware of the choices and possibilities open to them and more confident of their judgments in making clothing decisions.

Widespread education lessens the fears that so often inhibit fashion change.

Figure 5.5 A lightweight covering for roller skating.
Figure 5.6 A jogger's uniform.

Figure 5.7 In Japan today, the dress of both men and women is dominated by Western styles, but not everyone has abandoned the kimono.

Figure 5.8 A mixing of styles is evident in this blending of traditional Eskimo dress with modern ready-to-wear.

Culture Contact

Just as geographic isolation tends to slow fashion change, increased communication and contact with various cultures increases the rate of change (Figure 5.7). Although the language of another country may be difficult to learn, the outward symbols of clothing are easily transmitted from one culture to another. The eagerness with which the once-isolated communities adopt Western ways can readily be seen, especially among the younger generation (Figure 5.8). Before the arrival of Europeans, for example, Eskimo clothing was always made of animal skins; now nylon windbreakers replace the skin parkas, and rubber boots are worn instead of mukluks.

The intermingling of cultural elements in the modern world can be seen in almost every country (Figure 5.9). Even in the United States adaptations are found of the Oriental cheongsam, the Indian sari, the African burnoose, Micronesian sarongs, primitive jewelry, Tyrolean hats, Spanish toreador pants, peasant blouses, Middle Eastern caftans, and so on and on. Ethnic

clothing has been accepted by the American middle-class, middle-aged suburbanite and it is no longer a symbol of the youth culture. Ethnic is in, found in Bloomingdale's, and i⁺ refutes the "trickle-down"

Figure 5.9 The impact of culture contact often is responsible for incongruities. These women in Gabon wear miniskirts but carry their babies in the tradition of their culture.

theory of fashion adoption. It worked its way up the economic and status ladders and was expensively worn by the top of the social hierarchy and, for the most part, discarded by those who "discovered" it. Such cultural diffusion is facilitated, of course, through increased travel and improved communication, as well as through the inevitable exchange brought about by war. Vestiges of American G.I. uniforms are seen in all parts of the world, and soldiers and sailors return home with souvenirs from their distant stations.

Increased cultural contact, made possible by improved transportation and communication, speeds up the rate of change in fashion movements.

Youth

A way of life that emphasizes a reverence for custom, age, and tradition gives little chance for fashion changes. Conversely, a society that places high value on youth tends to be oriented in the direction of change and progress (Figure 5.10). In the sixties and seventies, retail clothiers became more and more aware of the dollar value of the teenage market. With increased incomes and few family responsibilities, young people in that period invested heavily in cars and clothes.

The assumption of fashion leadership by the younger generation led to development of a male couture that started when Carnaby Street overtook London's conservative Savile Row. The result was a revolution in men's finery that spread throughout the world. Pierre Cardin, a French couturier, began designing men's suits. American women's wear designers quickly followed: Bill Blass, Oleg Cassini, Geoffrey Beene, Oscar de la Renta, John Weitz, and many others put out a men's line. Thus, in the decade from 1960 to 1970, expenditures for men's and boy's clothing went from $9.7 billion to $18.6 billion.[7]

When fashion caters to youthful tastes, more radical changes are likely to be introduced.

Figure 5.10 A youth-oriented society has increased the variability seen in young men's and boy's wear. Sales doubled in a decade.

[7]Walter McQuade, "High Style Disrupts the Men's Wear Industry," *Fortune* (February 1971), 75.

Social Agitation

A thorough study of the history of costume and the social events of each period makes it clear that fluctuations in fashions indicate the pace of social change that occurs within the society in general. In the Far Eastern civilizations that maintained rigidly structured, unchanging caste systems, little innovation in clothing styles is noted from one century to the next. In recent years, political and social changes in India have resulted in self-determination instead of British rule; a less stringent, although still existing, caste system; and emancipation and franchise for women. The traditional Indian dress, both dhoti and sari, is beginning to disappear from the major urban centers.

The historical periods marked by social agitation, tension, and strain show intense variation in fashion departures from the basic pattern.[8] England's seventeenth-century political and social history provides a ready reference for comparing social change and fashion change, dramatic changes in a relatively short time. The century began with James I, the first Stuart king. He was a weak, inept monarch who made little change in government, and so the Elizabethan mode of dress continued into the first quarter of the century. The fact that his wife, Queen Anne, inherited over 2,000 of Elizabeth's gowns helped retain the style of the former monarch. By the 1620s the High Renaissance had given way to the Baroque style in the arts and so fashions became a visual expression of the attitudes and values of the Baroque period. Jewels and ruffs (hard and stiff) gave way to buttons, bows, and laces (soft and curved). Political events reached their peak during the Puritan Revolution and the resulting Commonwealth. This development had a decided effect on dress; ornamentation became associated with royalty and was finally banned. The Cromwell upheaval introduced the austere Puritan dress. The middle-class Puritan dissenter, to indicate his disapproval of morals and politics, adopted a somber coat, wide plain collar, woolen stockings, and a black, wide-brimmed felt hat. These Puritans who fought and won the civil war believed in hard work and individuality and although they paved the way for eventual political democracy, they doomed Englishmen's dress to joyless obscurity. The Commonwealth ended with Charles I's triumphant return from the court of Louis XIV, who ushered in an era of showy dress unsurpassed in the history of costume. The frivolity of the court and the political and social life in the last half of the century were reflected in bows, ribbons, laces, and curls, all competing for a place on the gentleman's costume.

The sociopolitical tensions that surround wars, revolutions, social upheavals, and struggles over human rights appear to cause fashion to violate the fundamental contour: normally wide skirts may become narrow or short, and slender waists may become thickened or dislocated in position.[9]

Thus, fashion's sensitivity to social problems provides a visible index of agitation and unrest. Drastic changes in clothing patterns are evidence of changes else-

[8]Jane Richardson and A. L. Kroeber, "Three Centuries of Women's Dress Fashions, A Quantitative Analysis," *Anthropological Records*, 5, No. 2 (Berkeley and Los Angeles: University of California Press, 1940), 111–153.

[9]A. L. Kroeber, *Style and Civilization* (Ithaca, N.Y.: Cornell University Press, 1957), pp. 10–18.

where. In 1953, Mandelbaum predicted that if women's evening dress should suddenly "take the form of tight trousers or should present standards of propriety in skin exposure be abandoned, sober observers of our society may well take it as a token of a truly major social upheaval."[10] Interestingly, when the counterculture demonstrations reached their peak after the Vietnam war ended, that is precisely what happened.

The rate of fashion change is related to the degree of social change that occurs in any given period.

Emancipation of Women

A radical change in women's position in society has the same effect as other types of social upheaval (Figure 5.11). The accepted form of dress in cultures that keep the female subservient to the male remains static for generations, sometimes for centuries. Men have hobbled women, politically, socially, and sartorially, since the cave men tied their women near the fire to keep them from running away. Conversely, in periods in which women refuse to accept an insignificant status and seek to put themselves on an equal footing with men, feminine dress modes change more swiftly. The wardrobe of the Victorian lady, for example, indicated clearly that she could not possibly indulge in strenuous physical exercise of any sort. The abundance of sportswear in the feminine wardrobe a hundred years later proves the exact opposite. Cunnington claimed that if we had no

Figure 5.1 Labor-saving devices freed women from home responsibilities. Here an emancipated wife reads a 1914 newspaper while an early washing machine does clothes for her. Women's increasing involvement in other activities implemented fashion.

other source of information but the typical clothing of the period, we could reconstruct much of the wearer's habits and outlook. We would know, for instance, that the early Victorian lady's

physique was poor, her chest compressed, her health delicate; that she took no real exercise and spent most of her time indoors; always cold, with bad circulation, in spite of hot rooms and shut windows. Her tiny hands would be fit only for "elegant accomplishments," at which by long practice she would excel. In this shut-in existence her mental outlook would be trivial and petty, sustained by daydreams of the Cinderella sort. We can picture her as a doll-like, ineffective, kittenish creature, innocent and picturesque. A Dora Copperfield, in fact, emerges simply from an analysis of the costume. This sort of woman was not only usual, but the ideal of the day.[11]

[10]David Mandelbaum, "The Interplay of Conformity and Diversity," in *Conflict and Creativity*, Part 2, ed. S. Farber and R. Wilson (New York: McGraw-Hill, 1963), p. 248.

[11]C. W. Cunnington, *Why Women Wear Clothes* (London: Faber and Faber, 1941), p. 28.

Feminine dress in the twentieth century has moved toward greater similarity to masculine attire (Figure 5.12). Women's increasing use of bifurcated garments is only one index of this trend. Women have of course worn shorts and slacks for several decades, but it was not until Norman Norell designed the trend-setting culotte suit in 1960 that divided garments moved from sportswear to sophisticated town wear. By 1964, even the French designers were decreeing more trousers for women. André Courrèges gave the trend another boost in the sixties when his tight-legged, hip-slung pants were shown in every fabric from flannel to lace. He stated that he designed for the woman who is "active, moves fast, works, is usually young and modern enough to wear modern, intelligent clothes."[12]

In the past sixty years, women have gained the right to vote; labor-saving devices have freed them from home responsibilities and moved them out into the work force. During World War II they took over the work of men in the factories and achieved further status as members of the armed forces. They have become increasingly involved in the political and economic affairs of the country, and their avid participation in sports has contributed greatly to their freedom—both physically and socially. The Equal Rights Amendment (ERA) will remove the last legal vestige of discrimination. No one may be denied civil rights because of sex. All people will receive equal treatment under law without bias because of sex. Functionalism already is and will continue to be a major motivation in clothing design for both sexes.

Figure 5.12 When sexual equality is achieved, differences in male and female clothing become less distinct.

The maxi was a flop, countless small businesses went under, and women emerged in complete control of their wardrobes for the first time in history. Clearly, women no longer turn pale and surrender when charged with being unfeminine. A lot of us have long suspected that it was an ancient device to keep us "in our place"—and out of the best jobs.

And maybe it should be pointed out to the fashion experts that femininity is not what you wear—not a plunging neckline, a bit of sparkle or a puffed sleeve. If you are female, it's what you are. (Seven-foot women basketball stars notwithstanding.)

The truth is we like the comfort of low-heel shoes and easy-care fabrics, the convenience of pants. Even a sexy dress has to be uncomplicated and priced right, which explains the huge success of designer Diane von Furstenberg. Voluminous satins and taffetas are old hat, no longer in harmony with our way of life.[13]

[12]"The Lord of the Space Ladies," *Life*, May 21, 1965, p. 54.

[13]Geri Joseph, "Peasant Chic and Femininity," *Washington Post*, August 16, 1976.

Women's independence from male domination is increasing economically as well as socially. Fashion historian James Laver notes that whenever women can afford to choose husbands who attract them as men rather than as providers, the clothing of both sexes becomes much alike. The corollary in modern men's wear is a trend toward higher fashion in masculine dress. Men have begun to take on gaily colored vests, shaped jackets, ruffled shirts, and fashionable shoes. Their use of jewelry and perfumed toiletries has increased threefold within the last decade. In 1975, retailers in department stores and specialty shops reported increased sales in body jewelry, an important new item in men's fashion accessories. Designed to accessorize sportswear and for the man forty and older, necklaces, bracelets, and medallions, primarily of puka and sterling silver, sold from $5 to $60 with little price resistance.[14] Ernest Dichter referred to this increased interest in clothing by men, as the peacock revolution. He said that young men seventeen to twenty-five were the peacocks of the future because they are less inhibited than their elders and also more verbal about their apparel likes and dislikes (Figure 5.13). Because of their relative affluence they have become a major influence on men's wear markets.[15]

It is apparent that when the women are confined to the more or less graceful bondage of the home, their contours become more softly rounded and their style of dress becomes relatively static. Given freedom and status, the feminine mode moves much more swiftly and the differences between male and female clothing lessen.

Figure 5.13 Many men now wear clothing their fathers would not have been found dead in.

The rate of fashion change has a direct relationship to the degree of freedom and status assigned to women in society.

Technology

Chapter 2 discussed the impact of changing technology on the evolution of styles. Here it is important to consider how such progress in tools and machinery hastens the fashion process. Invention of the sewing machine gave tremendous impetus to fashion, since it not only laid the foundation for the ready-to-wear industry, but increased the speed with which high fashions could be copied by the apparel industry and the skilled home sewer. As new machines were perfected, manufactured clothing was produced at lower and lower prices, making fashion goods available to more and more people. The introduction of the cutting knife replaced the tedious method of hand cutting a few layers of cloth at a time (Figure 5.14). The invention of the zipper—a gadget taken so for granted today—caused a minor revolution in garment construction. In modern

[14]Margot Raven, "Body Jewelry Shows Muscle in Stores," *Daily News Record*, September 8, 1975.

[15]Ernest Dichter, "The Peacock Revolution," *Department Store Economist*, May 1966.

Figure 5.15 A technician tests textile finishes in a plant laboratory.

Figure 5.14 Modern electric cutters can rip through more than a hundred layers of cloth at a time, greatly speeding up the process by which ready-to-wear fashions can duplicate the changing modes.

industry, specialized machines for literally every aspect of the construction process operate at high speed to produce low-cost fashions.

In addition to mechanization, change has been hastened by the chemical revolution. Before the turn of the century, silk was a luxury commodity available only to the wealthy. But with the invention of artificial silk—later known as rayon—in 1892, garments with the appearance of silk became accessible to the masses. This invention was followed in rapid succession by the development of other man-made fibers that not only simulated the costly status items but introduced a whole new field of fabrics that influenced the design of the finished product. So great was the impact of nylon on the women's hosiery industry that the common name for stockings was changed to "nylons." New fibers and chemical finishes now yield minimum-care, wash-and-wear, and permanent-press fabrics as well as adding anti-cling, water repellancy, stain resistance, and other desirable properties to apparel. Synthetic "fun furs" and reptile skins are less expensive than the real thing and so increase the adoption speed of new fashions, and they also protect endangered species. Trends toward the natural look in clothing in general increased the demand for leather. Because of a new process that produces leather that can be conventionally dry cleaned, rather than cleaned by costly leather-cleaning methods, leather is now widely used for many end uses that were prohibitively expensive in the past.[16] As technology continues to alter the functional and aesthetic quality of clothes, fashion continues to take advantage of its new and improved products (Figure 5.15).

In a less direct way, fashion also has been modified by technical advances in communication and travel. We have already seen how they increase culture contact, and when communication is slow, fashion change is also slow. When the first mass-produced automobile appeared on the market in 1908, fashion followed with dusters, caps, goggles, and motoring veils (Figure 5.16). Increased air travel heightened the demand for lightweight, packable, and crease-resistant clothing, and

[16]Annette Polyzou, "New Developments in Clothing and Textiles," *Family Economics Review* (Summer 1977), 5.

heavy, bulky garments became passé. The movies and television also play a part in accelerating fashion change. Since seeing is the first prerequisite for wanting to buy, the latest fashions worn by the popular idols of the day condition mass tastes and the resulting consumer demand.

Technical improvements in automatic heating and air-conditioning provided all-season environmental control. Labor-saving equipment in the home and in industry released people from long hours of toil and contributed to the country's mass leisure. People have more time for relaxation, entertainment, and sports. All these factors are interdependent, each having an amplifying effect on the other to produce rapid fashion change.

Fashion change is accelerated by technological advances.

Figure 5.16 Early automobile travel required special attire.

Planned Reform

Whenever fashion reaches such an extreme that it appears either to endanger the health of the wearer or to threaten the moral standards of the day, some individual or group attempts to initiate an organized reform movement. Such crusades have been made in the names of health, hygiene, practicality, utility, comfort, decency, and beauty. Numerous references in the Bible denouncing the extravagance of fashion indicate that open criticism of clothing practices is not confined to the modern world. During the Middle Ages, the church waged constant war against the evils in dress. The deeply cut armholes of the medieval surcote were named *fenêtres d'enfer* ("windows of hell"), and the Gothic hennin was regarded as a tool of the devil (Figure 5.17). In 1555, the bishop of Frankfurt distributed inflammatory pamphlets against the masculine mode of *Pluderhose*, which he claimed were causing scandal and creating a bad example. In the early part of the twentieth century the V-neck dress was denounced from the pulpit as immoral and by physicians as likely to lead to pneumonia.

Other attempts at planned reform were progressive in outlook and advocated changes that were far ahead of their time. After the French Revolution, the painter David was commissioned to design a "republican costume" that would express the reaction against the old regime's excesses. The men never adopted his styles, but the next decade saw development of neoclassical sentiments in the feminine dress of the period made famous by the fashionable Mésdames Tallien and Recamier. Women tried to copy, as closely as possible, the appearance of the ancient Greek and Roman statuary. They drenched themselves with water to make the sheer cotton

Figure 5.17 These medieval styles were subject to severe criticism from the church. Left, German *Pluderhose* with paned and slashed codpiece. Center, a surcote with large armholes worn over a long-sleeved tunic. Right, the Gothic hennin.

fabric cling to the body. So many people died of pneumonia from wearing soaked clothing that the government had to intervene by making the practice illegal. In 1851, an American, Amelia Jenks Bloomer, advocate of women's rights, urged the feminine readers of her paper to renounce their cumbersome dress for a costume consisting of a knee-length tunic worn over Turkish trousers (Figure 5.18). But few ladies adopted this revolutionary style, and it was not until the turn of the century with the advent of cycling for women that "bloomers" came into their own. Sports, that great emancipator, achieved what Mrs. Bloomer and her followers could not fifty years earlier.

However rational the concept, attempts at dress reform that run too far ahead of the natural evolution of the times are rarely successful. Men's dress, hoop skirts, short skirts, trailing skirts, corsets, low necklines, high heels, pointed shoes, and

Figure 5.18 The Turkish trousers and tunic introduced by Mrs. Bloomer in the 1850s did not make much headway until the arrival of cycling at the turn of the century.

AMELIA BLOOMER, ORIGINATOR OF THE NEW DRESS.—FROM A DAGUERREOTYPE BY T. W. BROWN.—(SEE PRECEDING PAGE.)

bathing suits all have been the subject of crusades for change at one time or another. Few, if any, made much headway in their day, although many indicated changes that evolved in later years as the spirit of the times allowed their expression. Many of the suggestions for improving men's wear made by Wilde in 1870, by Jäger in 1890, and by Flügel in 1930 are just now beginning to take hold in a few limited categories of masculine dress. The leaders of revolts against fashion rarely achieve more than the kind of fame that comes through ridicule and abuse.

Fashion change usually parallels change and progress in other spheres of human activity.

SUMMARY

Agents of Change

The acceleration of fashion change in contemporary society has been explained in terms of the coexistent and interdependent factors of

1. an open class system
2. abundance and diffusion of wealth
3. increased leisure
4. the growing influence of sports
5. extended education
6. greater culture contact
7. the emphasis on youth
8. concurrent social agitation
9. the improved status of women
10. advances in technology

Various attempts at planned reform in dress, although seemingly futile at the time they are made, often have long-term effects as forerunners of change in the direction of greater utility and practicality.

Those who would eliminate fashion by adopting an enduring and constant style of life make the mistaken assumption that our clothing habits exist as independent phenomena, totally unrelated to the social setting. One cannot stem the tide of fashion without halting progress in other aspects of our daily lives as well.

The accelerated changes that take place in fashion today are the direct result of the democratization of fashion. In our society, fashions are quickly copied into low-priced lines, and only a relatively small number of people are economically unable to copy fashion if they so desire. A slowdown in fashion change, therefore, would require a restriction on upward mobility in the class system.

FORCES THAT SHAPE FASHION CHANGE

By definition, the concept of fashion implies continuous change. We have discussed the forces that affect the rate of such change. Aside from the influence of sports (where the need is for greater utility and functionalism), and the status of women (where equality with men is related to equality of dress), such factors do not explain fashion change.

Several theories of fashion adoption, change, and variations have been suggested. Gibbons proposed five and classified them as follows: the boredom theory, the progress theory, the conspiracy theory, the status conformity theory, and the "spirit of the age theory."[17] The last theory was originally proposed by James Laver. He believed that fashions of a particular period reflect the "Spirit of the Age." Still another plausible reason used to explain the varieties of fashion concerns its cyclical nature. Since theories are not facts, simply possible explanations of phenomena based on observation and analysis, all the above theories are tenable, all have proponents, but all have faults and weaknesses, too.

Two theories, however, appear to be dominant in the analysis of fashion variation. One is that fashions follow an unchangeable, ordered pattern from one extreme to the other. The second is that fashion develops from a kind of cultural determinism, which defines fashion as a reflection of the political, economic, intellectual, and artistic events of the times (Figure 5.19). The cyclical nature of fashion will be discussed in a later chapter, but

here the focus is on the cultural determinants or what James Laver called the "Spirit of the Age."

Dominant Ideals

Many variations are possible within a typical style for any period. A tubular silhouette, for example, may be one that reveals the body form beneath it by use of sheer, supple materials and the combination of a deep décolletage with an empire waist, as in 1810. Or it may use heavy-bodied fabric to cover a rigid frame with the neck encased up to the ears in whalebone, as in 1910. Even though many elements of a costume from a given period and culture may be revived in later eras,

Figure 5.19 Afro garb, a symbol of independence to black Americans, became popular at the peak of the civil rights movement. Versions of the African styles are worn by both men and women.

[17]Kenneth Gibbons, "Social Psychological Theories of Fashion," *Journal of the Home Economics Association of Australia* (1971), 3–18.

THE SAFEST WAY OF TAKING A LADY DOWN TO DINNER.

Figure 5.20   The enormous skirt of the French court costume cannot be confused with the equally large Victorian skirt.

the total effect produced by the combined details creates a look that is unique and characteristic only of the time in which it developed. If this were not true, the bustled gowns of the 1690s would not be distinguishable from the bustle-backed costumes of the 1790s and 1880s; yet even with a slight knowledge of fashion history, one has no difficulty whatever in making the distinction (Figure 5.20). It is obvious that the underlying features of the styles of the day are molded by specific kinds of cultural influences.

We can trace certain similarities of dress among the cultural periods in which similar social ideas were evident. When religious values are dominant, dress tends to enshroud the figure in a relatively loose garment of simple design. The enveloping tunics, wimples, and head veils of the early Gothic period were carried on in the habits of Catholic nuns.

The rise of Puritanism in England during the early seventeenth century stripped clothing of its ornamentation and brought the sober, drab costume that spread to America in the dress of the early colonists (Figure 5.21). The same influ-

ence persists today in the dress of the Amish and the Mennonites. Eighteenth-century costume, on the other hand, was a creation of the sophisticated, extravagant, and artificial world of the French nobility; it was elaborate and profusely decorated, the dress of idleness, frivolity, and pleasure. The same elements can be seen in the

Figure 5.21   Puritan costumes of the seventeenth century. When religious values are rising, dress becomes austere.

eighteenth-century costumes of the American South before the Civil War. There is a relationship between the mentifacts of culture and dress, and we can see how ideals of patriotism, frugality, order, beauty, and youth all are expressed through clothing whenever such concepts become the dominating theme of a period. Because such ideals seldom exist in isolation, they blend with others that are also characteristic of the times. This unique blend produces the typical costume, which may indeed be imitated but never duplicated in succeeding periods.

The important point is that fashion is never arbitrary and meaningless. This can be plainly seen by looking at the fashions of the past. Every style seems completely appropriate for its age. So, too, will the fashions of today and of the future, whatever they may be. We cannot imagine Madame de Pompadour, or the Empress Josephine, or the Victorian lady in anything but what they wore. Each completely represented the ideals of her times. Properly evaluated, fashion is never a frivolity. Paul Nystrom said,

If we could understand the full significance of a woman's hat we could prophesy her clothes for the next year, the interior decoration of the next two years, the architecture of the next ten years, and we would have a fairly accurate notion of the pressures, political, economic, religious, that go to make the shape of an age.[18]

The dominant ideals that shape the thought and action of a cultural period also influence the character and direction of fashion movements.

[18]Paul Nystrom. *Economics of Fashion* (New York: Ronald Press Company, 1928), p. 125.

Economic Conditions

Economic conditions are reflected in clothing. In times of depression or recession dress is somber and simple. When the economy prospers, clothes are likely to be lavish and elaborate. The wealth that poured into England after the defeat of the Spanish Armada increased the ornateness of court dress in Elizabethan England. The worldwide depression in the early 1930s is portrayed in the drab, dull, uninspired clothing of that period. Only when President Roosevelt's New Deal improved the economy did clothing perk up.

From time to time there have been attempts to show a parallel between the rise and fall of hemlines and the rise and fall of the Dow Jones average (a reflection of the economy through the activity on the stock market). Interesting articles have been written and theories have been proposed, but the issue has not been subjected to serious investigation or scientific research. Some logic is involved. Because the textile industry is so large, a shift in fashion, such as longer skirts, in the mass market would provide a large boost to the entire economy. Two or three inches for each skirt is not much fabric, but multiplied by the thousands of skirts produced in this country yearly, increases in yardage needs and production would be only one result.

The uncertain economic conditions of the 1970s, particularly the unique combination of recession and inflation, was reflected in clothing in a return to the earth and a nostalgia for the past, an interest in the olden days when life seemed simpler and safer and more secure. Young people saw those times as not only free from financial uncertainties but also free from environmental pollutants, from carcinogenics, and from nuclear bombs. Bib overalls, denim work jackets, and jeans, originally worn by farmers and railroad men, were so much in demand that a market for used jeans developed. Eventually used jeans were the fashion and brand-new denims were treated to give them just the right worn, faded look considered fashionable. On the Russian black market "genuine" American jeans sold for $80 a pair. "Old" became synonymous with "in" for the high school and college crowd as they looked for antique clothes, pre–World War II clothes, old sweaters, baggy pants, calico prints.

Economic uncertainties are reflected in fashion. Sometimes the reflection is in the form of new styles designed to boost the economy; at other times, it is interpreted by a nostalgic return to clothing of a more prosperous era.

Events

During periods of actual conflict there is little time for fashion change; war activities usually make for more austere and functional clothes, with perhaps an emphasis on mannish or militaristic elements. The real change comes after the conflict. Wars and revolutions appear to trigger more radical changes than would occur under ordinary circumstances.

Other historical events often exert a strong influence on the fashion image of a period. The famed Garibaldi's Sicilian expedition in 1860 inspired a flood of Garibaldi jackets and Garibaldi shirts. The Panama Canal was opened in 1904, and American men adopted the custom of wearing Panama hats from the beginning of May until Labor Day each year. The Centennial Exhibition held in Philadelphia in 1876, the World's Fair in Chicago in

1893, and the 1925 International Exposition of Industrial and Decorative Arts in Paris all had profound influence on the shaping of public taste in their respective eras. When outstanding treasures of Russian costume were exhibited at the Metropolitan Museum of Art in New York City in 1977, the look perpetuated in fashion was that of the Russian peasants, fine embroidery and hand-woven bandings duplicated in rickrack and commercial trim. Outstanding fairs and exhibits of recent years also have called attention to the major artistic and industrial movements that help to characterize the spirit of the times. Mickey Mouse appeared on T-shirts, jewelry, hats, and bed sheets after Disney World opened in Florida. In an election year donkeys and elephants vie with red, white, and blue motifs on many apparel and accessory items.

Because a more sophisticated American populace had leisure time and affluence, the latest exhibit of Tutankhamen's treasures in 1977-1978 was seen by millions as it toured the major cities in the United States (Figure 5.22). A passion for all

Figure 5.22 A fourteen-carat gold pendant inspired by the 1977–1978 King Tut exhibit.

things Egyptian developed. "Tutmania" and "Mummy Madness" gripped visitors as they ended their tours in museum gift shops. Items on sale ranged from T-shirts that proclaimed "Love My Mummy" to reproductions of the golden statue of Selket priced at $1,500. Other stores had Tut tacos, Tut sheets and pillowcases, Tut toaster covers; Bloomingdale's offered a whole line of household linens with an Egyptian theme.[19]

Important historical events trigger public interest and enthusiasm for fashion change.

Figure 5.23   Peace negotiations in Vietnam and initiation of cultural relations with China in 1972 touched off renewed interest in Oriental styles.

International Relations

Political sentiments are also reflected in fashion change. Strained relations with unfriendly countries automatically make their national styles and art forms extremely unpopular. Political approval or acceptance, on the other hand, is often accompanied by a revival of interest in the fashions derived from the folklore or national dress of friendly countries.

The recurrent appearance of Oriental elements of dress—turbans, mandarin coats, coolie hats, kimonos, Nehru jackets, Mao tunics—mirror our on-again-off-again attitudes of association with nations of the world (Figure 5.23). At various times throughout history, fashion has helped to foster U.S. relationships with South America, Russia, Mexico, India, China, Japan, as well as the countries of the Middle East.

Fashion adaptations of art forms and clothing of other nations reflect the political sentiments characteristic of the times.

Entertainment and the Arts

The relationship of art and clothing is treated in Chapter 14, but it is noted here as an important factor in determining the direction specific fashion movements take. The forces that give rise to development of certain styles in painting also operate in the field of fashion. Manifestations of the Bauhaus philosophy, abstractionism, nonobjective art, surrealism, pop art, and op art have all been observed in the fads and fashions of contemporary dress.

One of the most outstanding influences from the performing arts was the 1909 Russian Ballet, which took Paris by storm. Settings, dancing, and costumes were all of equal importance, and especially in *Schéhérazade*, the most memorable ballet of all. The voluptuous Oriental decor and costumes burst forth in brilliant crimson, gold, and orange, in harem skirts, tunics, turbans, and veils. So lasting was its influence that the surge of Orientalism survived World War I and was brought back to a boil by Rudolph Valentino, who

[19]Amei Wallach, " 'Mummy Madness' Ending Its Run," *Washington Post*, January 31, 1978.

starred as "The Sheik" in movies of the twenties. Ladies bedecked themselves in Persian pantaloons, slippers with turned-up toes, and turbans garnished with egret and ostrich plumes. Theda Bara and Pola Negri, their eyes blackened with mascara, their bodies slinking in gold lamé, personified the look of the day. The era of the vamp was launched (Figure 5.24).

The overwhelming success of the musical hit *My Fair Lady* with its 1912 settings and costumes by Cecil Beaton created the "Fair Lady Look" of the 1950s. The publicity surrounding Elizabeth Taylor's filming of *Cleopatra* in 1963 had everybody going Egyptian again. Albert Finney's smash hit, the British film *Tom Jones*, gave rise to the long, white, beruffled blouse that bore the same name. *Bonnie and Clyde* and *The Sting* put young Americans into gangster clothes for a while: *Annie Hall* revived the clothing styles of a pre-World War II America.

To be successful, such fashion revivals must come at a time far enough removed from the original time that the styles appear new, not old-fashioned (Figure 5.25). Moreover, the tastes of the times that make people respond enthusiastically to a particular type of painting, play, or music are the same tastes that support fashion movements. Another *My Fair Lady* produced in the twenties instead of the fifties might have been a complete flop. The styles that succeed are those that are somehow in harmony with the spirit of the age.

As we look back over fashions of the past, we see that every era had its characteristic line and form, very relevant to the *Zeitgeist*. Yet to define this in advance is quite different from viewing the relationship in retrospect; it is difficult indeed to pinpoint the essential elements in the varied and seemingly unrelated design of contemporary life.

Fashion movements and revivals are given focus and impetus through the appeal of art and the different types of entertainment.

Figure 5.24   Theda Bara personifed the vamp look.
Figure 5.25   Movies like *Bonnie and Clyde* and *The Great Gatsby* inspired a revival of twenties and thirties styles.

SUMMARY

Forces That Shape Fashion Change

In attempting to explain the nature of fashion movements, we see that they are, by and large, determined by the same dominant forces that mold other aspects of the culture in any given period. Ideals like equality, piety, modesty, frivolity, and so on, all are expressed in the clothing of an era whenever such concepts are ascendant. Public sentiments and tastes are often shaped by important historical events as well as by national and international relationships. Further influences that stem from the arts, the theater, the movies, and other entertainment media may be noted. These influences give focus and impetus to the spirit of the times.

FOR FURTHER READING

Boyer, G. Bruce. "How the Three-Piece Suit and the Modern World Began," *Horizon*, 18 (Winter 1976), 112.

Carter, Ernestine. *The Changing World of Fashion: 1900 to the Present*. London: Weidenfeld and Nicolson, 1977.

Curtis, Mary, "Amelia Bloomer's Curious Costume," *American History Illustrated*, 13 (June 1978), 10–15; also reprinted in *Dimensions of Dress and Adornment: A Book of Readings*, pp. 73–75, 3rd ed. Ed. Gurel and Beeson, Dubuque, Iowa: Kendall/Hunt Publishing Co., 1979.

Glynn, Prudence. *In Fashion: Dress in the Twentieth Century*. New York: Oxford University Press, 1978.

Lockwood, Allison, "Pantsuited Pioneer of Women's Lib, Dr. Mary Walker," *Smithsonian*, 7 (March 1977), 113–114; also reprinted in *Dimensions of Dress and Adornment: A Book of Readings*, pp. 76–78.

Solomon, Stephen. "Ride to Golconda in a Wavy Sole Shoe," *Fortune*, 100 (July 30, 1979), 104–106.

Sproles, George B. *Fashion: Consumer Behavior Toward Dress*, pp. 55–69. Minneapolis: Burgess Publishing Co., 1979.

Stanfill, Francesca. "Decoding the Styles of the 70s," *New York Times Magazine*, December 30, 1979, pp. 24–27.

Wass, Betty M., and S. Madujse Broderick, "The Kaba Sloht," *African Arts*, 12 (May 1979), 62–65.

Part Two

CLOTHING AND
HUMAN BEHAVIOR

Chapter 6

CLOTHES AND THE SELF-CONCEPT

Theories from the root disciplines of psychology and sociology are often used to explain the relationships between clothing and human behavior. Central to any discussion of this relationship are those theories that encompass the idea of personality.

One aspect of the personality complex that is especially appropriate to a discussion of clothing and human behavior is that of the self-concept, the ideas and feelings one has about oneself. At the very beginning of the twentieth century, sociologists and psychologists speculated about clothing and how it might be affected by personality, and, conversely, how personality might be affected by clothing. These early scientists focused their interest on the self and the possible effects of clothing on the self.

William James was one of these early psychologists. Much of what he wrote about the self and the self-concept is still quoted today. He considered the self the center of one's personal identity and divided the me, or the self perceived by the individual, into three parts: "the material me," "the social me," and "the spiritual me."

The old saying that the human person is composed of three parts, soul, body, and clothes—is more than a joke. We so appropriate our clothes and identify ourselves with them that there are few of us who, if asked to choose between having a beautiful body clad in raiment perpetually shabby and unclean, and having an ugly and blemished form always spotlessly attired, would not hesitate a moment before making a decisive reply.[1]

Ryan also separated the self, but into only two parts. The first she called the

[1]William James, *Principles of Psychology*, Vol. 1 (New York: Holt, Rinehart and Winston, Inc., 1890), p. 292.

Figure 6.1 A padded jacket gives the wearer a feeling of extended body boundaries.

"somatic self," all the perceived physical characteristics of our bodies. The ideas of extensions of the self, body image, and body cathexis (individuals' feelings of dissatisfactions and satisfactions with various parts of their bodies) can be discussed under the concept of a somatic self.

The second aspect of the self, the "social self," Ryan further divided into the "sort-of-person-I-am-self" and the "self as a member of a group."[2] The personal concept or sort-of-person-I-am-self is a very important determinant of behavior and of role assumptions. Group belongingness and social participation are influenced by individual feelings about the self as a member of a group. Each of these selfs requires clothing that is used at times for different purposes. Thus, padded, bulky, or extended clothing (Figure 6.1) changes

[2]Mary Shaw Ryan, *Clothing: A Study in Human Behavior* (New York: Holt, Rinehart and Winston, Inc., 1965), pp. 82–83.

our body image boundaries; the frills of evening wear (Figure 6.2) or the sleek efficiency of tailored business clothes project the sort-of-person-I-am-self to others; conformity to peer clothing fads identifies us as members of a group.

The explanation of self Cooley gave many years ago has become known as the "looking-glass self":

As we see our face, figure, and dress in the glass, and are interested in them because they are ours, and pleased or otherwise with them according as they do or do not answer to what we should like them to be; so in imagination we perceive in another's mind some thought of our appearance, manners, aims, deeds, character, friends, and so on, and are variously affected by it.

A self-idea of this sort seems to have three principal elements: the imagination of our appearance to the other person; the imagination of his judgment of that appearance, and some sort

Figure 6.2 The special effects of evening clothes affect the wearer's feelings and actions.

of self-feeling, such as pride or mortification. The comparison with a looking-glass hardly suggests the second element, the imagined judgment, which is quite essential. The thing that moves us to pride or shame is not the mere mechanical reflection of ourselves, but an imputed sentiment, the imagined effect of this reflection upon another's mind.[3]

The **self**, then, is the object to which we refer with the words *I, me, mine, myself;* the **self-concept** is how I think and feel about "me" or "myself."

The concept of self is an awareness of one's existence as an entity separate from other selves. This self-awareness is learned through an individual's interactions with society. It is made up of values, needs, wants, emotions, ideas, and ap-pearance, as well as the awareness of the attitudes of others toward the self. The degree to which an individual is able and willing to live with the personal characteristics that make up the self is a measure of self-acceptance and adjustment. Individuals must define for themselves what they are, and be and appear to be unified wholes. The degree of integration of the several selves is an important determinant of the stability of the self-concept. The disintegrated personality is one whose several selves pull in opposite directions or give conflicting messages both to the person and to others. Before we see how theories related to the self and self-concept can be applied to the study of clothing, let us consider how such ideas about the self are likely to develop.

DEVELOPMENT OF THE SELF-CONCEPT

Although we do not actually know, we can guess how the world must look to a newborn baby. At first, babies can make no distinction whatever between themselves and the blur and confusion of the surrounding environment. We can observe them as they "discover" hands and toes and examine these body parts much as they examine other objects—a rattle, a toy, or even a finger that belongs to somebody else (Figure 6.3). They gradually distinguish the things that are "me" and the things that are "not me." If you ask a child of three, for example, who he is, he will probably reply with his name, "John." If you point to a table and ask, "Is this John?" he will say,

"No." If you point to his sweater, he may answer yes or no; if you point to his leg, he may say, "No, that's my leg!" If you tease

Figure 6.3   Development of the self-concept begins in infancy when the baby "discovers" fingers and toes.

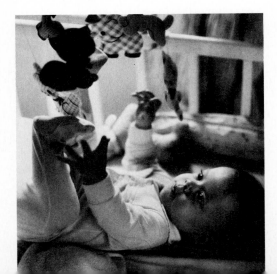

---

[3]Charles H. Cooley, *Human Nature and the Social Order* (New York: Charles Scribner's Sons, 1902), p. 152.

him about taking away his nose, he responds as if his nose were indeed an object that could be separated from his body. It is clear from such observations that the image of what constitutes the self must be learned.

Clothing and the Boundaries of the Self

It is common to assume that the entire self is contained within the body, and that the skin marks the distinction between the self and the environment. But in most societies, almost from the moment of birth on, some form of clothing separates the body from the surroundings. Dorothy Lee described this relationship between clothes and the self:

The body is never naked, or perhaps, only when absolutely necessary. Mothers often arrange to bathe and change the baby without undressing it all at once. The new pediatric practices and the new books on child care demand immersion, but it is all a matter of hygiene; no joy of the naked body is mentioned anywhere. Conversely, dress, and particularly festive dress, "dress of splendor" and ornamentation, are of great importance, and in fact, are essential to complete the body. When beautiful girls are described, their clothing and their jewelry are given at least as much place as their bodily charms, and are not treated separately; and when a brave youth is mentioned, his trappings are part of the picture. . . . And the lower world which holds no joy is a place where there are no ornamental trappings. The naked body, like the naked word, is stark and incomplete.[4]

[4]Dorothy Lee, *Freedom and Culture* (Englewood Cliffs, N.J.: Prentice-Hall, 1959), p. 147.

Is it so surprising, then, that children should have difficulty in learning the distinction between themselves and their clothing? Is it not logical that a body extremity, such as an arm or a leg, would appear to the child as belonging less to the self than an article of clothing, which is somehow closer and more functional in establishing who one is?

Throughout life, clothing functions as an extension of the bodily self. Whenever an object is brought into contact with the body, the conscious existence of the self is extended into the object's extremities, thereby giving the individual an increased sense of size, power, weight, movement, rigidity—whatever the characteristic of the object.

Thus, the corset-wearer takes on the strait-laced qualities of the garment (Figure 6.4), the dancer seems to have greater mobility from the graceful movements of

Figure 6.4 The Edwardian woman was well defined by boned, stiff necklines and straight-laced corsets. How could she relax her decorum when she could not even bend at the waist?

Figure 6.5 The dancer's action is not only extended but magnified by the movement of her costume.

Sex and Role Identification

At every stage of development, clothing helps to establish the identity of individuals not only to themselves, but to those with whom they interact. In the past clothing helped the child very early in life with sex identification. By dressing the baby in blue we signified to others that he was to be called a boy and treated as one. Dressing the baby in pink told everyone she was a girl and was expected to be sweet, gentle, dainty, and fragile. Such stereotyping of sex roles is a thing of the past. Now little girls and boys often dress alike, although boys still do not wear skirts. And, just as sex roles are blurred in general, so, too, we can no longer rely on clothing for cues to sex identity. Clothing does, however, facilitate the enactment of other roles and helps children learn appropriate patterns of behavior defined by their particular culture.

The self-concept is developed through assuming a series of social roles, and the individual learns the set of behavior patterns other people expect in performing such roles. Role identity is subject to constant modification, although the individual tends to integrate various role experiences into a unified pattern of responses: the woman who goes through life as "daddy's little girl" becomes the childlike, naive, dependent wife and may present herself in most situations in frilly, fussy clothes in pastel colors and dainty details. It is highly unlikely that this same woman would be comfortable in casual, rough-textured clothes in strong or earthy colors, even though the latter may be appropriate for certain activities.

Gradually a person takes the commonalities from experiences in many different role categories and integrates them into a unified feeling toward the self. Clothing

the floating chiffon dress (Figure 6.5), and the knight assumes the steel-plated strength of his armor. The individual becomes taller in a high hat, more forceful in striking colors, less refined in coarse fabrics.

Research has shown that individuals vary in the degree to which they extend their self-feelings beyond their body boundaries.[5] Compton's work was done with psychotic patients, but her findings suggest that clothing does indeed function in strengthening or weakening the individual's image of the boundary of the physical body.[6]

Clothing as an extension of the body acts as a "second skin" in establishing the physical boundaries of the self.

[5]S. Fisher and S. Cleveland, "Body-Image Boundaries and Style of Life," *Journal of Abnormal and Social Psychology*, 52 (1956), 373–379.
[6]Norma H. Compton, "Body-Image Boundaries in Relation to Clothing Fabric and Design Preferences of a Group of Hospitalized Psychotic Women," *Journal of Home Economics*, 56 (1964), 40–45.

functions most purposefully if it is consistent with the personal feelings an individual has about life in general and about the role assignments that are a part of everyday existence.

Clothing is a necessary "prop" in establishing and maintaining sex and role identities; it reflects what individuals think of themselves.

Individual and Group Identification

An understanding of the process of identification is essential in analyzing development of the self-concept (Figure 6.6). Children are likely to identify with their same-sex parents early in life. The parent's

Figure 6.6 The self grows by imitation and identification.

appearance, behavior, and feelings are imitated and, in so doing, children learn to play the role and they learn to see themselves through the parent's eyes. In acting out the role of mother, for example, the little girl demands for the child (in this case, herself) the same standards of conduct she thinks the parent holds for the child. Taking on the mother's dress helps the child take on the accompanying gestures, values, and orientations of the parent as well as the attitudes held toward herself. Thus, in taking on the role of the other, the individual learns to evaluate personal appearance and behavior according to the norms and values the other holds.

As the child's social contacts expand, choices of models also expand. The ideal person the child chooses to imitate may be an older sibling, an aunt, an uncle, a friend, but it usually is a person who possesses something the child wants, such as love, recognition, prestige, or power. Gradually the identification process spreads from single persons to groups of people, and the individual learns to play a role by learning the group values and norms for appearance and behavior. The idea of the "other," as Mead calls it, involves an organization of attitudes held by everybody else on the team; the social group that gives to the individual unity of self may be called the **generalized other.**[7] Thus, a whole pattern of responses may be determined by a particular group with which the individual identifies. Various writers have designated this group by such terms as *model, referent, generalized other,* or *significant others*.

[7]George H. Mead. *Mind, Self and Society* (Chicago: University of Chicago Press, 1934), p. 154.

Figures 6.7 and 6.8 In the late sixties and early seventies, young blacks identified with leaders like Angela Davis by adopting the Afro hairstyle as a symbol of angry militancy and pride in their African ancestry.

Figure 6.9 Young blacks experimented with new ways to retain their cultural identity through such styles as this.

Although the identification process is easily observed in children's imitative play, it is probably displayed most prevalently and overtly in adolescence when peer groups are the most common generalized others. The groups individuals choose to copy are usually those to which they want to belong. The person selected as a model usually is a peer or a near-peer who is slightly older, or popular, better looking, or skilled, or who has an attribute or power the individual would like to have. A second group used for identification can be called "mass media celebrities"—the Hollywood, television, or sports figures who influence teenagers with their distinctive dress.

Significant others can be defined in still another way, which relates to the manner in which patterns of dress are evaluated. When adolescents were asked the question, "Whose opinion counts most when you are deciding what to wear?" mothers and peers were designated as the most influential persons in determining how clothing behavior would be evaluated. It is significant that less than 4 percent considered their fathers' opinions about clothes important. Acceptance of the mothers' opinions, however, was strongest among eighth graders, and it diminished as the teen-agers grew older.[8] Older adolescents begin to see themselves in different social roles, and as new persons become significant to them, the old influences fade in importance. Such changing roles usually produce a marked change in the concept of the self.

The specific person or group chosen as the model (Figures 6.7–6.9) is not as important as is the recognition that the imitators see themselves through the eyes of the referent group and select their clothing to meet that group's expectations. If the group norm dictates that men should appear to be completely indifferent to clothing, it becomes extremely important for group members to select clothing that gives the impression that they really do not care how they look. Thus, as the individual takes on the attitude of the other, appearance and behavior are appraised in relation to various role partners and groups; a constellation of attitudes that represents concept of self is formed.

The imitation of clothing behavior is a direct and tangible means of identifying

[8]A. M. Vener and C. R. Hoffer, *Adolescent Orientations to Clothing*, Technical Bulletin No. 270 (East Lansing, Mich.: Michigan State University Agricultural Experiment Station, 1959), p. 21.

oneself with a model person or group. It facilitates the learning of new social roles and also is an important process in forming the concept of self.

Clothing and Body Image

Body image is one part of the self-concept and as such was included in James's "material me" and Ryan's "somatic self." The picture individuals have in their minds about how they look to others may be called their **body image**. Body image as a psychological concept is neither good nor bad, it just is. It represents what we think we look like and takes on values only when seen in a cultural context. Thus, a body may be pretty/ugly, fat/thin, tall/short, good/bad, but only within a society that places values on certain body dimensions or attributes and thus determines what a desirable body should look like. In other words, there is nothing especially good or bad, pretty or ugly about a body. It becomes so only within the framework of a culture. Whether consciously aware of it or not, everyone has a body image, for each person "cannot exist without the body image any more than a house can exist without walls."[9]

The cultural influences on body image can best be illustrated by referring to the wide variety of **corporal decoration** practiced around the world. People have painted, tattooed, and mutilated their bodies in order to achieve the standards of beauty set by their society. They have further adorned the decorated body with beads, shells, feathers, fabrics, skins, and furs. If all this is not done to achieve the desired body image for their time and place, then what other explanation can there be? "The importance of body image to our culture as a whole is obvious in terms of the widespread expenditure of time and effort that is given to altering the body's appearance."[10]

Although everyone in a society does not strive for the ideal body image, most people make some effort to conform, at least to their peers. Hair is colored, not just because blondes have more fun, but to overcome the negative image of aging. Plastic surgeons lift faces, de-bag eyes, add to or subtract from bust measurements, and straighten noses, all in the name of beauty. Further, a negative self-image results when one wants to, but is not able to achieve this societal ideal. If thin is "in" and society devalues obesity, those who are overweight may develop negative images of their bodies. The same is true of other physical features. Being "odd man out" in a conforming world does not help those who are different and cannot help it. Some problems of the physically handicapped stem from a distortion of body image and their deviation from the norms.

The difference between ideal body image and perceived body image is often used as a measure of adjustment. The less difference there is between the two, the more likely individuals are to be content with themselves both physically and emotionally. Since most people think of their bodies with clothes on, clothing becomes part of the body image. Often it can be used to bridge the gap between perceived and ideal self-image. We can, therefore,

[9]F. C. Shontz, "Body Image and Its Disorders," *International Journal of Psychiatry in Medicine*, 3 (1974), 461–467.

[10]Seymour Fisher and Sidney E. Cleveland. *Body Image and Personality* (New York: Dover Publications, 1968), p. 23.

change our clothing to conform to or at least come closer to our perceptions of what is considered ideal. By careful selection, clothes can be used to cover physical defects or call attention to desirable features; they can be used to expose, conceal, enhance, or emphasize parts of the body in order to help an individual create a more desirable self-image.

Closely related to the concept of body image is that of **body cathexis**, satisfaction or dissatisfaction with the physical body in whole or in part. Body cathexis is also related to behaviors associated with clothing and can be measured by asking questions concerning attitudes about one's body.[11] A study of high school-age boys and girls showed that, at least among the girls, those who were satisfied with their bodies were more interested in clothing and used clothes to attract attention, particularly to attract the attention of the opposite sex (Figure 6.10).[12] Body cathexis also has been shown to relate to feelings of self-acceptance and self-esteem.[13] Individuals who express a high degree of satisfaction with the physical self also tend to score high on measures of psychological security.[14]

Body satisfaction has been found to be related to race and sex also. Among a group of college women, blacks were more

Figure 6.10 High school students dress primarily to attract and please the opposite sex.

satisfied with their bodies than were the white subjects; college women of both races were more satisfied than high school students were with their body size.[15] Fisher, also interested in body satisfaction, noted that in American culture slimness is desirable. Femininity is associated with smallness in all body areas except the breasts.[16] Concern with breast size is a preoccupation at all ages, but particularly so for the young teen-ager and even the preteen who may be slow to develop physically. By bringing this ideal of femininity into every household, mass communication media places a heavy burden on many people to conform to an unrealistic

[11]P. Secord and S. Jourard, "The Appraisal of Body-Cathexis: Body-Cathexis and the Self," *Journal of Consulting Psychology*, 17 (1953), 343–347.

[12]Anna M. Creekmore, *Clothing Related to Body Satisfaction and Perceived Peer Self*, Research Report No. 239 (East Lansing, Mich.: Michigan State University Agricultural Experiment Station, 1974).

[13]Ann Elizabeth Snyder, "Sensuous Clothing in Relation to Self-Esteem and Body Satisfaction." Master's thesis, University of Tennessee, 1975.

[14]D. Torreta, "Somesthetic Perception of Clothing Fabrics in Relation to Body Image and Psychological Security." Ph.D. diss., Utah State University, 1968.

[15]Elizabeth Ann McCullough, "Attitudes of Black and White College Females Toward Sensuous Clothing, Selected Body Attributes, and the Use of Sensuous Clothing." Master's thesis, University of Tennessee, 1975.

[16]Seymour Fisher, *Body Consciousness, You Are What You Feel* (Englewood Cliffs, N.J.: Prentice-Hall, Inc., 1973).

body shape. Most female bodies are not slim in hip and waist and large in breast. Artificial means, in the form of girdles, stays, waist cinchers, and padded bras, have molded the figure in both past and modern times.

Clothes, then, become a part of the body image, and the same concerns that are attached to the body are often attached to clothing. Particularly at puberty, adolescents become acutely aware of changing body dimensions and are often troubled if their growth does not parallel the growth of others of comparable age and status. These young people seem to become obsessed with their clothing and appearance and spend a great deal of time and effort finding out what "they" are wearing, how "they" are cutting or styling hair, so they may present the same or similar image as their peers.

Although many psychologists question the validity of "somatotyping," as it is called, the body's external appearance is a relatively fixed aspect of the self, and it certainly influences how individuals think of themselves and how others may respond to them. Physical characteristics are important factors in the process of stereotyping in which we often are apt to think of all fat people as jolly, all thin people as wiry and energetic, and all muscular types as athletic and outgoing. Stereotyping is usually an error but it is quite possible that the chubby child who is expected to be jolly will grow up with the realization that the most positive responses from others can be obtained by being "jolly" in disposition.

Body image is strongly influenced by cultural forces. Clothing can be used to bring perceived and ideal body images closer together by concealment, enhancement, or exposure.

Physical Constituents of the Self

The emphasis thus far on the social nature of the self, however, does not deny the existence of inborn physical differences among individuals that may have a direct relationship to personality. Precise measurement of the organic traits of individuals is yet to be achieved.[17] Attempts to relate personality traits to body constitution date as far back as the ancient Greeks, and at least two modern studies have identified significant links between body type and behavior. Sheldon's constitutional types (Figure 6.11) include the *endomorph*, predominantly round in body contour with soft body tissue; the *ectomorph*, characterized by a long, slender shape with stringy muscles; and the *mesomorph*, the typical athletic type with a hard muscular build.[18] Every body type represents some combination of these three extremes. The center figure (Figure 6.11) shows a physique with the three components in equal balance. Women, on the average, tend to be somewhat more endomorphic.

Individuals work toward a consistent way of looking at themselves, and this "style of life" must be at least compatible—if not in true harmony—with the set characteristics of the physical body types. It would be difficult, for example, for a male predominant endomorph to reconcile his body type with aspirations of becoming a sophisticated fashion plate. A large-boned muscular female would also find it hard to fill the role of a demure, dainty damsel. Realistic perception and appraisal of one's physical characteristics

[17]For a more detailed explanation see Fisher and Cleveland, *Body Image and Personality*.
[18]W. H. Sheldon, *Atlas of Men: A Guide for Somatotyping the Adult Male at All Ages* (New York: Harper & Row, 1954).

144

Figure 6.11 Sheldon's constitutional types: the *endomorph* is predominantly rotund in body contour with soft body tissue; the *ectomorph* is characterized by a long, slender shape with stringy muscles; the *mesomorph* is the typical athletic type with a hard muscular build. Every body type represents some combination of these three extremes. The center figure shows a physique with the three components in equal balance. Women, on the average, tend to be somewhat more endomorphic.

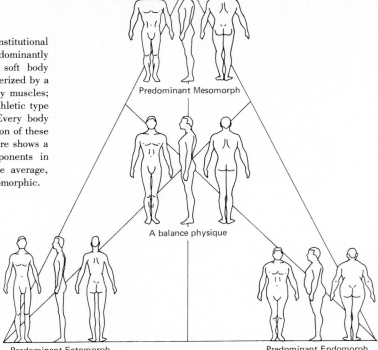

Predominant Mesomorph

A balance physique

Predominant Ectomorph   Predominant Endomorph

is basic to attaining harmony in the presentation of the self.

Even though the relationship between body type and personality is somewhat unclear, considerable evidence shows that body type affects the way we feel about ourselves. In our culture at least, most females want to be taller or thinner than they actually are, and most males desire to be heavier or more muscular. Even among male children, the mesomorph is clearly the preferred type, and children as young as eight years old appear to be able to report self-perceptions of their body images quite accurately.[19] Among men, the large mesomorphs tend to like their bodies better than other physical types do, and tall, thin men put the lowest value on their bodies, basketball players notwithstand-

ing. Apparently, potency and physical strength are associated not with height alone, but with height and bulk. Among women, those with ectomorphic body types are significantly more accepting of their self-images than are endomorphs.[20]

Studies have demonstrated significant relationships between body build and preferences in clothing but the analysis of physical characteristics in relation to suggested patterns of line and design will be made in Chapter 16. The emphasis of physical typology here pertains to its relevance in establishing rather fixed and stable aspects of the self.

Body type is a relatively fixed aspect of the self and exerts a significant influence in development of the self-concept.

[19]J. R. Staffieri, "A Study of Social Stereotype of Body Image in Children," *Journal of Personality and Social Psychology*, 7 (1969), 101–104.

[20]W. R. Alexander, "A Study of Body Types, Self-Image and Environmental Adjustment in Freshman College Females." Ph.D. diss., Indiana University, 1967.

SUMMARY

Development of the Self-Concept

Although physical body type contributes to its development, an individual's self-concept is derived largely from the social situation. Because the self is rarely presented in the social situation without some form of clothing, the body boundaries often are extended to include clothes in the body image. At every stage of development, clothing helps to establish the identity of individuals to themselves and to others with whom they interact. It sets the stage for rehearsing the roles one will be expected to play in life and also assists in portraying such roles more convincingly. Clothing contributes to the process of identification by which the individual takes on the attitudes and values of "the other," and self-feeling is shaped by the imagined judgments of these significant other persons.

CLOTHING AND EVALUATION OF THE SELF

We have seen how ideas about the self are socially derived. Thus far we have dealt primarily with the **cognitive** component of the self, that is, the recognition of "who and what I am." A nine- or ten-year-old child may respond with such answers as "I am a boy. I go to school. I have a mother, father, and little sister. I'm not as tall as other kids my age. I like to wear jeans and T-shirts most of the time." Such responses may not be made verbally, but they establish the individual's identity and characteristics. How people feel about their identity and characteristics is usually called the **affective** component of the self, that is, the person's own estimation of worth.

Achieving Unity

It is useful here to refer to the principle of **operant conditioning** in explaining how such feelings develop. In simple terms, operant conditioning means that you do, or

continue to do, those things for which you are rewarded and refrain from doing those things for which you are punished or not rewarded. If a little girl, for example, examines herself in the mirror, smooths her skirt and adjusts her sash, and the family members who observe this behavior respond in a positive manner, openly enjoying the demonstration and calling attention to the child as they do so, such behavior is reinforced and likely to be repeated by the child. It is very probable that the same behavior on the part of a little boy would not be reinforced in the same manner. On the other hand, children who are continually criticized or ridiculed about their clothes, or who feel their clothes are inadequate, soon become overly self-conscious about them.

According to Sullivan, the self is made up of a series of "reflected appraisals."[21]

[21]Harry Stack Sullivan, *Conceptions of Modern Psychiatry* (Washington, D.C.: William Alanson White Psychiatric Foundation, 1947).

By the time children are nine or ten, they have had many experiences of noting other people's reactions to their behavior, and they have a fairly good idea of the usual reaction they can obtain. The little boy who is reminded continually that he is a bad boy because he gets his clothes dirty comes to see himself as a bad boy. Thus, at age ten, he can make a number of evaluative statements about himself: "I don't do what my mother says. I'm careless and sloppy about my clothes. I never put things away where they belong."

The problem of achieving a consistent way of looking at one's self would be relatively simple if the individual's social contacts did not extend beyond a limited number of people who tended to respond in a uniform manner. But as we said earlier, people develop many different identities and perceive themselves as being evaluated differently by different groups of "significant others." A girl from a small town, for example, may consider herself particularly well dressed because she perceives that other students in her high school think she is well dressed. If she attends a large university as a college freshman, she may find other students there do not have the same high regard for her taste in clothes. What adjustments, if any, does the individual make in the concept of self?

Secord and Backman present a theory that suggests that the individual may use any one of a number of techniques to maintain the established self-concept.[22] A person may simply *misperceive* what the others actually see. The college freshman may see herself through rose-colored glasses, misperceive the judgment of the new

college group, and continue to think others regard her in the same way she was regarded in high school. Or, she may *select to interact* only with people who do consider her well dressed. A third possible response might be to *devaluate the opinions* of those who do not agree with her self-concept and convince herself that their views are not important because none of them knows how to dress anyway. Another possibility would be to *devaluate the importance* of being well dressed and find other outlets in athletic achievement or scholastic performance. Or, she may make a more conscious effort to select her clothes with particular care so as to create the impression that she is well dressed; in other words, she is careful to *control the cues* she presents to others for evaluation.

This theory is very similar to Festinger's theory of **cognitive dissonance**, which centers on the idea that people will do a variety of things to achieve consistency in their psychological worlds.[23] If two pieces of information do not "fit together," individuals will make certain alterations in the information, which Festinger calls "dissonance-reducing changes." A person can restore consistency by (1) changing opinions, (2) changing behavior, (3) changing the available information, or (4) distorting perception. The person will resort to mechanisms that will not require changing the original opinion or decision.

Here it is interesting to consider at what developmental stage an individual is likely to achieve unity or stability in the self-concept. The very young boy is apt to shift his identities in rapid succession, being a cowboy one minute, a firefighter the next, in a kind of trying-on of roles, before he

[22]Paul F. Secord and Carl W. Backman, "Personality Theory and the Problem of Stability and Change in Individual Behavior," *Psychological Review*, 68 (1961), 21–32.

[23]Leon Festinger, "Cognitive Dissonance," *Scientific American*, October 1962, 93–102.

decides who he is really going to be. In early adolescence, as we have seen, the patterns of identification tend to shift from parent to peer, gradually giving way to a more "generalized other." It is apparent, however, that many individuals have not yet achieved a high degree of stability in the self-concept, even at college age. Ryan asked college women to describe the type of person they considered themselves to be, and the majority of respondents were unable to do so.[24] They described their clothing preferences in terms of the simple tailored clothing that represented the prevailing campus style. Even though their clothing preferences were clear in terms of their likes and dislikes, they had not yet consciously recognized their most striking self-characteristics.

A similar study was made of women students enrolled in clothing courses at the University of Nevada. By and large, the majority of the students could not describe a core of feelings that represent the self in a distinctive way, and clothing preferences usually were stated in terms of the existing norm. About one-third expressed rather clear-cut impressions of themselves as "feminine and dainty," "classic," "wholesome," "original and different," "outdoorsy," and the like. About 10 percent openly acknowledged variations in the self-concept.

Such variations certainly are not uncommon, particularly at an age when new social roles must be assumed. Erikson describes this diffusion of the self as a common problem of adolescents, who have not quite given up childhood identities

and have not yet mastered adulthood identities.[25] Lack of a well-defined self-concept may also be due to the fact that in our culture introspective behavior is not generally encouraged. Given the opportunity to think about and verbalize their self-feelings over a period of time, the college women described above often could work out more distinctive patterns of feelings about themselves. This self-clarification was usually accompanied by a more consistent style of dress.

In a later study by Ryan, students' personality traits were compared with feelings of being well dressed.[26] The findings indicated that women who were high on the trait of "dominance" as measured by the personality inventory tended to rate themselves high on feelings of being well dressed. Women who were submissive rated themselves lower in their clothing appearance. Another notable finding of this study was that a high correlation existed among the ratings on the various scales. For example, if an individual rated herself high on feelings of being well dressed, she also rated herself high in her evaluation of physical characteristics, individuality in dress, and her own self-confidence. Moreover, the same kind of correlation was found in the group evaluation of a given individual, that is, if the group rated a woman high on appearance, the group also rated her high on physical characteristics, individuality, and self-confidence. This "halo" effect in the ratings gives some real evidence that a generalized impression of

[24]Mary S. Ryan, "Report of Interviews with a Selected Sample of College Women," *Psychological Effects of Clothing, Part III*, Bulletin No. 900 (Ithaca, N.Y.: Cornell University Agricultural Experiment Station, August 1953).

[25]E. H. Erikson, "The Problem of Ego Identity," *Journal of the American Psychoanalytic Association*, 4 (1956), 56–121.
[26]Mary S. Ryan, "Perception of Self in Relation to Clothing" *Psychological Effects of Clothing, Part IV*, Bulletin No. 905 (Ithaca, N.Y.: Cornell University Agricultural Experiment Station, August 1954).

the self is gradually derived from one's experiences with other persons.

Rewards or punishments received in connection with clothing behavior tend to reinforce the generalized feeling toward the self. Clothing contributes to stabilization of the self-concept.

Self-Enhancement

Most theorists agree that people in general have a strong need for self-enhancement, and clothing as an instrument in the beautification of the self is so commonplace that it is usually taken for granted. Few aspects of the self call forth as much open admiration as one's clothes, since there are rare opportunities, for casual acquaintances at least, to comment on one's gestures, facial expression, posture, speech patterns, intellect, and other character traits, even though these, too, are all parts of the self.

Thus, because clothes are such a visual part of the self, they are often included in the conscious evaluation of self-characteristics. For most people, clothes are more often a source of positive feeling toward the self than of negative feelings (Figure 6.12). In a study of black and white adolescents, Lott discovered that teenagers of both races who had a high degree of confidence in their adornment behavior also had high self-concepts of their physical attributes (Figure 6.13).[27] Jersild's earlier work also indicated that clothes were often mentioned in descriptions of

Figure 6.12 Positive feelings about the self are facilitated by attractive clothing. Conversely, attractive clothing enhances one's self-concept.

Figure 6.13 In most cases, clothing does project an individual's self-concept. It conveys an impression of what a person is like and likes to do.

[27]Isabelle Lott, "Self-Concept and Related Adornment Behavior of Negro and White Adolescent Girls." Master's thesis, Michigan State University, 1966.

what children and adolescents liked about themselves.[28]

For some people, however, clothing may be a source of embarrassment, discomfort, or belittlement, even though this is not the dominant or generalized pattern. Considerable empirical evidence shows that feelings of clothing deprivation have a significant relationship to lack of social confidence and to low self-concepts.[29] Some students in Ryan's study felt less well dressed than average and they indicated that they were likely to feel self-conscious and tried to keep from the center of group attention. In such cases, individuals react with negative feelings to the imagined judgments of the referent group and measure their self-esteem against the clothing expectations of "significant others." The greater the difference between the self-feelings and the imagined group-feelings, the more difficult it is for the individual to fill the required social role.

Clothing is also involved in restoring feelings of self-worth. Rather startling examples can be observed in the behavior of the mentally ill. Doctors and other hospital personnel have increasingly recognized the fact that personal appearance is one clue to mental health. **Fashion therapy** is usually used to designate programs geared to helping patients improve their physical appearance. One of the first such projects developed at a state hospital in California in 1959. With the help of the California Fashion Group, a dress was designed for each woman patient, and she was then helped to make it for herself. With renewed pride in their appearances, most patients began to improve, some responding to fashion therapy after all other attempts to reach them had failed. One such case was described by a member of the hospital staff:

We took a very classic example of one patient who, no matter what you would put on her, was able to get her dress up to her mouth and start eating at the neckline and she would eat as many as sixteen or eighteen dresses a day. We tried putting leather around the neck. Somehow she would manage to get to the stitching between the leather and the material and was still able to eat her dresses. We took her in and talked to her and told her that we were going to dress her up in the nicest of things: silk stockings, shoes, and either nylon or cotton print dresses. This may sound fantastic, but this has been going on for three years now and she hasn't eaten one dress. She goes to the shows; she goes to the dances, and she is just one of the crowd.[30]

Since one overt expression that often accompanies a mental disorder is that of a negative self-concept, the idea of using clothing both as a treatment aid and as a diagnostic tool with those who are mentally handicapped is not a new one. Many writers have suggested this link, particularly between self-concept and depression, but there has been little empirical evidence of the connection. Ryan described clothing as being an intimate part of ourselves and acting as a direct expression of one's

[28]Arthur Jersild, *In Search of Self* (New York: Teachers College, Columbia University, 1952).

[29]See Vener and Hoffer, *Adolescent Orientations to Clothing*. Also, Mary Brawley, "Feelings of Clothing Deprivation As Related to Self-Concept and Peer Acceptance Among Black and White Fourth Grade Girls"; and Mary Edwards, "The Relationship Between Feelings of Clothing Deprivation, Self Concept, and Peer Acceptance Among Low and Middle Socioeconomic Status Fourth Grade White Male Students," both Master's theses, University of Tennessee, 1971.

[30]Reported by Robert H. Tuttle, Supervisor of Nursing Services, Mendocino State Hospital in Ukiah, California.

self-concept. It is logical to assume, then, that changes in one's self-concept would bring changes in one's clothing habits, and that changes in one's self-concept as a result of the depressive illness would also affect one's interest in appearance and clothing. In two research studies, such a relationship was found. What was surprising was that the direction of the relationship was counter to what had been expected. Worrell, investigating depression and clothing interest, found that as depression rose so did interest in clothing.[31] Since the interest in clothing that was measured described the use of clothing to enhance one's self-concept, a logical explanation for the results was that people, at least at the mild and moderate stages of depression, do indeed use clothing to help boost morale.

In another study with slightly different variables, Johnson found that those who were more depressed had a higher self-image in clothing and appearance than did those in the less depressed groups. Here, too, the speculation was that those who are feeling depressed do actively use clothing to help them over some of the manifestations of their depressed mood.[32] Again, this finding demonstrates the significance of clothing in formation of attitudes and feelings toward the self.

Clothing is a significant force in the enhancement of the self, and when used positively, it contributes to one's feelings of self-acceptance, self-respect, and self-esteem.

[31]Jacqueline Anne Worrell, "Relationship Between Clothing Interest and the Mental State of Depression." Master's thesis, Virginia Polytechnic Institute and State University, 1977.
[32]Mary Lynn Johnson, "An Exploratory Study of the Relationship of Clothing Self-Concept to Depression" Master's thesis, Virginia Polytechnic Institute and State University, 1979.

In Defense of the Self

Even with (1) a thorough understanding of societal symbols, (2) the recognition of the possibilities inherent in role playing, (3) an acceptance of the limitations of the perceiver variables, (4) an awareness of deliberately fraudulent and misleading cues, and (5) the use of dissonance reduction, there is still another reason we cannot make definite conclusions regarding someone else based only on appearance and behavior. In order to defend itself against anxiety, frustration, and trauma the self has several ways of making exterior events appear different. Unconsciously, disturbing elements are changed to make life more bearable. Freud called these changes or denials **defense mechanisms**, mechanisms or methods used to defend the self against unpleasantness.[33] As a part of psychoanalytic theory, this defense system provides the individual with a variety of ways to keep from acknowledging unpleasant truths about the self.

Freud used the term *ego* for a concept that may be considered similar to that aspect of a person others have called "self." He said that when the ego had difficulty in handling pressures from society and the unconscious, it uses these defense mechanisms for protection. Although they operate differently, all defense mechanisms have two common characteristics. Like cognitive dissonance, another way in which individuals resolve conflicting evidence, defense mechanisms also change or distort reality, and they operate unconsciously, that is, the person is usually not aware of using them. The drive to defend the self is most powerful when one's

[33]Sigmund Freud, *The Origin and Development of Psychoanalysis* (Chicago: Gateway Editions, 1965).

self-esteem is threatened. Since clothing is such a convenient means of self-expression and, therefore, of protecting self-esteem, it is not surprising that the self uses it as a means of defense in many situations. Some of these defenses are more easily recognized than others.

One way to maintain self-respect is to have logical and socially acceptable reasons for doing the things we do. The process of **rationalization** involves inventing excuses for your behavior when you do not have an excuse ample enough even to satisfy yourself. Of all the defensive mechanisms, rationalization is probably the one that is used most commonly and most consciously. Due to the widespread popularity and familiarity of Freud's theories, it is not uncommon to hear people say that they are rationalizing. The process provides logically acceptable reasons for often illogical behavior, and logical but false reasons for impulsive behavior. An expensive clothing item can be justified by need, a questionable choice because it was a good buy or it was all the store had in stock. The woman who says she doesn't care if the line shows where she lengthened a dress to accommodate a fashionably lower hemline may care deeply but be unable to buy new clothes and unwilling to be "out of fashion" in a short skirt. The woman who "simply cannot keep warm" in a cloth coat rationalizes her desire for the mink she saw on sale last week. The home economics student tells her father that she "must" have a new sweater to match the skirt she just made or she will receive a poor grade in her clothing class. By giving the self false excuses we may retain a higher self-concept than the group is apt to ascribe to us.

The process of **identification** is a positive mechanism used in learning role behavior. However, it also may be responsible for misjudgments about one's self-concept. In copying the actions and attitudes of another person, individuals may also claim to have the admirable traits of the model, which in reality they do not have at all. Dressing up like the latest Hollywood sex symbol may impart to the wearer's self a semblance of the sex appeal of the originator, but the observer may be unable to perceive any such changes.

The mechanism of **projection** is just the reverse of identification. Instead of assuming the desirable traits of another, we assign our own attributes, usually undesirable ones, to other people. Doing so gives the self the assurance that others are equally or worse off than we are: in a world of sloppily dressed people, my own sloppiness will go unnoticed; if everyone else is too fat to be wearing shorts, it is acceptable for me to wear them because "She is as fat as I am and she can wear them." Projection is an indirect way to bolster one's self-esteem, and it may also account for discrepancies between the self and the group judgment.

Under ordinary circumstances, it is quite natural and desirable for people with deficiencies of one kind or another to compensate with superior performance in some other area or activity. Few people would refrain from covering up physical deficiencies with clothes—camouflaging hips that are too full, shoulders that are too narrow, arms that are too thin, or a waist that is too thick. These, of course, are all minor forms of compensation. A good job of camouflage obviously will influence the group judgment away from the reality of the self. In more extreme cases of frustration, an individual may use **overcompensation** to handle feelings of inadequacy. People labeled by the group as being conceited—

that is, those who hold unwarranted high opinions of themselves—are very apt to be covering up rather deep-seated feelings of inferiority. The woman who feels socially inferior may overcompensate by wearing conspicuously expensive clothes, or the salesman who lacks real skill on his job may find that he can gain acceptance and attention with flashy suits or unusual ties.

Some individuals find comfort and security in falling back to childish patterns of behavior. **Regression** is a mechanism by which the individual returns to earlier habits that may have brought positive responses from others at another time in life. The supposedly mature man who finds satisfaction in donning his old college sweater; the teen-ager who reverts to the messy habits of childhood when mother took care to see that clothes were clean and well pressed; the middle-aged woman who subconsciously believes that her "baby doll" dresses will recapture the protective concerns of others that she enjoyed as a little girl—such are the manifestations of regressive behavior.

Another behavior pattern that may be adopted is commonly known as **repression**. Some writers define it as "motivated forgetting," a process in which one's eyes are closed to reality. If early experiences with clothing caused humiliation, embarrassment, or discomfort, all thoughts about clothes may be put out of mind and the person may pretend that clothes hardly exist at all. A person may have a strong desire for clothes that will enhance personal appearance, but the requisite purchasing power or the knowledge to achieve a goal is lacking. This person may then adopt the attitude that clothes are really very unimportant. Because too wide a discrepancy between what one has and what one wants results in a

situation that is intolerable, the self is defended against such an occurrence.

A response similar to repression is called "goal substitution" or **sublimation** by the Freudians. Sublimation enables the individual to substitute socially acceptable patterns of behavior for desires society considers taboo. Fundamental sex drives, for example, are restricted by well-established conventions that block overt satisfaction of sexual desires. Such drives are quite commonly rechanneled into clothing behavior. It is perfectly acceptable to be attractive by virtue of one's clothes, but it is very unacceptable to attract attention with one's body.

A type of reaction that becomes habitual with some excessively shy people is that of **insulation**. They are so insecure in their social participation skills that they seek to withdraw from even the slightest bit of public attention. Inconspicuous clothing, of course, is a perfect shield for their seclusion. Clothes provide both physical insulation from heat and cold and psychological insulation as well.

Although it is impossible to categorize all types of human responses to conflict and frustration, one final mechanism should be mentioned in relation to clothing behavior. **Reaction formation** is a process that seriously interferes with the accuracy of group judgments of an individual, since it is an attempt to conceal one's real motives by displaying attitudes that are exactly the opposite. The person obsessed by obscene thoughts and desires may exhibit extreme prudishness in dress and protest the "indecency" of modern fashions. Or people who spend most of their money on clothes and most of their time deciding what to wear may claim that they have absolutely no interest in dress whatsoever and that their appearance is purely "accidental."

There are still other defense mechanisms. Those mentioned are most often and appropriately applied to clothing inconsistencies, although the others may be used also. Here, it is enough to know that they exist, that some are used at some time by most people, certainly not all defenses are used by all people, and that they do help protect the self in a sometimes hazardous, frustrating, and anxiety-producing world. We need to understand that this elaborate camouflage system exists to help us "save face," even with ourselves. One must be keenly perceptive to see through such a camouflage. The person who is able to develop some understanding of the actions motivated by the defense system may well be able to recognize certain clothing behaviors and practices as indicative of more deeply seated problems. Such an understanding may help in relationships with others and also in maintaining a well-integrated personality structure. It is important, therefore, that we be alert for indications of a defense or cover-up, both in ourselves and in others.

In most cases, clothing provides a real clue to personality since it conveys an impression of what one is, what one does, and what one believes. The majority of people tend to see themselves in much the same way that others perceive them. We must be cautious, however, in forming opinions about the underlying motives of behavior, since an individual may employ any one of several mechanisms that defend the self from detection. Moreover, the impression one may wish to create through clothing may not be perceived in the same way that one would like it to be (Figure 6.14). This may be attributed in part to a person's ignorance of the cues communicated to others through dress, or it may be accounted for by the fact that people tend

"Quick! Your gut reaction."

Figure 6.14 Clothing may or may not convey the impression the wearer intends. Drawing by Frascino; © 1980, The New Yorker Magazine, Inc.

to see what they are looking for—that is, they perceive and evaluate the other's appearance by their own expectations.

Thus, in terms of operant behavior, behavior resulting from rewards and punishments, clothing is both a *stimulus* and a *response*. It stimulates the wearer as well as the beholder. It stimulates the social and the sexual appetite. It calls forth responses of admiration, approval, acceptance, rejection, condemnation, or ridicule. Clothing is also a response in that it registers conformity to group expectations, rebellion to parental control, and satisfaction of psychological needs.

Unconscious use of defense mechanisms prevents observers from making definitive conclusions about someone else based only on behavior and appearance.

⊕ SUMMARY

Clothing and Evaluation of the Self

The effects of operant conditioning in relation to clothing behavior have been discussed. Positive attitudes expressed toward one's clothes tend to reinforce a generalized positive feeling toward the self, and negative responses contribute to self-deprecation. A unified, consistent way of looking at oneself develops gradually from the "reflected appraisals" of others. Changes in these feelings are common, especially on assuming new social roles.

For most people, clothing provides a positive means of satisfying the need for self-enhancement. It can beautify the appearance, make the physical self more desirable, increase acceptance by the group, and prevent rejection. It may be a source of overt admiration, resulting in increased self-esteem, self-respect, self-confidence, and security.

Clothing is a cue to personality in that it gives an impression of what one is, does, and believes. But this impression is not always perceived as one wishes, since others perceive clothing in terms of their own self-concepts and expectations, and individuals may not know the meanings conveyed by clothes. Further, defense mechanisms, such as identification, projection, rationalization, overcompensation, regression, repression, sublimation, insulation, and reaction formation, may be involved. Such mechanisms may further confuse perception.

CLOTHES, SELF, AND SOCIETY

"Clothes make the man," the saying goes. What seems at first to be a flippant appraisal of the importance of dress takes on added depth of meaning as we analyze the close relationship between clothing and developmental processes. Hurlock explained how the careful selection of clothes for children can satisfy some important needs: autonomy, attention, individuality, as well as peer group and sex identification.[34] We have already discussed how behavior patterns established in the early years of life are apt to carry over into adulthood. The continuing importance of dress even in later life is emphasized by Stone's contention that

1. every social transaction must be broken down into at least two analytic components or processes, appearance and discourse,

2. appearance is at least as important for establishment and maintenance of the self as is discourse,

3. the study of appearance provides a powerful lever for formulation of a conception of self,

4. appearance is of major importance at every stage of development.[35]

---

[34]Elizabeth E. Hurlock. *Child Development* (New York: McGraw Hill, 1972), pp. 406–408.

[35]Gregory P. Stone, "Appearance and the Self," in *Human Behavior and Social Processes*, ed. A. Rose (Boston: Houghton Mifflin Company, 1962), p. 87.

Figure 6.15 Left: Clothing also conveys to others what one does.

Figure 6.16 Right: Clothes maketh the man.

Subidentities

Stone's insistence that appearance is at least if not more important than language in communicating impressions of the self to others is corroborated by studies that have shown that the initial or primary impression individuals create is likely to be an important and lasting one.[36] First impressions are largely derived from outward appearances and established by nonverbal cues and symbols of the kind clothing provides. The way in which a person is first perceived is particularly important in establishing the self in new social roles. Every individual maintains a series of such subidentities that are defined and delimited by the boundaries of specific roles (Figure 6.15).

Thus, the identity established by the college freshman among juniors and sen-iors in a sorority house is apt to differ in many respects from the identity that same student enjoys among old high school friends at home. Each of the subidentities may require conformity to a different set of clothing expectations, and the individual is likely to make a more conscious effort to control the clothing cues in the less familiar situation. The clothing requirements of a man's role as a department manager may differ only slightly from those required as a member of the executive board, but both sets of requirements are put aside when he gets home in the evening and changes to his "husband-and-father" clothes. Various subidentities contribute to the changing and flexible qualities of the self (Figure 6.16). The self gradually absorbs or accommodates the requirements prescribed by the social groups in which membership is sought or claimed.

Clothing requirements for various subidentities are defined within the context of specific or separate roles, and they contribute to the changing nature of the self.

[36]See, for example, S. E. Asch, "Forming Impressions of Personality," *Journal of Abnormal and Social Psychology*, 41 (1946), 258–290, and N. H. Anderson and A. A. Barrios, "Primacy Effects in Personality Impression Formation," *Journal of Abnormal and Social Psychology*, 63 (1961), 346–350.

An Emerging Lifestyle

In spite of the fact that the self is developmental in nature, most individuals tend to respond with one generalized mode or pattern of behavior. Adler's phrase for this fixed expression of personality is "style of life."[37] The implication is that one type of response becomes dominant in an individual's life experiences, and a central, unified style emerges (Figure 6.17).

A "style of life" applied to patterns of clothing behavior will reveal that some men respond to almost all situations with attire that expresses a high degree of inconspicuous conformity—"he is the best-dressed whose dress no one observes." Other men (by far the minority in our society) exhibit a "style of life" through clothes that is built on the philosophy of "fine feathers make fine birds."

The point is that one's preference for different styles is not just a random adoption of a set of values. It is no accident, for example, that many black leaders are among the best-dressed politicians and athletes in the country. To black men, avant-garde dressing is rarely considered an affectation. Clothes are considered a symbol of pride—a legitimate masculine concern—and the source of personal compliments.

It is probably safe to say that the development of a lifestyle is an unconscious phenomenon and quite difficult for most people to see in themselves. The messages broadcast by other people's attire are often easier for us to receive and to understand than are our own.

A number of unique patterns of clothing behavior have been identified by Symonds

"I wish we had a life style."

Figure 6.17 For most people, the development of a lifestyle is an unconscious process. Drawing by Lorentz; © 1973, The New Yorker Magazine, Inc.

through her experience as a psychoanalyst. If you are like most people, she explains,

you have some clothes in your closet which you never wear, even though they're perfectly good. You also have some you're always wearing. That's because some clothes fit your inner picture of yourself, while others don't. Unconscious factors guide your choices of clothing as surely as though you were following a blueprint and you wear what satisfies your true feelings about yourself—whether you consciously know it or not. . . .

Your state of mind may change from day to day, or year to year, and your clothes will reflect it. This phenomenon has proved most helpful to me as a psychoanalyst in understanding the person I'm trying to help.[38]

[37]Heinz and Rowena Ansbacher, *The Individual Psychology of Alfred Adler* (New York: Basic Books, 1956).

[38]Alexandra Symonds, M.D., "A Psychoanalyst Reveals Why You Dress the Way You Do," *This Week*, May 27, 1962, pp. 18–22.

This comment seems to suggest that we often approach the problem of clothing selection from the wrong direction. Instead of trying to analyze one's personality (which is difficult with or without objective tests or devices), Symonds proposes that we analyze one's clothes, which may in turn tell us more about the self than do direct approaches to personality assessment. Clothing types are certainly easier to identify than personality types, and they can be looked at with considerably greater detachment and objectivity.

However it is achieved, understanding the self is a prerequisite to development of a "style of life" that is consistent with one's recognized values and aspirations. For, as Symonds concludes, it is only after you acknowledge what is really *you* and have accepted yourself, with your own particular idiosyncrasies, that change is possible.

Consistent patterns of clothing behavior emerge as a type of dominant response and gradually evolve into a "style of life."

SUMMARY

Clothes, Self, and Society

We have seen that the self is a configuration of (1) the cognitive components, of intellect, character traits, and various subidentities; (2) the affective aspects, of feelings and emotions about the self that are conditioned by the social environment; and (3) the somatic constituents, representing rather fixed physical characteristics. Clothing affects all these aspects of the self and is a powerful medium through which the self is presented to and perceived by significant others in the social world. It is only as the self is analyzed, as one develops a vocabulary for expressing feelings about the self, and as one brings values and aspirations to the conscious level of recognition, that resulting patterns of clothing behavior can be modified or altered to a "style of life" that will achieve optimal satisfaction and reward.

FOR FURTHER READING

Kneitel, Ken, Bill Maloney and Andrea Quinn. *The Great American T-Shirt*. New York: New American Library, 1976.

Sabol, Blair. "A Clothes Encounter." *New York*, 12 (January 29, 1979), 97–99.

"Secrets from Our Clothes Closet." *Glamour*, 76 (December 1978), 58.

Sproles, George B. *Fashion: Consumer Behavior Toward Dress*. Minneapolis: Burgess Publishing Co., 1979, pp. 141–154.

Thurman, Judith. "How to Get Dressed and Still Be Yourself: Finding Your Personal Style." *Ms*, 7 (April 1979), 49–51.

Chapter 7

CLOTHING SYMBOLISM

In daily life, people commonly form immediate impressions of those they meet for the first time. A quick scan of an individual's appearance communicates a wealth of information about the person's character, position, and status in life. Allport describes the process as follows:

With briefest visual perception, a complex mental process is aroused, resulting within a very short time, 30 seconds perhaps, in judgment of the sex, age, size, nationality, profession and social caste of the stranger, together with some estimate of his temperament, his ascendence, friendliness, neatness, and even his trustworthiness and integrity. With no further acquaintance many impressions may be erroneous, but they show the swift totalizing nature of our judgments.[1]

Although first impressions are sometimes altered as additional information about the person is collected over time, we can no more prevent the formation and rapid growth of these initial judgments "than we can avoid perceiving a given visual object or hearing a melody. We also know that this process, though often imperfect, is also at times extraordinarily sensitive."[2]

Clothing is part of the "silent language" communicated through use of visual or nonverbal symbols.[3] Goffman described such symbols as "sign-vehicles" or "cues" that select the status to be assigned to individuals and defines the ways others are

[1]Gordon Allport, *Personality—A Psychological Interpretation*, (New York: Henry Holt & Company, 1937), p. 500.

[2]S. E. Asch, "Forming Impressions of Personality," *Journal of Abnormal and Social Psychology*, 41 (1946), 258.

[3]Edward Hall, *The Silent Language* (Garden City, N.Y.: Doubleday, 1959).

to treat them.[4] These visual short cuts to person perception enable us to categorize an individual, at least tentatively, and set the stage for further interaction (Figure 7.1).

Therefore, it is important to understand the meanings clothing symbols convey in order to present the self in such a way that the desired impression is achieved. In today's mobile, urbanized society, a great many of our person-to-person contacts are impersonal and temporary. First impressions often are the only ones formed and, for all practical purposes, clothing becomes an intimate and inseparable part of the perceptual field within which a person is located. Clothing gives clues to self, role, and status, and it also helps to define the situation within which a person is perceived.

© 1965 by NEA, Inc.

"No, man—this isn't my wife and daughter—it's my husband and son!"

Figure 7.1 An effective clothing symbol would make it possible for a stranger to determine the social category to which the wearer belongs and thus avoid actions that would be considered social errors.

SYMBOLIC INTERACTION THEORY

The symbolic effects of clothing on the interactions of people are as ancient as dress and adornment, but only in the last hundred years have social scientists, primarily sociologists, consciously thought about clothing and the ways in which it is used as a nonverbal communicator. Many theories have been suggested to explain clothing behavior in general; one of the most fruitful to the study of clothing symbolism and to understanding the communicative aspects of clothing is symbolic interaction theory.

Some scientific theories are systematically formulated by one person (psychoanalytic theory) or by a group of people (learning theory). Some grow slowly over a

long period of time and have many contributors. The ideas and assumptions that make up symbolic interaction theory have such a history. Some of its basic ideas can be traced back to the writings of William James and others concerned with ideas about the self, but the theory was formally developed much later. Its main architect and the man whose name is most often associated with the theory is probably George Herbert Mead.[5]

Basically, symbolic interaction theory states that people live in a symbolic environment as well as a physical one and that behavior is stimulated by symbols as well as by physical acts. Practically all the

[4]Erving Goffman, "Symbols of Class Status," *British Journal of Sociology*, 2, No. 4 (1951), 294.

[5]George Herbert Mead, *Mind, Self and Society* (Chicago: University of Chicago Press, 1934).

symbols that are learned are acquired through communication (interaction) with other people. These ideas may not seem strange today, but in the late nineteenth and early twentieth century when symbolic interaction theory was developing, the natural scientists had become quite successful in understanding, predicting, and controlling the physical world. Social scientists were greatly influenced to copy the resulting scientific methods in examining the social world. Mostly behaviorists, they tried to reduce human behavior to the mechanisms found in the subhuman animal world. Only overt behavior was studied and no reference was made to the distinctive characteristics that differentiate human and animal behavior. A great deal of psychological theory was grounded in animal research. The result was that a good deal of knowledge about human behavior was based on the behavior of animals.

Humans, however, share another's behavior instead of simply responding to it as animals do. They do not respond mechanically to stimuli but are active participants in a highly organized, cooperative society. Mead therefore felt the need for a sociological theory based on human characteristics with research dealing with humans instead of animals.

The interactions that make society function depend on large networks of symbols. These symbols have a common or shared meaning within a culture. Although most symbols are communicated verbally, some are transmitted through sight, such as gestures, motions, and objects. Clothing and adornments are primary objects used symbolically in human interactions.

Appearance carries symbolic meaning to the observer, but the received message may not always be the intended message (Figure 7.2). The degree of consistency

Figure 7.2 Similarities of clothing in its infinite variability carries symbolic meaning within a culture. Swimming trunks convey symbolic messages about intended actions.

between the two messages is a measure of the effectiveness of the interaction. Within fairly homogeneous cultural units, this differentiation will be slight. However, many ineffective cross-cultural communications occur because the symbolic messages are incorrectly interpreted. In applying the basic ideas of symbolic interaction theory to clothing symbolism we shall consider: first, the qualities of clothing that present stimulus information to the perceiver; second, some of the variables in the perception process that determine the accuracy or inaccuracy of the impressions formed; and third, the consequences of impression formation in the social interaction process.

The interactions of people in a society depend on a large network of symbols. Symbolic interaction theory can be used as a theoretical framework for studying clothing symbols.

CLOTHING CUES

We always hesitate to accept the validity of judgments based on outward appearances because we have been told that "you can't judge a book by its cover." In other words, we are wary of stereotypes in forming opinions of others (Figure 7.3). We know stereotypes do not spell out the wide range of variability that occurs within a given role or status. They ignore the fact that every individual has a unique, complex set of characteristics, and the error of stereotyping is an error of oversimplification. Another difficulty is that cultural stereotypes are neither true nor false: stereotypes are always based on fact. They were true at one time or in one place, or with one group of people; they are no longer true. If they were true, they would be facts, not stereotypes. Stereotyping often occurs along with first impressions, or conversely, first impressions are often stereotypes. Instant impressions are formed from a name, a smile, a handshake, and other symbolic cues, and if the message conveyed fits a preconceived idea, the stereotype is applied. The fact that clothing plays an important role in this process has been demonstrated by empirical studies. During the late 1960s and early 1970s many long-haired, bearded young men were assumed to be politically radical and part of the drug culture. These opinions were based on a stereotyped idea—all long-haired and bearded men were hippies; all hippies smoke pot; all hippies are radicals. In an attempt to measure these stereotypes associated with clothes and appearance, students on a Berkeley, California, campus were asked to respond to drawings by determining which of the photographs "comes closest to the way you usually look when you're on campus" as well as associ-

Figure 7.3 Young people often are judged without sufficient information and with a good deal of stereotyping.

ating the figures with political activism (liberal or conservative) and the use of marijuana (Figure 7.4). The figures ranged from "Off-campus Clean cut, well groomed with conventional off-campus wear: jacket and tie," to "Earthy Distinctly—if not aggressively—unkempt, deliberately unconventional: scruffy work shirt and jeans,

Preppie   Earthy   Arty-Ethnic
                       Grubbie   Hippie

Figure 7.4 Groups differentiated by clothing are not only stereotyped as to behavior and beliefs, but given group names as well.

long disheveled hair." The two middle positions were "collegiate" and "shaggy." As was expected, stereotyping of dress was demonstrated; those dressed conventionally were considered conservative and the unconventional dressers were classified as liberals. There was a close correspondence between the activism of the students and the stereotyping of the figures as activists. Although the accuracy of these stereotypes cannot be determined, "it is nonetheless clear that a student's style of dress communicates his political position with considerable accuracy." Identical results were found when marijuana was used as an indicator of cultural conservatism.[6]

Stereotypes may also be an overgeneralized composite representing a kind of statistical norm for particular roles and statuses. At a governor's conference, for example, the typical "head of state" was described as a white male, a Democrat, age forty-nine, who has been a soldier, is an attorney, and a holder of some other public office. He would be married, the father of three children, recipient of a university degree, a Protestant, and have been born in the jurisdiction he serves.[7] Probably no governor in the country has all twelve of those characteristics, but the description is more right than wrong.

Several other problems are associated with the acceptance of clothing symbols as positive and accurate indexes of self, role, and status. One is that the value of a symbol changes over time, thereby altering its meaning. Generations of children knew

the good guys from the bad guys by the clothing they wore, thus symbolism in clothing often had more to say than did the words. The characters and plots change inevitably over the years, but the basic themes remain. We stereotype characters in fiction by clothing, and theatrical people, knowing that we do so, use clothing as part of the story line. Today bug-eyed monsters do what the Indians used to do when the good guys wore white hats and the bad guys wore feathers.[8]

Many people now can afford the symbols that have traditionally been associated with a particular social class. Others who may be bonafide members of the upper social stratum may reject the symbols because they are no longer marks of distinction. Moreover, the extended educational opportunities now available make it possible for all people to become knowledgeable in manipulating such symbols. Goffman refers to the organized teaching of symbol manipulation as "institutionalized sources of misrepresentation."[9]

On the other hand, a number of factors restrict the use of symbols in fraudulent ways. First, there is the **intrinsic restriction** imposed by one's inability to attain the symbol; if a mink coat costs several thousand dollars, there are relatively few paths to the goal unless one has several thousand dollars. But assuming that a woman has somehow acquired the money to purchase a mink coat—and she would in fact like to own a mink coat—she may still refrain from indulging her desires on the basis of some inner **moral restriction**. She shuns the possibility of being a "Mrs. Commonplace" trying to

[6]Jonathan Kelley, "Dress and Ideology: The Non-Verbal Communication of Political Attitudes." Manuscript, Department of Sociology, Columbia University, November 1970.
[7]"What Governors Are Made Of," *Nevada State Journal*, June 5, 1973, p. 14.

[8]Joseph McLellan, "New Sci-Fi Series: 'Battlestar Galactica,'" *Washington Post*, September 10, 1978.
[9]Goffman, "Symbols of Class Status," p. 303.

look like a "Mrs. Gotrocks" by a conscious recognition of her rightful place in society.

The restrictions of **cultivation** and **socialization** make it difficult for people to acquire the social style and manners of a class to which they do not actually belong. Thus, the woman described above might, in fact, be recognized by others as out of place if her speech as well as her mannerisms and deportment were inconsistent with the role and status the coat signified. Further, if the accompanying details of her dress and grooming did not show a cultivation of taste equal to the quality of the coat, misuse of the symbol would be suspected. Such restrictions usually require considerable time and experience to overcome; this is particularly the case in understanding the subtleties of restraint in dress that are required to achieve a distinctively refined appearance.

Finally, **organic restrictions**—such as the condition of the hands (Figure 7.5), face, or body—betray lifelong exposure to the elements, to diet, and/or to work. No beauty treatment can eliminate the lines, calluses, and muscles that develop from many years of manual work. The terminolo-

gy used to label these restrictions was suggested by Goffman.

In other words, taking on the symbol without the accompanying patterns is revealing, and the inconsistencies detected between the clothing symbol and other characteristics of the stimulus person usually leave some doubt in the perceiver's mind as to the person's actual pretension.

As another illustration, the cowboy's dress is part of a way of life that has been handed down for many generations. His clothes are designed to stand the stress of work in rough country, and most features have a practical purpose (Figure 7.6). The hat with its wide brim protects the neck and head from rain, sleet, and sun and it also serves as a good water bucket and a place to store portable belongings. Waved vigorously in the air, it will steer a cattle herd toward the railhead, and, tipped over the face during a midday snooze, it will keep off the bugs and provide the only shade for miles around. They say there are sure ways to tell a genuine cowboy from a dude. For one thing, the dude wears his pants short to show off fancy boot tops; the authentic working type wears his long for

Figure 7.5 The condition of the hands, face, or other parts of the body tells of life-long exposure to the elements.
Figure 7.6 To the experienced eye, a Western man's hat tells a good deal about him—its style, color, crease, angle, degree of dirtiness, and how it is doffed.

protection from the brush. "And then notice whose hands have done a good day's work. It takes a pretty good man to flank a 300-pound calf."[10] He has no time for the fancy fringed shirt or the bright polished boots. His Stetson will have "accumulated fingerprints on a certain spot on the front of the brim. To the knowing, this marks him as a true cowhand. For he always takes his hat off with the same fingers in the same place. Dudes don't."[11] And once the hat is removed, there is always the telltale line between the white forehead and the sun-bronzed face beneath it.

In less obvious cases, clothes have been found to be fairly accurate indicators of the personalities and lifestyles of the people who wear them. In a study of university men, for example, Kness found that conservative dressers had a greater concern for clothes and attached more status symbolism to appearance than did hippie-type dressers. Those who were conservative in dress also tended to hold more conservative social and political beliefs than did their hippie counterparts.[12]

Cultural stereotypes often result in false interpretations of clothing cues. However, several restrictions limit the use of symbols in fraudulent ways.

Cues Related to Personality

Considerable evidence indicates that people do make judgments about the personal-

ity of an individual based solely on appearance. Just as an individual develops a generalized mode of behavior, the perceiver in the situation is also apt to form a generalized impression of the stimulus person. Asch's experiments revealed that the perceiver tends to organize an individual's various traits into a relatively consistent impression. In the process, some characteristics are determined to be central, while others are seen as peripheral. Numerous theories have been advanced about the particular qualities of a costume that are judged to be indicative of the wearer's personality traits.

Many years ago, Northrup adapted the ancient Chinese concepts of **yang** and **yin** to dress and personality.[13] The terms represented extreme opposites, yang denoting the characteristics of strength, forcefulness, dignity, assurance, and the like, and yin indicating delicacy, gentleness, warmth, and submissiveness. Various writers have described the individual with a predominance of yang characteristics as tall, large-boned, large-featured, with strong or vivid coloring, erect posture, sleek hair, slightly coarse skin, and vigorous in movement and temperament. The yin person is described as petite, small-boned, dainty-featured, with delicate coloring, graceful walk, softly curled hair, finely textured skin, and light in movement, pliant in temperament. Styles of clothing exhibiting yang characteristics are described as having straight unbroken lines with few details, patterns that are large in scale, colors that are bold and in striking contrast, and textures that are heavy, rough, and stiff. Clothing representing yin

[10]Comments from a College of Agriculture Graduate, *Sagebrush,* University of Nevada, June 24, 1969.
[11]"Where the Hat Is the Man," *New York Times* Service news release, May 27, 1973.
[12]Darlene Kness, "The Clothing Attitudes and Social-Political Beliefs of University Men Identified as Conservative and Hippy Dressers." Master's thesis, Pennsylvania State University, 1971.

[13]Belle Northrup, "An Approach to the Problem of Costume and Personality," *Art Education Today,* Vol. 2 (New York: Teachers College, Columbia University, 1936), 94–104.

qualities is softly curved in silhouette, with broken lines that produce dainty, small details; patterns are small in scale in closely related tones, colors light with limited contrast, and textures that are soft, pliable, or sheer. A number of intermediate types and variations of the yin and yang extremes have been described in considerable detail, with descriptions of dress that relate to corresponding personality traits.[14]

Douty studied the influence of clothing in the formation of impressions of personality and used the dimensions of the yang and yin classifications. Four women were used as stimuli-persons and were presented to groups of subject-judges. Each appeared first in a costume selected from her own wardrobe and then a second time in a control costume consisting of a plain blue smock. The wardrobe costumes were also rated with the heads of the stimuli-persons blocked out. Findings indicated that the personalities of the four women were perceived quite differently when they wore costumes from their own wardrobes than when they wore the control smocks. Further, there was a strong positive relationship between the costume ratings and the ratings of the persons.[15]

A high score on the yin-yang continuum indicates that a person is perceived to be forceful, assertive, self-assured, and dignified in nature. A low score indicates an impression of gentleness, receptivity, and submissiveness. On the assumption that warm colors have always been considered bold and advancing and cool colors quiet and receding, Mahannah combined the variables of costume color and personal coloring in a study of the influence of color on personality assessment. Four photographs of the same stimulus-person were shown to groups of subject-judges. In one, the model was photographed wearing a brunette wig and a bright red costume; in another, she was photographed in a blonde wig and a pale blue costume. The third and fourth pictures combined blonde wig and red costume, and brunette wig and blue costume. The results showed that impressions of yinness and yangness were greatly influenced by the interaction of wig and clothing colors: the brunette in the red costume was perceived to be significantly more yang than were the other three combinations.[16]

So it is not costume alone that determines our impressions, but costume combined with specific body cues and facial expressions. Secord and Muthard reported that in rating women, a generally well-groomed appearance contributed to impressions of social acceptability, and narrowed eyes and full, relaxed lips were associated with sexual attractiveness. Bowed lips appeared to create the impression that a woman was conceited, demanding, immoral, and receptive to the attentions of men.[17] Berelson and Salter concluded that fair coloring and blond hair usually were associated with the heroes of fiction stories, while dark hair and swarthiness were most often ascribed to the

[14]See for example, Harriet McJimsey, *Art and Fashion in Clothing Selection* (Ames, Iowa: Iowa State University Press, 1973), pp. 74–99; and Grace Morton, *The Arts of Costume and Personal Appearance* (New York: John Wiley & Sons, 1964), pp. 48–65.

[15]Helen Douty, "Influence of Clothing on Perception of Persons," *Journal of Home Economics*, 55, No. 3 (1963), 197–202.

[16]Lynn Mahannah, "Influence of Clothing Color on the Perception of Personality." Master's thesis, University of Nevada, 1968.

[17]P. F. Secord and J. E. Muthard, "Personalities in Faces: IV. A Descriptive Analysis of the Perception of Women's Faces and the Identification of some Physiognomic Determinants," *Journal of Psychology*, 39 (1955), 269–278.

villains.[18] Another study revealed that the character traits of warm-heartedness, honesty, intelligence, responsibility, self-confidence, and refinement in men were perceived as related to such facial features as bright, widened eyes that had a direct gaze, a straight nose of average width, well-groomed hair of average waviness, an up-turned mouth with lips of average fullness, and eyebrows of moderate heaviness set against a smooth brow. Conversely, the less desirable character traits of ruthlessness, brutality, hostility, boorishness, and vulgarity were associated with close-set narrowed eyes in downward or averted gaze, either a wide or narrow nose with distended nostrils, slicked down or disheveled hair, thick or thin lips with the corners turned down, and heavy eyebrows set against a knitted, wrinkled brow.[19]

Again, such associations are the result of a form of cultural stereotyping, and cultural ideals are subject to change over time. Public opinion in the 1960s ran strongly against the long-hairs. Hairiness among males was generally associated with uncleanliness, rebellious behavior, and a radical lifestyle. In 1973, an inquiring photographer for a San Francisco newspaper got the following answers to "Do you distrust the clean-cut type?"[20]

Yes. Short hair, like the crew cut, is from another era. And they're usually that way in their thinking, too.

The clean-cut types are always very up-tight. Not open minded at all. They're not able to see anyone else's side. They're very conservative.

I'd just think he was terribly old-fashioned. Outdated. When they have those real short hair cuts, they're always kind of straight. I'm not comfortable with them.

Only squares have crew cuts.

I just feel they're terribly boring people. Anyone with really short hair, the clean-cut type, is very conservative, very self-righteous. I don't care for them.

So rapidly do fashion changes associated with social change occur that by the late 1970s hair was scarcely an issue. The long and the short, for males and females, coexisted with scarcely a ripple, no longer truly symbolic of left or right, conservatives or liberals, dissenters or establishment. Even the United States armed forces relaxed their former rules on hair length, head and face. Military men still do not sport full-length beards or shoulder locks, but those raised in the tradition of military crew cuts find it strange to see a variety of long and short hair worn with uniforms.

In another research study, Rosencranz attempted to assess the symbolic meanings attached to clothing through the use of a projective technique.[21] (A projective test is one that is relatively unstructured so that subjects project their own attitudes, beliefs, and values into their responses.) A modified Thematic Apperception Test (Clothing TAT) was devised in which a series of seven drawings showed incongruities between the clothing worn and the actions of the characters in the pictures (Figure 7.7). Subjects were asked to tell a

[18]B. Berelson and P. Salter, "Majority and Minority Americans: An Analysis of Magazine Fiction," *Public Opinion Quarterly*, 10 (1946), 168–190.

[19]P. F. Secord, "Facial Features and Inference Processes in Interpersonal Perception," in *Person Perception and Interpersonal Behavior*, ed. R. Tagiuri and L. Petrullo (Stanford, Calif.: Stanford University Press, 1958), pp. 300–315.

[20]"O'Hara, the Question Man," *San Francisco Chronicle*, May 11, 1973.

[21]Mary Lou Rosencranz, "Clothing Symbolism," *Journal of Home Economics*, 54, No. 1 (1962), 18–22.

Figure 7.7 Test items from the Rosencranz Clothing Apperception Test.

Figure 7.8 Modified Clothing TAT test used by Beeson to measure clothing apperception.

dramatic story about each picture. No comments were made about clothing in administration of the test. However, most subjects referred to some clothing cue in analyzing the drawings. About one fourth of the total comments made by the average subject related to dress, and, for some, the clothing comments ran as high as 50 percent.

In another modified Clothing TAT test, Beeson used line drawings of clothed figures instead of photographs (Figure 7.8). With no background details, the focus was on the clothed figures of people in a variety of occupational roles and activities.[22] Again, the purpose of the drawings was to elicit stories. By counting the times clothing was mentioned by the subjects, the person's clothing apperception could be determined. By "clothing apperception" Beeson referred to the mental process by which clothing is used to identify social, occupational, and activity roles as well as age levels, environmental settings, emotional states, or personality traits as they relate to clothing.

In order to demonstrate that observable differences in dress reflect something about the psychosocial makeup of adolescents, Gurel investigated the clothing behavior of high school students living in the affluent suburbs of Washington, D.C. She found that those who were discernibly different in dress were also measurably different in conformity as a personality variable; that clothing choices are, at least in part, determined by the kind of person one is and the groups to which one belongs. Those who most conformed in personal ideology were the clothing group identified

[22]Marianne S. Beeson, "Clothing Apperception among High School and College Students." Master's thesis, Louisiana State University, 1965.

as "greasers," and the "hippies" were found to be the least rigid in their beliefs. The "straights" and "mods" were less concerned with conforming attitudes and scored in middle positions. The surprising finding was that the hippies were least conforming. They had, at the time, been accused of rigid conformity, but to unconventional standards, in other words, conformity to their nonconformity. This was not demonstrated and their "do-your-own-thing" attitude toward clothing was a genuine expression of an inner disposition toward individuality and nonconformity.[23]

There is no doubt that in studies such as Gurel's, as well as that of Kelly (p. 162) styles and group names used change over time and are different in different parts of the country. These two studies took place at approximately the same point in time but in widely separate places. Although the group names were different the clothing styles represented in the four groups were surprisingly similar, even considering the fact that Kelly's group was made up of college students and Gurel used high school–age subjects. However much the names and styles change due to time and place, there is little doubt but that the group structure exists, differentiated at least in part by clothing, and similar studies done today would produce similar results.

Research in which clothing and some aspect of personality are the major variables has not been extensive. However, two basic conclusions can be drawn from what has been done to date. One is that judgments of an individual's personality traits are influenced by the clothes worn. The second is that judges usually agree on the symbolic meanings conveyed through dress. Whether or not such judgments are accurate evaluations of the individual's character is another matter entirely. Although some studies, such as those by Gurel and Kness, have demonstrated positive relationships between a person's beliefs or lifestyle and the clothing actually worn, results in general have been inconclusive.

Knapper's research tested the relationship between personality and style of dress in a group of male subjects. Assessments of dress made by the wearer himself correlated significantly with many of the personality dimensions, but there were relatively few correlations between personality traits and ratings of dress made by peers. Knapper concluded from this that the wearer's notion of how he dresses does not always agree with the way he is perceived by others, and that perceivers who use clothing as a cue to personality are apt to make inaccurate judgments.[24]

Such findings are entirely consistent with the theories set forth by people like Symonds, who suggest that the most direct approach to personality assessment is to ask the wearer to analyze both the clothes worn and the factors that guided the particular choice of clothing.[25]

Clothing is an important cue in forming impressions of other persons, and it is particularly significant when contact with others is limited.

[23]Lois M. Gurel, June C. Wilbur, and Lee Gurel, "Personality Correlates of Adolescent Clothing Styles," *Journal of Home Economics*, 64 (March 1972), 42–47.

[24]Christopher Knapper, "The Relationship Between Personality and Style of Dress." Ph.D. diss., University of Saskatchewan, Canada, 1969.
[25]Alexandra Symonds, M.D., "A Psychoanalyst Reveals Why You Dress the Way You Do," *This Week*, May 27, 1962, pp. 18–22.

Cues Related to Role and Status

In this section, **role** is used to designate an individual's position or category in social relationships. It includes occupational roles (teacher, doctor, rancher, barber), family roles (mother, sister, uncle), and age-sex roles (a young man, a teen-age boy, an old woman). **Status** refers to an individual's place on a scale or continuum of prestige, that is, the degree of social value attached to a given capacity. Thus, a person is perceived and evaluated on the basis of how well he or she fulfills the requirements of a specific role, and that role in turn is assigned a relative status position.

In a study of occupational clothing, the main cues used to identify men in particular occupations were clothing symbols.[26] Manual workers were readily identified by their overalls, coveralls, aprons, or other work uniforms, whereas suits and sport clothes were mentioned in relation to the white-collar workers.

Many other cues were used to distinguish occupations that were almost as important as the type of clothes worn. The condition of the fabric, for example, was often noted, such as paint, grease, or dust markings on the garments, and whether the clothes were clean or dirty. The expensiveness or quality of the fabric was generally used to identify office personnel. Men also detected differences in taste, garment upkeep, and the expressive quality of the clothes. Office workers tended to identify their own group as "conservative," "subdued," or "well-tailored" dressers, whereas clothes that were "flashy," "loud," or

"frilled" were most often associated with the manual workers. Rather subtle differences were also noted in terms of being "well-dressed" or "dressed up," "neatly dressed" or "presentable." Additional cues included the cleanliness of the hands and the type of shoes worn.

The shoe appears to be a particularly expressive item in identifying roles and statuses. An interesting case of shoe symbolism was reported many years ago in *Life* magazine. On the assumption that people's feet reflect the faces to which they belong, photographer Burt Glinn presented a series of pictures of eleven men and three women separate from pictures of their shoes, which were arranged in random order. Readers were invited to test their skill in matching feet and faces. A number of readers had difficulty in making the correct choices, but several thought they could identify the person's occupation solely on the basis of appearance. University of Nevada students consistently scored 100 percent in matching the feet of the three women with their faces; scores for the eleven men were considerably less accurate.[27]

In a take-off on the same theme, pictures of men's feet wearing alligator shoes and loafers were presented to groups of students at the University of Nevada over a period of four years. Students were asked to identify the role of the person wearing the shoes using a free response technique. The alligator shoes were associated with some type of business executive by 43 percent of the respondents. Another 20 percent identified the shoes as those of a salesman, while 15 percent used such terms as

[26]W. H. Form and G. P. Stone, *Social Significance of Clothing in Occupational Life*, Technical Bulletin No. 247 (East Lansing, Mich.: State University Agricultural Experiment Station, June 1955), p. 18.

[27]"Speaking of Pictures," *Life*, December 4, 1950, pp. 26–28, and subsequent letters to the editor in the December 25, 1950 issue.

"playboy," "gay blade," or "man about town." An additional 10 percent assigned the wearer to a "wealthy" or "rich" category. The remaining 12 percent responded in terms of idiosyncratic cues that were highly specialized, such as "diplomat," "lawyer," "sportswriter"—but none was inconsistent with a monied class of people.

Even greater agreement was found in the responses to loafers. Over 56 percent of the respondents classified the wearer as a student, 28 percent thought the shoes looked more like a young businessman, and 12 percent identified them as belonging to a teacher or professor. Only 4 percent of the responses in this case were single or idiosyncratic in nature.

In this same study, universal agreement was found in the responses to pictures of a rodeo rider, a nun, a policeman, and a bride. The rodeo rider was usually called a "cowboy" or "ranch hand," and the nun was sometimes called "a sister." And although all respondents designated the picture of the bride by that term, or "new

wife," or "newlywed," not a single respondent recognized the same model when she appeared later in the series wearing a pair of pink stretch pants, sheer ruffled blouse, and mules. In this latter capacity she was classified as an artist's or photographer's model by 59 percent of the subjects, and as some kind of actress, dancer, or entertainer by another 39 percent.

The close range of responses to all these illustrations emphasizes the similarity of meaning and the surprising agreement among those who perceive such symbols. The extent to which such cues are assigned correct or erroneous meanings depends not only on the clothing variable itself, but on the fidelity of the symbol. For example, the gentleman in Figure 7.9 is usually perceived as a high-status businessman or professional, and in almost half of the cases the words *English* or *British* are attached to the role description. The man is, in fact, a well-to-do Englishman. At the other extreme, most people see the character in Figure 7.10 as a wealthy old lady or

Figure 7.9 A model of the typical Englishman.

Figure 7.10 Fraudulent cues: is she perhaps an eccentric dowager who runs an antique shop?

Nouveau Riche   Insider   Reverse Snob

Figure 7.11 Because many people now can afford the status symbols of the upper class, the symbolic meanings of things are adjusted accordingly.

grandmother, and not a single respondent has ever identified it as the familiar face of Alfred Hitchcock! The cues of wig and apparel (in this case, false) are so powerful that they obscure even the sex of the wearer—a role that is normally assumed to be not only fixed, but obvious.

When the cues presented are either confusing or in conflict, the range of interpretations is much greater. Most perceivers detect the inconsistencies between details of dress and the total expressive quality of the costume. Statements such as, "She's trying to look like a lady of the upper crust, but she isn't really," or, "She's better dressed than she should be in this home," are based on incongruities of dress with apparent status or surrounding environment.

Vance Packard once said that historically "clothing has been one of the most convenient, and visible, vehicles known for drawing class distinctions" (Figure 7.11).[28] In 1961 Kittles asked a college population to identify specific apparel items that would be considered status

symbols. Most often mentioned were such items as fur coats, fancy hats, expensive jewelry, and well-tailored suits. At that time, nearly all the status symbols mentioned proved significant in distinguishing between white and black women of comparable income levels, that is, white women at that time actually owned more of these status items than did the black women.[29]

The shifts in status during the 1960s are mirrored in Hunter's 1967 study. She found that black women owned greater numbers of all types of dresses than did white women. The blacks thought clothes were more important and felt they were judged more often by clothing than white women did.[30]

The stimuli-persons in the Douty study mentioned earlier were rated on a status scale as well as on personality traits, and it was concluded that clothing was a strong influence in determining role and status impressions of unknown persons. Rosen-

[28]Vance Packard, *The Status Seekers* (New York: David McKay & Company, 1959), p. 131.

[29]Emma Kittles, "The Importance of Clothing as a Status Symbol Among College Students." Ph.D. diss., Ohio State University, 1961.

[30]Marilyn Hunter, "A Comparison of Clothing Between Negro and White Women of Low Socio-Economic Status." Master's thesis, University of Missouri, 1967.

cranz's subjects also often used clothing cues in identifying status incongruities. All these studies point to the importance of clothing symbols in forming role and status impressions (Figure 7.12).

Clothing is a significant factor in determining the role and status of unknown persons.

Cues Related to Sex and Age

With the exception of some occupational clothing, particularly where an obvious uniform provides almost universal recognition, the most used and useful clothing cues are those related to sex and age. According to Allport, in our thirty-second appraisal of strangers, sex and age are not only the first judgments made, but they are also likely to be the most accurate. Although differing widely from culture to culture, there are accepted symbols of sex in the clothing of all societies. The norm in most of the Western world for centuries was skirts for women and pants for men. Pants or skirts for women are now accepted but skirts for men are not. Exceptions are found only in some folk or national costumes, as the Scottish kilt, but not in everyday dress. In cultures in which the bifurcated garment is not the only or even major item for men, there are other differences. The ornamentation and accessories, the materials used, and even the corporal decorations, such as tattooing or scarification, are differentiated by sex. In some parts of the world the traditional costume for both sexes may seem alike to the untrained eye, but differences exist. The cut of the kimono and its color and designs show the wearer's sex. The basic garments of Eskimo women and men are parkas, but

Figure 7.12 Clothing indicates the role and status of individuals.

"the difference is that women's parkas are longer, generally almost ankle length, and they have an enormous hood with a sack in back in which Eskimo children spend the first year of their lives."[31]

In the recent period of long-haired boys and short-haired girls in the universal uniform of jeans and T-shirts, many members of the older generation felt that "you can't tell the boys from the girls these days." However, with very rare exceptions this feeling is inaccurate. Figure, posture, gesture, as well as cut and style of garment, still make it possible to determine sex by appearance, at least within one's own culture. No one could mistake the large masculine Tuareg horsemen for women, even though they wear veils, but cross-cultural differences may make the distinctions more difficult if one does not know local practices.

Some blurring of sexual symbolism in clothing may have developed due to the

[31]Lois M. Gurel, "Eskimos: Clothing and Culture," in *Dimensions of Dress and Adornment; A Book of Readings,* ed. L. M. Gurel and M. S. Beeson (Dubuque, Iowa; Kendall/Hunt Publishing Co., 1979), p. 41.

political, social, and economic gains made by women in the 1960s and 1970s. Women no longer are slaves to fashion and the fashion press. They have chosen their own styles but have continued to dress as women. They decided that pants were comfortable, that corsets, girdles, and even bras were uncomfortable, and that hats, gloves, and handkerchiefs were not necessary. They even tried the traditional three-piece gray flannel suit, but with the subtle symbolism that has always distinguished the sexes. The softer, more rounded contours of the woman's body were still obvious beneath the layers of gray flannel.

Although many traditional culturally defined symbols of sex differentiation in American society are changing, they continue to exist. A complete lack of sexually oriented symbolism in clothing and other areas may lead to confusion of sex roles, particularly for children, but it is unlikely to occur. Sexual roles are changing; the traditional symbols will change but some of the old symbolism will continue to exist and new symbols will be developed.

The symbolic use of clothing as part of a society's communication system has probably changed the most in the area of age. These changes resulted in more conformity and less differentiation, until by the middle of the twentieth century many obvious characteristics of clothing formerly used to denote age had largely disappeared from Western society. However, subtle distinctions remain for the observant eye to see. Changing values have lessened the distinction of age roles in our society and where roles are not sharply defined, clothing symbolism also is not.

The attitudes and values American society placed on youth created a youth culture and a reversal of the traditional flow of ideas from up to down. The flow is now from youth to age. No longer do young girls await the magic day when they, too, can wear pantyhose, high-heeled shoes, and eye and lip make-up. Instead, mother wears jeans and T-shirts (probably borrowed from daughter). Grandma wears a pant suit and the true color of her hair is known only to her hair stylist.

Historically, children were treated like miniature adults and dressed accordingly. The study of historic costume in the Western world indicates no particular emphasis on children's clothing until the last four or five decades. The children portrayed in the fashion plates of *Godey's Ladies Book* in the nineteenth century are remarkable for the intricate details of their exactly duplicated costumes of the adults in the pictures. Now, clothes with growth features and clothes that teach certainly symbolize the emphasis modern society places on children's needs and rights (Figure 7.13).

Many societies still have clothing symbols associated with the rites of passage into the adult world, but most industrial nations of the world do not. Little boys no longer go from short pants to knickers to long trousers. Little girls, instead of graduating from short skirts to floor-length gowns, pull their hemlines even higher. Specialty stores cater to the clothing needs of infants and children, and many boutiques stock only the fad items associated with the preteen and teen-age shopper. Clothes are sized for infants, toddlers, children, girls and boys, preteens, subteens, junior misses, and juniors. Beyond these categories, however, all women's clothes are made in only two categories, misses' and women's.

In several subcultural groups age can be determined from the cut and size of the hat (the Amish), the head and facial hair

Figure 7.13 In the nineteenth century children were dressed as miniature adults. Today, clothing for children emphasizes simplicity and utility.

(Hasidic Jews), the length of the skirt (Indian sari), and other far more subtle symbols, some of which are distinguishable only to those who are part of the "in group." In American society in general, with the exception of children's clothes, there is little difference in clothing based on age and it is harder to differentiate by age within relatively short spans. It is easier to tell the fine differences in age among those nearer to the age of the perceiver. Thus a thirteen-year-old girl can tell a fifteen-year-old from an eleven-year-old with far greater accuracy than she can tell a thirty-year-old from a forty-year-old. However, many organic restrictions prevent the older person from exactly duplicating the youth culture.[32] Posture, figure, skin, and hair change inevitably with age and, even with the technology available to camouflage some of these features, the aging process cannot be halted.

Age and sex are usually the first judgments made of strangers. They are also likely to be the most accurate.

[32]See page 162 for a discussion of the restrictions placed on the symbolic use of clothing.

Cues Related to the Situation

Clothing provides stimulus information for determining personality, role, status, age, and sex, and it also helps to define the social situation in which it appears (Figures 7.14 and 7.15). The adaptation and use of clothing to demonstrate situational change is explained by Stone and Form:

Visible objects and gestures provide cues in defining situations, and clothing is one of the most crucial of these cues. Thus, for example, every change in a significant life situation—birth, entering school, graduation from school, getting a job, marriage, parenthood, and even death—requires a change of wardrobe. Even in the course of daily life, situation after situation requires a change of dress to facilitate and symbolize the situational changes.

A change of dress indicates to others that a person's situation has changed, thereby assisting everyone (including the person) in defining the new situation. The soldier's change of uniform for the dress parade and the civilian's change of "uniform" for the dress ball provide extreme examples of these general observations.[33]

[33]Stone and Form, *Local Community Clothing Market*, p. 8.

Figure 7.14 Clothing symbols provide the situation cues in these pictures. Verbal descriptions are not needed to understand the events occurring.

Figure 7.15 When asked to describe the situation shown in this picture, most perceivers note the incongruity in dress between the two men.

Appropriateness or inappropriateness in dress is determined primarily by cultural and situational factors. A costume that would be entirely acceptable on the beach would be considered out of place at an afternoon reception. Probably the most common cue presented by clothes relates to observed differences in degree of formality or informality: "You're all dressed up! Going some place?" The sole purpose of verbal cues such as "formal," "semiformal," or "informal" at the bottom of written invitations is to tell guests how to dress for the occasion. Although the proscriptions attached to situational appropriateness have been greatly modified in recent years, dress still sets the stage for most social activity.

Missed signals or misinterpretations of situational cues often can cause considerable embarrassment. Differences in cultural patterns often have made it difficult for Americans abroad to anticipate incongruities between dress and situational requirements. A State Department wife returned from an assignment in the Far East concerned about the image Americans were creating by their casual dress in Oriental communities. "The Oriental believes that the more richly you dress, as a guest, the more honor you do your host. Silk is still their highest status fabric. You can see how these simple wool dresses seemed a direct insult, to them."[34]

In other words, we *expect* clothing to set the stage for the kind of social interaction that is to take place. Moreover, clothing is used in a variety of ways to announce or describe an event or occasion. Witness the "widow's weeds" and mourning bands that

[34]Karlyne Anspach, "The American in Casual Dress," *Journal of Home Economics*, 55, No. 4 (1963), 256 ff.

symbolize in very exact terms the passing of a family member; the bridal gown that can be worn for no other event save the wearer's own wedding; the wearing of green on St. Patrick's Day; the Shriner's fez that tells everyone of the convention in town; the formal riding habit that announces even to the fox that the hunt is about to begin.

Clothing is a means of defining the situation in which social interaction takes place.

SUMMARY

Clothing Cues

Clothing is one of the significant nonverbal symbols that communicates and defines certain aspects of personality, age, sex, role, status, and situation. Such cues may be true or false expressions, depending on the way in which they are used or manipulated. Fraudulent use of clothing symbols is limited by a number of restrictions that have been called intrinsic, moral, socialization, cultivation, and organic. Lack of congruence in clothing cues usually creates suspicion or confusion in the perceiver's mind.

Research has demonstrated that changes in clothing alter the impressions formed of an individual's personality traits. Several studies have shown that rather high agreement is found among judges in assigning persons to role and status categories on the basis of dress. In addition, clothing is an obvious key in the perception of situational factors that set the stage for subsequent social interaction.

PERCEPTION AND PERCEIVER VARIABLES

Clothing provides cues about the wearer to the perceiver, or observer. The observations and interpretations of these cues, as well as the judgments formed from them, largely depend on the observer and are accomplished through the mechanism of perception. **Perception** refers to the awareness of objects and people through the stimuli received from the senses. The accuracy of judgments made on the basis of clothing cues or symbols depends on the information presented, the way the perceiver receives and interprets the information, the perceiver's characteristics, and on the interaction situation.

Some people can list with high accuracy what everyone with whom they interacted yesterday wore. Others cannot even give a general description of what the person they are sitting beside is wearing. This ability to remember fairly accurately what we have seen depends on what and how much we saw in the first place. Some people see little; others can perceive and recall with high accuracy. Individuals who are trained to perceive and recall, such as police officers, are examples of the second category. As we have seen, there is more universal agreement on some types of cues and more variation with others. Ambiguous cues, that is, unclear or confusing cues, are apt to be interpreted in ambiguous ways, but some of the ambiguity may be attributed to the perceiver's personality and disposition.

Levels and Modes of Perception

Research has shown that individuals vary in their degree of sensitivity to stimulus information. Further, their responses appear to be differentiated in terms of concreteness and complexity. Let us compare the responses of different students to one picture in the Clothing TAT (Figure 7.16).[35]

One student simply described the characters in terms of their outward appearances: "The masculine female on the left is dressed in masculine clothes and has a boyish haircut. The feminine female on the right is dressed up, with hat and beads. These people are both women."

A second student perceived the difference between the two characters in terms of their deviation from a single or central trait: "Each girl is sloppy but in a different way. One needs her hair combed and needs to pay a little more attention to her appearance. The other one is overdressed and overly made-up. It's a case of either too much or too little."

The response pattern of still another student seemed to conform to personality descriptions that were congruous with the

Figure 7.16 One of the stimulus pictures from Rosencranz's Clothing TAT.

masculine or feminine traits suggested by the difference in clothing cues: "These two girls have just met and are conversing for the first time. The girl on the left is very plain; she likes tailored clothes, a short, simple hair-do, and never wears any make-up. The other girl always dresses nicely, takes a great deal of pride in her personal appearance, and enjoys wearing the latest fashions. Neither girl can quite understand the other, since their tastes are so widely divergent."

A fourth student was obviously able to resolve certain incongruities perceived in the picture and inferred that probably more was involved in the situation than one could fathom from casual observation: "These two young people seem to be having a rather serious time together. Their eyes are sad and troubled. The hat on the girl makes her look much older than she really is; perhaps she wears it to attract the attention of the boy in hopes that he will think she is more sophisticated and grown up. Their whole appearance portrays an involvement above their maturity level."

These four responses demonstrate differences in the level or complexity of perceptual abilities, ranging from a very simple mode of perception to observations

[35]These data were derived from administering the Clothing TAT to groups of University of Nevada students. They were not taken from the original study.

of a complex order.[36] Probably the degree of complexity with which one perceives the stimulus person is directly related to the intelligence and maturity of the perceiver, although this has not been tested empirically.

Another way to define such levels is in terms of the degree of concreteness or abstraction that is represented. One person may perceive others in very concrete or specific ways, making extreme distinctions between what is good and what is bad, and refusing to accept any possible ambiguity. Such a person usually relies on some external set of rules in making a judgment rather than the process of reasoning. Following is an example of such concreteness in reference to the same picture: "The woman on the right is very well dressed, and she is obviously giving the girl on the left some advice on how to dress like a young girl should. Apparently this girl is a tomboy and likes to wear mannish clothes, but underneath it all she really envies the woman who is pretty and feminine."

Greater abstractness in a person is characterized by increased tolerance of ambiguous situations. Such an individual sees many side aspects in particular clothing cues and tries to take the role of the stimulus person in an attempt to evaluate several possible explanations: "One might almost suppose that the figure on the left were a male, except for the definition of the bustline, which is clearly discernible. She may be wearing a school uniform of some kind—perhaps as a member of the band or a team. Of course, she could simply like plain, tailored things. In any case, the two have distinctly different tastes in dress."

[36]These levels of person perception have been outlined by Secord and Backman. See P. Secord and C. Backman, *Social Psychology* (New York: McGraw-Hill Book Company, 1974), pp. 15–16.

Another factor relating to modes of perception was described previously in connection with the development of the self-concept as the "halo effect." This principle operates as a kind of bias in our perception of others, that is, we tend to see a person as a "package" and make a judgment in terms of a total impression of goodness or badness. For example, one student's interpretation of the figure on the right in the picture was: "You can tell from the cut of her dress that she's a woman of ill repute. She's just returning home after being out all night, and her son is confronting her with the facts. She lies and tells him she had car trouble, but he knows better than to believe her."

Also mentioned earlier were the effects of "primacy" or first impressions on the accuracy of person perception. The way in which a person is first perceived may have lasting consequences in regard to evaluation in later situations, even though more information about the stimulus person is then available.

Inferences made from clothing cues depend, at least to some extent, on one's level or mode of perception.

Perceiver Characteristics

The fact that the same person is perceived in different ways by different individuals may be due not only to differences in level or complexity of perception and to the variation in awareness and accuracy, but also to certain aspects of the perceiver's own personality.

Thus we see that every perceiver has a particular set of standards and a particular pattern of past experiences that condition impressions of other people. One person may stress cleanliness, neatness, simplicity, modesty, and constraint in dress and will emphasize these criteria in sizing up the other person. Another individual may judge the stimulus person against such categories as smartness, sophistication, becomingness, distinctiveness, and suitability. Some preliminary research seems to indicate the following:

1. People tend to have a core or set of central consistent categories against which they measure other persons.
2. People use a rather limited number of such perceptual categories.
3. There is a strong positive relationship between the categories people use to describe others and the categories they use to describe themselves.

Some research suggests that the perceiver's personality traits are highly influential in the way clothing symbols are judged. Dickey found that the personality syndromes of self-esteem and security affected the way in which an individual evaluated pictures of clothed figures.[37] Individuals high in levels of self-actualization also have been found to be more analytical in their perceptions.[38] Those who have a high degree of self-insight (that is, those who rate themselves as others rate them) also tend to judge other people more accurately. Whether the judgment is accurate or not, the fact remains that perceivers view others in light of their own idiosyncrasies.

Selective Perception

If people were to perceive all possible stimuli presented by another individual's appearance, they would be burdened by the overload of information. In actual practice, observers select certain aspects of the person that are considered particularly relevant. Berelson and Steiner explain this phenomenon in concise terms: "We look at some things, ignore others, and look away from still others ('selective exposure'). Beyond that, only a fraction of those stimuli that have gained effective entry to a receptor ever reach awareness ('selective awareness')."[39] This statement brings to mind the "inconsiderate" male who crushes the woman's spirits by failing to notice her new dress. Or, when the wife asks him what Mrs. Jones wore when she visited his store yesterday, the husband replies, "How should I know?"

The Clothing TAT was originally designed as a measure of clothing awareness, and significant differences were found among the respondents with respect to the number of clothing cues perceived. The degree of clothing awareness was statistically related to such factors as social class and all of its indexes (occupation, income, education, organizational membership, and magazine readership) as well as verbal intelligence.[40]

Another simple measure of clothing awareness designed by Rosencranz consisted of twenty-five words that have double or triple meanings. One meaning of each word had a clothing connotation, as for the word *alligator*. The test is based on the assumption that people with a high clothing

[37]Lois Dickey, "Projection of the Self Through Judgments of Clothed Figures and Its Relation to Self-Esteem, Security-Insecurity and to Selected Clothing Behaviors." Ph.D. diss., Pennsylvania State University, 1967.
[38]Linda Boehme, "Persuasability and Visual Perception of a Dress Design as Related to Selected Personality Characteristics." Ph.D. diss., Pennsylvania State University, 1970.

[39]Bernard Berelson and Gary Steiner, *Human Behavior—An Inventory of Scientific Findings* (New York: Harcourt, Brace & World, 1964), p. 100.
[40]Rosencranz, "Clothing Symbolism," p. 22.

awareness will interpret the words in terms of their clothing implications. When the test list was administered to several hundred students, it was found that students majoring in the arts, the humanities, and the social sciences had higher clothing awareness scores than did those majoring in engineering and the physical sciences. As would be expected, women had significantly higher scores than men did.[41] Other studies have shown a high degree of relationship between awareness of dress and awareness of other aspects of the popular culture, such as painting, sculpture, music, movies, theater, and the like.[42] Research in general has shown that girls are more aware of clothing than boys are.[43] Over the years, children of various age levels have been tested, and the conclusion is that sensitivity to clothing is already well established by the time pupils reach the eighth grade. Data also reveal that boys and girls who are more other-directed (that is, sensitive to the feelings and opinions of others) tend to be more conscious of factors related to dress than those who are not so directed.

Further, if previous feelings and cognitions in relation to clothing behavior have been positively reinforced in the perceiver's past experience, it may be assumed that clothing stimuli will have a fairly high degree of relevance.[44]

The extent to which an individual uses clothing symbols in forming impressions of others depends on the relevance of clothing stimuli to the perceiver.

SUMMARY

Perception and Perceiver Variables

Some clothing symbols elicit meanings that have more universal agreement than others. Clothing cues interpreted in a variety of different ways may lack fidelity or be incongruous with other cues presented, but such variation also may be accounted for by the perceiver's personality.

Different individuals may describe stimulus persons at varying levels of complexity, ranging from a simple or concrete impression to a mode of perception that is highly complex or abstract. Further, individuals tend to exercise the economizing process of "selective awareness" in determining

[41]Rosencranz, *Clothing Concepts*, p. 62.

[42]See Judith Orkus, "Fashion Awareness of Men as Related to Aspects of the Popular Culture." Master's thesis, Pennsylvania State University, 1971; and Janice Patterson, "Fashion Awareness as Related to Aspects of the Popular Culture," Master's thesis, Pennsylvania State University, 1968.

[43]See A. M. Vener and C. R. Hoffer, *Adolescent Orientations to Clothing*. Technical Bulletin 270. (East Lansing, Mich.: Michigan State University Agricultural Experiment Station, 1959); and Katherine Merrick, "Clothing Awareness: A Comparison of Fifth Grade Boys and Girls in a Middle School and an Elementary School," Master's thesis, Pennsylvania State University, 1970.

[44]For additional details on this theory, see A. Hastorf, S. Richardson, and S. Dornbach, "The Problem of Relevance in the Study of Person Perception," in *Person Perception*, eds. Tagiuri and Petrullo, pp. 54–62.

which of the many cues presented will be recognized. Other variables discussed relate to the personal characteristics of the perceiver. The way in which one perceives others depends on one's own particular set of expectations and frame of reference.

CONSEQUENCES FOR SOCIAL INTERACTION

Clothing symbols that are (1) true representations of the self, (2) presented in an explicit, clear manner, and (3) consistent with other cues are apt to be perceived fairly accurately. The more ambiguous the cue, on the other hand, the more the perceiver is required to interpret its meaning in light of personal idiosyncrasies. Individuals may use a number of processes in making inferences from limited stimulus information. These will be discussed in the following section as judgment processes. In addition, the perceiver's interpretation depends to some extent on socially structured expectations and on the relationship between the judge and the person judged.

Judgment Processes

The influence of first impressions on sustained social interaction often has lasting effects. A person who is first perceived to be slovenly and poorly dressed often is thought to have little concern for personal appearance and little regard for the opinions of others. Sometimes this appraisal is extended, so that the person is assumed to be unfriendly or even rude. Although later contacts with the stimulus person may contain perceptible elements of friendship and courtesy, the judge has already been conditioned to look for the opposite characteristics. Studies in perception have shown that people tend to see things in terms of a

"relevant direction," that is, as they want or need to see them. Thus, particular clothing cues may be linked to other characteristics that, to the perceiver at least, seem interdependent and logically related. These characteristics, in turn, may be regarded as enduring attributes.

An inference process is usually based on some "logical" method of reasoning. For example, a person who wears glasses probably suffered from eye strain; eye strain is often caused from too much reading; a person who reads a lot is apt to be very intelligent; consequently, it is "logical" to assume that people who wear glasses are intelligent. Whether or not the association of such attributes is accurate and truly descriptive of the person being judged is not as significant as the fact that judges usually show rather marked agreement in evaluation of such stimulus information.

Sometimes the association is made between two similar individuals rather than between or among analogous traits. A new acquaintance may remind us of someone else: "That fellow looks just like Joe Johnson!" And, consciously or unconsciously, we assign Joe Johnson's traits to Bob Smith. The transference of personality characteristics from one individual to another is a fairly common although involuntary process.

Stereotyping is another process used in making inferences from limited stimulus information. A person is categorized and then assigned a whole set of characteristics that are typically associated with that role, status, or classification. For example, we saw in one student's response to Figure 7.16 that the feminine-looking figure was categorized as "a woman of ill repute"; not only do women of ill repute wear tight dresses and low-cut necklines, but they also stay out all night, and they lie about their activities, even to their own sons. The gaudy, bedecked American male (Figure 7.17) is the Englishman's stereotype of the typical American tourist. Responses to Figure 7.9 show that Americans also stereotype the Englishman; he wears a conservative suit and bowler and carries a rolled umbrella. Even though stereotypes are neither true nor false, the image of the "typical" freshman, professor, athletic coach, spinster, or politician is always there to provide a basis for identification.

Figure 7.17 Some people find anonymity when away from home and wear clothes they would never think of wearing on the main streets of their home towns. Sculpture by Duane Hansen.

Individuals use certain inference processes in making associations with clothing symbols.

Relation of the Judge to the Judged

People are well aware of the fact that they are likely to be judged on the basis of their appearance by people who do not know them intimately. There is less compulsion to be on our "best behavior" with lifelong acquaintances than with those with whom contacts have been more limited. However, the value we place on the other person's opinion will affect the degree to which we find it necessary to control our clothing signals. Hurlock's early study of motivation in dress provided some data in this regard. In answer to the question "in which case do you care most about your appearance?" almost 56 percent of the respondents indicated that concern for their appearance was greatest when they were with friends. Forty-three percent said it mattered most with strangers, and only 1 percent thought it important with one's own family. None of the respondents deemed clothing to be of importance when one was alone.[45]

Even though we care about their opinions of us, our families and our most intimate friends know us too well to judge us on the basis of clothing. Friends who know us less well are still forming their opinions about us, and since we value their opinions, we find it important to dress for their approval. The opinions of strangers, even if judgmental, may or may not be valued. Office workers in the occupational study cited earlier found it extremely

[45]Hurlock, "Motivation in Fashion," p. 41.

important to dress up for strangers, especially if they were likely to be potential customers or high-prestige people. Conversely, manual workers dressed more for the approval of their fellow workers, since strangers would have little influence over their success on the job. In like manner, some people who go to a different city may pay greater attention to their dress than they would if they were in their hometown. A woman going to shop in San Francisco, for example, may dress up in the belief that her appearance will affect the service she receives from the store clerks. Other people often experience a sense of anonymity in being far away from home and relax their standards of dress in places where they know no one will recognize them. The extremely casual dress worn by many Americans away from home has resulted in a rather unflattering stereotype of the typical U.S. tourist.

The consequences of judgment or inference processes have also been shown to be related to feelings of liking or disliking for other persons (Figure 7.18). Several studies have supported the theory that perceivers are inclined to like those whom they judge to be *similar* to themselves and dislike persons whom they see as very *different* from themselves. Legal experts often claim that court judges, as well as juries, are influenced by clothing in assigning penalties and criminal sentences. A study of misdemeanor cases in Detroit's Recorder's Court found that defendants who appeared in court in work clothes had a much greater chance of going to jail than did defendants who wore suits or sports coats and ties.[46]

Figure 7.18   We all make judgments on the basis of appearance. Drawing by Lorentz; © 1970 The New Yorker Magazine, Inc.

Some people believe that justice should indeed be blind. One man proposed that "every defendant should appear before the bar clothed in total anonymity accomplished by requiring each to be completely enshrouded in a litigant garment."[47]

Moreover, the characteristics that bring recognition in one role may bring rejection in another. One high school youth attracted considerable attention from his peers through extreme forms of dress, long hair, and a beard. On graduation, however, he found it difficult to find a job. When he checked back with personnel heads, all told him that his qualifications were good but his appearance was against him.

[46]Glynn Mapes, "Unequal Justice: A Growing Disparity in Criminal Sentences Troubles Legal Experts," *Wall Street Journal*, Sept 9, 1970.

[47]Burke Rummler, "Toward Justice," *Reno Evening Gazette*, July 23, 1969.

Obviously a number of problems arise from inaccurate associations between role or status categories and assigned traits. A receptionist in a large business office who failed to recognize an esteemed customer was taken to task by her boss. The writer of an advice column defended the secretary by writing: "Clergymen who insist on walking about in casual mufti cannot complain when they're herded like hoi polloi. The moral is, if the customer is so valued and esteemed, but dresses in a manner not associated with his august presence, he should be prepared to identify himself and not expect hard-working secretaries to discern his invisible 'Roman collar.' "[48]

The consequences of inaccuracies in judgment can be disappointing for both the judge and the judged.

Effective relations between the judge and the judged are influenced by an understanding of the meanings dress communicates to others.

SUMMARY

Consequences for Social Interaction

Clothing cues that are clear, consistent, and accurate representations of the self are likely to be perceived more correctly than cues that are fraudulent or ambiguous will be. Individuals employ certain judgment processes in associating meanings with given clothing symbols. These include (1) extension of clothing characteristics to other "logically related" personality traits, (2) transference of personality characteristics from one individual to another, and (3) role and status stereotyping.

The relation of the judge to the judged determines not only how individuals are perceived, but how individuals seek to present themselves. Clothing symbols are considered more important in situations in which the individual is recognized but not too well known and considers the perceiver's opinion valuable. Relatives or friends who have intimate knowledge of an individual's personality are not apt to use clothing cues in judging the stimulus person.

FOR FURTHER READING

Rosencranz, Mary Lou. *Clothing Concepts: A Social-Psychological Approach*, pp. 61–94. New York: Macmillan, 1972.

Ryan, Mary S. *Clothing: A Study in Human Behavior*. New York: Holt, Rinehart and Winston, 1966, pp. 8–39.

"The Pure Physician: Why Doctors Wear White." *Human Behavior*, 8 (May 1979), 49.

[48]Abigail Van Buren, "Dear Abby," syndicated column, August 1972.

Chapter 8

CLOTHING EXPECTATIONS:

ROLE AND STATUS

Clothing as it relates to the learning of new social roles functions in development of the self-concept. Additionally, an individual's clothes furnish significant cues the perceiver uses in determining that individual's role and status. An analysis of the clothing expectations connected to role and status requirements combines these ideas within a broad framework that sociologists call role theory.

ROLE THEORY

Role theory is concerned with role as a unit of culture, status as a unit of society, and self as a unit of personality. As an interdisciplinary study it therefore involves anthropology, sociology, and psychology. Role theory attempts to show the interrelationships among these three units, that is, the way roles, statuses, and the individual are related. Clothing is an obvious visual symbol by which an individual learns to identify others' roles and to identify personally with specific roles. Therefore, the many ideas social scientists express about role theory are combined into important frameworks for clothing researchers.

The term *role* may be defined as a particular position or category occupied by an individual in social relationships and all the behavior associated with that role. The word *status* refers to an individual's place on a scale of prestige when the person occupies that position. It refers to the degree of social value placed on that position or role. For example, a teacher would be considered a role position. A set of behavioral expectations culturally determined and enforced by society goes with the role of teacher. As a teacher, a person also occupies a status position on a hierarchy of prestige from university president on down to instructor or lecturer. There are also sets of expectations for various status positions within the hierarchy.

Role and status have been defined differently by different writers. Linton, for example, used status to mean an individual's position in each of the social systems, and he did not restrict the definition to a prestige continuum. He described role as the "sum total of the cultural patterns associated with a particular status," including the attitudes, values, and behavior ascribed by society to all occupants of that status.[1] More recently, writers have used role to define both the position and its related behavioral expectations.

Roles may be **ascribed**, that is, assigned, generally at birth, with the individual having little choice. These roles may remain constant over a lifetime, as sex, or as age, can change in the course of time. Roles may also be **achieved** through choice (group membership) or training (occupational roles). Some roles seem to occupy a middle position between ascribed and achieved. They may be originally assigned at birth, but due to circumstances or conscious effort by an individual they

may change to the achieved category. Socioeconomic class is an example of a role that can change from ascribed to achieved. A person is born into a certain economic level of society, so originally any social class role is ascribed. In a free and democratic country, a person's economic situation can change, at least in theory, and through work, education, or even luck an individual may achieve membership in a higher economic class. Thus, the new role is an achieved one. The concept of social mobility is firmly embedded in American society, although because of differential life chances it may be outmoded. People can also move down the social class ladder. The issues of social class and social stratification will be discussed in a later chapter, as will the matter of clothing as a facilitator of change or transition in particular roles and statuses. The point here is that although most roles are either ascribed or achieved, they may change from one to the other.

Each role has a set of behavioral expectations, many of which are accomplished through the use of clothing. How an individual learns what is expected and whether or not the choice is made to fulfill such role obligations are also matters of concern in the analysis of clothing behavior.

TRADITIONAL ROLE PERFORMANCE

Implicit in the definition of role are the associated rules or norms of behavior to which the role occupant is expected to conform. The way in which such group

norms are established was discussed in general terms in Chapter 4. It is clear that no society can operate effectively without giving its members some guide or consistent patterning that will insure accomplishment of specific social tasks. Roles are therefore something like job descriptions,

[1]Ralph Linton, *The Study of Man* (New York: Appleton-Century Co., 1936), p. 116.

and group members usually share notions of what is desirable or appropriate behavior in any given situation.

In many cases there is rather wide-spread agreement on the privileges and obligations associated with particular roles; in other cases, the expectations may be unique to a particular group or individual. If a person learns what is expected in a social situation and conforms to the anticipated behavior, rewards are made through **positive sanctions** (approval, acceptance, admiration). On the other hand, if the knowledge to perform the role adequately is not obtained, or if proper performance is disregarded and behavior is contrary to group expectations, **negative sanctions** are likely to be employed (ridicule, indignation, dislike, rejection). Specific expectations in regard to clothing are discussed below in relation to sex and age roles, occupational roles, and other social roles.

Sex and Age Roles

Differentiation in roles on the basis of sex is probably the most universal determinant of social behavior. Although vastly different, all societies ascribe a different set of obligations and expectations to males and to females. Such ascriptions are usually rationalized on the basis of physiological characteristics, but the actual restrictions that evolve are almost entirely determined by the culture.[2] In practically every society the world over, there is a marked distinction in the typical dress of men and women, and strict taboos are often maintained against wearing garments assigned to the opposite sex. "In our own society," Brown explains, "women may wear men's clothing but there is the strongest kind of feeling directed against the man who wears feminine attire."[3] The division of sex roles by means of clothing is so deeply embedded as a social norm that in most states and some countries it has become a part of the penal code. There are numerous city ordinances against transvestism, some of which go so far as to prohibit impersonation of the opposite sex on the stage.

In Western civilization, the most predominant cultural norm with respect to sex differentiation in dress has been that the female is supposed to have an interest in dress, while the male is supposed to have little or none. The woman has been expected to be soft, round, colorful, delicate, and decorative and the man to be hard, vigorous, strong, drab, and inconspicuous. Interestingly enough, such secondary sexual characteristics are by no means universal in nature. In the animal kingdom, the male of the species usually inherits the decorative plumage, while the female is most often plain and subdued. Even in human life, the male member of most primitive tribes is more highly ornamented than his female counterpart.

As a matter of fact, this particular distinction between the sexes has not held even among the higher orders of civilization. Prior to the eighteenth century, for example, the most sumptuously dressed members of society were the knight, the priest, the prince, the lord, the dandy, and the macaroni, and their ribbons and laces were rarely associated with effeminate traits (Figure 8.1). Since the French and the Industrial revolutions, however, we have gradually become accustomed to a

[2]Linton, *The Study of Man*, p. 116.

[3]Ina C. Brown, *Understanding Other Cultures* (Englewood Cliffs, N.J.: Prentice-Hall, 1963), p. 26.

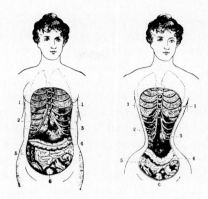

Figure 8.2 The ideal female shape at the turn of the century could be accomplished only with the help of a corset. Tight lacing compressed the waist (and the internal organs), rounded the hipline, and emphasized the bosom.

Figure 8.1 A seventeenth-century gentleman. Men's clothes have not always been dull.

world of "dingy men and bright women."[4] By the end of the nineteenth century, men no longer had to demonstrate through their dress the fact that their riches did not depend on their manual labors. The rising moneyed manufacturing class could dress themselves more solemnly and at the same time show their wealth by dressing their women to display their status. (See a discussion of Veblen's concepts of vicarious and conspicuous consumption on p. 30.)

Some writers contend that distinctions in dress were intended primarily to increase sexual characteristics. The corset, for example, not only reduces waist circumference, but it also increases the size of bust and hips. Further, the breathing activity is displaced upward, thereby rendering the breasts even more prominent (Figure 8.2). In masculine dress, tights, breeches, and trousers supposedly emphasize most effectively the male attribute of

energy and activity as represented by the lower limbs, the organs of locomotion.[5] At least one researcher claims to have identified a positive correlation between tight trousers and western heroes and has concluded that, historically, tight pants have always been a badge of masculinity. Psychologist Murray Sherman reported a study of the Freudian aspects of male attire as part of a motivational research project. He concluded that the adult male in tight pants has never shed his childhood admiration of the cowboy and "has a deep-seated unconscious desire to remain eternally young."

Havelock Ellis maintained that "the extreme importance of clothes would disappear at once if the two sexes were to dress alike."[6] A case in point was the virtual loss of sex identity in postrevolutionary Russia. Women, having achieved full equality with men, adopted the same uniformlike jackets, shirts, and boots, and

[4]Quentin Bell, *On Human Finery* (London: Hogarth Press, 1947), pp. 91–92.

[5]Ernest Crawley, *Dress, Drinks, and Drums*, ed. T. Besterman (London: Methuen and Co., 1931), p. 129.
[6]Havelock Ellis, *Studies in the Psychology of Sex*, Vol. 4 (New York: Random House, 1936), p. 209.

both sexes rejected all forms of dress that would in any way add to their physical attractiveness. Their shabby, drab, and "mildewed" suits became a badge of self-sacrifice to the state.[7] It was not until the late 1950s, as standards for the "classless society" were relaxed and more consumer goods became available, that a renewed interest in clothes began to develop. Western-style fashion shows were initiated in Moscow, and the Soviet woman gradually recaptured her desire to look feminine. Fashion was evident in the Soviet Union in the late 1970s, even though "a typical off-the-rack dress from Gum, Moscow's major department store, is apt to be a gaudily colored polyester sheath with short sleeves and round neck."[8] Some designers—Slava ' Zaitsev, for example—catered to the typical overweight Russian women. His designs were not for direct sale. They were produced in clothing factories, more or less like the originals. The apparel manufacturers still considered Zaitsev's creations "too far out" to be successfully mass-produced. But for a country that officially had adopted a unisex approach to most social issues, even this much interest in clothing design suggested a possible change in traditional sex-role patterns.

The close relationship between the status of women and the expression of sex roles through dress can be demonstrated in almost every period of fashion history. Clothes that restrict or hamper the female's movements have always been prevalent in cultures or periods in which the woman's position was inferior and her sphere of activities confined largely to the home. In

Figure 8.3 Although jeans still predominate, the college woman's wardrobe has other types of pants. Cotton velour is used for both day and evening wear.

periods of greater freedom and emancipation, feminine dress tends to take on more of the characteristics of male attire. The wearing of bifurcated garments, for example, has increased steadily in America since the suffragette movement of the late nineteenth century. There are notable exceptions to the correlation between female status and the wearing of bifurcated garments, but in all such cases some other element of dress restricted mobility, as, for example, when Chinese women wore trousers, their feet were bound and deformed. As early as 1965, research showed that more than one third of the average college woman's wardrobe consisted of bifurcated garments, a trend that increased dramatically during the late sixties and seventies.[9] In a 1978 survey of college women's wardrobe plans for the coming year, 47 percent said that they planned to purchase four or more pairs of jeans, adding to the average of six pairs they already owned.

[7]John Gunther, *Inside Russia Today* (New York: Harper and Brothers, 1958), p. 41.
[8]"Russia's Women Buy Bulky Styles," *Roanoke Times and World-News*, December 17, 1978, p. E–6.

[9]Betty L. Davis, "The Relationship Between Masculine-Feminine Personality Traits and the Feelings Associated with the Wearing of Bifurcated Garments" Master's thesis, Pennsylvania State University, 1965.

Figure 8.4 By age three, a child is indoctrinated with the fact that she is a girl or that he is a boy, and appearance becomes a vehicle through which sexual identity is reinforced.

And these were just jeans (Figure 8.3). They already had an average of five pairs of other type pants and planned to buy five more during the 1978–1979 school year. Compared to the three dresses and three skirts reported, one can readily see that even in the late seventies, when dresses were making a "come back," bifurcated garments still made up a major portion of the wardrobe of college women.[10]

Young children begin to learn the differences in sex roles very early, so that even by the age of two or three, distinctions in attitudes and interest may be noted. Patterns in child rearing reveal that parents strongly influence sex role ambiguity. Little girls are often dressed for play in overalls or shorts (Figure 8.4), and a certain amount of tomboy behavior is regarded with amusement by parents (Figure 8.5). Little boys, however, have less freedom, and tendencies toward feminine behavior are given immediate disapproval. Pitcher noted that fathers especially tend to emphasize a kind of exclusive masculinity in their sons.[11]

Figure 8.5 Top: A certain amount of tomboyishness in girls is reinforced through positive sanctions.

Figure 8.6 Bottom: The standard for what is "masculine" has changed over the years. Many little boys today are mistaken for little girls, and vice versa. Which of these children can you identify as male or female?

Thus, the cultural definition of appropriate sex-role behavior tends to be more ambiguous for females than it is for males (Figure 8.6). On the surface, this kind of role flexibility might seem to give women the advantage, but studies have shown that our culture gives greater priority to masculine qualities, and females are quick to

[10]"College Survey: Women's Market," *Retail Week*, May 1, 1978, 184–185.
[11]Evelyn G. Pitcher, "Male and Female," *Atlantic Monthly* (March 1963) 87.

Figure 8.7 As an army doctor during the Civil War, Dr. Mary Walker dressed in a somber three-piece black suit. She is the only woman ever to win the Congressional Medal of Honor.

their adoption of male attire—were admired more often than scorned. Today, the real breakthrough in dress is a growing permissiveness in the standard for what is accepted as manly.

Some people like designer Rudi Gernreich have believed that unisex clothing would be the style of the future. In 1970, he designed miniskirts, leotards, and pant suits for men and women alike, eliminating all sexual variations in dress. Unisex clothing was a fad for a short time among a small segment of the population, but Gernreich's prediction has not yet come true. Although differentiation of sex by dress is not as obvious as it was in the past, there is still a difference between male and female attire in our society (Figure 8.8).

Others maintain that whatever the age or era, children will always have to learn appropriate sex roles and that clothing

perceive this fact. In an analysis of adolescents' self-concepts, Ehle discovered that girls more often than boys considered their appearance to be less desirable than that of their peers, and they more often desired a change in the way they looked.[12]

With diminishing differences in sex roles in recent years there are corresponding signs of diminishing differences in dress between the sexes. Despite the fact that the women's movement emphasized changes in the woman's role, the real change has been in the cultural definition of masculinity. Women have always been free to take on male dress symbols without much social criticism. Women like Joan of Arc, George Sand, and Dr. Mary Walker (Figure 8.7), the Civil War army physician—all of whom were famous for

Figure 8.8 The diminishing differences in dress between the sexes requires a whole new cultural definition of what is masculine and what is feminine.

[12]Kathleen Ehle, "Adolescent Self Concept and Appearance." Master's thesis, University of Wisconsin, 1971.

gives strong support to one's sense of identity in being a girl or in being a boy. This point of view was expressed by Broderick as

Times change and cultural definitions of what is masculine and what is feminine change. What does not change is the need in each individual to feel secure in his own identity and that includes his sexual identity. However the symbols may evolve which reassure me and others that I am a man and my mate is a woman, there will be such symbols and they will matter.[13]

Although clothing is not as distinguishable with respect to age as it is to sex, every society maintains some differentiation in clothing norms for each stage in the life cycle. Most often these are broadly defined in terms of dress that is considered appropriate for children, adults, or the aged. In our own complex system, we make age-grade distinctions in size and in style, and for both males and females. The high value placed on eternal youth prohibits use of any commercial category that extends beyond clothes for mature men and women, although the growing proportion of elderly people in the population has given impetus to increased study of the clothing needs of the aged.

Clothing expectations for various age categories are seldom enforced as rigidly as they are for sex roles, but we quickly identify the black velvet strapless as too sophisticated for the teen-ager's first formal dance, and the woman past forty who continues to wear gay bouffant styles and ribbons in her hair rarely escapes social criticism. Incongruities between age and

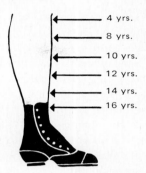

Figure 8.9 "The proper length for little girls' skirts at various ages." Like little boys' pants, the length of girls' dresses was precisely ordered. The standard in the 1860s is shown here.

dress are obvious because they highlight the individual's physical differences and because they essentially violate the normative expectation.

Not very many years ago, a boy's age had a direct relationship to the length of his pants (Figure 8.9). Boys under six or seven were usually clothed in shorts. Prepubescent boys wore knickers, and the first pair of long trousers really marked initiation into manhood. Bush and London attempted to account for the disappearance of these age-role symbols by analyzing the fundamental changes that have occurred in the prepubescent boy's social role.[14] Greater permissiveness in child growth and development theories has gradually removed Victorian ideas of children's proper place in society. Today, they have greater freedom; the fewer restrictions placed on their activities, the less structured their roles become. Fewer restrictions in age-role expectations lead to greater variation in acceptable forms and styles of clothing. Hence, the prepubescent boy is no longer

[13]Carlfred Broderick, "The Importance of Being Ernest—or Evelyn," *Penney's Forum*, Spring/Summer 1973, 17.

[14]George Bush and Perry London, "On the Disappearance of Knickers: Hypotheses for the Functional Analysis of the Psychology of Clothing," *Journal of Social Psychology*, 51 (May 1960), 359–366.

restricted to wearing knickers and the six-year-old to short pants.

A similar analysis could be made of women's age-role expectations. Improved health and widespread use of cosmetics have blurred the distinctions among young adult, middle aged, and elderly. Grandmothers are no longer confined to the image of Whistler's mother. It is highly probable that if age-roles were more specifically defined, corresponding clothing expectations would be more explicit.

In spite of the increased variability in role and clothing expectations, discernible patterns associated with age-role and dress remain. In early adolescence, rigid conformity to the peer group is expected. A twelve-year-old girl is not content with a sweater similar to her friend's—it must be an exact duplicate. But among adult females, an exact duplicate of a costume in the same social set means disaster.

The age-role standards of dress for men in our society have changed the most, however. It is still permissible for a young man in his twenties to engage in activities that will attract the attention of numerous members of the opposite sex. Therefore, he may spend a higher proportion of his income on clothes than may men in other age brackets (Figure 8.10). Generally, the young man pays particular attention to the latest changes in fashion and has the privilege of wearing bright colors, fancy patterns, and extreme styles. His clothing behavior is in keeping with fashion, though, rather than the fad behavior of earlier years. The former restrictions on showy, extravagant dress for middle-aged and elderly men have changed. A married man with three children may not be able to afford to keep up with the latest fashion items because of other priorities, but if he can manage financially to dress in splen-

Figure 8.10 Although more subdued in overall dress, the twentieth-century man can still display status through details of custom tailoring and choice of elegant fabrics.

dor, there is little likelihood of general societal disapproval. The expectations of middle-aged conservatism and of old-aged disinterest, at least in clothing, have become stereotypes. Men in their sixties and seventies are still interested in physical comfort in clothes, but they also are interested in their overall general appearance and many are enjoying a greater freedom in dress than they did when they were younger.

In two parallel studies directed at investigating the general and the specific interests in clothing of men from college age to elderly, a finding was that overall clothing interest increased with age. Five age groups were studied: college freshmen; college seniors; postcollege businessmen, twenty-five to thirty-five; young adult, thirty to forty-five; middle years, forty-five to sixty-five; and elderly, sixty-five to eighty. The postcollege businessmen were more interested in their appearance than were either the college freshmen or the college seniors.[15] This finding may be explained, at least in part, by the occupational role of these men in their twenties and thirties. They had just left the casual environment of college and were competing in a business world in which one is assessed on personal appearance as well as on ability. They also had, perhaps for the first time, discretionary income, that is, funds over and above what is needed for essentials, and they could indulge in fancy dress if they so desired.

When men of middle years were compared to the elderly group, again the older group exhibited more interest in clothing.[16] Perhaps the older man is more interested in matters of dress because of age-role expectations; he must not be more fashionable than the norm allows yet at the same time he desires to maintain a fashionable appearance; therefore, he must consider his clothing selections carefully.

Age and sex roles are thus arbitrarily ascribed to individuals on a biological basis, and each is associated with a particular set of clothing expectations, which are defined in varying degrees of specificity. Sex roles tend to be more clearly defined than age roles since they are determined immediately at birth and remain fixed throughout life. Age roles also begin at birth, but they follow a pattern of constant change as the individual gradually progresses through a series of chronologically determined stages.

[15]Amy Lee Charron, "The Clothing Interest of Three Groups of Young Adult Men Differentiated by Stage of Life." Master's thesis, Virginia Polytechnic Institute and State University, 1977.

[16]Doris H. Drake, "Clothing Interest of Young Adult, Middle-Aged, and Elderly Men." Master's thesis, Virginia Polytechnic Institute and State University, 1978.

Occupational Roles

Clothing expectations for particular occupation roles were discussed in Chapter 7 in connection with clothing symbolism. The study by Form and Stone of white-collar and manual workers revealed a rather clear-cut pattern of established clothing norms. The acceptable dress for office workers was a business suit or a sport jacket worn over shirt and slacks, while manual workers wore uniforms, overalls, or various combinations of old clothes on the job. Office workers tended to evaluate their clothing in terms of a well-groomed appearance and good taste standards. Manual workers' orientations were structured in terms of the functional aspect of clothes, that is, garments were supposed to be efficient and comfortable to facilitate maximum work performance and contribute to safety on the job.

In a very early study, Zweig noted similar standards in workers' ideas of dress. Manual workers did not believe in wearing heavy clothes and seldom wore hats or gloves. Men in positions of authority, however, such as foremen or supervisors, were expected to wear better clothes than the laborers did, although nothing that would make the distinction too great.[17]

Even though the white-collar workers admitted that they liked to wear new clothes on the job, most felt more at ease if they could "break in" such items in a social situation first. Having a positive group reaction to their new articles of dress gave them greater security in wearing the new clothes later on the job. Laborers had to wear new clothes first "to get the starch out" of them, so they would be comfortable at work.

[17]Ferdynand Zweig, The British Worker (Harmondsworth, Middlesex; Penguin Books, 1952), pp. 157–165.

Differences also were noted between these same groups of workers in their clothing expectations for a job interview and specific social situations. When applying for work, office personnel usually dressed up in their best suits, while the majority of manual workers wore overalls, work clothes, or trouser and shirt combinations. When asked what they would wear to church or to public meetings, many respondents in both groups suggested that a "best," "blue," "dress," or "conservative" suit would be appropriate. However, a much larger proportion of manual workers did not feel that the suit had to be "best," "blue," "dress," or "conservative," and almost a third considered sports outfits, trouser and shirt combinations, or simply clean, pressed garments acceptable attire for such occasions.[18]

As general values began to change at the end of the 1960s a more permissive attitude, less bound by tradition, could be seen in many aspects of life. It was particularly evident in clothing, probably because clothing is highly visible. The "do-your-own-thing" attitude toward clothing of the flower children and the hippies filtered up the social class structure as did fashion in general, from young to old, from poor to rich. The general lack of faith in institutions, governments, and the "military/industrial complex" during and after the war in Southeast Asia, and culminating in the Watergate exposures, made many established traditions part of the general distrust of the Establishment. Standards of dress for business and professional people were less formal. The gray flannel suit became the stereotype that represented all that was bad about business, and this trend

continued well past the middle of the next decade.

However, even in a more permissive atmosphere, appearance, including dress, was still important to employers, in initial contact interviews and for continued employment as well. Hiring agents in forty-six southern urban communities said that "Appearance could be a determining factor in employee selection if skills of several candidates were equal."[19] Adherence to appearance norms during everyday work was important both to retain a position and for advancement within the company. Employers looked for people who were "neat and conservative" in appearance. Outfits that were "revealing, overly accessorized, boldly printed, extreme in length, and unkempt were unfavorably regarded."[20] Most interviewers stated that hair styles, make-up, and grooming were more important to them than actual apparel items.

Another report noted that future employees and employers differed in their perceived image of the proper attire for student retail executive trainees. Employers described the appearance they desired as "businesslike"; the students used the term "fashionable." This employer attitude illustrates a continuing demand for appropriate attire for employees (Figure 8.11).[21]

By the end of the decade the importance of appearance for business situations was again emphasized, this time by the press. Dress for success influenced not only the

[18]Form and Stone, *Social Significance of Clothing*, p. 28.

[19]Susan Jones, "Hiring Agents' Perceptions of Appearance Norms Used by Their Organizations to Judge Female Employees in White-Collar Positions During the Interview and Daily Work Situations." Master's thesis, Auburn University, 1974, p. xii.

[20]Ibid., p. xii.

[21]Jo Ann Miller, "Student and Employer Perceptions of Appropriate Business Dress and Its Importance in Hiring Retail Executive Trainees." Master's thesis, Florida State University, 1976.

Figure 8.11 Women in management tend toward a conservative skirted suit. The softer bowed blouse is still acceptable.

apparel industry, but the publishing business as well. Numerous books and articles based on the general assumption that success and appearance were positively related appeared. And since women were entering the corporate world in greater numbers, books were for both sexes.[22]

In a period of tight jobs and an oversupply of trained people in some occupational areas, guarantees implied by a formula approach, which is espoused in most of these books and articles, seem particularly attractive to a person entering the job market or to someone feeling trapped in a job dead end. In other words, A (you) plus B (the success looks in dress and accessories) equals C (securing the job or the promotion), and ultimately or preferably instantly, come success, power, leadership, fame and fortune. It's a lot easier to change one's clothes and acquire a few symbols of status and authority than it is to earn another degree, to serve another

apprenticeship, or otherwise to improve one's real qualifications or level of expertise.[23]

The times were ready for a change back to more formality. Casualness and permissiveness in matters of dress had gone about as far as they could without resorting to rags or nudity (and some people had tried both). Even those on college campuses were getting tired of "the uniform" (T-shirts and jeans).

There is another factor, common to the background of most of today's young people who are seeking to make their way in business careers—that is the absence of dress regulations in the education experience. Dress codes in colleges and universities are almost entirely past history. A student today would be outraged, or at least baffled, if the student handbook contained a rule requiring him or her to "dress for dinner" in the dining hall, or to wear coats and ties, for the men, or skirts, for the women, to such a casual occasion as a class! Such rules were very common on campuses 20 years ago.

This generation of graduates is leaving the most permissive college environment ever, where blue-jean-sloppy is expected and revered, and trying to enter a business world where there are indeed rules. And shockingly enough there are rules for what was formerly a personal and private matter, namely *dress*. Then, adding insult to injury, *disregard of or failure to comply with these dress rules brings about undesirable consequences.*[24]

[22]See, for example, John T. Molloy, *Dress for Success* (New York: Warner Books, 1975); John T. Molloy, *The Woman's Dress for Success Book* (Chicago: Follett Publishing Co., 1977).

[23]Marianne S. Beeson, "In the Gray Flannel Mold," p. 128. Reprinted from Gurel-Beeson: *Dimensions of Dress and Adornment*, Third Edition. Copyright © 1979 by Kendall/Hunt Publishing Company. Used by permission.

[24]Marianne S. Beeson, "In the Gray Flannel Mold," p. 229. Reprinted from Gurel-Beeson: *Dimensions of Dress and Adornment*, Third Edition. Copyright © 1979 by Kendall/Hunt Publishing Company. Used by permission.

Considerable evidence shows that anticipated clothing behavior in many occupational situations has a close relationship to the statuses of the employees. Roth's observations of protective clothing worn by the medical personnel of a state hospital is a case in point.[25] The investigator noted the percentage of doctors, nurses, and other staff members wearing surgical caps, gowns, and masks in their contacts with communicable disease patients. If the use of such garments is effective in preventing spread of disease to others, it is logical to assume that no distinctions should be made in the categories of individuals required to wear them. Fewer than 5 percent of the doctors, however, wore the surgical clothes in their contacts with patients. Roughly a quarter of the professional nurses and about half of the practical nurses were so clothed when entering patients' rooms. Aides and student nurses were the only categories who wore the garments faithfully. Thus, the data showed an inverse relationship between the wearing of protective clothing and occupational status level. The lower the status of the employee, the more frequently protective clothes were worn. One possible explanation, of course, is that the threat of criticism for not dressing properly increases progressively down the status scale. No one would enforce the rule for a doctor, but every employee in a position superior to the aides and students could censure them for not protecting themselves.

Most occupational positions, however, can be defined in terms of the general type of attire that is acceptable or anticipated. A police officer is supposed to wear a blue uniform, the salesperson must keep pants pressed and shoes polished, and lawyers must look prosperous enough to inspire confidence in their clients. Low-cut dresses, tight sweaters, and conspicuous jewelry generally are considered inappropriate for the secretary; college teachers find that their image is enhanced if they dress in a fashion that is consistent with a professor's role.[26] At least one study has shown that people who look like professors are judged by others as being more successful in this role than those who fail to meet the appearance expectation.[27] Thus we see that an individual learns to play the role of a doctor or businessperson and in the process, learns the definition of the accompanying statuses and the behavior patterns appropriate to such statuses.

A new category of occupational clothing developed in the seventies, called career apparel (Figure 8.12). Worn primarily for identification rather than protection of personal clothing, promoters of these specially designed business clothes claim that they give a company a corporate fashion look that suggests efficiency and stability. Although they do eliminate competitive dressing among employees and cope with the problem of extreme fashion that might distract from professionalism, that is not their main purpose.

The production of career apparel may be just a new term for what was once the old uniform business, which is as ancient as war and work and as modern as manufacture of a flight attendant's uniform. The first work clothing probably was the knight's armor in medieval times. From it

[25]Julius Roth, "Ritual Magic in the Control of Contagion," *American Sociological Review*, 22 (June 1957), 310–314.

[26]Yvonne Bishop, "Perception of Professionalism Based on Dress." Senior honors thesis, Virginia Polytechnic Institute and State University, 1980.

[27]R. A. Ellis and T. C. Keedy, "Three Dimensions of Status: A Study of Academic Prestige," *Pacific Sociological Review*, 3 (1960), 23–28.

Figure 8.12 Left: Career apparel has been "sold" on the basis that it gives a company a recognizable public identity and suggests efficiency and stability. It also eliminates competitive dressing among employees and deals with the problem of extreme fashions that may distract from job professionalism.

Figure 8.13 Right: Military uniforms have always been a symbol of occupational role.

came military uniforms in vast proliferation and splendor, marking the inability of human beings to live in peace with each other (Figure 8.13).

Work clothing for peaceful occupations was rare until the end of the nineteenth century. Exceptions were found among mining and smelting workers, who wore protective leather aprons as early as the fifteenth century. In fact, the apron is probably the original model of all work clothing. In preindustrial times many manual workers wore it to protect the few items of clothing they could afford to own. More recently, the apron evolved into overalls, coveralls, and protective garments of many specialized types.

At the same time, or at least from the Middle Ages on, a different type of work clothing developed, a type worn for identification rather than protection. The clothes of monks and priests and still later of doctors, lawyers, and academicians are examples. A judge in court still wears the

robes patterned after the academic gowns of the Middle Ages. When craft guilds arose in England in the late Middle Ages their members adopted special clothing to identify them with their organizations. These were called liveries and were highly respected emblems of the status attached to the guilds. Eventually livery evolved into servants' dress, with the style, color, and fabric showing the master's status. Red is still the color worn by the servants of the British royal family (Figure 8.14). Thus the wheel of fashion has come full circle and the concept of liveries, that is, of career apparel to identify different groups of employees, is once again popular.

Investigating the attitudes of users of career apparel, Dirksen found that among the bank employees she interviewed, older women were more accepting of the new idea and their acceptance in general was based primarily on convenience and money saved. There was, however, no relationship between acceptance and cost. Those who

Figure 8.14 Career apparel carried down over generations: a sergeant-major of the Yeomen of the Guard at Buckingham Palace.

Figure 8.15 Evolving social patterns effect transitions in clothing expectations associated with given roles. The traditional attire of the Irish Dominican Order, carried over from the thirteenth century, is shown at the left. On the right, a member of the Mission Sisters of the Holy Ghost, whose order calls for habit-updating every five years.

had to buy their own were just as happy users as those who worked for banks that furnished and maintained the uniforms. The bank officers' opinions on the value of the clothing is particularly interesting in light of the reasons given for career apparel in the first place. They felt the program was a success. "Some admitted that it was hard to measure morale, but all felt relieved to have the problem of dress settled in such an attractive and amicable way."[28] No mention was made of corporate image or group identity.

Although scattered attempts have been made to standardize dress for people in occupations not traditionally associated with a uniform, the new look in career apparel really began in banks in the early 1970s. This adoption, occurring when many traditionally uniformed groups were

changing to less rather than more uniformity, is particularly surprising. The Vatican Council edicts on dress for religious orders resulted in widespread reforms in habits, and today many nuns dress conservatively, but in contemporary styles (Figure 8.15). Nurses' uniforms are so varied that they can scarcely be called a uniform and many have even given up the traditional cap. In most hospitals patients have to read the name badges worn by hospital personnel in order to identify the R.N., the L.P.N., the M.D., and the technician. Even the police have experimented with variety in uniform in an attempt to improve their public image. Colors other than "police blue" and styles ranging from blazers to bomber jackets can be found. While the military still wear a standardized uniform, it too, has been updated. A change in the visual image was part of the new recruiting program efforts of an all-volunteer army.

[28]Louise Dirksen, "Career Apparel: The Relationship Between Its Acceptance and Selected Socio-economic Variables." Master's thesis, Northern Illinois University, 1974, pp. 47–48.

Figure 8.16 The social role this man's clothing seems to indicate is not in line with his posture and location.

colleges tend to differ from Western colleges, and clothing norms on campuses in the center of a large city are apt to be quite different from those in a small college town.

Another factor that interferes with a predictable set of clothing expectations is the rapid, continuous change that occurs in the social patterns of any dynamic society. Since the end of World War II, America has experienced an increasing degree of informality in social behavior patterns. The roots of such change lie in economic factors that bring a greatly improved standard of living and increased leisure time to large segments of the middle and lower classes. Middle-class living standards have been shown on television screens, tempting the ambitions of those in lower statuses. At the same time, the rapid and relatively inexpensive reproduction of what once were exclusive styles of dress now brings fashion within the reach of the majority. Life in America has become characterized by an endless striving to obtain the material possessions of the next higher social status, while occupants of the upper class find it is no longer smart to live lavishly (Figure 8.18).

In spite of the gradual merging of class lines in American society, there are still the inevitable distinctions that must be made between groups or individuals who are widely separated on the status continuum. Even the "common sense" books of etiquette are directed toward those who have some opportunity to give formal dinners, attend the opera, fox hunt, or travel abroad. Because such activities are beyond the reach of those in the lower strata, mannerisms taken from the same social code are considered "putting on airs."

Social problems arise when norms are not clearly defined. Americans have been

Figure 8.18 Traditionally, clothing expectations for the male role in society have been rigidly explicit. Compliance to such prescribed patterns of dress produced a picture of multiple carbon copies.

taught to place such a high value on individuality that they resist the idea of any fixed standards for social behavior. Yet the most embarrassing moments occur when an individual does not accurately anticipate the group expectation or in some way fails to meet the expectation. Some clarification of the social code is necessary to avoid the confusions that stem from our diverse ethnic origins and class mobility. We are prone to pity members of a society who are restricted to prescribed statuses of class or caste, but because their lives are fixed and precisely arranged, they know exactly what is expected of them. "Membership in a rigidly organized society may deprive the individual of opportunities to exercise his particular gifts," Linton wrote, "but it gives him an emotional security which is almost unknown among ourselves."[29]

The fact that norms develop in virtually every aspect of human activity seems to indicate that people need to check their opinions and behavior for correctness against the opinions and behavior of other individuals and groups in their social setting. Knowing the society's ground rules

[29]Linton, *The Study of Man*, p. 131.

Figure 8.19 Adolescents feel they must look exactly alike.

enables individuals to live more comfortably and operate more efficiently in it than they could without such rules to guide them. It takes time to learn social codes and using them requires judgment in the many situations found in a varied social system. Adolescents have particular difficulty in learning the rules fast enough to keep up with their changing status. They rely on absolute conformity to peer group behavior to protect themselves from social errors (Figure 8.19). Thus a boy of thirteen must have jeans of a particular size and color, with a particular brand name and model, and the brand label must be clearly visible, fastened to the back hip pocket. Only then can he be sure the jeans will meet the required expectation in every detail.

Wass and Eicher studied clothing norms in relation to the role behavior of ninth-grade girls. In the school studied, students selected their own attire since no dress regulations were enforced. But when students were questioned, 83 percent were under the impression that the school did have rules and 80 percent felt that all schools should have rules. These teen-age girls conformed closely to the norm, and

although they indicated that a wider range of garments would be appropriate for each role, the range in garments actually worn was quite limited. Respondents thought a student should dress more casually for a basketball game than for school, unless she happened to attend the game with a boy. She would then play the role of somebody's "date," so they believed that dressier clothes would be required. Moreover, these ninth graders felt that certain roles were so specific on dress requirements that they often did not take part in an activity because they lacked the appropriate costume. In many cases, the girls indicated that they had gone to places where their dress was inappropriate and then wished they had not gone. This study showed that clothing was chosen in relation to specific roles, often changed when the roles changed, and frequently influenced the wearer's behavior. In addition, when no formal dress code operated, the group established its own.[30]

A similar survey was conducted informally almost fifteen years later and, as was expected, the results were remarkably similar. Again, ninth-grade girls were asked about clothing: Who influenced their choices; what they thought about dress restrictions; and what they would wear for special occasions. By 1978, they knew the school did not have any dress restrictions, other than that for no short shorts or bikini tops. Further, they did not believe there should be any restrictions. They did not seem to have any self-imposed regulations either, other than the general desire for peer approval. When asked whether they

[30]Betty Wass and Joanne Eicher, "Clothing as Related to Role Behavior of Teen-age Girls," *Quarterly Bulletin*, 47, No. 2 (East Lansing, Mich.: Michigan State University Agricultural Experiment Station, November 1964), 206–213.

would wear something their friends were not wearing, they said that not only would they not wear such things, but that they wouldn't buy them in the first place.

The only change from the earlier study was in regard to "date" clothes. Most said it wouldn't make any difference if boys were in the group; some said they might wear better jeans. The concept of "date" did not seem to be an important one; their associations with boys were in groups rather than in paired couples. Many said they would not go someplace if they didn't have appropriate clothes; however, just as many stated flatly that they had clothes for any situation they could think of and "If not, I'd just go buy it." Since these interviews were with relatively affluent upper-middle-class students in a fairly sophisticated college town, perhaps the answers were not typical for all young people their age.

SUMMARY

Traditional Role Performance

Common notions of appropriate dress for a variety of social situations help an individual learn the behavioral expectations for particular role categories. In our society, the most obvious distinctions in dress are made on the basis of ascribed sex and age roles. Virtually all societies assign a different set of clothing expectations to males and to females, and violation of established norms by either sex may result in negative sanctions, although the costs are usually greater for the male than for the female. Although clothing expectations for various age categories rarely are enforced as rigidly as they are for sex roles, society maintains some differentiation in clothing norms for each life-cycle stage.

Most occupational roles may be defined in terms of the general type of attire considered appropriate for the position. Part of the training for an occupation or profession is learning the clothing behavior that will project an accurate image. Suitable or proper attire is defined largely in terms of specific social activities, but the degree of consensus on what constitutes the current norm varies with the group. Factors that interfere with the establishment of predictable clothing expectations include

1. the influence of regional customs and local patterns
2. the rapid and continuous social change in American society
3. inevitable distinctions among classes of people widely separated on the status continuum
4. qualifying circumstances peculiar to the situation

In spite of the high value many Americans place on individuality, most people instinctively desire to conform to group expectations.

ROLE LEARNING AND PORTRAYAL

The composite of expected behaviors associated with a specific role must be learned. These appropriate behaviors may be acquired through formal educational processes but more commonly they are learned through imitation and identification. Costumes designed for the stage must reinforce the character played and help the audience visualize the dominant traits of the role; so, too, appearance, both clothing and grooming, helps the individual in defining life's roles. From early childhood on, the individual in society learns and rehearses the social roles that will be enacted in life, and clothing is as essential to the successful performance of these roles as the costume is to the actor. Just as the costume designer must be able to identify the distinctive features of the part and translate them into visual symbols of dress, the individual must learn to identify the role and acquire the appropriate symbols of dress and behavior.

Role Differentiation and Identification

In the last section we discussed sex roles as one of the first categories to which an individual is assigned. One of the earliest distinctions children learn to make about themselves and others is that some are boys and others are girls. Clothing and dress, although increasingly similar for young children, are still used by them to make such differentiations. Many preschool youngsters find it impossible to make sex distinctions without these symbols.

Everyone recalls the tired joke about one child asking another how he could be sure that the infant in the crib was a baby brother and not a baby sister. The response of pulling down the covers and saying, "See, blue booties!" was not at all unusual in light of the fact that small children were very apt to make distinctions in sex on the basis of clothing symbols rather than actual physical differences, even when appraising adults.

A number of investigations have been conducted that shed some light on the way in which children begin to discern specific role distinctions. Weese studied the preschool child's capacity to recognize the sex appropriateness of selected items of dress and appearance.[31] Data from the study indicated that both boys and girls were able to identify female articles (lady's blouse, brassiere, hosiery, and so on) more accurately than masculine articles (man's shirt, necktie, socks, and so forth). Girls were found to be more accurate than boys in the sex designation of such appearance items, and boys were more accurate in the sex designation of task items (egg beater, iron, wooden spoon; wrench, screw driver, pliers, and so forth). These findings suggest that the feminine role is more readily identified because preschool children spend most of their days in the female environment of the mother or nursery school teacher, while the father works away from home. This is coupled with the fact that American mothers often take on elements of masculine dress, but the reverse pattern is rarely true. Moreover, in the basic process of role learning, children begin to think, feel, act, and become like

[31]Audray L'H. Weese, "Cultural Objects and Apparent Symbols as Sex Discernment Factors Among Preschool Children." Master's thesis, Michigan State University, 1964.

the *significant other* person(s) in their environment; in most cases, this is the parent of the same sex. Through such identification, girls take on the mother's attitudes and interests and boys take on the father's identity. Thus, it appears that by the age of three or four, girls have developed more of the mother's interest in clothes, and boys seem to be more aware of the symbols of work orientation.

Children tend to develop sex-role impressions early in life. The tendency to show strong opposite-sex preference or mixed masculine-feminine preferences is more frequent in girls than in boys—that is, boys tend to show a more clear-cut preference for masculine roles than girls do for feminine roles. This is not surprising in view of past child-rearing practices and parental sanctions involving the child's behavior, much stricter for boys than for girls. A little girl's tomboy activities are often rewarded as much as her ladylike behavior, but boys experience no such freedom in assuming ambiguous roles.

This also helps to explain why appropriate men's attire is defined in such specific detail. When punishment is consistently applied for not conforming to the appropriate role behavior, the expectations attached to a position or category are clarified. If an individual understands clearly what is expected, role learning is greatly facilitated. The female, on the other hand, has a more difficult time learning the behavior appropriate to her role because she is confronted with an ambiguous set of expectations. Her clothing, therefore, reflects a much wider range of acceptable patterns. This relationship between clarity of the role and its expression through clothing is obvious in a number of other cases. The nun's role, for example, is sharply defined, and in spite of the varia-

tions in habit that occur from order to order and the modernization and fashion orientation of many new habits, nuns are recognized almost anywhere in the world. A fairly high degree of consensus exists in regard to the type of behavior expected of them. Wearing any uniform, in fact, indicates that the individual has given up some rights to act freely and independently and must behave in accordance with the rules and limitations specifically defined for the group.

The expectations assigned to the age role of adolescents is another case in point. Their role behavior is ambiguously defined and they find themselves treated like children one minute and like adults the next. Adoption in rapid succession of numerous odd fads reflects the instability of their roles and the lack of consensus surrounding expectations from them.

Thus, we see that "proper" attire can be more explicitly defined when role expectations are clear-cut. A sensible approach to the study of suitable or appropriate clothing requires a logical pattern of reasoning. First, the role to be played must be identified. This is not often as simple as it sounds, for all people play a number of overlapping and sometimes conflicting roles. Second, a method must be devised to determine the degree of consensus that exists regarding the norms associated with that role. And third, the individual must develop the ability to visualize the role requirements in terms of appropriate clothing symbols.

Role Learning

It is not enough for an actor to identify the part in the play; somehow the look, the mannerisms, the gestures, the skills, and

Figure 8.20 The costume is the fastest way to declare a role.

a deliberate copying of behavior of other persons in the immediate environment. Both terms are used here to indicate observational learning based on the behavior of a model.[32]

Very early in life the child imitates the parent of the same sex, thereby learning the appropriate attitudes, values, and behaviors. The process may be observed most easily in the children's game of "playing house." The child dons the attire of the mother or the father, and in effect *becomes* the mother or father. Stone studied adult men and women in their recollections of childhood play, and at least 65 percent of his respondents could remember "dressing up" in adult costumes when they were children. The play costume most frequently chosen was that of a parent of the same sex, that is, little girls dressed in mother's clothes, and little boys in daddy's.[33]

Gardner Murphy explained how the process of such identification involves enacting the other person's role:

The child dresses up to *play* pirate, not just to *be* pirate; he wants daddy's hat and cane not merely to look like daddy, but to aid in immersing himself in the daddy round of activities. It is likely, indeed, that the psychology of clothing has too often been conceived in terms of a simple narcissistic delight in one's appearance; clothing is largely a means of making real the role that is to be played in life.[34]

the feelings of the character to be portrayed must be acquired (Figure 8.20). The performer learns a single role in a relatively short time. The individual in society often learns several roles simultaneously, and the process extends over the entire lifetime.

The task of role learning is accomplished in a number of ways. We have discussed the process of identification in relation to formation of the self-concept. Another process used in role learning is imitation. Many writers make a distinction between *identification* and *imitation*. Identification involves the process of imagining oneself in the role of the other; imitation is

[32]T. R. Sarbin, "Role Theory," in *Handbook of Social Psychology*, Vol. I, ed. G. Lindzey (Reading, Mass.: Addison-Wesley Publishing). 1954, pp. 223–255.
[33]Gregory P. Stone, "Appearance and the Self," in *Human Behavior and Social Processes*, ed. A. Rose (Boston: Houghton Mifflin Company, 1962), p. 111.
[34]Gardner Murphy, *Personality: A Biosocial Approach to Origins and Structure*, (New York: Harper and Brothers, 1947), p. 494.

Some roles cannot be assumed in life without the "props" or a costume (Figure 8.20). The cowboy's role is much easier to play in boots and chaps, spurs and hat, but a three-year-old cannot play it at all without at least guns and holster. Because clothes symbolize the very early distinctions a child is able to make in sex roles, clothing serves as an important aid in the subsequent designation of many other role categories and their accompanying characteristics. This process of imitation is not confined to childhood, however, and individuals continue to pattern their behavior after desirable (and sometimes undesirable) models. This imitative nature of the human organism accounts for much of the fad and fashion phenomena. In learning new social roles, the beginner identifies with an experienced occupant of the same position, and by copying the latter's actions, soon acquires an understanding of the appropriate norms and values. A college freshman, for example, usually looks to those in upper classes for cues to guide her clothing behavior. Through observation, she learns what female students wear on campus to study in the library on Saturday afternoon, to eat breakfast in the dining hall on Sunday morning, to attend a sorority meeting Monday night, and to go to a movie on Friday.

The principles of operant conditioning also apply to the process of role learning. The same system of rewards and punishments shape the individual's behavior to fit the position's requirements. The social reinforcements for appropriate clothing behavior are many—a smile, a caress, acceptance, admiration—and inappropriate attire brings responses that range all the way from mild disapproval to possible arrest and imprisonment.

Direct instruction is another method of role learning. Each generation is responsible for teaching their children the customs and mores of their culture. The rules and regulations regarding appropriate clothing for specific roles are among the information passed down. This learning process may take place at home, at play, in the classroom, or at informal gatherings. Thus the fraternity brother who instructs the new pledge that "No Sigma Nu dresses like that" is tutoring by giving him verbal instruction. Such instruction, coupled with the opportunity to practice the new role, can lead to performance of the correct behavior.

Thus, in the process of learning to be a doctor, a teacher, a businessperson, or a nurse, one must learn the definition of the accompanying statuses and the behavior patterns appropriate to such statuses. In most cases, the more opportunity one has to become familiar with the norms and values of the particular group, the more apt one is to conform to them. It also follows that the greater the conformity to group expectations, the greater will be the acceptance by the group. However, factors other than dress operate in the group interaction process to influence acceptance or rejection, liking or disliking. Yet clothing behavior is a very obvious component of normative group activity. The degree to which clothing values take precedence over other values varies with the composition of the group, the primacy of the group, and the intimacy of the group. As a person's status in the group increases, the more behavior becomes a model for others to follow. This circular pattern of imitating, conforming, and example-setting works to continue the norms of the group in stable fashion.

Role Enactment

An actor's success in conveying a role's meaning to the audience is greatly enhanced by skillful costuming. In describing his approach to the designs for Kate in Shakespeare's *The Taming of the Shrew*, a costumer explains how he focused on the character's dominant trait. Her volatile temper was symbolized throughout the play by the repeated use of red, beginning with a rich cherry red velvet gown in the first scene. As the action progressed, the tones of red for her successive costumes became more and more subdued and

when the (final) curtain rises, we see Kate in a soft pink chiffon gown, the decolletage rounded and softened with pearl trim, her hair falls softly down her back. We feel reasonably sure that Petruchio, her husband, has finally tamed the shrew. . . . Petruchio quizzes her about her constancy, we see her chin tip up jauntily—then she turns quickly on her unsuspecting husband, and we see as she turns, a brilliant red petticoat peek from beneath the cloud of pink chiffon making the final statement, as Shakespeare does, that one never really tames a shrew.[35]

Role enactment, then, refers to the actual role performance that either validates or invalidates the expectations associated with it—in other words, the ability of the individual "to carry it off." And so

the function of clothing in its gross aspects is readily discernible in this regard (e.g., it would be difficult to accept a man wearing overalls in the role of the business executive), but trifling

"This daily metamorphosis never fails to amaze me. Around the house, I'm a perfect idiot. I come to court, put on a black robe, and, by God, I'm <u>it</u>!"

Figure 8.21 In each new role the beginner is seen through the eyes of the role partners. The "props" of costume can bolster one's self-image in enacting such roles—real or imaginary. Drawing by Handelsman; © 1971 The New Yorker Magazine, Inc.

details often reveal palpable incongruities. Even the majesty of the male can be shattered by an inch in the wrong direction; a judge with a wig awry, and where is his dignity then? Tip a man's hat backwards and he ceases to look even respectable, for half an inch too far turns him into a buffoon.[36]

The ability to perform convincingly depends on both the ability to perceive the role's exact dimensions and the skill in projecting such perceptions into observable behavior (Figure 8.21). In addition to the obvious wearing of certain forms of dress, costume, and ornamentation, it also involves "gross skeletal movements, the performance of verbal and motoric gestures, posture and gait, styles of speech and accent" (Figure 8.22).[37]

Role enactment also implies interaction between the role and the self. We have seen how the self develops from a series of

[35]Leon Brauner, "Character Portrayal Through Costume," speech given at Western Regional Clothing and Textiles Meeting, Logan, Utah, October 1964.

[36]C. W. Cunnington. *Why Women Wear Clothes* (London: Faber and Faber Ltd., 1941), pp. 128ff.

[37]Sarbin, *Role Theory*, p. 232.

Figure 8.22 The cogency of one's performance in a role is clothing-related. It would be difficult to accept a man in the attire pictured here in the role of a business executive.

role-taking experiences in which the individual is placed in various counterpositions to significant others. The self is thus evaluated in terms of how well the individual enacts a given role. In each new role beginners see themselves through the eyes of role partners and in the process, add another dimension to their concept of self. For example, fashion merchandising students gradually learn and take on a fashion buyer's clothing behavior. As others recognize them as fashion buyers, they begin to see themselves as fashion buyers. If they are unable to develop the associated clothing behavior, few people recognize their role assignments and their self-image is weakened.

SUMMARY

Role Learning and Portrayal

Clothing is an obvious and visual symbol by which an individual learns to identify and differentiate specific social roles. When a high degree of consensus exists about the definition of a role, the associated clothing expectations tend to be fairly explicit. Appropriate attire for men, therefore, is more narrowly prescribed than it is for women, because the masculine role is more consistently and rigidly defined. A study of what is considered suitable or proper dress may be approached through (1) identifying the role, (2) surveying the clothing norms associated with the role, and (3) ascertaining the degree of consensus surrounding such norms.

The learning of roles and accompanying patterns of clothing behavior is accomplished through a variety of processes, such as imitation, identification, direct instruction, and operant conditioning, which includes the rewards and punishments used to reinforce clothing behavior either intentionally or accidentally. Belief in one's performance in a given role depends on the accurate perception of clothing expectations and their subsequent translation into observable and appropriate clothing behavior. In the process of role enactment, the interaction that takes place between the role and the self causes individuals to evaluate themselves through the eyes of their role partners, and the concept of self is altered accordingly.

VARIATION IN ROLE PERFORMANCE

Conflict often arises from the fact that an individual always occupies more than one role in society. Liz Smith, for example, is not only a woman; she is also an attorney, a wife, a mother, a church worker, a sorority alumna, a PTA member, a musician, and a participant in numerous other activities in the community. Tom Jones is a man, a college professor, a husband, a father, an artist, a Boy Scout leader, a member of a fraternal organization, and an active participant on community affairs. Whenever the requirements for any two of these roles conflict or are incompatible, problem situations develop. When clothing is involved, such problems are usually resolved by compromise or deviation from the normative expectation.

Clothing Compromises

Incompatibility between certain role requirements and the self may result in conflicting attitudes toward clothing. Maryellen, for example, aspires to be a fashion coordinator. Fashion coordinators represent people who have a talent for combining costumes, colors, and accessories in new and unusual ways. Their refinement of taste should be coupled with an inventiveness one expects to see reflected in their own attire. Maryellen is considerably overweight; she refrains from buying new clothes because she vows to go on a diet and does not want to invest in clothing that will soon be too big for her. She never did like extreme styles because they only call attention to her figure, and she prefers to be inconspicuous anyway. She would rather conform to the group than be an innovator. She knows she does not look like a fashion coordinator but she argues that this should not interfere with her ability to do the work. The wide discrepancy between Maryellen and the expected image may lead to difficulty. Brophy's study of the self and role requirements led him to conclude "that congruence in the intrapersonal relationship between the self concept and the ideal self is one of the most fundamental conditions for both general happiness and for satisfaction in specific life areas."[38]

Another form of conflict arises when the requirements of one role are incompatible with the requirements of another. Women are commonly subjected to conflicting expectations in their adult sex roles. A girl's family or teachers often exert pressures toward professional pursuits and expect her to make maximum use of her capacities. Her desire for male friends encourages a leaning toward the typical homemaker role, and she may even perceive scholastic achievement as a threat to her femininity. The opposing pressures create a desire for fussy, feminine clothes one day and a tomboy's clothes the next.

Fortunately, all roles do not have to be played simultaneously. When a man comes home from work he usually sheds his work clothes and puts on his "family clothes"—perhaps a comfortable pair of slacks, a sport shirt, and a sweater. His role as a worker drops aside and his family roles begin. If it happens to be a lodge night, he sets aside his family roles, puts on his fez, and becomes a Shriner for three hours.

[38]Alfred L. Brophy, "Self, Role, and Satisfaction," *Genetic Psychology Monographs*, 59 (May 1959), 300.

When conflicting roles are separated by a time interval, the individual usually can handle both successfully. The · career woman can be efficient and detached sitting behind her desk in a smartly tailored suit but after five o'clock, she can slip into something different and appear as she pleases.

Additionally, people play their roles with varying degrees of involvement, ranging all the way from casual or minimal interaction to intense participation. A woman in a supermarket, for instance, performs her shopper's role with a minimum of involvement. She is a shopper for an hour or so, she collects her groceries automatically, and she is not particularly concerned about the opinions of the people she may meet in the market. If it rains, or if a friend happens to come visiting, she may even postpone her shopping role to another time. But in her professional role, she is apt to be considerably more involved.

Thus, in almost all role enactment, the individual establishes priorities of importance and decides which role will have priority over another. The teen-ager's pants style or hair style may be frowned on by parents, but the high school boy will wear them anyway because he is more intensely involved with his social role in his peer group than he is as a student.

Deviation in Role Performance

Earlier in this chapter we saw that considerable variation may exist in the clarity or consensus with which roles are defined. Certain roles and statuses expressed through clothing, such as those of an army captain or Eagle Scout, are defined in highly specific terms. However, with the increase in adult and continuing education programs, the role of student can be defined in terms of almost any individual over six years of age. Since the category is so broad, it includes a wide range of acceptable clothing behavior. Indeed, distinguishable clothes universally associated with the role of student may no longer exist.

Usually when consensus about appropriate role behavior is high, even the slightest departure from the norm is regarded as a deviation. Deviance is a matter of social definition rather than a characteristic of behavior in itself. The definition of what one "should" wear may be interpreted differently by different people. The mother of a high school tean-ager nearly went into shock when Jimmy arrived to pick up her daughter. He wore swimming trunks, drove an open convertible in midwinter, and it was beginning to snow. To the daughter, Jimmy was simply conforming to the norms of the Polar Bear Club, whose members take midwinter dips in Lake Michigan.

Most individuals make an honest effort to meet society's role expectations. Some groups of individuals consider themselves "above," "beneath," or "beyond" fashion dictates. The "underdressed snobs" described long ago by Russell Lynes are an example; they "wouldn't be caught dead at a cocktail party" in cocktail dresses.[39] It is all a matter of conforming to the clothing expectations of the group with which we identify. However, new social situations present some problems to newcomers, who have not had the chance to clarify the roles they must play. It is far easier to conform to explicitly defined dress standards than it is

[39]Russell Lynes, *Snobs* (New York: Harper and Brothers, 1950), p. 43.

to guess at the limitations of roles that are not clearly defined.

We recently saw limited adoption of what was called "identity clothing," that is, a kind of unspecialized dress worn for all occasions. Charles Reich described such "new clothes" as expressing a

wholeness of self. . . . There is not one set of clothes for the office, another for social life, a third for play. The same clothes can be used for every imaginable activity, and so they say that it is the same person doing all these things—not a set of different masks or dolls but one many-sided, *whole* individual.[40]

By the same token, Reich claimed, the individual is not limited to a single role, but can pick up "whatever new and spontaneous thing may come along."

According to this philosophy, an individual may be a court jester one day, a cowboy the next, a sheik the next—whatever happens to suit the fancy. Psychologist Erik Erikson saw this constant thirst for novelty and newness as an identity crisis for the whole nation. The many changes in everyday lifestyles in dress and behavior, he said, "are in some circles on their way to becoming a matter of obsession, as if any more defined identity were only too much conformity, and only absolute choice were freedom."[41] He believed that this greatly disturbed our sense of reality.

While some groups avidly sought a release from formalized role expectations, many more found new ways to meet the social requirements of dress. The rental and sale of formal wear, for example—particularly men's wear—expanded enormously in recent years. The fact that the big chains like Sears, Roebuck, and Montgomery Ward entered the formal wear rental business is sufficient indication that the demand for such clothing has grown among mass consumers.

Everyone deviates from clothing norms to some extent, because one cannot always know exactly what is expected. Or, people may know what is expected, but the pressure of conflicting role requirements makes them decide to deviate from one set of norms in order to conform to the requirements of the more valued role.

The most obvious deviant is the person who knows the requirements and deliberately sets out to violate them. Some research evidence shows that such individuals demonstrate a general disorientation to society. Even within a so-called normal population of college women, consistent clothing preferences were found to be highly related to social maturity and positive feelings toward society, and people who had mixed feelings toward society tended to fluctuate in their clothing behavior.[42] In another study of adolescent boys, nearly one third of those who deviated from the clothing norm were found to be social isolates.[43] It should be noted that in this study, clothing deviants included fashion innovators and independents as well as counterconformists.

[40]Charles Reich, *The Greening of America* (New York: Random House, 1970), p. 235.
[41]Erik Erikson, quoted in "Truth Is Newness in America," *Washington Post* news service release, June 13, 1973.
[42]Donna Ditty, "Social-Psychological Aspects of Clothing Preferences of College Women." Ph.D. diss. Ohio State University, 1962.
[43]Patricia Lee, "The Relation of Deviation from Clothing Norms of Eleventh Grade Male Students and Peer Acceptance." Master's thesis, University of Nevada, 1969.

Transitions in Role and Status

Thus far we have treated role and status as relatively stable elements in the social system, with variation caused largely by the way in which individuals or subgroups meet the associated clothing expectations. Roles and statuses themselves, however, undergo certain changes. In addition to the daily shifts in role occupancy, transitions occur as a person passes through the successive life-cycle stages. Long-term social changes also alter the way in which roles and statuses are defined.

As we have seen, an individual's role occupancy may shift several times a day, as well as from day to day, and many of these shifts require a change of attire. In most cases, such change provides a welcome relief from monotony. Other shifts occur as the person passes from childhood to adolescence to adulthood and old age. In adolescence, role requirements are redefined in terms of the peer group, and values attached to former patterns established in the family context no longer seem appropriate. As was mentioned earlier, the unclear definitions on adolescent roles and the conflict between peer and family expectations confuse the teen-ager. On the other hand, clothing sometimes helps to clarify new status: the first dark suit for the boy's confirmation or bar mitzvah and the girl's first formal dress or first pair of high-heeled shoes are the badges of advanced status and greater privilege.

A larger wardrobe or a new fur coat may show changes in the family economic status. Increased upward mobility of large population segments requires redefinition of many roles in terms of changing social statuses. A family may move from a rural area to a city or from a city to suburbs. Each of these changes leads to a different set of clothing expectations.

Changing social patterns also affect gradual transitions in the attitudes and expectations associated with given roles. The deliberations of the Pope's Ecumenical Council in the 1960s resulted in a radical revision of Roman Catholic doctrine, and the impact will be felt for many years to come. The habits of various religious orders have been modernized and most nuns have returned to secular dress in executing their more worldly responsibilities. Despite future councils or papal decrees, they are unlikely to return to the discomfort of the old habits.

Clothing once served to separate the aristocracy from the lower working classes; appropriate clothing for a black slave, for example, was fairly well established a century ago. Progress in the civil rights movement, coupled with a rising standard of living for all classes of people, has greatly reduced the distinctions that formerly were made in clothing expectations.

Increased leisure time and the mass move to suburbia produced a greater demand for casual, informal clothes, and at the same time created an unprecedented participation in active sports. Woman's entrance into sports and her increased acceptance in the business and political worlds had tremendous influence in reshaping the clothing expectations of women's roles. The same kinds of social changes have produced accompanying alterations in men's dress.

Changes in an individual's clothing indicate changes in that person's social roles and statuses.

SUMMARY

Variation in Role Performance

People occupy a number of social roles, some of which may be incompatible in terms of their clothing requirements. If an individual cannot separate conflicting roles by a time interval the tendency will be to favor the requirements of the role in which involvement is more intense. Some roles may be inconsistent with one's self-concept; in this case, the person usually attempts to resolve the conflict by resorting to one or more of the ego defense mechanisms. Such role conflict often results in deviation from the expected norms of clothing behavior. Everyone deviates to some extent from clothing norms because many role requirements are not clearly defined; thus, people cannot always know precisely what is expected. In addition, norms are shared by different individuals and subgroups, so the degree of consensus on normative behavior may vary widely. Those who know the rules of clothing behavior and deliberately set out to violate them show a negative response to social expectations.

Role occupancy shifts from day to day and changes as the individual passes through successive life-cycle stages. Role requirements are usually redefined in terms of a new reference group. Other shifts, such as those connected with class mobility or change in location, also result in a changing set of clothing expectations. Over the years, numerous transitions in social patterns have modified conceptions of what constitutes proper dress.

FOR FURTHER READING

Beeson, Marianne S. "In the Gray Flannel Mold." In *Dimensions of Dress and Adornment: A Book of Readings*. 3rd ed. Dubuque, Iowa: Kendall/Hunt Publishing Co., 1979, pp. 128–132.

"Foodservice Fashions on the Move." *Institutions*, 85 (August 1, 1979), 49–52.

Molloy, John T. *Dress for Success*. New York: Peter H. Wyden Publishers, 1975.

Molloy, John T. *The Woman's Dress for Success Book*. Chicago: Follett Publishing Co., 1977.

Sloan, Pat. "Whatever Happened to the Gray Flannel Suit?" *Advertising Age*, 50 (September 24, 1979), sec. 2, S22.

"Uniform Look: Career Apparel Does It with Style." *Savings and Loan News*, 100 (January 1979), 60–64.

Chapter 9

CONFORMITY AND

INDIVIDUALITY IN DRESS

All people seek an identity and a sense of belongingness through conforming to a given set of norms, and yet at the same time they strive to achieve some distinction as individual human beings.

The personal dilemma rises from the fact that a person must be, and wants to be, a conforming member of some social groups and he wants to play a part as himself, as a distinctive individual. . . . The more benign aspect of diversity—at least in our usual parlance—includes creativity, originality, adaptability. The other range of meanings for diversity takes in abnormality, delinquency, chaos. One face of conformity is identification, loyalty, solidarity; another is monotony, totalitarianism, rigidity. The fact is that both conformity and diversity are inevitable in social and personal life and that one must always complement the other.[1]

Nowhere is this paradox of human nature reflected more visibly than it is in dress. These two social tendencies—conformity and individuality—form the basis for all fashion behavior. Simmel emphasized that both are essential to the establishment of fashion and that "should one of these be absent, fashion will not be formed—its sway will abruptly end."[2]

[1]David Mandelbaum, "The Interplay of Conformity and Diversity," in *Conflict and Creativity, Part 2,* ed. S. Farber and R. Wilson (New York: McGraw-Hill Book Company, 1963), pp. 241 ff.
[2]Georg Simmel, "Fashion," *American Journal of Sociology,* 62 (May 1957), 546.

Either one, carried to an extreme, is incompatible with human social existence; complete order and rigidity contradicts the need for new experience, but complete freedom or normlessness may lead to a state of chaos. The basic question is how much freedom is desirable within what degree of conformity or control. In attempting an answer, this chapter will be concerned with the forces that motivate innovation, conformity, and deviation in clothing behavior.

NORM FORMATION

In Chapter 4 we discussed the process of norm formation in relation to folkways, customs, mores, and laws. Fads and fashions are also a part of the normative system, but they represent clothing practices that fall at the opposite end of the continuum in terms of strength, duration, and sanctions. This transitory nature of fashion, however, makes it the ideal medium for the study of norm formation, norm replacement, conformity, and deviation. An analysis of conformity versus individuality in dress will be facilitated by first defining the terms used to describe various kinds of clothing phenomena.

Definition of Terms

The wearing of trousers by men is a custom deeply embedded in the normative system of Western culture. It is also customary for men's trousers to be pressed into a lengthwise crease in front and in back or, in the case of jeans, with no crease at all. Although many men may wear trousers in which the crease has almost disappeared, few would wear trousers in which the crease had been pressed from side to side. We can, of course, cite a number of societies in which a bifurcated garment is *not* the "normal" or typical style of masculine dress. More important, perhaps, is the fact that trousers as we know them today have existed for less than two hundred years. Viewed against the span of man's recorded history, they may some day be regarded as a "fleeting fashion of the times"—but certainly not as fleeting as "ivy-leagues," "bell-bottoms," "baggies," or "flares."

The point here is that definitions of terms are relative rather than absolute. What may appear to be a contradiction in the comparison of a fluctuating fashion with an enduring custom is in reality the comparison of two extreme cases selected from different points along the same continuum. As already explained, a **clothing norm** represents the typical or accepted manner of dressing shown by a social group. By **conformity**, we mean acceptance of or adherence to a clothing norm, that is, dressing in accordance with the norm of a specified group. With the exception of the term *style*, all of the following may be considered clothing norms.

Style is a characteristic or distinctive form of dress; it has certain recognizable qualities or features that distinguish it from other forms. Styles exist independent of fashion. They may be part of the current normative behavior and, therefore, fashionable. Or they may be very unfashionable, seen perhaps only in history books. The popularity of a style varies, but the style itself is unchanging. The bouffant skirt, for example, is one style of dress that was considered fashionable in the 1860s and the 1950s, but it was definitely *un*fashionable in the 1920s, 1930s, and 1960s. The style of pants called bell-bottoms remains essentially the same. The popularity of the pants as well as the amount of flare (or fabric) in the bell may vary but the shape of the silhouette, thus the style, does not. In general, the styling of a garment refers to its design or cut, a quality that can be described in terms of its line, form, or proportion. There are styles of coats (box, redingote, balmacaan, chesterfield, trench, wraparound), styles of sleeves (bishop, dolman, kimono, raglan, leg-of-mutton), styles of hats (beret, bowler, fedora, cloche, Homburg), styles of shoes (oxfords, sandals, pumps, boots, sneakers, Dr. Scholls, espadrilles), and styles of collars (mandarin, peter pan, shawl, turtleneck, cowl).

Mode is a statistical word used here to represent the most common form of clothing worn among a given group of people, or, to say it another way, the greatest frequency of a style. If we were to observe the apparel of a population, we could count the number of times each variation of dress was worn. Such a counting procedure would give us two kinds of measurements: the range of differences in dress, and the style of highest frequency (the mode).

Universals, alternatives, and specialties help us describe the extent of a norm's applicability. A **universal** norm generally applies to every member of the society. Most societies, however, permit some degree of variation from the modal pattern. In a campus population, for example, Levis may be the mode, but ivy-leagues, high-waisted, french-cut, and corduroys may also be acceptable **alternatives**. Each is a

Figure 9.1 By 1970, the miniskirt had become a popular fashion.

norm, but one does not exclude the other. **Specialties**, on the other hand, are norms that are restricted to a particular subgroup. When micro-miniskirts were the mode for young females between the ages of thirteen and twenty-five, they were not the norm for all females (Figure 9.1).

Fashion represents the popular, accepted, prevailing style at any given time. In this sense, it means the same thing as mode. However, fashion is further characterized by its cyclical nature, that is, the gradual rise, high point, and eventual decline in the popular acceptance of a style. On its way into popularity, a particular style is worn by the relatively few who can afford financially to be different or are secure enough psychologically to try something new. As its popularity spreads, more and more people hop on the bandwagon until the style finally snowballs to the peak of acceptance, and no one wants to be different. But once everyone has it, the attraction is gone, and there is nothing for the style to do but slip gradually out of sight. The forces that cause the rise and fall of fashion are identical with the tensions that exist between conformity and distinction in dress.

Classic (sometimes "fashion Ford") is an occasional fashion that is so universally accepted that it gradually crystallizes into a conventional norm of dress (Figure 9.2). Such styles remain popular for so long that they rest on the borderline between fashion and custom. Over the years, styles like the shirtwaist dress, skirt and shirt combinations, and cardigan sweaters became classics. Similarly, T-shirts, jeans, and turtleneck sweaters, more recent styles, are headed toward the classic category.

High fashion is found only at the beginning of the very first stage of the normal fashion cycle. It has the snob appeal of exclusiveness; once it is no longer confined to restricted consumption, it loses its status as a high fashion. The

Figure 9.2 Classics like this tweed suit with pleated skirt have a certain timeless quality. Actual vintage: 1969.

rapid spread of high-fashion copies today considerably shortens the life span of such items. The potential success of a high fashion, however, must be reasonably assured before manufacturers will mass-produce it.

Not all high fashions mature into full-blown fashions. Some, because they depart too radically from the convention patterns of dress, fade away before the bandwagon rolls by. Others, because of prohibitive cost or availability, continue in restricted use. Thus the mink coat remains both a high fashion item as well as a clothing classic.

Fad is a kind of miniature fashion, usually more trivial or more fanciful than the normal fashion. Often it reaches fewer people and it sometimes is confined to a subculture. Fads have a sudden burst of popularity, enjoy a bandwagon plateau for several weeks or months, and then drop out of existence as quickly as they came in. Fads have included plaid shoestrings, colored tennis shoes, decorated sweatshirts, beer jackets, love beads, raccoon coats, striped blazers, shoe boots, message T-shirts, penny loafers, hooded blouses, charm bracelets, elbow patches, and so on. Fads sometimes cluster around a particular person, group, or event. The popularity of the Beatles gave rise to Beatle shirts, Beatle jackets, and Beatle haircuts. Bo Derek's braided hair was an early 1980s fad, but because of the skill required to achieve the look and the expense to have it done professionally, it was limited to those who could afford such extravagance (Figure 9.3). In a few rare instances fads survive the usual rapid decline and develop into enduring fashions (for example, the bobbed hair of the 1920s, the 1950s pearls worn with sweaters, T-shirts of the 70s, and gold status chains of the 1980s), but the vast

Figure 9.3   Left: Bo Derek's braided hair, a fad of the early 1980s.

Figure 9.4   Right: Message T-shirts: fads of the 1970s and 1980s.

majority last little more than six months (Figure 9.4).

With the exception of style, each of these concepts depends on varying degrees of conformity. The classic is widely accepted and worn for a long time. The fashion, usually initiated as a high fashion worn by a very select group of people, reaches its peak of mass acceptance and then gradually fades into obsolescence. A fashion represents the mass taste, what "everybody" wears; it becomes the property of a large, varied group in the total society for a period of time. Fads usually reach fewer people and are very limited in duration.

Conformity is expressed by the degree to which individuals follow the norm formations of the times. Styles, classics, fads, and fashion are all part of the normative formulations of a society. Expressed in specific types of clothing, norms may be differentiated on the basis of their relative endurance and the magnitude of their acceptance in the society.

The Cyclical Nature of Fashion

The term *fashion cycle* refers specifically to the gradual rise, high point, and decline in the popularity of a given style. The theoretical representation of the stages in the fashion cycle shows symmetrical bell-shaped curves. Since actual observations always represent a sample of the total population, statistics obtained from fashion counts almost never produce a smooth curve (Figure 9.5), although they yield a fairly accurate measure of the duration and magnitude of a style's acceptance.

If we were to make similar numerical tabulations on a regular basis and in different places, the fashion count would enable us to estimate the relative position of a style in terms of its anticipated cycle. Let us say, for example, that we want to determine the acceptance of narrow skirts with deep side slits. We can stand on the corner of Broadway and Main in Small-town, U.S.A., and count the number of women wearing them. At the end of an hour or two, we may have observed that six women out of one hundred and fifty turned out to be narrow-slit-skirt wearers. This

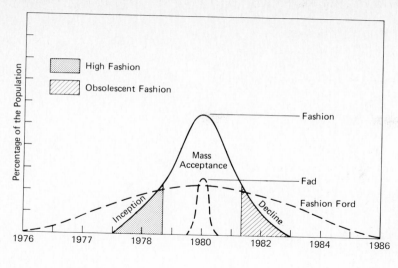

Figure 9.5 Theoretical representations of the rise, highest point, and decline of the average fashion, the "fashion Ford," and the fad.

does not tell us very much, except that this style of skirt has been adopted by roughly 4 percent of the Smalltown women. If we stand on the same corner every Saturday afternoon for the next six months, however, we get a picture of increasing or decreasing acceptance. Another dimension would be added to this analysis were we to have scouts make similar tabulations during the same time intervals in several large cities, such as San Francisco, Chicago, and New York. A third comparison could be made if we could count the number of women wearing them in the fashionably elite resorts. Figure 9.6 shows a theoretical representation of the fashion cycle at each of these levels.

It is entirely possible, of course, that a small but particularly fashion-conscious community may adopt high fashions before they are generally worn by large segments of the population in bigger cities. Fashion counts are useful in determining the degree to which this is so. There is an understandable time lag, however, between the introduction of the original high fashion and the availability of copied-down reproductions. In earlier days, it took almost two years for a high-fashion design to be worn universally by the average person on the street. Today, the ready-to-wear industry can turn

out copies in a matter of months; with some items that are easy to reproduce, the time lag may be reduced to weeks.

From our theoretical model, we can see that if the percentage of people wearing a given item in high fashion circles exceeds the percentage at the local level, it is a fair indication that the fashion has not yet reached its peak of popularity. On the other hand, if more women on Main Street are wearing narrow slit skirts than they are on Fifth Avenue, chances are that this fashion has begun its downhill trip. This kind of comparison also can be made by counting illustrations in magazines instead of actual people in various locations. Other sources such as newspaper advertisements and the clothing worn by television personalities could also be counted. Then, in order to determine the fashion followership of women on your campus, you could plot the curve of the incoming fashion against comparable fashion counts made in popular and high-fashion magazines, newspapers, and television (Figure 9.7). These curves can be compared with the theoretical model in Figure 9.6.

The time required for a fashion cycle to run its course obviously varies with the type of norm the fashion demonstrates. A fad may disappear in a matter of weeks or

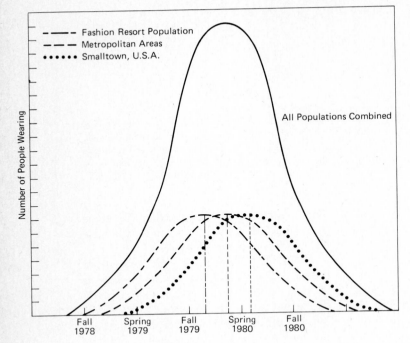

Figure 9.6 Theoretical representation of the fashion cycle in different areas.

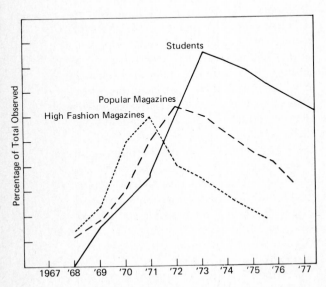

Figure 9.7 Observations of men's flared trousers, 1967–1978.

months, a classic may remain popular for fifteen or twenty years. The average fashion usually lasts from seven to nine years, from inception to its ultimate obsolescence. There is some evidence, however, that the duration of the fashion cycle is becoming progressively shorter, which is to be expected in times of rapid social change.

Aside from the fact that fashion counts provide valuable information in predicting a style's life span, they are a means of producing graphic evidence of the degree of conformity to local or national norms that exists. Every fad or fashion can be traced from its inception, through validation by fashion leaders, growing influence, mass acceptance and decline, to final obsolescence (Figure 9.8). Fads are even more dramatic than fashions in this respect because the cycle is so short; they snowball rapidly and approach their peaks like

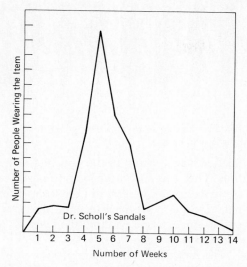

Figure 9.8 Actual observation of a fad curve: 1979, Dr. Scholl's sandals.

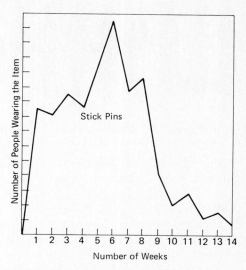

Figure 9.9 Actual observation of a fad curve: 1980, stick pins.

epidemics from which no one is immune. Many become grossly exaggerated. If full skirts are the rage, one or two petticoats are good, but seven or eight are better. If narrow trousers are "in," one must be "in" even further with a pair several sizes too small and reaching halfway up the calf. This kind of frenzied enthusiasm results in the vulgar excesses that sound the death knell. When the people who imitate fashion are far removed from those who set the fashion, they often have a vague and incomplete understanding of the boundaries. In attempting to imitate, they overreach, and thereby destroy the fashion they seek to adopt (Figure 9.9).

Another dimension of the cyclical nature of fashion relates to the principle of **recurring cycles**. Independent studies of costume characteristics over the centuries indicate that certain styles or patterns of dress tend to recur at fairly regular intervals. The analysis by Richardson and Kroeber, for example, pointed out that the

basic dimensions of feminine dress alternate between minimum and maximum measurements approximately every fifty years, taking a full century for the silhouette to complete the cycle from wide to narrow and back to wide again.[3] Thus, in terms of general contour, we can see peaks of fullness at about 1570, 1660, 1750, 1860, and 1950, with silhouettes that gradually shrink to the slender tubular shape in the intervening years. Young maintained that the transition from wide to narrow always passed through a period of back fullness.[4] Although the theory seems to hold true for fashions from 1760 through the early 1950s, it has not held for the changes that have occurred in the last decade or so.

[3]Jane Richardson and A. L. Kroeber, "Three Centuries of Women's Dress, A Quantitative Analysis," *Anthropological Records*, 5, No. 2, University of California Press, Berkeley and Los Angeles, 1940.
[4]Agnes Brooks Young, *Recurring Cycles of Fashion* (1760–1937) (New York: Harper and Brothers, 1937).

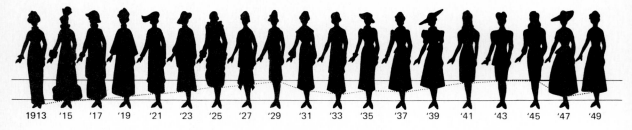

Figure 9.10 The recurring cycle in skirt lengths. Try this with other aspects of dress, such as the width of men's trousers, shoulder width, shoe proportions, and the like.

Still, the dominant elements of fashion (for instance, length and fullness of the skirt, size and placement of waistline, width of sleeve) progress through waves of continuous evolution. The typical fashion must always be different from that of the preceding year, yet it rarely differs in any marked degree. Each year's fashion is built on the past and can be seen as an outgrowth or modification of the previous style (Figure 9.10). In addition, the pendulum of fashion must swing from one extreme to the other. Normally, it cannot move from an extremely narrow sleeve to a moderately full one, then jerk back to a moderately narrow one before it continues its way to extreme fullness. Skirts of the 1860s became so full that at their peak it was almost impossible for the wearers to squeeze through doorways. The silhouette then began its slow progression back toward narrowness until some fifty years later a skirt was so tight about the knees and ankles that a lady could barely take a comfortable step. Many writers who attempt to interpret all body adornment in terms of its sexual significance see the 1912 hobble skirt as a masculine attempt to dominate women by impeding their movements. In terms of the cyclical theory of fashion change, the hobble skirt was nothing more or less than the logical conclusion to the diminishing fullness of the preceding fifty years. The farther the pendulum begins from dead center, the farther it will swing in the opposite direction. The extremes of elongation observed in the late Gothic period in the form of tall hats and pointed shoes reached the opposite in the extreme width of the fashions of the Renaissance.

The fact that both full and narrow skirts may exist during the same year does not contradict this basic assumption. Each season many new designs are introduced and undergo a period of experimentation before a trend is clearly discernible. This is why current fashions are difficult to analyze with accuracy; one often needs the benefit of historical perspective to identify the typical or dominant theme of an era. Moreover, one can always observe deviations from the theme; the degree of variability from the ideal norm of any period is an important index of the stability or instability of the times.

Thus, the cyclical nature of fashion may be explained in terms of the rise, highest point, and decline in the popularity of a style and long-term cycles of recurrence (Figures 9.11 and 9.12).

Clothing norms are subject to continuous change; each year's fashion is different from the last but without any radical departure from it. When observed over a period of time fashion cycles are clearly discernible. Historical perspective is necessary in order to see that the nature of fashion is cyclical.

'51 '53 '55 '57 '59 '61 '63 '65 '67 '69 '71 '73 '75 '76 '77 '78 '79 '80

Conformity

Conformity is the process by which individuals adapt their behavior to some preexistent norms. It is a form of social interaction in which one tries to maintain standards set by a group. Although often subjected to value judgments, excessive or overconformity tends to evoke negative feelings.

Conformity is neither good nor bad. Emerson said "To be a man is to be a nonconformist," and the German poet Goethe called for all men to be conformists. Although nonconformity or individuality contribute interest and change, conformity lends stability to our lives and to society.

Figure 9.11 Below: The pendulum of fashion swings from one extreme to the other.

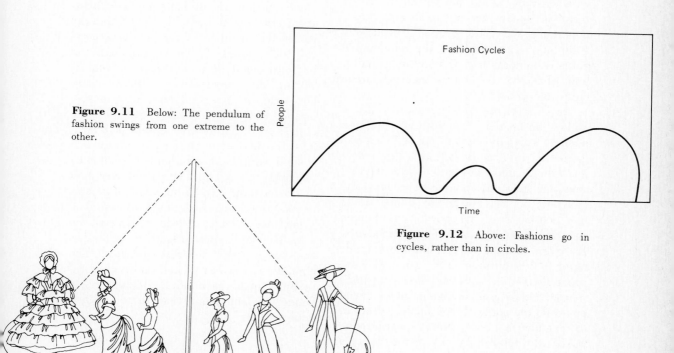

Fashion Cycles

People

Time

Figure 9.12 Above: Fashions go in cycles, rather than in circles.

1860

1870

1880

1890

1900

1910

Pressures Toward Conformity

No society in human history has ever been a "free society" in the sense that its members were free to do exactly as they pleased in all respects. There are some areas of activity in which society maintains rather rigid controls over human behavior. In others, conformity to or deviation from the accepted norm is a matter of choice left up to the individual; in still others, non-conformity may even be encouraged and rewarded. In the United States, there are few institutionalized controls over clothing behavior and considerable deviation from the norm is tolerated. Fashion leaders, however, are *expected* to depart from the established norm, and their status increases when they do so. But within the broad range of human activity related to dress, adherence to clothing norms is largely voluntary. To what extent, then, do people actually conform in their clothing behavior, and what are the factors that encourage such conformity?

As children we all played the game of Follow-the-Leader. The child who is quick enough to be the first to shout "Leader!" gains the privilege of initiating the behavior others must imitate. Obviously, if everyone insisted on being the leader, the game would fall apart; the whole fun of the action is seeing how many people can duplicate the innovator's maneuvers. Everyone but the leader, therefore, must agree to be a follower in the game. You are probably familiar with the following experiment in behavioral contagion: take a friend or two to the corner of the busiest street in town; stand in a conspicuous spot and look quizzically toward the sky or the top of a building. See how many passing strangers follow your glance skyward. Or, follow the sales in the bargain basement of the local department store, and watch the customers fight to reach the edge of the most crowded counter without even knowing what items are for sale behind the figures of the mob.

This same kind of contagious behavior causes innovations in clothing norms to flourish into fads or fashions. The desire to conform—consciously or unconsciously—to the established norms of the group appears to be strongly reinforced in human behavior. Several groups of undergraduate students at the University of Nevada were asked to analyze their motives in clothing behavior by ranking a list of ten phrases describing the ways in which an individual might prefer to dress or wish to appear.[5] The weighted rankings of these students are represented in Figure 9.13. In first place, almost all students ranked "neatness" and "cleanliness," both of which are values long held by Americans as second only to "godliness." "Appropriateness" can be interpreted only in terms of what is "fitting" or "proper," that is, the acceptable form of dress. Being "luxuriously" dressed was the least valued of the possible choices and the one that would have been most inconsistent with the group norms. It is significant that few students wished to be "inconspicuous," but neither did they want to be "striking" or "dramatic." Most students interpreted "fashionably dressed" to mean "in the height of fashion," that is, the same as high fashion rather than fashion as the terms were described earlier. The combined rankings placed "individuality" in dress near the middle, although not a single student rated this value as first choice.

[5]The phrases were adapted from Harriet McJimsey, *Art and Fashion in Clothing Selection* (Ames, Iowa: Iowa State University Press, 1973), p. 5.

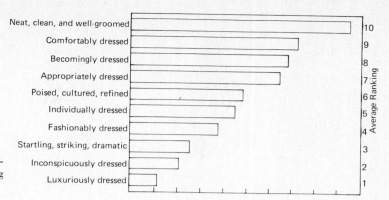

	Average Ranking
Neat, clean, and well-groomed	10
Comfortably dressed	9
Becomingly dressed	8
Appropriately dressed	7
Poised, cultured, refined	6
Individually dressed	5
Fashionably dressed	4
Startling, striking, dramatic	3
Inconspicuously dressed	2
Luxuriously dressed	1

Figure 9.13 Student responses to phrases describing appearance values.

All these examples merely indicate that the phenomena of contagion and conformity are present in most forms of clothing behavior. One might ask *why* these forces seem so deeply embedded in human response patterns, more so than drives toward creativity, individuality, or distinctiveness. Much of our social behavior is imitative. In the child's early life, the ability to discriminate among many environmental cues is limited, and appropriate responses are learned by imitating the actions of older siblings and parents.

Conformity is an important part of a person's personality structure at all stages of life. It is first learned in childhood in the form of obedience to parents and teachers who are, for the most part, great believers in conformity. Society and schools have tried to force individuals to conform to a single behavior pattern. It is easier to run organizations that way, to have rules, standards, and behavior codes. However, the rules must be flexible enough and the codes broad enough for individuals to fulfill their personalities. Some children learn the lesson of conformity too well, and they grow up to be adults who are incapable of thinking or acting for themselves. The complete conformist is afraid to think different or original thoughts because they produce feelings of anxiety. Such people cannot learn in the true sense of the word and can only copy the behavior of others.

Excessive conformity is negatively related to creativity. Taylor found that college women who considered conforming dress behavior important placed a low value on aesthetics, creativity, and individuality. Those who conformed in their dress were not interested in whether or not it was beautiful but only in whether or not it was acceptable and like that of the students around them.[6] The mature person, in contrast, is one who can conform to the reasonable demands of society without giving up individuality and creativity.

Beyond this, there is considerable evidence that people have a rather strong need to be "correct," and they look to other people for validation of their own opinions. Several experiments in social psychology have indicated that the tendency to follow the suggestions of others is particularly strong if the expectations are unclear or if the individual has little self-confidence.[7] We might infer from this that a person is more apt to rely on the judgment of others if understanding of the right form of dress is

[6]Lucy C. Taylor, "Conformity in Dress and Selected Color, Design, Texture and Personality Variables." Master's thesis, Utah State University, 1967.

[7]See, for example, the series of experiments reported in Edward L. Walker and Roger W. Heyns, *An Anatomy for Conformity* (Englewood Cliffs, N.J.: Prentice-Hall, 1962). Although not specifically related to clothing behavior, the factors that make for a high degree of conformity in human behavior are clearly described.

Figure 9.14 Figures in the entertainment world appeal to different subgroups of the population. *Annie Hall* was a smash hit.

"I feel like a damn fool."

Figure 9.15 People have a strong need to be "correct." Drawing by Richter; © 1970, The New Yorker Magazine, Inc.

limited or incomplete. "Independent thinking typically involves a deliberate exposing of oneself to the challenges and discomforts of uncertainty, of confusion, of alienation,"[8] but imitating the clothing behavior of a high-status person gives a feeling of assured success.

Obviously, different population subgroups take their clothing cues from various categories of leaders (Figure 9.14). Young teen-agers are apt to copy the current idols of the entertainment or athletic worlds. Women have a variety of sources to copy, depending on their roles and values. The "ten best-dressed list" is still an important source of fashion information, particularly for those in the upwardly mobile middle class. Others may find suitable models among the wives of prominent men or successful business and professional women. Men, too, have their fashion models. Those already of high status—leaders in politics, business, and the professions—are often copied by men on the way up the occupational ladder (Figure 9.15).

In an experimental study of junior high school girls, Traub tested the relative influence of peers and parents upon the subjects' opinions of "appropriate" dress. Regardless of the accuracy of the norm information given, peer group preferences were found to be far more important than parental opinions in shaping the clothing choices of the adolescents studied. Some popular leaders of the past seemed to have a personal quality that appealed to almost all age groups and class levels. Rudolph Valentino was such a person in the 1920s, Grace Kelly in the 1950s, and President and Mrs. Kennedy in the 1960s. There are still occasionally popular leaders that inspire fashion emulation. They are fewer in numbers, their appeal is shorter lived, and they do not leave a mark on a decade as previous personalities did. It is difficult to isolate a figure from the seventies that had a significant impact on fashion. Jackie Kennedy Onassis may have been the last of the fashion leaders. Clothing norms are derived from persons or groups who have high prestige and/or attract emulation, but

[8]Richard Crutchfield, "Independent Thought in a Conformist World," in *Conflict and Creativity, Part 2*, ed. Farber and Wilson, p. 210.

their influence in the last two decades has been more fleeting than in the past.

Years ago, Riesman suggested that American society fostered the development of an increasing degree of "other-directedness," that is, sensitivity to and concern for the opinions of others.[9] Centers attempted to compare the conforming behavior of "other-directed" and "inner-directed" persons by first telling them the opinions of a number of well-known and important people, and then asking for their responses to a series of items. Other-directed persons were found to be more susceptible than the inner-directed group to social influences, as measured by the similarity of their responses to the opinions of well-known and important others.[10]

Rogers attempted to test Riesman's theory specifically in the context of clothing behavior. Other-directed individuals, when found to deviate from the norm, tended to deviate in the direction of fashion innovation. When inner-directed individuals failed to follow the norm, their deviations were more often described as obsolescent.[11]

Pressures toward conformity also are thought to be related to the need for maintaining harmonious relations with others. Taylor's research supported such a theory by demonstrating that interaction-oriented subjects emphasized maintenance of harmonious group relationships over individualism, and that those who were high in interaction-orientation were also high in conformity in dress.[12]

Following the dictates of group opinion obviously has its rewards. A number of studies have identified a positive relationship between conformity to group standards of dress and peer acceptance.[13] Of the wide variety of individuals who have been tested, the vast majority desire to copy the modal style of dress for their respective social groups. Thus, conformity appears to have certain positive social values. On the other hand, however, conformity has been associated with a variety of psychological and personality inadequacies. Crutchfield, for example, reported that individuals who were high in conformity-proneness displayed feelings of personal inferiority coupled with an intense concern for other people's suggestions and opinions.[14] Those who exhibit greater independence of thought tend to rely on their own judgments (Figures 9.16 and 9.17).

Thus we have a picture of a clothing style being introduced and approved by persons of social status or prestige, with such endorsement spreading inevitably to the vast majority of the population. Imitating clothing styles worn by the leaders functions to help individuals identify with prestige models, thus bridging the gap, psychologically at least, between themselves and the model.

[9]David Riesman, *The Lonely Crowd* (New Haven: Yale University Press, 1950).

[10]Richard Centers, "Social Character and Conformity: A Differential in Susceptibility to Social Influences," *Journal of Social Psychology*, 60, No. 2 (1963) 343–349.

[11]Jean Rogers, "The Relationship of Conformity in Dress to Riesman's Theory of Social Character." Master's thesis, University of Nevada, 1967.

[12]Lucy C. Taylor, "Conformity in Dress and Selected Color, Design, Texture and Personality Variables." Master's thesis, Utah State University, 1967.

[13]For examples, see B. Smucker and A. Creekmore, "Adolescents' Clothing Conformity, Awareness, and Peer Acceptance," *Home Economics Research Journal*, December 1972, pp. 92–97; and Shally VanDeWal, "A Study of the Relationship Between Clothing Conformity and Peer Acceptance Among Eighth Grade Girls." Master's thesis, Purdue University, 1968.

[14]Crutchfield, "Independent Thought," p. 225.

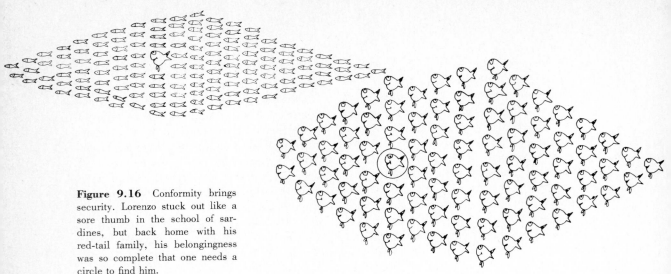

Figure 9.16 Conformity brings security. Lorenzo stuck out like a sore thumb in the school of sardines, but back home with his red-tail family, his belongingness was so complete that one needs a circle to find him.

The phenomenon of the fashion cycle can be explained in terms of social and psychological pressures toward conformity. When a new style is introduced, it is relatively easy to defend and maintain one's current tastes to one or two others, but more difficult to stand up against eight or ten. Yet there comes a point at which it

Figure 9.17 A human Lorenzo in a sea of homburgs. Find the man without a hat.

is no longer feasible to hold out against the tide of mass opinion. When fashion leaders adopt a new style, they are

objects of interest and excitement. . . . A few more follow, impelled to be *a la mode* by the need to assert their difference from those less fashionable. The bandwagon is gradually on and soon it begins to roll. In the end no one can afford to be different. The final blow comes when the woman standing aside appears ridiculous even to herself. "They" are no longer odd; she herself is. Popular taste, even one's own, has changed.[15]

Thus, fashion can be seen as a form of collective behavior in which people feel compelled to yield to a mass norm enforced by an anonymous multitude. The compelling nature of fashion is beyond the control of any single individual; its power lies in the collective definition of the clothing norm.

[15]Kurt Lang and Gladys Lang, *Collective Dynamics* (New York: Thomas Y. Crowell Company, 1968), p. 471.

SUMMARY

Norm Formation

Two social forces—conformity and individuality—form the basis for all fashion behavior. Conformity is both necessary and desirable to the extent that it provides for the transmission of functional normative patterns and gives the individual a sense of belonging. In the mass society, consumer demand for a style of dress often is enhanced by the mere fact that others are wearing it. This bandwagon effect may be demonstrated through a series of numerical tabulations called *fashion counts,* which help predict the life span of a fashion and also provide evidence of the degree of conformity that exists, nationally or locally, to a given clothing norm. Most fads and fashions reach their peak of popularity accompanied by an overeagerness in which people carry an idea to extremes.

The validation of new clothing styles by people of high status or prestige ultimately spreads the norm throughout the population. Conformity in dress appears to be widespread, and the desire to be like others is strongly reinforced in human interaction. Many people continue to rely on the judgment of others, particularly when their own understanding of the clothing norm is incomplete.

DEVIATION FROM THE NORM

The varieties of individuality are numerous, some socially acceptable and not only desirable but expected. In this category we can place those who start fashion, fashion leaders, and those who use individuality as true expressions of independent, creative minds. Nonconformity, on the other hand, may be seen as individuality, but it often results from unavoidable circumstances, such as marginality or minority status. Still other nonconformists may use individuality to express beliefs that differ from the norm, although they may adhere to a strict conformity of their own making. Subcultural and deviant groups may be included in the latter category.

Fashion Innovation

Just as clothing fashions provide an extraordinary opportunity to study contagion and conformity in mass behavior, so they provide a medium for observing the processes of innovation. Essentially, **fashion innovation** is a departure from the established norm and the creation of a new one.

For centuries, armchair philosophers have debated the question of where the source of fashion power really lies. Does it lie in the hands of a small group of dictatorial designers who push their styles on the helpless public without regard for people's needs and desires? Is it in the hands of the socially elite, the "fashion arbiters" of the upper class whom the masses seek to copy? Is the force controlled by those who spread fashion information, the publicists and editors of *Vogue, Harper's Bazaar, Mademoiselle, Women's Wear Daily,* and so forth who communicate, predict, and advise the public of the latest trends? Is the power restricted to the volume producers who choose from the designers' work only the models they care to promote and make available for mass consumption and who deliberately plan the premature obsolescence of products? Does the power lie with the ultimate consumer, the mass public, who in the end makes the decision to buy or not to buy, and whose changing tastes and craving for novelty create a demand for newness every season? Or is changing fashion a spontaneous reflection of other changes taking place in society, the "influence of the *Zeitgeist*," as Flügel calls it, "the climate of opinion, a sign of the times?"[16] The answer is as complex as the question. Each of the above plays an important role in the phenomenon of fashion, and each depends on the others.

Every style, of course, must have an origin, and the creation itself is the product of an innovator—an individual who designs for personal use or a professional who designs for others. To be successful, a professional innovator must know exactly how far departure from the current mode can be in any given year. Innovators remain in business only as long as they are able to net a profit, so they must somehow guess what people will buy before the people themselves are aware of it. If their styles run counter to the Zeitgeist, they are doomed to failure.

A number of people mistakenly believe that designers get together each season and plan the major style changes for the coming year. The clothing business is one of the most highly competitive industries in existence, and every house guards its new collections with the utmost secrecy. How is it then that such a marked degree of similarity is seen from one designer's collection to the next? For one thing, they are all subject to the same influences of the Zeitgeist: "it is inevitable that living in the same milieu, witnessing the same sights, selecting from the same fabric collections, subjected to the same influences, reading the same press, and meeting the same people, should result in similarity"[17] (Figure 9.18). Moreover, a designer must have accurate information about the market. Each season a careful stock-taking reveals which styles sold the best, how many of each were purchased and by whom, which ideas seemed to "catch on," and which models appear to have reached their saturation point. Most fashions are the result of slow evolutionary changes, and an analysis of the fashion cycle yields additional clues to the styles likely to become popular.

Fluctuations in the length of women's dresses may be used to illustrate the point. Skirts in the mid-1920s were the shortest they had ever been in costume history. From 1929 to 1932, skirts descended gradually, inch by inch, from knee level to bottom calf and remained at a low-level plateau for the ensuing three or four years. From 1936 to 1939, skirts inched their way back up to the knees. Three years later, when we might normally have expected another descent, Paris was under German occupation, and fashions in both the Unit-

[16]John C. Flugel, *Psychology of Clothes* (London: The Hogarth Press, 1930; reprinted 1950).

[17]Madge Garland, *Fashion* (Harmondsworth, Middlesex: Penguin Books, 1962), p. 54.

Figure 9.18 Professional designers must keep the Zeitgeist in mind.

"Hems are going down all over the world, Bradley. I fear they shall not go up again in our time."

Figure 9.19 What goes up must come down. Drawing by Carl Rose; © 1970, The New Yorker Magazine, Inc.

ed States and Great Britain were restricted by wartime fabric shortages. Fashion changes abruptly halted, and the short narrow skirt remained the accepted style of dress for over seven years, long enough to pass from fashionable dress to conventional dress. The distinction here is important because it helps to explain the mass resistance that met the *New Look* in 1947.

The *New Look* represented a revolutionary change from the broad-shouldered, straight-hipped wartime styles. It emphasized feminine curves, a tiny waist, a natural waist, a natural shoulder line, and, most conspicuously, a long full skirt that ended ten to eleven inches from the floor (Figure 9.19). The *Look* was attributed largely to the work of one designer, Christian Dior, whose fame and business skyrocketed as a result. Unfortunately, many writers use the *New Look* as the "classic example" of the way in which a designer superimposes ideas on a railroaded public. In actual fact, such drastic changes in dress have not occurred more than two or three times in costume history and have always been associated with other radical social or political change. The post-Revolutionary fashions in France and the *New Look* are the exceptions rather than the rule, although both were entirely consistent with the spirit of the times.

If the normal trend had not been interrupted by World War II, skirts probably would have made their evolutionary descent from 1942 to 1946, and a long skirt in 1947 would have been nothing at all unusual. Instead, having become so accustomed to their habitual short skirts, people protested strongly—and then went out and bought a new wardrobe anyway.

From 1947 on through the fifties and sixties, hemlines crept almost unnoticed back toward the knee—so slowly in fact, that the change only came when a woman put a new coat over an old dress and discovered that a half inch was visible beneath the coat bottom. Then, an incident occurred that seemed to demonstrate that the *New Look* would never have been successful in 1947 had the social climate not been ripe for a change. In 1963, skirts had been on the rise for fifteen years, and every good designer worth his salt knows that what goes up must come down. The trick, of course, is in knowing when the peak has been reached. At least one Paris designer felt the trend had been going on long enough, and Jacques Heim's fall collection that year came out in midcalf lengths. He was the only one—just as Dior had been the only one in 1947—but this time the guess was wrong. The current was too strong to stem the tide, and skirts continued on their upward course.

By 1970 it seemed that hemlines had reached their peak (both literally and figurätively), and fashion publicists began to push "the longuette" (otherwise known as the midi). Radical departures from the current mode always bring mostly negative reaction, and protests against the midcalf length were accordingly nationwide. True, the mini had reached its culmination, but the normal cycle had not been interrupted as it had been in the forties, and the drop was too abrupt. Consumers would not buy the midi—but neither did they buy more minis. For the first time in fashion history women chose to wear what they wanted. They wore their skirts at whatever length they chose or switched to bifurcates. By the end of the seventies skirts again stopped just below the knee, but the progression had been gradual, orderly, and widely accepted.

A radical innovation usually is required to change any style that has been firmly established for a long time. The cropped, "clean-cut" hair style for men was a universal norm for two thirds of a century. It took a few innovators with shoulder-length locks to shake the crewcut out of its rut. Extreme styles, however, rarely become the fashion. The innovation is nearly always modified before it is accepted by the masses.

In general, men's styles are more deeply entrenched and slower to change than women's, but the fashion cycle is there. Shoulders go from padded to unpadded, lapels and ties progress from wide to narrow, trousers move from tapered to full.

Designers provide the inspiration for clothing norms, but the consuming public makes the fashion.

Fashion Leadership

The **fashion innovator** plays an important role in the whole process of fashion change by assuming responsibility for introducing a new style. The innovator, however, rarely has the power to enforce mass acceptance of any creation. A new idea must progress through an established pattern of legitimization before it becomes the popular norm. Only a small percentage of a given population, not more than 15 percent, are early adopters, that is, those who will buy a new style in its beginning stages.

The vast majority of the population are **fashion followers**, the people who are responsible for the mass acceptance of a style. Some who fall into this category adopt a style before it reaches its peak, and others are among the last to take it on during its period of greatest popularity. Those who continue to wear a style long after its popularity has faded might be classified as **fashion obsolescents**.

In several studies, observations of fashion innovations have supported this theory of diffusion and acceptance. ZoBell's investigation, for example, began with the introduction of mid-length skirts in the fall of 1970. In every group she observed, a few tried out the new long lengths, but the number never exceeded 5 percent, even at the height of the midi's promotion in the current fashion magazines and papers.[18] Thus, the midi did not succeed immediately as a norm replacement. Most people, probably as high as 80 percent, are followers rather than initiators. They conform to the fads the leaders start.

There is a very clear distinction between initiators or early adopters and the small elite group of influentials who are truly the **fashion leaders**. The term *fashion leadership* is applied to the process of influencing others to accept a style innovation as a replacement for the currently accepted norm. Fashion leaders are the people who legitimize an innovation and make it a fashion item.

There always used to be fashion leaders. Status gives impetus to fashions, and the notion that the "best" people are wearing them (however you define "best") constitutes an endorsement for acceptance. In primitive societies, the successful warrior set the pattern in feathers, paint, and other forms of ornamentation. Until the end of the eighteenth century, new forms of dress were legitimized largely within the court circles; the kings and other royalty were the supreme dictators of fashion change. After the French Revolution, there were no ruling sovereigns with sufficient power or magnetism to exercise much influence, and fashion leadership fell to the well-known "dandies." Most famous among these was George Bryan (Beau) Brummell, who had

an eye for propriety and demanded perfection in fit and in workmanship.

By the beginning of the nineteenth century fashion leadership had passed from the ruling class to a set of socially elite men and women who had both wealth and influence. The important requisites generally were personal attractiveness, perfect taste, and enough money to allow an occasional mistake or misjudgment. Today, an additional requirement is a social life that gives the individual opportunities to be filmed and photographed. The last criterion is an important link in the whole communication network, because it keeps the leader in the public eye and illustrates the styles that are approved.

The vast majority still looks for a kind of symbolic leader, a person who sets the example. By copying the leader's style, the masses achieve an identification with and share in the leader's prestige. In the wake of an antimaterialistic ethic, however, prestige has faded from the wealthy elite and new mass communication media models have replaced them (Figure 9.20).

There is also growing evidence that such copying is not a direct process, but rather one that must pass the approval of a reference group before it is taken on by the individual. Rogers suggests that there are basically five steps in the process of adopting a new norm or practice.[19] First is the *awareness stage*, in which the individual is exposed to the new style, followed by the *interest stage*, in which additional information about it is sought and the opinions of others heeded. Third is the *evaluation stage*, when the possibility of trying it out is made. Fourth is the *trial*

[18]Toni ZoBell, "Fashion Diffusion: Influence of Mass Media and Prestigious Reference Groups." Master's thesis, University of Nevada, 1972.

[19]E. M. Rogers with F. Shoemaker, *Communication of Innovations* (New York: Free Press, 1971), p. 100. Rogers named the stages; the interpretations in relation to clothing have been added.

Figure 9.20 The social elite have gradually been replaced by mass communication media models. The symbolic fashion leader usually has admirers and followers who seek to identify with the prestige model by taking on the same manner of dress.

stage of testing the innovation by wearing it on a limited basis. Last is the *adoption stage,* when the decision is made to wear the new style on a broader basis.

Here we see an intermediate step in which the individual is influenced by certain key people in the environment. In other words, information about the new style (its "goodness" or "badness") filters first through the opinion leaders of the primary reference group and is then relayed to the less active individuals. In effect, the opinion leader in the smaller reference group exercises the greatest power in adoption of a new norm and the immediate social group can offer the rewards for conformity or apply sanctions to those who deviate.

In most cases, even the symbolic fashion leaders are not the very first to wear the new styles. They pick up somebody's innovative idea and give it status. Their departures from the current norm are regarded not as violations but as precedents for the proper and acceptable thing to do. Opinion leaders always know how far they can go without appearing ridiculous.

But unlike the innovators, they tend not to be highly creative themselves. It is not surprising, therefore, that the college women Kernaleguen tested who scored high on fashion leadership also scored significantly low in creativity.[20] In another study, Schrank found fashion innovators to have a relatively high degree of psychological security; fashion leaders, on the other hand, tended to express more conforming attitudes toward clothing and in general came from higher socioeconomic levels than the innovators.[21]

There is considerable evidence that leaders are popular, so it follows that the popular thing to wear is what the leaders wear. Whether they are symbolic leaders or leaders within a primary subgroup, they appear to share certain qualifications.

[20]Anne Kernaleguen, "Creativity Level, Perceptual Style, and Peer Perception of Attitudes Towards Clothing." Ph.D. diss., Utah State University, 1968.
[21]Holly Schrank, "Fashion Innovativeness and Fashion Opinion Leadership as Related to Social Insecurity, Attitudes Toward Conformity, Clothing Interest and Socioeconomic Level." Ph.D. diss., Ohio State University, 1970.

Figure 9.21 Presidents Truman, Kennedy, and Johnson had limited fashion effect. Loud sport shirts, the Harvard Look, and ten-gallon hats had Washington approval.

First, they must exemplify certain values, values that are held to be important by the individual. Second, they must be regarded as competent, that is, having more expertise or knowledge about dress and appearance than anyone else (this was Beau Brummell's claim to fame). Last, they must be in a strategic social location that gives them high visibility, public exposure, and a wide range of contacts. Many studies have demonstrated a high degree of relationship between fashion leadership and participation in social activities.[22]

Although they do not meet all the criteria in the last paragraph, American presidents have been known to exert some fashion influence (Figure 9.21). Harry Truman gave the stamp of approval to loud sport shirts worn outside the pants, and John Kennedy started the trend toward the Harvard Look. Lyndon Johnson improved the hat business considerably with his

preference for the ten-gallon variety. A modified form, in five-gallon sizes, brought renewed interest in a broader-brimmed hat for men. Gerald Ford probably set no fashion trends in motion but his nonconforming style provoked considerable comment by the press. He did make informality acceptable for both official and unofficial functions. According to the White House tailor, "the President's Middle American mod choice in clothes has been a bit too flashy for the White House."[23]

The crux of all fashion activity, however, lies in the complementary behavior of leaders and followers. Fashion innovations are made by those who wish to set themselves apart from others in the mass society. Fashion leaders select from those innovations the styles to which they give their approval and thereby legitimize them for the masses. The masses, in turn, seek to identify with the leaders' prestige and to copy them. As the fashion becomes available to all, its symbolic value of distinction

[22]One example is offered by Helen Allen, "Adolescent Fad and Fashion Leaders Compared with Fad and Fashion Non-Leaders on Selected Personality Factors and Social Participation." Master's thesis, University of Tennessee, 1971.

[23]"Coming On Like a Cocktail Cowboy," *Time*, November 3, 1975.

is lost to the person who started it. Thus, the first to accept the new styles are also the first to abandon them.

Taylor's study of fads at the high school level showed a relationship between fad adoption and status. Senior students were usually the first to take up a fad; by the time most of the juniors hopped on the bandwagon, the fad had already lost its novelty for the seniors, and they soon dropped it entirely.[24] This continual process of innovation, legitimation, and emulation marks the ever-present struggle by some to attain exclusiveness, and the compelling desire on the part of others to be current. "To look like nobody else is mortifying; to be mistaken for one of the rabble is worse."[25] The resulting product of this circular pattern is the phenomenon of the fashion cycle. High fashion has snob appeal to the leader, that is, its attractiveness lies in the fact that few other people can affort it. The true fashion, however, depends on the snowballing effect of the bandwagon; it is carried by the masses who cannot afford to be left out or to be different. Paradoxically, once everyone wears the fashion, it no longer offers distinction to anyone. As soon as it reaches its peak of saturation, everyone tires of the current fashion and it soon fades into oblivion. All fashions end in excess.

New styles are legitimized through the approval given them by people of prestige status. Such referent individuals may be symbolic leaders or opinion leaders within a primary subgroup.

[24]Anne W. Taylor, "An Investigation of Some Aspects of Clothing Fads and Fashions in Junior and Senior High School" Master's thesis, Cornell University, 1964.

[25]William Hazlitt, "On Fashion," in *The Complete Works of William Hazlitt*, Vol. 17, ed. P. P. Howe (London: J. M. Dent and Sons, 1933).

Diffusion of Fashion

If an individual or a group is to conform to a particular pattern of clothing behavior, information about the normative expectation must be spread.

All clothing innovations are not the exclusive possessions of professional designers, but for the bulk of the ready-to-wear industry the designer's showroom is the source of most new styles. Between designer and consumer, a number of mass media and interpersonal communications take place, each of which exerts some influence in the adoption of styles that ultimately become popular fashions.

Fashion and Trade Publications

Journalists who write for the daily newspapers and fashion magazines reach an immense public. "The fashion editor has two potent weapons: silence and space. She can ignore the collections she considers bad, and she can give the largest possible amount of space to those she thinks good, with priority in placing and the preference, if any, of colour reproductions."[26] Usually the fashion editor gives the style a name (that is, the A-line, the longuette, hotpants) that helps to identify the innovation. This initial filtering process has a tremendous influence on what the customer will look for in the shops the following season.

Misjudgment of consumer needs for ·change combined with overenthusiastic promotion can be disastrous when the influence of the press gears the industry toward a style that is not accepted. The fashion press, primarily the trade publications, were responsible, at least partly, for

[26]Garland, *Fashion*, p. 105.

the results of a major style failure in 1972. They predicted the midcalf and lower midi and maxi skirt lengths, which never caught on. Women either refused to reconstruct their wardrobes or just did not like the looks of the long skirts. They stuck to minis or turned to pants.

Similar predictions, but not on as large a scale, were made for longer skirts in 1978–1979. Women responded more favorably this time, perhaps because the shift was gradual. Skirts had been getting longer, whereas in 1972 the change was abrupt. Although more widely accepted, the longer skirts of 1978 really only lasted a season; by the fall of 1979 skirts were rising again.

Apparel Manufacturers

Since it is only through the ready-to-wear market that a style can become a fashion, the choices made by apparel manufacturers are crucial decisions. No manufacturer can afford to embark on large-scale production of a design without reasonable assurance that it will be widely accepted. In order to back up the choices made, therefore, advanced publicity for the selected models is immediately started to assure consumer demand.

Fashion Consultants

These are the reporters and interpreters of the fashion scene on national, international, and local levels. They cover everything from charity balls to rock concerts. They observe what people are wearing; they keep abreast of social, artistic, and economic trends that have an impact on fashion. They scout the local scene in cities all over the world. From this wealth of data, they sort, assimilate, evaluate, and then send a weekly report on fashion trends to their clients.

Central Buying Offices

Many retail stores use the services of resident buying offices located in the strategic market centers of the country. Staff in these offices make a daily check of the market and keep the retailers informed about national trends on fast-selling styles, daily and weekly price fluctuations, and supply conditions in general. In most instances, the buying offices do no direct buying but simply act as advisers, reporting on what is selling, looking for new items, placing reorders, and perhaps working on special promotions.

The Retail Buyer

The retailer of fashion merchandise is the person responsible for getting the kind of goods the customer wants into the store at the time the customer wants to buy them. Overall selections made by the retailer usually take into account both national and local fashion trends. Selections made by the buyer are certainly important in shaping consumer tastes. However, the retailer is also guided by the daily and weekly sales records. The actual purchasing of goods by the consumer influences these sales records.

Communication within these mass-media channels is a two-way process. There are a variety of ways in which the consumer feeds information back into the whole process. To be sure, an effective promotion and advertising campaign can contribute a great deal to the acceptance of a style, and within certain limits the journalists, manufacturers, and retailers are in a position to manipulate the mass taste. However, the critical decision to adopt or to reject an innovation is still made by the majority on an interpersonal, individual basis.

If we go back to the five steps in the adoption process, it becomes obvious that the mass-media communication channels are particularly effective in creating awareness of the innovation and in providing information about it to the potential adopter. Some research evidence shows that the early adopters or fashion leaders are inclined to use mass media rather than interpersonal contacts as a source of fashion information.[27] But for most people, some further legitimation of the style becomes necessary before they are willing to try it themselves. The opinion leader within the immediate reference group thus becomes the key agent of influence in the step toward mass acceptance.[28] The reference group, moreover, has the power to apply the sanctions for conforming or not conforming to the expected behavior.

Time is also an important factor in the fashion diffusion process. The time lag from the introduction of a new idea to its widespread adoption is one measure we use to differentiate among the various types of clothing norms. We also use the time variable to distinguish the fashion leaders from the fashion followers and the followers from the obsolescents. Further, by analyzing the time it takes for an incoming fashion to gain acceptance, we can estimate its life span with greater accuracy.

SUMMARY

Deviation from the Norm

Fashion changes are caused by the substitution of new clothing norms for established ones. The process through which such substitution is made may originate with the designer, although all successful innovations are based on a thorough understanding of cyclical trends and consumer demand. Fashions are spread through the work of fashion editors and reporters, photographers and illustrators, publicity campaigns of the volume producers, and retail store advertising. In this way, the average consumer is given the fashion information necessary regarding the potential norm replacement.

However, before a new style is accepted as a norm, it must progress through an established pattern of legitimation. The validation of new clothing norms takes place through the process of fashion leadership, in which persons of high prestige or status give their approval to particular styles. Even in the case of superficial fads, most of which are initiated locally, the power to start a fashion

---

[27]Margaret Grindereng, "Fashion Diffusion," *Journal of Home Economics* (March 1967), 171–174.

[28]In distinguishing between opinion leaders and their followers, Rogers noted that opinion leaders in a group have greater exposure to mass media, demonstrate a higher degree of social participation, enjoy a higher social status, and tend to be more innovative than their followers (Rogers, *Communication of Innovations*).

lies with those who have demonstrated opinion leadership. Fashion leaders depart from the established norm because they seek to set themselves apart from others in the mass society. As their styles are copied by the masses, the quality of distinctiveness is lost, so the first to adopt the new styles are also the first to abandon them.

NONCONFORMITY

Gradual acquisition of the knowledge necessary for an individual to do what is expected begins early in childhood and continues throughout life. Conformity provides a solid basis for transmission of the culture and preservation of civilization, but complete dedication to the status quo stifles the kinds of creative imagination and activity that are essential to progress and social diversity. Although the vast majority of people choose to dress as others dress, some members of society strive to be different. Fashion innovation is one form of deviation from the established norm, but other types of nonconformity also may be observed. Some individuals are able to make clothing decisions that are completely independent of the fashion norm. Still others belong to marginal groups that seek to replace the mass norms with norms of their own creation.

Marginal Groups

In preceding chapters, several examples were given of certain types of subcultural groups that tend to substitute counter norms for the norms of the larger society. Many minority groups find outlets for expression through their particular kind of deviation from clothing norms. Marginal groups are characterized by a degree of alienation from the general social structure, and consequently they are more prone to violate the conventional modes of dress. Groups that lack full acceptance often seek recognition by establishing their own group codes. Their dislike of society is reflected directly in their refusal to meet the standard clothing requirements.

Throughout history, there have always been groups that have considered themselves the symbols of nonconformity (the "incroyables" of the eighteenth century, the "aesthetes" in the 1880s, the "beatniks," the "hippies"). In any era, their style of dress is the exact opposite of the currently accepted mode. In other words, they demonstrate an acute sensitivity to society's norms and adopt a dress style that is deliberately counter to those norms. In the process they create norms of their own. As Crutchfield cautions,

the mere fact that the individual does sometimes express eccentric and deviant ideas is not necessarily proof of independent thinking in him. For one thing, this may simply reflect his conformity to the thinking of a socially deviant group. Or, for another thing, this may simply reflect his deliberate rejection of the majority group's ideas or the prevailing social norms.[29]

It is all a matter of conforming to the clothing expectations of the group with which we identify. Members of marginal

[29]Crutchfield, "Independent Thought," p. 211.

groups are usually those who experience similar problems of adaptation to society and find mutual support in a collective solution to feelings of powerlessness and isolation. Adolescents are among those who are especially susceptible to status problems.

Conformity among teen-agers is extremely high, particularly conformity to peer group norms. Those who try to be drastically different from other students either crave to be noticed or find that this is one way to defy the conventions of a society that has somehow discriminated against them. Many deviants have very low self-esteem; they are misfits trying to be something other than what they really are. Klapp contended, in 1969, that this was not confined to the adolescence stage; he felt that our whole society was undergoing what he called "identity dislocation."[30] He thought the dislocation developed as the result of a breakdown in status symbols, with a tendency for fashions to obscure classes in society rather than to mark differences between them. Overall, he said, we became a society of "made-up" people masquerading in search of identity. The extremes in faddism and exhibitionism in dress, so obvious at that time, were forms of ego-screaming that pleaded "Look at me, look at me!" (Figure 9.22).

Marginal groups, then, are both conformists and nonconformists. In the process of growing up, adolescents move away from parental influence and domination; they rebel. At the same time, they yield to the pressures of the peer group to which they cling for support and thereby conform. Thus, marginal and subcultural groups tend to seek recognition by conforming to countercodes of dress, and at the same

[30]Orrin Klapp, *Collective Search for Identity* (New York: Holt, Rinehart & Winston, 1969).

Figure 9.22   Liberace's red-white-and blue fringed and spangled hotpants, covered with beads and other jewels, were designed by the entertainer himself. *No one* could call Liberace a conformist.

time, refusing to conform to society's norms. A rigidly structured class system that encourages extreme conventionality in dress reinforces the subgroup. Greater tolerance for expression of deviant tendencies reduces pressures toward conformity.

Marginal and subcultural groups are nonconformists in the sense that they violate the dress codes of the larger society. They are conformists in the sense that they meet the counternorms created by the deviant group.

Individuality

Fashion leaders are nonconformists in that they constantly seek to be different from those who follow their actions. Like the counterconformist, their behavior is based on an awareness of the norm and a desire to set themselves apart from it. Neither one (fashion leader nor counterconformist) can operate independently from mass behavior; the fashion leader must be ahead of it, the counterconformist against it.

The true individualist, on the other hand, is one who can make a decision that

Figure 9.23   Bella Abzug's hats set her apart from other women.

is independent of group action (Figure 9.23). Such behavior requires an independence of thought and action that stems from a set of strong and internalized standards, and it is what Riesman describes as "inner-directed," that is, characterized by individual conscience and self-imposed goals. The ability to resist group pressure requires a high degree of psychological security as well as extreme faith in one's personal convictions. The individualist is often regarded as something of an eccentric and consequently must have the strength to withstand the criticism or ridicule brought on by deviations in dress.

Although research is limited, some evidence shows that the true nonconformist is more independent, more socially secure, more creative, and more intelligent than most conformists.[31] Conversely, there is also the suggestion that conformists tend to be more other-directed, more submissive, more conventional in values, less creative, and more dependent, with greater needs for social approval than nonconformists.

No one fits precisely and consistently into any one of these categories. Each of us finds that we conform to group standards in some situations and feel freer to express our individuality in others. Conformity tends to help people fit into their social roles; individuality fosters creative expression and facilitates an intelligent, rational, and free choice among the available alternatives in the selection of clothing. The ascendance of either set of values, with the accompanying consequences, depends on one's personal needs and desires.

Individuality in dress requires a strong sense of personal conviction and psychological security.

SUMMARY

Nonconformity

Several types of nonconformity may be observed in the clothing behavior of individuals and groups in society. Subcultural and marginal groups tend to substitute counternorms, which in turn dictate the dress standards followed by

[31]A broad generalization, but look at the findings of such studies as: B. White and A. Kernaleguen, "Comparison of Selected Perceptual and Personality Variables Among College Women Deviant and Non-Deviant in Their Appearance," *Perceptual and Motor Skills*, 32 (1971), 87–92; Elva Heidle, "The Extent of Conformity to the Modal Pattern of Dress as Related to Selected Student Variables for University of Tennessee Women," Master's thesis, University of Tennessee, 1970; and Judith Herk, "Clothing Conformity-Nonconformity as Related to Social Security-Insecurity for a Group of College Women." Master's thesis, Pennsylvania State University, 1968.

Figure 9.24 On a hot day in New York, this shopper attracted the stares of curious passersby. The individualist usually is regarded as something of an eccentric and must have a relatively high degree of psychological security to "carry it off."

their members. Wide discrepancies in dress between the subgroup norms and the general norms usually indicate the degree of alienation from the larger society. Members of such groups are nonconformists only in the sense that they do not meet the standards of society in general, but they are conformists to subgroup deviations.

Fashion leaders themselves are nonconformists in their striving to be different. Others, lacking the power to become leaders, openly defy the accepted dress standards by assuming a contrary position that will insure their being noticed. Their action, however, still depends on group opinion. The true individualist is guided by an independence of thought and action that neither relies on group opinion nor deliberately counteracts it (Figure 9.24). Conformity helps people to fit more easily into their social roles, but individuality is necessary for a completely rational choice among available alternatives.

FOR FURTHER READING

Darden, Norma Jean. "Harlem's Fashion Museum: Lois Alexander Traces Our Fashion Roots." *Essence*, 10 (November 1979), 82–83.

Hollander, Anne. "Vintage Clothes." *Vogue*, 169 (April 1979), 273 ff.

König, René. *The Restless Image: A Sociology of Fashion*. London: George Allen and Unwin Ltd., 1973, pp. 176–184.

Rosencranz, Mary Lou. *Clothing Concepts: A Social-Psychological Approach*, pp. 99–110. New York: The Macmillan Company, 1972.

"The Hat: Back After a Brief Disappearance." *Americana*, 7 (March/April 1979), 48–49.

Chapter 10

VALUES,
ATTITUDES, INTERESTS

Up to this point we have discussed clothing in relation to two major components of culture: the material artifacts created and used by people; and the sociofacts, or institutions and cultural patterns that govern behavior. The third major element of culture involves ideas—the mentifacts of life. This component holds the vast body of knowledge and beliefs that underlie or account for particular choices and judgments. These mentifacts include the values, attitudes, interest, goals, and ambitions that direct people as they follow any of several alternate courses of action.

Mentifacts are very important. They are not directly observable, but they may be identified by noting the choices people make, the attention they give to some things and not to others, what they say is

important or unimportant, and the kinds of behavior they approve or criticize. In this context, clothing reflects the ideas people hold to be of value. As an oversimplified illustration, we might say that the ever-increasing tendency toward greater uniformity in dress is tangible evidence of one of our strongest political beliefs, that all people are created equal, and that the wide discrepancy in styles of dress between nobles and peasants in feudal times reflected the conviction of that time that each person was born to a station in life, a place in the hierarchy of power and prestige.

Within economic limitations, people clothe themselves in the type of dress they think they should wear. The words *should* and *ought* express values because they imply that some judgment of relative worth is being made. Consciously or unconsciously, every individual reflects a set of beliefs through the clothing choices made. In this sense, the set of beliefs and values provides a central motivating force in human action and clothing behavior. Belief in the Wesleyan translation of religious doctrine that "cleanliness is next to godliness," for example, prompts the daily bath, the weekly shampoo, a regular change of underwear, and a clean shirt every day. Putting it into words, a person might say, "It really doesn't matter what you wear as long as it's neat and clean."

For some Americans, cleanliness does not come before other crucial values, but takes its place within a hierarchy of dominant to subordinate values. Such variation complicates the study of values but it does not rule out the possibility of identifying the typical pattern of beliefs and values that may characterize a particular culture, a historical era, a group, a family, or an individual.

THE CULTURAL SETTING

Like other aspects of culture, beliefs and values are not inherited. They are acquired in the process of living with others and sharing ideas. A culture's dominant themes are reflected in those values that are most commonly shared, and the socialization of the individual always occurs within the value patterns that prevail in the larger cultural group. Even in the pluralistic United States, a national character develops. It is unseen and unrecognized by the very people who show it but it is identified immediately by the people who are not subject to its uniformities. And although it changes continuously, some basic aspects of this national character seem to persist from generation to generation.

Although it is always dangerous to try to define a national "personality" or "type," there seems to be enough evidence of the difference in value patterns among various peoples and periods to note existence of certain dominant themes. Our purpose here is to illustrate a few of the ways in which clothing relates to the ideas and values in different cultures and in different periods.

Women in China

In Chapter 2, Chinese men's dress was used to show transitional variations in cultural patterns of dress. Chinese costume is a particularly good example because the country has had very marked changes in ideologies and because the current socialistic ideal represents a set of values that differs sharply from those of a democracy.

Up to the time of the 1911 revolution, Chinese women were expected to lead a secluded existence. The social restraints imposed on them were symbolized by their bound feet and cumbersome robes, both of which reflected a physical and mental withdrawal from the outside world. Little girls' feet were tightly bound from childhood on and the result was a small deformed foot that resembled a tiny hoof (Figure 10.1). This distortion led to the mincing steps and teetering gait that characterized the traditional Chinese woman. Abolition of this painful custom was among the reforms the revolution brought.

Reform in dress was the natural accompaniment to a reform in status. A great

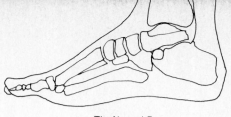

The Normal Foot

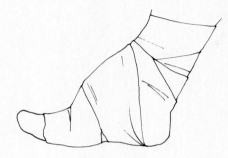

The Bound Lily Foot

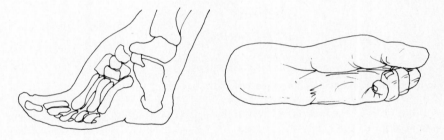

Changes in Structure of the Lily Foot

Figure 10.1 The deformed foot that resulted from tight binding. It was called the lily foot.

confusion of styles followed, mostly a mixing of Chinese elements like the short tunic with long, full skirts and Western shoes (Figure 10.2). Women groped for a dress style compatible with the demands of their new emancipated status without going too far from the traditional styles. Between 1912 and 1915, a modernized version of the old tunic and trousers appeared. It allowed a freedom of movement and became a step toward a new national style.

Two other factors influenced Chinese women during this period. Like their Western sisters, they began to take a more active part in the expanding world of sports, and the tubular, short-skirted fashions that evolved in Europe and America during the 1920s affected Chinese styles. The whole aim of Western dress seemed to be to display the leg and turn the body into a tube. The Chinese considered skirts above the knees altogether too immodest, so they achieved a similar effect by lengthening the tunic and keeping the slits up the sides. The resulting one-piece dress became known as the *ch'i p'ao*. Chinese women had at last achieved a basic style that represented the period's important

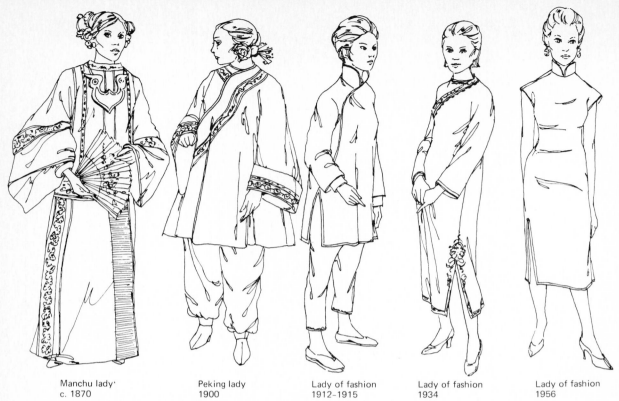

| Manchu lady· c. 1870 | Peking lady 1900 | Lady of fashion 1912-1915 | Lady of fashion 1934 | Lady of fashion 1956 |

Figure 10.2 Transition in Chinese women's dress.

values—a distinctive, recognizable national dress, a symbol of their active, progressive way of life, and a costume that was both fashionable and flattering to their racial characteristics.

When the Communists came into power in 1949, they brought a philosophy that recognized no distinction in rank or in sex. Men and women both wore the drab tunic, trousers, and soft, peaked cap. By 1950, the glamorous and feminine *ch'i p'ao* had entirely disappeared from the mainland, along with jewelry, cosmetics, and all other forms of decoration. The colorless uniform became an ideological symbol that expressed economic austerity, practical utility, and absolute classlessness. China was a worker state and life was shorn of frivolity. Faced with the more pressing problems of economic shortages, the Communists regarded dress, adornment, and

Figure 10.3 At the Nixons' official 1972 reception in Peking, Chinese women wore similar versions of the Nationalist uniform topped with black or navy coats.

beauty as not only dispensable, but even unpatriotic. Drabness became the national mode (Figure 10.3).

While all these changes were taking place, the country people working in the fields continued to wear their simple and loosely cut tunic and trousers. Their work, status, and values remained unchanged— and so did their dress. Because there was no shift in the dominant value patterns of the peasantry, there was relative stability in their national dress.

A hierarchy of values is represented by the particular forms of dress that become characteristic of a people. Clothing thus presents a value model in shaping national attitudes.

Fashion in the Nineteenth Century

Change in the dominant ideals of a culture occurs slowly and is frequently a difference in emphasis rather than a complete departure from earlier value patterns. The changes that seem so radical in revolutionary upheaval are expressions of feelings that have been smouldering for some time under the imposed cover of entrenched social and political institutions. Moreover, once the extremes of pent-up emotions are spent, the relationship to the historical past becomes reestablished.

The nineteenth century is no better example than any other century, except perhaps that it began just after a revolution. The preceding period was marked by an excessive lavishness of dress that symbolized an elegant, sophisticated way of life. Even before the French Revolution, French intellectuals had begun to admire the simplicity of the English country gentleman's costume. During the Revolution it

was not safe to appear in the streets in beautiful clothes, but it was not until the upheaval subsided that people had time to express their reaction through dress.

The most extreme stand was taken by the *incroyables* (the incredibles) and the *merveilleuses* (their feminine counterparts), who registered their contempt by a deliberate, contrived disarray of their clothes. Their uncombed hair hung in slovenly fashion from beneath their beaver hats, and their tight trousers, clumsy boots, coats with huge lapels, wrinkled cravats, and heavy knotted walking sticks all suggested the exact opposite of the sleek-groomed refinement of the earlier period. The mode was short-lived, however, and Frenchmen soon settled for the tastes of the English tailor, whose styles were simplified versions of the former court costume adapted to the outdoorsman's rugged life.

Women's fashions proved more flexible in reflecting the change in dominant ideals. The growing interest in classical forms resulting from discovery of the ancient cities of Pompeii and Herculaneum led to a revival of the Greek and Roman dress styles. Women did their best to look like antique statues, draping their cashmere shawls to effect a classical pose (Figure 10.4). This neoclassicism in dress symbolized a corresponding return to the political ideas of the early Greek democracy and republican Rome.

When the Bourbons returned to power following the defeat of Napoleon, they seemed to think they could restore the leisured and privileged days before the Revolution by reviving the styles of an earlier period in French history. Costume balls became the rage, and an odd mixture of period revivals characterized the styles of dress. Laver believes that the reappearance of the neck ruff helped to restore an

Figure 10.4 Influence of the classic revival (c. 1799). Except for the bonnet, she could have been an ancient Greek.

element of prudery to the value pattern of society:

After Waterloo the whole of French society was in conscious or unconscious reaction against the libertinage of the Revolutionary period and even of the Empire. Though Napoleon had done his best to introduce a more moral tone into his immediate circle, the example people remembered was that of Josephine, and Josephine had never been a prude. Gone were the days when ladies thought it permissible to bare their bosoms in the public street, to walk about bare-throated even in winter. . . . Now dresses rose to the throat, and a frill of lace seemed their obvious finish.[1]

[1]James Laver, *Taste and Fashion* (London: George G. Harrap & Company, 1945), p. 27.

The end of the 1830s marked the beginning of Victorianism, an age in which prudery seemed to be carried to all sorts of extremes. The nineteenth century catered to a new class of wealthy manufacturers who established their fortunes in the years following the Napoleonic wars. Such men were inclined to be hard-working and unpretentious, although somewhat puritanical in outlook, and these attitudes set the dominant tone of society. This, coupled with the growth of the democratic idea that all men were social equals, resulted in the somber, unattractive male apparel that continued for over a century.

The woman of this new class led the sheltered life of the gentlewoman. A lady had no responsibilities save her household duties, and a career was absolutely unthinkable. By far the most significant element in women's dress in the mid-1800s was the extended popularity of the crinoline. After the slender gowns of the Directoire, the silhouette was due for an increase in width, but the extreme skirt fullness that prevailed throughout the 1850s and 1860s could have occurred only through the added impetus given by the current social influences. The number of garments worn, for example, seemed to symbolize the material prosperity of the wearer, or at least that of her husband, and the difficulty with which fashionable ladies passed through doorways, entered carriages, and squeezed into church pews was enough to discourage anyone from straying far beyond the immediate surroundings. The skirt, moreover, created a physical barrier that kept men at "a proper distance."

The idea of the "liberated" woman began to take shape at the end of the century. The rise of a new attitude toward woman and her place in society gradually came about as the result of education and sports. In America, the passing of the Morrill Land Grant Act in 1862 brought the establishment of state universities throughout the nation, and the doors of higher education were at last opened to the daughters as well as to the sons of American families. No longer content to accept a life of dependency, women began to strike out for themselves. By accepting positions in offices and in the professions, they entered into a competition with men that was a new and purely economic kind.[2]

At the same time, a new mechanical invention called the bicycle appeared. The enthusiastic acceptance of cycling as a feminine sport created difficult problems for the moralists. Which was worse, hiking up skirts to reveal both ankle and calf, or enveloping legs in bloomers? Bloomers won out and went on to set a precedent for development of functional clothing in other areas of sport activities.

The body-revealing clothes that came about through the channel of sportswear conditioned society to a new set of values toward exposure of the female form, and in no small way contributed to freeing the modern woman from the conventionally circumscribed conduct of past generations.

Clothing has a reciprocal effect on social attitudes and values; it reflects the ideals already in existence and it also shapes ideas in the direction of change.

Fashions of the Flapper

In probably no other period of history has the fashion image of the woman been more symbolic of the spirit of the times than it was during the Roaring Twenties. Although the emancipation of women had been in progress for several decades, World War I gave it the final push. Women were on their own, and they liked it. Gone was the old ideal of the loving wife and mother; far from being admired, motherhood was to be avoided as long as possible.

The emphasis was on youth—a kind of eternal adolescence that indulged itself in extremes of dress and behavior. The flapper drank and, even worse, she smoked; her skirts grew shorter and shorter, revealing more than calves and knees when she sat down (Figure 10.5). All the attributes so long associated with the ideals of femininity were renounced. Women

Figure 10.5 This caricature by John Held, Jr., shows the famous flapper features: bobbed hair, painted lips, short skirt, rolled stockings, accent on legs.

[2]Ibid., p. 76.

cropped their "crowning glory" to a boyish bob; they all but abolished their breasts with a flattening brassière; and waists were completely hidden by a tubular silhouette that straightened out the natural female curves. If diet and exercise failed, women resorted to the corselet to achieve the hipless, bosomless, boyish figure that became the vogue. All attention was concentrated on the lower limbs, which, covered in flesh-colored stockings rolled to the knee, became the center of feminine seductiveness.

Feminine dress was, moreover, a frank expression of the stark functionalism that became the working philosophy of furniture designers and architects. Exposure of arms and legs was prompted by the same kind of thinking that exposed joints of the modernistic chair and the structural members of the contemporary house. The flapper so typified the ideals of the times that her name is synonymous with the age.

Clothing is a tangible, visual symbol of the ideas and values that typify the times.

SUMMARY

The Cultural Setting

Ideas and beliefs make up the third major component of culture. Mentifacts cannot be observed directly, but they are reflected in the clothes worn and the fashions that are typical of any given culture or period. Consciously or unconsciously, the choices made in selecting clothing reveal many of the things held important—democracy, equality, beauty, practicality, economy, extravagance, tradition, maturity, progress, individuality, austerity. These are the values and beliefs that are motivating forces in clothing behavior.

Value patterns differ from one culture to another and from one generation to the next. Dress in socialist China, for instance, is characterized by widespread uniformity, which contrasts with the rapidly changing fashions and great variety of styles that dominate democratic societies. Chinese dress, on the other hand, has been highly symbolic of women's changing status over the years. This has also been true in the Western world, where education (followed by economic independence) and participation in sports have been the natural forerunners of liberating fashions and increased social status.

GROUP AND INDIVIDUAL VALUES

Just as value patterns vary among cultures and between generations, so do they differ from one group to the next and from individual to individual. The chief agency

through which the individual acquires values is the family or kinship unit responsible for socializing the child in the early years. Children are quick to recognize those qualities that have high value and those that have none, behavior that brings reward or punishment, and actions that are admired or disapproved.

In most cases, the family experience is the most important in transmitting cultural patterns, but other agencies make significant contributions to idea formation and value orderings that eventually characterize the person as an adult. The school transmits attitudes and values as well as knowledge and skill and, at the same time, it provides a setting for the exchange of ideas within the peer group itself. In society today the influence of mass communication media is increasingly important in shaping the standards by which the younger generation will try to live. Movies, television, and the other forms of mass communication constantly present value models that either strengthen or weaken the teachings of the family and/or the school.

Values associated with clothing originate in the culture, are adopted by the family, and finally are transmitted to the child. However, in some cases the views—either of the family or of a subgroup with which the individual may identify—seriously conflict with those of the general culture. As children mature, the number of influences outside the family increases, and each exerts a varying degree of control over the children's thoughts and actions (Figure 10.6).

Theoretically at least, attitudes and values are significant because they represent an inclination to act. However, what a person thinks or says is not always consistent with what that person actually does. For this reason, researchers have divided values into component parts. One part represents an individual's conscious values, that is, the ideas that can be expressed verbally. These are sometimes

Figure 10.6 Belonging to Cub Scouts and wearing that uniform has an influence on the developing youth.

called **explicit** (or cognitive) **values** and they are what people say they believe. They may believe, for example, that others make judgments based on what is worn, or that clothing is not a valid criterion of one's real worth, or that the time one has to spend on clothes detracts from other more important things in life.

The behavioral component is inferred from what the person actually does. These are the **implicit** (or behavioral) **values,** which may not consciously be recognized by the individual. In actual fact, however, an observer may note that the individual wears inconspicuous clothes or may refuse to participate in certain social activities because of lack of appropriate attire. Implicit values are assumed to be conditioned by a third component, which is the way a person feels about a given object. These are **affective values**. With respect to clothing this could mean that an individual may be emotionally insecure or embarrassed about personal appearance, constantly worried or frustrated in an attempt to achieve the look desired.

Some research related to attitudes and values has been concerned with identifying the relationship among these three components—the cognitive, the behavioral, and the affective. Many studies have been limited to an assessment of attitudes held by particular groups or segments of the population. Still other researchers have concentrated on the larger value patterns into which individual attitudes are organized. This unique ordering of values ultimately helps us understand how people can resolve their value conflicts.

Clothing Values

Explicit values can be identified simply by asking people what factors influence their choice of clothes. Comments made by college women and collected over a period of several years have revealed attitudes similar to the following examples:[3]

In general, I refrain from extremes. Standing out in a crowd does not appeal to me.

I choose the conventional type of clothes that the majority of people are wearing.

I value being properly dressed for the occasion. Nothing makes me feel more uncomfortable than showing up in the wrong clothes.

These kinds of comments, and others about being "appropriately" or "simply" dressed, reflect a desire to conform to the general pattern of group dress; in terms of frequency, they constituted the type of comment made most often. Attitudes expressed often, but less frequently than

[3]Subjects were home economics students at the University of Nevada.

those illustrated above, pertained to a desire for self-expression:

I like to stand out in a crowd and have people notice me. Some of the clothes I wear I'm sure other people wouldn't think of wearing, but I enjoy clothes that are in some way different.

I'm continually searching for clothes that are new, different, and exciting. I make many of my own clothes because it gives me a sense of accomplishment, and more important, I don't see everybody else wearing the same thing.

Some researchers have defined this desire for self-expression as "individuality" or "distinctiveness" in dress. It is also like what some have termed the *exploratory* value in clothing, which refers to the use of clothing as a medium for experimentation.

Many statements showed a concern for beauty or becomingness, and these were categorized as aesthetic values:

I seek clothes in bright and cheerful colors, clothes that are becoming and flattering to my figure.

I feel that if a person has a few well-designed good-looking outfits that others will enjoy seeing her more than a person who wears a different costume every day.

Other comments referred to the prestige value of clothing:

I like to make a good impression on others. I'd like others to be able to tell that I know fashion and observe its rules.

In some studies this is called a *political* value in the sense that clothing is viewed as a vehicle for gaining prestige, leadership, or influence.

Some attitudes were centered around the desire for social participation and/or sexual attraction. This *social* value is directed toward a concern for the opinions of others:

Clothes are important to me in the way that others think about me; I believe I will have more social opportunities if I dress well.

I love clothes that are feminine. I must admit that I dress for the opposite sex, but then, who doesn't?

Comments relating to the values of comfort and economy also were made, but they were by far in the minority:

I consider first the economic and functional values. I don't feel I have to keep up with everybody else; I'd rather buy something a little less expensive and get more use out of it than waste money on clothes just because they're fashionable.

In general I choose clothes that are comfortable and practical. I avoid frills because they are neither functional or serviceable, and they require too much upkeep.

Economic values are usually thought of as those that emphasize conservation of time, energy, and/or money. The desire for comfort in dress is sometimes called a *sensory* value.

The dominant values reflected in these comments represent a very select segment of the population. Still, they do provide a framework for studying individual values as well as some basis for organizing them into broader value patterns.

Over the years, various measures have been devised to ascertain the relative importance of clothing in the individuals' lives. Several early studies seemed to indicate that women in general placed a higher value on clothes than men did. Silverman's work with adolescent girls, ranging in age from twelve to eighteen years, revealed a particularly high degree of interest among teen-agers; roughly 96 percent of those in the study expressed a willingness to sacrifice other values for the sake of clothes.[4] In 1949, Rosencranz reported findings on adult women. Females under twenty-five were found to attach greater importance to clothing than women over age thirty.[5] Baumgartner found that the amount of money college freshmen spent for clothes was observed to be higher among women than among men, and higher for members of sororities and fraternities than for independents. Measures used to establish the importance ascribed to clothing showed similar responses.[6]

A number of investigations have dealt not only with relative values, but with specific attitudes associated with clothes. One of the earliest of these was carried out by Hurlock in 1929.[7] At that time, the most prevalent attitude that seemed to determine whether or not a person spent a disproportionate amount of money on clothes was the feeling that clothes helped to put up a "good front," and thereby contributed to one's professional advancement. At the conscious level at least, people did not acknowledge that they used clothing as a status symbol, and men in

[4]Sylvia Silverman, *Clothing and Appearance; Their Psychological Implications for Teen-Age Girls* (New York: Teachers College, Columbia University, 1945).

[5]Mary Lou Rosencranz, "A Study of Women's Interest in Clothing," *Journal of Home Economics*, 41 (October 1949), 460–462.

[6]Charlotte W. Baumgartner, "Factors Associated with Clothing Consumption Among College Freshmen," *Journal of Home Economics*, 55 (March 1963), 218.

[7]Elizabeth Hurlock, "Motivation in Fashion," *Archives of Psychology*, 17, No. 111 (1929).

general claimed that a regard for modesty dominated their selection of apparel. Nevertheless, all the men studied believed that their estimate of a person was affected by the impression clothes made, and almost 97 percent of all subjects reported feelings of increased self-confidence when they were well dressed. About half of the women in the study indicated that they would deprive themselves of certain pleasures in life in order to be in fashion, and about a quarter of them would have foregone even necessities.

On the basis of the attitudes identified in Hurlock's survey, Barr went a step further in trying to determine the relative strength or importance of group attitudes toward clothing.[8] Results showed that the most fundamental attitudes associated with clothes were those related to the desire to conform, the desire for comfort and economy, the artistic impulse, and self-expression. These attitudes occurred so positively and so prevalently—cutting across differences in educational background, economic status, and other variable characteristics—that they were thought to be universal in nature. The desire to conform in matters of dress was the most widely diffused, varying only in intensity among the different groups studied. Warden's research, conducted almost a quarter of a century later, indicated that many of these same attitudes still persisted.[9] All the college women surveyed expressed a desire for clothes that would attract attention some of the time, but which would conform or be similar to those owned by

their friends. Although they regarded comfort and serviceability as important factors in clothing, they were not willing to sacrifice style or fashion for either one. It is interesting that Barr's analysis, made in the depression years of the early 1930s, perceived the "desire to appear prosperous" as being unimportant in the value patterns of her subjects. However, in the late 1950s, a period of economic prosperity, Warden's subjects wanted clothes to "be in large quantity" and to "look prosperous and expensive"—tangible evidence that attitudes and values are modified by changing conditions.

In 1958, Runbeck identified a number of different values college students held in selection of apparel, but most subjects believed that it was important to be fashionably dressed.[10]

A decade later, the interest in fashion appeared to subside, at least at the cognitive level. The young liberals were declaring that "fashion" was "out of fashion," and the values of "comfort" and "convenience" became the current catch words. To be lavishly dressed in the latest high fashion was even considered by the wives of political candidates in the 1972 election to be professionally hazardous.

The selling of the candidates' wives, 1972, seems to have been inspired by what might be called "the Pat Nixon cloth coat syndrome." . . . The fur coats, or at least most of them, have been left home in the closet. The skirt lengths are neither too midi nor too mini. The dresses smack of Paris, Ill., rather than Paris, France.[11]

[8]Estelle Barr, "A Psychological Analysis of Fashion Motivation," *Archives of Psychology*, 26, No. 171 (1934).

[9]Jessie Warden, "Some Desires and Goals for Clothing of College Women," *Journal of Home Economics*, 49 (December 1957), 795.

[10]Dorothy Runbeck (Stout) and Alpha Latzke, "Values College Women Consider in Clothing Selection," *Journal of Home Economics*, 50 (January 1958), 43–44.

[11]"Fashion: The New Political Taboo," *New York Times* Service news release, published in the *San Francisco Chronicle*, April 6, 1972.

Figure 10.7 The women's movement has been partly responsible for the waning interest in fashion.

BERRY'S WORLD

© 1970 by NEA, Inc.

"I, personally, resent their air of superiority because we're 'bums,' and they're 'street people'!"

Figure 10.8 Synthetic poverty often is not accepted by others as the most sincere statement of a person's true values.

Some believed that this was due partly to the state of the economy and partly to the Women's Movement (Figure 10.7). In London, fashion was hailed as a "capitalistic ploy" by British Communists who claimed that it was "merely a sales gimmick used by the clothing industry to persuade people to buy more clothes."[12] The feminists, on the other hand, complained that fashion put women on display and made them out to be nothing more than fragile, decorative sex objects.

Values, of course, are reflected not only in what people say, but in what they do. Like Baumgartner, Walker used actual expenditures made for clothing as a behavioral index of the importance attached to dress. There were highly significant relationships between subjects' expressed interest and the amount of money they spent for clothes.[13] In other instances, however, actual behavior has contradicted professed values. One of the most blatant examples can be found in the antimaterialistic philosophy expressed by the youth culture. Many give lip service to the triviality of appearance and in fact look as though their entire wardrobe was picked up at the Goodwill (Figure 10.8). But

if you check the label, you'll find the "surplus" jacket came off a rack at a hip little boutique just last week. The T-shirt is new, too; the tie-dyed version costs $2 more than the regular kind. The jeans are also brand new; you have to pay extra to get them all faded and tattered like that. As for

[12]"The Left's Fight Over Fashion," Associated Press news release, published in the *San Francisco Chronicle*, February 5, 1973.

[13]Norma Walker, "Clothing Expenditures as Related to Selected Values, Self-Actualization, and Buying Practices." Ph.D. diss., Pennsylvania State University, 1968.

the sandals, they're the new "tire-look" numbers. The knack of making them was picked up from impoverished South American Indians; you pay $10.[14]

This kind of inconsistency is bound to occur when a person adopts a set of synthetic values just to be "in" with the crowd. The process is often not a conscious one. How often do we parrot values that have been indoctrinated through public opinion and in fact do not reflect what we really consider important? In the matter of conforming to an accepted standard of dress, for example, there is rather overwhelming evidence that even though people do not consciously acknowledge the value of conforming, their behavior indicates extremely strong tendencies in a conforming direction. College students in particular tend to be negative about the notion of conformity in dress, men favoring nonconformity more than women. One study demonstrated, however, that when actual behavior was observed, both sexes actually conformed to a greater extent than they thought they did, and men were significantly more conforming in dress than women were.[15]

Even the early studies by Hurlock and Barr indicated very strong tendencies to prefer clothing that would be similar to or accepted by one's friends. Teen-agers have been found to give greater weight to clothing as a means of gaining acceptance and approval than do mature persons. The latter group tends to place a higher value

on the effects of physical enhancement.[16] The desire to conform to peer group norms seems to be highest at about the eighth grade.[17] By the time students reach senior high school, dressing in a more individual manner and dressing to attract the opposite sex become important values.[18]

In most groups, values usually change with advancing age. Interest in clothing is generally higher among young people, decreasing as age increases.

The importance of clothing as a means of achieving approval and acceptance is paramount in the value configurations of adolescents, but for those with greater maturity and/or self-confidence, it appears to decrease in favor of aesthetic or economic considerations.

Value Patterns

Values held about clothing, such as those just described, are meaningful only when placed within the context of an individual's total value pattern. Several researchers have attempted to analyze attitudes and values associated with clothing against a background of other behavioral or descriptive characteristics. Lapitsky's work, for example, dealt with the relationship between clothing values and general values. As would be expected, positive correlations were found between the specific

[14]Barry Newman, "Riches in Rags: Companies Find Profits in the 'Antimaterialism' of the Youth Culture," *The Wall Street Journal*, April 27, 1971.

[15]L. Anne Swanson, "Male and Female Conformity in Dress: A Study in Perception and Behavior." Master's thesis, University of Nevada, 1971.

[16]Olive Alexander, "A Pilot Investigation of the Motives Underlying the Desire to Feel Well-Dressed at Various Levels." Master's thesis, Cornell University, 1961.

[17]Sandra Ehrman, "Clothing Attitudes and Peer Acceptance." Master's thesis, Colorado State University, 1971.

[18]Shirley Kopitzke, "Aspects of Dress of Teen-age Girls." Master's thesis, Colorado State University, 1971.

values held about clothing and parallel general values, that is, subjects who emphasized the aesthetic aspect of dress also scored high in terms of general aesthetic values.

More pertinent, perhaps, to this discussion is the fact that aesthetic and economic interests were more important in the value configurations of the women studied than were any of the other clothing values investigated. When these results are compared with the findings of earlier experiments, some interesting points of agreement appear. Lapitsky's subjects were adult women; other studies of adult women also indicate that beauty in dress is of primary importance. The more mature female regards the social aspects of dress (that is, wanting clothes like others, desire for social approval) lower in her hierarchy of values than the desire for comfort and the conservation of time, energy, and money. Further, when Lapitsky's subjects were divided on the basis of anxiety measures, the emotionally secure group scored significantly higher in aesthetic values; those judged to be socially insecure placed greater emphasis on the social value of clothing.[19]

Creekmore also studied this relationship between general values and behavior.[20] Significant associations were found between certain types of clothing behavior and specific values. People who were strong in aesthetic values placed a corresponding degree of emphasis on the tactual aspects of clothing as well as on the symbolic meanings associated with particular styles of dress. Those whose economic values were high stressed the factors of cost, maintenance, and the general management aspects of clothing, whereas those who scored high in religious values tended to be concerned with modesty in dress.

The important point here is that values held in relation to dress and adornment do not exist in isolation. They are all interrelated with the other things we hold to be important, and they are based on some deep-lying assumptions about what is "good" and what is "bad." The term **value pattern** refers to a whole configuration of values, all of which we hold to be important but which fit together in some kind of orderly hierarchy.

Many of the value orientations in America today are outgrowths of what is commonly known as the "Puritan ethic." First and foremost in the value configuration of the early Protestants was an undying faith in God. Based on powerful religious sanctions, the drive toward hard work became a sign of grace. People oriented to the rewards of a life hereafter were also characterized by a willingness to "do without" in the present. Frugality and simplicity were natural accompaniments to their way of life, and comfort was merely incidental. Anything but a conservative mode of dress and ornamentation would be alien to such a value pattern.

For many Americans today, a growing affluence has lowered the value once placed on hard work and saving money (Figure 10.9). With more and more comforts of the "good life" and increased leisure time, the emphasis has shifted to a desire for peace and security, and to getting along with others. In 1970, *Life* magazine surveyed a cross-section of Americans on matters pertaining to goals and lifestyles. The poll asked people to

[19]Mary Lapitsky, "Clothing Values and Their Relation to General Values and to Social Security and Insecurity." Ph.D. diss., Pennsylvania State University, 1961.

[20]Anna M. Creekmore, "Clothing Behaviors and Their Relation to General Values and Basic Needs." Ph.D. diss., Pennsylvania State University, 1963.

Figure 10.9 With the growing threat to our natural resources, Americans have become increasingly concerned about grass, trees, and wildlife. These demonstrators are protesting the killing of animals for production of fur fashions.

Figure 10.10 Traditionally clad Amish of Indiana exchange glances with a California surfer.

choose the things most important to them. For the 4,047 respondents, the following percentages were reported:

Green grass and trees around me	95%
Neighbors with whom I feel comfortable	92%
A kitchen with all the modern conveniences	84%
To be at peace with yourself	82%
To be able to wear what I feel like wearing	82%
Having a full and relaxing time in leisure life	59%
Fixing up your house the way you want it	54%
Hard work and saving money	47%
Getting to the top in your work	38%

It was interesting that 78 percent of the people perceived that "traditional values are being torn down, and that's bad," and more than half (54 percent) thought that "new styles in hair and dress are a sure sign of moral decay in America."[21]

Values held in relation to clothing are integral parts of a total value configuration.

Value Conflict

Conflict always arises when the total value system gets out of adjustment. The bits and pieces cannot be changed without altering the whole arrangement. This is the basic reason why many religious sects view technological innovations with suspicion—because "progress," for whatever it is worth, is a threat to a total way of life.[22]

Lifestyles in American society today are so diverse that conflict is inevitable (Figure 10.10). The variety of subcultures makes it difficult to generalize about dominant value themes of the population as a whole, but we can at least look at the so-called traditional values in light of those that have been called antiestablishment.

In 1970, Charles Reich, a widely known proponent of the "new generation" values, held that "new generation" people had to reject the values of the current society and reassert rational control over encroachments by the industrial system and the corporate state. He felt that the clothes worn by the "new generation" expressed that philosophy and were an important symbol that represented a "deliberate rejection of the neon colors and artificial, plastic-coated look of the affluent society.

[21]Bayard Hooper, "The Real Change Has Just Begun," *Life*, January 9, 1970, pp. 102–106.

[22]Notably those of the Mennonite movement, such as the Amish, the Brethren, the Dunkers, and so on.

They are inexpensive to buy, inexpensive to maintain . . . (they) are worn with pride, as befits a statement of principles and basic values."[23]

The basic conflict in this philosophy lies in its incompatibility with our modern material culture. The sixties and seventies were a time in which people were concerned about exploding populations and the loss of individual identity. Rather than seek the faceless namelessness of the new philosophy, most people were searching for ways to achieve and maintain a semblance of individuality.

On an individual basis, problems often arise when two competing values lead to different courses of action. Value conflict appears to be particularly prevalent among youngsters of immigrant parents. When the family value patterns differ sharply from those of the larger culture, considerable tension may arise among the children, who find it extremely difficult to maintain loyalties to both parents and peers.

Even within the so-called typical American family, we have seen how values change at different age levels. We have only to observe the flood of problem letters in the advice columns to know that clothing is a continual source of conflict between parental and teen-age values.

An example is the case of a young woman who, in seeking independence from her affluent family, turned to a career in prostitution. "I've always had a split personality about middle class things," she confessed. "If I had $100 right now to spend on clothes, I'd still go to Altman's and blow it on a skirt and sweater, rather than to Macy's and two skirts and two sweaters. See my shoes—they're Gucci,"

(green suede platforms, worn with blue jeans and an old burgundy sweater).[24]

Or, take the girl who would like to attract the admiring glances and attentions of the male guests by choosing a backless black satin gown for Saturday night's party; but the dress is really beyond her budget, its use would be limited, and her father would have a fit. In most cases the individual can order values so that one takes precedence over the others. If it is difficult to accept one because it implies open rejection of the other, people usually find some socially acceptable reason for ignoring the one that they do. If the girl buys the backless black satin dress, she can save the needed money by skipping lunch for the next two months, and this will help her to lose a few pounds, which she ought to do anyway. Father will never know if she keeps the dress at school, and besides, his idea of suitable dress is strictly nineteenth-century.

Most conflict is resolved through the choice of one of several acceptable alternatives, but if no satisfactory solution to conflicting values can be achieved by choosing one over the other, the individual may follow a deviant course of action. A girl from a low-income family, for instance, strongly desiring the prestige and social recognition that new and expensive clothes will command but lacking the money, may sacrifice the value of integrity and develop a regular habit of shoplifting.

When two or more values lead to alternate courses of clothing behavior, the individual resolves the conflict through a unique ordering of alternate choices.

[23]Charles Reich, *The Greening of America* (New York: Random House, 1970), p. 234.

[24]Judy Klemesrud. "Former Prostitute Finds Going Straight Difficult," *New York Times* News Service Special, March 14, 1973.

Value Change

We have seen how the value patterns of societies, groups, and individuals are subject to change as they come under the influence of new sets of experiences and circumstances. Adjustments to a persistent, widespread conflict in general values inevitably leads to social or cultural change.

In American society today, it is easy to exaggerate the extent of such change. One reason for this is that conflict, when it occurs, is widely publicized, and we tend to generalize about what we see in the news media. A 1971 survey of young Americans between the ages of fifteen and twenty-one revealed a set of values the researchers described as "remarkably moderate, even conservative." In general the findings showed that the attitudes of the younger generation differed very little from those of their parents. "The majority of youth listens to the rhetoric of dissent, picks what it wants, then slowly weaves it into the dominant social pattern."[25]

In 1970, it was estimated that less than 7 percent of the youth population could be considered "radical activists," that is, those whose views are deliberately counter to the mainstreams of the established society. About 20 percent were described as "concerned liberals," and over half were found to be conservative, even reactionary.[26] Such statistics are supported by the fact that in the early 1970s, over 40 million families (60 percent of all Americans) had annual incomes under $10,000.

With respect to the potential appeal of an antimaterialistic ethic, one writer noted:

Certainly, the 20 million family units with incomes of less than $5,000 would like nothing quite so much as to "make it" into the middle class and its traditional values. An equal number of family units, moreover, find their energies bound up in the struggle to get more of—or merely to hold on to—the middle-class amenities they have only recently attained. Indeed, most of the ten million family units earning between $5,000 and $7,500 a year and many of the ten million in the $7,500 to $10,000 bracket would be surprised to learn that they have much discretionary income at their disposal.

For many years, Americans expected to discard garments before they were worn out, and patching and mending rapidly disappeared from women's lists of tasks. Buying on the installment plan was widespread, regarded as the normal state of affairs in many homes.

Values that were appropriate half a century ago could not survive when other situational factors changed. We can look back over time, see the gradual evolution of change in our value system, and wonder how long our present values will remain important. Even though the activists of the sixties and seventies were few in number, society will never again be quite the same. They contributed to the long-term shifts in values that will be occurring for many years to come. Additionally, the values will be altered in unforeseen ways by developments during the 1980s.

Persistent and widespread conflict in the general values related to clothing inevitably results in cultural change.

---

[25]Louis Harris, quoted in "Change, Yes—Upheaval, No," *Life*, January 8, 1971, p. 22.
[26]Walter Thomas, "Value Change and American Youth," *Penney's Forum*, Fall/Winter 1970, p. 7.

SUMMARY

Group and Individual Values

Clothing is an expression of both the dominant value-themes in American society and those attitudes and values held to be important by various subcultural groups and by individuals. In most cases, the family derives its values from the larger society and transmits these values to the child through the process of socialization. However, other agencies also make a significant contribution to the individual's value pattern: the school, movies, television, and all other forms of mass communication.

Several studies have demonstrated the relative importance different groups and individuals assign to clothing. In addition, investigations have shown that the attitudes most often associated with clothing relate to

1. a desire to conform
2. a desire for self-expression
3. a desire for aesthetic satisfaction
4. prestige values
5. the desire for social participation
6. physical comfort
7. economy

Decision making in regard to clothing choices is sometimes difficult because an individual holds competing or conflicting values. Most conflict is resolved by placing one value above another, although in some cases, the individual may follow a deviant course of action. Because all personal values must be viewed against the general cultural setting, a change in other circumstances—economic conditions, technological advances, and the like—often leads to a changed attitude about dress.

FOR FURTHER READING

Beeson, Marianne S. "Clothing in the Commune." In *Dimensions of Dress and Adornment: A Book of Readings*. 3rd ed. Dubuque, Iowa: Kendall/Hunt Publishing Co., 1979, pp. 93–95.

Dupree, Nancy Hatch. "Behind the Veil in Afghanistan." *Asia*, 1 (August 1978), 10–15.

Emerson, Gloria. "Your Clothes: What They Tell About Your Politics." *Vogue*, 169 (September 1979), 292–93.

"Resplendent Male: Fashions of the Hapsburg Era at the Costume Institute of the Metropolitan Museum." *Esquire*, 92 (December 1979), 105–7.

"The Commune Comes to America." *Life*, 67 (July 18, 1969), 16–23.

Chapter 11

CLOTHING: SOCIAL
CLASS AND SOCIAL MOBILITY

More than half a century ago, George Dearborn observed that one's social movements are determined more by clothing than many people have ever stopped to think or to realize.[1] He maintained that the clothes people wore influenced how much they went out, both into the street and into society in general; where people went and with whom they associated; the jobs they were able to hold and the jobs they missed or lost. Thorstein Veblen's observations on the relation between dress and social class were also made before the developing theories of social stratification found their base in empirical fact.

American society in particular has great difficulty with the concept of a social class system. The idea of a class structure is familiar to the public. Phrases referring to a class society are part of the everyday language; middle-class values, middle-class suburbia, lower-class ghettos. And yet the sociocultural context within which this country was founded rejects all notions of class. The inalienable rights of human beings and their inborn perfectability are clearly stated in the Declaration of Independence and the Constitution. The liberal interpretations of these ideals, the rags to riches stories of Horatio Alger, and the frontier democracy led Americans to believe that, although social class structures existed elsewhere, American society had left all that behind in the Old World. Such

[1]George Dearborn, "The Psychology of Clothing," *Psychological Monographs*, 24, No. 1 (1918).

differences as did exist were due to lack of motivation or perhaps educational opportunities. Following the rise of Marxian theory and the depression of the 1930s, new social theorists began to see class structure as objectively observable and classes as clearly separate. This picture of American society was also a false one. Recent sociological thought seems to follow a merging of these two viewpoints. Social class in America is seen as an informal arrangement of poorly defined groups, not recognized by all people and with loose boundaries that allow much mobility up and down the social class ladder. *Social class* generally refers to layers or levels of a population divided by factors related to the economic life of the community. In research, such stratification is generally based on income, occupation, power, or education—by a combination of the above criteria or by only one. Social scientists agree that it is not based on race, religion, or national background.

The extent to which people themselves identify their own class association is shown by their common references to "our kind of people." Members of the same social class intermingle because they tend to share the same values and have a certain unity of outlook. In this way, groups set themselves apart from others and form what we call a social class, that is, a group of people of similar status or prestige in the community whose members have intimate access to one another. This type of social stratification differs markedly from that of

the **caste** system, in which upward mobility is restricted and intermarriage between members of different castes is taboo. Caste distinctions usually are made more visible by such physical signs as skin color or symbolic differences in dress. Caste and class are similar in that they are both ascribed at birth. The major difference is that class membership can, and often does, change through achievement. In a society that operates under a caste system—India, for example—there is literally no change. Individuals are locked into their ascribed caste role for life. In any case, stratification is a reality in every community. People are ranked along some continuum from high to low.

Although behavioral scientists still argue a good deal over the precise definitions of class and status, there is fairly general agreement that (1) all people in society are ranked in terms of a prestige hierarchy, (2) everyone is a member of a social class, and (3) one's lifestyle is a criterion commonly used to make such rankings.

Clothes are an important part of the material possessions and patterns of behavior that constitute one's lifestyle. In this chapter we consider some of the ways in which clothing, as a symbolic indicator of status, both influences and reflects the caste and class distinctions observable in American society. We also shall be concerned with the function of dress as it relates to class consciousness, group identification, and social mobility.

CLOTHES AND CLASS DISTINCTIONS

In terms of the democratic ideal, social class distinctions may seem inconsistent with the philosophical declaration that all

men are created equal. Yet in every human society, some individuals stand higher than others in the community. Clothing, in the form of a wide variety of status symbols, is visible evidence of this stratification.

Prehistoric peoples used early status symbols to distinguish those with special skills—hunters, chieftains, and those who healed or cured through magical or spiritual powers. So, too, through all the centuries of civilization, people have had special forms of adornment or decoration for those held in higher regard than the masses. The difference between a bear-claw necklace and the stars on a general's uniform may be widely separated both chronologically and geographically, but the symbolic meanings attached to these items are similar. The individual wears a badge of rank, honor, or prestige.

In Chapter 1, Veblen's theories regarding the leisure class and their symbolic use of clothing to show status were discussed (see page 30).[2] Some critics of Veblen think his work is outdated, archaic for the twentieth century. Veblen was the first economist to write about dress and he did write about the world he lived in, primarily the late nineteenth and very early twentieth century. However, much of what he said still holds true today, even if we take into consideration the sociological changes brought about by modern technology.

Contemporary writers continue to use Veblen's nineteenth-century theories in attempts to explain current sociological phenomena. "No line of consumption affords a more apt illustration of conspicuous waste of goods than expenditure on dress. Our apparel is always in evidence and affords an indication of our pecuniary standing to all observers at the first glance."[3] In applying these ideas to the

[2]Thorstein Veblen, *The Theory of the Leisure Class* (New York: Modern Library, reprinted 1931).
[3]Ibid., pp. 170–171.

Figure 11.1 Sports, particularly those that require costly clothing and gear, and travel have become status symbols of the upper classes.

1980 social scene, the *Washington Post* noted that those with the money easily spend $20,000 to $40,000 a year on clothes, exclusive of furs and jewelry with the comment,

Clothes are very important for the up-and-coming climbers. But they're just not interested in being well turned out, though. They buy for status rather than aesthetics; when they walk into a room they want to be wearing a label that shouts, "This dress cost $2,000," even if it looks terrible on them. I think that's conspicuous consumption all right.[4]

The diversity of status symbols (Figure 11.1) that are part of American society include material items—automobiles, club memberships, and certain types of food and alcoholic beverage. Still others are less tangible but just as valid indicators of status—mate selection processes, sexual

[4]Sarah Ban Breathnach, "Embarrassment of Riches," *Washington Post*, July 23, 1979, p. 14.

behavior, family rituals, and even burial practices. Where no fixed symbols mark the socially elite (or if the customary symbols are blurred), then in a stratified society, clothing is often used. The kind, quality, and style of clothes reflect both cultural backgrounds and social positions. Clothing gives a quick visual clue to the wearer's social class, especially when other clues are missing.

Although mass production and mass consumption indicate the emergence of a mass culture in the United States, differences remain. The practiced eye can still distinguish hand-tailored suits, even from high-quality mass-produced ones. The idea that the increase in the extent of material possessions now available to the American people has somehow made them cultural and social equals is not valid.

Advertising one's position in society is often a motivation for dressing in a certain manner. Clothing and its relation to social class have received considerable attention from researchers. Both variables, social class and clothing behavior, are relatively simple to observe and measure, certainly more so than many personality factors. Therefore, considerable information is available about the clothing behaviors of people in different social strata. This information ranges from the obvious— clothing selection, performance, care, and management—to less obvious variables of clothing values, attitudes, or interests.

Indexes of Social Status

An index is a means of estimating the amount of some variable found in the real world. Usually it is an objective paper-and-pencil test or questionnaire used to determine how much of what the research-ers are interested in can be found in certain individuals or among specific groups. A status or social class index places a value on a person's position on a prestige scale. The index is based on questions people commonly ask others to approximate their social position: "What do you do?" or "Where do you work?" (occupation); "Where do you live?" (neighborhood); "What church do you go to?" (religion). The purposes of such indexes are many. They are useful in placing subjects into groups for various behavioral research projects. Then comparisons can be made among the groups in an attempt to account for behavioral differences. In an index, answers to the questions are given numerical values and, when these numbers are summed, a social class index is obtained.

Over the years several indexes have been developed and used with varying degrees of success. One of the first was Warner's Index of Social Status Characteristics.[5] This measure uses four population characteristics: occupation of head of household; source of income; house type; dwelling area. This index is seldom used today because of the changing values of the index items (how do you determine head of household where there is more than one?) and the time required to determine the last two categories. However, it is still considered one of the most accurate in assessing social class.

A short form of the Warner index has also been developed for use in situations where it is not feasible to obtain information on the location and type of house a person lives in. Using only the occupation, source of income, and education, the

[5]W. Lloyd Warner, *Social Class in America* (New York: Harper and Row, 1960).

information is weighted and the weights added. This short form, Index of Social Status, has been widely used because of its relative simplicity and its high correlation with the Warner index.[6]

Hollingshead's Index of Social Position uses area of residence, education, and occupation.[7] This scale is easier to use than Warner's because the place where data is to be collected is divided into areas beforehand so all the researcher needs to determine is residence, occupation, and number of years of school completed.

Most social class measures divide society into from three to seven groupings with variations of upper-upper, lower-upper, upper-middle, middle-middle, lower-middle, upper-lower, and lower. The most common are those that include two middle classes and one upper and one lower. However, as we shall see in discussing clothing, there is an important difference between upper-upper and lower-upper.

Social class may also be measured subjectively, simply by asking people where they place themselves and others. The problem is that most people put themselves in the middle class. The upper class is rarely selected descriptively, the lower class never. Lower class is regarded as inferior and lower-middle or low-income is as far as people will go in identifying themselves. It seems reasonable that if we have a middle and an upper of anything, we also have a lower, but an American lower class is scarcely if ever mentioned, in speech, in print, or, least of all, by

people who are obviously a part of it. A story about Thomas Jefferson comes to mind. When his gardener told him the rabbits were eating the cabbage plants in the outside rows he told his gardener not to plant any outside rows. "We solve nothing when, in our eagerness to soften the edges of hard facts, we resort to playing little tricks on ourselves. Grim it is, but all cabbage patches have outside rows, all skyscrapers have 13th floors, and all stratified societies have a lower class."[8]

Aside from the language and technical problems of expressing social class so that it is meaningful for all, there does appear to be a definite popular conception of the social classes as abstract demographic categories. There are people in one category who are rich and well educated, have small families, live long lives, and live in the right part of town. There are other people who are neither rich nor poor, have a high school or better education, live in an ordinary part of town, have medium-sized families, and live as long as anybody. And there are people who are poor, do not finish grammar school, live across the tracks, have huge families, and die early. These are social classes understood as demographic categories. There may be more than three or there may be fewer.

Although people are ultimately stratified into classes on the basis of a number of different criteria, each person acquires initial status from the position of the family of birth. Thus the kinship relationship is still another indicator of social class. The degree of value placed on these various indexes is a matter of local designation; classes are defined differently in Newport than they are in Newark; upbringing may be heavily weighted in Larchmont, but

[6]Carson McGuire and George D. White, "The Measurement of Social Status" Research Paper, Department of Educational Psychology, University of Texas, March 1955.
[7]A. B. Hollingshead, *Elmtown's Youth: The Impact of Social Class on Adolescents* (New York: John Wiley and Son, 1949).
[8]*Christian Science Monitor*, November 10, 1971.

money talks in Las Vegas. In small communities where people are well known, the emphasis is likely to be placed on family background and personal attributes, but in large cities the tendency is to rely heavily on the common criterion of money and what it will buy. For the majority of Americans, however, prestige is closely tied to occupation. In almost all studies of status characteristics, occupational rankings prove to be important determinants of social class ascription. Moreover, there is fairly widespread agreement on which occupations rank high in status and which rank low.[9]

Increasing evidence shows that education has become an equal or even more important indicator of social class. There is a close relationship, of course, between education and occupation, but this association is by no means perfect or universal. In many research studies using college populations, social class variables are measured solely by parental educational level. Even when actual income is asked for (and this is done rarely because people tend not to respond honestly to the question), the correlation between that figure and highest educational level attained is considerable.

The difference between the use of a person's position in the community as an index of general status and a description of the person is sometimes not considered. Substituting three- and four-dimensional models is sometimes very tempting to researchers, but human beings cannot be so easily reduced to these set forms. Models sometimes make more sense when statuses are scalable, that is, when they can be ranked and ordered. But some very

important personal positions cannot be ranked, as for example, marital status. In human society one deals with whole persons, not with abstract categories. An index of any sort is simply an indicator of the presence of something, nothing more, nothing less. And, indexes vary in their accuracy. A single-item category such as occupational level, or a complex index such as the Index of Social Status Characteristics may suggest the presence of general status, but that is all. Every individual exists in many ordered, nominal statuses.

No one has tried to summarize all the many statuses for any given person. However, a number of studies have tried to show relationships among the several statuses of individuals. Probably there have never been as many inconsistencies and contradictions in personal statuses as can be found now in the United States.

Analysis of Social Class and Clothing Behavior

Although the economic significance of occupation and education makes them the most reliable indicators of prestige, other ways in which money is used may, in the long run, be more important: "Even wealth and income are not in America the ultimate badges of belonging: they are currency to be converted in time into the 'right kind' of associations and thus into the 'right kind' of manners, clothes, behavior, in which each person shapes himself to the model of the class to which he aspires."[10]

One's lifestyle and accompanying consumption patterns, therefore, are the more visible indexes of status. Lynes agreed that

[9]R. W. Hodge, P. M. Siegel, and P. H. Rossi, "Occupational Prestige in the United States: 1925–1963," *American Journal of Sociology*, 70 (November 1964), 286–302.

[10]Max Lerner, *America as a Civilization*, Vol. 2 (New York: Simon & Schuster, 1957), p. 528.

class distinctions in the American social system are based not so much on wealth as on differences in cultural tastes. The "high-brows," he claimed, "are a class of elite intelligentsia who affect a shaggy indifference to dress in their comfortable (albeit not inexpensive) Harris tweed suits." The "low-brows," on the other hand, have no fashionable tastes whatever and would not recognize a Harris tweed if they saw it. By far the largest in number, the "middle-brows" conform to all the conventional codes in their search for culture and a better life. These comments by Lynes are over thirty years old now, and he is remembered for the words he coined rather than for the comments he made. Phrases such as *high-brow* and *low-brow* have become part of the common everyday language used to describe social class.[11]

In a classic study, Barber and Lobel analyzed women's fashions from 1930 to 1950 and gave some empirical support to such a theory of differentiation in dress among the social classes.[12] The investigators concluded that the women at the top of the American social class system—those from the "old money" families having an established position of status preeminence for several generations—had little need to demonstrate their superiority through conspicuously fashionable attire. Their tastes in dress were distinctly more British than French, with a preference for "well-bred" tweeds and classic woolens. Most of the high fashion was found in the social class just below the "old money" families. Paris

originals gave these women clothing symbols that were related to wealth and high living rather than to family connection. In the middle and lower classes, clothes were conservative but smart (where "smart" was interpreted to mean what everybody else was wearing). High styles were regarded with some distaste, and extreme or daring clothes were avoided. Similar findings were reported in another study. In an analysis of three different groups of homemakers, Francl found that the group holding the lowest status position made the most conservative fashion choices.[13]

Vener's findings also appear to be consistent with such observations. He showed that clothing increased in importance to the individual as the person's social status increased, although clothing was given the highest importance by the medium-high status group and was ranked as less important by the highest status group.[14] This same pattern was reported by Snow, who found that interest in clothing increased with education up to the level of college attendance and then seemed to decline as more education was acquired. There was a relatively high degree of clothing interest among attorneys, salesmen, and schoolteachers, and factory workers attached the least importance to clothes.[15]

In addition, personal estimates of clothing importance have been found to be

[11]"High-Brow, Low-Brow, Middle-Brow," *Life,* April 11, 1949, pp. 99–102; also Russell Lynes, *The Tastemakers* (New York: Harper and Brothers, 1954).
[12]Bernard Barber and Lyle Lobel, "Fashion in Women's Clothes and the American Social System," *Social Forces,* 31 (1952), 124–131.
[13]Janell Francl, "Fashion Choices Associated with Values of Homemakers." Master's thesis, Iowa State University, 1970.
[14]Arthur Vener, "Stratification Aspects of Clothing Importance." Master's thesis, Michigan State College, 1953.
[15]Janet Snow, "Clothing Interest in Relation to Specified Socio-Economic Factors of Men in Four Selected Occupations." Master's thesis, Texas Woman's University, 1969.

directly related to social participation, that is, those who tend to be more socially active place a greater emphasis on clothes. A fairly early study of social stratification described the lower-status woman as one whose activities were confined to housekeeping and child rearing. Her wardrobe was correspondingly limited. Upper-class women, on the other hand, were absorbed in extended social affairs, and their personal costumes were "multiple in number."[16] Similar relationships between clothing and social participation have been found among males as well as females,[17] among the elderly[18] as well as among the young.[19]

On the surface, it seems that the youth of the seventies openly rejected the use of clothing as a status symbol. Apparently, "Minimal wardrobes of jeans and shirts, worn until they fell apart, were a sacrificial purge of parents' overstuffed closets. The young were wearing the cumulative guilt of a rich society like a hair shirt." "This," said Johnston, "was a direct and dishevelled challenge to the impeccable dress of the establishment."[20] To be sure, there has always been a small yet influential minority of young people whose parents had suffi-

cient wealth for them to make a mockery of fine clothes. The "Pepsi Proletariat" costume consisted of "overalls, flannel shirt, and heavy work boots, the traditional accouterments of the working class."[21] The outfit could have been bought cheaply at the local Sears store, but, the wearers explained, "We buy all our clothes in New York. My work boots came from a groovy leather store, and we got our overalls at a hip boutique."

For the vast numbers of young people who later followed the lead, however, adoption of such clothing did not represent identification with the working classes. To them, bib overalls became the new status symbol of the upper classes.

Clothes are symbolic indicators of status and, as such, they obtain recognition, approval, or identification for the individual.

The High and the Mighty

Historically, the American aristocracy was built on a monied class of people who made their fortunes through a peculiar combination of good luck, personal ingenuity and dealing, as well as plain hard work. The men who achieved great financial success in the nineteenth century—the miners, manufacturers, merchants, and railroad builders—were a breed apart from the traditional European aristocracy that passed inherited wealth along the blood lines of a ruling class. American society was thus based on a strong philosophy of upward mobility.

There is, to be sure, a cluster of families in the United States that derives its prestige

[16]J. Useem, P. Tangent, and R. Useem, "Stratification in a Prairie Town," *American Sociological Review*, 7 (1942), 331–342.

[17]Elizabeth Harrison, "Clothing Interest and Social Participation of College Men as Related to Clothing Selection and Buying Processes." Master's thesis, University of Tennessee, 1968.

[18]Marian Moore, "The Clothing Market of Older Women." Ph.D. diss., Purdue University, 1968.

[19]Patricia Lindley, "The Relationship of Dress and Grooming to the Success of the Mexican-American Student in a Selected High School." Master's thesis, Texas Technological College, 1968.

[20]Moira Johnston, "What Will Happen to the Gray Flannel Suit?" *Journal of Home Economics*, 64 (1972), 6.

[21]Blair Sabol and Lucian Truscott, "The Politics of the Costume," *Esquire*, May 1971, p. 124.

from blood relationship to the "first families" of New York and Virginia or the Boston Brahmins of New England. The third and fourth generations of the industrial and business magnates also received a family heritage that ultimately emphasized lineage and kinship connections in the admission requirements to high society. In addition, numerous American heiresses earned their tickets to prestige positions by marrying into European royal families. Today there is hardly any royalty left, even for royalty to marry. Consequently, in more recent years, many status positions have been turned over to the celebrities of the mass communication media. Despite this shift in character of the upper class, these people are the tastemakers of American society. They have the money, the access to publicity, and the social prestige to make their lifestyles ones the masses seek to copy.

Certainly one of the most tangible measures of status and prestige so far as clothing is concerned, the annual Best-Dressed List publicly identified those individuals who had a significant influence on contemporary dress. Even to be considered for the BDL a woman had to spend between $20,000 and $100,000 yearly on her clothes, exclusive of jewelry. Jackie Onassis reportedly spent more than $1.2 million on clothes during the first year of her marriage to the Greek tycoon. Yet money is not everything: Elizabeth Taylor, with all her jewels and furs, never made the list.

Among those who achieved fashion "Hall of Fame" status over the years are Queen Elizabeth II, the Duchess of Windsor, Princess Grace of Monaco, Queen Sirikit of Thailand, Jacqueline Onassis (when she was Mrs. Kennedy), Mrs. William Paley, Gloria Guinness (wife of the British beer heir), Rose Kennedy, and

Figure 11.2 The symbols of status and prestige of the monied upper class.

Gloria Vanderbilt Cooper. Men named to the list include former New York mayor John Lindsay, film stars Robert Redford and Richard Roundtree, and film executive Robert Evans.

Some people would consider it a dubious honor to be acclaimed for what might be called such conspicuous consumption. Members of the upper classes, however, are not responsible for the BDL's falling into disfavor. The culprits are the members of the not-quite-so-upper classes who work all their lives to acquire the status symbols of the class above them. When status symbols fail to maintain class distinctions, their value is zero (Figure 11.2). The mink coat is an example; today with cut-rate assembly-line methods and department store credit, almost anyone can be swathed in fur.

Ostentation in dress has rarely, if ever, been considered "in good taste." If an outfit looks like something you have been waiting years to buy, chances are you really cannot afford it. Among the very rich who can afford just about anything, however,

Figure 11.3 Status is never cheap. These travelers have Vuitton luggage. The famous brown bags once bestowed instant good taste on its proud owners, but now people who don't know the correct pronunciation of the name (Vwee-tohn) use it.

ostentation is hard to achieve, although Liz Taylor did it with her 69.4 carat diamond and $125,000 Kojah coat. She eventually got some of the social position she had been seeking through her marriage to John Warner, member of an F.F.V. (First Families of Virginia). She even sold the diamond for a reported five or six million dollars to help finance her husband's senatorial campaign in 1978.

Instead of ostentatious dress, a more typical response among the highest income groups is to seek what may be costly but does not look it (Figure 11.3). As one Fifth Avenue furrier explained, his customers wanted mink that didn't look like mink. So he offered

for $2,500, a dyed variety that includes pink, yellow and blue-denim colored mink; shaved mink stenciled to look like tiger, cheetah and leopard; mink imprinted with assorted patterns; and even a rainbow coat made of vari-colored swatches sewn together like a patchwork quilt.[22]

Among the truly elite it is more fashionable *not* to be fashionable. One columnist

noting Happy Rockefeller's unstylish mode of dress commented, "Mrs. Rockefeller . . . is in casual, tried-and-true good taste. She's from the good skirt, good sweater, good string of pearls school. . . . Her look is the look of the typical well-dressed Philadelphia Main Liner, which is exactly what she is."[23]

Whether people qualify as upper-upper, lower-upper, or simply upper, they become "the arbiters of the 'proper' use of money, physical appearance and dress, etiquette, language, and aesthetic taste."[24]

The relatively few people in the upper classes of American society are in a position to set a standard of dress that others seek to copy. Those whose social positions have been established for generations are less likely to use fashionable attire as a symbol of their pre-eminence.

The Great Middle Mass

Of the three broad strata in American society (upper, middle, and lower), only the middle class has steadily increased in proportion to the whole. The very rich are, relatively speaking, not as rich as they used to be. From the 1940s on, the incomes of the richest 5 percent of all Americans have been falling, but the share of middle-class families has risen. Even more recently, the poor have been the big gainers, largely as the result of increases in social security, reformed income tax laws, and other government projects.

[22]"Sorry, New Canaan, but Now They Wear Mink in the Bronx, Too," *Wall Street Journal*, March 11, 1971.

[23]"Happy Rockefeller's Personal Campaign," *Cosmopolitan*, October 1963, pp. 58–59.
[24]Bernard Berelson and Gary Steiner, *Human Behavior—An Inventory of Scientific Findings* (New York: Harcourt, Brace & World, 1964), p. 488.

The composition as well as the size of the middle class has changed from a group of independent farmers and owners of small businesses to larger and larger numbers of salaried professionals, salespeople, and office workers. The original term *white-collar workers* came from the prestige associated with the type of clothing customarily worn by this group—white collars (on shirts or blouses). It is no longer the norm. With changing fashions, the white-collar worker is now apt to wear a blue shirt, the blue-collar worker probably wears the white shirt, and the person in jeans and denim shirt is likely to be the boss's son or daughter.

Because of the nature of the work done, the desk worker is clearly in a position to wear a different type of attire on the job than is the manual worker. This basic difference in clothing symbolism is probably the most important single criterion used to establish the dividing line of demarcation between middle class and working class. Salary alone is no reliable index, for the hourly wage of many workers today may equal or exceed the salary of white-collar employees. But if we compare the clothing budgets of workers and white-collar people of similar income, we will find that a much higher percentage is spent on clothes by the latter group.

Thus, the middle class is the consuming class; the stress placed on clothes and appearance reflects the continual striving for upward social mobility and the search for higher and higher status (Figure 11.4). The middle classes are the eager copiers, the "crucial audience," as Lerner called it, for the fashions set by the upper classes. The costly original designs the office worker sees in fashion magazines, movies, and newspapers are quickly copied into less

Figure 11.4 Genuine wool fleece has become a status item, particularly since upper-class life has become less formal.

expensive imitations, and despite the differences in quality and workmanship, the smartness and the look of a fashionable appearance may be had by all.

At times the middle class seems obsessed with the search for the right way to act and the right thing to wear. The number of possessions—including clothes—becomes a significant expression of social position, and the middle class is far more status conscious than either of the groups above or below. Because of their strict observance of convention, people of this middle stratum are not likely to adopt a new or daring fashion until they are sure it has been accepted by the class above them. Yet for all their insecurities, America's middle classes are the carriers of the culture and the group largely responsible for the great productivity that characterizes the nation as a whole. The middle-class image makes Americans the best-dressed people in the world.

Members of middle-class society constitute the bulk of fashion followers; their status is more dependent on the symbols of appearance and dress than is that of either of the other social classes.

The Working Class

The working class is most often defined in terms of its occupational characteristics to include those individuals and families in the semiskilled, unskilled, farm laborer, and custodial class positions. National polls taken as far back as the early 1940s show that well over three fourths of the people in this category call themselves "middle class" rather than "lower class,"[25] although Centers' survey revealed that almost 52 percent of the population identified with this stratum when the label was changed to "working class." In the broadest sense, these are the people who work for hourly wages (as distinct from a salaried position) and in the majority of cases wear some type of uniform or work clothes on the job.

We might remember here that with the advent of career apparel, many who formerly were called white-collar workers are now also in uniform—bank tellers, airline attendants, and others. This illustrates the arbitrariness of the word *uniform* and the impossibility of placing all people into neat little boxes with social class labels on them.

The process of stratifying individuals into social categories is always complex, and few individuals conform in every respect to the total class definition. There is in today's society the class-blurring effect of mass production, which makes the products of the ready-to-wear industry not only more available but at the same time less reliable as indicators of social class

position. One has to look harder for the subtle differences in cut, fabric, and workmanship that distinguish the hand-tailored suit from the mass-produced copy.

If we are to generalize anything at all from studies that indicate significant relationships between clothing behavior and social class position, it would be that clothing is decidedly important to those who are upwardly mobile in their aspirations. Because the worker generally is more concerned about economic security than about social position, little value is placed on clothing or its symbolic interpretation.

In two separate investigations, Delp[26] and Smith[27] found significant differences between children from advantaged homes and children from disadvantaged homes in their awareness of dress considered appropriate for different occasions. By the age of four or five, the child from the economically "advantaged" family has already been conditioned to the nuances of dress that would make one costume suitable for play and another costume suitable for parties. Children from the lower economic groups apparently have less opportunity to develop such sensitivity.

Similarly, the working-class woman does not find it necessary to spend large amounts for a high-fashion wardrobe. She has little social opportunity to be fashionably dressed, and she finds it more important to be "neat and clean" than "all dolled up with no place to go." Even within the

[25]See "The People of the United States—A Self Portrait," *Fortune*, February 1940; and G. Gallup and S. Rae, *The Pulse of Democracy* (New York: Simon & Schuster, 1940).

[26]Janice Delp, "Awareness of Clothing Differences for Age and Sex: A Comparison of Four-Year-Old Children from Advantaged and Disadvantaged Homes." Master's thesis, Pennsylvania State University, 1970.
[27]Velda Smith, "Awareness of Appropriateness of Dress Among Four- and Five-Year-Old Children from Advantaged and Disadvantaged Homes." Master's thesis, Pennsylvania State University, 1968.

"Oh, Edith we're only going around the block, for God's sake!"

Figure 11.5 Drawing by Stan Hunt; © 1969 The New Yorker Magazine, Inc.

the normative patterns of dress between women who shopped for clothing in the designers' salons of local stores and those who shopped in the fashion departments of discount houses.[29]

Thus we see that the importance of clothing appears to increase as one progresses up the social ladder until one finally reaches the top (Figure 11.5). Then, because there is no place left to go, the significance of clothing again diminishes.

Clothing tends to be regarded by workers as having limited importance to their social position, although they now have access to clothing commodities that symbolize a higher status.

context of a common activity like shopping, class differences may be noted.[28] Tucker observed highly significant differences in

SUMMARY

Clothes and Class Distinctions

In every society, individuals are ranked on some form of prestige continuum. Social stratification in America is based on an open-class system that permits fairly easy movement from one level to another. Clothing is an important part of one's style of life, and it is one of the visible indexes used to identify an individual's class affiliation. The fashion leaders in American society tend to come from the upper class by virtue of the fact that they have the money to buy high-fashion clothes, the social opportunity to display them, and the access to publicity so that they are noticed. Those at the very peak of the socioeconomic pyramid usually find it more fashionable *not* to be fashionable, and their use of clothing as a status symbol diminishes.

The majority of Americans in the middle class recognize that a "proper" appearance and "proper" dress are the keys to association with the "right crowd," which in turn opens the door to job advancement, increased income, success, and greater prestige. Thus, status for middle-class society members more clearly depends on the symbols of dress than it does for either the upper or the lower classes. Workers attach relatively little importance to the social

[28]Stone and Form, *Social Context of Shopping*, 1957.
[29]Susan Tucker, "The Relationship Between a Normative Pattern of Dress and Upward Social Mobility." Master's thesis, University of Nevada, 1969.

significance of clothing, even though mass production has made virtually all types of apparel available to them. In general, people tend to minimize the difference in dress standards between themselves and those in the next higher class, but they clearly set themselves apart from those below.

GROUP BELONGING AND CLOTHING BEHAVIOR

Objective descriptions of class characteristics alone cannot account for the sum total of group distinctions in dress that are seen in modern society. It is conceivable, for example, that people of different status positions could develop a group feeling of belonging through common interests and goals that may be completely unrelated to the social stratification system. In addition, a uniform pattern of behavior depends largely on a conscious identification with a given group or class (Figure 11.6).

Groups outside the norm are identified in many ways. There is no consensus in names, definitions, or composition. Without becoming involved in a controversy over the meanings of terms, we shall attempt to distinguish some of these groups

and discuss how their deviations from the norm affect their clothing.

Subcultures and Minorities

If any one term can be an all-encompassing one to describe these groups, *subcultural* would come the closest. A subcultural group may be defined as a segment of the larger society, made up of people who belong to a particular interest group and who operate in a social system more or less distinct from the rest of the community. They are, and at the same time are not, part of the larger social scene. A subcultural group's distinguishing characteristic, for our purpose here, presupposes some element of choice and a distinctive culture that truly sets it apart (Figure 11.7). It is a group that is ongoing within and beyond an individual's life span. Thus we eliminate from this category groups that are differentiated by age and by economic conditions.

A minority group, on the other hand, has a numerical connotation. A minority is less than a majority. In recent years, however, discrimination and prejudice have become part of the definition. A minority group may be defined as a group of people who, because of physical or cultural characteristics, are singled out from others in the society in which they live for differential, unequal, and/or inferior treatment.

Figure 11.6 A trip to the laundromat does not provide the social opportunity to wear fashionable clothes.

Figure 11.7 The Amish represent a religious subculture. Their clothing is a part of group identity.

Unfortunately the two words have become interchangeable in our society. Although it is true that many subcultural groups are also considered minority groups, all are not, just as all minority groups are not truly subcultural.

Over thirty years ago, Myrdal observed that among American blacks, a predominant characteristic at that time was a desire for flashy, unusual, and showy dress.[30] Denied the use of other status symbols in their social setting, they used clothing to compensate. This use helped them increase self-esteem and overcome some of the inferiority feelings built into the social structure. A 1963 report indicated that clothing, a portable and relatively less expensive item of conspicuous consumption, was more easily exhibited than were other status symbols.[31] A 1976 newspaper report stated that "wearing pretty clothes, bright colors, and expensive shoes was one way of being independent, being looked upon with admiration by our peers, and mostly, I guess, a way to make up for having nothing" among some blacks in the ghetto.[32]

Kittles's 1961 study of women's dress, mentioned earlier, also presented findings of that period. At that time, white women in general owned a greater number of high-status clothing items than black women did, but black women in the lower-income levels owned more of these items than whites grouped in the same category. As the income level of the blacks rose, ownership of high-status clothing decreased. The reverse was true for whites since the mechanism of compensation was not operant, and their pattern of clothing consumption followed a typical middle-class striving toward the lifestyle of the next higher class.

Other minority groups may use clothing to accentuate their subcultural characteristics and thereby carry on a style of life that might otherwise break down within the larger society. Among the religious Jews of New York, a number of internal discriminations in status, exhibited through the visual symbols of dress, are employed to encourage stricter conformity to religious practices. Social stratification within the Jewish community is based entirely on one's dedication to ritualistic observances. The common criteria of lineage, wealth, success, education, morals, and so forth have little to do with the prestige position to which an individual is assigned.[33] A variety of Hassidic garments serve to identify the relative position of each person in

[30]Gunnar Myrdal, *An American Dilemma* (New York: Harper and Brothers, 1944), p. 962.
[31]Jack Schwartz, "Men's Clothing and the Negro," *Phylon*, 24 (1963), 225.

[32]Earl Byrd, "Stylin' Out in the Ghetto," *Washington Star*, December 31, 1976.
[33]Solomon Poll, *The Hasidic Community of Williamsburg* (New York: Free Press of Glencoe, 1962).

the hierarchy. The lowest class of *Yiden* (that is, the least intense in their religious observance) wear the dark, double-breasted, outmoded suits that button right over left; these are considered to be the very minimum of Hassidic status symbols. The next highest class is permitted a beard and sidelocks in addition to the double-breasted suit. The third stratum may add a large-brimmed, black beaver hat, while a still higher status is indicated by wearing a long black overcoat in place of a jacket. Near the very top of the hierarchy, a man may wear—in addition to the beard and the sidelocks—the hat, the long overcoat, and a long silk coat with rear pockets. Only the *Rebbes*, the top-ranking and most religious community members, may wear the slipperlike shoes and white knee socks into which the breeches are folded. Through these external symbols by which each person is identified with his appropriate social position, the group is able to maintain control over its members and extend its religiosity. Thus, through a system of visible rewards, the Hassidic community succeeds in stemming the forces that might otherwise lead to assimilation into the secular society.

Clothing symbols that distinguish minority groups from the larger society inhibit the process of assimilation and increase the possibility of discrimination.

Reference Groups

In Chapter 6, we saw how a person's behavior is shaped by relationships to significant others. If we generalize "others" to the broader concept of the **reference group**, we will be able to understand the influence of group opinion in determining an individual's pattern of clothing behavior (Figure 11.8). A group functions as a frame of reference for an individual in one or both of two ways: it may set and enforce standards for the person by giving recognition or withholding it; and it may serve as the standard used for self-evaluation in comparison with others. In either case, recognition of one's relationship to the group must be made in order to be motivated by it. People seek the security of knowing that they belong to a particular social group, as well as the distinction within the mass society that such identification affords. Whether this identification is made within the large, varied status system of social class or within the context of a smaller, more intimate group depends on the person's orientation or point of reference. In terms of reference group theory, it would be a mistake to assign an individual to a given class solely on the basis of external criteria. People will be more strongly motivated to conform to the norms of the group to which they feel they belong, or should belong, than of the group

Figure 11.8 Group cohesiveness is greatly enhanced by wearing a conspicuous symbol of membership and giving the group a name. Like the Hell's Angels, this gang displays its insignia on the backs of their jackets.

to which they might be assigned by virtue of their income, occupation, birth, or other status criteria.

Awareness of one's own position within the system depends on knowledge of the class distinctions in society. Many wage earners, for example, tend to have limited perspectives of any social roles other than their own. They do not enlarge their view of society beyond their own immediate environment through extensive reading or social participation. In general, they think that people in the upper classes are there simply because they have more money. They see only the gross similarities in styles of dress, and to them, one outfit is just as good as another. Their capacity for making differential evaluations of the more subtle differences in clothing is limited, and consequently they are insensitive to the symbols that distinguish them from anyone else. In short, they tend to have very little class consciousness.

The increased availability of a college education today, coupled with widespread communication, brings a knowledge of "how the other half lives" to larger and larger segments of the population. In the process, one's own lifestyle can be compared with those of others in the social hierarchy, and the end result is a greater consciousness or awareness of class position.

A number of studies have demonstrated an increased awareness of dress as socioeconomic level rises. Bullock, for example, found greater fashion awareness among girls who came from higher economic brackets than among those from lower brackets[34], and Bloxham found a similar relationship between an awareness of dress norms and socioeconomic status.[35]

This kind of sensitivity among members of the upwardly mobile middle class stimulates their copying of the fashions of the upper class and helps them maintain their separateness from the lower stratum from which many have risen. Obviously, this produces a need for more rapid changing of styles among the upper-class fashion leaders, in order to maintain *their* separateness from the middle stratum. Thus we see that increased class consciousness results in greater degrees of status seeking. As one establishes identity, position is evaluated against the standards of the desired membership group.

Awareness of the subtle differences in dress is highly correlated with an individual's consciousness of class distinctions. People will try to conform to the norms of the group to which they feel they should belong.

Obviously, the importance an individual attaches to clothing is strongly influenced by the values of the group identified with (Figure 11.9). In the teen-age culture, the conscious association between clothes and group belongingness is perhaps the most pronounced. Social factors other than age-status, however, affect the prestige value assigned to clothing by particular reference groups. Patton compared college sorority women with nonsorority women, using a measure of prestige consciousness. Her findings revealed highly significant differences between the two groups. Sorority women were much more aware of the status

[34]Marilyn Bullock, "Fashion Awareness of Students in Selected Rural and Urban Areas." Master's thesis, Texas Tech University, 1970.

[35]Thine Bloxham, "Adolescents' Awareness of Dress Norms." Master's thesis, Washington State University, 1969.

Figure 11.9 The values of the group an individual identifies with influences the clothing worn.

value of particular items of dress than nonsorority women, and they recognized clothing as a way to "get in with" popular students on campus. She also found a higher prestige consciousness among women of the upper and upper-middle classes than among those in the lower strata.[36]

In another comparison of female college students' opinions on "appropriate dress standards," there was far greater unanimity among sorority members than there was among independents who lived in the dorms.[37] Apparently those who join organizations of this kind are more strongly motivated to conform to the patterns of a social reference group. The intensity of the need for belonging is directly related to the compulsion and eagerness with which the individual follows the group norms.

Vener and Hoffer attempted to demonstrate the kinds of persons or referent groups adolescents wanted to copy.[38] Of the students who responded, almost 58 percent indicated a peer or peer group as the model for emulation in patterns of dress. Typical responses cited in this category were: "There is a certain group of girls my age who are a clique. I like the way they dress." "If I could dress like any person I would like to dress like S. S. because I think she dresses nice." "D. B. because he always wears tight jeans and cat-shirts, so I'd like to wear that kind of clothes." "P. W. because he has nice clothes, not real flashy but they are nice and he also has a nice personality."

A second group of referents reported in the same study were classified as "mass media celebrities." Less than 12 percent indicated a relative or family member as their model, and about 7 percent chose some person or group from the community. Even though the latter categories were mentioned less frequently, they give some

[36]Elizabeth Patton, "An Analysis of the Prestige Factors in Clothing as Related to Selected Groups of Freshmen and Senior Sorority and Non-Sorority Women at the University of Alabama." Master's thesis, University of Alabama, 1964.

[37]Barbara Ross, "A Comparative Investigation of Conformity Patterns of Dress of Home Economics Students at the University of Nevada." Master's thesis, University of Nevada, 1970.

[38]A. M. Vener and C. R. Hoffer, *Adolescent Orientations to Clothing*, Technical Bulletin No. 270 (East Lansing, Mich.: Michigan State University Agricultural Experiment Station, 1959), p. 21.

evidence of the extent of adolescents' identification with reference groups or a single referent.

In most instances, the model or the ideal possesses some qualities that are not only desirable but socially approved. It is not uncommon, however, for individuals to identify rather strongly with referents who are not acceptable to the general society. Those who differentiate themselves from the masses, for example, maintain their visual identities via the symbols provided by clothing like black sweaters, leather zippered jackets, and tight pants. Such identification, though not socially approved, gives the individual power, importance, and approval of the referent group, which is, after all, the only group valued.

Clothing provides a conspicuous badge of group belonging. Therefore, the imitation of clothing behavior is a direct, tangible means of identifying oneself with a referent person or group. It not only facilitates learning of new social roles, it also becomes an important process in forming the concept of self.

SUMMARY

Group Belonging and Clothing Behavior

Individuals need the security and distinction of belonging to a particular group within the mass society. The extent to which people identify with any group or class depends on their own consciousness or awareness of the group's existence as well as knowledge of their own relative status or position. People are more strongly motivated to conform to the standards of the group to which they feel they *should* belong, rather than the group or class to which they might be assigned on the basis of external criteria.

Feelings of group belonging are greatly enhanced by giving its constituents a membership emblem, or by giving it a name, or by threatening its existence. Clothing is probably the most conspicuous and the most visual of all possible badges of group belonging. Criticism of group dress standards tends to increase group cohesiveness and the compulsion to conform to the established norms. Subcultural groups use dress symbols in maintaining a style of life that will preserve the identity of a group that might otherwise be assimilated into the larger society.

SOCIAL MOBILITY AND DRESS

Social mobility is the movement or shifting of membership that occurs between or within social classes. Although social class is assigned at birth, it is a role that can change through acquisition. Therefore, many societies, but American society in particular, are marked by a relatively high degree of vertical mobility, that is, move-

"Do you have something a little more garish? We're nouveaux riches."

Figure 11.10 Just knowing and affording the symbols of the class above may not be enough. Upward mobility requires that the wearer be comfortable with them. Drawing by D. Fradon © 1969 by The New Yorker Magazine, Inc.

ment up and down the ladder of income and prestige. As we have seen, there is an extremely close relationship between clothing and class consciousness and status seeking, both of which have significant relevance to social mobility.

In many ways mobility can be thought of as the opposite of stratification. Stratification refers to the unequal placement and reward of society members in the various available positions or roles. Mobility consists of movement in and out of these positions. Mobility may even be seen as the moral side of stratification. If stratification and its resulting inequalities are unfair, then mobility is the opposite side of the coin. Theoretically, there is an equal chance for everyone to improve the position they occupy, to advance to a higher status on the prestige scale.

Mobility implies change, and the change can be in more than one direction. Mobility is a part of all social life. Everyone moves through a life cycle, with resulting changes in age, marital status, educational levels, and jobs. Such changes represent horizontal mobility, since they do not imply that the individual is better or worse off than before. Changes in ordered statuses represent vertical mobility because they imply a change along a continuum on which various points have assigned values. Vertical mobility will most concern us in our discussion of the effects of clothing on changing social roles.

One's lifestyle is the major factor in both this ordinal ranking and any subsequent change. Clothing, an important part of the material goods that contribute to lifestyles, provides clues or symbols that aid in differentiating people in a mass society such as ours. Clothing, the lack of it, the amount of it, and the type, not only reflects the individual's present social class or status but also indicates the position on the social class ladder (Figure 11.10). In addition, clothing influences a person's ability to climb up or be pushed down, that is, into or out of social class positions. Copying practices of the class above has created a great deal of upward mobility. Such mobility depends on outward conformity to the standards of the class above.

Clothing is a symbol that can be manipulated by those who seek to get ahead. One must know the dress standards of the social class one desires to enter. Breakdown in many barriers makes this possible, even easy. Mass production, mass marketing, and communication have put most consumer goods into the hands of many who could not afford them in the recent past.

Barriers to Social Mobility

Three major barriers prevent the free upward shift from one status to a higher one. **Functional barriers** are those that relate to the person's ability to discharge the requirements of the higher position. If a person does not have the physical or mental ability to become a physician or an engineer it seems rational and moral to deny access to those professions. **Arbitrary barriers** are those imposed by virtue of sex, color, religion, former social position, or other essentially undemocratic and unrelated qualities. Increased concern for human and civil rights has done much to reduce the arbitrary barriers in our society, but one might still argue about the differential life chances predetermined at birth that deny access to the high social levels to many people. The third category might be called **interclass barriers**, which consist of anything that prevents peoples of different classes from associating with one another and so learning the passwords required for entry into the next class. These barriers may be physical, like living on the wrong side of the tracks, or they may be attitudinal. Inherent feelings of inferiority are often impossible for a person to overcome. Regardless of the means, upward mobility is only possible by entrance into the primary groups of a higher class.

Money, skills, and appearance are the major means of gaining entrance to a higher class. Education, associated with money and skills, seems to be an increasingly important means. Many capable lower-class students, however, do not aim as high occupationally and thus educationally as do upper-class students of similar capabilities. In fact, even the reverse is true. Students of higher social class backgrounds and lower abilities are less likely to aspire to inferior occupations than are lower-class students of similar or even higher scholastic abilities. Thus, lack of education is one reason for lower job opportunities; the fact that even capable students do not hope for more prestigious employment is another indication that even given the theoretical belief in upward mobility, differential life chances often keep lower-class students down. Several research studies have noted that socioeconomic status contributes to educational and occupational aspirations, independent of the contributions of intellectual abilities.

Movement Within the Mass

One of the favorite themes in American novels revolves around the struggles and disappointments of artless but wealthy prospectors whose wives seek access to high society: "Eventually they secured acceptance to such groups for their children by sending them to the 'correct' schools and dancing masters, outfitting them at the proper dressmakers and tailors, and providing them with the appropriate accouterments."[39] A second theme, which presents the other side of the coin, describes the hardships of the once-affluent upper-class family that strives to maintain its ancestral dignity in economic adversity. The problems in both situations arise from inconsistencies between class position and economic status, and both reflect the kind of social mobility that is characteristic of American society.

The greatest push, however, is not from the top down, but from the bottom up. Great numbers of people have been able to earn their way from the lower strata up to the ranks of the middle classes. By copying practices and values, attaining higher educational levels, and by a "keeping up with the Joneses" made possible by increased purchasing power, individuals motivated to do so have improved their relative positions. Acceptance into this

[39]Ely Chinoy, *Society* (New York: Random House, 1962), p. 135.

new way of life, however, depends on outward conformity to middle-class standards—the right kind of house, the right model car; the right style of clothes and manners.

Empirical data appear to support this assumed relationship between clothes and mobility. Vener's findings indicate that a person's estimate of clothing importance is directly and significantly related to vertical social mobility, that is, people who seek to improve their status positions place a higher value on clothes than do those who regard themselves as socially stationary.[40]

The investigation of clothing habits of white-collar and manual workers by Form and Stone revealed that low-level white-collar workers had much more concern for styles of dress and appearance than did manual workers of comparable income and that they were much more likely to believe that their clothes affected their chances for social and occupational advancement.[41]

The implication that may be suggested by all these studies is that clothing is consciously recognized as a symbol that can be used by those who seek to get ahead in the world. Knowledge of the standards of dress required on the varied levels of society is a positive factor in one's attempt to achieve the social position desired.

Clothing as an aspect of one's lifestyle facilitates movement within the class structure of society.

[40]Vener, "Stratification Aspects of Clothing Importance."

[41]William H. Form and Gregory P. Stone, *The Social Significance of Clothing in Occupational Life*. Technical Bulletin No. 247 (East Lansing, Mich.: Michigan State College Agricultural Experiment Station), June 1955.

Barrier Breakdown

Although many aspects of Veblen's theory of conspicuous consumption in dress still have validity in today's society, the clothing symbols that mark people as members of the leisure class are far less distinct than they were in the nineteenth century. In the early part of the twentieth century, the professional man was still recognizable in his black frock coat and silk hat, but the worker or farm laborer seldom exchanged bulbous-toed shoes for any more refined style of footwear. Differences in income were accompanied by sharp differences in both the symbols of wealth and available leisure time. Mass production and mass marketing have blurred the distinctions in dress and at the same time, increased mechanization, which led to a shorter work week, has provided leisure. The visible signs of stratification have become much more subtle, and both upper and lower categories have tended to converge toward a middle-class standard of living.

The big push for copies of high-fashion merchandise among the low-price companies has created an America with the best-dressed poverty the world has ever known. Harrington's classic statement, made in 1931, is still true. He said:

It is much easier in the United States to be decently dressed than it is to be decently housed, fed, or doctored. . . . There are tens of thousands of Americans in the big cities who are wearing shoes, perhaps even a stylishly cut suit or dress, and yet are hungry. . . . it almost seems as if the affluent society had given out costumes to the poor so that they would not offend the rest of society with the sight of rags.[42]

[42]Michael Harrington, *The Other America* (New York: Macmillan Publishing, 1962), p. 5.

These examples illustrate two important phenomena. One is that technological developments contribute greatly to the weakening of class lines; the differences in dress that reflect one's mode of living are still there, but the shadings are more elusive and imprecise. The other—and perhaps the more significant of the two—is that clothes can "make the poor invisible"; if one *feels* equal in visual appearance and dress, many psychological barriers that divide the inferior from the superior are greatly minimized. This simple fact explains the motivation that underlies much of our clothing behavior.

Clothing becomes a less reliable indicator of social class as similar styles of dress are increasingly available to all persons.

Diversity versus Conformity

We have described in rather general terms some of the values and practices that appear to be characteristic of clothing behavior within each of the broad social classifications in American society. The bulk of the upper class has the refinement of taste that comes through exposure to the skill and craftsmanship of creative designers and tailors; its members have both the security and social opportunity to exercise the kind of distinction in dress that can make them the fashion pacesetters for the rest of society.

At the middle level, individuality in dress is somewhat overshadowed by a widespread conformity to the "ideal" codes enforced by the opinion of the majority. People from the lower stratum may devalue the importance of dress, although those who are conscious of their positions often experience strong drives toward upward mobility. When such is the case, the functional value of clothing is often sacrificed for the outward, more ostentatious symbols that seem, at least to the wearer, to eliminate class distinctions in dress.

General statements such as these, however, present an oversimplification of a very complex organizational pattern. Elements of good and bad taste show in all levels of society. Dress, as a form of creative expression, is not necessarily limited to the upper classes, nor is conformity confined to middle-level living. A crisscrossing of clothing values and practices appears more obvious to the casual observer than does strict adherence to any of the social class norms.

To expect, or even to assume, that any single standard of dress would be the most desirable for everyone in society would be to contradict the acceptance of the diversity that is at the very core of the American cultural ideal. But conformity should not be interpreted only in the negative sense as a block to creative self-expression; it is a mechanism through which we keep our society intact. To the individual who asks, "Who am I, and where do I belong?" conformity to a given set of norms can give a sense of identity and group belongingness. To place such a high value on clothing that it obscures all other worthwhile facets of living seems to be no more or less desirable than failing to recognize the significance of dress to successful enactment of life roles. We may deplore the mass-produced tastes our highly developed industrial system imposes on us, but we can be grateful for a vastly improved standard of living that may bring us closer to elimination of widespread poverty.

The intelligent approach is to be fully aware of the choices open to us, not only in terms of commodity availability, but in terms of the values by which we prefer to be known.

Diverse patterns in clothing behavior reflect differences in tastes and values that often overlap class lines; no single standard of dress can be best for all of society.

SUMMARY

Social Mobility and Dress

American society is marked by a relatively high degree of vertical mobility. Upward movement is usually characterized by a consciousness of one's social position and greater emphasis on the importance of dress in affecting the transition. Class distinctions in dress have been greatly reduced by the wide variety of commodities available to all.

Clothing is a symbol easily manipulated by those who seek to get ahead. One needs to know the dress standards of the social class one desires to enter. Then technology, in the form of mass production and mass marketing as well as widespread communication, makes the clothing items available to anyone with the money to buy them.

FOR FURTHER READING

"Creative African Coiffure Catches On: Cornrowed, Braided Styles," *Ebony*, 35 (November 1979), 112ff.

Duka, John. "The Way We Wore." *New York*, 13: (December 31, 1979), 36–37.

Rosencranz, Mary Lou. *Clothing Concepts: A Social-Psychological Approach*. New York: The Macmillan Company, 1972, pp. 127–146.

"Status Symbols: U. S. Swings Back to Basics," *U. S. News and World Report*, 87 (November 26, 1979), 70–71.

Part Three

AESTHETICS AND DRESS

Chapter 12

ARTISTIC

PERCEPTION OF CLOTHING

Art may be approached in any number of ways. We may see the flowing, graceful lines of a Japanese woodcut, feel the vast proportions of space inside a Gothic cathedral, contemplate the rounded contours of a Maillol sculpture, perceive the tactile richness of an elegant fabric, or respond to the clouds of color in a Kandinsky painting. Whatever the medium, the same plastic elements of line, form, space, texture, and color are the basis for all visual design. These elements of design are the physical parts of an object that produce visual images that the creator can communicate to the perceiver. So, too, design consists of principles that organize these elements in a logical or unified fashion. Balance, proportion, emphasis, rhythm, and coordination in art affect our senses

and, therefore, our perception. Even though they are largely subjective, these design elements and principles have sufficient universality to override a particular artistic expression and therefore can be applied as readily to clothing as to other art forms. We may produce art, or we may merely look at it; we may enjoy it, appreciate it, or understand it.

Clothing is one means through which the components of art are illustrated, perceived, and experienced. Through clothing design, we can attune our eyes to subtle variations of line or of color, which in turn helps heighten our awareness of similar elements in other artistic forms. When we produce a complete design through garment construction, or when our composition takes form by assembling the various parts of a costume, we create a "picture" for others to see. A study of clothing design can contribute to the depth of our art understanding and increase appreciation of the visual richness of our surrounding physical environment.

ELEMENTS OF DESIGN

Just as chemical elements constitute the ingredients for all chemical compounds, all art is concerned with the combination or organization of the fundamental elements of **line**, **form**, **space**, **texture**, and **color**. These raw materials of design never appear in isolation, except in the abstract. In costume at least, every line and shape may have a character of its own, but such elements take on meaning only as they are seen within the context of the total appearance. In this section we shall study the plastic elements as separate aspects of design in order to sharpen our recognition of their use in costume.

Line

Line is often used as the simplest form of representation. Stick figures (Figure 12.1) illustrate both form and action utilizing the utmost economy of means. We can see how line functions to outline contour as it defines the shape of the body (Figure 12.2). In all visual design, line functions to outline contour, to connect shapes, and to divide space within a shape. When line predominates in a design, it may provide a path of vision along which the eye may travel. The route may be straight and direct, or it may wander in devious ways. Even when line is broken, the eye tends to connect points in space to form a linear pattern (Figure 12.3).

Various types of lines differ in their expressive qualities. **Straight lines** tend to be stiff and severe: "To most people the straight line suggests rigidity and precision. It is positive, direct, tense, stiff, uncompromising, harsh, hard, unyielding."[1] Straight lines in themselves contradict the subtle curves of the human form by giving it an angular quality. In stiff fabrics that maintain a rigidity of line, straight seams and edges may obscure body contour, but in yielding, pliable textures, the line loses its stability and takes on the shape of the curve beneath it.

Curved lines vary all the way from gentle undulation to full rounded convolution. A restrained curve is graceful, flowing, and gentle. The gradual transition in the change of direction imparts a slow but rhythmic quality to the line.

We see how straight line may take on aspects of the body contour; this effect is usually compounded in the case of curved line. A costume that appears to be restrained in line when worn by a slender person may seem to be excessively rounded on a fuller figure. The banded edge of the admiral's coat (Figure 12.4) exaggerates his fatness in a wonderfully humorous manner.

Lines that are vigorously curved tend to be more active in character, and for this

[1]Maitland Graves, *The Art of Color and Design* (New York: McGraw-Hill Book Company, 1951), p. 202.

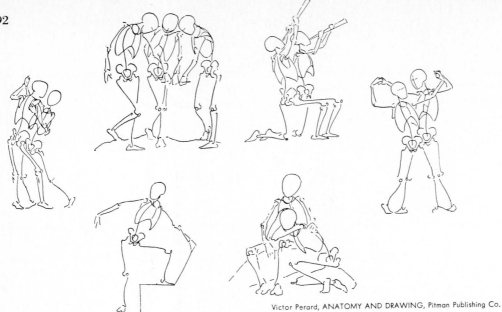

Figure 12.1 Line captures the form and action of the human body with simplicity and economy.

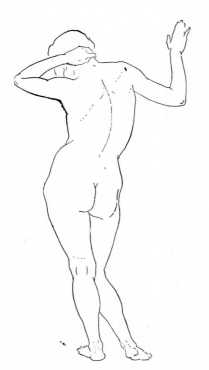

Figure 12.2 Line defines the contours of the human form.

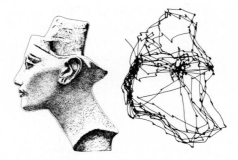

Figure 12.3 The eye tends to follow fairly regular pathways in perceiving objects within its field of vision. As a subject viewed the head of Queen Nefertiti (left), eye movements (right) were recorded by Alfred L. Yarbus of the Institute for Problems of Information Transmission in Moscow.

reason they can easily be overdone in costume (Figure 12.5). Wavy lines that constantly change their direction quickly become restless and aimless (Figure 12.6).

Zigzag lines force the eye to shift direction abruptly and repeatedly, with an erratic, jerky movement. Bold herringbones (Figure 12.7) are both startling and tiring under prolonged observation.

Figure 12.4   Curved lines predominate in this portrait of Admiral Keppel by the English painter, Reynolds.

Figure 12.6   Curved lines may be devised to exaggerate and to add fullness as well.

The direction of line contributes as much to its quality as the type. Each direction—vertical, horizontal, diagonal—produces a different effect on the person who beholds it.

Vertical lines predominate in the tall slender arches of Gothic interiors as well as in the architecture of modern skyscrapers.

Numerous examples of verticality in dress can be found throughout historical and contemporary periods (Figure 12.8).

Horizontal lines suggest the pull of gravity and parallel objects at rest or repose, such as the surface of the earth, a

Figure 12.5   Curved lines may vary from gentle curves to more exaggerated roundness.

Figure 12.7   Zigzag lines can produce a startling effect but may become tiring under prolonged observation.

Figure 12.8 The extreme verticality of these elongated figures expresses the austere, straining effect so characteristic of the Gothic.

quiet expanse of water, or a sleeping human figure. Line direction that causes the eye to travel along horizontal planes usually has the effect of increasing apparent width. Figures 12.9 and 12.10 show use of horizontal line in dress.

Oblique or **diagonal lines** give an impression of greater movement or action

Figure 12.9 Repeated horizontals form the basic theme of this mid-nineteenth-century ball dress. The puffs of the overskirt as well as the bands and rosettes diminish in size as they step up the figure, lending rhythmic progression to the total design.

than either vertical or horizontal lines do. "When running or otherwise very active, the body assumes a diagonal position, head thrust forward, balance somewhat precarious, elbows and knees forming angles."[2] This association with movement gives diagonal lines (Figure 12.11) an active, somewhat unstable quality.

In addition to its type and direction, line is characterized still further by other factors, such as strength versus fragility, tension as opposed to flexibility, or sharpness counter to blurred. Such qualities are expressed by the size and thickness of the line, its placement within the total composition, and the degree of contrast it enjoys with other plastic elements.

Form

We noted that one function of line is to define contour or shape. The distinction

[2]Ray Faulkner and Edwin Ziegfeld, *Art Today* (New York: Holt, Rinehart & Winston, 1969), p. 304.

Figure 12.10 In this painting of the Infanta Margarita by Velasquez, horizontal lines and forms predominate. The sweep of the peplum, the bertha, the accented bateau neckline, and the extended coiffure all accentuate the breadth of the composition. Even the length of outstretched arms does not exceed the extreme width of the silhouette.

Figure 12.11 The use of strong, unabashed line creates a forceful design.

In applying the concept of form to clothing, we are dealing with three basic shapes: the form of the human body itself; the external shape created by the costume silhouette; and the outline of individual parts within the silhouette. The beauty of any design is affected by the interrelationship among these three forms.

The human head, basically oval in shape, bears a unique mathematical relationship to all other parts of the body (Figure 12.12). The distance from the crown of the head to the bottom of the chin is called **head length**, and this measurement is used in considering other body measurements. The body is essentially rectangular in its total configuration, always taller than it is wide, without precise geometric shapes, and infinite in its subtle contour variation. Bodies that vary significantly from these expected proportions do not look aesthetically pleasing since the eye is accustomed to the norm. Clothing has the particular advantages of being able to camouflage body contours that are less than ideal and to add graceful forms of its own. A torso less than three heads in

between line and form is, therefore, quite arbitrary. Although the term *form* can be used in a broader sense to mean the visual arrangement and effect of all the plastic elements within the total design, we use it here as being synonymous with shape or contour. We will recognize line as having only the one dimension of length.

Figure 12.12 Relative proportions of the human form: each circle represents the length of a head from chin to crown.

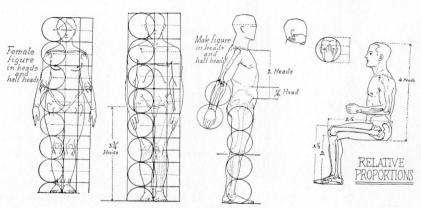

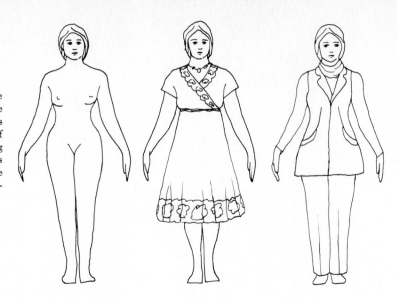

Figure 12.13 The empire line on this dress hides the short waist and camouflages the long legs and short torso of the figure beneath. The long tunic top of the pants suit is another way to disguise the same lack in body proportions.

length, for example, or legs longer than three and a half heads can be covered in such a way that these variations are not as apparent (Figure 12.13).

Every period in fashion history can be identified by the distinctive shapes that characterize its silhouette (Figure 12.14). In many design periods geometric forms

Figure 12.14 Shapes created by costume reflect the ideals of the era in which the design was created.

Minoan
c. 1400 B.C.

Gothic
c. 1460

Renaissance
c. 1540

Baroque
c. 1630

Baroque
c. 1665

Louis XVI
1778

19th C.
1825

19th C.
1895

have been superimposed on the human body with little regard for the structure they adorned. Other silhouettes have retained a beauty over time by emphasizing the most pleasing body proportions, and at the same time adding subtle areas of fullness that contribute to the overall harmony of design. Individual shapes within the silhouette may be seen in the collar outline, the sleeve contour, in lapels or pockets, and in shapes that form between seamlines and darts.

Form, like line, has an expressiveness that conveys feelings and emotions. The strained, elongated forms of the Gothic period are in sharp contrast to the stocky quadrilaterals of the Renaissance. In contemporary dress an endless number of examples of forms can be found that have such distinctive characteristics.

Space

In visual design, space becomes the background against which forms or shapes are seen. In the perceptual process, one part of the design emerges as the "figure" or form, and the remainder becomes the "ground." "Moreover, perceptual experience never

Figure 12.15 An early-nineteenth-century ball gown embroidered with rose blossoms and ears of wheat. The designs are formed by gilt wires, applied almost like pieces of jewelry.

continues at a flat level; there is always a differentiation of the 'figure' which is central in awareness from the 'ground' which is perceived vaguely if at all."[3]

Far from being what is "left over," space constitutes an important part of visual design, just as movements of silence are essential to the beauty of sound in music. Space provides relief from pattern, a kind of void against which decorative detail is highlighted.

A careful study of Figure 12.15 will show how the spacing of the pattern is calculated to accentuate the size and shape of the surface area it covers. Through the bodice, the shapes and spaces are small in scale, dainty and feminine in effect. As the design descends to the hemline, the ears of wheat and leaves are separated by broader spaces, and the pattern increases in weight and movement.

Sensitivity to space is probably more difficult to develop because the observer is

forced to reverse the figure-ground effect. The untrained observer usually pays no attention to the areas between shapes and sees them only as meaningless parts of the background. Yet a subtle interplay between positive figures and negative spaces in a design contributes to the unity of the total composition.

Texture

Texture is the plastic element most commonly associated with our sense of touch, although texture may be seen as well as felt. Every object in our environment has a surface quality that may be described in varying degrees of roughness or smoothness, hardness or softness. Most individuals could identify articles with their eyes closed simply by running a finger over the surface—the cold polish of marble, the warm softness of a fleecy sweater, the slippery gloss of patent leather, the coarse-grained harshness of sandpaper. Such tactile sensations impart a character to objects—and to clothing fabrics in particular—that makes them suited to different purposes.

All tactile sensations cannot be translated precisely into visual experience. Two beige coats, for example, may appear similar from a distance of two or three feet, but touching the cloth immediately would reveal the difference between wool and cashmere. Trained fingers can easily tell the cool, crisp feel of linen from the softer fuzziness of cotton, or the liveliness of silk from the slipperiness of acetate. The oldest test of quality in fabric is to close the eyes and rub a piece between the fingers. For the experts at least, the test is surprisingly reliable.

[3]M. D. Vernon, *A Further Study of Visual Perception* (Cambridge, Mass.: The University Press, 1954), p. 41.

Most of us learn to make certain associations between sensations of touch and sight. As Graves explains, "texture is perceived by our eyes as well as by our sense of touch, because wet or glossy surfaces reflect more light than dry, dull, or matt surfaces, and rough surfaces absorb light more unevenly and to a greater extent than smooth surfaces. Thus, by association of visual experiences with tactile experiences, things look, as well as feel, wet or dry, rough or smooth."[4]

This ability to *see* how a texture *feels* is thus made possible by the way in which fabrics absorb or reflect light. Short fibers made into yarns with many fuzzy ends are usually rough or coarse and result in dull-surfaced cloths that absorb light, as in denim, challis, homespuns, or woolens. Tightly twisted yarns produce fabric like crepe and voile that have a pebbly rather than a smooth surface. Light-reflecting fabrics are made either from long fibers that are naturally shiny or from lustrous filament yarns, or they are given a glossy finish that deflects light rays from the surface. Fabrics that are light-reflecting are satins, taffeta, and some cottons, linens, and even fine worsted wool. Many of the newer plastics fall into the light-reflecting category by virtue of the fact that they are not made from fiber at all but extruded into liquid smoothness.

Some fabrics both absorb and reflect light so that the edges appear almost white, while the folds are deeply absorbing and darker in color. Softly piled textures, such as velours, velveteens, and short-haired furs, have this characteristic.

Still another way to describe textures relates to their hang, or fall, or drapeability. The weight, bulk, and flexibility of a fabric will determine the degree to which it follows body contour. Chiffon, for instance, a very light, thin fabric, falls easily about the body in many folds, but gabardine, a heavier, tightly woven cloth, resists draping and holds a comparatively firm line.

Some textures, by virtue of their own stiffness, create forms that are independent of the body. If such fabrics are opaque, they may camouflage or totally obscure the line of the figure. Crisp fabrics, however, may also be transparent. From the tactile standpoint, they conceal the human form but visually reveal body contours if no backing or lining is used. In the luxury fabric category satin, taffeta, peau de soie, and ottoman are fabrics in the stiff, opaque category. Corduroy, pique, heavy denim, and suede cloth have similar characteristics but are more utilitarian. Dimity, organdy, voile, net, and organza are typical of the family of crisp sheers.

All sheers of course are not crisp. A totally different character is seen in the transparent softness of batiste, chiffon, and gauze cloth. The weight of the fabric is also important; rayon marquisette—both soft and sheer—may hang in heavy folds, and silk chiffon literally floats in the air when the body is in motion (Figure 12.16).

Every texture has a unique character in the sense that it may combine any number of qualities. Using the kind of profiles that individuals score on interest and personality tests, textures can be rated somewhere along a continuum on each of the polar traits in the chart on the next page.

Many textiles would not rate at either extreme but would probably show relative gradations nearer the center of the continuum. Textures that are neither rough nor smooth, coarse nor fine, of medium weight, thickness and luster, have a wide variety of uses as background materials, but they

[4]Graves, *Art of Color and Design*, p. 221.

Dull						Shiny
Rough						Smooth
Uneven						Flat
Grainy						Slippery
Coarse						Fine
Bulky						Gossamer
Heavy						Light
Compact						Porous
Bristly						Downy
Crisp						Limp
Stiff						Pliable
Hard						Soft
Rigid						Spongy
Inelastic						Stretchy
Warm						Cool
Scroopy						Waxy

lack the strength of character to become the focal point of a design.

Textures used in combination can be most effective when they share a unity of idea or character and are suited to a similar purpose. Textural harmony is achieved through a combination of consistent ideas. The lustrous folds of peau de soie, the luxurious softness of fur, a floating bow of organza, frivolous feathers, and curving lines, when put together in one costume are entirely consistent and express textural harmony.

Color

Many areas of study contribute to an understanding and perception of color. To the physicist, color is a form of energy. The psychologist is primarily concerned about perception; the physiologist seeks relationships between the eye and the brain. The artist is interested in the use of color to create designs and moods. Sensitivity to color may be instinctive in some people, but most require the experience of direct observation before they can recognize and appreciate the infinite variation of color in our environment. Children learn at an early age to differentiate among the bright, intense colors and the names of red, blue, green, and yellow. With increased exposure, they begin to note the difference between light colors and dark colors, bright colors and dull ones. To be knowledgeable in the use of color and articulate about its use, it is necessary to understand something about the color order system and develop a color vocabulary. Such learning experiences will also increase enjoyment of color.

The white light coming from the sun contains all colors. We can actually see this when nature breaks down rays of sunlight into a rainbow, displaying all the colors of the spectrum arranged in fixed order from red through orange, yellow, green, and blue to violet. This unvarying order is explained by a difference in wave length or rate of energy, with red having the longest wave length and violet having the shortest. This difference in wave length

Figure 12.16 When the wearer is in motion, silk chiffon literally floats through the air.

also accounts for the fact that red appears to carry greater distances than do other colors.

When the source of light changes, color also changes. At dawn and at dusk, the sun's position is low in relation to the earth's surface and its light rays therefore must penetrate more of the earth's surrounding atmosphere. Dust particles and moisture in the atmosphere interrupt the shorter blue wave lengths and scatter them before they reach us. Consequently natural light at these times of day is deficient in blue rays and it appears redder. Direct light from a clear sky, on the other hand, permits a greater proportion of blue light rays to reach us. In artificial light, incandescent bulbs emit more yellow rays than other colors and fluorescent tubes vary from orange to blue. Mercury lamps used for highway lighting are deficient in red and proportionately high in blue and green. Colored lights make an excessive amount of light rays of a particular hue available for reflection.

Objects in the environment appear colored because they absorb some of these light rays and reflect others. A ripe tomato, for example, absorbs all light rays except red, reflecting the red wave lengths back to the eye. The vine on which the tomato grows consumes most of the red, orange, and violet rays, reflecting equal amounts of blue and yellow, and most of the green, and therefore it appears green. The apparent color of an object then, depends on its ability to absorb or delete certain wave lengths, with its visual color becoming a combination of the hues that remain in the beam of light that is reflected back to the eye.

Obviously the quantity of any color that can be reflected by the surface of an object depends on the proportion of that color in the light source. Under incandescent light, which has an excess of yellow, the tomato will appear orange-red. In clear northern daylight it will seem nearer the blue side of red because more blue rays will reach its surface. Under a mercury lamp, extremely deficient in red, the poor tomato abstracts all the remaining colors from the light beam and ends up almost black. Costume colors are particularly affected by a change in the source of light. A lavender evening gown purchased in broad daylight may become a neutral gray under the yellow of artificial light.

Color Systems

Color systems are simply methods of arranging color so as to make color communication possible. A color system must be broad enough to be useful, have some means of standardization, and be both permanent and convenient.[5] "Only a method of color notation that is simple to understand and easy to remember can adequately fill the practical needs of modern workers in color and color media."[6]

Attempts to describe and classify color have a long history and today several color systems are available. All color systems are based on a cross-section of the rainbow, that is, a series of hues arranged in fixed order, each blending easily into the next with no distinct marks between them. The basic difference among the various color systems is that each designates a slightly different set of primaries. The commonly used pigment system begins with red, yellow, and blue. The color

[5]Victoria Kloss Ball, *The Art of Interior Design* (New York: Macmillan Co., 1968).
[6]*Munsell Book of Color* (Baltimore, Md.: Munsell Color Co., Inc., 1966), pp. 1–2.

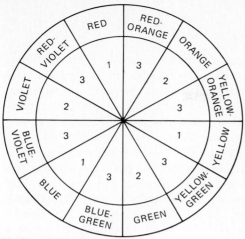

The Prang Color Wheel
1. Primary Hues
2. Secondary Hues
3. Tertiary Hues

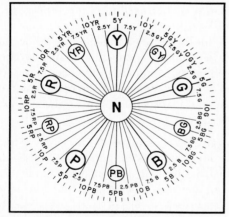

Figure 12.17 The Prang Color Wheel.
Figure 12.18 The Munsel Hue Circle.

printing process uses magenta, yellow, and cyan blue; the primaries in colored television are red, green, and blue. We shall use the Prang system and the Munsell system in our study of color, because they provide more precise scales than other systems for defining color qualities. These qualities are discussed below in terms of the three dimensions of color: hue, value, and intensity.

Hue refers to the name of a family of colors and is the term by which we identify reds, yellows, greens, blues, and purples.

Thus we differentiate between chromatic colors by their hues. Achromatic colors, white, black, gray, do not have hue. The eye can differentiate approximately 125 hues, but for convenience most systems divide the hues into five or six major families. If we were to cut a cross-sectional band of the rainbow and bend it into a circle, we would have the same arrangement of colors seen in these two color wheels (Figures 12.17 and 12.18). In this position certain hues fall directly opposite other hues that have, in fact, opposite properties. Any two hues that oppose each other on the color circle are called complements because together they reflect the full complement of the spectrum. If lights of complementary colors are mixed together, they will produce a neutral gray. If complements are not mixed but placed side by side, the eye, experiencing extreme contrasts, will see them as more intense than they really are. Thus, a bright turquoise sweater worn by a person with reddish brown hair will intensify the hair's red tinge. Viewed from a distance, however, small spots of complementary hues used close together may mix in the eye and appear neutral. This is the reason that many tweeds and prints, vibrant with contrasting color when close at hand, seem to lose their life when seen from greater distances.

Hues that are next to each other on the color circle, such as blue, blue-green, and green, are called analogous or related hues, because each family of colors is related through an intermediate offspring. The closer the interval between analogous hues, the more harmonious they will seem since there will be little contrast or conflict.

Hues may be distinguished further by their degree of warmth or coolness. Red, orange, and yellow have long been associated with the sources of heat—sun and fire. The blues, greens and violets, on the other hand, suggest cool waters, restful grass, shady trees, and distant hills. From a scientific point of view, the red end of the spectrum is actually warmer and the blue end cooler. Red, with its longer wave lengths, is an advancing hue and gives the sensation of warmth. Blue and violet, with short wave lengths, appear to recede and create a feeling of coolness. It is easy to see how this principle applies to dress. A figure or portion of a figure dressed in the warm hues will seem to advance into the foreground and appear larger, more important. Cool colors will cause it to recede into the distance and thereby seem smaller or less important by comparison.

The hue that is midway between the two extremes of red and violet is green, so that it usually is the mark between the warm and cool ends of the spectrum. Greens that fall toward the yellow side, such as apple greens, are warmer greens than those on the blue side. All hues, however, are considered to have a warm or cool cast. Even blue may seem warmer with a touch of green if compared with a blue that contains a small amount of purple.

Value may be defined as the lightness or darkness of a color, and it is determined by the total percentage of light rays absorbed or reflected. White objects may absorb less than 10 percent of the light rays that reach them, in contrast to black objects, which absorb over 95 percent. No wonder black suits seem hot in the summer! Any fabric that is dark enough to absorb a high percentage of light energy will have an actual temperature higher than that of a pale fabric of similar construction.

The natural order of values provides one of the fundamental principles of color harmony. When colors are combined, they are likely to be pleasing if they maintain their natural value relationship. For example, the combination of yellow, green-yellow, and green will result in greater harmony if the yellow is maintained as the lightest value in the scheme and green as the darkest. In some cases a reversal of this natural order of values will create a note of dissonance to produce unusual and exciting effects. A discord in color is analogous to its counterpart in music, in which a minor chord is introduced for brilliance or vibration. Value dissonance in costume can provide a touch of the unexpected, but unless it is done skillfully, it can be jarring and disturbing.

Value is the one dimension of color that can be seen independently from the other two (hue and intensity). The value pattern in a design is created by the distribution of light and dark areas into a pleasing arrangement:

A degree of value contrast is necessary to give structure to any design. It is difficult to see the boundaries between adjacent colors of the same value. Therefore, it is an important function of value contrast to define form and shape by making the boundaries between colors more visible. Similar values produce soft, vague boundaries, while sharp value differences cause hard, well-defined boundaries. Value contrasts also provide a welcome relief for our eyes from the monotony of seeing the same degree of lightness throughout a composition.[7]

The value key of a design may be predominantly light, medium, or dark, with value contrasts that are closely related or strongly contrasting. High-keyed de-

[7] F. R. Quinn, A. Linn, and W. N. Hale, *Consumer Color Charts* (Baltimore, Md.: Munsell Color Co., Inc., 1964) p. 11.

Figure 12.19 The costume of Mme. Mole-Raymond in this eighteenth-century portrait by Lebrun is an excellent example of textual harmony.

signs in close value intervals achieve a delicate quality of femininity. Light values that are sharply accented by black are usually more forceful.

An intermediate or medium value key is illustrated in Figure 12.19. The light scarf is placed close to the skin tones, lighting the face and making it the focal point of the

Figure 12.20 Medium values accented by black and white give a rich masculine quality.

composition. The patterning of low lights and high darks throughout the rest of the costume is created through the subtle contrast of highlight and shadow in the lustrous texture of hat and dress and the long-haired fur. A medium value also predominates in Figure 12.20, but the range in value is much greater. A black velvet ribbon is in sharp contrast against the silvery white wig in the same way that white stockinged legs are accented by black shoes. The suit, in medium value, lies halfway between the two extremes, with the richly embroidered design providing interesting gradations from light to dark and making a transition between the two areas of greatest contrast. Medium values with close intervals are somewhat subdued, but when accented forcefully with black and white they impart a rich, masculine quality.

Lack of value contrast in a design often leads to monotony. Some contrast is needed, and its location is of the utmost importance, for the eye will be drawn first to this point. When we look at objects in the distance the contrast in value is slight, and their outlines are blurred and somewhat vague. The outlines of objects that are closer to the eye are sharp and in focus. For this reason, strong, sharp value contrasts appear as though they were in the foreground, and closely blended values seem farther away. This principle has important application in costume for those who wish to increase or decrease apparent size. In like manner, the higher values, because they reflect more light, usually make objects and figures stand out and appear larger than objects of similar size in darker values. The latter phenomenon, however, depends on the degree of contrast between the object and its background. An overweight skier will be more conspicuous against the snow-covered slopes in a black outfit than in camouflaging white.

It is clear that the degree of contrast in the lightness or darkness of colors helps to determine the predominant expression of the total appearance.

Intensity is the third dimension of color, and it describes its brightness or dullness. Strong, brilliant, saturated colors are referred to as highly intense; weak, grayed, neutral colors are those that are low in intensity. The intensity of a hue is lowered by mixing it with its complement. Hues with similar intensities usually combine to create a pleasing relationship, although weak or moderate hues are more harmonious than two or more different hues at maximum intensity. Vivid colors tend to produce strong, dramatic effects; grayed, subdued tones tend to be soft, subtle, and conservative.

Intensity, like the other dimensions of color, has an impact on total appearance. Bright colors have much the same effect as warm hues; they tend to advance, attract attention, and thereby increase apparent size. Weak, subdued colors, like the cool hues, are receding, soothing, and less conspicuous than bright colors.

The Prang Color System.   The Prang system is probably the one most used in a beginning study of color. Color has been taught with this system for many, many years in primary and secondary schools. The basic color wheel of the system is made up of three primaries: red, yellow, and blue. Combinations of these produce the binary or secondary hues: orange, violet, and green. Intermediate hues are made by mixing primary and secondary hues. Thus, according to the color wheel (Figure 12.17), combining the primaries of red and yellow will result in orange; yellow

and blue produce green. So, too, red and orange result in the intermediate hue labeled RO (red-orange).

Colors that are opposite on the color wheel are called complements and when added together, tend to neutralize or gray the hues, creating colors of different values. Certain proportions of complements will, in fact, produce a completely neutral gray. So, too, adding white, or sometimes plain water, reduces the saturation and thus changes the intensity of the color.

The Prang system uses hue, value, and intensity as the three dimensions of color. The system is simple to use and sufficiently accurate for many design purposes. But lack of precision lessens its value for scientific and research purposes.[8]

The Munsell Color System.   In the 1890s a Boston art instructor began to standardize the three aspects of color—hue, value, and intensity (which he called chroma). Munsell was the first to illustrate these dimensions of color graphically on a three-dimensional model. The first charts were printed in 1905 and today the Munsell Color Company continues work in "standardization and improvement of the color charts along the line foreseen by their originator."[9]

The system uses five primary hues: red, yellow, green, blue, and purple. These are combined to make the intermediate hues: YR, GY, BG, PB, and RP. Steps between the primary and intermediate hues are assumed to be equal in distance and are numbered from one to one hundred around the outer rim of the Munsell Hue Circle

[8]Helen Marie Evans, *Man the Designer* (New York: Macmillan Co., Inc., 1973), pp. 41–42.
[9]*Munsell Book of Color*, pp. 1–2.

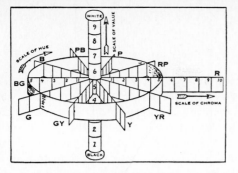

Figure 12.21 A three-dimensional projection of the attributes of color—hue, value, and intensity—in their relation to one another. The circular band represents the hues in their proper sequences. The upright center axis is the scale of value. The paths pointing outward from the center show the steps of chroma or intensity, increasing in strength, as indicated by the numerals.

(Figure 12.18). However, to simplify the numbering, primary and intermediate hues were given the number 5 and combined with a letter or letters. Thus 5R refers to red, and 5YR would be yellow-red. Similarly 5B is blue and 5PB, purple-blue. As you can see from the figure, intermediate steps are also numbered, so that 7.5GY would be halfway between 5GY and 10GY. Values are represented by a notation from 1/ to 9/ with near-black equal to 1/ and near-white at the upper extreme. An object that appears visually midway between black and white has a value notation of 5/. The lighter tints of a color are indicated by notations above 5/; the darker shades have numbers below 5/.

The home value level of a color is the step on the value scale at which the hue reaches its fullest intensity. The hues progress in a natural order of values from yellow (which is at full intensity at 8/) in both directions until they reach the complement of yellow (purple-blue), which is the darkest. The home value level for green is 5/, red 4/, blue 4/, and purple 3/. These are the levels at which the greatest number of intensity variations will occur, that is, the greatest number of yellows will be found at lighter levels; the greatest number

of purple-blues will be at darker value levels. These can be seen on the central pole in Figure 12.21.

In the Munsell system chroma is measured by the number of steps it departs from neutral gray. Starting with a neutral gray axis, intensity steps are numbered outward from 1/ up to the strongest saturation obtainable for any given hue. The three-dimensional representation in Figure 12.21 shows the relationship of hue, value, and intensity, but only at value level 5/. These same relationships exist at all value levels. The color chart in Plate I takes one set of complementary colors (yellow and purple-blue) and flattens out the sphere to indicate how hues depart from opposite sides of the neutral axis at various value levels. All the colors to the right of the neutral scale are of the same hue (a slightly greenish yellow). The two colors closest to the right of the neutral axis have the same hue (7.5Y) and the same intensity (/2), but they differ in value. At value level 8/ you see a progession in intensity of yellow from /0 to /12. All colors to the left of the axis are of the same hue (7.5PB); all hues in the third row are identical in value (4/); intensity increases from a dull gray-blue (/2) to a bright, electric blue (/14) at the outermost step.

The intensity of a hue is lowered by mixing it with its complement. Maximum saturation can be obtained only at the home value level for any given hue, and raising or lowering the value of a hue from that level automatically reduces its intensity.

The complete notation for any color is written with the number and letter of the hue first, followed by value over intensity (hue value/intensity). A vivid yellow, for example, might be written as 7.5Y 8/12. This would mean a yellow slightly on the greenish side, at the home value level of 8, in twelve steps of increasing intensity from the neutral axis. A color of the same hue and value which might be described as ivory, would be written 7.5Y 8/2. A deep olive green may have the same hue and intensity as the ivory, but be darker in value. Its notation would be 7.5Y 3/2.

You can readily see that such precision in notation is readily communicable to people in different situations and virtually all over the world. A Munsell notation of 5R 5/10 can be accurately matched as a hue of red with a middle value on the lightness/darkness pole and an intense chroma, since it extends far out on the chroma line.

The Munsell system is the most sophisticated of those available. It is a useful research tool facilitating communication even internationally. It is widely used in industry, business, and education. The system of notation allows accurate color matching of dyes by textile workers in both home furnishings and apparel. The system is used in laboratories, by food processors, medical technologists, and chemists working in such widely diverse areas as the automotive and textile industries. The system has been adopted by the U.S.A. Standards Institute, the American Society of Testing Materials (ASTM), and the National Bureau of Standards. It is the basis for the Japanese Industrial Standard for Color, the British Standards Institute, and the German Standards Color System.

Color Perception and Illusion

The perception of color is a complex process affected by many situational and environmental factors. The way we see color depends on: (1) the amount of light energy available, (2) conditions of light energy at the time, (3) the size of the

colored object, (4) the condition of the visual mechanism (the eyes), (5) the way the brain is working at the time, and (6) the "viewer's mental set."[10] "The eye is truly blind to what the mind cannot see."[11] We tend to see what we are accustomed to seeing.

Color illusions occur whenever two colors are next to each other. Since colors are rarely seen in isolation, it is important to understand how they affect each other when placed close together.

When two colors lie in the same hemisphere of a color circle (i.e., are similar in hue) they will push each other farther apart in hue and will weaken each other in saturation . . . when two colors lie in different hemispheres (i.e., are quite different in hue) they will push each other farther apart in hue and strengthen each other in saturation.[12]

If we study the two reds in Plate II, we get the impression that they are different. When surrounded by yellow, red moves toward the violet side of the spectrum; when seen next to blue, red appears to be more orange. This simple phenomenon is known as the principle of **simultaneous contrast**: "Whenever two different colors come into direct contact, the differences between them will be intensified. They will tend to push apart. The change will be greater in proportion to the degree that they differ in value, hue, or chroma."[13]

The effect of hue contrast is readily demonstrated in Plate II. Contiguous hues force each other apart on the color spectrum. A bright yellow dress worn by a cool blonde will impart greenish tones to the

[11]Ibid., p. 112.
[10]Ball, *The Art of Interior Design*, p. 109.
[12]Ibid., p. 111.
[13]Quinn, *Consumer Color Charts*, p. 10.

COLOR DIMENSION CHART

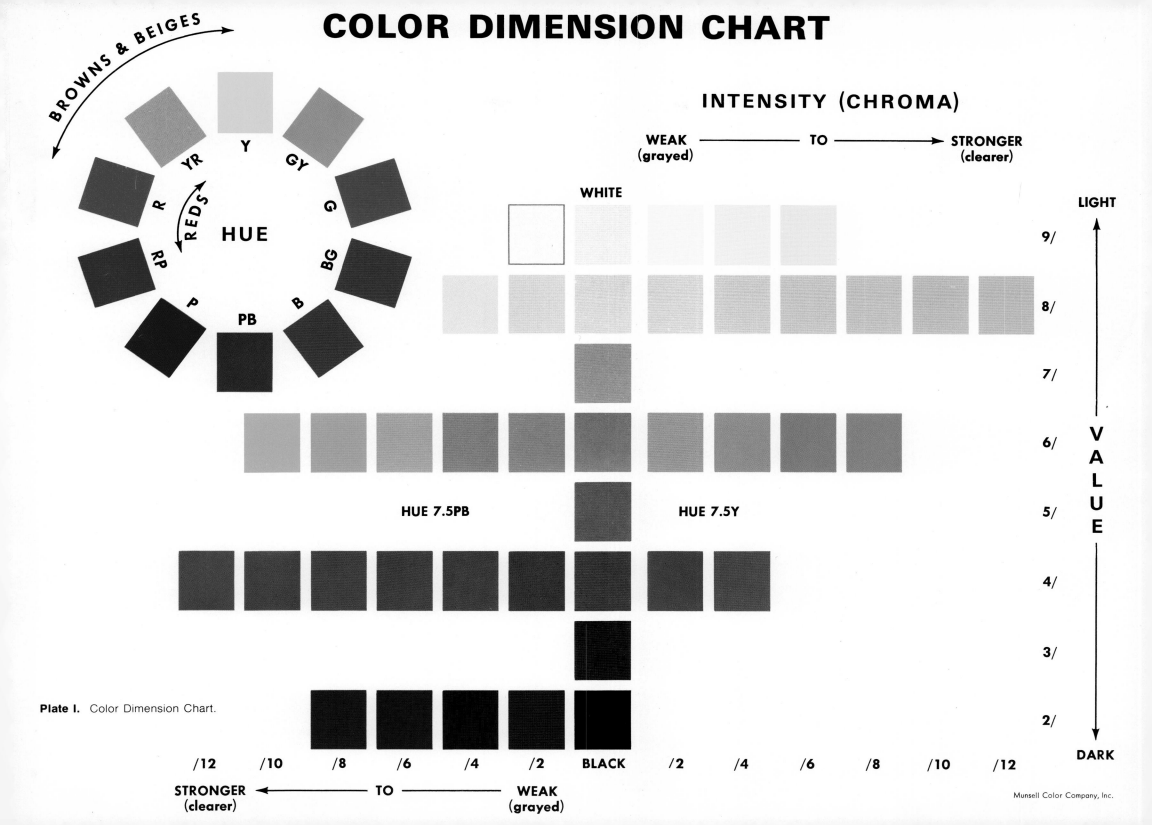

BROWNS & BEIGES

HUE

YR

Y

GY

R

REDS

G

RP

BG

P

B

PB

INTENSITY (CHROMA)

WEAK (grayed) ——— TO ———→ STRONGER (clearer)

WHITE

LIGHT

9/

8/

7/

HUE 7.5PB   HUE 7.5Y

6/

5/

4/

3/

2/

Plate I. Color Dimension Chart.

/12   /10   /8   /6   /4   /2   BLACK   /2   /4   /6   /8   /10   /12

STRONGER (clearer) ←——— TO ———→ WEAK (grayed)

DARK

V A L U E

Munsell Color Company, Inc.

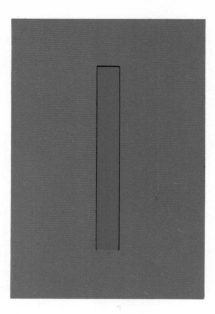

Plate II. These blocks of color show the effects of simultaneous contrast. In both blocks the reds are exactly the same, but the yellow forces the red toward a red-purple cast, while the blue makes the red appear to have an orange cast. In the blue block, the red seems lighter and brighter than it does when surrounded by yellow.

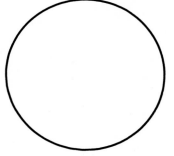

Plate III. Focus your eyes on the red circle and stare at it intently for a minute or so. Shift your gaze quickly to the blank circle on the right and maintain your steadfast gaze. What color appears?

hair. Turquoise next to green will appear blue, just as red will push purple toward blue.

In the case of value contrast, a middle value will appear lighter against dark colors and lower in value against light colors. Again in Plate II the same red looks darker when surrounded by light yellow than it does when surrounded with a medium blue. This is why light colors seem more luminous when combined with black, and why dark colors appear brighter when contrasted against white.

The interaction between different intensities also alters the frame of reference in which we see color. A weak blue worn next to a saturated blue will turn into gray. Old rose will make a medium red more intense by comparison. A dull brown suit will intensify the color of rich brown hair.

Another phenomenon that affects the way we see color is commonly known as the **afterimage**. If you gaze fixedly at the red circle in Plate III and then transfer your gaze to the white paper, you will see a pale blue-green spot of color, the complement of red. If you repeat this experiment with any other bright color you will find that a complementary afterimage will appear. This occurs because the nerve endings in the human eye quickly tire of strong color; sensitivity to that color is reduced and the complementary receptors in the eye become dominant. In other words, the eye provides its own relief from strong color. When the eye shifts its gaze from a bright orange sweater down to neutral gray slacks, it will superimpose an afterimage of blue, making the slacks appear bluish gray. A bright magenta worn next to white skin will impart a greenish tone to the skin.

When an intense hue is combined with the color from which it differs the most—its complement—a series of successive after-images are superimposed, increasing intensity to the point of vibration. This explains why it is difficult for the eye to look at strong complementary colors in close combination. The vibrating sensation is reduced when one or both complements are toned down or grayed. In costume, pleasing effects are difficult to achieve with intensifying opposites.

Color Expression

The **expressiveness** of color is evident in our common daily associations of color with mood or emotion. Even people who have a limited sensitivity to color talk about "feeling blue," being "in the pink" of condition, feeling "green with envy," or having a "rosy disposition." Individuals vary in their perception of color, and the meanings they attach to specific hues are usually found to depend on their past associations and experiences with color. A number of experimental studies, however, have identified some of the commonalities in the human reaction to color.

One experiment, for example, conducted in the pediatrics unit of the Teaching Hospital at the University of Florida, recorded the reactions of children between the ages of nine months and five years when approached first by a nurse in a white uniform, and then by a nurse wearing a softer pastel. The children were reported to be calmer, more relaxed, and amenable when nurses wore the tinted rather than the stark white uniforms. Similar studies indicate that wall colors have a decided effect on the mental outlook of patients.[14]

[14]The research on color associations, attitudes, and preferences is too extensive to be summarized here. If the reader wishes to pursue this aspect of color further, reference to the *Psychological Abstracts* will yield a

Color is used in many ways to relieve the traditional stark white in hospitals and other institutional settings. At numerous institutions, particularly for the chronically ill and disabled, interiors are decorated to be eye-appealing and interesting to look at. Ben Rose, designer of draperies and wall hangings, "says that color is even important to blind patients, who are extremely sensitive to the reactions of sighted visitors to the fabrics and colors around them."[15]

In general, studies have shown remarkable similarity in the characteristics attributed to particular colors by different individuals. The warm colors (yellow, orange, and red) are usually seen as cheerful, aggressive, stimulating, and exciting. The cool hues suggest quietness, aloofness, tranquillity, or serenity. It is important to keep the character of color in mind when judging or combining colors,[16] because

for example, a sad brown might be enlivened by

combination with a cheerful yellow, while a "strong, egotistical" purple overbears completely a "simpering, mild" blue. It is likely that this character aspect is inadequately grasped by many people in the combining of colours; and it would seem that some women in choosing dress colour schemes, whilst very sensitive to the clashing or blending of colours as such, ignore the more subtle beauty which is derived from a blending of this aesthetic character of the colours with their own characters and temperaments.[17]

Our sensitivity to color is sometimes conditioned by factors beyond our control. Some individuals, more usually men, are actually blind to one or more colors in the spectrum. Other rare individuals can "feel" differences in color with their eyes closed. Most people, however, can develop their sensitivity through a study of color attributes and gain an increased perception of color in their clothes and environment.

SUMMARY

Elements of Design

Clothing is at once so ever-present, so directly observable, and so personally relevant that it provides a common medium through which our sensitivity to the basic components of aesthetic expression can be developed. The five plastic elements have been defined as line, space, form, texture, and color. Variation in the qualities of each of these elements contributes to the overall effect of the total design. Line may vary in straightness, direction, and strength. Form is a

number of sources. Consult the subject index on color. A suggested text on the subject is C. W. Valentine, *The Experimental Psychology of Beauty* (London: Methuen & Company, 1962). See chapters 1 and 2 on "Colour and Colour Preferences," and "Attitudes to Colours and Combinations of Colours."

[15]*PPG Products*, 86, No. 2 (1978), p. 29.

[16]For the symbolic meanings usually associated with specific colors see Graves, *Art of Color and Design*, pp. 402–408; Morton, *Costume and Personal Appearance*, pp. 175–177; or Valentine, *Experimental Psychology of Beauty*, p. 57.

[17]Valentine, *Experimental Psychology of Beauty*, p. 62.

composite of the human figure itself, the silhouette of the costume, and the positive shapes within the boundaries of the silhouette. Texture may be described by its visual appearance, the tactile sensations it produces, and by its quality of "hand." Space varies in its relative size and shape. Color, probably the most complex of all the elements yet at the same time the most stimulating, varies greatly in its three dimensions of hue, value, and intensity. In costume, none of the elements exists in isolation, and each one is affected by the other four in combination. The creative process requires a knowledge and understanding of the nature of these tools in order to use them effectively in dress.

FOR FURTHER READING

Davis, Marian L. *Visual Design in Dress*. Englewood Cliffs,N.J.: Prentice-Hall, Inc., 1980, pp. 121–152.

Evans, Helen Marie. *Man the Designer*. New York: The Macmillan Company, 1973, pp. 18–51.

Itten, Johannes. *The Art of Color*. New York: Van Nostrand Reinhold Company, 1973.

Chapter 13

EXPRESSIVENESS

IN DRESS: APPLIED DESIGN

We may approach the study of costume at the logical, objective, descriptive level, that is, we may consider separately the various aspects of line, form, space, texture, and color, and we may analyze their function in the total design. And we may add to these design elements the special organizing principles of design—balance, proportion, rhythm, and emphasis. This level of human perception is limited to intellectual observations and produces an awareness of design qualities, an understanding of their effects, and perhaps an appreciation of their aesthetic unity.

Other phases of human perception, however, are not objective observations, they are, rather, subjective reactions. Clothing has the power to arouse feelings and thoughts in the observer's mind,

emotions that are not easily described but are keenly felt. The costume serves as a symbol—a kind of catalyst that evokes feelings that extend far beyond the costume itself. If the wearing of a bowler hat and a tweedy suit conveys the essence of the "typical" Englishman, such symbols may produce associations of political sentiments, social formalities, moral sensibilities—none of which can be visualized, but all of which can be deeply felt or experienced.

A clothing symbol stands for something beyond itself. Symbolism in dress is often unconscious, but a symbol used consciously can be more powerful: the designer or the wearer can, through careful manipulation, heighten the effect that is being created. A dynamic, forceful personality can be emphasized by strong angular lines, or by forms that are large in scale and widely spaced. The effect may be compounded further through the use of coarse, heavy, rough textures, and bold colors in striking contrasts. Thus, through a knowledgeable use of symbols, the communicator draws the communicant more closely into the intended mood. A truly artistic experience is one that requires a personal involvement, both at the level of creative expression and at the level of enjoyment, understanding, or appreciation. The creation of clothing, therefore, or the organization of dress, is a form of artistic expression through which feelings and ideas are communicated. This concept is embodied in the term **expressiveness**.

EXPRESSIVENESS IN DRESS

Every age has a distinctive flavor, just as every designer develops a characteristic style, and both these phenomena derive from expressiveness. Style is very closely allied to symbol making. Those who are familiar with the products of the couture designers can spot the earmarks of a gown or coat by Halston, a dress by von Furstenburg, or a suit by the tailors of Savile Row. In other words, designers impart their individual imprints to the products of their craft and in doing so reveal a part of their nature, their ideals, values, thoughts, and emotions. The product in turn evokes a similar or perhaps a widely different range of feelings and emotions in the observer. It is important to note here, however, that this two-way communication between designer and observer takes place whether or not the designer's work is recognized by name. Art communicates, sometimes negatively and sometimes positively, but seldom neutrally. It happens whether or not an artist is known by name. Dress as an art form has this same power to create moods, to provoke opinions, to produce reactions (Figure 13.1). We may like or dislike high fashion, but seldom are we, collectively, indifferent.

Why do some designers see woman as something ethereal—beautiful, constrained, statuesque—and others see her as being quite logical—uncompromisingly modern and stripped for action? The answer of course is that all designers project themselves into their work. Courrèges began his career as an engineer. He was profoundly influenced by the ideas of LeCorbusier, the architect, and maintains almost as much interest in architecture as he does in the couture.

Figure 13.1 Design *may* produce nonfunctional clothing, with the beauty in the object created devoid of utility.

In his own words Courrèges once said: "Luxury in clothes to me has no meaning. It belongs to the past. My problem is not rich embroidery, useless lavishness—it is to harmoniously resolve function problems—just like the engineer who designs a plane, like the man who conceives a car."[1]

Some observers have trouble in perceiving in a design the same meanings that the creator intended to convey. Particularly if designers are ahead of their time—as creative people often are—many people will inevitably view their work in the light of their own experience rather than in the light in which the designer sees it personally. The more we understand the artist's goals, the more we will share in the expressiveness of individual designs.

The creation of clothing is a form of artistic expression through which feelings and ideas are conveyed.

All people cannot express themselves through the actual creation of clothing. In our world of mass-produced ready-to-wear wardrobes, the opportunity for self-expression often seems limited. Technology to some extent reduces individuality, yet at the same time it has made available a much greater variety of products to more people than ever before. The elements of choice making become an increasingly complex problem. In this sense, every individual assumes the position of the artist; the extent to which the solution of a problem shows personal influence is an indication of expressiveness. Those who lack the ability to design individual appar-

el items can still experience expressiveness in combining component parts that make up a total outfit or wardrobe.

Johnny Carson became a powerful influence on the clothing tastes of American men with the clothes he wore on the "Tonight Show," and he later became involved in the apparel business. Considering himself a typical American man, he carefully avoids extremes of dress. Some years ago he said, "The average guy feels a little weird wearing costumes. Doc (Severinsen, the garishly dressed bandleader on his show) can carry it off. But people forget Doc is a musician, a personality."[2] Not all men, however, are so conservative. Some are elegantly flamboyant and dramatic.

[2]Carson as quoted by Howard Kissel in "Johnny Carson. The Comedian as Clothier," *Gentlemen's Quarterly*, November 1971, p. 70.

Figure 13.2   This sultry dress with exposed midriff is typical of the bone-sleek styles that made Cher Bono a fashion pacesetter.

[1]"The Lord of the Space Ladies," *Life*, May 24, 1965, p. 57.

Figure 13.3 and 13.4 The expressive power of dress can transform one's character.

Expressiveness can also be reserved and dignified, as shown by some of the wives of recent United States presidents, such as Pat Nixon, Betty Ford, or Rosalyn Carter. In contrast, the image singer Cher projects through what she wears is anything but "reserved." Her clothes, which are as lithe and bone-pared as her figure, made her a high-gloss sex symbol (Figure 13.2).

The expression of personality through the medium of dress comes about through development of an individual style, a style that becomes the person's symbol and gives the dominant external "tone" or expressive quality to that person's appearance (Figures 13.3 and 13.4). The symbol may not reveal all of one's traits, and, in fact, it may even camouflage some. Yet a distinctive style gives a summarizing effect to personality and solves an artistic problem that is unique to the individual.

Aesthetic expression of the self through clothing may lead to a deeper comprehension of one's most conspicuous characteristics.

SUMMARY

Expressiveness in Dress

Clothing is an ideal medium through which many people may fulfill creative needs and express individuality. The designer, as well as the person who selects and organizes the components of costume, may communicate moods, feelings, emotions, and ideas through the pervasive effects of applying the organizing principles of design to the elements of art. Expressiveness in dress is the quality of appearance that is intensifying, unifying, and summarizing. It is the underlining of traits that facilitates a shared experience between communicator and communicant, and it helps to create in the observer the same moods and emotions the artist intended.

BEAUTY IN CLOTHING

We have seen that the effect of individual elements in a design may be compounded or intensified in their impact when combined with other elements of like qualities. Stimulating line may be reinforced by stimulating color in extreme contrasts of dark and light so that the total effect is quite shocking. On the other hand, the effects of such elements may also be lessened or even hidden when combined with dissimilar elements. Thus, we use straight lines to counteract the curves of a full, rounded figure, and soft, bulky tweeds to camouflage the hard, bony angularity of the very thin figure.

By using art components in this way, we can alter the frame of reference in which we see the human form, and in so doing, we can create illusions or effects that would not be possible in any other way. By manipulating art elements, dress may be organized into a satisfying and meaningful whole in such a way that the whole becomes more meaningful than its parts.

But what is the ultimate goal of such organization? The terms *more meaningful, more effective, more beautiful* imply that there are some universal standards by which we are to judge the value of the total design. How do we resolve the fact that lips distended with discs are considered beautiful by the Suyá Indians and ugly by most Americans? Why is it that a costume that was regarded as the ultimate in beauty ten years ago appears hideous to us today? Are the standards of beauty ever-changing—

and often contradictory—from culture to culture, from era to era?

The evaluation of costume or dress can reflect all manner of criteria that may be only incidental to its aesthetic quality. We may judge it on the basis of the skill required to produce it. We may see it as valuable in one social context but not in another. We may place great weight on its symbolic value or on the power with which it communicates an idea. We may view it in terms of its cultural manifestations, that is, the extent to which it expresses the character of the times. Clearly, each of these approaches has some validity in determining the worth of a costume, and the final judgment probably will involve them all.

If, however, we confine our judgments to those qualities that delight the eye, to the organization of elements that makes the design comfortable or pleasurable to behold, we are then dealing objectively with the aesthetic attributes of clothing.

What Is Beauty?

For centuries philosophers have searched for a definition of beauty, a word that has such universal meaning, yet a concept that is difficult to express in objective terms. Reactions to aesthetic stimuli depend not so much on association and experience as they do on the psychological similarities in the minds of observers. Beauty has come to be synonymous with the human desire for order; people are made restless by discord and confusion and thus seek to systematize, organize, and categorize their experiences into something that is meaningful and satisfying to them.

Balance, for example, creates a feeling of rest or repose; it is a reassuring, stable quality. Lack of balance, on the other hand—or the fear of losing one's balance—becomes a disturbing factor and makes for insecurity. Simple action patterns, repeated over and over, become effortless when executed in time to rhythm or pattern. Rhythm means regularity—repetition on which one can depend—and, like balance, gives a kind of psychological reassurance.

The human need for order and stability, however, is divided by a corresponding need for interest and excitement. Thus, the principles of dominance and subordination, unity in variety, emphasis through contrast, all stem from an attempt to maintain a pleasing relationship between order and diversity, between stability and new experience.

The Organizing
Principles of Design

Nature has a habit of combining elements in a way that is never absolute, seldom regular, yet always logical. In the search for beauty, we attempt to simulate nature's way by mixing sameness with variation. Often there is disagreement over the precise terminology that best describes this concept, but the differences in wording seem to be not so important as the overall agreement on intended meaning.

Beauty involves **order** (unity, compatibility, consistency, relatedness, integration, harmony), without which human sensations are troubled and confused; and its counterpart, **interest** (call it variety, contrast, conflict, difference), without which our sensations cannot be fully stimulated. In general, people are bored with the obvious, excited by the unexpected, yet they are uncomfortable in disorder and secure in regularity.

The problem is knowing how to achieve the proper balance between order and interest. Many years ago, Birkhoff developed a mathematical formula that would yield a precise quantity of aesthetic merit. It was based on the theory that aesthetic measure (M) is equal to the order (O) divided by the complexity (C), or $M = O/C$. Thus, the value of M is increased if the complexity is diminished without altering the order, or if the order is increased without changing the complexity.[3]

This formula has been applied to clothing by adding points for costume details, such as lapel pin *and* necklace *and* contrasting bright buttons on the same outfit. A high score reflects a cluttered (or complex) appearance. A low score illustrates the concept of "elegant simplicity." Thus aesthetic merit (M) is increased if there is either less contrast (C) or complexity to the outfit, or if the overall order is maintained by well coordinating (O) or matched accessories.

In direct opposition to such absolute standards is the theory that standards of any sort have no meaning because they lessen the individual's freedom to respond to art objects.

Somewhere between these two extremes lies a logical set of criteria that can guide

[3]George D. Birkhoff, *Aesthetic Measure* (Cambridge, Mass.: Harvard University Press, 1933).

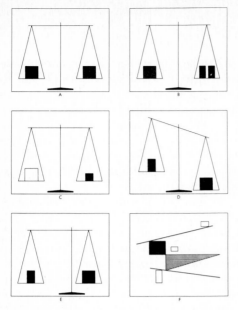

Figure 13.5 Balance can be achieved in a number of ways.

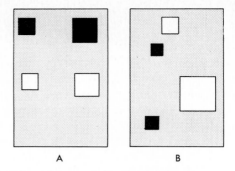

Figure 13.6 A design judgment problem in balance.

us in organizing, interpreting, and evaluating art experiences. The following principles may help the student in evaluating the organization of elements within a design.

Balance, the first organizing principle, is achieved through equal weights or forces on both sides of a central axis (Figure 13.5). If we observe the human figure in action, we find that the head is always balanced over the center of gravity. Were this not true, the figure would fall over without some external means of support. Visual balance is much like our physical balance. Loss of equilibrium is an uncomfortable experience.

Balance may be accomplished in any one of several ways. The scales in Figure 13.5 are abstract representations of formal and informal balance. Scale A illustrates formal or bisymmetric balance, which is the most obvious and probably the easiest to achieve, because one side is the mirror image of the other. It presents a stately, dignified type of symmetry, but it can easily become static and uninteresting if

other aspects of the design are not handled skillfully. Scale B is a variation of formal balance, in which one shape is replaced by two smaller shapes having a combined equal weight. Another variation in Scale C uses a much larger object on the left, but because it is so much lighter in value it can still be placed at the same distance from the axis. Obviously, all designs are not balanced designs. If unequal weights are used at equal distances from the center, equilibrium will be lost, as it is in Scale D.

Informal or asymmetric balance brings unequal weights into equilibrium by arranging them at different distances from the axis, as is shown in Scales E and F. The latter is a more complex arrangement, and it requires greater skill in identifying the visual weight of dissimilar elements. Usually the darker values, the stronger intensities, and the warmer hues carry greater visual weight than light, dull, or cool elements of comparable size and shape. The heavier areas of a design, therefore, need to be reduced in size or placed nearer the center and bottom.

Balance affects the relationship between individual shapes and the background or field of a design. This is shown in a simplified way in Figure 13.6. The larger shapes in A are placed to the right of the center and almost at the same distance as the smaller shapes on the left. In addition, the dark, heavy shapes are at the top,

1931 1915

Figure 13.7 Top- and bottom-heaviness produce a lack of equilibrium in design.

making the whole effect not only lopsided but top-heavy. The rearrangement in B eliminates the overpowering dark and increases the weight of the white square by enlarging it. The dark accent is small, high, and farther from the edge of the field. The design has been stabilized, and at the same time the forms have been brought into relationship with the ground.

A similar top-heaviness can be observed in Figure 13.7. But this also shows that merely transferring the weight to the bottom is not the answer, for a costume can easily become bottom-heavy. A reduction in size or area is usually required as well. It is this top-to-bottom balance that is often destroyed by a large bright hat, a dark blouse worn with a light skirt, or white shoes with a middle- or low-valued costume. Men's dress provides a standard formula for achieving balance: pocket handkerchief to the left, hat tilted slightly to the right.

Most types of informal balance provide greater interest than bisymmetric arrangements, but asymmetry is not achieved just by making two sides of a costume unalike.

Proportion is the principle of design that deals with relationships or ratios. When we talk about the proportions of a room, we are referring to its length in relation to its height and width. The spatial dimension of one measure is impossible to comprehend visually except in comparison with another. The human figure appears heavy or thin, short or tall, on the basis of its width/height ratio, which for the average person is 2:7.5.

Two basic design problems deal with proportion. One is the planning of shapes, sizes, spaces, or areas within the figure rectangle in such a way that each part bears a relationship to each other and to the whole. The second is the problem of creating the illusion of pleasing proportions with costume when the spatial dimensions of the body are not pleasing. The latter function of proportion will be discussed in Chapter 16, and we will concern ourselves here with an analysis of space division within the silhouette and the relationship of forms within the total design.

In Figure 13.8 we see that the body rectangle is subdivided into shapes, some of which are related to anatomy, and others that are dictated by fashion. Waistline placement and hem, jacket, and trouser lengths are the major horizontal divisions that fluctuate from year to year. An increase in hem width will also alter the visual dimension of height, just as shoulder padding and wide trouser cuffs create different width/height ratios. It is important to identify the proportions of these basic shapes before going on to the more complex relationships.

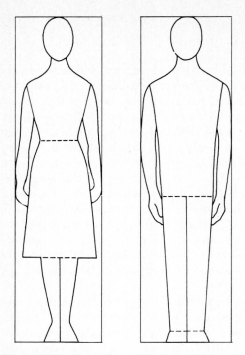

Figure 13.8 Basic shapes within the body rectangle.

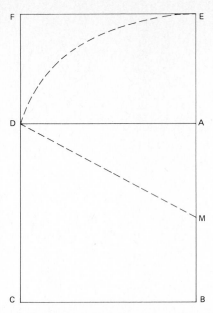

Figure 13.9 The Golden Mean Rectangle. (ABCD = perfect square; M = ½AB; MD = radius of arc to E.)

Problems in proportion parallel those within the larger organization of interest in order. How can the figure be divided into shapes that give variety and at the same time maintain a relatedness to the whole? The Greek laws of proportion give us a clue that is embodied in the *Golden Mean*. The Golden Mean Rectangle has a width equal to the side of a square, and its length is equal to half that measure plus the diagonal of half the square. This produces a ratio in which the smaller part (BC) is to the larger part (BE) as the larger part is to the whole (BC + BE). Rectangle ADFE also has the same proportions as the larger BCFE (see Figure 13.9).

In effect, this creates a relationship that is not too difficult for the eye to perceive, yet not so obvious that the eye dismisses it without further exploration. The body rectangle itself does not conform to this proportion; body proportions are far more complex, but no less pleasing in their relationships. Many shapes within the silhouette, however, take on a visual relationship that approximates it.

Taking the lower left designs in Figure 13.10 as an example, we can see that the upper block of garment B has a ratio of width to length that is roughly 5 to 8. The skirt block is almost square but it does not give an impression of boxiness because it is divided vertically, creating a center rectangle (EFGH) with the same proportions as the total garment block (ABCD). Illustration A, on the other hand, creates a bodice rectangle that is nearly 1 to 2 in ratio, and a skirt block that is broader than it is long. The total skirt rectangle in A, however, has the illusion of squarishness because the vertical divisions break the width and bring the four sides into visual equilibrium.

This does not imply that all good proportion must conform to a mathematical formula. And of course *all* forms have proportions, pleasing or not. For this reason, it is probably more accurate to talk about **related proportions**, as opposed to equal and to unrelated proportions, than it is to use the term **proportion** alone as an organizing principle. If we could use as precise a measure as a scale, we might be able to say that a design either had balance or did not have balance. Aesthetic judgments can never be that absolute, however, and the best that we can do is to say that design X is "more nearly balanced" or "less well balanced" than design Y. Such judgments are always relative.

Another aspect of proportion concerns the sizes of different objects used in combination with the total costume. It is usually expressed by the more specific term **scale** and refers to the size relationship between different parts of the costume and the wearer. A handbag that may in itself be designed with good proportions but scaled to a large figure can look like an outsized shopping bag when carried by a small person. The sizes of hats, collars, pockets, and buttons all present problems in scale relationships. This also extends to surface patterns of fabrics. A small-scaled print that would be suitable and attractive on a petite woman often makes the large figure seem larger because of the heightened contrast in size. Details of costume and articles worn as accessories will ap-

Figure 13.10   Space divisions in A illustrations result in equal measures that lack interest. Proportions have been improved in the B illustrations to create space relationships that are somewhat more pleasing. It is easy to see how raising or lowering skirt length alters the entire affect of the design.

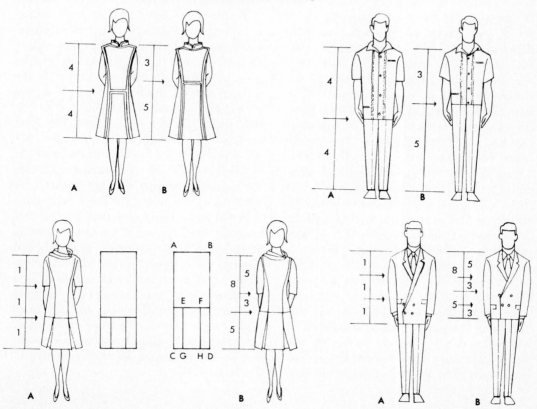

pear to be more related if their sizes are scaled to the wearer's size.

Rhythm is that quality of design that imparts a graceful, flowing movement throughout the costume. A dancer who lacks rhythm is clumsy and awkward; music without rhythm is aimless and incoherent; a costume without rhythm is static and disjointed. Words become poetic when they are combined with a planned interval and a beat or accent. This same concept of orderly, related movement applies to visual design. Just as rhythm in music helps the ear to make an easy transition from one note to another, rhythm in costume leads the eye from line to line, from shape to shape, from color to color.

Rhythm, like balance, can be achieved in a number of ways, and it may vary from very simple to more complex forms. *Repetition* of lines or shapes, textures or colors, can produce a rhythmic pattern. Like the simple waltz, it has a regular beat, but without some variation it becomes very repetitious and monotonous.

Greater interest can be generated by introducing some variety in the repeat. Note the increasing size of skirt puffs and rosettes in Figure 12.9 as the bustle cascades to the floor. The horizontals become wider and wider as they move down the figure, giving the silhouette the shape of a great cone, with the head of a woman at the apex. This type of gradual transition from the wide to the narrow, from the large to the small, is known as *gradation* or *progression*. Music that becomes progressively louder has a way of building up attention that is somewhat more dynamic than a composition that maintains the same volume throughout. In like manner, progressions in the art elements can build greater interest by increasing or decreasing one or more quality.

Colors may progress from hue to hue, from light to dark, from bright to grayed; textures may go from dull to shiny, rough to smooth.

Movement also can be created by the use of continuous line that may carry the eye throughout the design.

Emphasis is the fourth organizing principle. Emphasis helps to focus attention on the most important areas of a design, creating a center of interest through the dominance of a particular art element. The eye is disturbed and confused when confronted with equally strong conflicting ideas; the conflict cannot be resolved until one idea is allowed to dominate all others. Dominance of one kind of line, shape, texture, or color simplifies the appearance of an ensemble and helps to create an impression of unity.

Emphasis is illustrated in a simplified form in the comparison of the two designs in Figure 13.11. Design A has a dominant vertical direction; the repetition of the perpendicular can be seen in the background shape, in the lines and shapes having the longest dimension, and in the placement of elements within the total composition. Horizontals are used for contrast, but they are kept subordinate to the vertical and are grouped together to create the major focal point. The eye travels from there along the zigzag path to a secondary interest area, the five small circles that contrast in shape with the predominantly straight lines and shapes. Their size and placement, however, do not alienate them from the other elements. Design B lacks a dominant form and direction. Verticals compete with horizontals, straight lines equal curved lines, diamond rivals disk; the same degree of contrast exists throughout the arrangement so that a center of interest is lost.

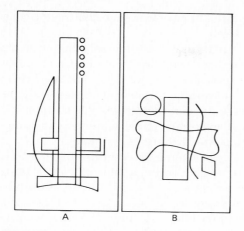

Figure 13.11 A design judgment problem in emphasis.

Men's costume provides a standard though somewhat static formula for attaining emphasis. The center of greatest contrast usually occurs near the face, with the tie making the transition to the dominant area of the suit. A less monotonous effect is achieved when the value contrast at the neck is supported through repetition in subordinate centers created by buttons at the waist and sleeve. At the same time, a pleasing rhythm is developed by using stitch-trimming on pockets and lapels, connecting major and minor centers of interest in their proper sequence of importance, and providing an easy path for the eye to follow.

Thus, emphasis can be achieved through strong contrasts in value, but the contrast can also come about through bright intensities of color, unusual shapes, the use of different textures, a boldness of size, or a juxtaposition of contrasting lines. Such contrasts create effective centers of interest only if they are seen against a background of dominant elements that give unity to the design. Too much contrast

results in disorder; lack of contrast produces monotony.

When the art elements are combined according to the organizing principles of balance, proportion, rhythm, and emphasis, the overall effect is a unity of design that permits effortless enjoyment for the beholder. A design must be evaluated with *all* the principles in mind. An outstanding example of rhythm may be sadly lacking in balance; emphasis can often be achieved by sacrificing scale or good proportion. The final analysis will depend on our ability to integrate these ideas into a total pattern.

Aesthetic integration in dress requires a satisfying balance between order (without which human sensations are confused) and interest (without which human awareness cannot be fully stimulated).

Organization in Color

The fundamental principles underlying the aesthetic use of color in dress are the same as those that apply to the other art elements. Because color is somewhat more complex in its dimensions, however, it merits special consideration. Three basic factors control the effectiveness of costume colors.

Choice of the Predominant Hue

Unity in color organization begins with selection of a hue that will be allowed to dominate in the design. Any color can be beautiful if combined skillfully, but in costume at least, the major hue will probably be more effective if it is related and flattering to the individual's skin tones, hair, and eyes. The predominant hue sets the mood or feeling of the design. It may be warm or cool, subdued or striking, but whatever the choice, it will be the one color around which the harmony will be built.

The predominant hue may or may not occupy the largest area in the design. It will maintain ascendency as long as the colors combined with it are shifted toward that hue from their normal position on the color circle. For example, if the major theme is to be yellow, reds that shift toward the orange side and blues that are on the greenish side, when used in combination, will produce an overall effect of yellow regardless of the amount or saturation of yellow actually used. In other words, if all hues take on a yellowish cast an impression of unity will be achieved.

A predominance of hue is thus made possible by suppressing colors within the range of its complement. This does not mean that complementary hues can never be used together; a touch of red or orange is often needed to warm a predominantly cool color scheme, and the warm hues may require bits of blue or green for accent. If used in controlled amounts, opposite colors will not destroy the unity of a design.

Restricting the Color Range

In costume, a limited number of colors can be used together successfully. Most people will find that an organized plan provides a starting point for color harmony.

The simplest type of mechanical color scheme is the **monochromatic**, in which all colors in the scheme are value or intensity variations of the same hue. A monochromatic color scheme may be made entirely of greens (pale green, gray-green, forest green), or oranges (beige, apricot,

brown), or any other single hue on the color circle.

Analogous hues are neighboring colors that have some basic hue in common. For example, blue-green, blue, and blue-violet all have blue in common. In general, the related color harmonies (monochromatic and analogous) produce quiet, restful combinations that are easy to wear.

Color chords based on contrasting hues are at once striking and difficult to bring into harmony (Figure 13.12). **Complementary** color schemes are those that combine any two hues that are opposite each other on the color circle. Greater variety is introduced by including the two hues on either side of the complement, for example, orange with blue-green and purple-blue. This type of color chord is called **split-complementary** because the complement is split into two components. A double complementary color scheme uses two adjacent hues with their respective complements.

The greatest variety in hue is created in **triad** color plans, which use any three colors that are equidistant on the color circle.

Almost any combination of hues can be made to seem pleasant or unpleasant if the values and intensities of the hues are carefully controlled. A close range of values will produce more harmonious combinations than will strong contrasts. Increased unity also will be achieved if colors are combined in their natural order of value.

Restricting the range of hues, values, and intensities used together will provide a relatedness or unity in the color plan. Conversely, attraction is basically a matter of contrast, and contrast may be produced by any of the three color attributes. The degree of contrast that is desirable in any

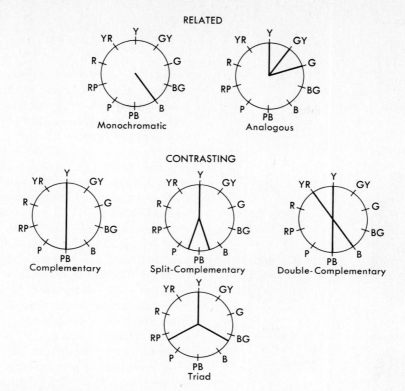

Figure 13.12   Various types of color chords.

scheme is determined largely by the overall effect one wishes to achieve.

Determining the Color Areas

The use of equal amounts of different colors in a costume cancels the principle of hue predominance. Another reason for avoiding equal areas of color is that some colors are visually "heavier" than others, and some are more demanding in their attention-getting qualities.

Unity in color organization can be achieved by allowing one hue to predominate and by restricting the range of colors that are combined with it.

Large areas of low-intensity colors are balanced by small areas of bright color. Research in color psychology seems to bear out the fact that most people prefer saturated colors in smaller quantities and larger areas of the less intense hues. As colors progress toward neutrality, their specific hue is less well defined. By increasing the size of the color area, a greater stimulating effect is produced and the uncertainty of its actual color is diminished. Stronger hues are less apt to lose their identity even when reduced in size. In some cases, therefore, an extremely brilliant color can be used effectively with weaker ones, providing that its relative area is sufficiently restricted.

All the qualities of color are relative, that is, colors are relatively warm, relatively bright, relatively light in contrast with the other colors with which they are used. The greater the contrast in any of these dimensions, the greater the attraction will be. Closer intervals will produce a greater feeling of unity in the composition.

Figure 13.13 Changes in the line of the silhouette are accompanied by subtle changes in the lines of the accessories. (A) The curved line of the bicorne hat repeats the button-trimmed edge of the coat. (B) The slightly concaved line of the top hat flows gracefully into the S-shaped vertical that sweeps along the front edge of the frock coat and into the trouser stripe. (C) Crown lines straighten as the silhouette loses its curves. (D) The straight horizontals of the skirt are echoed in the banded hat. (E) The softly rounded curves give way to (F) deeper convolutions in hat and bell-shaped skirt.

Coordination in Dress

Every article of clothing is composed of lines, shapes, spaces, texture, and color. Harmony in costume begins with the ability to create or select a suit, a dress, a coat, or separates that are balanced designs with good proportions, rhythmically related parts, and pleasing emphasis. The beauty of a garment, however, can be destroyed completely if it is combined with accessories that either lack beauty in themselves or are incompatible with the basic garment. Each component of the costume may be a well-designed object in itself, but it is the complete ensemble that gives the total effect—including the form, coloring, and personality of the wearer. The whole is therefore different from the sum of its parts because each component of dress has either an enhancing or a modifying effect upon every other component.

The terms *overdressing* and *underdressing* relate in part to the suitability of a costume for a particular occasion, but they are also used to describe too much variety, on the one hand, and plain monotony, on the other.

Line Coordination

Accessories chosen to complete an ensemble will enhance the major structural lines of a garment if they are similar in character (Figure 13.13). A broad-brimmed hat, for example, will reduce the perceptual stimulus of predominantly vertical lines in a suit or dress. Rhythm can be achieved through repetition of line in various parts of the costume. Turn back to Figure 12.19 and observe the harmonious relationship achieved through the repetition of softly curved lines in hat, muff, fichu, and dress. Remember that strong contrasts in line will capture the eye; competing centers of interest will detract from a major focal point if line detail in accessories creates attention-getting contrasts.

Figure 13.14 Size and shape coordination in this *Portrait of a Man in Black* by Ter Borch is produced by consistent repetition of pyramidal forms in different dimensions. (Collection, The National Gallery, London)

seem completely unrelated to the rest of the costume. A box handbag, for example, geometric in form, will bear little relationship to the rippling shapes created by a softly draped silhouette. There is a consistent repetition of form in the *Portrait of a Man in Black* (Figure 13.14). The pyramidal shape of the cloak is echoed in the crown of the hat, the skirted breeches, and the fanning ruffles below the knee.

Size and Shape Coordination

The degree to which we consider an accessory large or small is influenced somewhat by fashion, but even if large hats are the current mode, a huge hat will appear incongruous on a small person. We are quick to note the inconsistency that exists between the large brawny man with a full face and a tiny hat with a very narrow brim. Size ratios are also important in selecting purse size, collar widths, and the scale of jewelry and prints. A distinct difference in shape can make an article

Texture Coordination

Articles chosen to be worn together will appear more related if they have a common purpose and a unity of idea or character. A slippery-smooth satin tie will be incompatible with a rough textured tweed unless other elements, such as line or color, give them some relationship. Harmonizing textures are generally those that provide some degree of variation without extreme differences in surface quality. Review Chapter 12 to reinforce your understanding of textural harmony.

In the organization of dress, the whole transcends the sum of the parts, for each component either reinforces or modifies the effect of all others with which it is combined.

SUMMARY

Beauty in Clothing

The evaluation of dress may reflect all manner of criteria in determining the ultimate worth of a garment, but if we confine our judgments to those qualities that please the eye we can identify certain universal responses to beauty that appear to have a firm grounding in an individual's psychological make-up. The human mind is made restless by discord and confusion and thus seeks order in its environment. The need for stability, however, is controlled by a craving for interest and excitement. The organizing principles of balance, rhythm, proportion, and emphasis develop out of the opposing forces of order and interest, unity and variety.

These same principles are employed in the organization of color. One method for achieving a unified color scheme consists of selecting a predominant hue, restricting the range of colors that are used together, and carefully weighing of relative color areas.

Evaluation of dress is made not on the basis of the garment alone, but on the combined effect of all articles that are worn with it. A further perceptual interaction occurs between the costume itself and the form, coloring, and personality of the individual who wears it. Since each component of dress affects all others with which it is combined, the whole of one's appearance takes on greater meaning than the sum of its parts.

WHAT IS TASTE?

Few people, if any, are willing to make their selections of dress solely on the basis of aesthetic criteria. Attitudes, feelings, emotions, and preferences determine to a large extent what we like and what we dislike, what we choose to wear and what we refuse to wear. Any attempt to dress oneself in a manner that is radically different from that of an immediate circle of friends, or from the majority of people in the society, is equivalent to alienating oneself from group values and the standards of the culture. Taste, simply defined, is what we like. It implies a preference among alternatives that have aesthetic implications, but it may or may not be based on objective aesthetic criteria. For the most part, our tastes are shaped by the time and place in which we live, yet each individual has a unique set of experiences that condition personal preferences. Taste is both cultural and individualistic in nature.

Individual Taste

We have seen that there are certain innate reactions to beauty in design. Infants and young children show sensitivity to balance, and the regularity of rhythm—particularly in sounds—produces a soothing, hypnotic effect. The extent to which individuals experience these "normal" reactions, however, depends on their perceptual abilities. People possess varying degrees of sensitivity to rhythm, balance, order, and so forth. Some may be sensitive to certain colors and not to others; a number of people are wholly blind to color.

Individuals also differ in their perception of elements and wholes. Young children and untrained adults tend to become absorbed in the parts of design rather than in the effect of the total composition. One beautiful line in a dress that is otherwise ugly, or a beautiful color in a suit that lacks distinction in general, may often produce such a strong liking that it becomes the main factor in evaluating the costume as a whole. Sensitivity to the techniques of construction influences the skills-oriented person to become absorbed with the technical product rather than the beauty of the design.

Familiarity is another factor that shapes the individual taste. People tend to like the things to which they are accustomed. Studies have shown that the development of taste and judgment is highly correlated to exposure. After an object has been around for a while, one gets used to it. The initial exposure to a new art form is rarely accompanied by sufficient comprehension for full appreciation, but after repeated study the hidden meanings emerge and the beholder finds enjoyment in the more complex forms of art that at first appeared to have no significance or value.

Valentine explains the contradictions of the soothing versus the stimulating qualities of art with "If our attention is to be held for more than a few moments some complexity must be found. . . . Yet the unity and structure of the object must be such that apprehension is facilitated and not frustrated by undue difficulties. Here, as we have just seen, familiarity is a supreme help."[4] Valentine's findings indicate that training in art is linked to an increased liking of more complex figures. Judgments of design made on the basis of familiarity or on the purely personal associations with selected parts of the design are found to be more common among children and adults with little aesthetic training. They also have less concern for overall unity and make their evaluations on the

basis of their own subjective feelings toward the art object rather than any objective analysis of its aesthetic excellence. It also has been shown that individuals with extended art experience and high levels of perceptual awareness tend to exhibit a greater tolerance of experimentation in dress than do those with limited exposure and lower perceptual ability.[5]

Our tastes also are affected by the fact that matters of clothing and appearance (or beauty) are weighted differently in an individual's unique value patterns. For example, some studies seem to show that women who place greater value on the aesthetic and economic factors in their environment tend to have greater interest in dress, whereas the women who place greater value on religious and theoretical factors are relatively disinterested in clothes. Disinterested or not, clothing still reflects the wearer's values. One's tastes, therefore, become synonymous with a sensitivity to the kind of dress that is appropriate to one's outlook and personality. In this sense, the individual's approach to art and clothing becomes a form of self-expression.

The world is full of people with vastly different perceptual abilities, educational levels, value patterns, and cultural backgrounds. Individual taste is a product of all of these combined. We can, however, see degrees of at least three generalized patterns of response to art forms.

There are people whose tastes remain untrained and uncultivated. Largely because they are insensitive to the elements of form, they have very little positive identification with any kind of art. They are

---

[4]C. W. Valentine, *The Experimental Psychology of Beauty* (London: Methuen & Company, 1962), p. 420.

[5]Edith Pankowski, "Perception of Clothing and Selected Areas of Tolerance for a Group of College Males." Ph.D. diss., Pennsylvania State University, 1969.

not attuned to "culture" in general. (Note that we use the word *culture* in a different context here, as general refinement and appreciation of the arts.) Those who do not perceive the relationships between the arts and daily life are indifferent to beauty, and they therefore feel that their clothes need not be beautiful as long as they are comfortable.

At the opposite extreme are those who have a high degree of perceptual awareness of art in many forms, and who experience a genuine enjoyment of beauty. Because they have been exposed to a wide range of aesthetic experiences, they can develop an intellectual and objective approach that enables them to appreciate the more subtle, complex creations. The vast majority of Americans fall somewhere between the two extremes, which of course is what makes "popular taste" popular. It is a taste that is conditioned by majority opinion, based on the principle that when in Rome it is best to do as the Romans do.

Popular taste can be determined by vote. Samplings of public opinion on issues of taste often are conducted by organizations such as the Gallup Poll. Popular opinions, however, are rarely based on objective analysis, and in most cases they bear little relationship to aesthetic criteria. The tastes of aesthetically oriented people are more closely allied to standards of beauty; for such people, *taste* and *beauty* are more nearly synonymous.

Individual tastes are conditioned by one's perceptual abilities, education, value pattern, and cultural background.

The Tastes of an Era

Any form of art must be judged not only on the basis of aesthetic criteria, but in light of the culture and the era in which it is produced.

The ruins of antiquity were just as available in the twelfth century as in the fifteenth, and there were esthetically sensitive people at both times. The twelfth-century people remained much more aloof to the classical remains because they lacked the underlying affinity of outlook needed to make the classical forms seem vital, not because they were unexposed to the forms or lacked the esthetic capacity for their appreciation.[6]

Tastes are varied and they are changing, and like the other forms of artistic expression, clothing reflects the cognitive, moral, and social aspects of the times. The immediate reaction to radically new fashions is usually one of dislike. But as the eyes become accustomed to a new idea through its frequent appearance in fashion magazines and newspapers, as manufacturers pour hundreds of thousands of dollars into production, as fashion leaders are seen and photographed in the controversial style, and as more and more ready-to-wear garments appear on the market at prices that make them available to all, the once prevalent value of modesty becomes less and less important.

The revolution in male wardrobes that began in the 1960s reflected a changing social pattern that went far beyond the length of the hair and the cut of the suit. It reflected what some writers called "the spirit of the NOW." For the decade of the sixties, that spirit included

. . . a whole generation with no memory of global war, an internationality that increases

[6]Frank Seiberling, *Looking Into Art* (New York: Henry Holt & Company, 1959), p. 242.

daily ("You can't" complains one sociologist, "tell American teenagers from European ones until they open their mouths"), the final shedding of prewar morality, freedom of movement in clothes as well as travel, affluence, vitality and a wholesale blossoming of idiosyncrasy in the face of big problems and bland governments. At no time since the 1930s have so many elements—books, dances, art, slang, movies, dress, everything—coalesced into the same mood.[7]

Out of that mood of the sixties grew the tastes of the early seventies—in many ways a kind of blanket acceptance of anything that defied what had once been considered as the "canons of good taste." The term *funky* (originally something that was considered offensive) was applied to things that were really extreme and distasteful. One student described it as "old stuff that's new now; like wedgies, Jean Harlow satin dresses, ankle straps, and red nail polish." Even though it started out as a big joke, funky flowered into fashion, and tastes changed accordingly.

As a result of the sobering world situation in the late seventies, clothes became conservative and functional. Generally in times of economic uncertainty colors tend toward neutrals and clothes become more versatile. For instance, one beige jacket can be coordinated with last year's pants, skirts, and sweaters. Mix-and-match became the predominant method of assembling a wardrobe. A decade that continued the rebellion of the sixties at its beginning ended with the man *and* the woman in gray flannel suits. It was marked by a nostalgic look backward and taste in dress was anything that had been: cowboys, Indians, Russian peasants all became design inspi-

rations. By the decade's end there was even talk of reviving the seventies.

Reshaped attitudes toward clothing, begun in the seventies, continued into the eighties. Catalogue shopping and buying at discount became both socially acceptable and something to brag about.

If the 70's didn't show us much worth framing . . . it certainly reshaped attitudes towards clothing that will continue to develop in the 80's. Catalogue shopping became an instant and easy shopping tool. Energy became an influence in clothing design and purchase. Needed were clothes offering warmth with indoor thermostats down, cool comfort with air conditioners off. Cheap chic became an admired practice and at the same time expensive. . . . Feel-good fabrics soothed Me Generation sensitivities with satin undies, silk shirts, cashmere sweaters, leather pants and the like. Comfort became the common ground rule for clothes. . . . The Anti-fashion attitudes of the 60's spilled into the last decade as fashion independence—do your own thing, but do it with a designer label. Even if you never jogged . . . wearing jogging clothes and sneakers showed you thought about it. Success dressing offered a formula for board room chic. Even if you never got the job, the fashion industry gained a purchase.[8]

Changing tastes are all a part of the changing times. Fashion historian James Laver submits that the same costume will likely receive the following evaluations at different times throughout its fashion cycle:

Indecent	10 years before its time
Shameless	5 years before its time
Daring	1 year before its time

[7]Gloria Steinem, "The Ins and Outs of Pop Culture," *Life*, August 20, 1965, p. 75.

[8]Nina S. Hyde, Fashion Notes, *Washington Post*, January 6, 1980.

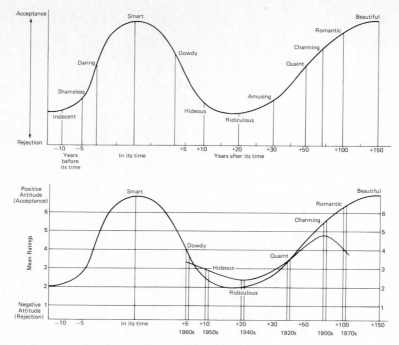

Figure 13.15 A theoretical model of Laver's Law.

Figure 13.16 Mean ratings of the six costumes plotted against Laver's Law.

SMART

Dowdy	1 year after its time
Hideous	10 years after its time
Ridiculous	20 years after its time
Amusing	30 years after its time
Quaint	50 years after its time
Charming	70 years after its time
Romantic	100 years after its time
Beautiful	150 years after its time[9]

A group at the University of Nevada set out to test the validity of Laver's theory.[10]

[9]Laver, *Taste and Fashion*, p. 202. Laver is somewhat inconsistent in estimating how long it takes for a style to become "dowdy." In his 1969 publication *Modesty in Dress*, he states that the same dress is "dowdy *three* years after its time, hideous *twenty* years after its time." Since the acceptance of a well-established fashion is likely to span a period from five to seven years, and its total cycle from inception to obsolescence may take up to ten years or more, it is difficult to pinpoint exactly the year in which a style should be considered "after its time."

[10]M. J. Horn, M. Amis, and T. ZoBell, "Ecology and Fashion: A Test of Laver's Law." Manuscript, November 1973.

A conceptual model was developed that showed in graphic terms the relative levels of acceptance connoted by Laver's adjectives (see Figure 13.15). The most negative attitudes were represented by the terms *hideous* and *ridiculous*; the most positive reactions were assigned to the words *smart* (the current fashion) and *beautiful* (a 150-year-old style). Six dresses from a historic costume collection were chosen that epitomized the fashion of each of the following periods: 1960s, 1950s, 1940s, 1920s, 1900s, and 1870s. The costumes were worn by live models, photographed in color, and shown to a sample of female subjects.

Subjects were given Laver's list of adjectives and asked to select the word they thought best described each of the six costumes. Each adjective was arbitrarily assigned a numerical value from one to six that was approximately equivalent to its position in the theoretical model of Laver's

Law. In this way, it was possible to calculate mean ratings on a positive to negative continuum for each costume. These values were then plotted and superimposed on the theoretical model (Figure 13.16).

The most widely accepted style was the costume from the 1900s, a white cotton batiste accessorized with picture hat and parasol, not unlike many of the "romantic" adaptations seen in the current retail market at the time. Almost half of all respondents chose the adjective "romantic" as most descriptive of this seventy-year-old fashion. Another 30 percent thought it was "charming" or "quaint." Conversely, the style from the 1940s was considered either "hideous" or "ridiculous." Its broad padded shoulders and very tailored straight skirt was almost the exact opposite of the 1900s costume in design.

The astonishing "fit" of the two curves—the average ratings of the six costumes and the theoretical model—lends empirical support to Laver's Law. The greatest divergence from the model occurred in the evaluation of the hundred-year-old style, a bustle-backed gown in purple taffeta. According to Laver's theory, it should have been considered at least "romantic" if not "beautiful," but the subjects generally thought it "quaint." Many writers today contend that the fashion cycle has been greatly accelerated. If we accept this proposition, it is not unreasonalble to assume that the cyclical popularity of certain styles would be affected in a similar manner. In other words, the downward trend in appreciation after a hundred years may indicate a shortening of the fashion cycle itself.

In any case, it is clear that evaluations are made within a time perspective. The tastes of an era express a whole way of life. In whatever ways their manifestations may deviate from the accepted forms of beauty, the tastes of this era represent an outlook that typifies the here and the now. This relationship between the aesthetic character of clothing and the cultural forces that shape it will be discussed in greater detail in the next chapter.

Standards of taste are subjected to powerful cultural changes and reflect the varied and changing spirit of the times.

SUMMARY

What Is Taste?

Tastes are shaped by the time and place in which people live, yet each individual's tastes are conditioned by a particular set of perceptual abilities, education, and values. Familiarity has a significant influence on artistic preferences; most people know what they like, and they like what they know. Popular taste centers on art forms that are widely recognizable and preferred by the majority of people in a society regardless of aesthetic merit. Cultivated taste is developed through a broad exposure to many art forms coupled with a high degree of perceptual awareness.

Tastes vary not only with the individual, but with the changing times. The aesthetic values of dress must be judged in light of the culture and the era in which the clothing is produced. Attitudes, feelings, emotions, and preferences that dominate the tastes of a people at any given point in time merge into a spirit that reflects a total way of life, the flavor of an epoch.

FOR FURTHER READING

Evans, Helen Marie. *Man the Designer*, pp. 52–66, 303–311. New York: The Macmillan Company, 1973.

Rosencranz, Mary Lou. *Clothing Concepts: A Social-Psychological Approach*. New York: The Macmillan Company, 1972, pp. 223–232.

"The Textile Study Room," *American Fabrics*, No. 115 (Spring 1979), 40–45.

Chapter 14

CULTURE: CLOTHES AND ART

In Part One, culture was defined as the sum total of people's social inheritance, derived partly from the past and partly from contemporary innovations. Clothing was discussed in its relation to technology, morals, customs, beliefs, values, and the structure of the society in which it was worn. All these factors contribute to the cultural climate in which art forms develop, and the forces that are exerted on the creators of dress are the same forces that influence architects, painters, sculptors, composers, writers, poets, and interior designers. The major art forms of each period have a way of exaggerating the essential lines and elements that make it express the needs and aspirations of the times. Even the aesthetic deficiencies of a style mirror the image that is favored by a society at any given point in time.

CLOTHING AND OTHER ART FORMS

Illustrations of the interrelationships between clothing and other art forms—paintings, sculpture, architecture, and even furniture and other home furnishings—can be found in most historic eras (Figure 14.1). The aesthetics of the classical world and those of the medieval period were discussed in Chapter 5. Little imagination is needed to see the emphasis on height in the Gothic cathedrals reflected in the hennin, pointed shoes, and lengthy sleeves of Gothic dress or the relationship between the chitons and columns of ancient Greece. Examples may be seen in

Figure 14.1 The aesthetic unity in the art forms of an era can be seen in the similarity between the Gothic headdress and its architectural counterpart, the spire on the cathedral.

Figure 14.2 David's portrait of Madame Récamier shows the Directoire style in its purest form.

some representative periods from more recent times.

Neoclassism

In the middle of the eighteenth century, the ancient cities of Pompeii and Heraculaneum were discovered. And so, at the beginning of the nineteenth century, the Western world was steeped in neoclassicism, a revival of the philosophy and styles of the ancient Greek and Roman cultures of some two thousand years before. The essence of that spirit is captured in painter David's portrait of Madame Récamier (Figure 14.2), a summary of the Directoire style in its purest form. David drew every detail of his pictures with the utmost precision in line, borrowing his forms exactly from the bits of painting and sculpture found in the excavated Roman cities. In this same period Josiah Wedgwood made exact reproductions of Roman glass and pottery to create the neoclassic dinnerware that is still highly prized by collectors, and Robert Adam created his delicate furniture in forms copied directly from the wall paintings in Pompeii.

Women's fashions reached their peak of slenderness in 1800. The predominant character of the line was strictly classical, so that dresses made of softly draped white muslin had high waists. Flat slippers or sandals replaced the high-heeled shoes of the Rococo period, and a draped shawl—reminiscent of the Roman *palla*, a loose, wrapped cape—became an indispensable accessory. Even the hair styles imitated the Greek coiffures. In short, costume was entirely in tune with the aesthetic philosophy that permeated all forms of the day.

Romanticism

The spirit of the new century, however, was too strong to be held in check by the intellectual purity and sterile styles of the classical for very long and soon it gave way to nineteenth-century romanticism. The romantics dreamed of adventure in faraway places and exotic lands and drew on all past periods as rich sources of inspiration. The German poet Schiller completed his work on *Maria Stuart* in 1800; soon after that the neck ruff in women's costume was revived, and dress designers went back to the second half of the sixteenth century for much of their inspiration. Even Goethe's

Faust created a renewed excitement in the modes of the German Reformation.

In their emotional attraction toward all things antique, people were out to produce the picturesque. Architecture in church design returned to medievalism, and Queen Victoria commissioned the present Houses of Parliament to be built in the popular style of the perpendicular. In dress, the pointed forms of the Gothic, the neck ruff of the Renaissance, the full sleeves and wide, falling collars of the Baroque, even turbaned headdresses from the Orient were popular. The masculine silhouette took on an hourglass shape, with widened shoulders and hips and a narrowed waist. Men also wore side curls that corresponded to the hair arrangement of the ladies with ringlets at the temples.

When steel construction made light, open architecture possible, the same technology was applied to women's wear. The famous Crystal Palace in London was created from an open web of metal girders covered with a glass skin to produce a spacious, open interior. The framework of metal hoops used to create the dome-shaped skirts of the 1850s was a practical substitute for the great weight of layers of petticoats (Figure 14.3). Both were practical solutions for illogical extremes.

The Romantic period was an age of revivals. Never before had people been so style-conscious and yet at the same time done so little to create a unique style of their own. Still, the confusion and wide assortment of styles seemed to fuse into a character that was truly expressive of the romantic.

As the Industrial Revolution gained momentum at midcentury, clothes and furniture increasingly were factory made rather than hand crafted. Designs were dictated by the largely uneducated tastes of the majority, and a "rich, costly look" seemed the dominant standard.

Figure 14.3   The same principles of prefabrication and steel construction were applied to the architecture and the costumes of the day.

Figure 14.4 This lady's fashionable cape was not very different from a lampshade counterpart in 1895.

The most significant element of the Victorian period probably was the consistent, recurring conflict between the ideals of tradition and reform. Popular tastes favored the revival of Grecian, Elizabethan, Rococo, and Gothic forms, but reformers were reacting against the shoddy vulgarity of commercial designs on the basis of aesthetic, moral, or rational criteria. William Morris was one of those who led the reform movement in furniture and architecture, believing that if the shape of an object was adapted to its purpose the object would be not only practical but beautiful as well. Oscar Wilde campaigned for the aesthetic movement in dress (Figure 14.4). But such literary and artistic philosophies that ran counter to the conventions of the age had limited acceptance, and the influence of men like Morris and Wilde was not felt until much later.

Eclecticism

By the last quarter of the nineteenth century, styles were hopelessly confused. Renaissance dining rooms, Oriental smoking rooms, leopard-covered divans, and drooping potted plants abounded. The world's newly rich industrialists travelled all over and brought back bits of "culture" from every known civilization. The resulting hodge-podge of forms became known as "artistic broadmindedness." Basic structures invariably were covered with ornamentation. The "architecture" of a building usually was applied after the structure was completed. Basic shapes of furniture were concealed under upholstery, drapery, tassels, and fringes, and costume followed the same general principle (Figure 14.5). The late Victorian age has the distinction of being labeled the ugliest in history as forms, shapes, and colors clashed and competed for attention.

Art Nouveau

By the end of the century, the styles had run their course, and the time for rebellion was ripe. The revolt was expressed in the art nouveau movement, which in many respects was clearer in terms of what was *not* acceptable than it was in regard to development of a distinctly new style. Art nouveau was characterized by a sensuous curvilinear shaping applied to many art forms. Designers, dissatisfied with the ornateness and chaos of the Victorian era, shaped and decorated art objects with a natural symmetry inspired by botanical and other biological forms. Relationships

Figure 14.5 The slashed and bombasted breeches of the Renaissance found their match in the carved and bulbous supports of cupboards, table legs, and bed posts.

creations showed an Oriental influence, but the effect was heightened by the success of the Russian Ballet in 1909, which was mentioned in Chapter 5. Its stage settings in brilliant colors and Oriental splendor had a profound influence on public taste. It led Poiret to introduce new violent hues in costume—purple, cerise, vermillion, and emerald green—and, in so doing, he revitalized the textiles industry. Poiret's first theatrical production of *Minaret* in 1913 was a milestone in fashion history. The Minaret silhouette took on the lines of the Japanese kimono. Sleeves were no longer separate tubes set into an armscye, they were extensions of the garment body. The simplicity of cut made the corset obsolete, for the costume contours obscured figure lines.

Functionalism

Development of the art nouveau style foreshadowed the swing toward an extreme doctrine of functionalism. Architects and designers renounced all extra ornamentation, stripping their designs down to the most basic forms and exposing the structure to view. Costume, furniture, architecture, even literature, fused into an excessively simple, practical style. Women's

between the soaring curves of structural steel and the fluid lines of flowers and foliage were noted. This treatment of line was reinforced by a growing interest in Japanese art (Figures 14.6 and 14.7). The Oriental use of color and line was a revelation to the art nouveau designers, and the extreme simplicity of form and fluid ornamentation spread into costume, furniture, and architecture. The streamlining of the feminine form was never more apparent than in the sway-backed figure of the first decade of the twentieth century, with its slender skirt swinging into spirals around the feet (Figure 14.8).

The leading fashion designer of the day was Paul Poiret. From the beginning, his

Figure 14.6 The fluid lines of Japanese art provided much of the inspiration for art nouveau designers at the turn of the century.

Figure 14.8 The soaring curves and fluid lines of L'Art Nouveau produced this "streamlined" clothing of 1910.

Figure 14.7 The Japanese kimono was adapted in the styles of dresses, coats, and tunics. These two evening wraps are from 1912.

dresses were short and simply cut in the straightest lines possible; hair was severely cropped and worn uncurled. Deeply under the influence of cubism that sought a geometric purity of outline, interiors became arrangements of rectangles and cubes, extremely rigid in line and without any softening curves. The steel furniture was unadorned and unrelieved by pattern or decoration (Figure 14.9).

Functionalism reached its peak near the end of the 1920s and gradually declined in popularity during the next decade. It was replaced by a style that once again accentuated the curves of body and form. Artistic movements and countermovements continued to follow one another in search of the final victory of "good" over "bad." The first half of the twentieth century moved through waves of expressionism, cubism, and abstract art, along with the counterrevolutions of surrealism and dadaism.

Pop Art

Just as the art movements of the early twentieth century tended toward greater and greater abstraction, pop art, their exact opposite, swung to literal realism by making the false, the ugly, and the deplorable even uglier than they really were. Pop art has been regarded as a significant reaction against the sterility of abstract expressionism (Figure 14.10). Even those who denounce it as a complete aesthetic failure are forced to recognize it as a movement that dominated the artistic world of the 1960s. Lichtenstein's adaptations of comic-strip motifs and Warhol's now-famous Campbell soup cans typify the pop approach to art. The latter, painted in endless sequence, were hailed as an expression of the "archetypal 20th century nightmare" in "up and down narrow aisles between high walls of brand-name uniformity, with the lights glaring down and the canned music boring in, as we search desperately for one can of Cream of Mushroom where every label reads Tomato."[1]

[1]Calvin Tomkins, "Art or Not, It's Food for Thought," *Life*, November 20, 1964, p. 144.

One argument defenders of pop art give is that it intensifies the cheapness and shoddiness of the man-made world to which we have become calloused through exposure.

The essence of pop is to create an illusion that either fools or confuses the observer into thinking that the fake beer can is a real one. Translated into costume, we find fabric prints with strands of beads

Figure 14.9 The severely straight lines and rectangular shapes of functionalism dominated costumes, furniture, and buildings in the 1920s. (Collection, The Museum of Modern Art, New York) Le Courbusier, (Charles-Edouard Jenneret), Armchair with adjustable back, 1929, The Museum of Modern Art, New York, Gift of Thonet Industries, Inc.

painted around the neckline, belt lines that are not belts at all, and conspicuous zippers gliding down the fronts of dresses that really open down the back.

Op Art

The illusory aspect of pop art makes it akin to op art, which began to ascend over the school of pop and abstract expressionism in the late 1960s. Op (short for optical) art achieves eye-teasing three-dimensional effects by juxtaposing the simplest of lines, shapes, contrasting values, and pure spots of color in such a way that they create visual motion. Forms (Figure 14.11) seem quite literally to pop, jump, quiver, wiggle, vibrate, and flicker in a manner that is so disturbing to the eye that it can "induce elementary hallucinations, bring on hypnotic spells, throw an epileptic into severe seizure and cause persons susceptible to motion sickness to reel from the room in spasms of nausea."[2] Almost the exact

[2]Tom Robbins, "'Op' Goes the Easel," *Seattle*, 2, No. 16 (1965), 15.

Figure 14.10 An example of pop art: *Soft Toilet* by Oldenburg was created from a large piece of white vinyl.

Figure 14.11 The eye-teasing effects of op art are even more striking when they are close together.

opposite of the universal aesthetic principle, it creates chaos out of order.

Op art developed out of a scientific age in which an attempt was made to break down every element of the environment in search of increased understanding of the laws of nature. Op is an outgrowth of recent studies of visual experience that catalogue and analyze the infinite responses of the human eye to colors, lines, and shapes. It also suggests that art, like other mass-produced products of our age, may one day be scientifically determined and mechanically created. To many people it represents "a healthy departure from the meretriciousness and superficial existentialism of much Pop art and from the shabby technique of much abstract expressionism. It calls, above all, for a precision of technique, for meticulous execution."[3]

The influence of op art on clothing can be more readily seen in textile design than in garment design or construction. Vibrant-colored stripes and checks that seem to move and shimmer of their own volition are made into relatively simple forms. Traditional fabrics, such as herringbones and houndstooth checks, can produce similar effects. The simple A-line dress was often the medium for using fabric to create the illusions associated with op art.

The movements described here represent a limited sampling of the infinite number of ways that art has been approached in the thousands of years of aesthetic expression. The point that should be clear is that fashion mirrors a society's aesthetic philosophy; it is not an unpredictable invention that operates isolated from the forces around it. Clothing and textiles are as much a part of art history as pottery, furniture, buildings, and wall paintings.

SUMMARY

Clothing and Other Art Forms

Clothing, like architecture, literature, music, painting, and sculpture, is an art form that develops from a particular set of cultural circumstances and reflects the needs and aspirations of the society for which it is created. Fashions in dress over the last hundred and fifty years have mirrored the spirits of

[3]C. Lubell, "Op Art—The Responsive Eye," *American Fabrics*, Spring 1965, p. 83.

neoclassicism, romanticism, eclecticism, functionalism, cubism, expressionism, and abstraction. Even the more recent developments of pop art and op art have found immediate expression in the fashions of the day.

☙ CLOTHING AS A VALUE MODEL

Fashionable dress is more than a journal that records events after they occur. Clothing as an art image registers emotion, meanings, and social criticism, which in turn become value models for the members of society as a whole. Most people are convinced that the gradual evolution of fashion represents continual progress toward a style that is more versatile, more functional, more practical (and therefore more beautiful) than the fashions of the era that preceded it. This may be true of the older generations. However, recent years have brought a new development, that of the younger generation looking backward to antique clothes, to costumes from grandma's attic. Designers picked up this trend and the late 1970s brought a tendency to look backward with nostalgia to the clothes of twenty or thirty years before. The generation that actually wore those clothes in their youth wonder how they could have worn such ridiculous garb. Clothes from the past, to be popular again, have to be far enough removed or sufficiently changed so that they are not remembered by their target buyers. When the narrow skirts and padded shoulders of the 1940s reappeared in the late 1970s, their appeal was to those under fifty, too young to have worn them in their youth. The younger generation, to whom the style was new, accepted it with enthusiasm.

Thus clothing shapes and at the same time reflects societal values, but this delusion is not confined to youth. Any individual with a deep-rooted concern and desire to be in tune with the times is susceptible to indoctrination in the values and virtues of the current mode and all it stands for. Clothes are pieces of visual propaganda that shape our ideals of the good and the bad, the sensible and the stupid, the moral and the immoral, the right and the wrong.

Changing Values in the East

Little more than fifteen years ago it was considered unpatriotic for a citizen of the Soviet Union to indulge in the corrupt capitalistic extravagances of fashion (if indeed any citizen could afford them!). Clothing was strictly utilitarian and uniform in dark browns, dreary grays, and mournful blacks. Women's costume for the most part consisted of a long suit-jacket worn over a drab print dress, coarse stockings, flat-heeled shoes, and the ever-present head scarf. It was not entirely a matter of poverty. The suppression of individuality in dress was a constant reminder that the worker served the state.

Then a number of changes took place. Gradually Russia began to emerge from its desperate economic condition. Communication with the Western world increased. In 1963, the Russian national newspaper *Izvestia* reported that a group of French designers had come to Moscow for inspiration in styling fashion boots for women. Nothing had given a greater boost to the

Russian feminine ego since Valentina Te-reshkova took off into outer space. Women began to notice their feet—and other parts of their anatomy as well. Today, in Moscow and Leningrad at least, one can see stylish skirts, ever-deepening décolletages, and beauty salons doing a thriving business. The GUM department store is fairly well stocked with cosmetics and toiletries, most of them imported from East Germany. Of course, the store has always sold cosmetics of a sort, but

one must compare the old days with the new. Lipstick used to be like taffy, the powder like flour, and old timers recall when the only perfume in the entire Soviet Union was called Svetlana's Breath (after Stalin's daughter) and was powerful enough to restore consciousness to a dying man.[4]

Fashions spread into male attire as well. Young men were seen in fashionable trousers and shoes, with their hair combed in the latest mode. What had happened to the Communist philosophy? If fashion was a corrupt capitalistic influence a decade ago, why was it not still corrupt?

Immediately after diplomatic relations were established between the United States and the People's Republic of China in January, 1979, the *Washington Post* declared in a list of "ins" and "outs" that Peking was in and Paris was out. One wondered whether that should be interpreted to mean that soon the Chinese peasant's uniform would be seen on Fifth Avenue or whether the re-opening of China to the West would result in Chinese clad in T-shirts and Levis.

In the spring of 1979 beauticians from Hong Kong were allowed to demonstrate modern hair styling and foreign make-up to Chinese women. "But after the demonstration, the young Chinese models were made to wash their faces and redo their hair in plaits or pigtails. For a few short months this year, Chinese women were allowed to have permanent waves. But not any longer."[5]

Clearly, in both Russia and China, the old communism excluded individualism. The evolving communist doctrine, however, tolerates a wider range of ideas and allows for changing tastes. Clothing played a significant role in affecting the transition of attitudes in both instances.

Changing Values in the West

Consider the "revolutions" of the past twenty years or so. The "nude look" got underway in the sixties with Gernreich's topless bathing suit. Ungaro's backless styles and Cardin's suggestive cutouts then seemed pretty mild. By the time St. Laurent showed his transparent chemise worn over a flesh-colored body stocking, the "nude look" was well on its way. By the 1970s, it was commonplace for women at fashionable resorts to swim and sunbathe in monokinis. Taste had absolutely nothing to do with modesty. Compared with exposed breasts in public, premarital cohabitation seemed not so bad after all. Clothing was part and parcel of the experimentation with new lifestyles and a new morality.

Revolution was by no means confined to women's wear. The gaudy styles from London's Carnaby Street spread to the

[4]Geoffrey Bocca, "The Revolt of the Russian Women," *Family Weekly*, May 30, 1965, p. 5.

[5]"Corrupting the Chinese," *Washington Post*, Parade, June 24, 1979, p. 19.

Figure 14.12 The greatest social change of the twentieth century—the Women's Movement. Cartoon reprinted by courtesy of NEW WOMAN magazine. Copyright © 1978 by NEW WOMAN. All rights reserved throughout the world.

United States with amazing speed. Young American males adopted the "rakish, thin-shanked, high-heel booted, broad-belted, narrow-hipped and epauleted variations of attire" that were the biggest change in men's clothes since the subtle Ivy League style invaded the fashion field. A Chicago retailer claimed that American boys were spending up to $150 a month on new wardrobes. Although this figure would be surprising even in feminine fashions, the phenomenon was all the more bewildering in the men's field "where change has always been measured in quarter-inches per decade."[6] The peacock revolution in men's wear threatened to wreck the whole he-man image of the American male.

Then came the women's movement. Its advocates objected to any differentiation made on the basis of sex, causing a rejection of clothes that highlighted sexual distinctions. The female's wholesale switch to pants in the early 1970s was not just indecision over proper skirt length. The

growing trend toward unisex clothing was observed in all articles of dress, including hairstyles.

The style changes in men's and women's fashions were mild compared with those advocated by the gay liberation movement, which brought homosexuals out into the streets. Their deliberately contrived styles attempted to erase sex-role definitions of appropriate dress. Part of their platform was the freedom to dress as they pleased—as a male, as a female, or both (Figure 14.12). Even though such values may have been confined to the homosexual subculture, they helped set the stage for heterosexuals' adoption of less restrictive dress codes.

The growing complexities of a highly industrialized society also contributed to the revolution in lifestyles. The establishment of agricultural communes, the popularity of folk music, and the adoption of a casual, homespun variety of clothing were among the more obvious manifestations of the search for the simple life. The association between casual clothes and country music was described in terms of the development of a "looser attitude."

[6]"Face It! Revolution in Male Clothes," *Life*, 1966, pp. 82A–90.

First you wear the clothes, and then you find other things that make you comfortable. . . . The music fits the clothes, and the clothes fit the music. Both are simple and natural. For example, jeans and a checkered shirt are worn because they are comfortable, and they allow the wearer to be less uptight. . . . People that dress this way are geared to discover country music sooner or later.[7]

The one thing all these examples have in common, and the thing that qualifies them for revolutionary status, is their flagrant disregard for anything that had been established as proper, fashionable, or tasteful. In this sense, we witnessed a whole series of "revolutionary" movements in the anti-aesthetic philosophies. Pop art has already been described as a rebellion against the hyper-aestheticism of abstraction. Another kind of opposition to fashionable tastes came to be identified by the single word, **camp**. Camp was difficult to define because it could be anything as long as there was something grotesque about it. A typical camp comment was: "Isn't it awful? I just love it!"

Camp always had something of a tongue-in-cheek air about it, and it could be "a thing, a person or a fashion that is so bad that it is good . . . or so boring that it is entertaining . . . so banal that it is sophisticated."[8] It involved a kind of shared joke whenever the conventional was being upset. The term *camp* itself came from the tastes and attitudes of the homosexual subculture, which has always considered itself the vanguard of forces against the standards of the bourgeois society. In the sixties the word came to mean a kind of exaggerated style that was anti-fashionable, anti-tasteful, and anti-aesthetic.

Funky was a kind of updated version of camp, except that it applied specifically to outmoded styles. Anything definitely *out* of fashion could not possibly be considered *in* fashion; hence it was an anti-fashion fashion. In this same category, the term **kitsch** was used by the avant-garde to mean anything considered to be in bad taste.[9] Kitsch was defined as anything copied from a work of art but done in another medium, form, or setting. The Parthenon copied in plastic and a replica of Venus de Milo made into a cigarette lighter are examples of kitsch. The Mona Lisa's face printed on a sweatshirt is a pure example, but the term *kitsch* probably also would cover a $6,000 mink coat design made in authentic Orlon or vinyl alligator shoes.

Oscar Wilde once said, "Fashion is that by which the fantastic becomes for a moment universal." At first, pop art was purchased just for fun by people who could afford to follow a funny fad. "Many a cocktail party that would otherwise have died a natural death has been saved by a piece of Pop art hanging on the wall (or lying on the floor, as much of it does)."[10] But gradually, pop art found some serious collectors, and, in the process of changing American tastes, instead of looking "like comic strips or highway restaurant signs,

[7]"Country 'N Fashion," *Daily News Record*, May 25, 1973.
[8]"What Is Camp?" *Women's Wear Daily*, August 12, 1965.
[9]Gillo Dorfles, *Kitsch: The World of Bad Taste* (New York: Universe Books, 1969).
[10]John Canaday, "Pop Art Sells On and On—Why?" in *Pop Culture in America*, ed. D. M. White (Chicago: Quadrangle Books, 1970), p. 237.

highway restaurant signs and comic strips are now beginning to look like Pop art—which is an improvement of sorts."[11]

Anti-aesthetic movements such as these do not in the least deny existence of an underlying set of aesthetic criteria. Quite the contrary, if there were no standard to react against, there would be no purpose to the whole movement. If a beautiful object is to be "pleasing to the eye," or "easy to behold," then the psychedelic effects of clashing colors and visually baffling designs are anti-aesthetic. Needless to say, every revolution breeds reaction. Impressionism was revolutionary in its day, and reaction against it was strong. Reaction against a revolutionary fashion in dress is equally strong. However, once the eye becomes accustomed to such change and the mind begins to read meaning into the new forms, the innovations lose their revolutionary status and their attraction to the avant-garde as well.

The point we cannot miss here is that clothing is a powerful tool of communication. As an art image, it registers attitudes and emotions; it manifests social criticism; it provokes reaction. Not only does it reflect and interpret the patterns of culture, but it establishes visual value models that can help to show the way the wind is blowing.

SUMMARY

Clothing as a Value Model

Through its design and meaning, clothing creates a visual impression that is expressive of philosophical ideals and attitudes. Like other forms of artistic endeavor, fashion is subject to revolution and reaction. Changing aspects of the Communist doctrine, for example, were facilitated and symbolized by the clothing image, and revolutions in men's wear and in women's fashions have mirrored the disregard for tradition that is characteristic of rebellion. Clothing as an art image registers attitudes and emotions, manifests social criticism, and provokes reaction.

FOR FURTHER READING

Battersby, Martin. *Art Deco Fashion: French Designers 1908-1925*. London: Academy Editions, 1974.

Dorfles, Gillo. *Kitsch: The World of Bad Taste*. New York: Universe Books, 1969.

Hollander, Anne. *Seeing Through Clothes*. New York: Viking Press, 1978.

Langner, Lawrence. *The Importance of Wearing Clothes*. New York: Hastings House Publishers, 1959, pp. 241–282.

[11]Ibid., pp. 239–240.

Part Four

CLOTHING AND
THE PHYSICAL SELF

Chapter 15

CLOTHING AND
PHYSICAL COMFORT

Human beings, by nature, are unclothed creatures and therefore might be better off both morally and physically to expose their skins to the sun and air and permit the body's regulatory processes to make the adjustments necessary for thermal comfort. A wealth of anthropological data attests to the fact that the human body is capable of adapting to a wide range of environmental conditions, often without the aid of protective clothing. Chapter 1 pointed to the fact that there were and still are peoples in the world who apparently manage quite well with little or no clothing even in extremes of temperature. The Australian aborigines and the inhabitants of Tierra del Fuego at the southern tip of South America survive in the nude at temperatures below freezing. They sleep on bare ground at night and their small fires are used for cooking, not warmth. Since physiologically there is no reason to believe that they are different from other humans, their lower sensitivity to cold probably is due to a thicker layer of body insulation; their "relatively bloodless skin ["skin clothing"] extends deeper into the body."[1]

The physical need for clothing depends on a number of factors, the most obvious of course being temperature extremes. The kind and amount of clothing required is affected by physiological condition, food intake, physical activity, and the length of exposure. Beyond the factor of thermal comfort, however, we must consider the effects of clothing as it restricts or facilitates body movement, causes or prevents skin irritation, and protects from or exposes to infection by disease-producing organ-

[1]"The Physiology of Clothing," *Ciba Review*, 4 (1964) 35.

isms. Although the exact limits of human tolerance to any one or more of these factors has yet to be determined, scientific knowledge has progressed beyond mere conjecture. In this chapter we will consider the components of body comfort and the physical properties of fabrics and garments that contribute to corporal well-being.

FACTORS AFFECTING BODY COMFORT

Physical comfort is affected by a number of variables that originate inside and outside the body. Considering first the matter of thermal comfort, the body has an elaborate mechanism that attempts to keep the internal organs at a constant temperature in spite of heat fluctuations in the immediate environment. The mechanism calls for production of heat by the body at the same rate that heat is lost from the body. Such balance can be achieved by either consuming enough food and engaging in physical activity sufficient to produce the required amount of heat, or preventing heat loss from the body by using clothing as a protective barrier. To utilize clothing as an effective means of heat insulation, one must understand the principles of heat exchange. Body comfort is also affected by a wide variety of environmental factors, climatic, mechanical, chemical, and biological. These will be discussed in turn, along with some unique ways in which humans have adapted to their environments.

Principles of Heat Exchange

Optimal thermal conditions occur when the amount of heat produced by the body equals the loss of heat from body surfaces. Just as we use oil, gas, or electricity to produce the units of energy that heat our buildings, food serves as the fuel for heat production in the body. The 2,000 to 3,000 calories a day consumed by the average person are oxidized in the tissues, producing heat as a result of the internal and external work performed by the body. When the individual is at rest, 80 percent or more of the total body heat is produced in the combined work of respiration, circulation, and activity in the brain, liver, and intestines.[2] If the individual engages in physical activity, more calories are expended in the muscle tissues, and a greater amount of heat is liberated. Muscles constitute about 45 percent of the body, so that no other factor so powerfully influences the amount of energy liberated in the body as the activity of the skeletal muscles. A person lying in bed may generate from 70 to 75 calories per hour; in a sitting position, between 90 and 100 calories per hour. A slow walk will more than double the quantity, and a brisk walk uphill will triple it.

Heat thus generated leaves the body surface through four major channels: radiation, convection, conduction, and evaporation. **Radiation** is a transfer of heat or energy from a hot object to a cooler one by means of electromagnetic waves. The areas of the body exposed to the environment lose the most heat by radiation; the skin between the fingers, under the arms, between the legs, and under the chin

[2]H. C. Bazett, "The Regulation of Body Temperatures," in *Physiology of Heat Regulation and the Science of Clothing,* by L. H. Newburgh (Philadelphia: W. B. Saunders Company, 1949).

radiate heat to adjacent skin areas, not into the environment. A person in a spread-eagle position will lose more heat through radiation than when curled up because the radiation area is increased.

The direction of heat flow, of course, may be negative instead of positive, that is, from the environment to the body rather than from the body surface into the surrounding air. Radiation from the sun or from a red-hot stove may increase body temperature. The amount of radiated heat the body absorbs depends on its emissivity, the degree to which it emits radiant energy. As our study of color showed, black objects absorb most of the rays that strike them. A perfect reflector, such as a highly polished metal, rejects the rays that strike it. Thus, surfaces that are good radiators are poor reflectors, and vice versa. The skin is a very poor reflector. White skin, for example, reflects about 30 to 40 percent of the sun's radiation; black skin reflects less than 18 percent.[3]

Most clothing reflects appreciable amounts of environmental radiation. A nude person sitting in the sun gains an average of 143 calories per hour. White clothing, by reflecting the sun's radiant heat, will reduce that heat gain to about half.[4]

Heat transfer by means of **convection** occurs through the actual flow or spread of warm molecules from a warm object to a cooler one. This flow, called convection current, is stirred up by the slightest body movement, so that waving or swinging the arms and legs greatly increases heat loss by convection. Air movement or speed determines the amount of air that comes in contact with the body surface, so that heat transfer is increased with increased air speed.

Conduction refers to heat flow through a medium without the actual physical transfer of material. The molecules that make up all matter are always vibrating. Adjacent molecules strike frequent blows on each other, and in the process the fast-moving molecules transfer some of their energy to the slow-moving molecules, so that in time, molecules far removed from the heat source receive some of the transmitted energy by conduction. Heat is conducted in this way from within the body, across tissues, to the skin surface, and from the skin into any cooler object that may come in contact with the body.

Ordinarily, thermal conductivity is a slow process, although some objects conduct heat more quickly than others. Energy will spread rapidly through metals that have a high heat conductivity, as compared with still air, which transmits heat very slowly. Thermal conductivity values (representing calories per second per square centimeter per degree Centigrade per centimeter thickness) give some basis for comparing the relative insulating qualities of widely different substances.

Silver	0.99
Glass	0.0025
Human tissue	0.0005
Leather	0.0004
Paper	0.0003
Wool felt	0.000125
Pure wool	0.000084
Still air	0.000057

The muscle and fatty tissues of the body have relatively low thermal conductivities, as do many textile fibers. Wool and entrapped air are two of the poorest conductors, and hence two of the best insulators.

[3]J. D. Hardy, "Heat Transfer," in Newburgh, *Physiology of Heat Regulation*, p. 85.

[4]Sid Robinson, "Physiological Adjustments to Heat," in Newburgh, *Physiology of Heat Regulation*, p. 195.

The slow process of conduction is considerably hastened by convection, in which air currents constantly remove the heated molecules and replace them with cold molecules.

Heat loss by **evaporation** is the only way to dissipate heat from the body when the environmental temperature is greater than skin temperature. When the surrounding air is not cool enough to receive heat from the body through radiation, convection, or conduction, sweating becomes the chief protective mechanism against overheating. Liquid sweat is transformed into vapor at the skin surface, and it passes into the environment to cool. Evaporation of moisture from the skin surface is tremendously effective in disposing of body heat because each gram of water thus evaporated carries away 578 calories at skin temperature. Perspiration is actually a cooling process, and it brings a large measure of relief to the overheated body. Unlike the first three methods of heat transfer, evaporation is primarily a mechanism for disposing of body heat. Only under rare circumstances (such as steam burns) is heat acquired through the reverse process.[5]

Environmental Factors

Obviously, conditions in the immediate environment affect the physical comfort of the human body. Thermal comfort is influenced by air temperature, humidity, air movement, and radiation intensity.[6] **Air temperatures** with upper limits of 27°C to 95°C (79°F to 95°F) and lower limits of 18°C to 23°C (64°F to 73°F) (depending on humidity) provide the most comfortable range. At higher temperatures increased evaporation from the skin surface occurs.

The amount of such evaporation also depends on the vapor pressure of water on the skin and that in the air. A high **relative humidity**, that is, a high percentage of water vapor in the atmosphere, will reduce the rate of moisture uptake by the air and limit the evaporative cooling process. In hot, humid atmospheres, most people perspire profusely, but because the air is already saturated with moisture, much of the sweat drips unevaporated from the skin surface.

We have mentioned the effects of **air movement** in the discussion of convection. The displacement of large masses of air increases the rate of heat transfer.

The effects of radiation depend not only on the temperature of the radiating body, but on the temperature and emissivity of the surrounding areas. Indoors, for example, the radiation heat exchange is affected by the character of the walls, ceiling, floor, and other objects in the room having different emissivities. Outdoors, the factors of solar radiation, sky radiation, and reflection from the terrain are involved. Human skin is an excellent radiator and a very poor reflector. If the body were placed in a large sphere made of highly reflecting materials, nearly all the radiant heat the body emitted would be reflected back to and be reabsorbed by the skin. Even if the surface of the sphere were very cold, the body would lose little heat to it through radiation.[7]

Atmospheric pressure in itself has an effect on body comfort beyond its relationship to heat transfer. At high altitudes,

[5]W. H. Forbes, "Laboratory and Field Studies—General Principles," in Newburgh, *Physiology of Heat Regulation*, p. 321.

[6]P. Yaglou, "Thermometry," in Newburgh, *Physiology of Heat Regulation*, p. 70.

[7]Hardy, "Heat Transfer," p. 83.

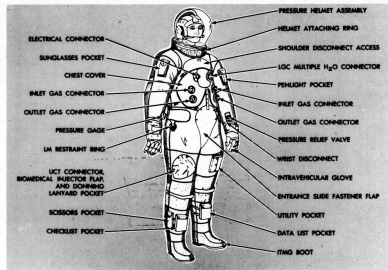

PRESSURE HELMET ASSEMBLY
HELMET ATTACHING RING
SHOULDER DISCONNECT ACCESS
LGC MULTIPLE H₂O CONNECTOR
PENLIGHT POCKET
INLET GAS CONNECTOR
OUTLET GAS CONNECTOR
PRESSURE RELIEF VALVE
WRIST DISCONNECT
INTRAVEHICULAR GLOVE
ENTRANCE SLIDE FASTENER FLAP
UTILITY POCKET
DATA LIST POCKET
ITMG BOOT

ELECTRICAL CONNECTOR
SUNGLASSES POCKET
CHEST COVER
INLET GAS CONNECTOR
OUTLET GAS CONNECTOR
PRESSURE GAGE
LM RESTRAINT RING
UCT CONNECTOR, BIOMEDICAL INJECTOR FLAP, AND DONNING LANYARD POCKET
SCISSORS POCKET
CHECKLIST POCKET

Figure 15.1 Left: The astronaut's thermal underwear has ribbed sections that allow circulation under the next layer of pressurized, rubberized nylon.

Figure 15.2 Right: The space suit pressure garment assembly provides a total environment in which the astronaut is encased in pressurized oxygen.

there is less oxygen to breathe and the rarified atmosphere does not provide enough counterpressure to balance the internal pressures of the body. At an altitude of 25,000 feet air pressure is only a third of that at sea level, so that the body begins to swell. Airline companies furnish uniforms with self-expanding features for flight attendants. At altitudes of 5,000 feet and above, clothes with elasticized waistbands and button adjustments provide relief for swelling abdomens.

Modern aircraft are pressurized, as are the suits worn by deep-sea divers and astronauts (Figures 15.1 and 15.2), but there is considerable variation in atmospheric pressure in sea-level towns and in those at higher elevations. The normal individual readily adjusts to such changes in atmospheric pressure, but for those with abnormally high or low blood pressure, such change often brings discomfort. Some articles of clothing (elasticized stockings, for instance) help to increase the internal pressure on the body and often are used to

improve the circulation in low blood pressure cases. In a few rare instances, a person's blood pressure may be so low that the simple act of rising from a prone to an erect position causes the blood to drain from the brain, and the individual faints immediately—a phenomenon comparable to a pilot's blacking out in steep climbs and dives. Wearing a pressurized suit that squeezes the lower extremities and forces blood upward through the body restores fairly normal circulation.[8]

The environment may also produce various kinds of hazards or irritants that cause body discomfort. An infinite number of **mechanical agents** (for instance, sharp instruments, nails, thorns) cause abrasions and cuts of the skin. Besides the effects of heat, cold, and solar radiation, other **physical and chemical agents** act on the skin in various ways, such as burns from electrical wires, or dermatoses from acids,

[8]"Medicine: New Garment Raises Blood Pressure by Squeezing," *Life*, October 7, 1966, pp. 73–74.

alkalis, and other chemical irritants. **Biological agents**, which include bacteria, fungi, viruses, and numerous parasites and insects, can produce skin lesions and other harmful reactions. Many poisonous plants (poison ivy, for example) produce blisters or rashes.

Properly designed protective clothing is one of the most effective means of reducing the danger from environmental hazards such as these. Closely woven cotton fabrics are often a sufficient barrier. Protection from solar radiation, on the earth's surface at least, is afforded by broad-brimmed hats and garments that cover the torso, arms, and legs. Impervious materials, such as rubber or synthetic films, give adequate protection against liquid irritants, and leather gloves and sturdy shoes are good safeguards against mechanical dangers. Air-proof suits fitted with mittens, boots, and helmet, and air conditioned for adequate ventilation are used for more extreme occupational hazards (Figures 15.3 and 15.4).

Human Adaptations to the Environment

We have seen that climatic conditions, activity, a person's state of health, and clothing are all important modifying factors in regard to our physical comfort. Nature has given the human body an excellent thermostat that automatically regulates the internal temperature. One adaptive response that occurs almost immediately takes place in the **circulatory system.** When overheated, the blood vessels dilate, permitting increased flow of blood and raising the skin temperature, which in turn increases the heat loss from the skin through radiation, convection, and evaporation. Following exposure to the cold, constriction of the blood vessels decreases heat transfer by decreasing the quantity of blood flowing through veins close to the skin and other surface tissues.

Two other nervous responses are **sweating**, which speeds up the heat loss by evaporation when the body is exposed to

Figure 15.3 Elaborate protective clothing is used against the more extreme types of occupational hazards.

Figure 15.4 The miner's hardhat and headlamp are other examples of specialized occupational clothing designed for a specific function.

heat, and **shivering**, which consists of simultaneous muscle contractions that greatly increase heat production in the body. Shivering is usually preceded by goose flesh that roughens up the skin surface and causes an erection of hairs, thereby diminishing air movement and consequently improving the layer of air insulation around the skin. This kind of insulation is considerably less for cylinders than for flat areas, which is why the skin temperature in the fingers, toes, hands, or feet serves as an effective thermostat in activating other physiologic responses to heat and to cold. At high environmental temperatures, much body heat is given off by evaporation by way of the hands and feet, and, in moderately warm temperatures, mainly through convection.

Continued or prolonged exposure to extremes in temperature induces another phenomenon known as **acclimatization**. The British, for example, appear to be particularly resistant to the cold, and easily become overheated in rooms that most Americans find comfortable, whereas the natives of tropical climates seem to be relatively unaffected by heat extremes. Chronic exposure to cold does in fact cause an elevation in basal metabolism and a resulting increase in heat production, enabling an individual to withstand low temperatures with less discomfort. Acclimatization to heat may also develop over a period of time in which the basal metabolic rate is lowered.

Some adjustments to the environment are learned human responses rather than reflex or motor mechanisms. Through **accustomization**, people gradually learn many techniques that increase the protective value of their clothing.

SUMMARY

Factors Affecting Body Comfort

Calories provided by daily food intake are oxidized in the tissues to produce heat or energy, which in turn is dissipated from the body surface through the processes of radiation, convection, conduction, and evaporation. Clothing serves as a barrier to heat transfer in either direction, that is, it reduces the amount of heat lost from the body to the atmosphere and decreases the amount of heat the body absorbs from the environment. Textile fibers and entrapped air, both poor conductors of heat, are excellent insulators.

Thermal comfort of the body is influenced by the environmental factors of air temperature, humidity, air movement, and radiation. Other environmental conditions that affect physical comfort include atmospheric pressure and various kinds of hazards capable of producing body irritations.

In addition to the immediate nervous or motor responses made by the body to variations in temperature, the human body adjusts to prolonged exposure through a process of acclimatization over a period of time. Beyond this, the individual learns certain techniques of adjustment known as accustomization.

CLOTHES AND PHYSICAL WELL-BEING

The two major responses that human beings make voluntarily to the stresses of cold are increased food consumption, which facilitates a greater energy output, and use of adequate clothing. The two may be compared for relative efficiency in accomplishing the task because food can be measured precisely in terms of caloric value, and the insulative value of clothing can be determined by the unit of measurement called the **clo**. One clo is defined as the insulation necessary to maintain body comfort in a sitting-resting position, in a normally ventilated room where air movement is 20 feet per minute, temperature is 21°C (70°F) and humidity is less than 50 percent.[9] The typical business suit has an insulation value of about one clo, but our requirements vary from less than .5 clo in midsummer to 4 or 5 clo in winter.

The food requirements for the average man doing moderate work have been estimated at 2,880 calories per day if he is clothed, and at about 4,100 calories unclothed. Caloric requirements for women in similar situations are slightly less. In other words, if we did not wear clothing, our average food intake would need to be increased approximately 42 percent.

Clothing also conserves body energy in warm climates. As early as 1937, studies confirmed the fact that men sitting in the sunshine fully clothed produced 130 to 180 grams per hour less perspiration than when nearly nude.[10] A study of the physical properties of fibers and fabrics will help us to use clothing more effectively in achieving and maintaining thermal comfort. Beyond this, we will consider the uses and function of clothing in relation to physical health.

Physical Properties of Fibers and Fabrics

Much of the research relating to the functional properties of clothing was stimulated by the extreme demands of military service in which the supreme objective was survival rather than beauty. Although in most circumstances clothing is chosen on the basis of criteria relating to appearance and durability, some knowledge of the principles of physics and physiology as they relate to dress will improve one's ability to select appropriate clothing.

Our chief concern here is with the structural properties of fabrics that affect the passage of air, heat, and water vapor between the body and its environment. The following characteristics of fibers, yarns, fabrics, and garments are pertinent to the thermal qualities of clothing.

Fiber—absorbency, resilience, density
Yarn—smoothness, degree of twist
Fabric—flexibility, porosity, recovery from compression, thickness, weight per unit area, finish, texture, color
Garment—number of layers, design, fit

Since still air is the poorest conductor of heat, the insulating value of any garment or fabric depends on its capacity to entrap air. Even without clothing, the body is surrounded by a thin layer of relatively still

[9]J. F. Hall and J. W. Polte, *Thermal Insulation of Air Force Clothing*, Wright Air Development Division Report 60-597, Wright-Patterson Air Force Base, Ohio, September 1960, p. 3.
[10]E. F. Adolph, "Heat Exchanges of Man in the Desert," *American Journal of Physiology*, 123 (1938), 486–499.

air, as is each surface of cloth that envelops the body, hence the more layers of clothing, the greater the insulation. For example, a suitable "layering" for extremely cold weather might include:

	Thermal Value in Clo
First Layer:	
Insulated underwear (T-shirt and pants), wool socks	.50
Second Layer:	
Wool shirt and trousers, shoes	1.15
Third Layer:	
Coveralls, wool knit gloves, wool helmet	1.30
Fourth Layer:	
Insulated parka with hood, mittens, fur-lined boots	1.80
Total clo	4.75

It is seldom feasible to wear more than 4 to 5 clo because the fabric bulk hampers physical activity (Figure 15.5). Moreover, insulation has been found to stay essentially the same for nine-layer as for five-layer assemblages.[11] Besides, there is the problem of ventilation. Even at rest, the body gives off a certain amount of moisture through perspiration. With increased activity, the individual may sweat considerably, getting the underlayers of clothing wet, thus greatly reducing its insulating value. When fabric sticks to the skin, the surrounding air layer is removed. The greatest disadvantage to sweating is that it stops when the activity stops. The body then produces little heat and needs to conserve all it has, but wet clothing is a high heat

[11]Deanna McCracken, "Thermal Insulative Values of Certain Layered Assemblages of Men's Wear." Master's thesis, Kansas State University, 1967.

"Mom, I'm home—peel me."

THE SATURDAY EVENING POST

Figure 15.5   Too many layers of clothing will hamper physical activity.

conductor that goes on dissipating heat at a great rate through evaporation. For this reason, it is best if clothing can be peeled off layer by layer as the activity level increases, or at least opened for ventilation to avoid sweating. The layers then can be put back on as needed when the activity lessens or stops.

For maximum insulation, garments should be designed with close-fitting openings around the neck, wrists, and ankles, but the garment itself should be loose enough to permit easy formation of the air layer. Clothes that fit too tightly and cling to the skin reduce the effectiveness of the air surrounding the body. Conversely, garments for warm weather will be more comfortable if they have large openings around the legs, arms, and neck so heat can escape easily while the body is protected from radiation.

Thickness is probably the most reliable single indicator of a fabric's insulation value, but it is often difficult to produce a fabric that is both thick and lightweight. Quilted fabrics (Figure 15.6) and foam

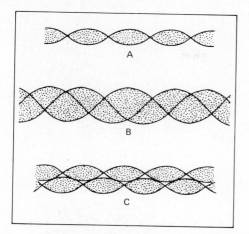

Figure 15.6 Three types of quilt constructions showing different thickness and layering effects. Stitching is necessary to hold the fill of insulation in place, but type A is the least effective because there is no insulation at the seams. Type B is better, not only because it is thicker, but because cold spots are eliminated. Type C has the additional value of built-in air pockets between the baffles.

laminates provide high levels of insulation. The small pore size of the foam makes it more efficient than an equal thickness of fabric in immobilizing air.[12]

Still, a very thick fabric does not solve the ventilation problem and the need to adjust the insulative capacity to varying activity levels. Further, a fabric must maintain its thickness after repeated crushing and bending. The ability to recover from this type of compression is very important. A person wearing a very thick but easily compressible garment, such as a down-filled parka, will lose heat rapidly by conduction through the packed layers if the wearer leans against cold stone or ice. The flexibility of a fabric also influences its effective thickness and its

relationship to the personal atmosphere of surrounding air. Stiff clothing that does not conform to the body shape will contribute to heat loss through convection, pumping air out of the interlayer spaces during body movement. Limp fabrics are no better because they collapse onto the skin and air spaces between clothing and body are minimized.

Many new fabric constructions developed as part of the space program are available for consumer use. One is a lightweight nylon with aluminum on the reverse side and urethane used as a laminating agent. The fabric has the warmth of a quilted garment but weighs a mere ounce-and-a-half per square yard and is used chiefly for ski wear.[13] Another fabric has metallic particles bonded to it on the theory that they will reflect back to the body heat that would otherwise be lost through radiation. To be effective, the metal must be exposed, either to the skin or as the outer surface of clothing. If inserted as a lining between other layers, its function as a radiation barrier is lost.

Dyes also differ appreciably with respect to absorption or radiation of heat from sunlight. As we have already seen, white garments are cooler in summer than dark or black ones. But white fabrics often require more shadow-proofing than do black, and an added layer of cloth can easily offset the advantages of lighter colors.

Fabric that is not porous is an important consideration as wind velocity increases. A fabric could be thick, but be made with dense yarns that left wide-open spaces through which air could pass quickly. A great deal of heat would be lost from the body through convection. Dense fabrics

[12]C. J. Monego, et al., "Insulating Values of Fabrics, Foams and Laminates," *American Dyestuff Reporter*, 52 (January 7, 1963) 21–32.

[13]Bob Spector, "Skylab Fabrics to Warm Skiers," *Daily News Record*, June 7, 1973.

with tightly packed yarns afford good protection against the wind.

Finishes on fabrics sometimes fill the spaces between yarns, making the fabrics less porous. Plastic coatings on the surface of fabrics, for example, decrease the amount of heat lost through convection. Laundering also affects air permeability of fabrics.[14] By removing some of the finish, washing may make a fabric more porous and thus more comfortable in summer.

The **texture** of a cloth is largely a matter of the type and spacing of the yarns in weaving (Figure 15.7). Smooth, tightly twisted yarns form a fabric with fewer air spaces surrounding the fibers and the surface of the cloth. Raising the ends of loose fibers through finishing processes of napping or brushing increases the number of free fiber ends capable of holding air. Fuzzy yarns thus create an outer fur of projecting ends that entrap warm, still air. This also accounts for the fact that fuzzy fabrics, such as velour and flannelette, feel warmer to the touch than does a sleek fabric like satin. Since most fabrics are at room temperature, which is almost always lower than that of the skin, heat passes from skin to fabric until the surface reaches skin temperature. In smooth fabric, more surface is in contact with the skin and hence more area must be warmed, but the skin touches only tiny sections or ends of fibers in the fuzzy fabric, and the fiber volume to be heated is minimal.

Resiliency, weight, flexibility, and texture depend on the choice of fiber, as well as the fabric construction. Continuous filaments of silk and the man-made fibers, such as rayon and nylon, produce more

[14]Sharon Frankenberry, "The Effects of Laundering and Layering on Air Permeability of Selected Cotton and Man-Made Fabrics." Master's thesis, Kansas State University, 1970.

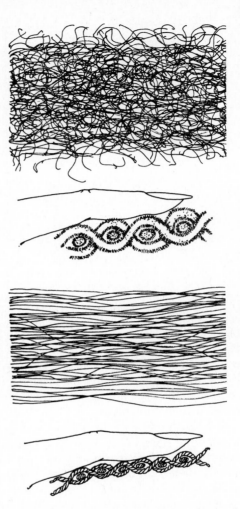

Figure 15.7 The type and spacing of the yarns in the weaving process are important factors in determining a fabric's insulation value.

compact yarns. Short, staple fibers with natural crimp or man-made fibers that have been cut into staple length or texturized to produce crimp give a loftiness or fuzzy characteristic to fabrics without a great deal of weight. Wool has particularly good insulating qualities because of its natural crimp or twist (Figure 15.8), which has the effect of creating a fiber-to-fiber repellence

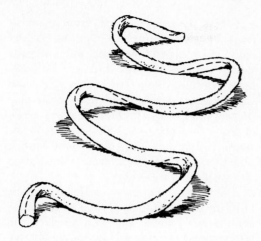

Figure 15.8 The three-dimensional crimp of the wool fiber.

with dead air spaces between the fibers. This assures the greatest amount of free fiber area within the yarns and fabrics.[15] Wool also has a high resiliency that enables it to maintain its loft; it tends to spring back rapidly after being crushed. Linen with its long, straight fibers feels cooler to the touch than a similar weight fabric of fuzzy, short, staple, cotton fibers.

Another fiber property that is closely tied to insulating value is capacity for moisture absorption. If excess perspiration can be absorbed by the fiber without wetting the surface of the fabric, the cloth will not stick to the skin and the clammy feel of a wet garment is less likely to develop. Wool has the highest moisture absorbency of any textile fiber. It can hold almost 30 percent of its weight in moisture without feeling wet to the touch. The low absorbency of nylon and the other man-made fibers causes excess moisture to accumulate on the fabric surface rather than being taken up by the fiber.

[15]Giles E. Hopkins, *Wool as an Apparel Fiber* (New York: Rinehart & Company, 1953), p. 71.

In absorbent fibers, such as cotton, linen, and wool, water absorbed from the body or atmosphere and stored in the fiber also helps to discourage the accumulation of static charges that cause fabrics to cling tightly either to the skin or to adjacent layers of clothing. Cotton, rayon, and silk, although they have fairly high absorbency rates, lack the resilience that would give them an insulation value comparable to that of wool. Especially when sweating takes place, the fiber-to-skin repellence imparted by wool's crimp enables the fabric to stand away from the skin, creating that all-important air space; cotton, once saturated, collapses on the skin.

Another way to keep fabric from collapsing on the skin is through the use of ventilating net underwear. The open square mesh construction permits perspiration to evaporate, with the vapor-laden air escaping out the neck or sleeve openings. Even in cold climates, this is an effective way to keep body moisture from entering the clothing.

Clothing for Different Climates

Heat loss from the body is not substantially affected by conventional clothing in moderate temperatures, but it may provide considerable protection beyond the range of the optimal comfort zone. When the air is below 25°C (77°F) skin temperature is higher than the surface temperature of clothing, indicating that heat loss from the body has been retarded.[16]

[16]A. P. Gagge, C. Winslow, and L. Herrington, "The Influence of Clothing on the Physiological Reactions of the Human Body to Varying Environmental Temperatures," *American Journal of Physiology*, 124 (1938), 30–50.

When air temperature is higher than that of the skin, it is important to use fabrics that are not only highly absorbent but relatively impermeable to air currents so that heat from the hot air is not transferred to the body by convection. The greatest protection in hot, dry climates is the insulation from solar radiation provided by clothing. The Arab, accustomized to desert heat, wears a full covering of loose, flowing garments that are usually white. The robe is often made of wool, which offers both protection against the hot wind and insulation against the cold at night. Headgear that provides some shade for the face is extremely important.

When the atmosphere is both hot and moist as it is in the tropics, clothing should offer very minimal resistance to evaporative cooling from the skin. Since evaporation from the skin is more efficient than evaporation from wet clothing, fabrics that will not absorb water vapor seriously hinder the cooling process. In humid high heat, an absolute minimum of clothing is desirable as long as the person can remain in a shaded area out of the sun's direct light. Natives of hot countries (including the ancient Egyptians and many of the peoples of South America and Africa) removed body hair, either by shaving or plucking, permitting the sweat to run off or evaporate more easily from the surface of the skin. Sandals are better than an enclosed shoe for the same reason.

In cold regions, clothing must prevent body heat loss from exceeding the metabolic heat production. The biggest problem is the accumulation of moisture during periods of activity. Water then condenses in the intermediate layers of the clothing, and if the body vaporizes water faster than the outer layer of garments does, the clothing becomes wet and insulation is reduced.

One of the most difficult climatic conditions to handle through clothing is wet cold. Special outfits made for undersea work, both utilitarian and recreational, have been developed (Figures 15.9 and 15.10). However, similar discomforts may be experienced in cold weather when clothing is soaked through in the rain, or when feet get wet and cold. Waterproofing both the inner and outer layers of insulation often becomes necessary.

Maximum efficiency of insulation is built up rather quickly on the extremities, such as the hands, feet, and head. When feet are getting cold, it is far more effective to add additional insulation around the

Figure 15.9 An outfit such as this is highly functional. It provides warmth and water-repellency for work and recreation.

Figure 15.10 One of the most difficult climatic conditions to control through clothing is wet cold. This uni-suit is made of foam neoprene, but water seepage is always a problem. Civilians may experience similar discomforts in cold weather when clothing is soaked through in the rain or when feet get cold and wet. Waterproofing both the inner and outer layers of insulation is necessary.

trunk of the body than to put on additional footgear. The excess heat thus produced in the trunk will warm the blood sent to the extremities, and as a consequence, they become heated. Waterproof material keeps out wind as well as external moisture, but it contributes to the problem of internal moisture accumulation. In areas of damp or wet cold, however, a moisture-proof exterior is essential.

For survival in cold weather, we can learn a great deal from the Eskimos. Their costume consists of two layers of animal skins and furs. The outer layer consists of a long, loose, hooded parka, trousers, boots, and mittens, all worn with the hair side out. The inner layer of undershirt, underpants, and socks is worn with the hair side in. Caribou and seal skins are the most widely used materials. Eskimo clothing is shaped to the body but it actually fits very loosely. The undershirt and parka are worn outside the trousers, gathered in at the waist with a belt when extra warmth is needed, and unbelted when activity in-

creases. In order to avoid sweating, the Eskimos loosen their clothing when working and begin to remove them first by taking off the mittens, then throwing back the hood, and finally removing the outer parka. When indoors, they strip and sit almost naked because they know that their clothing must be kept absolutely dry when not in actual use.[17]

Health and Sanitation

Clothing is healthful to the extent that it helps to regulate body heat and protects the skin against insects, injury, and environmental irritants. It may also be unhealthful to the degree that it causes skin irritations, encourages bacterial growth, or restricts the body in such a way that deformation results.

Allergies

The incidence of skin irritations caused by wearing apparel is small, although occasional cases have been reported due to sensitivity to certain fibers and fabrics.[18] Allergenic reactions to the protein fibers, wool and silk (and occasionally other animal hairs), may cause contact dermatitis in a few individuals. Unprocessed vegetable fibers, such as cotton and linen, are not considered sources of allergies, and man-made fibers made from cellulose (acetate, rayon, and triacetate) as well as the truly synthetic ones (nylon, polyester, acrylic) are also nonallergenic.

[17]F. R. Wulsin, "Adaptations to Climate Among Non-European Peoples," in Newburgh, *Physiology of Heat Regulation*, pp. 9–10.

[18]L. Schwartz, L. Tulipan, and D. J. Birmingham, *Occupational Diseases of the Skin* (Philadelphia: Lea & Febiger, 1957), p. 370.

Irritations reported as being caused by fabrics made from these fibers have usually been the results of allergenic reactions to the finishes or the dyes used, not to the fiber itself. The low absorbency of the synthetics is often responsible for accumulation of moisture on the skin, which is a source of discomfort to many people, but it cannot be thought of as a sensitivity to the fiber. There have been some reports that nylon pantyhose cause irritations, but this again is attributable to the fact that nylon does not "breathe." The addition of a cotton crotch or cotton soles in stockings usually provides sufficient absorbency to eliminate the problem. The problem is usually not caused by fiber irritation, but rather by disease-bearing organisms, since these areas of the body, without proper ventilation, are warm and moist and provide excellent breeding areas for a wide variety of fungi, bacteria, and viruses.

The glass fiber, used for insulating purposes, may cause a mechanical irritation of the skin because of the sharp fiber ends, but it will not cause any irritation from allergy to the glass.

Items of wearing apparel made from rubber or spandex—girdles, dress shields, gloves, and so forth—have been reported to cause dermatitis, but in all cases the cause of irritation has been chemicals used in processing the material rather than the rubber or fiber itself. Resins and other finishes applied to fabrics or to leather are the chief causes of such irritation. The National Allergy Foundation reports an increasing incidence of skin problems associated with soaps, detergents, softeners, and rinses as well as dry-cleaning solvents used to keep clothing clean.[19]

Bacterial Growth

In general, clean textile fabrics—especially those that are laundered at high temperatures—can afford good protection to the skin. Soiled clothing, however, often contains large numbers of microbes, many of which may remain alive on fabrics for extended periods of time. Research studies of laundry hygiene have identified as many as five million bacteria per square inch in the underarm areas of a cotton T-shirt.[20] Many of these microorganisms are harmless, but some, such as *Staphylococcus aureus* and *Pseudomonas*, can cause skin lesions, pneumonia, or kidney infections, and paracolon bacteria may infect the intestines. Microbes, both harmless and infectious, may be transferred from the clothing to the skin or to other articles of clothing during laundering. Extremely hot wash temperatures provide one of the best ways of destroying these microorganisms. Unfortunately, the water in many home washing machines never goes above 54°C (130°F), which is considerably lower than the boiling temperature of 100°C (212°F) needed for sterilization. Outdoor drying in direct sunlight has a certain germicidal effect, but the only sure way to reduce the numbers of bacteria to a safe level is to add a disinfectant directly to the wash or rinse water. Chlorine bleach (hypochlorite), phenolic, pine oil, and quaternary have been found to be effective for these purposes.[21]

Although special antibacterial finishes can be applied to cloth, their effectiveness tends to diminish after repeated launderings. There is some evidence that a regular permanent-press finish inhibits bacterial growth, and in this sense it may serve an

[19]"Textiles," *MD Medical Newsmagazine*, 18 (April 4, 1974), 99–110.

[20]Ethel McNeil, "Laundry Hygiene," in *Consumers All*, The Yearbook of Agriculture, 1965, pp. 371–373.
[21]Ibid, p. 372.

antibacterial as well as a permanent-press function.[22]

In cases where sanitation is of particular concern, disposable garments have much to offer. Disposable diapers and hospital gowns have been familiar items for many years. Developed for convenience, their usefulness for sanitary purposes in bacteria-communicating areas has far outweighed their original function. A much larger market in disposable underwear may be predicted for the future.

Restrictive Clothing

Fashion history has many examples of clothing that must have been sheer torture to wear. Infants' heads have been wrapped to conform to an elongated shape, feet have been bound, necks have been stretched, breasts have been depressed, and waists constricted. Few fashions have been fatal, but many have been the subject of much controversy. Doctors are still arguing the pros and cons of girdles and shoes. There is no doubt that many elasticized garments give healthful support to sagging muscles and tissues. However, any article of clothing that causes flesh to bulge above and/or below it can be said to be too tight. Round garters used to hold up stockings, for example, can have a tourniquet effect and restrict the flow of blood in the legs.

As far as feet are concerned, there is no disputing the fact that unshod primitive peoples are freer from foot troubles than are "well-heeled" civilized folks who pound the city's pavement, often in ill-fitting shoes. The corn is strictly a product of cultivation caused by shoe pressure

[22]Judith Redekopp, "Effect of Permanent Press Finish on Bacterial Growth." Master's thesis, San Fernando Valley State College, 1969.

against the counterpressure of the bony joint of a toe. To fit properly, the shape of the shoe should conform to the shape of the foot, with sufficient width across the ball of the foot to allow for spread when the foot is in action. Low heels with a broad surface give the best support. But the woman's foot and ankle have long been regarded as erotic attractions more than a means of locomotion, and, although her feet may be more comfortable in sensible shoes, her mind is not.

Safety

In spite of all the protection that clothing may provide, at times it can also be amazingly hazardous. Long, flowing garments, such as full skirts and wide pant legs, can get caught in doors, escalators, and bicycle wheels, or they can trip the wearer on stairs and curbs. Beside all the rationalizing about miniskirts in the early 1970s, there *were* a few safety factors in their favor. They never tripped the wearer; but beyond that, their shortness forced women to bend at the knees rather than at the hips (as so many do), thereby avoiding potential back injury.

Anything that dangles from the body— long scarves, ties, flowing sleeves, jewelry—is hazardous in the sense that it is apt to get caught on something (or *in* something, like the closing door of a bus). As well as causing foot problems and back problems, shoes also can be safety problems. Spike heels were notorious for getting stuck in floor cracks and street pavement, and they also caused many a turned ankle. But the "killer clogs," and the "perilous platforms" that replaced them were not much of an improvement from the standpoint of safety (Figure 15.11). A New York osteopath said: "The new shoes elevate the

feet and thereby elevate the center of gravity also. The higher the center of gravity, the less stable the victim. When you combine a high center of gravity with the almost nonexistent support these shoes give you and the fact that most of us have weak ankles anyway . . . what you get is an accident waiting to happen."[23]

Unfortunately, most textile fibers, as well as fabrics, burn, and when they burn directly next to the skin the damage done is frequently fatal. The most highly flammable fibers are pure cotton or other cellulosics, such as rayon and acetate. Wool is inherently flame retardant, that is, it will burn, but slowly, and once the source of flame is removed, it is self-extinguishing. Although the synthetic fibers rarely burst into flames, they frequently melt into hot sticky globs that can stick to the body and result in severe skin destruction. Fabrics with a brushed or pile surface, such as velour and flannelette, are particular fire hazards because of the air entrapped between the fibers. In tests of flammability, untreated all-cotton plissé has been shown to have one of the fastest burning rates, as do cotton flannelette and batiste.[24] These fabrics are often used in infants and children's sleepwear.

The Flammable Fabrics Act was first passed in 1953 after a number of fatalities resulted from the so-called torch sweaters made from brushed rayon. The standards were later amended and flame-retardant fabrics are now required for all children's sleepwear, sizes 0–14. To pass the regulations imposed by the Federal Trade Commission, these fire-resistant finishes must

Figure 15.11 A broken foot resulted from the fatal combination of wide-cuffed pants and platform shoes. After the accident, the victim discarded the pants but continued to wear one shoe—because it balanced the cast on the other foot.

withstand fifty washings. Using bleach or low-phosphate detergents and commercial laundering removes the flame-retardant finish. In time, similar standards may be applied to all clothing. Until then, the consumer must keep these dangers in mind when purchasing potentially highly flammable apparel items.

Utility and Convenience

Sensible clothes should provide for freedom of action. From the standpoint of muscular activity, most clothing is hampering to a certain degree at least. The weight of clothing alone may add to the metabolic cost of walking and running. Regular street clothing weighs about six or seven pounds more than a pair of running shorts and sneakers. Heavy arctic clothing weighs about fifteen pounds more. In addition to the load imposed by this added weight, the hampering effects of heavy clothing on body movements could increase the work load about 10 percent.[25] Under most conditions, however, the utility and convenience of clothing far outweigh these minor disadvantages. In many situations ordinary clothing lacks both utility and convenience and garments must be designed to meet the special needs.

[23]Dr. Richard Bachrach as quoted in "The High Heels Trip," *Moneysworth*, April 30, 1973, p. 1.

[24]Annette Johnson, "A Comparison of the Flammability of Three Types of Fabrics Used in Girls' Sleepwear." Master's thesis, Oklahoma State University, 1968.

[25]Newburgh, *Physiology of Heat Regulation*, p. 447.

SUMMARY

Clothes and Physical Well-Being

Clothing functions to conserve body energy in the thermal regulation of physiological processes. The structural properties of fibers that relate to the thermal characteristics of clothing are absorbency, resiliency, and density. The smoothness or fuzziness of the yarns, in turn, contribute to the textural quality of the fabric. Fabric characteristics that contribute to thermal behavior include flexibility, porosity, compressional recovery, thickness, weight, finish, and color. The design and fit of the garment as well as the number of layers also help to determine the insulating value of clothing, which is expressed in terms of the unit of measurement called the clo.

When the air temperature is higher than that of the skin, garments should be highly absorbent, light in color, and impermeable to air currents. If the atmosphere is both hot and humid, a minimum of clothing will permit more efficient evaporation of perspiration from the skin. When the temperature is lower than that of the skin, the most effective barrier to heat loss from the body is a protective layer of still air. The ability of a garment to entrap air is the most reliable index of its potential warmth.

In most cases, clothing contributes to the health and comfort of the body, but it can also be the indirect cause of skin irritations, infections, or other physiological problems. Functionally designed clothing greatly increases human versatility and enhances performance in various kinds of activity.

FOR FURTHER READING

"Best Clothes for Cold Weather." *Changing Times*, 33 (November 1979), 42–44.
　　Saving Energy with Clothing and Textiles. Reference Leaflet PE 2206. Coats and Clark Inc., Consumer Educational Affairs Department.
Fourt, Lyman, and Norman R. S. Hollies. *Clothing Comfort and Function*. New York: Marcel Dekker, Inc., 1970.
Helgeland, Glenn. "Camouflage Clothing." *Outdoor Life*, 164 (October 1979), 141–142.
Hollies, Norman R. S., and Ralph F. Goldman. *Clothing Comfort: Interaction of Thermal, Ventilation, Construction and Assessment Factors*. Ann Arbor: Ann Arbor Science Publishers, Inc., 1977.
"How to Keep Cool at the Office." Interview with John T. Molloy. *U.S. News and World Report*, 87 (July 30, 1979), 52.
"Look is Layered and Down is Up." *Time*, 114 (December 24, 1979), 56–57.
Weathers, Diane. "America Bundles Up." *Newsweek*, 94 (November 26, 1979), 96–97.

Chapter 16

CLOTHING AND

PHYSICAL APPEARANCE

Some years ago, Loudon Wainwright gave an entertaining account of his experience in acquiring his first London-tailored suit. The original story gives the full flavor of Savile Row and particularly the characterization of Mr. Perry, the courteous tailor. However, to summarize, Mr. Wainwright felt splendidly rejuvenated in his elegant suit, which covered up what he called a "substantial secret." Before leaving the shop, he asked Mr. Perry if any special problems had arisen in making the suit. Evasive at first, the tailor finally admitted after considerable prodding, "Well, sir . . . you have rather a long body, and that's the thing we had to minimize. We had to lengthen your legs, so to speak, and shorten your body. Nothing serious, really, and it worked out quite well." This was the first time I'd heard of this particular defect in my structure, and I took another look in the mirrors. Mr. Perry was right. It was impossible to tell now where my short legs ended and my long body began."[1]

Unfortunately, few individuals have perfect body proportions, and most people look better when their structural defects are camouflaged with clothing. Effective use of the art elements in costume can alter visual sizes and contours by modifying the frame of reference in which we perceive the human form. Attributes of the physical self can be maximized by an understanding of the cultural ideals to which we aspire and a knowledge of the perceptual responses of the human eye. Skillful applications of these principles to clothing can control the impression the eye picks up and the brain subsequently interprets.

[1] Loudon Wainwright, "Disguising the Man," *Life*, April 2, 1965, p. 33.

THE PHYSICAL SELF

Contemporary figure ideals are culturally induced and not only change over time, but, as we have seen, differ from place to place. Thus, what is considered beautiful in body proportions varies from culture to culture and within a culture, from time to time (Figures 16.1–16.3). Ideals may exist as goals to be attained by few people, whereas cultural standards of beauty, different from the ideal, are real, tangible, and achievable by many. Standards may be measured and quantified. People can actually record how well they measure up to a standard. No such measurement can be used to determine ideal physical forms.[2]

For centuries the ideal of feminine beauty was the ancient Greek model of perfection. Shown primarily in statuary, artists have used it as the example of physical perfection. History shows recurring periods of a return to this Greek concept of pleasing proportions. Recent research indicates that what we have known intuitively is empirically true. Greek figure proportions do not depict beauty in fashion illustrations. "Any relationship existing between the configuration of the currently fashionable ideal of beauty and the Greek ideal of female beauty is probably due to chance."[3]

Over the centuries, the human body, amazing in its plasticity, has been molded into an infinite variety of shapes, each of which in its day was considered to be the most desirable combination of proportions

[2]Mary Ellen Roach and Joanne B. Eicher, *The Visible Self* (Englewood Cliffs, N.J.: Prentice-Hall, 1973), p. 94.

[3]Anna M. Creekmore and Elaine Pedersen, "Body Proportions of Fashion Illustrations, 1840–1940, Compared with the Greek Ideal of Female Beauty," *Home Economics Research Journal*, 7, No. 6 (July 1979), 388.

(see Figures 16.4–16.6). In addition to the manipulations possible through such devices as corsets, waist-cinchers, shoulder

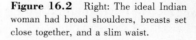

Figure 16.1 Left: The Venus von Willendorf. This prehistoric female figure was a fertility symbol and it demonstrates differences in cultural ideals at different times and in different places.

Figure 16.2 Right: The ideal Indian woman had broad shoulders, breasts set close together, and a slim waist.

Figure 16.3 Egyptian ideals of the male and female figures, c. 1350 B.C.

1600 BC   1600   1640

1840   1860   1900

Figure 16.4 Changing ideals in men's body proportions.

Figure 16.5 Left: Twentieth-century ideal in women's body proportions.

Figure 16.6 Right: Fifteenth-century ideal: *Eve* by Van Eyck, c. 1425.

pads, and bust developers, certain physiological changes have taken place over the years as a result of improved dietary habits and changes in physical activity. In general, Americans are slightly taller than they were a generation ago, have broader shoulders, narrower hips in relation to waistline circumference, and bigger feet.

It is difficult to present a tangible model of an ideal figure, even within the limits of a particular fashion era. For one thing, it depends on whether tastes run toward the voluptuous figure, as represented by many curvacious television personalities, or the long, lean, almost unisex tall (or short), thin, flat-chested figure. Furthermore, actual tape measurements are not nearly as important as the visual proportion. Three figures with exactly the same bust, waist, and hip measurements can appear to be quite different in size if the length dimensions vary, or if the form is deep from front to back or wide from side to side (Figure 16.7). The international beauty contests, however, seem to indicate that the criteria

Figure 16.7 Length and depth variations in the human form.

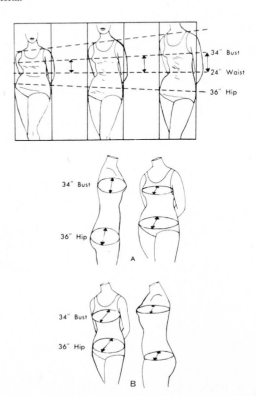

34" Bust
24" Waist
36" Hip

34" Bust
36" Hip
A

34" Bust
36" Hip
B

for "ideal" proportions, at least for the second half of the twentieth century, are becoming quite universal in nature. Beauty queen measurements seem to cluster around a height of 5 feet 5 or 6 inches and a weight between 115 and 120 pounds. Bust, waist, and hip measurements are in the vicinity of 36, 24, and 36 inches, respectively.

However, a figure of any height can appear to be in good proportion. Therefore, we will concentrate here on relative proportions rather than on the actual measurements.[4]

Figure Proportions

The classical Greek proportions were considered the ideal for centuries. In this model the unit of measure used in Figures 16.8 and 16.9 is head length. The average figure, both male and female, is approximately seven and one-half heads high, with the fullest part of the hipline at wrist level dividing the total length exactly in half. The neck is about one-third the length of the head, and the shoulder line slopes a distance of a half head length from the level of the chin. The fullest part of the bust or chest is located two head lengths from the crown, and the smallest part of the waist (which coincides with the bend of the elbow) is two and two-thirds heads from the crown. Fingertip, knee, calf, and ankle positions are indicated on the figure charts.

Male and female proportions differ only in circumference ratios. The female figure, front view, has a hipline that is visually

[4]For a comparison of specific measurements according to height and weight, see Henry Dreyfus, *The Measure of Man* (New York: Whitney Publications, 1959) and Grace Morton, *The Art of Costume and Personal Appearance* (New York: John Wiley & Sons, 1964), pp. 38–40.

equal to shoulder width. Masculine hips are also one and one-half heads wide, but they appear more slender because they are balanced by a broad shoulder line (two heads wide) and a thicker waist (one and a quarter heads). There is also a greater difference in depth ratios from front to back in the female figure than there is in the male with respect to bust/waist and waist/hip relationships.

Body alignment is indicated by a perpendicular line falling from the ear lobe to the inside of the heel, passing through the center of the shoulder and hipline and slightly to the front of the leg at knee level. The body weight at chest, waist, and hip levels is thus balanced on either side of the plumb line in profile view. Looking at the figure from the front, straight legs meet at upper thigh, knee, calf, and foot.

Few figures correspond to these models in all respects, but the illustrations are useful for identifying major departures from the physical norm of individual physiques. Comparisons are facilitated by dividing the figure into head-length squares, beginning with a plumb line down the centerfront, and marking the chin level with a horizontal line at right angles to it. The distance from the chin to the crown (not the top of the hair) can then be used as the unit of measure to grid the rest of the figure. Figures 16.10 through 16.13 show some common deviations from the norm.

The Face and Head

The size of the head is significant in establishing the visual height of the body. Large heads tend to dwarf the body, and small heads increase the apparent span even though the individual may not be very tall in actual inches. Again, male and female proportions of the face and head are

370

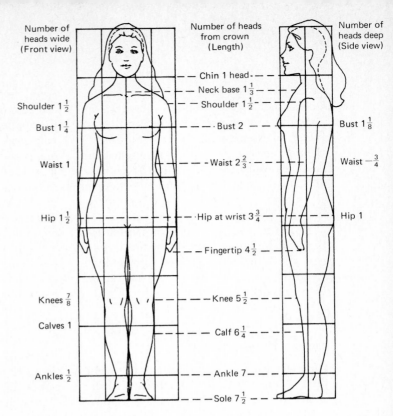

Number of heads wide (Front view)
Shoulder $1\frac{1}{2}$
Bust $1\frac{1}{4}$
Waist 1
Hip $1\frac{1}{2}$
Knees $\frac{7}{8}$
Calves 1
Ankles $\frac{1}{2}$

Number of heads from crown (Length)
Chin 1 head
Neck base $1\frac{1}{3}$
Shoulder $1\frac{1}{2}$
Bust 2
Waist $2\frac{2}{3}$
Hip at wrist $3\frac{3}{4}$
Fingertip $4\frac{1}{2}$
Knee $5\frac{1}{2}$
Calf $6\frac{1}{4}$
Ankle 7
Sole $7\frac{1}{2}$

Number of heads deep (Side view)
Bust $1\frac{1}{8}$
Waist $-\frac{3}{4}$
Hip 1

Figure 16.8 Average proportions of the female figure.

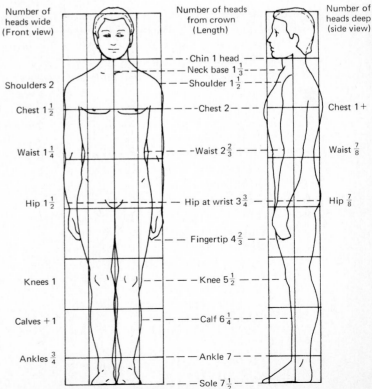

Number of heads wide (Front view)
Shoulders 2
Chest $1\frac{1}{2}$
Waist $1\frac{1}{4}$
Hip $1\frac{1}{2}$
Knees 1
Calves +1
Ankles $\frac{3}{4}$

Number of heads from crown (Length)
Chin 1 head
Neck base $1\frac{1}{3}$
Shoulder $1\frac{1}{2}$
Chest 2
Waist $2\frac{2}{3}$
Hip at wrist $3\frac{3}{4}$
Fingertip $4\frac{2}{3}$
Knee $5\frac{1}{2}$
Calf $6\frac{1}{4}$
Ankle 7
Sole $7\frac{1}{2}$

Number of heads deep (side view)
Chest 1+
Waist $\frac{7}{8}$
Hip $\frac{7}{8}$

Figure 16.9 Average proportions of the male figure.

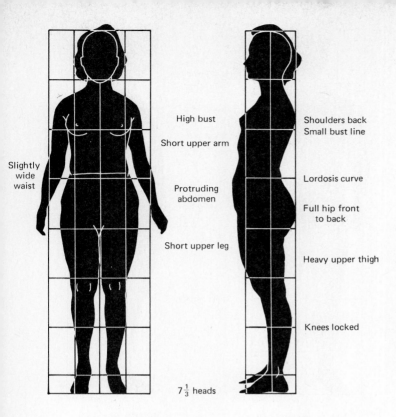

Slightly wide waist

High bust

Short upper arm

Protruding abdomen

Short upper leg

Shoulders back
Small bust line

Lordosis curve

Full hip front to back

Heavy upper thigh

Knees locked

$7\frac{1}{3}$ heads

Figure 16.10 This figure, less than seven and one-half head lengths, is visually shorter than average. Most of the length is lost in the upper leg since the torso is about a third of a head longer than the leg span. Shoulder line is more curved than usual; there is a fleshy roll near the waist; the right hip is irregular in contour. Legs meet from thigh to knee but do not touch at calves and ankles. In profile, body weight is forward with a lordosis curve caused by thrusting shoulders and buttocks back and stiffening knees.

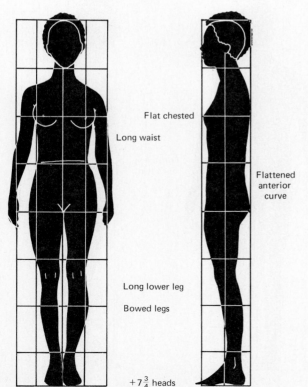

Flat chested

Long waist

Flattened anterior curve

Long lower leg

Bowed legs

$+7\frac{3}{4}$ heads

Figure 16.11 This figure is taller and more slender than average, with body length equal to more than seven and three-quarter heads. The torso is long-waisted but in proportion to the leg span. The lower leg is longer than average; legs are slightly bowed. Right shoulder is higher than the left with a correspondingly flatter hip on the right side. In profile, the body is in fair alignment but curves are flat.

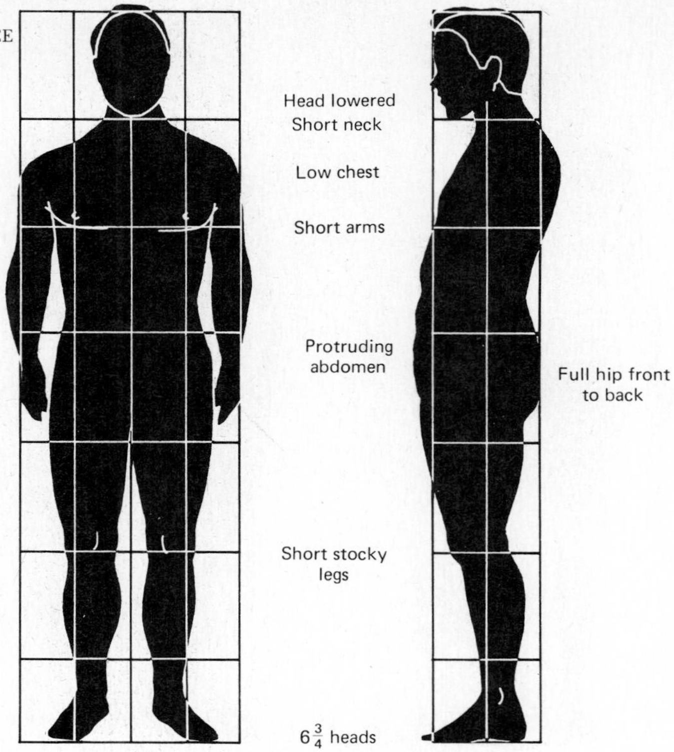

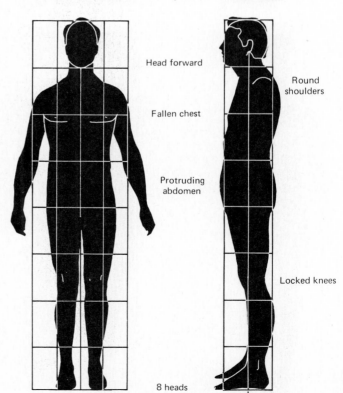

Figure 16.12   This figure, less than seven heads tall, gives a short, stocky appearance. The legs and arms are both quite short and the torso is average in proportion. Shoulders are fairly broad, the left one higher than the right, with a correspondingly flatter hipline on the right side. In profile, body weight is slumped forward, with chest fallen and abdomen protruding.

Head lowered
Short neck

Low chest

Short arms

Protruding abdomen

Full hip front to back

Short stocky legs

$6\frac{3}{4}$ heads

Figure 16.13   This is a tall, well-proportioned, eight-head figure, with only slight variation in shoulder heights and hipline contours. In profile, body balance is destroyed; the head is held forward, chest fallen, abdomen relaxed, and knees locked.

Head forward

Round shoulders

Fallen chest

Protruding abdomen

Locked knees

8 heads

surprisingly similar, except that male contours are usually more angular, and the neck is thicker.

Figure 16.14 illustrates the relative size and placement of the average facial features. Many faces that are considered beautiful or handsome do not conform to this ideal, but an understanding of average facial contours will help to identify the features one may wish to emphasize through dress (Figures 16.15 and 16.16).

Composite Coloring

Theoretically, the color of the skin could be identified anywhere on the body, but it is the most consistently exposed in hands and face, and, in the face, skin tones are in closest juxtaposition to the colors of the hair and eyes. We have already seen how neighboring colors affect each other. The three color areas should be studied carefully and given a color notation in order to determine the degree of contrast in the composite of individual coloring.

For example, there would be little hue contrast if a golden skin were combined with pale blond hair and hazel eyes, whereas a blond, blue-eyed person with predominantly pink skin would demonstrate a maximum contrast in hue. If the pale blond with the golden skin had topaz eyes there would be little contrast either in hue or in value. Maximum value contrast would be found in the combination of near-white skin and raven hair.

Intensity patterns are also critical. Clear strong colors such as bright blue eyes or vivid Titian-red hair are more forceful determinants of costume colors than the neutralized smoky tones of drab blond or brown hair, gray eyes or olive complexions.

In very general terms, individuals fall either into warm or cool types of composite

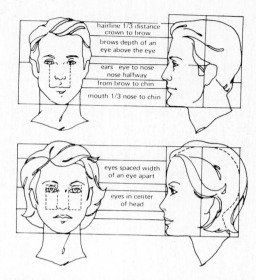

Figure 16.14   Average proportions of the human head.

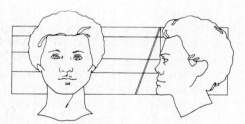

Figure 16.15   The full, round face is almost as wide as it is long. Eyes are widely spaced and set high in the head. Nose and neck are both short; chin protrudes into a jutting jaw line.

Figure 16.16   In the long, narrow face, the head is shallow in depth of the crown. Forehead and chin are slightly receding. Other features are average in proportion.

coloring. The **warm type** has a predominance of red-orange or yellow-orange pigmentation, with brown, sometimes greenish shadows or overtones. Eyes are usually brown, black, or a little on the greenish side, and the hair may vary from red to dark brown. **Cool types** combine blue, violet, gray, or green eyes with skin tones of yellow-orange that lean toward the yellow side. Skin shadows are blue or red-violet, and hair may be blond, black, or somewhere in the range of the cooler browns.

Texture should also be considered in the overall analysis of physical attributes. Skin may be smooth, clear, and transparent, or it may be rough and blemished. The textural quality of hair may vary anywhere from fine, straight, and lustrous to coarse and tightly curled. These characteristics may be masked or exaggerated through the choice of dress.

In visual appearance every individual is a unique combination of contours, proportions, textures, and colors.

SUMMARY

The Physical Self

Cultural ideals of the human form have been studied as a basis for identifying the unique attributes of individual physical conformations. Anthropometric data indicates that the relative proportions of the human face and figure are approximately the same for both sexes, varying only in circumference measurements and angularity of contour. Actual measurements are less significant in conveying a visual impression of size than the ratio of head size to other body proportions. Hue, value, and intensity patterns in the composite coloring of an individual establishes a distinctive set of characteristics that influences the effect of costume colors that are combined with it. The textural qualities of skin and hair are additional aspects of the physical self that may be obscured or enhanced by the visual elements of dress.

ILLUSORY RESPONSES OF THE HUMAN EYE

Most people believe what they see. Scientific studies of visual perception, however, indicate that we do not always see things as they actually exist. What is seen is not merely a matter of visual images picked up by the retina of the eye, as a camera receives images through its lens. Rather, the optical image is transmitted to the brain for interpretation of its meaning. Seeing is combined with judgment, and the human being looks for cues or clues in making discriminations about the size, color, and shape of objects.

If we were to see a figure floating in space, we would have no way to judge its approximate size. But if the figure is placed in connection with common objects of known dimensions (Figure 16.17), we can

Figure 16.17 This normal-sized actor seems tiny in combination with the huge scissors created for this set.

at least guess its relative size. Thus, our judgments of the visual shape, size, and color of objects are made in relation to the total perceptual field in which the objects are found.

Perhaps most important of all is the fact that the human brain seeks to establish some order or meaning among the visual stimuli it receives. This tendency to organize our perceptual field into a meaningful whole is demonstrated in Figure 16.18. The shape represented in A combines nine straight lines in a configuration we can easily recognize as a cubic rectangle. Even though the same form is contained within B, the simple figure of the cubic rectangle becomes imperceptible because the additional lines in the more complex figure change its meaning entirely.

This search for unity, or sensory organization as the Gestalt psychologists call it, also causes us to "see" illusions. If you cover the right illustration in Figure 16.19, you will perceive the solid black bar as rather large. If you cover the left illustration, the dark bar looks short. In effect, we have organized the elements in each of these units and made a visual judgment on the basis of size comparisons. In like manner, all our visual discriminations are

made in relation to the total field in which objects seen are found. In order to see anything as "big" or "small," "straight" or "curved," "red" or "orange," we must have some basis for comparison. Illusions occur as a result of assimilation or contrast. Assimilation illusions are those that minimize or camouflage the different parts by increasing the similarity of relationship of the parts to the whole. Contrast illusions are those that exaggerate the separate parts by placing them next to elements that are extremely dissimilar. In the following sections we will examine some of the ways in which optical illusions occur in line, shape, size, texture, and color.

Illusions in the apparent length, direction, or curvature of lines are quite common. The best known perhaps is the Müller-Lyer illusion (Figure 16.20) in which a line is divided into two equal segments. Observers consistently see segment A as being shorter in length than B. One explanation is that the eye tends to

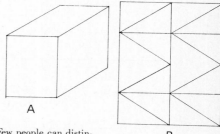

A

B

Figure 16.18 Few people can distinguish the simple figure A in B, demonstrating that the parts are less meaningful than the unified whole.

Figure 16.19 Sensory organization.

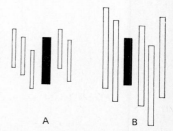

A

B

Figure 16.20 The Müller-Lyer illusion.

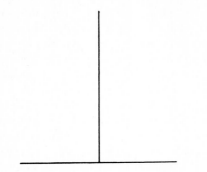

Figure 16.21 The horizontal-vertical illusion.

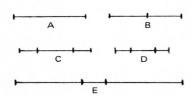

Figure 16.22 The effects of subdivision.

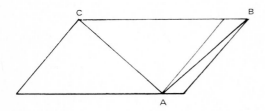

Figure 16.23 The Sander parallelogram.

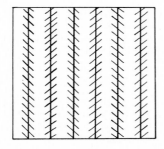

Figure 16.24 Zollner's illusion of direction.

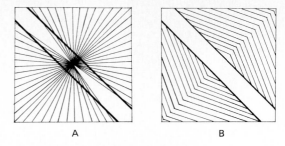

A   B

Figure 16.25 Illusions of curvature.

follow along the path of a line. In segment B, the eye continues along a path that exceeds the actual length of the line, whereas in A, the eye is forced to reverse its direction abruptly at the ends and thus travels a seemingly shorter distance. The effect is compounded by the fact that the observer sees each segment as a whole, including the angles; as a unit, B is really longer than A and this impression carries over to the parts of the whole that the observer imagines is the element to be judged.

Another illusion is that vertical lines are often perceived to be longer than horizontal lines of the same length. This has been explained by the theory that the eye moves more easily along a horizontal plane, and because it requires greater effort to ascend the vertical, the distance seems longer. In Figure 16.21, the horizontal is also bisected by the vertical. In terms of the eye movement theory, travel along the horizontal is interrupted before reaching the other end and diverted in an upward direction. The effects of line interruption are obvious in Figure 16.22. Subjects consistently take lines B and C to be shorter in length than A, and at the same time believe that the middle segment of line C is longer than either section of B. The same illusion occurs in D and E; the middle segment in D appears to be longer than the middle segment of E. Segments that are adjacent to long line lengths seem smaller by comparison; segments adjacent to shorter lines appear longer.

Further error in judgment of line length is caused by our tendency to read perspective into a figure. The parallelogram in Figure 16.23 is usually seen as a slanted surface, and because we "know" that the left parallelogram is larger than the right one, we assume its diagonal CA is longer than the diagonal AB.

Adjacent lines and angles cause a distortion not only in the apparent length, but also in the direction and curvature of lines. The heavy black verticals in Figure 16.24, for example, appear not to be parallel. Cross lines slanting upward force the verticals to veer to the left; diagonals that slant down to the right make the vertical shoot up to the right. The illusion is increased if the page is turned at about a 45-degree angle. Straight lines can also be made to bend in one direction or another. In Figure 16.25, the heavy black lines in A appear to bow out in the center, and those in B appear slightly concaved. Such illusions have been explained by the theory of figural aftereffects that operate much like the phenomenon of the afterimage in color. If the eye is fixed on a field that seems to converge in the center, the aftereffect on the secondary figure is just the opposite, outward curvature. When the field bends outward from the center, as in B above, the aftereffect is an opposing inward curvature. (Also, because the field of B tends to be seen in perspective, the enclosed border does not seem square.) Experiments in figural aftereffects demonstrate that when a subject observes a slightly curved line in a vertical position for several minutes, a straight line shown next to it will appear to curve in the opposite direction. These same effects are observed when the hand follows a curved edge over and over again and then shifts to follow a straight edge.

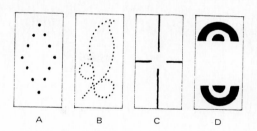

Figure 16.26   The emergence of shape.

Shape

Illusions in shape or contour are just as numerous. In Chapter 12 we discussed the emergence of a "figure" as distinct from the background of a design. Usually we think of shape as something defined by an outline, but figures often emerge as a result of the eye connecting points in space. The four illustrations in Figure 16.26 demonstrate this phenomenon. This tendency to see continuous closed figures is called the **law of closure**.[5]

Shape is also affected by the element of shading, which can give the impression of protuberances or indentations regardless of the outer contour of an object. The first illustration in Figure 16.27 appears as a flat disk, whereas the other two take on the third dimension of depth. This characteristic accounts for the fact that lustrous fabrics with brilliant highlights have a wide range of gradients and thus emphasize body bulges.

Contours that are parallel will be seen to reinforce one another in direct proportion to their nearness. In Figure 16.28 the oblique lines of the lower quadrilateral are closer together and reinforce the verticality of the shape. In the upper quadrilateral, the horizontals are closer together, and even though the sides are the same length

[5] K. Koffka, *Principles of Gestalt Psychology* (London: Kegan Paul, 1935).

Figure 16.27   The effects of shading on contour.

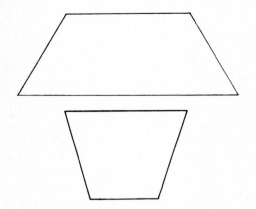

Figure 16.28   The reinforcement of parallel contours.

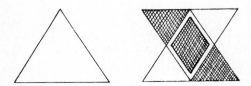

Figure 16.29   The masking of a figure.

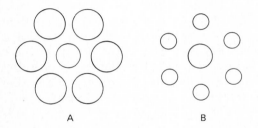

Figure 16.30   Illusions of size.

in both, the upper figure emphasizes width rather than verticality. It is also difficult to see that the top horizontal lines of both shapes are equal in length and the width of the lower shape exceeds its height.

Contours can be masked (Figure 16.29) as well as reinforced. In Figure 16.18 we saw how simple figures may be included and at the same time obscured by more complex additions. The transformation may be accomplished in a number of ways, such as continuing lines beyond projecting corners of the simpler figure, concealing flat sides by placing other lines beyond them, or dividing the interior space with contradictory lines. In short, the major characteristics of a shape may be concealed by the addition of new parts.[6]

The visual proportions of a shape are affected by the same comparisons and contrasts that affect the visual lengths of lines. In Figure 16.28 the upper quadrilateral appears as a wide shape and the lower one as a tall shape even though the heights of both are approximately the same. The oblique lines look short when put next to wider horizontals, and longer when next to narrower horizontals.

Size or Space

Difference in apparent sizes was demonstrated in Figure 16.19. The organization of similar elements of an object forces the dissimilar element further toward the extreme of its variant dimension. The center circles in Figure 16.30 appear to be different. Surrounded by larger shapes in A, the circle shrinks; next to smaller shapes in B, the circle swells.

[6]R. S. Woodworth and H. Schlosberg, *Experimental Psychology* (New York: Holt, Rinehart & Winston, 1963), p. 416.

Figure 16.31 Illusions of filled and unfilled space.

In addition to such size comparisons, the dimensions of an object are altered by the well-known illusions of "filled" and "unfilled" space. Generally, the filled space appears greater in magnitude than the unfilled space, as illustrated in Figure 16.31. The series of dots in A seem to carry the eye a greater distance than does the blank space between the two series. A similar illusion is perceived in B with the solid length of line appearing slightly longer than the same amount of unfilled space to the right. The effect is heightened in C, and it is most obvious in D. These illustrations clearly show that the size of the interval between the verticals influences the extent of the illusion. The wider the interval, the greater the illusion, that is, as the space between the short verticals increases, viewers tend to increase their estimation of the horizontal distance traversed. The illusion is lessened as the spaces between the parts become so numerous that they are regarded as a whole rather than as individual lines.

An extension of this principle is illustrated in Figure 16.32. The filled square (A) that is divided vertically seems broader than it is high, and the square divided horizontally (B) increases in apparent height.[7] The addition of the perpendicular

Figure 16.32 The effects of space division versus filled space.

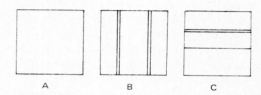

Figure 16.33 The effects of divided space.

line in square C superimposes the horizontal-vertical illusion on the total area and compounds the effect of increased vertical dimension. Illustration C also demonstrates the opposing effects of the principle of space division versus the principle of filled space. In Figure 16.33 the effects of space division are obvious. Large, unbroken areas (A) seem more expansive than equal areas divided into smaller segments. When the division occurs vertically, the vertical illusion is increased (B), and when the division occurs horizontally (C), the horizontal illusion is increased. The effects of subdivision are the same for spaces as they are for lines (see Figure 16.22). The important point is that space divisions are seen as individual parts of the whole, and filled space in terms of overall surface pattern.

[7]The extent of this illusion has been tested and reported in Lucy Stewart and Rose Padgett, "Interval Influence in Overestimation of Vertical and Horizontal Dimension," *Journal of Home Economics*, 57 (February 1965), 133–137.

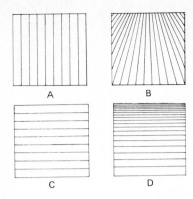

Figure 16.34 The effects of gradation on apparent size.

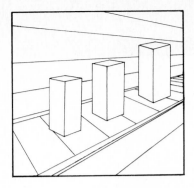

Figure 16.35 Size as determined by visual distance. The increasing size of the vertical blocks is illusory.

As soon as we combine the element of a gradient with the effects of filled space, we complicate the illusion of size by introducing imagined perspective. In Figure 16.34, the straight verticals in A produce the same horizontal increase that they did in Figure 16.32. But in B, because the width gradient is reduced along the top level of the square, we see lines fading away in the distance and receive an impression of continuous depth. In D, the effect of horizontally filled space is compounded by the gradation of lines from the bottom to the top of the square, creating the illusion of continuous distance. In B, the gradient counteracts the effect of filled space; in D, the effect is exaggerated.

The tendency to read perspective into a figure accounts for many illusions of size and space, just as it does in judging the length of lines. The most familiar of these is illustrated in Figure 16.35. Because we tend to perceive converging lines as the vanishing point in linear perspective, we expect objects of the same size to be correspondingly smaller in "the distance." When their size does not diminish in proportion to the angle, the result distorts our judgment of their actual dimensions.

Texture

Textural contrasts create illusions in much the same way that filled space contrasts with unfilled space. Visual texture is, in fact, a kind of filled space. Visually, we might define texture as being composed of raised parts or projections and depressions or areas between them. Large projections or wide gaps between them create deep, coarse textures; perfectly flat surfaces with no projections or depressions result in smooth textures that can be compared to unfilled space.

Obvious texture tends to extend the size of the area it covers. The principle also applies to the size of the dots or the scale of the figures in a printed fabric. Larger numbers of parts increase the apparent size of the whole, up to a point. As the number of projections (or figures) in the filled space increases, the visual area seems to increase until the parts become too numerous to be perceived separately. Then the entire surface is seen as one and not made up of separate parts.

Earlier we discussed the effects of gradual shadings on the visual impressions of contours (see Figure 16.27). Textures that have a close range of gradients, that is, diffused or equal brightness from the edges to the folds, produce soft, ill-defined contours that the eye has difficulty in seeing. But if the protruding elements in the texture contrast sharply with the depression, with the shadings covering a wide range from light to dark, the contour is more impressive and well defined.

Textural comparisons or contrasts are much like size comparisons. Coarse textures seen against smooth textures increase the effect of their difference. Smooth lustrous satin makes a porous skin appear grainy and pock-marked, but in comparison with rough-textured tweeds, the same skin may look smooth and clear.

Color

Color illusions were discussed in Chapter 12 but it will be helpful here to review the basic color principles that affect our perception of color and its influence on our visual impressions. Color perception involves the same kind of sensory organization discussed earlier, in which we recognize the similarity and dissimilarity among combined elements. Colors that are very similar in their dimensions of hue, value, and/or intensity will have their slight differences exaggerated when placed close together, and the contrasts between colors that are strikingly different will be emphasized still further.

The principle of simultaneous contrast describes the process whereby the eye adjusts itself to the predominant color of the field, accepting it as the norm and seeing all other colors as deviations from the norm in varying degrees. Try this experiment in simultaneous contrasts: cut out four identical figures from a blue-green color swatch that is medium in value and intensity. Place each one in the center of a larger field, one white, one black, and the other two of medium value and intensity but one yellow-green in hue, and the other, purple-blue. In the black field where the norm is darkness, the blue-green figure will appear lightest in value of all four figures. On the white field where the norm is lightness, it will appear darkest in value.

Seen against the yellow-green field, the figure will take on a bluish cast; against the purple-blue it will seem greener.

Afterimage is a response to a color stimulus so strong that satiation or fatigue overtakes the nerve endings in the eye. Strenuous activity on the part of one retinal area induces an opposing activity in an adjacent area—a kind of internal complementary chemical reaction. Effects of the afterimage can be demonstrated in another experiment: cut out a figure from a bright green color swatch that is medium to light in value, and mount it on a larger field of black to enhance its intensity. Prepare four other fields the same size as the black mounting, one a neutral gray, another a bright yellow, a third bright red, and the fourth light blue. Look fixedly at the mounted green figure for a minute or more and then shift the gaze to the center of the gray field and you will see a reflection of the figure's image in complementary magenta. Because the gray has no hue of its own, the complement is seen in its pure form. Repeat the experiment, transferring the gaze from the original green figure to each of the other three fields. On the yellow field, the magenta afterimage will mix with the hue of the field and appear orange; on the other two surfaces a similar mixture will occur—the magenta afterimage will mix with the red field to produce a darker, more intense red-purple figure, and with the blue field to create a purple figure.

Several other factors affecting our perception of color should be mentioned. Differences in light source, or the effects of colored illuminants were discussed briefly in Chapter 12. The eye readily adjusts itself to different levels of illumination after prolonged exposure. Everyone has had the experience of entering a darkened room after being in bright sunlight and suffering from momentary blindness. Gradually we begin to see differences between light and dark objects in the room and eventually we regain our "normal" vision in which all colors in the room take on their familiar relationship to one another. Standing in strong sunlight, we find it difficult to see clearly those objects that are in the shadows, but once in the shade the eye adapts to the reduced illumination and the overcast of shadow disappears, and then objects out in the sunlight become too bright for us to see comfortably.

Very strong contrasts of color repeatedly juxtaposed in large or equal amounts will produce what is known as flicker or chromatic vibration. Stark black and brilliant white, for example, combined into a large check or pattern will create a pulsating effect in which the figures seem to jump or quiver on the surface. Strong complements combined in similar fashion produce equally unstable images that the eye has difficulty bringing into focus. The illusion is reduced if the contrasting figures are separated by a neutral ground. The illusion is reversed if the figures are so small that the eye does not perceive them as individual units; contrasts fuse to give an additive mixture that moves toward neutral gray.

The "spreading" effect of colors that seem to "mix in the eye" results in the exact opposite of the principle of simultaneous contrast. Small spots of medium blue, for example, on a white ground will not appear darker and more intense as they would if they were seen as independent contrasts. Rather, the white will seem to mix with the blue and give a total impression of a lighter blue.

Experimental studies have also indicated that most subjects tend to perceive strong saturated colors and warm hues as being closer (and therefore larger), as opposed to the cool and/or grayed colors, which seem farther in the distance (and therefore smaller). Perspective can be considerably distorted by reversing advancing and receding colors in the visual field.

The combined effects of color are complicated by the fact that we rarely have the opportunity to judge a color against a single contrast. In a normal situation, our field of vision includes many colors, all of which have an effect on one another. In costume, it is not merely the garment color against skin, but skin against hair and eyes, and all of it together against a background. Regardless of the advancing or receding qualities of its color, any object will be less conspicuous if it is similar to its background in hue, value, and intensity. Objects that differ sharply from their backgrounds in any one of the color dimensions stand out in greater contrast.

Moreover, the average observer cannot isolate perception of hue from the other dimensions of lightness and brightness. It was noted that neutrals brighten colors by virtue of their intensity contrast; yet a dark neutral such as black will provide a minimum of contrast against a bright but dark blue because the values are so similar. At the opposite end of the scale, we might assume that black would intensify the pigmentation in the skin, but the greater contrast occurs in value rather than intensity; black makes the skin seem whiter by comparison, and as colors ascend the value scale they automatically decrease their intensity. Whenever two principles appear to compete, the one having the greater degree of contrast will usually take precedence.

The apparent size, shape, and color of an object are relative to the total situation in which they are found.

SUMMARY

Illusory Responses of the Human Eye

Illusion in the visual appearance of objects is largely a function of the sensory organization that takes place in the brain, through which we tend to perceive the similarities and the differences of juxtaposed elements in the visual field. Elements that are similar to one another, having a commonality of line, shape, size, texture, or color, tend to fall into a single configuration to which the law of closure is applied. Similarity or repetition of parts tends to reinforce or strengthen the total configuration. Conversely, single parts that are clearly differentiated from all the others that resemble one another will be conspicuous by their contrast.

Any abrupt change in line direction, contour, dimension, surface quality, or color will produce contrast. Illusions specifically related to line have been discussed in terms of the eye movement theory and the effects of bisection, perspective, and afterimages. Shapes may be altered through masking or the use of gradients and reinforced through concentric or parallel repetition. Size comparisons are affected by the principles of space division, and "filled" versus "unfilled" space, and also by the tendency to read perspective into visual impressions. Textural contrasts contribute to illusory responses in much the same way as size and space comparisons. The principles of simultaneous contrast and the afterimage account for the majority of illusions experienced in relation to color.

ILLUSION IN DRESS

Application of the principles of illusion to dress can alter the frame of reference in which we perceive the human form. Physical aspects of the body that cannot otherwise be controlled through balanced diet, adequate exercise, and/or corrective posture can be manipulated in the direction of the desired proportion by skillful use of the visual components of dress. We should be acutely aware of the importance of the organized whole. To concentrate on the sizes and shapes of individual body parts is to run the risk of camouflaging a minor problem with a solution that accentuates a major one. In practice, the most effective masking for a full, irregular hipline, for example, is a skirt that is full enough to obscure the contour completely. A widened hemline, however, also has the effect of diminishing apparent height, and unfortunately, broad hips and a short figure often go together. It may be helpful to demonstrate a systematic application of illusion principles to specific figure types.

The Full Figure

If we look back at the silhouette in Figure 16.10 we see a form with a totally unique combination of physical attributes. Assuming that the objective is to make the figure conform more closely to the visual proportions of the average model, we can then identify the illusions we wish to create. The major problem is that of organizing the whole into an illusion of increased height. Since the waist length is normal and the legs are slender and well-shaped below the knee, the alteration in visual length should be concentrated between waist and knee. Other desirable illusions of secondary importance would be: (1) decreasing the width of the waist, (2) increasing bustline contour, (3) straightening the shoulder line, and (4) reducing the width of face and neck.

Each of the two designs in Figure 16.36 were developed from the contours of Figure 16.10. (Note: The drawings in Figures 16.36 through 16.39 are proportionate to the body silhouettes of Figures 16.10 through 16.13.) Their proportions may be verified by comparing each drawing with the original figure. A comparison of the visual impressions made by each can be explained in terms of the optical illusions presented in the foregoing section. Application of the Müller-Lyer principle (Figure 16.20) is fairly obvious. In A, the eye travels along a vertical path that has no definite termination point. In B, the effects of the horizontal-vertical illusion (Figure 16.21) are totally obscured by the reinforcement of the waistline horizontal in contrasting value and extension into the cuff line. If the eye does in fact get started along the vertical path of the centerfront, it is quickly returned to the waistline via the downward angles of the arrow.

The effects of subdivision are utilized in A by dividing the figure vertically at the waist and continuing the line the full length of the figure (refer back to Figure 16.22, A

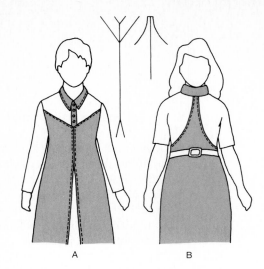

Figure 16.36 The full figure.

and B). The outwardly slanting V of the bodice and the set-in sleeve help to mask the curve of the sloping shoulders.

The use of gradients also may be noted in comparing the effects of the two designs (Figure 16.34). The outward radiation of lines in A gives increased width to the shoulders, and the gradient in B gives width to the waist and reinforces the pyramidal shape of the total figure. Further, the reinforcement of parallel contours in the high rolled collar of design B increases the illusion of width through the face and neck (see Figure 16.28).

The hair style in A also reduces apparent head size, contributing to the overall impression of added height. In short, design A more nearly meets the objectives of illusion outlined in our preliminary analysis of body proportions.

The Slender Figure

Figure 16.11 exhibits body proportions that are probably closer to an ideal than to the average or normal configuration. In our culture at least, a long waist and long legs are not usually considered disadvantages unless they shorten other body dimensions

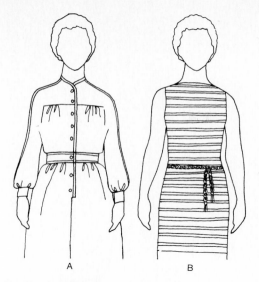

Figure 16.37 The slender figure.

by comparison. The fashion model is typically an eight-head figure, very slender and often flat-chested. However, if we use the same average standard that we applied to the preceding example, we might state the major goal of visual organization in this particular case as softening body angularity and emphasizing the feminine contours of bust and hip.

The two designs in Figure 16.37 both use horizontal lines as major constituents or elements. The total effects of the two are quite different, however, and illustrate the fundamental difference between the principle of space division and the principle of filled and unfilled space (Figures 16.31, 16.32, and 16.33).

Design A increases contour through bust and hipline by introducing added fullness in fabric and, at the same time, by increasing the contrast between bust and waist and waist and hip proportions (see Figures 16.28 and 16.30).

The horizontals in design B are used to fill space rather than to divide it (Figure 16.32). The figure appears cylindrical and lacking in contour, with little apparent difference in the bust, waist, and hipline measurements.

The Short Figure

Stockiness of build contributes to a dwarfing of the figure in 16.12. The torso is average in proportion, but the arms and legs are short. In Figure 16.38, design A avoids horizontal lines that will destroy any illusion of height. There is minimal contrast at the bottom of the coat, and the garment is cut a little on the short side to make the legs look as long as possible. The trousers are straight, pleatless, trimly fitted, and finished without a cuff, again to lengthen the legs.

The double-breasted blazer in B is cut just full enough through the waist to give a broad, boxy look to the torso, which is accentuated by the squarish placement of buttons and the wide flap pockets that draw attention to the sides of the figure. Trouser

Figure 16.38 The short figure.

A   B

legs are cut full enough to give a baggy effect, and width is again exaggerated by the double line of the cuff. Strong value contrast between jacket and trousers emphasizes horizontal space division and gives the figure a top-heavy appearance. Alternating values in dark tie and shirt, light blazer, dark pants, and light shoes create a spotty effect and, at the same time, present a series of rather powerful horizontal barriers. Design B is a prize example of contrast illusions; A illustrates the effect of assimilation illusions.

The Tall Figure

The body build in Figure 16.13 conforms closely to average proportions, although it is eight heads in height. In terms of our own cultural ideals, being tall is a decided advantage, particularly among males. The major "problem" in Figure 16.13 is largely a matter of posture, which could easily be corrected through practice and exercise. It is possible, however, to camouflage postural deficiencies with optical illusions in dress. Figure 16.39 shows two profile views that demonstrate the effects of the Zöllner illusion (Figure 16.24) on the alignment of the body. Oblique lines that contradict the perpendicular force the latter in the direction that will maintain its right-angle relationship to the crossbars. A figure that appears to be slumped forward, therefore, will counteract the slant by jacket lengths that are slightly shorter in back than in front, and pocket lines which repeat the angle, as in A. The slouch is exaggerated in B by pocket and jacket lines that slant downward from front to back and also by overfitting the back of the jacket. A round shoulder is improved by slanting the

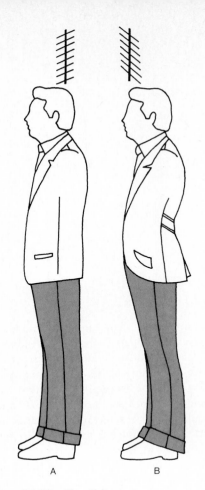

Figure 16.39   The tall figure.

shoulder seam back from neck to armscye, and it is accentuated by a seam that shoots forward, as in B.

Textures and Colors

It is important to remember that every texture has an independent effect on body size and contour. Bulky, heavy fabrics, such as tweeds, shetlands, wide-waled corduroys, and thick bouclés, add bulk to the figure and increase apparent size. They help to fill out a tall, slender figure and conceal its angularity. Stiff textures also increase size, but they often mask irregular contours effectively by superimposing their own firm shape over parts of the silhouette. Textures that have luster call attention to body contours by virtue of their wide range of gradients (see Figure 16.34). Supple fabrics tend to emphasize the figure if allowed to cling to body curves. Transparent textures are also figure-revealing; if they are stiff in addition to transparent (for instance, organdy, tulle, net), they add their own bulk and at the same time reveal the contour of the figure beneath them. Mediumweight textures without luster do the most to minimize figure size by making it as inconspicuous as possible. Keeping in mind the principle of filled and unfilled space, it is important to select prints, plaids, and checks that are scaled to the wearer's size.

In relating costume colors to personal coloring, the most related effects are achieved if the dominant hue of the costume enhances the skin color. Hair and eyes tend to be less important in determining which colors are most flattering, unless of course they are one of the individual's most outstanding attributes. Vivid red hair or luminous green eyes are certain to be noticed before skin tones. A healthy appearance, however, largely depends on the clarity and color of the skin. In general, the cool skin types look better in cool, dark colors, and the warm types wear warm colors best. Usually costume colors that are slightly darker in value than the skin will improve its clearness. However, if one wishes to enhance a deep suntan, the lighter tints will do this best, particularly the hues in the blue-green range, which provide a complementary contrast.

A florid complexion is minimized by warm colors that are low in saturation and dark enough in value to make the skin seem pale by comparison. Colors that are complementary to flesh tones (the blue-greens) will emphasize skin color and bring out the rosy tones in a pale face. Sallowness is exaggerated by hues in the blue-purple, purple, red-purple range, and reduced by yellow-greens. Individuals who lack strong contrasts in their personal coloring will find moderately bright intensities in the medium-light, medium-dark value range the most becoming. Strong, intense colors will weaken intermediate coloring, and drab neutrals in costume do not provide enough contrast to relieve the monotony.

Color tones for dark-skinned people range from black to almost white. A general division of skin color includes the following categories: black, red-brown, yellow-brown, and yellow. Those with truly black skin (almost blue-black) have very black hair and eyes as well. They can wear most colors but not at full intensity. Flattering tones are gray-pink, straw-yellow, and pale orange. Brilliant colors next to saturated skin tones either cast a glow over the face or reflect the color's complement.

For example, if scarlet red is used, a glow of red is cast over the skin and the person will appear much darker than she really is. If the red color reflects its complement, which is blue-green, the skin will assume an ashlike appearance. Since all strong hues produce the same effects, it is evident that all intense colors should be avoided.[8]

Those with red-brown skin tones can wear more colors with greater intensity, while the brown skinned person with a yellow-red cast looks best in warm colors.

[8]Charleszine Wood Spears, *How to Wear Colors with Emphasis on Dark Skins*, (Minneapolis: Burgess Publishing Co., 1974).

Yellow skin is perhaps the most prevalent. Often called olive, it is found among peoples in the Orient, in Southern Europe, in South America and among the American Indians, Mexicans, and American blacks. Medium values with strong chroma are most flattering. Pales, pastels, and neutrals need accent colors.

Variation in the use of art components alters the frame of reference in which we see the human form.

SUMMARY

Illusion in Dress

A systematic application of the principles of illusion to dress has been demonstrated, using four different figure types as specific examples. In general, figure irregularities can be camouflaged by increasing similarity to adjacent components; other qualities can be emphasized by increasing the contrast. The danger in attempting to camouflage or accentuate isolated parts of the figure lies in the possibility of destroying the unified effect of the whole. The desired illusions must be clearly identified through a comparison of actual proportions with those of an ideal.

Body areas that are judged to be too large can be subdivided into smaller areas or counterbalanced by increasing the visual size of the surrounding elements. Body proportions that are considered too small may be masked or increased in size through the use of perspective and gradient techniques, or by minimizing the size of adjacent elements. Lines can lead the eye along pathways that travel in the desired direction, which is usually away from problem areas, and toward the attributes that one can afford to emphasize. Attention will be drawn to the points of greatest contrast. Some people may, in fact, choose to draw attention to their most deviant characteristics in order to emphasize their individuality.

FOR FURTHER READING

Bergen, Polly. *I'd Love to, But What'll I Wear?* New York: Wyden Books, 1977, pp. 23–31.

Luckiesch, M. *Visual Illusions: Their Causes, Characteristics and Applications*. New York: Dover Publications, 1965.

Norment, Lynn. "Big Can Be Beautiful." *Ebony*, 33 (October 1978), 82–84.

Sloan, Pat. "Large-size Fashions Becoming a Growth Market." *Advertising Age*, 50 (June 25, 1979), 26 ff.

Spears, Charleszine Wood. *How to Wear Colors with Emphasis on Dark Skins*. Minneapolis: Burgess Publishing Company, 1974.

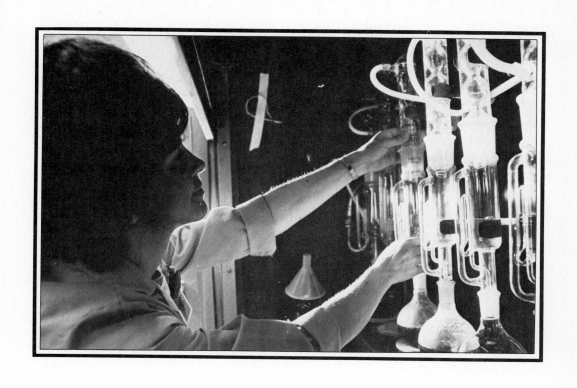

Part Five

CLOTHING
ECONOMICS AND CONSUMPTION

Chapter 17

THE AMERICAN
CLOTHING INDUSTRY

In a land of freedom and abundance, consumers are apt to believe that what they buy (and wear) is nobody's business but their own. Very much to the contrary, however, the economic unit of the private household never operates isolated from the surrounding economic system. The independent family—as well as the independent business—makes daily decisions on the use of its resources. These decisions, in turn, determine the character of local, national, and international markets. In this sense, the consumer is both the beginning and the end of all economic activity.

In the American enterprise system, the economy is largely based on private ownership of businesses with varying degrees of competition in the marketplace. However, the interests of all citizens are not alike.

Some, in fact, are in serious conflict. When there is disagreement between or among various special-interest groups, whether farmers, manufacturers, processors, retailers, importers, or consumers, the government must make a decision that will benefit the largest number of people. Sometimes a governmental decision that benefits one group is a detriment to another.

Most clothing manufacturers agree that the apparel business is a highly uncertain one. Fashion is fickle; it changes rapidly, often without apparent cause. Fashion requires a kind of hand-to-mouth buying and speedy delivery of goods. Fashion demands are seasonal, creating labor market problems. Tremendous rivalry exists among the many small mills and manufacturing firms, and competition from foreign

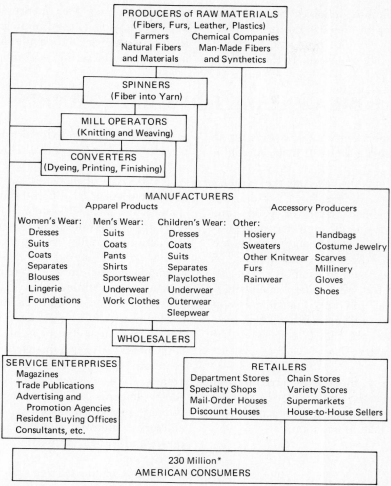

Figure 17.1 The complexity of the clothing industry creates an interdependence among its segments throughout the distribution production.

imports grows. As if these problems were not enough, the complexity of the industry creates an interdependence among its various segments all along the chain of production and distribution (Figure 17.1).

Despite the headaches, the production of textiles and clothing combined consti-

tutes one of the five largest industries in the United States. Americans spend over $81 billion annually for clothing and shoes.[1] Part Five in this book will show the impact

[1]*Family Economics Review*, U.S. Department of Agriculture, Winter–Spring, 1978.

individual clothing choices have on the total economy by demonstrating the relationship between business and personal economic decision making. In this chapter we will look at the importance of the apparel industry to the American economy in terms of fiber and textile production, apparel manufacturing, and retailing.

SOME GENERAL ECONOMIC CONCEPTS

Ideally, Western democracies strive for an economic climate that will make possible

1. *efficiency* in the use of the nation's resources
2. *equity* in distribution of goods and services among all society members
3. *growth* in the national output and elimination of short-term fluctuations in employment and production
4. *freedom* for all society members— consumers, laborers, businesspeople —to make independent decisions within a framework that is consistent with social welfare

Needless to say, these goals have not been fully met, even though in America we have come closer than have most nations to achieving a mature economy.

Types of Economic Systems

All countries work out some economic system for production, distribution, and consumption of goods and services. In the less economically developed countries of the world, tradition has long been the regulator of economic activity. Under a **traditional system** goods are produced and exchanged according to a pattern that varies little from generation to generation. Totalitarian societies, on the other hand, operate under a **command system**; a central authority decides what shall be produced, and the individual consumer has very little influence on the nature of goods and services that are available.

A third type of economy is known as the **market system**. It differs from the traditional and command system in that it both encourages innovation and operates without central authority or supervision. It is based on the interaction of supply and demand, that is, it is a system in which consumers determine what shall be produced by virtue of their behavior in the marketplace. In actual fact, each of the three economic systems has some elements of the other two. Even though the American economy comes closest to the market system, we have some mix of tradition and some elements of the command system through such regulatory devices as wage and price controls, quotas, tariffs, subsidies, and other artificial incentives or restrictions.

Success of the market system depends largely on the opportunity for open competition. This means that there must be (1) many firms competing with one another, (2) ease of entry and exit (it must be fairly easy to get into the business), and (3) no differentiation in products. In reality, there is no such thing as pure competition. For the most part, we operate in a market situation that is characterized by imperfect competition. As we shall see, various segments of the industry meet the conditions of the market system in different ways. The apparel industry includes many

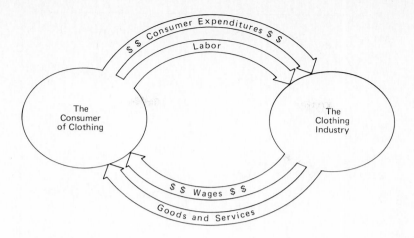

Figure 17.2 The circular flow in a market economy. The individual consumer of household and the individual firms that make up the clothing industry are linked together by a series of expenditures and receipts. The consumer buys goods from an individual firm. The consumer also sells labor to the industry in exchange for wages, which enables him or her to buy more goods and services.

firms, all having relatively easy entrance and exit; but each firm tries to sell a product that is different from that of every other firm. The man-made fiber industry, on the other hand, is composed of relatively few companies. Access is limited by demands for large capital investment, but the companies tend to manufacture undifferentiated products.

Economic Indicators

It is important to keep in mind that the flow of money in the national economy is circular (Figure 17.2). The individual consumer or household and the individual firms in the clothing industry are joined by a series of expenditures and receipts. The consumer buys goods from an individual firm. The consumer also sells labor to the industry in exchange for wages, which are then used to buy more goods and services. Although all persons are consumers of clothing and, therefore, make some monetary input into the clothing industry, obviously not everyone contributes labor and withdraws wages from the clothing industry in itself. But as in other areas of production, the needs and wants of those who are themselves not producers must be provided for. The success of the clothing industry is of great significance to the economic health of the nation as a whole because of the supplies and services it buys and the wages and taxes it pays. The industry's economic significance thus can be assessed in terms of such factors as number of people employed, level of wages and salaries they receive, and contribution the industry makes to overall national income.

TEXTILE PRODUCTION

Production of textiles has often been one of the first steps taken by developing nations toward industrialization, and this was certainly true in America. The production of

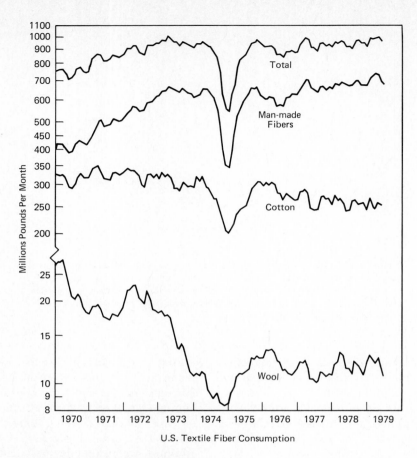

Source: *Textile Organon* September, 1979.

Figure 17.3 United States textile fiber consumption.

Table 17.1 U.S. Textile Fiber Production

	Million Pounds	Percentage
Polyester	3,580	29.3
Cotton	3,170	25.9
Nylon/aramid	2,350	19.2
Glass	790	6.0
Acrylic/modacrylic	650	5.3
Olefin	650	5.3
Rayon	600	4.9
Acetate/triacetate	270	2.2
Wool	134	1.0
Other man-made fibers	10	.008
Silk	1	.006
Total	12,205	99.2

(Source: Textile Organon, March 1978.)

cotton and wool fiber was important in the early agricultural development in the colonies, and at his inauguration George Washington wore an American-made suit of homespun broadcloth to promote the young textile industry. The first textile mill began in Pawtucket, Rhode Island, in 1790, so manufacturing textiles is one of our country's oldest industries.

Historically, many small operators have always engaged in one or more of the major processes by which the raw material is produced and transformed into finished cloth: spinning the fibers into yarn, weaving or knitting the yarns into cloth, and finishing the fabric to give it color, pattern, or other desired characteristics. The flow chart in Figure 17.1 represents these operations as separate divisions of the industry, but many large firms integrate all processes.

Size and Scope

The United States textile industry today is the largest in the world. Until recent years it was typified by small, family-owned businesses and partnerships, generally set up by independent farmers, spinners, weavers, dyers, and finishers to cover single end-use trades. There are still many small producers of the natural fibers (cotton and wool) who strive to get the best possible price for their product in the marketplace. Prior to the 1960s, cotton was the leading fiber percentagewise, but since the mid-sixties both cotton and wool comprise less and less of the end-use consumption each year (Figure 17.3 and Table 17.1). The 1979 figures, for example, showed cotton's share of the market at 24 percent, compared with almost 75 percent for the man-made fibers. Wool constituted less than 1 percent of all fibers consumed;

silk and linen combined (neither of which is produced in the United States) probably accounted for less than 0.006 percent.[2]

These figures are for the United States only. On a worldwide basis, cotton still holds a dominant position. It will probably not be long, however, before the spectacular growth rate of the man-made fibers will overtake cotton's present lead all over the world as it already has in the United States. The tremendous growth in the man-made fiber field after World War II shifted production focus from agriculture to the giant chemical corporations, such as DuPont, Tennessee Eastman, Monsanto, and Celanese. In 1978, for the first time in history, American textile mills used more polyester than any other fiber including cotton. Polyester represented 29 percent of all United States man-made fiber consumption.[3]

Fewer than seventy-five companies operate about one hundred fifty plants that make all the man-made fiber produced in the United States (Table 17.2).[4] This yield amounted to over 9½ billion pounds of fiber in 1979. By the spring of 1981 the industry plans to expand capacity by 6 percent to 10,295 million pounds. More than half the expansion is expected to be in polyester fiber.[5]

Mergers have made many of these chemical companies multiple-fiber producers. Celanese, long-time maker of cellulosic man-made fibers, acetate and triacetate, is the principal owner of Fiber Industries, which produces nylon, polyester, and olefin. American Enka, a rayon producer, now also manufactures polyester and olefin

[2]Man-Made Fiber Producers Association, Inc., 1979.
[3]*Focus on Man-Made Fibers*, Man-Made Fibers Producers Association, Inc., No. 5 (1978).
[4]*Textile Organon*, September 1979.
[5]*Textile Organon*, June 1979.

Table 17.2 Location of U.S. Man-Made Fiber Product-Producing Plants

States & Area	Rayon & Acetate	Non-Cellulosic						Textile Glass	Grand Total
		Acryl	Nylon	Olefin	Polyester	Other	Total		
New England									
Connecticut				1			1		1
Maine				1			1		1
Massachusetts				2		1	3		3
Rhode Island				2			2	1	3
Vermont			1		1		2		2
Total N.E.			1	6	1	1	9	1	10
Mid-Atlantic									
Delaware			1		1		2		2
Maryland	1		1	2	1	1	5		6
New Jersey				3			3		3
New York			2	4	1	1	8		8
Pennsylvania	1		1	2	2	1	6	1	8
Total Mid-Atl	2		5	11	5	3	24	1	27
Piedmont									
N. Carolina			4	7	10	1	22	2	24
S. Carolina	1	1	10	5	9	1	26	2	29
Virginia	2	2	8	3	3	3	19		21
West Virginia	1		1		2		3		4
Total Piedmont	4	3	23	15	24	5	70	4	78
South									
Alabama	1	1	2	3	3		9		10
Florida		1	1	1			3	1	4
Georgia			1	11			12		12
Louisiana				3			3		3
Tennessee	3	1	3	3	4		11	3	17
Texas				1			1	2	3
Puerto Rico			1	1		1	3		3
Total South	4	3	8	23	7	1	42	6	52
Mid-West & West									
California				3			3	1	4
Iowa			1	1			2		2
Kansas				1			1		1
Michigan				1			1		1
Minnesota				1			1		1
Missouri				1			1		1
Ohio				1	1		2	3	5
Washington				1			1		1
Wisconsin				1			1		1
Total West			1	11	1		13	4	17
Total # of Plants	10	6	38	66	38	10	158	16	184
Total # of States	7	5	15	27	12	8	30	9	30

(Source: *Textile Organon*, September 1979.)

through Fibron, Inc.[6] Nearly one third of these fiber-producing firms are listed among the five hundred largest industrial corporations in the country.[7] By the late 1970s, well over 100,000 workers were employed in man-made fiber producing plants. In the decade from 1960 to 1970, their gross annual payroll more than doubled, reaching an estimated $865 million in 1970. It doubled again to $1660 million by 1976.[8]

The primary producers of cotton and wool, on the other hand, still tend to be small independent farmers and ranchers. Most of the cotton is grown in the southeastern part of the United States or in other states, such as Arizona, California, New Mexico, Oklahoma, and Texas, where the climate is suitable. Most of the wool comes from the ranch areas of California, Colorado, Nevada, Texas, Utah, and Wyoming. Wool growers usually market their product through a cooperative association, although sometimes a mill representative buys directly from ranchers, especially if they have developed a fiber with special qualities. Cotton growers often sell to wholesalers, who in turn bargain with mill representatives in a central market. In any case, before sale, both wool and cotton are graded as to quality and then sold to the highest bidder.

Originally mills produced textile products from only one kind of fiber. Now most plants process several fiber types, singly or in blends. Cotton mills combine synthetics in varying percentages: woolen mills blend cotton, silk, fur fibers, and man-mades into a wide variety of fabrics. Within individual plants there is still further specialization; some process the raw fiber, spin it into yarns, and ship it on to another mill to be woven or knitted into cloth (Figures 17.4–17.8). There are also a number of independent converters who buy unfinished goods, dye or print the fabric, and apply durable-press, water- or soil-repellent, flame-proof, or other types of special finishes.

During the 1950s, however, the American textile industry was faced with growing competition from foreign producers, many of whom built modern up-to-date plants after World War II. The U.S. mills began a series of mergers and acquisitions that eliminated many of the smaller plants and increased the size of many larger ones. An industry that had operated traditionally on small amounts of capital and huge amounts of labor gradually moved toward integrated operations that took over spinning, weaving (Figure 17.9), dyeing, and finishing, as well as control of the sale of the finished product. Private ownership gave way to corporations, and, as a result, the vertically integrated plants became the fastest growing companies in the country. The impact of vertical integration can be seen in the gradual decline in number of textile mills from over 8,000 in the early 1950s to 7,500 in the mid-1960s. They have dwindled even more, to fewer than 7,000 in the late 1970s. Burlington Industries, for example, began in North Carolina in 1923 as a small mill. Gradually it acquired interests in a number of converting plants until it now comprises over thirty divisions that perform every operation from converting raw fiber into yarn to selling the finished product. Because of its annual sales record, Burlington is rated among the hundred largest industrials in the nation. It is the

[6]*Textile Organon*, September 1979.
[7]"Fortune's Directory of the 500 Largest U.S. Industrial Corporations," *Fortune*, May, 1978.
[8]*Man-Made Fact Book* (Washington, D.C.: Man-Made Fiber Producers Association, 1978).

Figure 17.4 and 17.5 Raw materials. The cotton boll represents a large portion of the farming economy and provides the fibers for nearly a third of all textile mill products. The man-made fiber emerging from the spinneret is either twisted into yarn or blended with other fibers. It now constitutes almsot 70 percent of all fiber consumption and continues to provide an increasing share of total production.

Figure 17.6 Spinning fiber into yarn. Short fibers are drawn out and given a twist to form a fine, continuous length of yarn.

Figure 17.7 Modern machinery and computers produce fabric at remarkable speeds and in intricate patterns.

Figure 17.8 A very modern loom that does away with the conventional powered shuttle.

Figure 17.9 Finishing processes. They include a number of chemical and mechanical treatments, such as bleaching, dyeing, Sanforizing, printing, embossing, and applying crease-resistant finishes. Here a plain fabric is printed with a colorful floral pattern. The design is engraved on copper cylinders and a separate cylinder is used for each color.

largest textile producer. Next to Burlington, the five largest mills in terms of annual sales are J. P. Stevens, M. Lowenstein, West Point Pepperell, Springs Mills, and Cannon.

The vertical operation of the American textile industry is also shown by the fact that the relatively large number of plants mentioned above are run by fewer than seven hundred companies. In the last three decades, many of the larger companies abandoned the small mills in New England and invested large amounts of capital in new plants and equipment concentrated in the Southeast where land and labor were cheaper than in New England, as well as readily available.

At first, the increased efficiency of the new plants reduced the total number of workers, but with vastly increased production requirements, the industry again employs over 1.3 million people.[9] These

employees, in turn, are important to the entire national economy. They earn billions of dollars, pay millions in personal taxes, and spend their incomes for a wide variety of consumer goods and services. Sales from the goods they produce amount to over $22 billion annually.

Most of the larger integrated firms produce fabric for apparel manufacture and home sewing, loom carpeting, and turn out a wide variety of finished products for the home—sheets and other bedding, towels, blankets—and other furnishings, such as curtains, draperies, and rugs. Over 50 percent of all goods manufactured goes into apparel. The home furnishings market runs a close second, accounting for about one third of the textile output. The remaining textiles manufactured in this country go into industrial uses (17.3 percent) and exports (2.8 percent). Small amounts are used in miscellaneous consumer goods, such as piece goods and luggage.[10]

Another important economic indicator that reflects the performance of an industry is related to prices. The Producer Price Index (PPI), previously called the Wholesale Price Index (WPI), measures average price changes of wholesale products in all stages of processing. All commodities produced in the United States or products imported for commercial sale are included, broken down into three categories. Finished goods are products that are ready for sale to the ultimate consumer, either individuals or businesses. No further processing is necessary. Intermediate materials are those that are partly processed but require more processing before they become finished goods. Crude materials are

[9]*U.S. News and World Report*, April 9, 1979.
[10]*Textile Organon*, November 1978. 1978 figures were the latest summary statistics available at this writing.

Table 17.3 Producer Price Index

Commodities	December 1979	Percentage Change from December 1978
All finished goods	225.9	12.8
Foods	230.5	8.9
Apparel	162.9	4.9
Women's and Misses'	142.5	
Men's and Boys'	188.4	
Children's and Infants'	162.2	
Textile Home Furnishings	194.6	7.9
Footwear	227.3	18.3
Cosmetics	165.8	10.2
Costume Jewelry	106.4	
Intermediate Materials		
Synthetic Fibers	124.9	12.9
Finished Fabrics	108.5	3.5
Leather	319.8	14.7
Crude materials (for further processing)		
Plant and Animal Fibers	215.4	1.8
Hides and Skins	447.6	7.3

(Source: *Producer Prices and Price Indexes*, U.S. Department of Labor, Bureau of Labor Statistics, January 1980).

products entering the market for the first time; they have not been previously manufactured or fabricated in any way but will be processed into finished goods. This third category does not include crude or raw materials that may be used as is. Textile products appear on the PPI list in all three categories. In recent years the price of textiles at the wholesale level has been consistently below the average for all industrial commodities as a whole. The price increases that have occurred were due largely to the record increases in raw agricultural fiber prices. In 1979, for example, the PPI for all finished goods was 225.9. The index for finished fabrics was 108.5 and for synthetic fibers, 124.9 (Table 17.3).

Activities of the Textile Industry

The small independent producers of natural fibers have little control over the end-use products that utilize their raw materials. Whatever advertising is done to promote the use of cotton or wool is usually handled through a trade association such as Cotton, Inc., the National Cotton Council, or the Wool Bureau. Imported natural fibers also are represented by organizations like the International Silk Association and the Belgian Linen Guild. Although the large man-made fiber corporations also have trade associations, they can use heavy competitive advertising to make the consumer conscious of their respective brand names or trademarks. They carry out much of their promotional activity in cooperation with fabric and garment manufacturers, through whom they subsidize local and national advertising. Celanese, for example, paid $3 million just to sponsor the "Tonight Show," and Hoechst and Burlington have spent many millions of dollars on big-name, prime-time television shows.

The trend among the textile mills toward big business has also put an emphasis on brand names, but consolidation has brought other benefits as well. Larger amounts of money have been channeled into research and product development. As a result, new impetus has been given to technological changes and innovations, both in terms of greater efficiency of output and in terms of new fibers, fabrics, and finishes. DuPont, as an example, budgets more than $100 million a year for research and development.

According to a report by the Council on Wage and Price Stability (COWPS), prices increased by 6.4 to 7.5 percent a year to pay for research and development as well as plant modernization to keep pace with innovations in all phases of the industry. This increase was possible because in the past ten years inflation within the textile industry was only one-half that recorded by industry overall.[11]

The industry also has stepped up its market research in order to gear its production more closely to consumer needs and desires. Several firms have employed home economists in their educational departments. More recently, companies initiated consumer advisory groups to analyze consumer trends and advise the industry on how it can respond most effectively to consumer needs and desires.

Future consumer demand predictions are essential for efficient operation of the textile industry, particularly predictions concerned with the consumption of natural versus man-made fibers. Thus other information from COWPS on this subject is important for future planning. The group predicts little likelihood of shortages in cotton fabrics in the next decade. Short supplies of cotton, particularly for apparel, have often been mentioned in connection with increased cost of land and the need to use it more productively for food crops. The rationale behind COWPS's reasoning

came from the facts of decreased consumer demand coupled with an underutilization of existing capacities that may well offset any reductions necessary because of differing land use.[12]

Much as consumers may want to return to the comfort features of cotton and other natural fibers, it may not be economically feasible to do so. The big issues of the 1980s undoubtedly will be energy, consumption, and inflation. A study reported in 1978 concluded that production and maintenance of an all-cotton garment uses 88 percent more energy than a polyester-cotton blend. This report came as a surprise since it had been known that it takes more energy to produce a pound of polyester fiber than to produce a pound of cotton fiber. However, this information by itself is misleading. Consumers do not use raw fibers. Fibers must be made into cloth or garments to be useful to the public. In the long chain of production from raw fiber to finished end-product, the one step in which cotton production does use less energy is in the fiber production stage. In the Yale study all aspects of garment production and use were considered: fiber production, fabric and garment manufacture, maintenance (washing, drying, ironing), and durability or wear life. The 65 percent polyester/35 percent cotton shirt when compared to a 100 percent cotton shirt used less energy from the point of fiber production through useful wear life. It lasted one and one-half times longer, required 25 percent less fiber to produce, and saved half the energy required to home launder. "Since 73% of all fibers used in America today are man-made, it does not appear practical to advocate going back to nature and animals as major fiber sources,

[11]*Purchasing*, Vol. 85, No. 6 (September 1978), 27.   [12]Ibid.

particularly with consideration for future food needs."[13]

In view of the above it is interesting to note that of the 480 million shirts produced in 1977 for men and boys, more than 80 percent contained man-made fibers. Blends of polyester and cotton, in which polyester was the predominant fiber, accounted for 48 percent; other fibers blended with cotton (nylon, acetate, rayon, and wool) made up 24 percent, with cotton the predominant fiber. Fifteen percent were made of 100 percent cotton, and 13 percent were mostly knit shirts of 100 percent polyester.[14]

The fabric producers work so far ahead of the consumer market that they must be extremely adept at anticipating fashion trends. For this reason, most companies retain style specialists and market reporters who sound out leaders in the fashion field for hints of styles that are headed for popular acceptance in the coming season.

Fabric designers determine what will be on the market next year and they also provide the inspiration for much of the design in the clothing trade. New developments in textiles greatly influence garment construction. Laminates, stretch fabrics, and permanent-press finishes, for instance, forced a number of changes in both design of clothes and in production techniques. Long-range planning in the textile industry must provide for a wide variety in color, weight, thickness, texture, and finish to meet the needs of a diversified market. At the same time, it must be flexible enough to respond to sudden changes in consumer demand.

Integration among firms and increased technological and market research have characterized the textile industry in recent years.

SUMMARY

Textile Production

The textile industry has been characterized by a decreasing number of smaller firms and an increasing diversification and efficiency in the larger companies.

Research leads to technological innovations in fiber, fabric, and finish that increase the versatility and serviceability of fabrics used for clothing. At the same time, market research reduces the errors in judging the market potential and helps the textile producer gauge output more accurately in relation to consumer demand. This in turn reduces the inventory of unsold stock and passes price savings on to the consumer.

Because fabrics are often the source of inspiration for clothing designers, decisions made in the mill on color, texture, and pattern influence the design of the garments that ultimately appear on the market.

[13]*Focus on Man-Made Fibers*, Man-Made Fiber Producers Association, Inc., No. 5 (1978).
[14]*Focus on Man-Made Fibers* (1978).

APPAREL PRODUCTION

The apparel industry—also known as the ready-to-wear industry, the garment makers, the cutting-up or needle trades, and sometimes as the "rag business"—is little more than a century old. As in the textile industry, some of the greatest changes have taken place within the last twenty years. Traditionally a highly fragmented industry consisting of thousands of small, independent firms, the trend has been toward larger companies and greater diversification of production, and from proprietorships or partnerships to corporations. These developments have taken place largely as a result of the increased competition from the growing industrialization abroad, and the challenge of new materials, new processes, and new markets.

Development of the Industry

In Colonial days textiles were produced by the cottage system; practically every home was a factory, with its own spinning wheel and loom and the nimble fingers of family members to hand-stitch the homespun into wearable garments. It was not until the early 1800s that a small group of New England merchants conceived the idea of having ready-made trousers and shirts available for the sailors who had only a few days in port. By the 1840s the demand for ready-made garments was spurred by the rush to the West for gold. Inexpensive clothes were needed by laborers, plantation slaves, and the many bachelors who had no wives to sew for them. Still sewn by hand, the ill-fitting clothes were hurriedly made.

The invention of the sewing machine and the Civil War gave further impetus to the ready-mades after the middle of the century. Women went to work in central places to make uniforms for the soldiers, and from this concentrated effort a standardized system of sizing developed that was later adapted to civilian requirements. By 1880, the men's ready-to-wear business was well established.

The manufacture of women's clothing was first noted in about 1859, when the census figures reported a total of 5,739 workers engaged primarily in the production of cloaks, mantillas, and hoop skirts. In the 1880s and 1890s, heavy immigration from eastern Europe contributed many eager workers to the clothing industry, many of whom had developed tailoring skills in their native countries. The 1890s brought the Gibson Girl, and the demand for women's shirtwaist blouses helped the newly established ready-to-wear movement. By 1900, 2,070 manufacturers of women's clothing employed a total of 96,000 workers.[15]

The development of the clothing industry is significant from another standpoint in that it was one of the first enterprises to offer large-scale employment to women outside the home. Of the 5,739 workers reported in the 1859 census, 4,850 were women. Although men gradually took over the cutting operations, and the waves of immigrant tailors displaced many women, the apparel industry still has a high concentration of women workers.

The earliest ready-mades were usually farmed out to workers who sewed in their homes (Figure 17.10). Some firms maintained their own factories, but working

[15]*The Dress Industry*, Market Planning Service, National Credit Office, New York, March 1948.

Figure 17.10 Early sewing was given out to people who worked in their homes and were paid by the "piece."

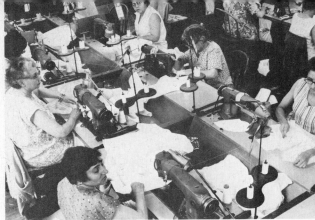

Figure 17.11 A sewing room in a modern apparel factory.

conditions in these "inside" shops were deplorable: "Unsanitary conditions, long hours, and low wages helped to give the sweat shop its unsavory name. Public opinion became aroused when epidemics broke out, and women objected to having their clothes made in tenement rooms, where people cooked, ate, and slept."[16]

It was in this atmosphere that the International Ladies' Garment Workers' Union was founded in 1900. Thereafter, the economic situation of the garment worker continued to improve. Today, the I.L.G.W.U. has a membership of over 442,000, of which 80 percent are women. Garment workers in the men's wear industry are also highly unionized, organized under the Amalgamated Clothing and Textile Workers Union.

Location of the Garment Centers

New York City became the dominant manufacturing center early in the history of the garment·trade (Figure 17.11). The industry found a pool of skilled labor in the endless

flow of immigrants that streamed into New York Harbor. New York was strategically located between the southern cotton mills and the New England woolen mills. Once the industry was established there, the city attracted other related enterprises that made it the mecca of trade for buyers from all over the country. So much of the business is concentrated in midtown Manhattan that the term *Seventh Avenue* has come to mean women's fashionable ready-to-wear (Figure 17.12).

New York still produces almost 60 percent of all women's and children's wear sold in the United States, and over 40 percent of the men's and boys' wear. Other cities, such as Boston, Philadelphia, Chicago, and St. Louis, have long been established as manufacturing centers, but none rivals New York in terms of product diversity or volume. California is growing as a leading center for sportswear, with Los Angeles ranking second only to New York in apparel production. Dallas and Atlanta have rapidly developing apparel centers and merchandise markets that attract buyers from all parts of the country. Atlanta has been called "the New York of the South," at least as far as fashion is concerned. Almost every state has some part in the clothing industry, but manufac-

[16]Florence S. Richards, *The Ready-To-Wear Industry 1900–1950* (New York: Fairchild Publications, 1951), p. 8.

Figure 17.12 Racks of dresses are pushed along in New York's Seventh Avenue district. Adding to the congestion, delivery trucks always are doubleparked so that the streets are virtually closed to traffic.

ture tends to concentrate in the urbanized industrial areas in or near large cities. The only states with *no* commercial apparel production are Idaho, Montana, Nevada, North Dakota, and Wyoming.

Economic Significance

In round figures, the apparel industry comprises about 20,000 clothing factories, of which over 12,000 are concentrated in the New York metropolitan area. The next largest area, Los Angeles, has about 1,800. Most of these enterprises are small establishments that employ on the average of fifty people each. There are a few large companies, but less than 1 percent of them employ more than five hundred people, and many have fewer than ten workers apiece. Plants producing men's and boys' apparel tend to be much larger than those making women's clothing. In the last decade, as total employment in the United States rose, the number employed in the textile and clothing industries represented a decreasing proportion of the total labor force (Table 17.4).

Although the apparel industry employs over 1.3 million workers, the weekly paycheck of the apparel worker is considerably less than the average wage of all manufacturing production workers (Figure 17.13). Although hourly wages for apparel workers and textile workers are nearly comparable, weekly gross earnings of textile workers are generally higher because they work over forty hours a week, as compared to an average thirty-six hour work week for the apparel worker. Wages of both are significantly lower than wages of workers in all other manufacturing industries (Table 17.5). Profit rates in the garment business are also lower than those in textile production or in all manufacturing as a whole (Table 17.6). Low wages and low profits can be explained by intense competition within the ranks and the threat of the low-wage manufactures from abroad. Foreign competition is so important that the next chapter is devoted to this topic.

In addition to employment, wages, and profits, the economic significance of any business may be evaluated in terms of its contribution to the national income. The **national income** refers to the total earnings of the country as a whole. If we examine the national income figures over a period of time (Table 17.7), we see that the textile and clothing industries combined contribute many billions of dollars a year to the national income, although their proportionate share over the years has declined, as did the share of all manufacturing industries. The actual dollar amounts of income contributed by textiles and apparel have risen, but the wholesale price of clothing (Table 17.8) has not increased at the same rate as that of other goods and services, and the proportion of national income derived from services (as opposed to the total value of goods) has gone up.

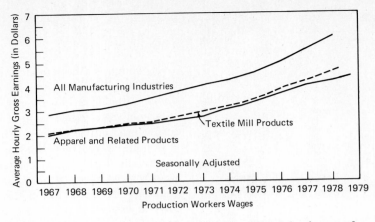

Figure 17.13 Production workers' hourly wages. Although hourly wages for apparel workers and textile workers are nearly comparable, weekly gross earnings of textile workers are generally higher because they work over forty hours a week, as compared to an average thirty-six-hour week for the apparel workers. Wages of both are significantly lower than wages of workers in all other manufacturing industries.

Table 17.4 Employment in the Textiles and Clothing Industries (in Thousands)

	1960	1970	1971	1975	1976	1977	1979
Total U.S. Labor Force	72,104	85,903	86,929	24,793	96,917	99,534	105,534
Total employed in all manufacturing industries	16,796 (23.3%)	19,369 (22.5%)	18,608 (21.4%)	18,347 (19%)	18,956 (19.5%)	19,554 (19.6%)	21,106 (20%)
Number in textile mill products	924 (1.3%)	997 (1.1%)	962 (1.1%)	902 (1%)	966 (1%)	982 (1%)	893 (1.1%)
Apparel and related products	1,233 (1.7%)	1,372 (1.6%)	1,361 (1.5%)	1,235 (1.3%)	1,299 (1.3%)	1,288 (1.3%)	1,300 (1.2%)

(Source: *Statistical Abstracts of the United States*, 1972, 1979; U.S. Dept. of Labor, Bureau of Labor Statistics, January 1980.)

Trends

Although there are still many hundreds of small garment manufacturers, the really small firms have been disappearing, and the big companies have cornered an increasing share of the total apparel market. In the past decade, the number of establishments shrank by nearly 3,000. It is estimated that somewhere between four hundred and five hundred firms go out of business each year. It is not possible to keep an exact count because the industry is characterized by a high degree of business turnover, and the same firm may be reported as entering and leaving the industry twice in the same year.

Many more firms have been consolidated through mergers and acquisitions. For example, General Mills, Inc., is a giant conglomerate whose fashion division includes David Crystal, Inc., Kimberly Knitwear, Alligator outerwear, Knothe Pajamas and Belts, Siltex double-knit fabrics, and Monet costume jewelry. The subsidiaries retain their separate identities. In addition,

Table 17.5 Employment Hours (Per Week) and Wages (Per Hour)

	Employment Hours Per Week			
	1949	1959	1969	1979
All manufacturing industries combined	39.1	40.3	40.5	40.0
Apparel retail stores	37.0	35.0	31.9	29.0
Apparel manufacturers	35.4	36.3	35.9	35.1
Textile mill production	37.7	40.4	40.8	40.2

	Wages Per Hour			
	1949	1959	1969	1979
All manufacturing industries combined	$1.34	$2.14	$3.19	$6.58
Apparel retail stores	1.06	1.44	2.15	4.11
Apparel manufacturers	1.21	1.56	2.31	4.33
Textile mill production	1.18	1.56	2.35	4.85

(Sources: U.S. Department of Labor, Bureau of Labor Statistics, January 1980, *Handbook of Basic Economic Statistics*, Economic Statistic Bureau of Washington, D.C., January 1980.)

Table 17.6 Corporate Profit Data

	Net Profits as % of net sales								
	1967	1968	1969	1970	1971	1972	1977	1978	1979
All manufactured nondurable goods	5.0	5.1	4.8	4.0	4.2	4.3	5.0	5.0	5.2
Textile mill products	2.9	3.1	2.9	1.9	2.4	2.6	3.4[1]	3.5[1]	3.6[2]
Apparel and related products	2.3	2.4	2.3	1.9	2.3	2.3			

[1]Composite for Textiles and Apparel Manufacturing. (Source: *Business Week*, July 1979.)
[2]Composite for Textiles and Apparel Manufacturing Projected. (Source: *Business Week*, January 1980.)
(Source: *Textile Hi-lights*, American Textile Manufacturers Institute, Inc., December 1973.)

Table 17.7 National Income in Billions of Dollars

	1950	1960	1970	1975	1977	1978	1979[1]
Total	241.0	418.0	804.4	1,244.6	1,554.8	1,724.3	1,924.2
All manufacturing	76.2	125.4	215.4	312.5	408.9	459.5	511.0
	31.6%	30.0%	26.7%	25.0%	26.0%	27.0%	26.5%
Textile mill products	4.4	4.5	7.5	8.8	11.8	13.8	14.4
	1.8%	1.0%	.9%	.7%	.7%	.8%	.75%
Apparel	3.5	4.9	8.7	10.8	13.2	15.5	16.35
	1.5%	1.1%	1.0%	.8%	.8%	.9%	.85%

[1]1979 figures are projected.
(Source: *Survey of Current Business*, U.S. Department of Commerce, Bureau of Economic Analysis, January 1980.)

Table 17.8 Wholesale Price Index

	1960	1967	1970	1975	1977	1978	1979
All commodities	94.9	100.0	110.4	174.9	194.2	203.3	225.9
All industrial commodities	95.3	100.0	110.0	171.5	195.1	203.6	Finished goods[1] 227.3 Intermediate 259.8 Crude materials 302.5 124.5[2]
Textile mill products	—	100.0	103.2	102.2	104.1	106.4	109.3[3]
Apparel	94.9	100.0	110.8	133.4	147.3	150.0	162.8

[1]In 1979 the WPI was changed to the PPI and industrial commodities broken into categories.
[2]Synthetic fibers.
[3]Finished fabrics.
(Source: *Survey of Current Business*, U.S. Department of Commerce, Bureau of Economic Analysis, January 1980.)

the traditional partnership arrangement is gradually giving way to the corporation. By expanding operations, manufacturers have been able to reduce the unit cost of production through volume sales.

Despite this trend toward bigness, the largest garment companies still cannot compare in size with the giant corporations that dominate other fields of manufacturing, or even with the larger textile mills. Jonathan Logan is probably the largest dress manufacturer. There are several larger apparel firms, but they tend to produce a more standardized product, such as men's shirts, suits, and uniforms. The very nature of fashion behavior puts an automatic lid on the volume of any one design that a manufacturer can expect to sell. People who seek individuality in dress do not buy a garment that hundreds of others are wearing. In high-fashion merchandise, the advantages of volume production are seriously curtailed.

Instead of producing more of the same kind of garment, therefore, the growing companies tend to diversify their output. For example, some men's wear firms have branched out into women's wear; blouse companies have started lingerie divisions;

and dress concerns have expanded into sportswear. Some larger establishments have decentralized their sewing operations and have moved to less urbanized areas.

The manufacturer is caught in a fiercely competitive, low-wage, low-profit business. The only acceptable way to stay afloat is to capitalize on the consumers' desire for newness and tasteful clothes. More and more, attempts are made to do this through market research and promotion, developing increased communications with retailers and consumers through national advertising programs and increasing emphasis on brand names.

From Textile to Garment

Most apparel firms produce a new line of merchandise twice a year, although in the more fashionable categories like women's dresses, there are often spring, summer, fall, holiday, and resort collections—five lines per year. The designer begins work about six months before the garment is to appear on the racks of the retail store. For some firms, "designing" means copying or

Figure 17.14 Modern technological innovations like these speed up production and reduce labor costs, but they require large investments of capital and are generally useful only for standardized products. Many small operators go into business with only a modest investment in a few sewing machines and a small work space.

Figure 17.15 The trend is toward bigness in the apparel business. This photograph shows the interior of a very large garment factory.

adapting styles from higher priced merchandise or updating the best sellers from the previous season. The designer's sketches are then translated into cloth garments, either muslin or finished fabric, and checked against yardage requirements, ease of construction, and other production points to keep them within the firm's price range.

Designs approved "in the muslin" go to the patternmaker and are made up in the sample size to be modeled at the openings when the line is shown during the market weeks to prospective retail buyers from all over the country. On the basis of orders received, manufacturers plan their production schedules. In most cases, almost a third of the line is eliminated because the orders are too few to warrant production. A garment that retails for $175 may not be put into production unless there are orders for a hundred or more. At higher prices, the manufacturer may go into production on several dozen of a particular style.

Once this decision has been made, the original pattern is graded and laid out for cutting (Figure 17.14). Garment pieces are then bundled according to size and moved on to the sewing operations. At this point a firm may hire a contractor and send the bundles out to be sewn in an "outside" shop. If a manufacturer runs an "inside" shop, it means the entire garment is produced, from start to finish. Technically, manufacturers who contract with "outside" shops are known as jobbers; they do everything but the sewing.

In higher-priced lines, a single operator may do all the sewing on a garment, but in most cases, section work prevails in which each worker completes a single operation before passing the bundle on to the next station (Figure 17.15). Garments are usually returned to the manufacturer (if a contractor is involved) for final pressing, inspection, and shipment to the retail stores.

In either case, the industry is locked into a system of union wages, and even though apparel workers have a lower pay scale than do those in other industries, the labor cost is several times the materials cost. A zipper may cost the manufacturer only seven or eight cents, but putting a zipper in the neck of a sweater can triple the labor costs.

Manufacturers depend heavily on reorders for their profits, that is, volume production on popular styles that continue to sell month after month. Known in the trade as "hot" items or "runners," styles that gain extensive consumer acceptance can be cut in quantity in a wide range of fabrics at a much lower unit cost. A great deal of the manufacturer's success depends on the speed with which reorders are filled while consumer demand is at its peak.

The Fashion Creators

The most important person in the hectic business of fashion is the designer. No matter how well or how fast a garment is constructed, it will not sell if it has no style appeal.

The fashion creator in the United States has always been limited by the economics of mass production. Even those who have achieved fame in the design field—Bill Blass, James Galanos, Pauline Trigère, Diana Von Furstenberg, and others—are not custom couturiers but ready-to-wear manufacturers. Their designs may be as creative and as expensive as anything from Paris, but they still sell at wholesale prices to retail stores rather than directly to the customer. Bill Blass, Ltd., one of the few designer-owned firms in the country, manufactures exclusive women's wear with prices ranging from $200 to $2,000 an item. In addition to women's fashions, however, the company also licenses Blass designs for men's clothing, swimsuits, rainwear, hosiery, scarves, watches, luggage, furs, and sheets and pillowcases. Early in the 1970s, Blass launched a line of men's cosmetics.

The name of a firm's designer used to be treated as a trade secret—never advertised in connection with the product. During World War II, however, when Paris fell to the Germans, the fashion scene shifted to the United States and American designers gradually achieved recognition in their own right. After the war, the Americans remained leaders in sportswear and casual clothes, a category of dress in which the French had little interest until recent years.

Unlike the French coutouriers, however, who are subsidized by the government and protected by copyright laws, American high-fashion designers are completely on their own. European houses can make their money by selling designs to manufacturers for copying. American designers do not have this option, since the most successful designs are copied anyway, and sometimes the cheaper imitations can be turned out faster than the originals can be.

This also happens in the couture to some extent. A manufacturer with a keen eye and a good memory may buy a model or two at a Paris opening but come home with enough ideas for a dozen or more adaptations. A model may be copied at almost any price level, with certain modifications: complicated cuts are often simplified; construction details like linings, interfacings, and hand work may be eliminated; and yardage may be reduced. Style piracy in the fashion business is a fact of life.

Fashion imitation is the mechanism that keeps the fashion cycle moving and makes fashionable clothing available to those of limited means. Further, the "knockoffs" stimulate consumer buying, which is good for the entire industry.

The men's wear industry used to be relatively insulated from rapid fashion fluctuations. In the days before the Peacock Revolution, a man's white dress shirt was probably one of the most uniform products on the market. Volume was not only high, it was predictable. It was no accident that firms like Hart Schaffner & Marx (men's suits) and Cluett Peabody (shirts) had larger sales figures than the biggest dress manufacturer. But high style penetrated the men's wear field. The sale of suits has gone down, and that of haberdashery items—shirts, slacks, belts, ties—has gone up.

Professionals classify men's suits "according to the quality of the fabric used and the amount of handwork that goes into the construction."[17] Suits are graded from one to six, and the highest grade indicates the finest quality and the highest prices. A Grade Four suit may sell from $175 to $300. The Grade Two suit may be a sound machine-made product and sell for under $100. The Grade Four suit of similar fabric would have hand-set chest pieces, collars, and lapels, and handmade buttonholes. It would sell for $175 and up. Its female counterpart might cost as much as $400.

The news in men's wear styling in 1979, and predictably the trend for the 1980s, is the "sportswear-made suit." Slacks, blazers, jackets, and vests were introduced first by the giant jeans and pants manufacturers, such as Levi Strauss and Blue Bell, and were originally made of traditional suit fabrics. To the untrained eye they look like conventional two- or three-piece suits. They are not made with the same precision of construction and finishing that characterizes the well-tailored man's suit, but they are far less expensive, about half

the price. They can also be mixed and matched, thus providing the versatility and expandability that women long have been able to use to stretch their clothing dollars. The sportswear-made suits were not intended to affect the traditional suit market, but many premium-made clothing manufacturers have been forced to compete as the price of traditional suits has gone up. The sportswear-made suit is similar in concept to the leisure suit, introduced in 1974, but

the difference, however, lies in the inherent flexibility of the former. Although initially conceived as separates, leisure suits could not effectively be merchandised as such. Men thought of them as suits and bought them accordingly. The concept of mixing and matching the top and bottom components of the leisure suit was not adequately imparted by the industry to the consumer.

With sportswear-made suits, however, no such education process is critical. Men wear sport coats and vests both for casual and for dressy occasions. Since, unlike the leisure suit, the sportswear-made suit offers no radically new silhouette, men will be equally at home wearing it separately as sportswear or together as a suit.[18]

"Based in part on an inflationary economy which requires a reduced revolving wardrobe,"[19] this new concept in merchandising for men resembles the women's ready-to-wear market. Some observers predict that in another decade or two men will not wear suits at all, they will have

[17]*Washington Post*, September 1, 1979.

[18]"Sportswear-Made Suits Gathering Strength in U.S. Menswear," *American Fabrics*, No. 113 (Summer 1978), 8–9.

[19]Susan Loder, "Collections: Building Fashion for the 80's," *Daily News Record*, San Diego Issue, March 14, 1979, Sec. 2, p. 4.

untailored clothing as light, casual, and varied as women's.[20]

While more and more women's wear designers (Blass, Beene, Cardin, and so on) turned out lines for men, traditional men's wear companies (for instance, Levi Strauss) branched into women's wear. In the past, traditional men's wear manufacturers presented only two lines of merchandise a year—spring and fall. Usually the order for piece goods was made nine months in advance, and actual construction of tailored garments took about eight weeks. At the same time that many women's wear designers were eliminating their summer lines, a few innovators in the men's wear business added "holiday lines" and "cruise lines." Little by little, the men's wear industry has turned toward the women's wear concept of a quick turnover business to meet rapid fashion change.

Unpredictable consumer response to fashion change imposes a high degree of uncertainty on the apparel producer.

SUMMARY

Apparel Production

The ready-to-wear industry grew from the sweatshop working conditions of the late nineteenth century. The stream of European immigrants to the United States provided a skillful, low-cost labor pool for the trades and helped to establish New York as the garment production center. Now highly unionized, garment workers have improved standards of work and wages, although their pay scale is still below that of many production workers in other manufacturing industries. Still, domestic labor costs are so high that the United States cannot compete with the low-wage countries on a worldwide basis.

Although the general trend is toward larger, more diversified companies, the apparel industry as a whole is still characterized by many small, independent, and highly specialized firms. Most of these revise their lines of merchandise twice a year, but those that deal in more fashionable items do so five times a year. The American economy is geared to volume production. Even the most influential designers are ready-to-wear manufacturers rather than haute couturiers. Many firms resort to copying the styles that are doing well in the upper price lines.

The manufacturer who anticipates consumer acceptance accurately is rewarded for risk-taking through volume sales; those who guess wrongly suffer economic losses on unsold inventories and drastic markdowns on merchandise. The apparel industry remains an intensely competitive, low-profit business that can thrive only on the basis of fashion obsolescence and a constant flow of fresh ideas.

[20]Walter McQuade, "High Style Disrupts the Men's Wear Industry," *Fortune* (February 1971), 71.

RETAILING OF CLOTHING

In most cases, distribution of clothing merchandise is a direct transaction between manufacturer and retailer. In some staple lines, however, such as utility or work clothes, underwear, and pajamas, a wholesaler may work as a middleman between the garment maker and the independent retailer (see Figure 17.1). A few of the biggest apparel manufacturers have moved into the retail business by buying out chains of independent retailers. Hart Schaffner & Marx, one of the largest suit makers, now owns about two hundred fifty retail outlets. Another example is Phillips–Van Heusen, operating many stores throughout the country. In recent years, there have been many mergers in the retail field just as in the textile and apparel industries. Outwardly, the stores appear no different to the average consumer. They usually continue to operate under the same name, but they enjoy the advantages of pooled assets.

Types of Retail Stores

Taken as a whole, there are more than 1,950,000 retail stores of all kinds in the United States today. It is difficult to tell exactly how much of the retail business can be attributed to clothing or fashion, but we can understand some statistics better if we distinguish among the various types of retail outlets.

The **department store** evolved from the old dry-goods store of the early nineteenth century. Its growth paralleled the growth of cities and the concentration of people in urbanized areas. A department store may be either independently owned or part of a chain, but characteristically it sells a line of home furnishings in addition to clothing, household textiles, and yard goods. It also offers a number of customer services, which in addition to the sales personnel, includes such conveniences as charge accounts, mail and phone orders, delivery of merchandise, return privileges, and gift wrapping.

Over the past five years, department stores have consistently accounted for just under 10 percent of the total retail sales in the United States.[21] These stores have strong competition from new-style retailing establishments and, therefore, they are unlikely to take any larger share of the consumer market in the future. Ten percent may very well be their top level and they could even experience some decline in the next decade.

Variety stores sprang up around the department stores once the downtown area became established as a center for shopping. In the early days they were essentially discount stores, offering low unit–priced merchandise to customers who happened to be in the shopping area anyway. Today, variety stores such as Woolworth's, Murphy's, and Hill's provide mass outlets for lower-priced ready-to-wear, and their price range has been broadened to include items considerably above the original five-and-ten-cent categories. By far the largest is F. W. Woolworth's with 5,000 stores, 23 percent of the total variety stores.

The name **chain store** was applied whenever a group of variety or specialized stores became centrally owned. The Lerner Shops, for example, and the big shoe chains have a tremendous sales volume with stores in almost every major city of the

[21]*Retail Trade International*, 1978–1979.

country. Department stores that may have several branches are not recognized as chains, although in many ways the difference is hardly perceptible to the consumer. Chains tend to be characterized by highly standardized merchandise, and they are managed remotely from a central or regional office. J. C. Penney is probably the largest of the chains. With an annual gross sales of over $9 billion, it is the nation's third-largest retailer. In 1976, the corporation lost its long-held position as number two in retailing revenues to K-Mart Corporation, a large chain of discount stores.[22]

Mail-order companies grew from the need to service isolated rural families who did not have access to convenient shopping areas. Everyone thought that the mail-order business would decline as farm population decreased, but as the automobile increased the mobility of the buying public, city and rural alike, mail-order houses opened retail stores that in many cases catered to the driving public. Usually located in a suburban area, they expanded into automobile tires and accessories, garden equipment, and home improvement supplies. Mail-order catalogs traditionally had featured the time-tested variety of housedresses and work clothes, but today buyers from stores like Sears can be found at many European fashion openings, and the haute couture copies, manufactured especially for catalog sales, are now the most prominently featured items of merchandise. Sears operates eight hundred fifty department-type stores and accounts for 10 percent of the United States department store trade. Additionally, they have over 2,000 other retail outlets, such as mail-order centers and discount stores. They employ over 440,000 people in this

country alone.[23] With the inevitable overseas connections and many subsidiaries, Sears is the largest retailer in the world, with an annual volume of business of over $14 billion.[24]

Discount stores appeared in increasing numbers during the 1950s, although many stores had operated on a discount basis for a number of years. Some discount stores are single operations but many, like Zayre's, Woolco's, and K-Mart, are similar in concept to the chain stores. The phenomenal growth of the discounters may be attributed to a number of factors. One was the shift of population from cities to suburbs. The discounter took the cue from those who had been successful with the driving public and built in outlying areas that provided ample parking space. Large assortments of merchandise were offered under one roof and the customer could make selections supermarket style and check out purchases in short order. Additionally, many consumers during that period were reacting against the retail methods of the conventional store, where they were helping to pay for high rentals, salespeople, elaborate store fixtures, credit, and other customer services, but were not getting any more merchandise for their money. The discounter stepped in, started selling goods right from the packing boxes on a self-service basis, and reduced overhead enough to sell below the prevailing price level. Stores such as Orhbach's and Loehmann's, located in the most congested areas of New York City, have been selling fashion goods on a self-service, cut-rate basis for years. The idea of discount, however, is still spreading.

[22]*Business Week*, January 16, 1978.

[23]*Retail Trade International*, 1977–1978.
[24]"Think Twice About Sears," Sears, Roebuck and Co., p. 5.

A growing number of companies specialize in what has been called cut-rate haute couture. Such stores buy surplus stock from designer-manufacturers, cut out the labels to protect the producers, and sell the garments at rock-bottom prices. The customer must know how to read garment quality without a label's help and be willing to try on garments in crowded community dressing rooms.

Specialty stores may vary all the way from the posh atmosphere of a Bergdorf Goodman or a Henri Bendel to a modest small store selling lingerie and blouses. Stores that specialize in related categories of merchandise—children's wear, men's furnishings, women's apparel, and so on—may be independently owned or part of a chain. They may even be discounters. The specialty store was the major retail operation of the seventies because "it was a concept with which customers instantly identified and it allowed stores to zero in on a particular kind of shopper."[25]

Obviously, there is considerable overlap in concept, image, merchandise, and definition among the various types of retailing establishments mentioned. There are, of course, many other types of retail outlets for clothing merchandise. Many supermarkets carry standardized lines of children's play clothes, hosiery, and underwear, and some have expanded into work clothes, shorts, slacks, and blouses, and even drug stores carry some apparel items.

Beyond this, the number of **second-hand clothing stores** is on the increase. Nearly everyone is familiar with the typical Goodwill thrift store, but not many people know of the shops that deal in high fashion. "Encore," for example, is a three-story shop in New York, with another operation in Washington, D.C., where the designer clothes of the rich are resold at about one third of the original retail price. The proprietor may resell a $1,000 de la Renta for $333 and split that with the original owner of the dress. This procedure gives a better incentive for disposing of worn-once clothes than does a tax deduction for contributions of clothing to the Salvation Army.

Economic Significance

Omitting local supermarkets, drug stores, and second-hand shops, there are probably close to 180,000 retail outlets for fashion merchandise in the United States today. The largest number of these are the specialized apparel and accessory stores, although the big general merchandise companies have a greater number of employees by far. Over 2.3 million people are on the payrolls of department and variety stores and the large chains, while only 733,000 work in specialty shops.[26] Together, they earn over $8 billion a year in wages and salaries.

Obviously, the general merchandise stores (the chains, department, and discount stores) also have the largest volume of retail sales. Early in the 1960s, the apparel trade was almost evenly divided (55 percent general merchandise, 45 percent specialty shops and other). A decade later, the chains, department stores, and discount houses were doing 62 percent of the business with an annual sale of apparel merchandise of $25 billion as compared to the $11 billion's worth of goods sold in

[25]"Marketing Will Provide the Competitive Edge," *Homesewing Trade News* (February 1980), 4.

[26]*Statistical Abstracts of the United States*, U.S. Department of Commerce, 1978.

Table 17.9   Comparison of Wholesale and Consumer Price Indexes (1967 = 100)

	1960		1967		1970	
	WPI	CPI	WPI	CPI	WPI	CPI
All commodities	94.9	88.7	100		110.4	116.3
Apparel and upkeep	94.9	89.6	100		111.0	116.1
Footwear	87.6	85.1	100		113.0	117.7

[1]PPI: Producer Price Index.
[2]Information not available.
(Source: CPI Detailed Report, PPI Detailed Report, U.S. Bureau of Labor, Bureau of Statistics.)

apparel and accessory stores. Growth rate was highest among the four big chains. In 1963, Sears, Penney, Grant, and Ward accounted for $3.1 billion in apparel sales. A decade later, their sales were more than doubled ($8.0 billion in 1973). In 1979, chain stores, defined by the U.S. Department of Commerce as all commercial establishments with eleven or more retail outlets, had apparel sales of $14.0 billion.[27]

Prices and Profits

Price lines and merchandise markups clearly vary with the type of store. The average markup on goods may vary anywhere from 17 percent over wholesale in the discount houses, to 70 percent for a high-priced designer dress sold in a fashionable specialty store. This does not necessarily mean that the specialty shop makes a bigger profit. In a typical department store, the markup is usually between 35 and 40 percent of retail. Even at that, the average profit on sales rarely amounts to more than 2 or 3 percent. Let us say that a store does a million dollars' worth of business a year. It costs the store about

[27]*Handbook of Basic Economic Statistics*, Economic Statistics Bureau of Washington, D.C., January 1980.

three cents to make every transaction, and if a customer returns a piece of merchandise, it costs another three cents to remove the sale from the books. Obviously, these kinds of costs must be absorbed in the sales price. So from the gross sales of $1,000,000, the store must deduct about $100,000 for returns and other allowances plus the wholesale cost of the goods (which would be close to $600,000), leaving a gross margin of $300,000. Out of this must come employee wages and salaries, as well as rent and other operating expenses. These may amount to 25 percent or more of the gross sales, or $250,000, leaving a net profit of $50,000, on which the retailer must still pay taxes. If lucky, three cents on the dollar of gross sales may be the profit margin.

Small retailers face a serious threat from the mass merchandisers and factory-outlet operations. The big chains like Sears and Penney have upgraded their fashion image in recent years, and for volume-produced clothes their retail prices are hard to match. It is difficult for them, however, to offer a high degree of style differentiation. The top of their lines may be a $50 sportcoat or $35 dress, and clothes that retail at $200, let us say, are not available in chains. The specialty store can offer the type of service and merchandise some customers demand. "The business execu-

	1971			1977			1978			1979	
	WPI	CPI		WPI	CPI		WPI	CPI		WPI[1]	CPI
	113.9	121.3		194.2	186.1		203.3	199.4		225.9	229.9
	112.9	119.8		147.3	158.2		150.0	162.7		162.9	172.2
	116.8	121.5		—[2]	159.6		—[2]	168.3		227.3	184.2

tive who wants to buy expensive, well-tailored clothing, for instance, wants a certain amount of service and expertise to go along with the product. He wants to be called by name when he walks into a store; he wants a professional clothier to wait on him—not a clerk."[28] In short, some consumers are willing to pay for service and a pleasant shopping environment.

All stores have certain fixed overhead expenses. Obviously, retailers in low-rent districts who hire inexperienced sales personnel at minimum wages have lower operating costs than those who have higher maintenance expenses, pay higher salaries, and offer more services. The type of merchandise also influences the profit potential. If a cocktail dress has to be marked down from $60 to $40 at the end of a season, the retailer is just barely meeting costs. On clothing that is marked off 50 percent or more, the store is actually taking a loss.

The retail price of clothing has gone up in recent years, although it has not increased at the same rate as have other commodities (see Table 17.9). There is, nevertheless, a greater difference between wholesale and retail prices than there used to be. Stores have had to raise their markups because they have to pay more today for office and sales help, delivery

services, advertising, and window displays. Another factor that contributes to higher price tags is the increase in stock shortage, otherwise known as shoplifting. Stores were increasingly troubled by this problem during the seventies, to the extent that figures on stolen merchandise were outdated in six months' time.

The actual dollar increase in shoplifting between 1962 and 1977 was $4 billion, from $2.5 billion to over $6.5 billion. The estimated cost to each family in the United States is somewhere between $50 and $160 each year because retailers are forced to add the cost of shoplifting to their cost of doing business and pass the ultimate cost down to consumers, even those who do not engage in shoplifting. The cost of surveillance equipment (Figure 17.16) needed—two-way mirrors, guards, and closed circuit television—is also added to the price of merchandise. This may amount to as much as $80,000 to $100,000 per store each year. Professional estimates place the amount of shoplifting each week as high as $150,000 in department, food, drug, and discount stores.[29]

Trends in Retailing

Trends in retailing have followed the trends in social structure and organization throughout the country. The movement of

[28]Sanford Josephson, "Challenges Beset Smaller Retailers," *New York Daily News Record*, February 14, 1973, p. 36.

[29]"Shoplifting Has Some Hard Consequences," *Blacksburg* (Virginia) *Sun*, August 15, 1979, p. B–10.

the population into the suburbs, coupled with the universal dependence on the automobile, gave tremendous impetus to the growth of shopping plazas of varying sizes. As many large chains built modern facilities in the outlying centers with plenty of parking space, other stores moved out to join them. Parent stores opened branches, and specialty shops improved their locations. In some cases, severe losses were suffered by the downtown stores, many of whom had large capital investments and/or long-term leases that prevented them from moving out. However, urban renewal projects in many major United States cities have included refurbishing existing downtown stores. Corporations with sufficient capital are modernizing structures to include built-in parking facilities. City governments are supporting downtown shopping malls with free transportation, better lighting, and other safety features in an appeal to both city dwellers and suburbanites. In some cities the idea has worked so

well that stores that originated in the suburbs or in small towns surrounding the metropolitan areas are actually opening new downtown branches. As suburban property becomes scarce and increases in cost and as mass transit improves the eighties may be marked by a return to the inner city for major shopping.

Consumer shopping habits have influenced retailers in another respect, which relates to the peak shopping times. With more women working during the day, families often go shopping together in the evening. Many stores have found it necessary to remain open several nights a week as well as on Sundays to compete.

Mail-order buying has increased. Sears, for example, can do business anywhere without having to worry about plant location and without the consumer having to worry about parking.

Installment buying, prevalent for many years in the automobile, furniture, and large appliance lines, is now widely used for clothing purchase. The majority of department, specialty, and chain stores have developed some plan of extending credit to their customers. For many retailers, the charges made for credit service constitute a substantial proportion of their net profits. Stores without the financial assets to carry credit accounts can take advantage of the many multipurpose bank credit card systems now available. Both VISA and Mastercharge plates are accepted everywhere in this country and in most foreign countries as well. Without these credit competitors, small stores would lose sizeable amounts of business to the larger firms that carry their own credit customers. Most major department, chain, and variety stores use their own charge accounts and the bank credit systems as well. It is now

Figure 17.16   Some retailers invest in elaborate surveillance systems like the one shown above, to monitor shoppers throughout the store.

Table 17.10 Retail Trade: Apparel and Accessories in Billions of Dollars

Stores	1967	1970	1975	1977	1978	1979
Total retail trade	292,956	368,403	584,776	724,020	789,813	798,117
Total nondurable goods	204,231	259,208	403,508	476,188	520,902	566,380
Apparel and accessories	16,342	22,110	30,291	34,341	37,828	39,876
Apparel retail firms (11 or more stores)	4,862	5,475	6,834	10,631	13,071	21,764

(Source: *Handbook of Basic Economic Statistics*, Economic Statistics, Bureau of Washington, D.C., January 1980.)

possible to buy a shoelace or a mink coat with a VISA card.

The same trend toward bigness that was observed in the textiles and the apparel industries also is evident in the retail establishments. Mergers and acquisitions are on the increase. The independent, family-owned store is gradually being bought out by larger establishments. Even the larger department stores have consolidated. The May Company, for example, owns the May's stores in Cleveland, Denver, Los Angeles and San Diego, and it also owns the Hecht Department Stores in Washington and Baltimore, Kaufmann's in Pittsburgh, Meier & Frank in Portland, Strouss-Hirschberg in Youngstown, Ohio, and Famous-Barr in St. Louis (Table 17.10).

The central buying operations that are possible through large-volume sales make fashion merchandise more quickly available to consumers in all parts of the country. By the same token, many people view the clothing market as one with less and less product differentiation each year. The same knitted pantsuit can be found in stores from Washington, D.C., to San Francisco, with not more than a two-dollar variation in retail price. Many larger stores have computers that evaluate retail activi-

ties on a day-to-day basis. Daily analysis of store sales provides a fashion profile of the sizes, fabric textures, silhouettes, color preferences, and other style features favored on the local market. The retailer can draw many conclusions about consumer acceptance locally from customers' purchases, requests for merchandise, complaints, and returns. In this sense, customers' behavior in the marketplace is quickly assessed, and it becomes a useful guide to the retailer in gearing store merchandise to consumer demand.

Related Activities

In addition to the merchandising function, the retailer contributes taxes to local, state, and federal governments and, through advertising, to the cost of newspapers and other advertising media. Further, many, many people are engaged in fashion-related activities that also figure in the overall economics of the clothing business. Fashion advisory services and resident buying offices operate as intermediaries between manufacturers and retailers. Fashion publications are also a big business. In early 1977, more than $30.4 million was spent for national newspaper advertising of wearing apparel, $70 million for magazine advertising, and $47 million for television advertising.[30]

Advertising and public relations firms prepare the newspaper and magazine ads, plan large-scale promotional campaigns, and often conduct marketing research on consumer preferences and shopping habits. Probably more than 15 million people in the United States depend in one way or another, on the clothing industry for their livelihoods.

Successful retailers must make rapid adjustments in their business practices to meet consumer demands and preferences.

SUMMARY

Retailing of Clothing

The retailer is the last link in the chain from the fiber producer to the ultimate consumer. The retailer has the responsibility of stocking the combination of styles, textures, colors, and sizes the customer will demand. The retailer's purchases, in turn, constitute feedback to the manufacturer concerning consumer acceptance of products.

The consumer who knows the retail market is better prepared for selective shopping than one who does not know it. Department stores and specialty shops offer a variety of customer services along with a wide range of merchandise. Discount stores can offer clothing items on a self-service basis at a much lower markup. Mail-order houses offer the convenience of shopping at home, and these—along with many apparel chains—are now offering more fashionable merchandise. The individual consumer must weigh the relative value of each of these advantages, including the quality of the merchandise, the privileges of return on unsatisfactory purchases, the willingness of the merchant to stand behind goods, and the convenience of shopping itself. A knowledge of the retail stores in your community and how they operate will increase your competence and satisfaction as a clothing purchaser.

INDUSTRY RESPONSIBILITY

Most firms count on the repeat sales that will occur if a customer is satisfied with the merchandise. It goes without saying that all manufacturers and retailers are in business to make money. There are, no doubt, some businesspeople who will sell an inferior product for as long as they can get away with it, but they usually do not stay in business very long. Not more than thirty years ago, the average American consumer had to be content with shirts that wrinkled, dresses that shrank, colors that faded, and

[30]*Statistical Abstracts of the United States,* 1978.

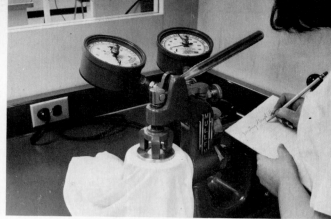

Figures 17.17 and 17.18 Many retail stores maintain their own test laboratories for quality control. Durability of fabric is tested with a hydraulic machine. Colors, specifically treated to resist fading from air pollution, also are tested.

many fabrics that could be cleaned only once, if at all. Today, consumers not only get an improved product, but they expect satisfactory performance as a kind of legal right.

For many years the clothing industry has engaged in research for development of better products and has regulated its output through a quality-control system. When such voluntary controls proved inadequate, or in cases where business practices were fraudulent or harmful to the consumer, the government usually stepped in to regulate the industry through legal processes.

Voluntary Standards

Many instances could be cited in which various segments of the clothing industry have demonstrated their social responsibility. Many manufacturers maintain their own quality control on textile and apparel products through testing and research in company-owned laboratories (Figures 17.17 and 17.18). For years, men's suits and coats have been graded on a numerical scale according to the quality of the material and the tailoring that goes into each garment. Today, with the scarcity of wool and the high cost of labor, these

quality standards have become economically unfeasible for all but the top of most manufacturers' lines. The mass merchandisers, for example, have stopped handling men's business suits altogether. Retail companies, as well, operate their own laboratories to keep their merchandise up to certain minimum standards.

As early as 1956, the American Standards Association, under the sponsorship of the National Retail Merchants Association (NRMA), led the way in establishing a set of performance standards for wearing apparel and home furnishings. The American Apparel Manufacturers Association (AAMA) has also worked toward establishment of voluntary standards for apparel within the industry itself.

Government Regulations

One of the earliest pieces of legislation that attempted to insure a competitive market for American consumers was the **Sherman Antitrust Act** of 1890. Essentially, the goal of the act and its subsequent amendments was to protect the market from monopolistic price fixing by a few large firms. Even though the clothing industry is generally characterized by a high degree of competition, there have been a few cases of antitrust violations. In 1972, for example, the Federal Trade Commission opposed the purchase of New York's Bergdorf Goodman by the Broadway-Hale Stores. Broadway-Hale had previously merged with Emporium Capwell and already operated forty-eight department stores in the Southwest, plus four Neiman-Marcus stores in Texas. The FTC maintained that the California firm would have an unfair competitive advantage over other New York retailers. The sale was subsequently approved, however, on the grounds that it was a unique situation in that Bergdorf's would have gone out of business if it were not sold.

Although antitrust laws forbid the manufacturer or retailer to fix prices, the **Miller-Tydings Act** of 1937 and state fair-trade laws allowed manufacturers of name-brand goods to set the retail price for their products. Such fair-trade laws are clearly incompatible with a market economy. Many discount stores have ignored such prices, and lawsuits have followed. Nevertheless, collusion among enterprises to control prices is prohibited. On these grounds, four swimsuit makers were indicted a few years ago for attempting to force retailers to hold to the prices the manufacturers set. The Justice Department claimed that competition had been eliminated by fixing prices at artificial levels and that retailers had lost their freedom to set their own retail prices.

The **Wheeler-Lea Act** of 1938 is directed against false or misleading advertising. A garment must live up to claims made on the label, and failure to reveal facts about the product is considered false advertising. In other words, if the advertising is written in such a way that the consumer is led to believe that a fabric

behaves in a certain manner when actually it does not, the practice is considered deceptive.

The **Wool Products Labeling Act** of 1939 requires that a product containing any amount of wool—virgin wool, wool, reprocessed, or reused wool—must be labeled to show the fiber content by percentages. Before this statute was enacted, manufacturers could pass off products made from shoddy, reclaimed wool, or of no wool content at all, as "virgin wool" or "pure wool." Textile mills now are required to keep records that will enable them to identify the particular lot of yarn and fibers that went into each piece of cloth. Lot number labels sewn into most wool garments will connect with manufacturers' cutting tickets that can be then traced back through the weaving, spinning, and blending records to the original raw stock.

The **Fur Products Labeling Act** of 1951 prohibited use of such names as Hudson seal, Mendoza beaver, mink-dyed muskrat, mountain sable, and a host of others, all of which were deceptive titles for various grades of opossum, muskrat, and rabbit. The fur act requires that every article made of or trimmed with fur bear a label that includes (1) the true name of the animal from which the skin was taken, (2) the country of origin, (3) whether the fur is natural, dyed, or otherwise artificially colored, and (4) an identifying mark by which the fur product can be traced back to its source. Many retailers as well as consumers are thus protected from deceptive practices on the part of manufacturers or wholesalers.

The **Textile Fiber Products Identification Act** of 1958 is the third "truth-in-fabrics" statute to be passed by Congress. This act covers the labeling of all apparel textiles that were not covered by the Wool Act. The Textile Act requires that all products be labeled as to fiber content by percentage, in the order of predominance by the weight of each fiber in the fabric. Prior to this legislation, a product could have been falsely advertised as "silk," when it may have contained only 3 or 4 percent silk and 96 or 97 percent rayon. In order to avoid the confusion of a proliferation of new man-made fibers sold under a wide variety of trade names, the Federal Trade Commission adopted a set of generic classifications that designate man-made fibers according to their chemical characteristics. These are acetate, acrylic, anidex, aramid, azlon, glass, lastrile, metallic, modacrylic, novoloid, nylon, nytril, olefin, polyester, rayon, rubber, saran, spandex, triacetate, vinal, and vinyon. Azlon and vinal are not currently produced in the United States; nytril is not currently produced in the world; and lastrile has never been produced commercially. These names may be used along with the names of the natural fibers, such as cotton, wool, silk, and linen (flax).

Many of these generic names, however, proved to have little meaning to the average consumer. For a number of years the apparel industry had been working voluntarily toward a program of care labeling. The Federal Trade Commission held discussions with members of the industry and with consumers, and the result was the **Federal Trade Commission Ruling on Permanent Care Labeling** that went into effect in July 1972. The rule requires that all textile apparel products and piece goods have a permanently legible care label affixed for its useful life. Products *not* covered are hosiery, hats, gloves, footwear, fur, leather, remnants, disposables,

see-through items, and garments that retail for three dollars or less. In July 1979, the Federal Trade Commission approved in substance "a new type of label telling consumers more specifically how to care for textile garments and piece goods and how to avoid damaging them."[31] This action will amend the 1972 ruling and extend the coverage to draperies and curtains, upholstered furniture and slipcovers, carpets and rugs, household linens, and suede and leather garments. Other substantive items of the new ruling will place the burden of recommendations for care on the manufacturers. If they affix a label stating that a garment requires washing, they must also recommend the method, including temperature, unless all methods can safely be used. Similar constrictions will apply to ironing, drying, and bleaching. The new ruling will "require that the manufacturer have a 'reasonable basis' for the recommendations on the care label."[32] (see examples of labels in Figure 17.19). This ruling represents a big step for the textile industry. "It will not only cost the manufacturer anywhere from $2.50 to $35 a thousand to print the labels, but up to 2½ cents to sew them in. One big apparel maker estimates this cost at about a half million dollars a year."[33]

The **Flammable Fabrics Act** was originally passed in 1953 and amended in 1967, 1972, and 1975. The act prohibits the manufacture or sale of wearing apparel made from fibers or fabrics that are dangerously flammable. The 1972 amendment

[31]"FTC Moves Toward New Care-Label Rule; More Specific Instructions Mandated," *FTC News*, July 26, 1979, p. 1.
[32]Ibid., p. 2.
[33]"Message from the FTC: We Always Knew You Cared," *American Fabrics* (Summer 1972), 64.

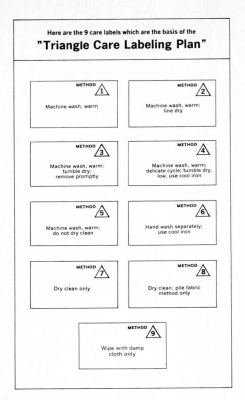

Here are the 9 care labels which are the basis of the
"Triangle Care Labeling Plan"

METHOD 1
Machine wash, warm

METHOD 2
Machine wash, warm:
line dry

METHOD 3
Machine wash, warm:
tumble dry;
remove promptly

METHOD 4
Machine wash, warm;
delicate cycle; tumble dry,
low; use cool iron

METHOD 5
Machine wash, warm;
do not dry clean

METHOD 6
Hand wash separately;
use cool iron

METHOD 7
Dry clean only

METHOD 8
Dry clean; pile fabric
method only

METHOD 9
Wipe with damp
cloth only

Figure 17.19 Coded labels developed by the Textile Distributors Association for use with retail fabrics.

was essentially a flammability standard involving children's sleepwear, sizes 0–6X (the 1975 amendment extended the size range to 14), which required that five specimens of every item of sleepwear in these size ranges be selected for testing. In effect, this means that the industry must produce fire-retardant sleepwear whether it wants to or not, since all merchandise that does not meet the standard is banned from the market. Some estimates are that the cost of testing plus the application of the finish adds as much as 50 percent to the cost of the article and reduces the wear-life of the garment by as much as 50 percent. Inability to retool to meet the stringent requirements forced some of the smaller manufacturers out of the market.

The consumer is protected from fraudulent business practices and products by a number of voluntary controls within the industry itself and by federal legislation.

SUMMARY

Industry Responsibility

The Federal Trade Commission administers a number of acts designed to protect the consumer from deceptive practices by unscrupulous manufacturers or merchandisers. Most reliable firms willingly comply with the statutes because they seek the repeat sale that comes with customer satisfaction and because they find that labels are a good way to promote their trade name. In many cases, compliance to federal regulations means additional expense, which is passed on to the consumer in the form of a higher retail price.

FOR FURTHER READING

"Apparel's Last Stand," *Business Week*, May 14, 1979, pp. 60–63.
Buck, Rinker. "The New Sweatshops: A Penny for Your Collar." *New York*, 12 (January 29, 1979), 40–46.

Conway, Mimi. *Rise Gona Rise: A Portrait of Southern Textile Workers*. Garden City, N.Y.: Anchor Press/Doubleday, 1979.

Council on Wage and Price Stability. *A Study of the Textile and Apparel Industries*, pp. 1–3, 5–20, 53–74. Washington, D.C.: U.S. Government Printing Office, 1978.

Crippen, Kaye. "Tris on Trial." *Journal of Home Economics*, 70 (January 1978), 29–31.

Dean, Ailene, and Elizabeth M. Dolan. "Clothing Flammability Alternatives." *Journal of Home Economics*, 70 (January 1978), 32–33.

"How California Got to Be No. 2 in Apparel." *Business Week*, November 6, 1978, p. 188.

Kidwell, Claudia, and Margaret C. Christman. *Suiting Everyone: The Democratization of Clothing in America*. Washington, D.C.: U.S. Government Printing Office, 1974.

Scott, Mark. "A Day in the Life: Menswear Buyer for Bloomingdale's Saturday Generation Shop." *Esquire*, 91 (December 1979), 119–20.

Chapter 18

CLOTHING AND
THE INTERNATIONAL MARKET

The interactions of supply, demand, and purchasing power are by no means confined to the domestic production, distribution, and consumption of consumer goods. From a worldwide standpoint, the attempt to achieve a balance of interests is even more complicated. International trade is highly desirable because it enables people to enjoy products not otherwise available, it fosters competition and greater efficiency within an industry, and it advances cultural and political relations among countries.

On the other hand, preventing the deterioration of our own national wealth is important. Any nation seeks to maintain a high employment level, protect home industries, and retain self-sufficiency. Furthermore, the economic security and prosperity of any one country is affected by conditions existing in other countries. The United States has the highest per capita income in the world and by far the greatest consumption of textile products per person. In many other countries, particularly in the developing nations, availability of raw materials as well as the power to purchase them are far below the need. The differences between human wants and the means for satisfying them are a major problem in all economic activity. In this chapter we will consider the role textiles and clothing play in the international market.

INTERNATIONAL TRADE

The United States is both the largest producer and the largest consumer of textiles and clothing in the world market. Based on a 1978 population of over 218 million persons, the level of fiber consumption in this country was about 71.8 pounds per person. By way of comparison, the per capita fiber consumption in developing countries is about 13.3 pounds and in the socialist countries of Eastern Europe, 21.5 pounds.[1] Some of the same ships and planes that bring foreign-made fibers, fabrics, and apparel to our shores carry American textile products to other countries. We ship millions of dollars worth of textiles and clothing abroad and at the same time we import over several billion dollars in goods from other nations (Tables 18.1 and 18.2). As an example, according to the United States Department of Commerce, American consumption of raw cotton fell to its lowest level in fifty years in 1978. However, record high imports of cotton manufactured products brought domestic consumption of cotton above the 1977 level.[2] We import more cotton manufactured goods than we export; we export more man-made finished products than we import. This excess of lower-cost imported apparel is partly balanced by the export of woven fabric, tire cord, home furnishings, and industrial textiles.

Those who favor a permissive policy toward imports believe that this trade situation is as it should be. Establishing protectionist policies at the beginning of the textile line of production may protect the process-inefficient industrial operations. If the countries that have cheap labor handle the labor-intensive industries, such as raw fiber production, our country may devote its manufacturing to the sophisticated stages of production, such as in chemical fiber, fabric, finishing, and apparel manufacturing.

Increased Variety of Goods

Foreign imports greatly extend the variety of merchandise on the local market. Through a combination of native skills and availability of raw materials, many national products have a unique quality that cannot be duplicated in other parts of the world. Oriental designs from Hong Kong, batiks from Indonesia, bleeding Madras from India, Belgian lace, and Italian knits are a few examples of the many textile and apparel items that are easily identified with their place of origin.

There is a certain status appeal to American consumers of labels that read "100% imported cashmere" or "pure Irish linen." By the same token, the United States sells large quantities of American goods abroad because the "Made in U.S.A." label has prestige on many foreign markets. In some cases the "snob appeal" is accompanied by increased quality. The well-known Harris tweed is a good illustration. The Highland Blackface sheep raised on the island of Harris in the Outer Hebrides yield a long staple wool that is characteristically rough, tough, hairy, and durable. This, coupled with the weavers' unique fabricating techniques, produces a

[1]*Textile Organon*, March 1979.
[2]Ibid., January 1979.

Table 18.1 Raw Fiber Equivalent of Imports & Exports of Man-Made Fiber, Cotton & Wool Manufactures (Million Pounds Per Year)

Commodity	Man-Made Fiber							Cotton	
	Annual Average 1965-1969	Annual Average 1970-1974	1974	1975	1976	1977	1978	Annual Average 1965-1969	Annual Average 1970-1974
Imports									
Semimanufactured Products									
Yarn, Thread, etc.[1]	10.0	25.4	14.0	14.5	19.2	39.7	59.7	52.0	27.1
Cloth[2]	47.1	102.5	75.8	75.1	84.2	87.9	109.6	221.6	281.1
Subtotal	**57.1**	**127.9**	**89.8**	**89.6**	**103.4**	**127.6**	**169.3**	**273.6**	**308.2**
Manufactured Products									
Wearing Apparel[3]	73.2	253.4	252.1	289.6	344.4	366.1	425.6	132.7	158.7
Industrial[4]	2.4	7.6	6.6	0.7	0.2	2.7	0.1	3.8	8.3
House Furnishings[5]								33.5	36.9
All Other[6]	25.7	30.6	22.8	20.5	31.5	34.3	47.6	11.6	14.4
Subtotal	**101.3**	**291.6**	**281.5**	**310.8**	**376.1**	**403.1**	**473.3**	**181.6**	**218.3**
Total imports	**158.4**	**419.5**	**371.3**	**400.4**	**479.5**	**530.7**	**642.6**	**455.2**	**526.5**
Exports									
Semimanufactured Products									
Yarn, Thread, etc.[1]	8.7	23.3	47.6	27.7	36.9	39.5	37.7	15.4	20.7
Cloth[7]	76.9	113.0	174.8	166.3	165.6	153.2	187.5	117.3	170.0
Subtotal	**85.6**	**136.3**	**222.4**	**194.0**	**202.5**	**192.7**	**225.2**	**132.7**	**190.7**
Manufactured Products									
Wearing Apparel	9.1	21.5	33.1	31.8	34.4	40.3	48.6	25.0	32.9
Industrial[4]	17.5	11.2	26.2	17.8	25.6	35.5	63.9	10.4	17.8
House Furnishings[8]	8.1	24.3	48.9	44.6	51.9	56.6	43.8	15.2	23.5
All Other[9]	15.2	36.8	60.1	34.2	37.8	42.5	60.2	11.1	21.8
Subtotal	**49.9**	**93.8**	**168.3**	**128.4**	**149.7**	**174.9**	**216.5**	**61.7**	**96.0**
Total Exports	**135.5**	**230.1**	**390.7**	**322.4**	**352.2**	**367.6**	**441.7**	**194.4**	**286.7**
Net Exports (+) or Net Imports (−)	**−22.9**	**−189.4**	**+19.4**	**−78.0**	**−127.3**	**−163.1**	**−200.9**	**−260.8**	**−239.8**

[1]Includes sliver, tops, roving, plied (textured and other), thrown and spun yarn, sewing thread and handwork yarns. Yarn singles (textured and other) are not included here.

[2]Includes broad & narrow woven fabrics and knit cloth, except that cotton narrow fabrics and wool knit fabrics are included in All Other.

[3]Wool includes lace and lace articles, veils and veilings, and nets and nettings.

[4]The man-made fiber data are tire cord and tire cord fabric.

[5]Includes carpets and rugs. Lace window curtains are in All Other.

[6]Includes such products as lace and lace articles, lace window curtains, braids, tassels, polishing and dustcloths, etc. Wool includes knit fabric in the piece, but not lace and lace articles, which are in Wearing Apparel.

[7]Includes broad and narrow woven fabrics and knit cloth. Cotton also includes table damask, tire cord and fabric. Cotton knit fabrics and narrow fabrics are included in All Other.

[8]Includes carpets and rugs.

[9]Includes such products as lace and lace articles, polishing and dustcloths, braids, tassels, etc. Cotton also includes knits and narrow fabric.

Note: In the case of blended or mixed fiber products, the poundages of each of the component fibers have been estimated and included in the proper category, e.g., in a polyester and cotton fabric, the polyester portion is tabulated with man-made fiber and the cotton portion with cotton. A waste factor has been included to bring the data to the equivalent raw fiber consumption.

	Cotton					Annual Average		Wool				
1974	1975	1976	1977	1978	1965-1969	1970-1974	1974	1975	1976	1977	1978
13.4	11.7	26.2	13.5	30.8	17.8	8.2	5.9	4.4	5.8	6.6	6.1
267.1	226.4	325.2	244.6	299.9	27.3	13.2	9.3	8.4	12.2	18.7	25.8
280.5	**238.1**	**351.4**	**258.1**	**330.7**	**45.1**	**21.4**	**15.2**	**12.8**	**18.0**	**25.3**	**31.9**
168.3	223.0	293.2	348.3	430.2	36.4	30.4	23.9	22.9	33.0	44.1	44.9
6.8	4.7	6.1	5.6	6.7	Nominal Poundages Included in other						
35.2	23.5	38.4	39.4	57.7	14.3	11.7	12.9	11.8	14.4	15.3	14.5
11.9	12.0	19.5	18.0	20.1	2.1	2.4	1.3	1.1	1.3	1.2	0.9
222.2	**263.2**	**357.2**	**411.3**	**514.7**	**52.8**	**44.5**	**38.1**	**35.8**	**48.7**	**60.6**	**60.3**
502.7	**501.3**	**708.6**	**669.4**	**845.4**	**97.9**	**65.9**	**53.3**	**48.6**	**66.7**	**85.9**	**92.2**
24.0	17.0	18.5	16.9	32.0	0.8	14.0	13.9	11.8	5.7	3.2	2.6
231.1	217.4	248.4	204.0	187.8	0.6	0.7	0.9	1.3	1.0	0.9	1.2
255.1	**234.4**	**266.9**	**220.9**	**219.8**	**1.4**	**14.7**	**14.8**	**13.1**	**6.7**	**4.1**	**3.8**
40.1	42.5	54.3	65.3	61.8	1.0	1.8	3.4	2.2	2.2	2.4	5.5
22.3	17.8	25.5	24.5	23.8	Nominal Poundages included in Other						
39.4	31.9	41.0	37.3	32.2	0.9	1.7	2.8	2.4	2.9	2.7	0.8
35.6	27.1	25.5	21.5	18.1	2.0	1.5	2.0	1.5	2.1	2.3	1.5
137.4	**119.3**	**146.3**	**148.6**	**135.9**	**3.9**	**5.0**	**8.2**	**6.1**	**7.2**	**7.4**	**7.8**
392.5	**353.7**	**413.2**	**369.5**	**355.7**	**5.3**	**19.7**	**23.0**	**19.2**	**13.9**	**11.5**	**11.6**
-110.2	**-147.6**	**-295.4**	**-299.9**	**-489.7**	**-92.6**	**-46.2**	**-30.3**	**-29.4**	**-52.8**	**-74.4**	**-80.6**

(Source: *Textile Organon*, March 1979. Data from U.S Department of Agriculture, Cotton and Wool Situation.)

distinctive fabric that offers superb protection against the elements.

Sometimes the added value lies in the quality of design. Marimekko fashions from Finland have been status symbols for intellectual young Americans, but the designs also have a sophisticated simplicity that accounts for much of their popularity. They were brought into this country primarily for the home furnishings industry, but they have been widely accepted as unique apparel fabrics as well.

In addition, the extent to which one textile fiber will substitute for another has limits. No fiber has quite the degree of warmth, resilience, or tailoring qualities as wool; none has aesthetic crispness that compares to that of flax; none is as versatile and as cool as cotton; none has a more beautiful luster than silk. Because natural fiber production is limited to certain geographical areas of the world, trade is necessary if we are to enjoy the benefits of diverse qualities.

Table 18.2   Imports and Exports of Textile and Apparel Products, 1960–1978 (in Millions of Dollars)

	1960		1965		1970		1974		1975	
	Imp.	Exp.	Imp.	Exp.	Imp.	Exp.	Imp.	Exp.	Imp.	Exp.
Textiles other than clothing	582	478	800	528	1135	603	1615	1795	1219	1624
Yarns	36	114	66	131	223	145	190	407	126	298
Fabric, not cotton	275	102	423	135	499	151	528	413	433	386
Fabric, cotton	97	142	134	98	173	103	356	384	219	376
Apparel	304	140	541	143	1269	198	2331	400	2562	403

(Source: U.S. Department of Commerce, Industry and Trade Administration, *Overseas Business Report*, *Foreign Trade*, published periodically.)

Specialization in Production

Technological advances have greatly increased the production of fibers, fabrics, and wearing apparel throughout the world. Still, geographic and economic conditions in all countries create an excess of some products and a scarcity of others. The United States produces millions of bales of cotton for export to other countries, but produces no silk and virtually no flax. Japan and India, on the other hand, have both the supply of mulberry leaves and cheap labor that allow cultivation of silkworms, whereas Ireland and certain parts of Russia have ideal climates for production of flax. Wool requires suitable pasture land for sheep, and the cotton plant thrives only in restricted climatic regions. Even some man-made fibers are created from raw materials that have an agricultural base.

As a result of differences in natural resources as well as the availability of labor and machinery, over 60 percent of all the cotton consumed throughout the world is grown in only four countries—the United States, China, Russia, and India. Japan, India, and Italy furnish 70 percent of the world's supply of silk, and the principal wool producers are the countries of New Zealand, Australia, and Argentina.

Even though a country could produce a variety of textiles and clothing, it may pay to concentrate on one or a few and buy the others from foreign countries. In the case of some products, a country may have what is known as an **absolute advantage**, meaning that it can produce something at a lower cost than another country can. At the same time, it may have a **comparative advantage** in the production of one or two particular items. Let us suppose that China could produce both cotton and wool clothing more cheaply than the United States could. It might pay to concentrate on production of cotton goods and let the United States concentrate on production of wool, if China's comparative advantage in cotton were greater than in wool. To state it another way, the United States would have the **least disadvantage** in producing wool.

There are any number of reasons why, in a particular country, specialization in production may be more economical than diversification. In addition to the difference in natural resources, there may be

1976		1977		1978	
Imp.	Exp.	Imp.	Exp.	Imp.	Exp.
1635	1971	1736	1970	2200	2225
192	374	225	417	246	370
521	423	569	399	719	472
390	499	345	438	427	426
3634	510	4100	608	5657	677

considerable difference in the productivity or wage rates of labor. If low wage rates reflect only a low productivity, it may not give a country any competitive advantage in foreign markets; but if low wages are accompanied by high productivity, such producers have the advantage in selling to other countries. Besides this, there may be differences in the amount and quality of capital equipment available, or certain advantages in terms of the competence of business management.

With the exception of silk, flax, and a few specialty fibers, the United States could be relatively self-sufficient in raw materials since we produce surplus fibers to export. Production does not stop with the fibers, however. As recently as the mid-seventies Japan was our biggest purchaser of raw cotton. This is no longer true, although we still provide the largest outlet for Japan's manufactured textiles. With its high concentration of population and limited natural resources, Japan is forced to export large quantities of merchandise manufactured by its low-cost industries in order to sustain its economy. What has changed dramatically is the nature of those exports. In the past, textiles were their largest export products, but now the Japanese have branched into more sophisticated industries, such as electronics, automobiles, and manufacturing equipment. Holland is another country that depends heavily on foreign sources for its supply of raw materials and, like the Far East, must export great volumes of manufactured goods to maintain an even balance of trade. Large quantities of low-cost cottons from the Far East are finished in the Netherlands and then reexported to countries outside the Western European community.

In former years France was a good example of a country immune to the problems encountered by trade deficiencies and trade balances. France, highly self-sufficient in textile production, also exported very little in the way of yard goods. The government protected its home market from outside competition through a system of high tariffs and trade restrictions. However, as in the United States where the apparel industry had losses in employment, most European countries, including France, experienced as great or even greater losses. Many of these governments enacted assistance programs and trade policies to protect domestic industries. Although at the beginning of the decade most European countries had positive trade balances, by the mid-seventies, despite new protectionist policies, they had growing trade deficits also. The reason was the same, an inability to compete favorably with the lower-cost imports from the Far East.

International Relations

The United States government recognizes the importance of foreign trade not only to our national economy, but to our foreign relations as well. Increased international trade promises a rising level of consumption in all parts of the world. The United States has long been committed to a policy of liberal trade. Since 1934, for example, import duties have gradually been reduced, and, at the same time, imported goods have become a larger percentage of our total domestic consumption.

Although foreign trade is necessary for a balanced world economy, the United States government is also mindful that a prosperous domestic textiles and clothing industry contributes to maintenance of a technically balanced national economy. Essentially, there are three ways to control international trade. One is to place a tariff or import tax on goods brought into the country. The second is to place limits or quotas on the total volume or value of goods that may be imported in a given year. The third way involves government subsidy payments to the home industry, thereby making it possible to sell domestic products at lower comparative prices both at home and abroad.

The **Trade Expansion Act** of 1962 gave the president unprecedented tariff-cutting powers in an attempt to enlarge our foreign markets and strengthen our economic and political relations with foreign countries. Obviously, the United States is placed in a less advantageous competitive position if the tariff differential is high. International trade is essential to the American economy because it provides an outlet for our own products, and also because imported products enable us to maintain a high standard of living. Beyond this, the sharing of cultural traditions fosters both individual and international friendships, which may help to avoid world conflict in the future.

Another important aspect of our international economic relations involves the **European Economic Community** (EEC), better known as the Common Market. Created in 1957 with six member countries (Belgium, France, West Germany, Italy, the Netherlands, and Luxembourg), it admitted the United Kingdom in 1973. Essentially, the aim of the Common Market is to engage in economic disarmament that eliminates tariff barriers and provides for free movement of goods, capital, labor, and services among the cooperating countries. At the same time, the EEC applies uniform external tariffs on imports from nonmember nations. This tremendous consolidation of interests represents the world's largest single economic unit, with huge bargaining power.

The EEC further has less restrictive trade agreements with the countries of the **European Free Trade Association** (EFTA).[3] Economically, the EFTA is less powerful than the EEC, but the tariff reductions on EFTA goods make American exports less competitive in EEC markets.

The United States has not pursued an aggressive policy toward exportation of textiles in general and apparel specifically. The apparel industry has asked for government assistance in both promoting apparel abroad and protecting apparel imports, and government-sponsored programs in 1979 and 1980 were specifically directed toward these ends. As a result of direct government intervention or of industry promotion, there was a 45-percent increase over 1978 in textile and apparel exports in 1979. Although imbalance still existed, the trade

[3]The EFTA includes Austria, Denmark, Norway, Portugal, Sweden, and Switzerland. Thus, the only Western European countries outside EEC and EFTA are Finland, Greece, Ireland, Spain, and Turkey.

Table 18.3   U. S. Cotton, Wool and Man-Made Fiber Textile Imports (in Millions)

Product Group		Calendar 1978		1979[1]		% Change	
		SYE	$	SYE	$	SYE	$
Yarn	Cotton	122	30	44	11	−57%	−56%
	Wool	10	19	5	11	−38%	−31%
	Man-Made	841	160	337	89	−56%	−38%
	Total	973	209	386	111	−56%	−40%
Fabric	Cotton	933	440	589	314	−25%	−13%
	Wool	26	87	19	74	−17%	− 3%
	Man-Made	518	486	342	378	−23%	− 9%
	Total	1,477	1,013	950	766	−24%	−10%
Apparel	Cotton	942	1,700	779	1,600	− 4%	+10%
	Wool	97	537	73	440	−18%	− 8%
	Man-Made	1,862	2,443	1,405	2,050	−13%	− 2%
	Total	2,901	4,680	2,257	4,090	−10%	+ 2%
Made-Up	Cotton	229	141	181	124	− 6%	+ 4%
and	Wool	11	168	9	134	0	− 7%
Misc.	Man-Made	171	111	168	101	+25%	+19%
	Total	411	420	358	359	+ 7%	+ 3%
Total	Cotton	2,226	2,311	1,593	2,049	−16%	+ 4%
	Wool	144	811	106	659	−18%	− 8%
	Man-Made	3,392	3,200	2,252	2,618	−24%	− 4%
	Total	5,762	6,322	3,951	5,326	−21%	− 1%

[1]1979 figures are through October.
(Source: *Apparel Import Digest*, American Apparel Manufacturers Association, January 1980.)

deficit in these products was reduced by 25 percent in one year. Textile imports in 1979 amounted to over $7 billion with a remaining deficit of over $3.5 billion (Tables 18.3 and 18.4). Major markets for textile exports, 70 percent of United States mill products, were the European Economic Community, Canada, Japan, and Australia.[4]

In the past, protective tariffs helped to reduce the flow of foreign merchandise into the American market, but even when

calculated at 50 percent of cost in low-wage countries, the American-made product was still at a disadvantage. The United States has virtually the highest tariff level in the world and those who study the international market no longer believe that protective tariffs are enough to limit imports. Leaders from the American textiles and clothing industries therefore have pressured for government restraints on the soaring textile imports. Imports hit the United States the hardest in labor-intensive industries. Domestic producers of textiles and clothing are generally worse off than

[4]*Women's Wear Daily*, February 27, 1980, p. 15.

Table 18.4   U.S. Imports of MMF, Cotton, and Wool Apparel by Country (in Millions)

	1978		1979[1]		% Change	
	Units	$	Units	$	Units	$
MMF Apparel *SYE*[2]	1,862.4	2,443	1,405.4	2,050	− 13%	− 2%
Dominican Rep.	25.2	34	29.1	43	− 47%	− 59%
Haiti	44.5	35	38.0	34	+ 4%	+ 21%
Hong Kong	249.3	356	172.1	284	− 19%	− 4%
Italy	26.2	46	13.3	30	− 42%	− 23%
Japan	109.8	134	47.5	61	− 52%	− 49%
Korea	416.6	565	328.7	490	− 10%	0
Mexico	78.8	135	57.1	114	− 15%	0
Philippines	116.3	103	95.7	95	− 2%	+ 12%
Singapore	56.5	55	40.6	45	− 12%	+ 2%
Taiwan	548.5	721	402.7	600	− 16%	− 4%
Thailand	34.4	28	24.3	24	− 12%	+ 9%
Total Above	1,706.1	2,212	1,249.1	1,820	− 15%	− 4%
Cotton Apparel *SYE*	941.8	1,700	778.5	1,600	+ 4%	− 10%
Hong Kong	410.0	720	300.6	657	− 15%	+ 8%
India	74.3	124	55.9	119	− 18%	+ 4%
Japan	54.9	110	29.8	72	− 39%	− 26%
Korea	26.4	49	19.5	45	− 18%	0
Macao	16.2	30	15.1	34	+ 9%	+ 36%
Mainland China	48.6	50	85.7	99	+107%	+130%
Mexico	12.4	30	12.0	31	+ 13%	+ 24%
Philippines	41.0	56	31.3	48	− 14%	− 2%
Poland	15.0	30	9.8	25	− 27%	− 7%
Singapore	28.2	60	26.3	55	+ 11%	+ 8%
Taiwan	54.9	106	50.3	124	+ 6%	+ 38%
Total Above	781.9	1,365	636.3	1,309	− 7%	+ 11%
Wool Apparel *SYE*	97.6	537	73.2	440	− 18%	− 8%
Canada	3.7	16	3.2	14	+ 3%	0
France	4.0	53	3.1	45	− 6%	+ 5%
Hong Kong	35.7	168	28.0	133	− 15%	− 14%
Italy	5.8	64	3.9	56	− 24%	+ 2%
Japan	4.9	17	2.5	10	− 47%	− 38%
Korea	15.2	47	11.4	46	− 22%	+ 5%
Taiwan	4.1	11	4.0	11	+ 5%	+ 10%
United Kingdom	4.1	43	2.6	33	− 28%	− 11%
Uruguay	4.2	20	3.3	16	− 6%	− 6%
Total Above	81.7	439	62.0	364	− 17%	− 7%

[1]1979 figures through October.
[2]Square Yard Equivalent.
(Source: *Apparel Import Digest*, American Apparel Manufacturers Association, January 1980.)

the steel and automobile industries, but not as bad as manufacturers of televisions, radios, and phonographs.

The National Retail Merchants Association has reacted with listed reasons as to why added costs of imports make them competitive with domestic-made goods and so are not really a threat to domestic production. For one thing, buying expenses are greater and a longer lead time is necessary between purchase of unfinished goods and sale of finished products to the ultimate consumer. There is also no recourse for defective merchandise. The fluctuation and thus uncertainty of costs due to currency exchange, as well as freight charges, also add to the cost of imports.

Nevertheless, in the middle of worldwide recession it is difficult to argue the point that this country, because of its high relative standard of living, should broaden its import allowances and lower both import quotas and tariffs. When this happens, it is often the low-income consumer who bears the burden of higher costs for domestic goods. Imports permit higher markups. It has been said that those who buy imports subsidize consumers who buy domestic goods.

Recent trends indicate that the quantity of imports will continue to increase, and controls on imports imposed by government do not seem to be the solution to the problem of import competition. Perhaps consumers and retailers need to be made aware of the consequences of imported apparel on domestic industry. One partial solution would be resistance to imports at the purchase level. Although this may or may not be a good idea, considering the pros and cons of international trade, it would have a significant effect on the volume of products brought into the United States.[5]

Balance of Trade

Most people favor importation of goods that are not readily available in our own country, but there is considerable disagreement surrounding imports that sell for less than our own competitive products. Whenever we import foreign-made textiles and apparel, we are essentially providing work for labor in other countries. Many groups, such as the International Ladies' Garment Workers' Union, have held out consistently against imports of ready-to-wear clothing because they pose a threat to our own domestic apparel industry.[6] Many American textile mills have had to reduce their production or close down completely in the face of competition from abroad. An import treaty or quota is made in terms of sales, of course, but Americans see it primarily in terms of jobs. High import quotas means fewer jobs for American workers. The American Textile Manufacturer's Institute estimates that 208,000 textile/apparel jobs would be lost if tariff on industrial products were reduced by 50 percent. The American Apparel Manufacturers Association projects a loss of 100,000 to 150,000 jobs in the apparel industry alone by 1984 if tariffs are cut.[7]

[5]Kitty G. Dickerson. "Consumers' and Retailers' Attitudes on Buying Imported Textile and Apparel Products." United States Department of Agriculture Experiment Station Research Project No. 614340, 1980–1982.
[6]General Executive Board Report, International Ladies' Garment Workers' Union, 1977.
[7]Clothes, Etc., PRADS, Inc., April 15, 1978.

By the early 1970s the value of American textile imports reached over $3.2 billion, whereas exports were less than $1 billion, leaving a deficit of over $2 billion in the United States textile trade balance. By 1978, textiles and apparel imports together made up 17 percent of the American trade deficit, an increase of 48 percent over the previous year.[8] The value of apparel imports alone was up 37 percent over 1977.[9]

Textiles and clothing account for nearly one third of the total United States trade deficit. Here the labor inequity is one factor, and another is that the textile and apparel industries in rapidly growing countries like Japan are more vertically integrated than are those in America. Many giant Japanese firms have more than 10,000 workers apiece and they produce a whole line of products, from raw fibers to finished apparel items. This is in direct contrast to the United States, where textile plants may be large and a relatively small number of firms do more than 70 percent of all the textile business. But the apparel-manufacturing business has many small plants that do not have the advantages of the economics of scale. This is due to a great extent to the nature of the fashion product, in that consumers do not want everyone in the country to have the same items that they wear.

Public policy in the matter of regulating or controlling apparel and textile imports must draw a fine line between protecting domestic industry from the effects of uncontrolled foreign competition and outright public assistance to aid affected companies that see import competition as a threat to survival. The greatest threat from imports to the United States industry occurred prior to 1971; since then the import pressure has been lessened. This was due to various limiting trade agreements regarding textile imports as well as the devaluation of the dollar. Imports were down 18 percent and 20 percent over 1972 levels in 1973 and 1974, respectively.[10]

However, since 1975 imports are on the rise again and 1976 showed a 20-percent increase over 1973 despite the Multifiber Arrangement (MFA) effective in January 1974. The MFA also set quotas restricting import growth levels per year for most major apparel categories. The eighteen bilateral textile agreements, most of which expired in 1977, have been or are in the process of being renegotiated.

The virtues of a free trade policy are historically American. In a truly free and equal economic utopia such a system might work. But with worldwide recession and unemployment, "to maintain that the United States should accept as an economic fact that its mature industries [in this case the textile and apparel industries] will be lost to low-cost developing country producers is tantamount to political suicide in today's economic climate, regardless of the merits of that position."[11] Instead, consumers pay the price for tariffs and quotas when they purchase goods in the marketplace.

[8]U.S.A. Textiles/Apparel Newsletter, Prent Thomas Textile Consultants, Greenville, S.C., February 1979, p. 8.
[9]"U.S. Textiles: Pawn in World Trade Game." Textile World (August 1978), 32.

[10]"The Search for Import Bargains," Business Week, September 21, 1974, 104.
[11]"The Challenge for Public Policy," in Corporate Responses to Import Competition in the U.S. Apparel Industry, ed. Jose de la Torre et al. (Atlanta, Ga.: Publishing Service Division, College of Business Administration, Georgia State University, 1978).

One thing is clear; no country can live in economic isolation from the rest of the world. Economic decisions made in Tokyo and Paris become the concerns of business-people in San Francisco and New York. The clothing and textile industries are enmeshed not only in the foreign-trade policies of the United States, but in the welfare of peoples in all corners of our shrinking world.

The complex interaction of the clothing industries in a global economy affects the variety, cost, and quality of goods available to consumers in all parts of the world.

SUMMARY

International Trade

The trading of goods and services between and among the nations of the world is desirable for three basic reasons. It gives the consumer a wider range of choice and often provides unique commodities that cannot be produced in a highly industrialized economy. Differences in climate, natural resources, native talents, the cost of labor and availability of machinery result in the excess production of some commodities in most countries, and at the same time a scarcity exists in others, so that some goods may be acquired at a lower price abroad than they can be produced domestically. Liberal trade policies make for improved foreign relations and promise a rising level of consumption. Limitations on free trade through tariffs, quotas, and subsidies tend to penalize the consumer by generating higher prices. On the other hand, they protect our domestic industry, which in turn contributes to a technically balanced national economy.

THE INTERNATIONAL
COUTURE AND READY-TO-WEAR

Since the dawn of history, fibers and fabrics have been used as important items for barter, first between neighbors within a community, and gradually extending to include wide areas of trade. Over two thousand years ago, Phoenician merchants sold fine-textured woolens and linen along the trade routes of the Mediterranean, and it is probable that weavers' guilds existed among the ancient Babylonians. With the rise of the factory system and improvements in transportation and communication, the exchange of textiles and clothing among the nations of the world became a common and daily occurrence in international trade.

All countries have a history of clothing production, even though it may be limited to those people who grow, spin, and weave fibers into cloth in their own homes. The development of fashionable clothing as we know it today has a related but somewhat different background. Prior to the French Revolution, the extravagances of fashion were confined to the nobility and to that small segment of the population having extreme wealth. The common people had no part in fashion; their garments were simple in design, made from coarse home-spun fabric, with men often wearing leather breeches that lasted for much of their lifetime.

Wealthy American colonists ordered their suits from London, where their measurements were kept on file in the English tailor shops. The ladies kept in touch with fashions via *les fameuses poupées*, the French costume dolls dressed in the latest designs. The dolls were sent from Paris to London every month, and from there to friends in America, where a local seamstress was employed to copy the style.

Throughout the Industrial Revolution, home production of clothing was gradually replaced by mass-produced apparel that made the luxury of fashion available to the great masses of people who had once enjoyed little more than bare subsistence. The factory system, coupled with the unprecedented opportunities for economic advancement during the nineteenth century, gave tremendous impetus to the growing market for fashionable merchandise.

The French couture—center of the fashion world for more than a century—is now threatened by the economic competition of the ready-to-wear industry. American apparel manufacturers are researching the style preferences of European consumers, and many established European sales offices as well as foreign factories in England, France, Holland, Belgium, Northern Ireland, and Italy. At the same time, European manufacturers are studying American production methods, and many retain American consultants to promote their sales on this side of the Atlantic.

France

Paris has been a world center of fashion since the days of Louis XIV, but the modern couture began about the middle of the last century with a designer named Charles Frederick Worth, an Englishman by birth, who was the first dressmaker to show made-up samples on living models. Before the days of Worth, dressmakers suggested a design through a sketch or fashion doll. The garment was then cut to the individual client's measurements, with no intention of making more than one of a kind. Worth's business sense, coupled with the perfection of the sewing machine in the 1850s, led to the development of a large-scale dressmaking establishment and the initiation of wholesale relationships with foreign trade buyers.

Paris designers have held an enviable position of fashion leadership ever since. Their enduring influence may be attributed to a combination of factors, not the least of which is the continued support of the French government, which subsidizes the couture houses on an annual basis. Beyond this, the French tradition of perfection is a matter of national prestige. The teaching of sewing skills begins at an early age, so that a great number of skilled seamstresses are available for work in the ateliers (workrooms) of the couture. The related industries, such as the makers of French textiles, accessories, buttons, and other findings, cater to the requests of the creative designer. The couture itself is highly organized under the *Chambre Syndicale de la Couture Parisienne,* a trade association that deals with various labor and administrative problems in all segments of the industry. In addition, the Chambre registers the designs of its members to insure against fashion piracy; unauthorized producers of registered designs are prosecuted under French law.

In spite of its financial difficulties in recent years, the couture still brings in over a billion dollars a year in retail turnover, although this figure now covers the sale of everything that bears the couturier's name—including perfume, scarves, hosiery, ready-to-wear (rtw), and other boutique items. There are probably not more than twenty or twenty-two successful couture houses in Paris today. Each shows a sample collection twice a year to clothing manufacturers and retail store buyers, who in turn purchase models to reproduce in their own countries. Following the openings, designers cater to individual customers, for whom they make custom copies of any model in the season's collection.

The commercial buyers pay an entrance fee or *caution* to view the collection (Figure 18.1). The caution may range upward from $1,500 per person and may be applied toward the purchase of a model. In the popular houses, a dress, suit, or coat is likely to sell for several thousand dollars; an elaborate evening gown may easily be twice that much. Individual customers pay somewhat lower prices, since they do not buy the copying privilege, but still the houses could never survive financially on the custom business alone. A dress usually requires three fittings on the customer and up to ninety hours of labor. On a $2,000 dress, the designer probably has to pay for the materials, labor, taxes, sales commissions, and overhead. This leaves a profit of about 4 percent if the house is lucky enough to sell thirty or forty copies of the same design. If a number is reproduced only three or four times, the house loses money.

Most couture houses maintain their custom salons for the international prestige it brings to the designer, but almost all are forced to seek other sources of income to remain financially solvent. In addition to the government subsidies, some houses are backed by various textile firms, but more often they sell other commodities—notably perfumes—that bring a sizable profit. The luxury trade of the haute couture is gradually losing out to mass production. With the revolution in masculine fashions, some designers went into men's apparel lines. Pierre Cardin was one of the first to venture into a complete collection for male clientele. He was so successful that he now

Figure 18.1 A model on the runway at a Cardin showing.

distributes his men's wear and accessories not only in Europe and the United States, but in South America, Asia, Africa, the Near, Middle, and Far East as well. His men's wear line has grown into a multimillion-dollar business; his women's fashions, both couture and rtw, account for about half that amount a year.

Other houses report similar transitions in terms of their source of sales. In the seventies, Dior did a $60 million business, exclusive of perfume, with only $2.5 million coming from the couture. At Givenchy's salon, one of the largest couture houses in Paris, couture sales amount to a small percentage of the total profit; perfume sales reached over $70 million.

More than 30 percent of the couture's private clientele comes from the United States. Nevertheless, the number of couture customers has dropped. Probably not more than three hundred women still buy couture, and only twenty-five to thirty really big customers are left in the entire world. There are fewer big spenders, and even the big spenders are spending less on clothes. In today's economic world, extravagant consumption seems as out of place as a baroque chariot on a California freeway. Although the most creative talent still may be going into the couture, businesswise the big emphasis these days is on ready-to-wear.

Aside from the couturiers, there is, of course, a growing French ready-to-wear industry. The rtw designers show their collections twice a year at the Porte de Versailles exhibition hall in Paris. In spite of its growth, which has more than doubled in the last decade, the French ready-to-wear industry still has some production problems. Many of the firms are too small to turn out big orders, and U.S. retailers find their delivery schedules unreliable.

American manufacturers are adept at copying styles.

As a result, the French ready-to-wear industry is big in influence but relatively small in dollar volume. That's partly because French production is fairly small-scale, but the French also have a right to blame it on the American stores and manufacturers who prefer to steal ideas rather than buy French merchandise.[12]

In self-defense French firms, beginning in the mid-seventies, laid the groundwork for expansion into the American market. The French Apparel Center, Inc., encouraged them to establish New York showrooms, and many of them do a million-dollar business in the United States. Gradually the men's wear industry organized itself along lines similar to its feminine counterpart. Independent designers like Cardin have their own men's wear showings; other manufacturers from all over Europe show their collections together at the Salon European de L'Habillement Masculin in Paris.

Italy

Following World War II, Italy set out to rebuild its shattered economy. Emilio Pucci, who scored a hit with American consumers with his new look in sportswear, was one of the many Italian nobles who turned their refined tastes and creative talents to the fashion field. In the early 1950s, G. B. Giorgini, an Italian merchant who dealt in antiques and handcrafts, organized a group of nine couturiers and invited American buyers to his home to view their collections. From this begin-

[12]Joan Chatfield-Taylor, "The Great Idea Ripoff in Paris," *San Francisco Chronicle*, April 13, 1973.

ning, the Italian couture developed into an industry that now rivals the French in terms of its export trade. Three national organizations receive government support in promoting Italian fashions, and the couturiers, like those in France, are subsidized with state monies.[13]

By 1970, more than forty haute couture designers showed their collections every January and July in Rome. Buyers and reporters battled for seats at the openings. Business was so good that top designer Valentino could afford to toss out half a dozen representatives from the largest newspapers in the EEC and the U.S.A. because he disliked their copy on the previous season's line. But the couture in Italy, as in France, proved to be just too costly. Many designers began to cut their collections to fewer and fewer models. Some closed shop completely, and others continued only their ready-to-wear lines. The houses that continue to present regular collections do so with financial aid from the government. In fact, because of these government subsidies Italy is the only country in Europe where employment in the apparel industry did not decline during the seventies.

The high-fashion rtw collections are shown twice yearly in Florence along with knitwear, leather goods, and furs. The Italian government provides the historically famous Pitti and Strozzi Palaces for showrooms and trade center. Italy has always been famous for its knitwear and leather. Names like Missoni (knits), Gucci, and Ferragamo (shoes) are popular in American stores. Leather gloves, handbags, and other accessories are all a part of

[13]The Centro di Firenze per la Moda Italiana in Florence, and the Camera Nazionale della Moda Italiana and Italian Institute for Foreign Trade in Rome.

the industry that has become one of Italy's most important national assets.

The Italian showings include both men's and women's fashions. Men's wear collections are scheduled right along with the others. American males also find Rome a good place to buy custom-made suits, especially in the summer weights of Italian silk. The average cost of a completely hand-tailored suit is less than its counterpart in the United States, and it takes about five days to make one up.

The fashion industry (textiles, apparel, and accessories) is second in Italian export trade and brings into Italy's treasury over a billion dollars a year in foreign exchange. Italy is Europe's biggest exporter of fashion to the American market.

United Kingdom

Britain ranks second to Italy in terms of the volume of European fashion exports shipped to the United States market. The British couture designers operate much like those in France and Italy, showing their collections regularly to American and other foreign buyers, and then existing as custom salons for private customers. The couture is considerably smaller in England than in France or Italy, and the models are considerably less expensive. English designer Hardy Amies—like France's Cardin—has a men's ready-to-wear line that is distributed in retail stores throughout the United States.

The London tailors of Savile Row, however, are to the well-heeled fashionable gentleman what the Parisian couturiers are to the international feminine socialite. The quality workmanship, superb fit, and individual attention given each customer still draws prominent men from all the world.

British tweeds and woolens have been traditional import items on the American market for generations, but the ready-to-wear industry is a relatively newcomer to the export field (as is true all over Europe). The wholesale manufacturers got their greatest boost during World War II, when the British Board of Trade ordered drastic cuts in yard goods consumption. Up until that time, ready-made clothing was poorly designed and lacked quality, but the government commissioned the country's leading designers to come up with simple, tasteful styles that could be mass-produced.

Gradually, the British learned to tailor their lines to American tastes, using lighter weight fabrics and improving the sizing, and as a result, the United States became Britain's biggest ready-to-wear customer. The competition from English goods is still in the upper price bracket, just as it is with French rtw. Usually the workmanship is very high. In the past prices were lower than the highest-priced American rtw because labor costs were considerably lower than those in the United States, but this is no longer true. European labor costs are roughly comparable to ours and so this economic advantage no longer exists.

Israel

In the early 1960s, Israel's Ministry of Commerce invested many millions of dollars in construction of textile plants, particularly in the outlying areas of the country where labor was plentiful. There are now textile workers all over Israel, but they are primarily in the areas where agriculture is not as profitable. Israeli manufacturers concentrate on fashion goods that have a high profit.

Of all Israel's textile exports, approximately two-thirds is in apparel. Well over half of these apparel exports go to the United States and Canada, facilitated by and large by American Trade and Industrial Development with Israel, Inc. (ATID), a nonprofit organization based in New York that works as a liaison between Israeli manufacturers and American stores. ATID sponsors a semiannual trade show of Israeli fashions in New York, and it also establishes working arrangements with American manufacturers to have their lines produced in Israel where labor is cheaper. Another plus factor is that the Export Institute established a quality-control system to insure that all exported goods meet the standards of comparable merchandise produced in American factories.

Israeli fashion apparel is geared to a moderate-priced market. Israeli knitwear sells for less than Italy's, although it still cannot compete with the Far East in prices. Israeli fashions reportedly retail in the United States at three times the price paid to the manufacturer. The United States is not Israel's only customer, however; the country made a concentrated effort to get its products into the world market. Manufacturers developed special-sized clothing for sale in Japan, for example, where they hold fashion exhibitions to promote their products. Because clothing brings export dollars into the country, apparel manufacturers are subsidized for every dollar they earn outside Israel.

Other European Countries

A number of other European countries developed their talents in terms of both designing and marketing in order to enter the U.S. fashion field. In addition to the exports of Irish crochet lace, linens, and tweeds, Ireland has a growing rtw industry, particularly in men's wear. The Spanish capitalize on up-to-date versions of their traditional beadwork, laces, and leathercraft, and their designs sell well in the more exclusive American specialty shops. Sweden does a good export business to the United States in coats, jackets, and sportswear. Wool sports sweaters are a specialty of the top Swiss knitwear firms.

Although many European manufacturers already have sales outlets in the United States, representatives from Austria, Sweden, West Germany, Switzerland, France, and Finland display their wares to American buyers twice a year at the European Fashion Fair in New York. As a kind of return favor American manufacturers are invited to participate in the Overseas Import Fair held in West Berlin. They are encouraged to display samples of their lines to test the market for U.S. products in Europe.

The 1970s also brought the beginning of trade negotiations with some of the European socialist countries. After the Nixons' visit to Russia in 1972, Americans took the initiative in seeking out fashions produced in the U.S.S.R. A Pennsylvania department store was the first to purchase four evening outfits made in Moscow. If an American woman wanted to buy one, the price tag was $900, but the store was not particularly interested in selling the clothes—they were purchased more or less as Russian "showpieces."[14]

For many years the typical pattern in Europe was for most of the retail shops to sell fabric, and the consumer then made the clothes at home or had them made at a local tailor shop. Now, almost all countries are into ready-to-wear production of some kind.

European couture houses have found it increasingly difficult to continue in business because of their increasing economic problems.

SUMMARY

The International Couture and Ready-to-Wear

In terms of clothing production, world societies pass through successive stages. First, all family clothing is produced at home and luxury clothing items are available only to the wealthy few. At some point thereafter, a ready-to-wear industry develops, and ultimately, a wide range of fashionable, good quality merchandise is available for all.

Competition in American apparel markets from the fashion rivalry of European goods is no longer the economic factor it used to be. The European couture serves mainly as a source of ideas and is a stimulus, to some extent, to American fashion.

[14]Nine S. Hyde, "Peekaboo—From Russia, With Love," *Washington Post* News Service, March 8, 1973.

THE FAR EAST AND THE UNITED STATES

In many emerging nations of Asia and Africa and in South America, one of the first steps taken toward industrialization was the processing of textiles. Entry into the apparel industry is ideal for less industrialized countries with larger labor supplies: it is still the cheapest and easiest way to put many people to work. For example, in Nigeria, South Africa, and the Sudan, countries that have always been big importers of cotton fabrics, local industries have begun to produce millions of yards of cotton goods annually. Apparel manufacturing in developing countries proceeds in stages. At first, very simple garments are copied, and innovative styling appears very gradually. "Generally, as the technological developments become more sophisticated, the apparel which it produces becomes more complex and more appealing to potential wearers. The industry also becomes more sensitive to fashion changes and responds to these changes."[15]

Clothing production has been the passport to industrialization all over the Far East. Starting in the fifties with Japan, Hong Kong joined the group in 1960, and by the end of the sixties apparel manufacturing was a force to be reckoned with in Korea and Taiwan. In the early seventies, the Philippines and India became major sources of apparel and in the last two years Sri Lanka's products appeared on the American market. Even more recently the countries of Central and South America entered the textile and apparel markets.

In 1979, with the opening of diplomatic and business relations with the People's Republic of China (PRC), new foreign competition emerged. China has the potential to rival all other sources of imports, both because of its size (sheer numbers of people) and its extremely low hourly work rate (20 cents or less). Prior to direct trade agreements, in 1975 and 1976, China was the seventh-largest supplier of textile/apparel imports to the United States. Their total exports to this country were greater than those of many countries with whom we have bilateral trade agreements. In 1977 "400,000 dozen slacks and enough cotton work gloves to capture 20% to 30% of the domestic market" were imported, according to the Work Glove Manufacturers Institute. In the first year of direct trade with the PRC, 1979, imports from China rose by 115 percent to $63 million, primarily in gloves, men's suits, and work trousers. China can underprice American-made apparel even though its imports are burdened by duties roughly twice those levied on all other apparel imports. United States apparel and textile executives are worried. "The 17 million Chinese in Taiwan and the 4 million Chinese in Hong Kong presently produce 45% of all our apparel imports. With 950 million Chinese on the mainland, they have the capacity to wipe us out in a decade."[16] Export of labor-intensified products—apparel and other textiles—will pay for a good deal of technology. American trade officials, primarily in the State Department, continue to negotiate with China and other exporting countries in hopes of settling on quotas, the cornerstone of the industry's strategy for competing with foreign-made apparel.

[15]Kitty G. Dickerson and Mary E. Barry, "The Textile and Apparel Industry in World Trade." Manuscript, 1980, p. 6.

[16]Ellis E. Meredith, president of the American Apparel Manufacturers Association (AAMA), 1979.

Asian Producers

Although the United States wholesale apparel market has grown by one-third since the 1975 recession (38.3 billion), the Far East low-wage countries of Taiwan, Korea, and Hong Kong have more than doubled their output ($8 billion). Imports now make up 22 percent of the apparel market, up from 13.7 percent in 1975 and 6.9 percent in 1967. More importantly, these new imports are increasingly of better-quality and higher-priced products. "Made in Hong Kong" is no longer synonomous with shoddy merchandise. "Many experts are now predicting that imports may well capture half of the market during the 1980s and cut the number of domestic apparel makers at least in half by the end of the decade."[17] Seventy-two percent of the total man-made fiber apparel imports came from Japan, Hong Kong, Korea, and Taiwan. These four countries also accounted for 57 percent of the cotton apparel imports and 63 percent of the wool imports.[18] The extremely low labor costs in the Far East make it more economical for us to ship the raw materials to these countries for fabrication and then buy the apparel back than to produce the apparel in this country.

Bilateral agreements with low-wage countries of the Far East established import quotas on a country-by-country basis on textiles, shoes, and apparel. These bilateral agreements on textiles were set at 6 percent in 1971/72. An average annual import growth of 6 percent was allowed on United States imports from the eighteen countries involved. These agreements have not kept imports down due to many factors—interpretation of the categories of imports, loopholes in the law like Item 807 of the Tariff Schedule of the United States, and lenient enforcement of the quotas by the Federal government. Item 809.00, part of the 1964 tariff law, makes provisions for contract work to be done abroad and goods sewn there from fabrics cut in the United States. These apparel items can enter the United States on payment of lower custom duties. When this law was first adopted, apparel imports equaled less than 1 percent of all imports. By 1976, imports brought in under Item 807 alone accounted for 10 percent of all shipments from abroad. Of all imports of apparel into the United States in 1977, 86 percent came from ten countries: Taiwan, Hong Kong, Korea, Japan, the Philippines, Singapore, Mexico, Haiti, India, and Thailand, all countries covered by the bilateral quotas agreements of 1971–1972.[19] In 1978, imports of cotton, wool, and man-made-fiber apparel amounted to 241 million square yards, well above the 1977 level of 208 million square yards. This represents an increase of 37 percent in dollar value. Cotton took the major share at 37 percent, followed by wool at 24 percent, and man-made-fiber apparel products at 19 percent. According to the United States General Accounting Office, the 1974 bilateral treaties cost American consumers $350 million in textile goods from Japan, Hong Kong, Korea, and Taiwan.

Japan exports to the United States an almost equal amount of fiber, but finished textile products—apparel and home furnishings—are included as well. Therefore, when all textile and apparel products are combined, Japan easily outranks all other countries in the amount of these

[17]"Apparel's Last Stand," *Business Week*, May 14, 1979.

[18]*Apparel Import Digest*, August 1, 1978.

[19]*Clothes, Etc.*, p. 57.

imported goods sent to the United States.[20] In apparel products only, the big four exporters to the United States are Taiwan, Hong Kong, Korea, and Japan with Japan ranking fourth now. Originally our export exchange was mainly in silk and in made-up cotton blouses. It was not until the 1930s, for example, that the Japanese began to wear any Western-style clothing at all. Their phenomenal growth in fashion was explained by a Japanese in his own words:

Tie-ups with overseas makers have helped Japanese clothes manufacturers to catch up with overseas makers, who are advanced in fashion, thus enabling Japan, once backward in fashion, to attain the international level in fashion. Everything from designs and patterns to technical know-how imported from overseas, therefore, served as textbooks for Japanese fashion designers and pret-a-porter makers. The Japanese were extremely diligent and brilliant in learning and mastering the textbooks they had bought from foreign countries. Tokyo and Osaka, as a result, have grown into big fashion-consuming centers comparable to New York, Los Angeles, London and Paris.[21]

At the same time that the creations of Japanese designers (Figure 18.2) are marketed in American and European retail stores, most of the leading department stores in Japan have marketing arrangements with overseas suppliers. You can buy Pierre Cardin in the Takashimaya Department Store, St. Laurent and Louis Feraud at Seibu's, and Oleg Cassini designs at Mitsukoshi. Many French rtw designers have lucrative contracts to have their lines adapted, manufactured, and

sold in Japan. Japanese apparel manufacturers today contract with overseas companies. Jantzen and Catalina swimsuits, Munsingwear, and Big John blue jeans are just a few of the name brands adapted to Japanese sizing and produced in Japan.

Taiwan, Hong Kong, and Korea have growing fashion industries that export millions of dollars worth of clothing to the United States annually. Their biggest asset is an army of skilled workers available at unbelievably low wages. American merchants can buy silk in Thailand and have it converted by Chinese dressmakers into styles that were purchased from the Paris couture. The more handwork required in constructing the garment, the greater the advantage the Hong Kong manufacturer has. Although affected by the declining value of the American dollar, Hong Kong is

Figure 18.2 A design by Japanese designer Ichiro Kimijima. Black velvet trousers with a bouffant black taffeta top for evening.

[20]*Textile Organon*, September 1979.
[21]Makoto Urabe, "Internationalized Japanese Fashion," *Japan Illustrated*, Autumn 1972, p. 7.

still the mecca of American tourists for custom-made suits, shirts, and shoes of all kinds. Thousands of custom tailors measure clients, both male and female, day and night, and produce replicas of almost any design. An American can buy a good quality tailor-made suit for a fraction of what it would cost at home, and in most cases the customer has the pick of the world's fabrics: English worsteds, Irish tweeds, and Italian silks. Custom-made shirts in Sea Island cotton and English broadcloth sell for a low price.

Effects of Far
Eastern Competition

The American apparel market seems to be harder hit than most by foreign imports because our apparel industry remains one of the least automated and most labor-intensified manufacturing endeavors in the United States. Labor accounts for 27 percent of the cost of a garment. The fabric itself accounts for 44 percent of the cost. Although grossly underpaid, compared to United States workers as a whole, the average pay of $4 an hour for textile and apparel workers is still well above the $1 an hour paid to most Hong Kong garment makers. In Taiwan and Korea, the average wage is fifty cents an hour and in Sri Lanka, the fastest-growing source of apparel imports in the United States, workers receive the grand sum of twenty-five cents an hour for their labors. Imported apparel, even with amounts added on for import duties, can be sold in the United States for 20 percent less than the cost of American-made goods.

While foreign countries were taking advantage of their surplus of cheap labor, the American apparel industry was often unable to modernize and mechanize their operations for more efficient production. Many operate on such low-profit margins that they simply have not had the capital necessary to do so. Textile production in general is heavily affected by recession and inflation. Being a labor-intensified industry, it is particularly vulnerable to minimum wages. Physical plants are affected by the rising costs of building; overhead is susceptible to energy price increases; capital for automation and further mechanization is limited.

Far Eastern manufacturers, on the other hand, put their profits back into modern equipment and machinery and by doing so have eliminated much of the technological advantage American firms previously had. This enabled the foreign importers to produce high-quality merchandise, and they were even able to lure older American companies like Sears and Saks and Co. to set up shops in the Orient to produce and purchase foreign-made goods directly. In fact, some governments in the Orient and other developing countries have also provided financial subsidization to develop these industries in a way in which the United States has not been able to do. It is somewhat ironic to think that many developing countries, as well as those reconstructing following World War II, built their newly competitive textile industries with United States financial assistance, such as the money available under the Marshall Plan in Europe, occupational assistance in Japan, and AID (Agency for International Development) funds in many South American and African countries.

Now, with the American apparel industry running scared of foreign competition that seriously threatens it, there has been a dramatic change toward mechanization. However, despite many new machines developed in the last decade to design and cut fabrics and improve the productivity of the apparel mills, a 1979 study concluded that 62 percent of the apparel manufacturers were undermechanized. They still were not using the more productive machinery now available and affordable. Low profits, unavoidable because of import competition, have in many cases not enabled people in the manufacturing industries to "think five years ahead like the people in the aerospace industry."[22]

Representatives of the textile industry, from fiber and textile producers to finished apparel manufacturers and retailers, suggest that by the middle of the 1980s 50 percent of the apparel sold in the United States could be foreign made. As much as 70 percent of Bloomingdale's designer apparel is already made of imported fabric.[23]

Although the American apparel industry increased one-third in the three-year period following the 1975 recession, optimism is not in order. A gloomy picture is presented by an industry that foresees its current 2.4 million employed persons as "a shadow of its former self a decade from now" if the domestic industry does not increase productivity to meet overseas competition.[24]

A plentiful supply of skilled labor, low wages, and high productivity give the Far Eastern countries a tremendous competitive advantage in the international market.

SUMMARY

The Far East and the United States

Competition in the apparel markets of the United States has come from the lower-cost products of low-wage countries of the Far East, primarily Taiwan, Hong Kong, Korea, and Japan. The same problems plague apparel manufacturers the world over: inflation causing ever-increasing wages, petroleum shortages for both energy consumption and man-made fiber production, low profit margins, and scarcities of natural raw materials for fibers that cause sky-rocketing prices for cotton, wool, and silk.

THE UNITED STATES ABROAD

All together, imports of foreign-made apparel to the United States take increasingly larger percentages of the total consumer expenditures for clothing and accessories made by the American public. Imports are rising steadily each year in millions of dollars, and more important is the fact that our apparel imports greatly exceed our exports.

[22]*Business Week*, April 14, 1978.

[23]*Clothes, Etc.*, April 15, 1978, p. 55.
[24]Ibid., p. 59.

U.S. Imports

Historically, the European couture, rather than posing a threat, actually served to increase our domestic apparel production. We now have an American couture and many designer-owned firms in the United States, but most of our leading creative artists are in high-priced ready-to-wear, not in custom production.

The business of reproducing "line-for-line" copies of Paris apparel is still a powerful asset to American retailers and manufacturers. Twice a year buyers from America's leading retail stores attend the European couture openings to buy the models they think will appeal most to American women. Twice a year a jet airliner carries more than half a million dollars' worth of Paris originals into the United States, delivering the precious cargo to its respective purchasers. In the weeks that follow, there is a frenzied duplication of each model that varies all the way from exact replications to cheap adaptations. The biggest buyers are stores like Ohrbach's, Macy's, and Alexander's, who maintain a worldwide reputation for their couture copies. Ohrbach's, for example, contracts with about thirty New York manufacturers to produce many copies between the time the models arrive (in winter, the last week in February) and the second week in March, when the copies go on sale. The processing is so amazingly fast that some of the cheaper, less complicated mass-produced models are ready in a matter of days.

In most cases, the copies sell at a fraction of the original cost. The counterpart of a St. Laurent gown purchased in Paris for thousands of dollars can often be found at Ohrbach's for under $100. At one store, all two hundred copies of a Chanel suit were sold before the end of the first day of sales. The explanation, of course, is volume sales, but the margin of profit is extremely small. If retailers sell a hundred copies of a dress they must deduct the amount paid for the original and the expense of a trip to Paris, as well as the cost of manufacture from the total sales.

Not all couture originals come from Paris or are produced in volume. The couture models, imported or domestic, reproduced are made with all the fine details of workmanship that were once available in the custom salons of many exclusive American specialty stores. Today, I. Magnin in San Francisco is the only store left in the United States that still makes custom copies of haute couture. Because custom work is done to individual measurements and labor costs are high, a copy made in San Francisco could easily be higher in price than the original bought in Paris.

The European models are brought into the country "in bond," which means that buyers do not pay duty (which may be as high as 60 percent of the cost) if they do not resell the garment in the United States. Within a year, therefore, the models are shipped off to Canadian and Latin American stores that specialize in "secondhand" couture, where a St. Laurent gown may be sold at a bargain basement price. The American store or manufacturer who buys in the European salons really pays for the privilege of copying a design, not for merchandise that is resold.

The amount of goods we import from Europe, however, is very small compared to the volume of imports from Asia, particularly in the low-priced field. The recent quota regulations have had a curious effect on the quality of the goods brought into this country. Since the quotas are based on units rather than dollars, manufacturers want to make the most out of their dozens. "In most countries in the Orient, apparel production is an economic mainstay, therefore, in some of these countries there is an effort to produce a better-quality, more fashionable garment."[25]

As yet, goods from the socialist countries—Russia, Rumania, China—have been considerably lower in quality than those from the Asian countries, and importers have to pay a double duty on their shipments. It may be some time before they will be able to make a significant input into the American market.

U.S. Exports

It has been said that the French design while the Americans make fashion. In short, the French have the Americans to thank for popularizing their styles. But if Paris designs are coveted by some Americans, the quality of United States ready-to-wear is treasured by Europeans. Many American lines, such as designs by Lanz of California and Jonathan Logan, sell like hotcakes in Europe, where it is a rarity to find well-made and well-fitting clothes available off the rack.

This unusual exchange of talents between Europeans and Americans has stimulated some of the most intensive market research in years. United States apparel manufacturers have investigated the style and fabric preferences of European consumers as well as the modifications in sizing required by the difference in national body types. In the 1960s, less than 0.5 percent of all male apparel produced in the United States was sold abroad. American manufacturers discovered a growing inter-

est among European men for lighter-weight suits and colorful sportswear, and no other market can compete with American products in these categories. European consumers have increasing amounts of disposable income, and they pay increasing attention to fashion in the purchase of items heretofore considered as luxuries.

Gradually the barriers between countries are being broken down by international trade. Physical distances are reduced by the speed of jets and the power of mass communication. The American market is rapidly becoming a world market.

Multinational Trends

Corporations that maintain a base of operations in more than one country are commonly known as multinational companies. In the past twenty years an amazing number of American firms have extended into foreign lands. The British, of course, have done so since the early 1900s, but American expansion has been relatively recent. The big retail chains were among the first to establish overseas outlets. Sears, for example, opened stores in Havana and Mexico City in the forties, and it has since spread to many other countries. Joseph Magnin opened a chain of stores in Japan in 1973, and now the Japanese can buy some of the same merchandise available in the Western JM shops. Italians can buy the same clothes from J. C. Penney in Milan as Americans can buy in Los Angeles.

As indicated earlier, a number of American apparel firms contract with manufacturers in Far Eastern countries to have their brand-name merchandise produced where labor costs are low. But the idea is spreading to American designers and manufacturers who plan to market their products abroad; Anne Klein, for instance,

[25]Dickerson and Barry. "The Textile and Apparel Industry in World Trade," p. 7.

opened a shop in Paris, and Jerry Silver-man has a boutique in London.

The biggest push toward multinational organization is among the textile produc-ers. The giant fiber producers are already well established overseas. Du Pont, for example, has plants in Brazil, Canada, Germany, the Netherlands, and the United Kingdom; Celanese is also in Brazil and Canada, and in Columbia, Mexico, Peru, and Venezuela as well. Many weaving mills have made similar kinds of overseas invest-ments. Burlington Industries has plants on all continents. Some apparel manufactur-ers have spread out and have their own manufacturing plants in low-wage coun-tries where apparel items are made and labeled with the American name and then sold in the United States.

In most cases the American company makes a direct capital investment in the multinational corporation abroad, thereby creating an entirely new operation. Manu-facturers seek to make such an investment for a number of reasons. First, they do so to secure new resources of raw materials. America is rapidly becoming resource poor, so textile plants are usually opened in areas with high resource potential. Second, manufacturers seek low-cost labor to produce more economically. Third, they capture the existing market of the country in which the goods are produced. Beyond this, however, the national company can give the developing foreign nation techni-cal expertise and an opportunity to learn modern management controls.

Many individuals and groups—notably the American labor unions—see this kind of investment as a threat to the American economy. They believe that we are export-ing both capital and technology and that by setting up operations overseas, we are shutting down American industries and creating unemployment here at home. In addition, they argue that by investing in foreign holdings multinationals avoid pay-ing U.S. taxes on foreign-earned profits.

In the face of growing competition from abroad, however, the multinational trend seems inevitable. Quite aside from the promise of lower labor costs and more efficient production, it also helps to over-come hidden international trade barriers. We may indeed be looking forward to a division of labor on a worldwide basis between advanced and developing nations. The biggest explosion of the world's popu-lation has taken place in Asia, providing an abundant supply of labor. High-wage coun-tries like the United States may be forced to discontinue their noncompetitive manufac-turing operations and transfer them to low-wage areas. The rich, industrialized countries may then concentrate on capital-intensive production, research, and prod-uct development; the developing countries make their greatest contribution in the labor-intensive areas.

The demand for textiles will continue to increase as world population increases. But increases will also come as consumers in developing nations acquire the financial resources that will allow them more than bare essentials. Added disposable income is accompanied by greater desires for a variety of clothing items. The changes in the textiles and clothing industry in the last century have resulted from continued growth and expansion based on consumer demands. It may well be that in the coming years the problems of expansion will give way to the problems of maintaining an ecological balance on our planet. A rising level of consumption in all parts of the world creates new outlets for United States goods abroad, and new sources of supply for American consumers.

SUMMARY

The United States Abroad

Domestic producers are affected differently by competition from foreign markets. In the developing countries, textile and apparel plants are the least expensive types to equip, and they can absorb a great deal of relatively unskilled labor. Consequently, the squeeze of competition is felt first among the small domestic firms, primarily those that make apparel. On the other hand, with increased wealth, foreign nations become better customers for United States merchandise, particularly in areas where they cannot compete with American technology.

Because of the efficiency and volume of the American ready-to-wear industry, its fashion products are in demand not only by our citizens here at home, but by an increasing number of people in all parts of the world. It may be, however, that workers in the highly competitive industries face eventual adjustment to other types of employment. The trend toward multinational corporations has the potential of eliminating many of our current trade barriers, and of tying nations closer together through cooperative production and international trade.

FOR FURTHER READING

Bancore, Marielle. "Issey Miyake Revisited." *American Fabrics*, No. 115 (Spring 1979), 84–87.

Brady, James. "Fashion." *Saturday Review*, (September 15, 1979), 34.

Bryan, Morris M., Jr. "A Time to Reach Out." in "America's Newest Challenge: Creating World Markets," *American Fabrics*, No. 117 (Fall 1979), 20–22.

Lewis, John. "Following Hanae Mori's Waves and Raves in Paris." *Far Eastern Economic Review*, 104 (June 22, 1979), 61–63.

Szuprowicz, Bohdan O., and Maria R. Szuprowicz. *Doing Business with the People's Republic of China*. New York: John Wiley & Sons, 1978.

Walkins, Josephine Ellis (compiler). *Fairchild's Who's Who in Fashion*. New York: Fairchild Publications, Inc., 1975.

Chapter 19

CLOTHING

CONSUMPTION PATTERNS

Every business that deals with the public is guided by consumer demand for its products. The fiber producers, the fabric and apparel manufacturers, and the clothing retailers make continual adjustments in their operations in light of the spending patterns, tastes, and preferences of American consumers. The quantity or quality of clothing individuals are ready and willing to buy is determined by a number of factors, including personal income, changing needs and desires, commodity price, and prices of substitute goods or services. Here we will examine some of the trends in clothing expenditures, the social and economic changes that may influence how much is spent for clothing in the future, and the consumer's power to force changes in the clothing industry, national and international.

WHERE THE MONEY GOES

The performance and growth of an economy can be measured in terms of its **gross national product** (GNP), which represents the total output of goods and services of a country for any given year. In 1979, the GNP of the United States reached $2,455.8 billion (Figure 19.1). In the process of this production, capital goods wear out, so if we deduct the allowance for capital depreciation and other indirect business taxes, we arrive at a figure described as national income (see Table

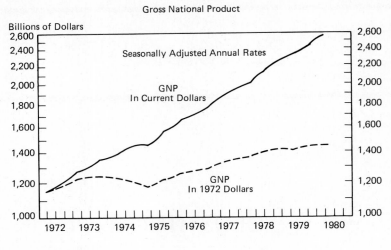

Gross National Product

Figure 19.1 Gross national product.

19.1). By subtracting corporate profits and contributions made for social insurance, and adding money earned through interest, dividends, and other transfer payments, we arrive at the total **personal income** for the population of the United States as a whole.

Disposable personal income is the amount left after personal taxes are deducted, and it refers to the money consumers are free to use as they wish. We pay for our standard of living with disposable personal income. In the period from 1970 to 1979, our disposable personal income rose from $685.9 to $1,678.8 billion, an increase of 144.7 percent. During this same period the American population increased from 203.8 million to 221.3 million people, so the per capita income increased from $3,348 to $7,586, or about 126.4 percent (Figure 19.2).

One factor that influences purchasing power is the price of goods and services.

Prices also went up in this period, so the dollar does not buy as much today as it did in 1970. In fact, $7,586 in per capita income in 1979 dollars is only $4,489 in 1972 dollars. The rise in the average cost of living can be measured by the consumer price index (CPI), which is a measure used to determine average price changes of the various goods and services purchased by households. By keeping the dollar value constant at some predetermined year, the fluctuations in the value of the dollar can be determined. The present CPI is measured by the 1967 dollar value of 100 cents (1967 = 100). Thus the 1960 CPI was 88.7, meaning that a person needed only 88.7 cents to buy a dollar's worth of goods. The CPI for 1970 was 116.3, which means that higher prices reduced the purchasing power of the dollar by 16.3 percent compared with the value of the dollar in 1967. The CPI in 1979 was 229.9, which indicat-

Table 19.1   Relation of Gross National Product, National Income, Personal Income, and Savings (in Billions of Dollars)

	1970	1979
Gross National Product (GNP)	$974.1	$2,455.8
Less: capital depreciation		
Equals: Net National Product	886.5	2,200.8
Less: indirect business taxes		
Equals: National Income (NI)	795.8	2,025.9
Less: corporate profits and social security payments		
Plus: interest and dividends		
Equals: Personal Income (PI)	803.6	2,000.5
Less: personal taxes		
Equals: Disposable Personal Income (DPI)	687.8	1,678.8
Less: personal consumption expenditures	633.7	1,622.8
Equals: *personal savings*	54.1	55.9

(Source: *Survey of Current Business*, U.S. Department of Commerce, Bureau of Economic Analysis, January 1980.)

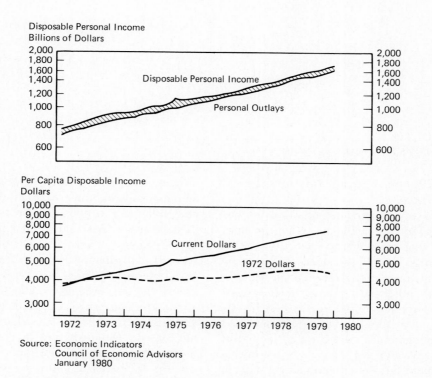

Source: Economic Indicators
Council of Economic Advisors
January 1980

Figure 19.2   Disposable personal income: national and per capita.

Table 19.2   Annual Expenditures on Clothing and Shoes, 1960–1977.

Year	Per-capita expenditures		Percent of expenditures for personal consumption		Aggregate expenditures	
	Constant dollars (1972)	Current dollars	Constant dollars (1972)	Current dollars	Billions of constant dollars (1972)	Billions of current dollars
1960	203	148	8.1	8.2	36.6	26.7
1961	203	149	8.1	8.2	37.3	27.4
1962	209	154	8.1	8.1	38.9	28.7
1963	209	156	7.9	7.9	39.6	29.5
1964	222	166	8.1	8.0	42.6	31.9
1965	227	172	7.9	7.8	44.2	33.5
1966	239	186	8.0	7.9	46.9	36.6
1967	236	192	7.8	7.8	46.9	38.2
1968	242	208	7.7	7.8	48.6	41.8
1969	245	223	7.6	7.8	49.6	45.1
1970	240	227	7.4	7.5	49.2	46.6
1971	249	244	7.5	7.6	51.6	50.5
1972	264	264	7.5	7.5	55.1	55.1
1973	281	291	7.7	7.6	59.2	61.3
1974	279	308	7.8	7.3	59.1	65.3
1975	288	329	7.9	7.2	61.5	70.2
1976	301	355	7.9	7.0	64.7	76.3
1977	306	373	7.7	6.8	66.2	80.9

(Source: *Family Economic Review*, Spring, 1980.)

ed a 129.9 percent increase over the 1970 dollar value.

For many people, personal income has not kept up with inflation. When incomes fail to keep pace with prices, living standards must drop. Less money will not buy the same amount of goods and services. In spite of inflationary prices, however, our real income continued to rise through the 1970s and the national economy was characterized by a relatively high degree of prosperity. Our total income is not evenly distributed, of course, and many groups in our society continue to suffer economic hardships. But as a total population we enjoy a higher consumption level than ever before in our history, and we are still better off economically than most of the other nations in the world. This is true even though the seventies ended on a downward or recessionary curve along with an unprecedented inflationary figure, measured in double digits. There is some pessimism as far as the economic outlook for the eighties is concerned, but most economic authorities consider it to be unfounded and temporary. Although inflation will undoubtedly stay high throughout the eighties, the increases in national productivity tend to cope with inflation. "Business investments in modern plants and equipment and a higher proportion of experi-

Table 19.3   Personal Income Disposition (in Billions of Dollars)

Period	Disposable Personal Income	Personal Saving	Services	Personal Consumption Expenditures			
				Food and Beverages	Durable Goods	Clothing and Shoes	Percent of Income for Clothing and Shoes
1960	$ 350.0	$17.0	$128.7	$ 80.5	$ 45.3	$27.3	7.8
1961	364.4	21.2	135.1	82.9	44.2	27.9	7.6
1962	385.3	21.6	143.0	85.7	49.5	29.6	7.6
1963	404.6	19.9	152.4	88.2	53.9	30.6	7.6
1964	438.1	26.2	163.6	92.9	59.2	33.5	7.6
1965	473.2	28.4	175.5	98.8	66.3	35.9	7.6
1966	511.9	32.5	188.6	105.8	70.8	40.3	7.9
1967	546.3	40.4	204.0	108.5	73.1	42.3	7.7
1968	591.0	39.8	221.3	115.3	84.0	46.3	7.8
1969	634.4	38.2	242.7	120.6	90.8	50.2	7.9
1970	687.8	54.9	261.8	132.1	90.5	52.0	7.5
1971	742.8	57.3	293.4	136.3	84.9	46.6	6.2
1972	801.3	49.4	322.4	140.6	97.1	50.5	6.3
1973	901.7	70.3	352.3	150.4	111.2	55.1	6.1
1974	984.6	71.7	391.3	168.1	123.7	61.3	6.2
1975	1,086.7	83.6	437.5	189.8	122.0	65.3	6.0
1976	1,184.5	68.6	488.5	209.6	132.6	70.1	5.9
1977	1,305.1	65.0	549.8	227.1	157.4	75.9	5.8
1978	1,458.4	72.0	619.8	246.7	178.8	82.4	5.6
1979	1,623.2	72.8	733.9	271.7	200.3	91.2	5.6

(Source: *Economic Indicators*, Council of Economic Advisors, January 1980.)

enced workers in the labor force"[1] make the long-term future look good.

Clothing Expenditures

In 1978, consumers spent over $81 billion for clothing and shoes. This figure represents an increase of almost $5 billion over the previous year's allocation to the nation's clothing budget. But despite the fact that our per capita expenditures for apparel are the highest they have ever been, consumer clothing expenditures in the last decade have averaged only 7.1 percent of total disposable income and dropped to 6.6 percent in 1979 (Table 19.2). By compari-

son, in 1955 the average American family spent over 12 percent of its income on clothing. Although the share of the total income absorbed by clothing today remains at less than 7 percent, annual expenditures for services have risen at a much faster rate than personal consumption expenditures have (Table 19.3).

While the percentage of family income spent on clothes went down, the per capita expenditures for clothing and shoes increased during the seventies. Two thirds of this increase was caused by a general rise in price levels, but only one third represented increase in buying—a real increase of 51 percent in dollars of constant value. This increase in per capita percentage but decrease in overall percentage can be attributed to rising incomes as well as to a

[1]*Changing Times*, March 1980, p. 7.

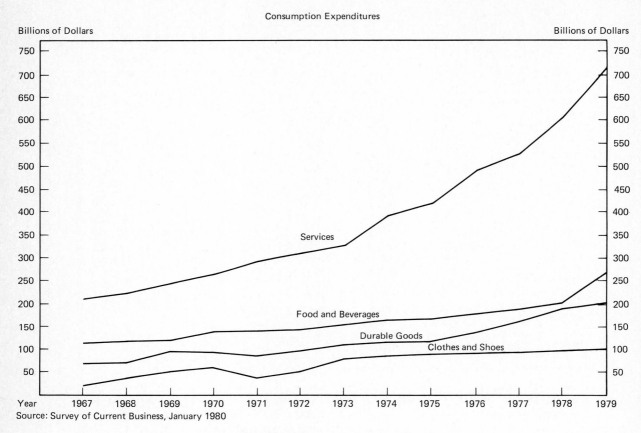

Figure 19.3   Personal consumption expenditures.

change in population make-up. An increased proportion of people were in the fourteen to thirty-four age group and they are individuals who typically have high clothing expenses. This is because of a need for new clothes associated with growth, sports, dating, beginning college, and new careers. This age group is generally more fashion oriented and spends a higher percentage of their income on fashionable or even faddish clothing items than other age groups. Projections for the early 1980s indicate that the composition of the population will not change much; the greatest proportion of people will remain in the high spending group as far as clothing is concerned. Personal clothing expenditures, per capita, are likely to continue at their present level or even rise slightly as real personal disposable incomes rise (Figure 19.3). "However, future increases are likely to be at a slower rate since projections indicate no further growth in the 14–34 age group."[2]

A number of opposing factors, however, may account for clothing's declining share of the consumer dollar. For one thing, the population growth has been largely at the

[2]*Family Economics Review*, Winter–Spring 1978, p. 34.

Table 19.4   Comparison of Income and Expenditures for Clothing and Clothing Related Services for Non-farm Families, 1978–1979[1]

Money Income (before taxes)	Dollars Spent (millions)	Percent of income
Under $3,000	187.39	6
$3,000 to $4,999	307.44	10
$5,000 to $7,499	479.59	16
$7,500 to $9,999	535.65	6
$10,000 to $14,999	687.51	5
$15,000 and over	886.94	3

[1]These figures include not only clothing and shoes, but also jewelry, jewelry repair, dry cleaning, and other costs of upkeep. The percent of income is therefore higher than the percentages listed in Table 19.3.
(Source: *Consumer Expenditures and Income: Survey Guidelines*, U.S. Department of Labor, 1971–1979.)

two extremes of the age scale, in the groups under eighteen and over sixty-five, and the clothing needs of the very young and the very old are considerably less than those of the young adult or the wage-earner. Since the end of World War II, moreover, there has been a significant trend toward casual dress, with a corresponding expansion of "separate" items in the wardrobe (for example, skirts, blouses, sweaters, slacks, sport jackets, and the like), and casual clothing in general is less expensive than is more formal wear.

The parallel development of synthetic fibers has made clothing lighter in weight, easier to care for, and longer wearing. Only a small percentage of our clothing today has to be replaced because it wears out.

Consumer interest in clothing for active sportswear, jogging suits, for example, for everyday wear has been another change in attitudes toward clothing that has affected overall demand. These items tend to be well made, versatile, and transcend fashion in that they do not go "out" but retain an "in" look for a longer period of time than do many clothing items. Interest has also shifted from faddish items to those of greater utility and permanence. "Trade sources expect consumers to purchase a

few higher priced, better quality garments with more durability for long-lasting wear rather than many lower quality faddish items."[3]

In general, the percentage of a family's income spent for clothing increases as the income goes up (Table 19.4). However, in successively higher income brackets over $15,000 clothing constitutes a diminishing proportion of total expenditures.

Clothing Prices

In 1978, per capita expenditure for clothing and shoes was approximately $373, which was a decline from the previous year. The actual dollars spent for clothing, however, must be viewed against the inflationary prices characteristic of the economy in general. Since 1970, the consumer price index for all apparel and upkeep was generally lower than that for all items (Table 19.5). Although the price of clothing went up markedly by the end of the seventies, it did not increase as sharply as did many of the other commodities and

[3]Ibid., p. 35.

Table 19.5   Consumer Price Index for Selected Commodities and Services (1967 = 100)

| Period | All Items | Food | Housing | Medical | Clothing | | |
					All Apparel and Up-Keep	Men's & Boys' Clothing	Women's & Girls' Clothing
1965	94.5	94.4	94.9	89.5	93.7	94.0	93.8
1966	97.2	99.1	97.2	93.5	96.1	96.5	95.6
1967	100.0	100.0	100.0	100.0	100.0	100.0	100.0
1968	104.2	103.6	104.2	106.1	105.4	105.7	105.9
1969	109.8	108.9	110.8	113.4	111.5	112.4	111.7
1970	116.3	114.9	118.9	120.6	116.1	117.1	116.0
1971	121.3	118.4	124.3	128.4	119.8	120.3	120.1
1972	125.3	123.5	129.2	132.5	122.3	121.9	123.0
1973	133.1	141.4	135.0	137.5	126.8	126.4	127.3
1974	147.7	161.7	150.6	150.5	136.2	136.4	134.9
1975	161.2	175.4	166.8	168.6	142.3	142.2	138.1
1976	170.5	180.8	177.2	184.7	147.6	147.2	141.9
1977	181.5	192.2	189.6	202.4	154.2	154.0	146.4
1978	193.2	209.3	202.4	217.6	160.0	159.5	149.0
1979	229.9	235.5	243.6	250.7	172.2	165.4	154.6

(Source: *Economic Indicators*, Council of Economic Advisors, January 1980.)

services, particularly housing, medical expenses, and hard goods.

One reason for this is that the apparel industry is one in which a large number of firms has created a highly competitive market situation; this is reflected, in part, in considerable price flexibility. Price inflation was generally stronger at the retail level than at the wholesale level (Table 17.8). The difference in the rate of increase in consumer prices is due mainly to the marked increase in retailing costs.

Another important factor that affects consumption of clothing is the price of other services and commodities that compete for disposable income. In the 1970s, for example, housing costs went up at a faster rate than costs for either food or clothing, and by 1979 housing costs had more than doubled in five years.

Most important, the price of clothing is affected by the forces of supply and demand. When supplies go down, prices go up. When the supply of raw cotton was extremely tight because of a poor crop in 1971, cotton prices went up 10 percent, compared to man-made-fiber textiles, which rose only 7 percent, and wool goods, which increased 6 percent. Then when the cotton crop was almost one-third larger in later years, the increase was partially offset by Japan's purchase of a large portion of the supply. On the other hand, wool production in the United States has steadily declined and we are forced to make larger imports of raw wool for apparel to meet the demand—of course, at higher prices. Similarly, the price of leather goods went up in the early 1970s because of the world-wide scarcity of hides. In 1970, for instance, we exported nearly one third of our entire production in cattle hides. By 1973, as the demand for beef reached its peak and more stock went to market, the supply of leather increased.

Beef prices are up again and the cost of feeding and shoeing a family are related. "Consumers need to realize that leather prices fluctuate with the state of the meat industry and in the current cycle, cattle are in short supply."[4] The economic law of supply and demand implies that as the supply of beef is limited, the supply of leather also will be limited since they come from the same source. Shoes that sold for $30 in 1979 sold for $40 in 1980. "Shoe customers can expect footwear to be affected by these conditions for at least the next three years. . . . All industries using leather as a source material—including makers of apparel, handbags, gloves and upholstery—will be affected by soaring leather prices."[5] For an example of how this statement is reflected in the economic picture, look at the consumer price index for footwear, leather, and hides and skins in Table 17.3.

This information points up another advantage of the man-made fibers in the apparel market. The producing capacity for man-made fibers is considerably higher than our actual production. Domestic production, moreover, is concentrated in a few firms that sell directly to the textile mills. They can gear their production schedules precisely to mill demands and thereby maintain a relatively stable, predictable price.

As we saw in the last two chapters, clothing prices have been kept down in relation to other commodities by the competition of low-wage countries abroad. In order to meet the competition, American clothing and textile workers are generally paid less than are workers in other industries. In effect, the textiles and clothing industry more or less subsidizes the rest of the economy.

[4]Beatrice Kalka, "Shoes' Cost Likely to Rise with Beef's," *Washington County* (Virginia) *News*, July 12, 1979.
[5]Ibid.

Categories of Apparel

Apportionment of the family clothing dollar has changed gradually over the years with respect to the relative amounts spent for various types of clothing. One of the most notable changes has been the steady increase in spending for women's and children's wear as compared with men's and boys' clothing. Half a century ago clothing expenditures for the man of the household exceeded those for his wife by almost a third. After World War I, the woman's wardrobe began to expand until early in the 1930s clothing expenditures for women and girls surpassed those for men and boys. By the 1960s, one out of every three workers in the labor force was a woman, compared to only one out of four in the 1940s. The working woman requires a larger wardrobe than the woman who stays at home and, as her earnings increase, more of her money goes for clothing. Since women now comprise almost 50 percent of the American workers, expenditures for women's clothing have continued to rise, greatly surpassing the sums spent on all other categories of clothing.

The largest expenditures for clothing occur in families with older children or among the young married group with no children. Unmarried consumers under age thirty-five spend more on clothes than do married consumers with families. Generally, proportionate amounts spent for apparel used to decrease with advancing age but indications are that the preconceived stereotypes of age are changing. Too, a longer life span now can be anticipated and the elderly members of the population take part in more social activities. It is therefore logical to assume that their clothing needs will increase also. The increased numbers of people over sixty-five already make up a financially important group to the clothing industry and every indication is that this group will continue to expand well into the next decade.

Men's and boys' clothing, excluding footwear, took $16.8 billion of consumers' income in 1971, as compared with only $9.9 billion in 1964 (Figure 19.4). In the last decade, however, this category consistently represented about 25 percent of the total expenditures for all clothing, accessories, and jewelry. Men's wear is following the same general trend toward more casual dress shown by clothing in general, moving away from formal wear and business suits to the more informal slacks, sweaters, and sport coats. The sale of men's suits sank 13 percent during this period and at the same time, the sale of jeans and dungarees rose 201 percent.[6] The average man today buys a new suit about once every three or four years (if at all); twenty years ago, he bought one every other year. The suits he buys are lighter in weight than they used to be, with an increasing proportion of fabrics that are blends of fibers. And even though recent figures show that men are spending more money for suits than in the past, these figures do not indicate the actual number of suits purchased, only the increased costs of suits in general.[7] Men's expenditures in the 1970s were way up on haberdashery items and furnishings, such as shirts, slacks, belts, and neckties. In spite of the fact that the male population has increased by several millions during the last decade, the consumption of socks remains about the same—another illustration of the effects of

longer wear imparted by such features as nylon-reinforced heels and toes. The fact that modern man does most of his traveling by automobile rather than on foot is reflected in the falling number of raincoats, overcoats, rubbers, and other types of protective clothing in his wardrobe. The number of hats purchased by men has also decreased appreciably, but items in the underwear and pajama categories are on the upswing. Underwear, incidentally, shows an unusual relationship to technological innovation; prior to 1920, all men wore heavy union suits, but in heated buildings and cars, long drawers became virtually extinct. On the other hand, cotton undershorts, practically unheard of sixty years ago, took over the underwear market almost completely for a while. The cotton was replaced by synthetics, mainly nylon, and then by fiber-blended fabrics, primarily polyester/cotton or polyester/rayon. Due to the bitter-cold winter of 1977 and the continuing rising price of fuel, long johns (and joans) came back in style. The new "old-fashioned woolies" were made of cotton, synthetics, and even wool blended with other natural fibers and with synthetics. The new long underwear is, however, more than utilitarian. It is a fashion item used not only for warmth, but for sleep, loungewear, and even outer body suits.[8]

The designer label epidemic also touched this very traditional apparel field. Christian Dior was the first to come out with a complete line of men's undies, all types and all styles included. What made them so different? They were all cotton and all expensive.[9]

[6]*Focus: Economic Profile of the Apparel Industry.* Arlington, Va.: American Apparel Manufacturers Association.

[7]*American Fabrics and Fashion*, No. 113 (Summer 1978).

[8]Barnard L. Collier. "Long John and Joan Join Energy Battle," *Parade Magazine, Washington Post*, December 2, 1979.

[9]Nina Hyde, "Fashion Notes," *Washington Post*, March 6, 1980.

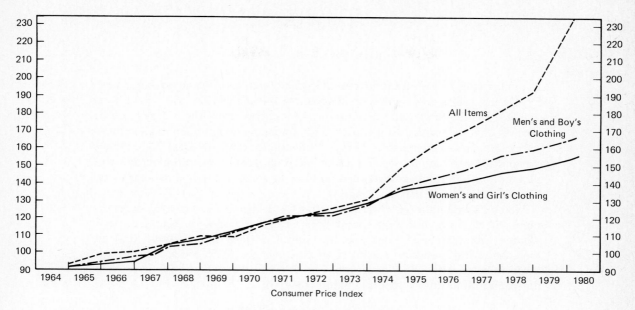

Figure 19.4 Consumer price index.

Women's and children's clothing accounts for about 46 percent of all the money spent by American consumers for items of apparel, shoes, jewelry, and accessories. As family incomes increased over the years, larger proportions of money went for women's clothes. In the past decade, the purchase of blouses, pants, and sweaters skyrocketed at the expense of dresses and suits. Today, leisure-wear and sport clothes account for a large portion of the modern woman's wardrobe.

Per capita production of dresses has dropped drastically. Throughout the first half of the twentieth century, dresses were the mainstay of a woman's wardrobe. Today, she buys fewer dresses in proportion to separates, and fewer house dresses in proportion to street dresses. Women's wear parallels men's wear with respect to a sharp decrease in the purchase of hats and heavy coats. The fact that fewer women wear hats today is another indication of the trend toward casual dress. Lighter weight, all-purpose coats have replaced the heavier, interlined variety.

College students' wardrobes provide an interesting area of study from the standpoint of clothing expenditures. More homogeneous than the total male or female populations, college students also represent an age group that not only demands greater variety, but is the most sensitive of all population groups to style obsolescence. In recent years there has been a tremendous increase in the buying power of consumers between the ages of eighteen and twenty-one. The growing affluence of young adults in today's society is clearly and tangibly reflected in their clothing purchases.

Expenditures for clothing have kept pace with the rise in total consumption expenditures, in spite of the fact that the general trend has been toward more casual dress.

SUMMARY

Where the Money Goes

In the last quarter of a century, annual expenditures for clothing have declined in relation to the sharp gains in disposable income for the population as a whole. For the last decade, however, American consumers have rather consistently spent about 10 percent of all personal consumption expenditures for clothing, accessories, and jewelry. While dollar amounts spent for clothing have increased each year, prices in general have been inflationary, and although apparel prices have gone up, they have not increased as sharply as those of many other commodities.

Women's and children's wear accounts for a larger share of total expenditures for clothing than men's and boys'. The wardrobes of both men and women show the trend toward lighter-weight clothing, casual wear, and an increase in the "separate" items of apparel over the suits, coats, and dresses (especially the dressy or formal type). The textile and fashion trades catering to the young adult have expanded enormously.

FACTORS AFFECTING DEMAND

How much money consumers are able and willing to spend on clothing depends on prices and income and also on a number of factors that originate in political, social, and cultural forces. It may be helpful at this point to review the summaries in Chapter 5 that deal with the relationship between sociocultural trends and fashion change, because some of those same trends are very relevant to the current economic situation.

Diffusion of Income

One important factor that influences expenditures for apparel is the amount of money we have available. The unprecedented increase in personal and family income in the last thirty-five years has resulted in a tremendous increase in the middle-income class of Americans. In 1950, less than a quarter of all families in the United States earned more than $5,000 a year. Today, more than 87 percent have incomes at or above this level, and almost 70 percent earn $10,000 or more (Table 19.6). Obviously much of this increase has been purely inflationary, but considerable evidence shows that America's wealth is also becoming more equally distributed. Before the 1940s, the 1 percent of the population at the very top of the economic bracket held almost 20 percent of the nation's wealth; today, their share is less than 5 percent.[10]

[10]The inequality in income distribution was reduced markedly during the 1940s. The trend toward greater equality has continued, but at a slower rate. For a more thorough analysis of the dispersion of personal income, see Sanford Rose, "The Truth About Income Inequality in the U.S.," *Fortune* (December 1972), 90.

Table 19.6   Percent Distribution of Money Income by Income Categories, 1950–1977

	1950	1960	1970	1977
Median income	**3,319**	**5,630**	**9,867**	**16,009**
	Percentage of All Families			
Under $3,000	42.5	21.7	8.9	3.6
3,000 to 4,999	34.3	20.3	10.4	5.7
5,000 to 5,999	9.0	12.9	5.8	3.5
6,000 to 6,999	5.2	10.8	6.0	3.7
7,000 to 7,999	5.8	20.0	19.9	10.9
10,000 to 11,999	—	6.5	12.7	7.2
12,000 to 14,999	—	4.1	14.1	11.3
15,000 to 19,999	3.2	—	—	17.8
20,000 to 24,999	—	2.8	17.7	13.9
25,000 and over	—	.9	4.6	22.4

(Source: *Statistical Abstracts of the United States*, 1978.)

Another current pattern that tends to equalize the money income is that young people tend to move away from the family and set up separate households. Formerly, most families had to pool their incomes to make ends meet. This change shows in the census data as an increase in the number of households at the lower end of the income range, when actually these single-persons households are not really as poor as their incomes would indicate. As mentioned earlier, more women are in the work force, and the American working woman, married or single, spends about a quarter of her income on clothes. In short, the mass market has shifted upward from the bottom of the economic scale to the middle. The exclusive market, once reserved for the economically and socially elite, has trickled downward. American secretaries are probably better dressed than most of Europe's top level of society.

Closely linked to the dispersion of wealth and high employment is the trend toward shorter working hours and paid vacations. This trend has contributed greatly to an increased taste for travel, growing participation in sports, and the switch to more casual dress.

For most of the American population, the dispersion of wealth has led to gradual elimination of dress differences between adjacent socioeconomic groups. Strictly speaking, the families at either end of the economic scale may be considered minority groups in that they represent increasingly smaller segments of the population. The discussion of our rising consumption level may seem to obscure the fact that sizable numbers of people still cannot afford mink coats and $500 dresses. Some individuals in the low-income bracket cannot afford to purchase any new clothing, and they rely on secondhand merchandise. Clothing is often discarded by its original owners before it is worn out and it subsequently is acquired by other individuals. This process of filtering is widely recognized in housing. When upper-income families trade up or move to more modern facilities, their vacated units become available to others. Secondhand automobiles also are commonly accepted as reusable items, as are refrigerators and stoves.

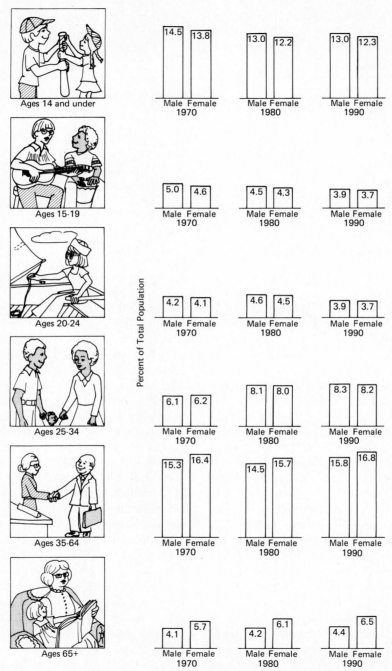

Figure 19.5   Population distribution by age and sex, 1970, 1980, 1990.

Table 19.7 Composition of Population by Age, Specified Years, 1960–1980

Year	Total population (in thousands)	Percent of population by age group			
		Under 14	14–34	35–54	55–65+
1960	180,671	30	28	25	18
1970	204,878	26	32	23	19
1976	215,118	22	36	22	20
1980	224,066	21	36	22	21

(Source: U.S. Department of Commerce, Bureau of the Census, 1977, Projections of the Population of the United States: 1977 to 2050, *Current Population Reports*, Series P-25, No. 704, table h.)

Considerable evidence shows that used-clothing sales are rapidly growing in number. Rummage sales and clothesline sales are fairly common throughout the country. Not all purchases of used clothing are made by low-income families, either.

Consumer credit also makes clothing accessible to those who do not have ready cash, and in part, it accounts for the fact that America has the "best-dressed poverty" in the world.

Population Shifts

We have already noted the gains in total population of the United States. Obviously, as the number of people increases, the need for clothing also increases. But just as important as the per capita figures are the statistics that describe the composition of the population (Figure 19.5). The baby boom of the late 1940s and 1950s created a population bulge at the lower end of the age scale. As these babies grew to maturity during the sixties and seventies, the clothing market expanded accordingly, since this age group represents the most clothes-buying, style-conscious segment. The proportion of 15- to 24-year-olds peaked in the seventies, and groups that fed into this market actually decreased as a result of the declining birth rate (Table 19.7).

The youth market had a tremendous impact on the clothing market as a whole. Young people had money to spend and their tastes influence all other market segments—young adults, parents, and older people in general. By 1980 these "boom babies" were in their early thirties, and by 1990 they will be in their forties. The age group from 25 to 34 showed the greatest increase of all population shifts in 1980 and the youth market decreased proportionately.

The greatest population increase in the eighties will be among the thirty- to forty-five-year-olds. Of the approximately twenty million population increase expected by 1990, it is estimated that three-fourths will be in this age group.[11] These consumers generally are more concerned with quality than the younger, fashion-oriented shopper. Some of this emphasis on quality items was already apparent as early as 1979 and 1980. With quality more important than style, and fashion obsolescence an outmoded concept, a more classic look will predominate.[12] Sales directed toward the thirty- to forty-five-year-old group will also be directed primarily to-

[11]"Retailing in the 80s," *Chain Store Age*.
[12]"Your Customer for the 80's," *Homesewing Trade News*, February 1980.

ward the woman consumer. In 1980 six out of ten women were employed outside the home. This figure is expected to increase through the decade to seven out of ten by 1990.[13] "Quite simply, the woman who gets out of the house and into the workplace sharpens her fashion awareness at the same time she earns the income to upgrade her wardrobe. Although she won't be as fad oriented as the 70's shopper, her value consciousness will increase."[14]

Studies seem to indicate that stage in the life cycle may be an even more important determinant of consumer behavior in general[15] and clothing consumer behavior specifically[16] than social class distinctions. The young shoppers of the last two decades have turned into the young marrieds with young children, and they currently provide the bulk of the business in the large chains and discount stores. Shoppers over age forty, especially those with no children, tend to prefer the department store for many of their clothing purchases.

Another factor that will continue to influence future expenditures for clothing is decreasing family size. Families with fewer children and higher incomes have more money available for discretionary spending. The rural population is also diminishing. In the 1940s, clothing purchases made by farm families were about half as great as those of city families.

Today, even those who live in isolated areas are familiar with urban tastes and habits, and the characteristic differences between urban and rural groups is fast disappearing.

Exogenous Forces

Changes in income and population statistics have a rather obvious relationship to economic activity, but clothing consumption patterns are also affected by a variety of noneconomic trends, such as education, lifestyle, the consumers' general mood, and the changing values. In a study of demographic variables related to family clothing expenditures, Daub found that education of the family head had the greatest relative importance to the proportion of family income spent for clothing.[17] The dispersion of wealth combined with an increasing level of education gradually results in a cultural sophistication that makes a more discriminating shopper out of the average consumer. This often means upgraded tastes and a greater demand for individuality in design.

The current revival of handcrafts in general and sewing specifically, in this the world's most industrialized nation, probably reflects this need for individuality. The increased cost of high-quality clothing in a depressed economy resulted, in the late seventies and early eighties, in more and more people turning to high fashion home sewing (Figure 19.6). Retail sales of fabrics, notions, patterns, and sewing machines more than doubled in this period. Although a few people say they sew primarily to save money, women sew for creative

[13]*Homesewing Trade News*, p. 4.

[14]Ibid.

[15]S. U. Rich and S. C. Jain, "Social Class and Life Cycle as Predictors of Shopping Behavior," in *Contemporary Marketing Research*, by A. P. Govoni (Morristown, N.J.: General Learning Corporation, Morristown, 1972).

[16]Amy Charron, "The Clothing Interest of Three Groups of Young Adult Men Differentiated by Stage in Life." Master's thesis, Virginia Polytechnic Institute and State University, 1977.

[17]K. E. Daub, "Demographic Variables and Family Clothing Expenditures." Master's thesis, Purdue University, 1968.

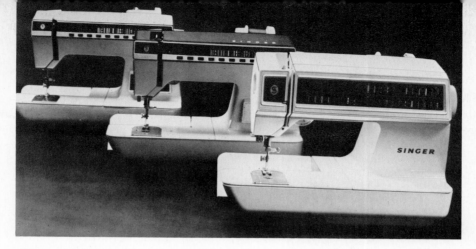

Figure 19.6 The sewing machine of the 1980s will be used to make high-fashion items at home.

expression as well.[18] Fabric sales enhanced rather than diminished the volume of business in the textile and clothing industry as a whole. Home sewers now look for high-quality merchandise and make high-fashion items rather than copy lower-priced goods. The emphasis is on fashion, not price.[19] Independent stores that specialize in couture fabrics and are oriented toward the professional consumer are now part of the retail scene in most shopping malls.[20] Consumers sew to save money, that is, large amounts of money on high-cost fashion merchandise rather than moderate amounts on lower-priced sportswear and casual attire.

The degree of confidence consumers feel about their economic situation is quickly reflected in their buying habits. Experienced retailers know that in periods of recession the sale of dresses drops and sale of separates increases. The skirts, shirts, pants, and other items often are mostly neutral in color, so they may be coordinated with other items in closets. When clothes on the racks in secondhand stores are more than five years old, it is usually a sign that people are holding on to their clothing rather than disposing of old fashions and buying new ones. Many people claim that this is a sure sign of hard times.

In earlier chapters we discussed how shifts in values alter lifestyles, and these same trends affect the relative importance we place on certain economic factors, such as the price and desirability of other goods, goals, and services that compete for the clothing dollar. Another example of how social values can influence economic decisions relates to our growing preoccupation with the quality of our physical environment. The textiles industry is particularly affected by demands to control the pollution of lakes and streams into which their wastes flow. But such control is extremely costly. Some industries can pass the cost of pollution control on to the consumer by raising prices, but others in highly competitive areas (especially those affected by imports) are forced to absorb much of these "social costs" by reducing capital investments and profits. Environmental concerns will force people to reform priorities when it comes to national growth at the possible expense of natural resources. Consumers

[18]Karen Joyce Chan. "The Relationship of Motivation for Sewing, Amount of Sewing, Perceived Depersonalization of the Job, and Creativity." Master's thesis, Oregon State University, 1976.
[19]Eunice Farmer, "Buying Techniques for a Changing Market," *Homesewing Trade News*, February 1979.
[20]Senta C. Mead, "Overview: 1980," *Homesewing Trade News*, January 1980.

will have the inherent ability to decide whether the benefits derived from such controls are worth it.

Changes in consumer values, tastes, and living habits force continual adjustments in the clothing industry.

SUMMARY

Factors Affecting Demand

In addition to the price/cost relationships discussed in the previous sections, socioeconomic trends that influence consumer expenditures include

1. the unprecedented increase in personal income coupled with a greater dispersion of wealth through the population segments
2. the overall growth in population that increases needs, plus the changes in age mix and family size
3. the consumer's education, lifestyle, and changing values

All these factors require constant adjustment by fabric producers, apparel manufacturers, and fashion retailers to match changing consumer demands.

CONSUMER SOVEREIGNTY
AND RESPONSIBILITY

Unconscious and irrational though it may be, the motivation underlying most of our fashion purchases cannot be explained in terms of dictates by the fashion industry and helplessness on the consumer's part. Many styles promoted by designers and publicists never got to first base on the consumer's popularity list. Whether we realize it or not, our behavior in the marketplace contributes to an economic decision that is reached by the multiple choices of millions of individual consumers acting independently. The choices we make as consumers thus affect not only our own welfare, but the welfare of our neighbors as well. They also help to shape the character of our economy on a local, national, and worldwide basis.

The Collective
Aspects of Consumption

The individual consumer casts a ballot in the marketplace with every clothing purchase. The records of daily and weekly sales kept by the local retail store constitute the election returns from one precinct. Let us say that the local merchant has stocked a small quantity of velour stretch knits and suddenly finds they are selling like hotcakes in men's sweatershirts and women's sportswear. The retailer calls the apparel manufacturer and orders more. The phenomenon is seldom restricted to one store, and if you multiply the reorders by the hundreds of retailers that may buy from one manufacturer, you get some idea of the volume of information channeled back to the maker in regard to consumer acceptance of the product. If a style has no reorders, chances are it will be found on the markdown racks in a number of stores, and both producer and retailer will have learned their lesson. The flow of information goes beyond the garment maker. If the manufacturer orders more stretch velour from the knitting mills, the fabric producers will have to order more nylon and cotton yarns, and so on all the way back to the fiber producer.

It is through this process that the collective power of the consumer is felt throughout the industry. The articles that are purchased (as well as those that are not) give tangible evidence of the acceptance or rejection of style, quality, color, fabric, fit, and/or price. The final result, though not immediate and direct, is that the collective behavior of individual consumers has a tremendous influence on the character of the merchandise that will appear on the market the following season. In most cases, the consumer's reaction is automatic and unconscious. Sometimes, however, a direct opinion is asked for. Much of the early research home economists conducted in the area of textiles and clothing related to consumer preference studies, and this continues to be an important area of investigation. One such study surveyed over 400 men in regard to their favorite and least-liked shirts. Women were also interviewed about their favorite garments, and subjects in each case were asked to explain their preferences. Women rated appearance over comfort and said that the most important reason for dressing attractively was to boost their morale. The majority of the men, however, referred most frequently to the temperature and absorbency features of the fabric.[21]

These kinds of findings have rather obvious implications for fabric and apparel producers. In the case of shirt fabrics, for example, the textiles people went to work to find the right blend of fibers and fabric construction that would combine maximum comfort with good wash-and-wear characteristics. The very core of motivational research is to find out what consumers want and then to design a product that will meet their desires.

Today, even retailers seek the opinions of their customers. Many stores sponsor high school or college fashion boards that bring in young people to react to new styles and predicted trends. Manufacturers and retailers who are really concerned actually encourage consumer complaints. It pays them to find out what is wrong with their merchandise. All too often consumers politely ignore their dissatisfactions and the real cause is never identified. The store may lose a customer and, in some cases even a reputation, and never know why.

Consumer Rights
and Responsibilities

In Chapter 17, industry responsibility toward the consumer was discussed. These

[21]*Consumer Satisfaction with Men's Shirts and with Women's Slips and Casual Street Dresses*, Bulletin No. 984 (Ithaca, N.Y.: Cornell University Agricultural Experiment Station, New York State College of Home Economics, July 1963).

responsibilities have been formulated into a list of consumer rights; however, a corresponding set of consumer responsibilities goes with these rights. Four basic consumer rights were proposed by President Kennedy in 1962: the right to safe and nonhazardous merchandise; the right to be informed about the goods and services purchased; the right to choose among alternatives in the marketplace; and the right to be heard by those who make and sell consumer products offered in the marketplace, as well as by those who provide needed consumer services. In 1975, President Ford proposed a fifth consumer right, the right to consumer education. Still another right has been proposed by writers and researchers in the field of consumer affairs, the right to redress, that is, the right to compensation, correction, or satisfaction for merchandise or services that prove to be unsatisfactory for any reason.

If these rights are to be assured in an effective manner, the consumer has corresponding responsibilities. These include the responsibility to

use products safely, in the manner prescribed by the manufacturer

become informed before or during purchase

select wisely from the vast array of goods and services available and comparison shop where practical

learn more about consumer products by careful study of labels and other promotional literature

be heard by complaining in a positive way to the proper sources, so as to assume logical redress of wrongdoings

Implementing such a philosophy obviously calls for effective communication between consumers in general and the American industry.[22]

Complaints should be made to the store, to the manufacturer, or to other appropriate groups when the merchandise does not give satisfactory service, otherwise, the manufacturer may never know that the product does not meet consumer expectations. It is also helpful to praise businesspeople when they improve their products or their services so that they may know what it is that pleases consumers. Let store personnel know, too, if there are things you want that they do not carry. They may be happy to stock them if they are aware of the demand.

The most effective way to register consumer opinion about clothing merchandise or any other type of merchandise, for that matter) is to write to the consumer relations department of the store in which the garment was purchased (a typed letter usually receives more attention than a handwritten one). State the facts clearly, without exaggeration or sarcasm, and explain exactly what is wrong with the article. If the store is a small, independently owned specialty shop, address your complaint to the owner. If the manufacturer's label is in the garment, write to the manufacturer directly and send a carbon copy to the retailer. Voicing consumer opinion is just as important as going to the polls to vote.

The old business motto, "The customer is always right," has been used so often that even the customer has come to believe it. It is easy to assume that when a consumer is dissatisfied, the culprit must be either the manufacturer or the retailer. Certainly the seller is at fault if goods are

[22]Jean M. Lown, "Development of a Consumer Issues Attitude Inventory Based on a Descriptive Framework of the Consumer Interest." Ph.D. diss., Virginia Polytechnic Institute and State University, August 1979.

misrepresented, by practicing deliberate deceptions, by taking advantage of the buyer's ignorance, or by being ignorant themselves about the quality of their products. Buyers, however, may be at fault by failing to state their needs accurately, failing to ask questions, not really knowing what they are looking for, or neglecting to follow the manufacturer's directions for use and care. The woman who demands an adjustment on a cashmere sweater because it shrank out of fit is abusing her privilege if she washed the sweater in hot water and tumble-dried it in the machine.

Comparison shopping should be done before you make a purchase, not after. If you buy a blouse and then find another down the street that you like better, you have no reason to expect the retailer to refund your money cheerfully. Remember, too, that the attitude with which you approach the salesperson will determine to a large extent the treatment you will receive. State your wishes in a pleasant manner and be conscious of your mood when shopping.

As a consumer, you should also be aware of market conditions and problems. When particular commodities are scarce, stockpiling goods will only help to bring about inflationary prices. Buying according to your normal needs will work to the benefit of the largest number of people.

There is a dual approach to good citizenship in the market economy of our nation. One is to educate ourselves not only to be discriminating shoppers, but to have a broad social intelligence about economic problems. The other is to develop an interest in consumer affairs and take an active role in organized movements that work toward the betterment of consumer welfare. Participation in consumer cooperatives, credit unions, and buying clubs not

only helps us get more for our money, but helps us to understand what is going on in business. The government has already taken action on the needs of the consumer. In 1962, a National Consumer Advisory Council was established by the president. This was followed by the appointment of a President's Committee on Consumer Interests and a Special Assistant to the President on Consumer Affairs. The consumer will find it advantageous to keep informed of their activities and cooperate with government and business in finding better solutions to common problems.

Improved Choice Making

It is estimated that seven out of ten buyers are habit shoppers, that is, they buy in the same manner, over and over again without much conscious attention as to how they do it. The production and marketing of quality merchandise at fair prices becomes the responsibility of manufacturers and retailers, but both will supply what the consumer demands.

A satisfactory wardrobe depends not so much on the amount of money spent as careful planning. The basic assumption underlying intelligent decision-making is that individuals know what they want or need. The teenager who claims she "needs" a new sweater, when she already has seventeen in her wardrobe, appears on the surface at least to be unable to recognize the difference between a "need" and a "desire." A rational choice of clothing is predicated on an honest evaluation of why we want the things we do. The basic difference between needs and desires may be illustrated by our physiological need for protection against the cold. People satisfy this need in a variety of ways. The Eskimo keeps warm by wearing an undershirt of caribou skin. The Mongol wears a long sheepskin gown that covers the hands and boots several sizes too large to permit the use of fur socks in winter. The Englishman is apt to wrap a long wool muffler around his neck and increase his activity by a brisk walk. Thick woolen stockings and warm boots are efficient insulators for the legs and feet in winter climates, but the majority of American women prefer to shiver in sheer nylon hose and thin pumps. These women may need to be warm, but for them fashion overrules need.

Our needs, of course, are not limited to the physiological. We have a variety of social and emotional needs that must also be satisfied in some way. For some people, clothing satisfies the need for creative self-expression. For others, it provides social status and prestige. Still others value the social approval and the feeling of belonging that can be achieved through dress.

Our desires increase as we are exposed to a greater variety of goods. Eskimos who know nothing but animal skins as a medium for clothing usually want nothing else, but through increasing contact with modern technology, many are coming to prefer jackets and boots made from synthetics, even though such clothing may be decidedly inferior to their traditional parkas and mukluks. Most Americans today are familiar with a wide variety of styles and materials, and the mere knowledge of such products tends to expand our desire for greater variety in our wardrobes.

The fact that wants change over time sometimes makes us dissatisfied with the clothes we already have, even though when purchased, they may have fulfilled the same basic needs. Desires, moreover, are not usually equal in importance. Everyone—to some extent at least—wants

clothing to do a number of things: keep them warm; make them more attractive; help them to feel part of a group; give them individuality; provide aesthetic satisfaction. Not all of these wants have the same value to the individual, and some may even be in conflict. Some wants must be satisfied immediately; others can be postponed. It may be very important to be warm now and attractive later.

For all these reasons, desires are often not very clearly defined, and people frequently have little understanding of what it is they really want. Everyone needs some experience in verbalizing desires and consciously evaluating them in order to make rational choices in selecting clothing. Although needs may be satisfied in a number of alternate ways, it is rarely possible to achieve all our desires.

Our clothing needs and desires are determined by the kind of life we choose to lead. There is really no average individual, because each person has a unique set of requirements that are bound to influence clothing purchases. Income, occupation, social participation, the climate, the way we spend our leisure time, our style of living—all these factors affect the logic of a clothing decision for a particular individual.

Standard of living usually is used to designate the way people believe they should live or want to live. It includes all the goods and services an individual or family considers important, along with some beliefs about the way in which the goods should be used. For some families, this might involve a comfortable home, abundant food, practical and suitable clothing, a new car, camping gear, a yearly vacation, adequate medical care, protective insurance, and a number of other wants. Through the use of such goods, people may hope to achieve the ultimate satisfactions of physical health and comfort, happiness, leisure, beauty, order, prestige, success—in short, the goals they regard as worth striving for.

It is not just the possession of certain kinds of goods that people desire, but the way in which they would like to use them that also determines the standard of living. Some people, for example, eat dinner in the same clothes they have worn all day. Others look forward to getting out of their work or business clothing and putting on something more comfortable. Still others believe in bathing and changing into more formal attire. One person may think a garment should be worn until it develops a hole or a tear and should then be discarded. Someone else may take the time and effort to repair or mend clothing and continue to enjoy its use.

Few people have the resources to achieve all their wants. Their **level of living** is different from their standard of living in the same way that what we want is different from what we actually have. As we progress toward our goals, our level of living gets closer and closer to our standard of living, although by the time the standard is approached, we have usually learned about other things we want, so the standard continually moves ahead of the level.

Level of consumption is still another phrase used to describe people's living conditions, but it refers to the actual consumption of goods rather than to the way people feel about what they use. Frequently we talk about a family or a society as having a "high standard of living," when actually all we can observe is their level of consumption. A standard of living cannot be accurately defined by anyone outside the group itself, because outsiders do not really know how the

individual or the family regards its possessions. We may think a person has a low standard of living because we see shabby clothes and an old car, but such an evaluation reflects our own standards, not the standards of the individual we are observing.

Standards are important here because they greatly influence the clothes we choose. Standards probably develop first from the family in which we grow up, where we learn how children "ought" to dress for school and how people "should" dress when they go to church, or to the grocery store, or out to play. Beyond this, standards evolve from actual use of goods. For instance, if we have had a bad experience with a nylon shirt that was uncomfortable to wear and became gray and dingy with washing, we probably would not want another nylon shirt. But if we received many flattering comments when wearing a blue sweater, we might tend to select other blue garments and our partiality to blue might even extend to items besides clothes.

In this section, we suggest a rational approach to choice making. It does not imply that wearing apparel should always be chosen on the basis of its quality or durability. These factors have a place of relative importance among the other criteria—comfort, appearance, fashion value, maintenance requirements, status or social significance, and price. Some of these factors will always rate higher than others in individual consumers' value patterns. For most people, however, the weighing of criteria will be slightly different in every situation. Few brides, for instance, would choose their wedding gowns with comfort, durability, and ease of care as prime considerations. And only a vain person would choose all clothing solely on the basis of appearance.

The purpose is not to dictate what values the consumer should have, but to replace haphazard, impulsive buying with conscious, intelligent, and informed behavior. Throughout this discussion, we have referred to agencies, groups, and laws intended to protect the consumer from fraudulent practices and inferior merchandise, but no one else can make decisions for us, and no amount of legislation will ever replace the perceptive consumer. If customers are sure of what they want, if they are reasonably well informed, if they ask intelligent questions, and if they make the best judgments they know how to make, their satisfactions as consumers of clothing will be greatly increased. Above all, they must be aware of how their actions and decisions affect the total economy.

Consumer behavior is a controlling factor in determining the character of goods that appear on the market. A rational approach to clothing needs and expenditures makes the consumer a more effective participant in the entire market economy.

SUMMARY

Consumer Sovereignty and Responsibility

The information that is fed back from individual consumers to all segments of the apparel industry takes place through the retailer and the daily record of sales and reorders. Every clothing purchase that is made is a ballot cast for the continued production of similar kinds of merchandise. Learning to voice individual opinions in an effective manner is an important contribution to the clothing industry as a whole.

Along with rights go responsibilities. Consumers have the right to product safety but they have a corresponding responsibility to use products according to manufacturers' directions. So, too, the consumer has a responsibility to become informed, choose wisely, learn more about products by reading labels and directions, and voice complaints to proper sources. Only by demanding rights and assuming responsibilities can the consumer be satisfied in the marketplace.

FOR FURTHER READING

Current spring report on textiles and apparel. In *Family Economics Review*. Consumer and Food Economics Institute, Agricultural Research Service, U. S. Department of Agriculture.

Sproles, George B. *Fashion: Consumer Behavior Toward Dress*, pp. 173–194. Minneapolis: Burgess Publishing Co., 1979.

The Customer Speaks About Her Wardrobe. A Fairchild Fact File. New York: Fairchild Publications, 1979.

Chapter 20

THE CONSUMER
AND THE MARKETPLACE

Intelligent consumer choice is a fundamental problem for people in almost all modern societies, but it becomes even more complex in a country in which goods are abundant and the number of alternatives increases each year. The quality of living achieved by any society as a whole depends largely on the actions taken by all the individual consumers in the marketplace.

THE INFORMED CONSUMER

Clothing is only one of the many goods and services that must be provided for the average household, be it an individual, a family unit, or a group of people living together. Through a study of clothing one source of wants and needs can be analyzed. By applying information obtained from this analysis to other areas of life, we can become more effective and discriminating managers of personal or family incomes and more intelligent users of our nation's resources.

Planning Clothing Expenditures

A personal approach to clothing needs is a practical way to start an assessment of the clothing purchase process. Listing the kinds of activities we engage in on a daily or weekly basis and then those in which we participate less frequently shows the types of clothing that are needed and worn most often. People usually find greater rewards in spending the bulk of their clothing budget for garments that are used regularly and less on the items that are seldom worn. An analysis of clothing requirements, then, is the first step in planning clothing purchases. Other important issues include how much to spend, the sources of clothing, where and when to buy them, and how to pay for them. This chapter is devoted to discussion of these aspects.

Analysis of Clothing Requirements

Once clothing needs are identified, the articles of clothing already on hand that are suitable for the activities listed can be evaluated. One way to do this is to list all clothing items owned currently, along with an estimate of the need for yearly replacement. This wardrobe inventory is a practical exercise for several reasons. It is a logical step in planning future clothing purchases and it forces the individual to weed out and discard items that are never worn or no longer suitable. It also shows what proportion of the total income goes for apparel and upkeep.

The wardrobe can then be checked against the activity list. Many items will be suitable for a number of occasions, particularly if they are basic in design. Some activities, however, will require specialized clothing. A uniform may be required for work, and participation in sports, such as skiing, swimming, riding, and so forth, may call for items that are more or less restricted in use.

Annual additions or replacements of clothing can be determined by the difference between clothing requirements and clothing already on hand. The inventory will also show those items that tend to be overstocked and so make further purchases unnecessary and probably undesirable as well. Further investment in categories of clothing that are already in full supply is a questionable practice at best and probably an unnecessary luxury.

The cost of each new article desired should be estimated as closely as possible so that an overall plan may be developed in which the total cost of all items is anticipated. Unsatisfactory purchases are often made because we see something on sale and buy impulsively. A bargain is never a bargain, whatever the cost, unless the garment has a purpose and fits into an overall plan. Impulse buying leads to overspending and a poorly coordinated wardrobe. Few people are in a position to buy a completely new wardrobe at one time; planning ahead usually enables a person to take advantage of sales when they come along and still buy the needed things. In fact, a special list of things that would be nice to have if the price were right is handy to have on hand. If this list includes the regular retail price of each item as well, a true sale price can readily be recognized. A wise purchase or a truly good sale value adds immeasurably to one's resources.

How Much Should One Spend on Clothing?

There is no one answer to the question. Just as individuals vary in their needs, wants, values, and priorities in all areas of life, so, too, do their clothing priorities differ and thus, their expenditures. The

Table 20.1   Consumer Expenditures

	Percentage of Total Expenditures			
	1950	1960	1970	1977
Food, beverages, tobacco	30.4	26.9	23.2	21.7
Household operations	15.4	14.4	13.9	14.7
Housing	11.1	14.2	14.8	15.3
Transportation	12.9	13.3	12.6	14.3
Clothing, accessories, and jewelry	12.4	10.2	10.1	7.9
Medical care	4.6	5.9	7.7	9.8
Personal business	3.6	4.6	5.8	5.0
Recreation	5.8	5.6	6.3	6.7
Personal care	1.3	1.6	1.6	1.4
Religion and welfare	1.2	1.5	1.4	1.3

(Source: *Statistical Abstract of the United States*, 1978.)

Table 20.2   Average Expenditures for Clothing, Accessories, and Jewelry

Year	Expenditures Per Capita in Dollars	Percent of Personal Consumption Expenditures
1950	$188	12.4
1960	178	10.2
1970	235	10.1
1977	426	5.6

(Source: *Statistical Abstracts of the United States*, 1978.)

percentage of total income spent on clothing varies considerably, although in general people spend an increasing proportion for apparel as incomes progress from low to middle levels. American families as a whole spend about 7 percent of their disposable incomes on clothing, accessories, and jewelry, and almost another 2 percent on personal care (see Table 20.1).

Looking at it another way, we might consider the average expenditure for clothing per capita and the proportion of one's total personal consumption that it represents (see Table 20.2).

Most college students spend a higher percentage of their income for clothing than the average figure indicated in Table 20.2. Knowing how much you have to spend, regardless of the actual amount, will result in a better wardrobe plan. If the list of wants greatly exceeds the purchasing power available, the wants must be reevaluated in light of the most urgently needed items. Sometimes a basic design will serve more than one purpose and thus extend the wardrobe at little additional cost. If one's purchasing power actually exceeds the list of wants, it may be possible to trade up in quality on some of the planned purchases. Investment in a better grade of merchandise often extends the wear life of a garment, and it can add immeasurably to the distinctiveness of the wardrobe. However, this too, is a very personal matter and value judgments should not be applied. Some people prefer the variation possible with many clothes even if the quality is inferior. Others prefer few items of better or even status quality. Most people fall between the extremes. However, planning does allow an individual to pursue either course instead of just accidentally ending up with a closet full of nothing to wear.

Sources of Clothing

People sometimes forget that the outright purchase of new ready-to-wear items on the retail market is not the only way clothing may be obtained. Many usable garments are passed on in good condition from one family member to another or from one family to another. In some cases, such clothing is actually of better quality than the individual might be able to purchase firsthand and with minor adjustments in fit or design, the item may be suitably adapted to the new owner's needs. Gifts are also an important source of new clothing, although like passed-on items, they may not always fit perfectly into the wardrobe plan.

Purchase of used clothing can be a very satisfactory way to obtain garments for a particular purpose without investing a great deal of money. Children's clothes, quickly outgrown, are common items on the used-clothing market, and many good values can be found. People with creative sewing talents often can find garments of excellent quality that can be updated to conform to the current fashion through simple renovation. Some shops offer clothing from individuals who have large expensive wardrobes and dispose of garments after very little wear.

Home sewing, of course, continues to be an important source of clothing for many individuals and families. Americans spent over $5 billion on fabric, patterns, notions, and sewing machines in 1979. The desire to save money is probably an important incentive to home sewing, but certainly not the only one. In a survey of home sewers 44 percent said that enjoyment was the primary reason they sewed, but 30 percent stated that they also made most of their own clothing in order to save money. This group of women included full-time homemakers as well as professional home economists employed in the clothing and textiles field.[1] In another study involving professional women working full time outside the area of home economics, 74 percent made their clothing in order to get a better fit. However, they also listed enjoyment and money saving as important reasons for sewing clothing.[2]

Money *can* be saved. A simple unlined designer skirt made of cotton with an elasticized waistband priced at $98 can be made at home in the best Swiss cotton ($9.98 a yard) for about $30 or less than a third of the purchase price.[3] The real question, however, is whether or not the time spent in home sewing could be used more profitably in other endeavors. In general, women who make most of their own clothing have much greater variety in their wardrobes, but they do not necessarily spend less money. As a matter of fact, annual expenditures of those who do make their own clothing in many instances are as

[1]Carolyn M. Lanier, "Reaction of Fabric in Encased Seams: The Relationship Between Fabric Thickness and Seam Modification." Master's thesis, Virginia Polytechnic Institute and State University, 1980.

[2]Sharon W. Gizzi, "Home Sewing Needs of Business and Professional Women." Master's thesis, Virginia Polytechnic Institute and State University, 1980.

[3]Jura Koncius, "Fashion: Those Sew-and-Sew Prices." *Washington Post*, March 27, 1980.

high or higher than the average expenditures for women in general.

Some people may pay a local seamstress or tailor to make their clothes. For those with special fitting problems or unique tastes, custom work or home sewing may provide the only satisfactory means of obtaining the desired clothing. But when labor cost is added to materials cost, both usually prove to be expensive ways to obtain new articles.

Where to Buy

Even if the decision is to buy ready-to-wear clothing in a retail store, the consumer is still faced with a number of alternatives. Department stores, specialty shops, variety and chain stores, discount and mail-order houses, and even the food supermarket all offer the customer different shopping advantages. By comparison shopping the customer should be able to find the store (or stores) at which the type of merchandise wanted can be found at a satisfactory price. The buyer should be aware of several factors in selecting a clothing store.

The range of merchandise offered for sale is one important consideration. A store may sell suits beginning at $100 and ranging upward, and another retailer may not carry any item priced higher than $50. A customer can lose a good deal of time looking through merchandise that is not within the right price range. Some stores also specialize in a restricted line of styles and sizes.

The types of service a store provides should also be evaluated. Efficient and courteous salespeople, delivery service, charge accounts, gift wrapping, and return privileges are all beneficial to the customer, but they add to the cost of purchases.

Some people prefer to shop in a store that has a pleasant atmosphere and attractive surroundings. To them, the shopping environment itself constitutes an added value for which they are willing to pay.

Convenience in shopping is a significant factor if the shopper considers time valuable. One's ability or willingness to travel distances in order to buy at a particular store depends not only on the time available, but on transportation cost. Mail-order houses offer the convenience of shopping at home, which in effect saves both travel time and cost, even when shipping or mailing costs are included.

The business practices of the store or retailer should also be studied carefully. One can learn a great deal by checking merchandise against a store's advertising to see if information has been presented honestly and accurately. An intelligent consumer who knows how to judge quality usually can tell whether salespeople are truthful and competent in presenting merchandise. A retailer who is willing to stand behind the products and services sold is the best protection a consumer can find against tricky or unfair dealings.

By patronizing a particular kind of store a vote of confidence is given to one group of merchants over another. Giving business to unprincipled competitors makes it harder for the reliable merchant to survive.

When to Buy

Another advantage of a wardrobe plan is that it enables the consumer to shop the sales. If one can anticipate the year's clothing needs, garments can often be purchased at the end of a season at considerable savings. The percentage of the markdown should always be considered in light of the store's profit margin. Higher-priced stores may have an original markup anywhere from 35 to 50 percent. Obviously, "one-third off" sales in this type of store would not be as much of a bargain as a 20-percent reduction in a store that operated on a 20- to 25-percent margin.

Clearance sales usually offer the biggest price reductions, and they are held to get rid of fashion items that have not moved. Clearance sales in men's and boys' wear are commonly held in January, and February is a good month for women's fashions, but end-of-season selling may take place any time after the demand has fallen off. Swimsuits, for example, can often be found at half-price near summer's end. If one buys basic styles or is familiar enough with the fashion cycle to gamble on styles that may be halfway through their fashion life, clearance sales offer good savings.

Annual sales generally do not afford the drastic reductions found in clearance sales, but they are considered more reliable because goods from regular stock go on sale for a short time. The purpose here is not so much to get rid of the merchandise as to attract customers to the store during a slack selling season. It is wise economy to wait for the annual sales to buy staple dress items, such as hosiery, underwear, men's white shirts, pajamas, and the like. Buying hosiery by the box instead of by the pair is always more economical because a sock will always have a mate until you get down to the last one.

Special-purchase sales come about as the result of a special price reduction in the wholesale market for large lots of a particular item. The price reduction is usually better than the markdown in annual sales but not as great as in clearance sales. The customer must be wary of some slight imperfection in special purchase merchandise that may detract from the sale price value.

Anniversary sales are most often storewide sales in which each department marks down a few items. Like annual sales, the anniversary sale is intended to stimulate business during slack periods.

Obviously, no one can fill all clothing needs through sale purchases, but if one plans ahead, considerable savings can be effected.

How to Pay

The decision on when to buy is closely tied to the payment method. Those who believe in the cash-and-carry system buy only when the money is available. Others may use some type of credit plan either to take advantage of sales or to have the clothing on hand when it is the most useful. Since clothing is a commodity that earns no money for the buyer and is generally nondurable in nature, it is wiser to pay cash whenever possible.

Credit plans include the familiar **charge account**. Usually there is no service charge for open accounts billed at the end of the month. Some banks issue credit cards that may be used in a number of stores, and the customer is billed once a month for all purchases. This type of credit is a convenience because it eliminates the need to carry large amounts of cash, and the monthly statements provide a valuable record of purchases. As long as the charge account is used in such a way that it does not encourage overspending, it has certain decided advantages. **Revolving credit accounts** and **lay-away plans** are slightly different in that they usually involve a service charge. Revolving plans establish a maximum credit level, and the customer has from six months to a year to pay for purchases. In using the lay-away plan, the buyer makes a small deposit to hold the merchandise until the full purchase price of the article is available.

Installment buying differs from the various types of charge accounts. The buyer makes a small down payment at the time of purchase and agrees to make regular payments until the balance is cleared. The customer has the use of the merchandise while paying for it, but failure to meet one installment often means the merchandise is repossessed by the store, and the consumer loses the entire investment. Whenever it seems necessary to purchase clothing on an installment basis, the individual should be thoroughly aware of how much extra the privilege of deferring payment costs, as well as what will happen if payments are not made promptly. Installment buying is usually very expensive in terms of the interest rates paid, and it should be avoided if possible. Clothing may very easily be worn out before it is paid for, and the individual will be in debt for something that can no longer be used.

PREPARATION FOR SHOPPING

Learning to recognize quality and good workmanship in clothing is an essential part of consumer education. Buyers should be well informed before they go into the market if they expect to get full value for the clothing dollar. Strange as it may seem, the people who shop the market, compare values, and look for the best buys are usually those with a fairly high standard of living. Studies have shown that low-income families tend to restrict their shopping to one store and favor the well-known brand names that often are priced at the high end of the line. Susceptibility to overselling by salespeople is greatly reduced when the customer is fortified with facts.

Recognizing Quality

Assuming that a garment meets the shopper's needs in terms of style, color, and fashion appeal and that it fits into the wardrobe plan, a further examination of its true value should be made before buying.

The following five points should be checked in judging fabric serviceability.

Fiber Content

A knowledge of the fiber content will help the consumer anticipate the care that will be required and help to determine whether the garment will be suited to its end use. This implies that the individual is sufficiently informed to be able to relate a fiber's generic name to a particular set of fiber properties or characteristics. Nylon, for example, is a very strong, long-wearing fiber with high elasticity and low absorbency. It washes easily, dries quickly, and requires little pressing. Socks made from nylon will hold their shape and resist holing. Because of their low absorbency, however, they may not be particularly comfortable to wear in warm weather. Cotton may be a better choice for summer, and wool would be warmer in winter.

Learning fiber properties is not difficult if one knows how to group them properly.

Cellulosic fibers (cotton, linen, rayon), for instance, have many characteristics in common; they tend to be highly absorbent, wrinkle easily unless chemically treated, and are subject to attack by mildew. Most of the synthetic fibers, on the other hand, do not absorb moisture and tend to build up static electricity, but they are sturdy and lightweight, resist wrinkling, usually retain their shape and size after laundering (they tend not to shrink at all, certainly not excessively), and are resistant to moths and mildew. When the customer is unsure of fiber terminology it is necessary to rely on the manufacturer's label to supply information about performance and directions for use and care. Several inexpensive booklets and educational materials are available to the public. They are published by the various fiber trade associations, by the American Home Economics Association, and by the federal government.[4]

Yarn Construction

It is more difficult for the consumer to evaluate yarn construction than any other component in an apparel product. Because of the fabric and the garment construction and many of the finishing agents used, individual yarns are often hard to see. Although in buying yard goods a single yarn can be isolated and examined, this is not possible in finished products. Sometimes yarn construction does limit the fabric's serviceability, however, and often it dictates its care. Very loosely twisted

[4]See, for example, Josephine M. Blandford and Lois M. Gurel, *Fibers and Fabrics*, National Bureau of Standards Information Series 1, November 1970 (available from the United States Government Printing Office); *Man-Made Fibers Fact Book*, Man-Made Fiber Producers Association, Inc., 1978; *The Textile Handbook*, The American Home Economics Association, 1980.

yarns may pick up soil more readily and fuzz or pill on the surface. And although pulling or snagging is generally classified under fabric construction problems, loosely twisted yarns can also be subject to snags because individual fibers, particularly long-filament fibers, catch on rough edges. Highly twisted yarns, on the other hand, such as those used in crepe fabrics, are subject to excessive shrinkage.

Fabric Construction

Whether the fabric is woven or knitted, laminated or bonded, further determines its wearing qualities. Open-weave fabrics in which the yarns are widely spaced usually snag easily and do not hold their shape as well as those with a higher thread count. Loose weaves often fray badly in the seams and pull out around buttonholes. Knitted fabrics have greater elasticity than woven fabrics and conform to the shape of the body, but, by the same token, they have less dimensional stability and may bag, sag, or stretch as well as shrink. Pliable or loosely woven fabrics are sometimes bonded to a lining fabric. Their shape retaining qualities are then about as good as the backing material. These fabrics must be examined carefully because problems occur when the bonding agents do not hold and the outer fabric separates from the lining.

Colorfastness

The label should carry some assurance that the color will hold up under light, washing, or dry cleaning, depending on the end use of the garment. In certain types of apparel, colorfastness to perspiration and to crocking (a rubbing-off of color) should also be determined. A bathing suit needs to be colorfast to chlorine bleach.

Finish

Finishes cannot be seen and labels must be relied on. This is one area in which the manufacturer's reputation is important. Almost all fabrics today are finished in some way to improve their sales appeal or to impart certain functional features that increase wearing qualities. Most common perhaps are the wrinkle-resistant finishes that cut down on the maintenance required. There should be some guarantee that the fabric has been sufficiently relaxed in finishing that residual shrinkage is minimal (Sanforized fabrics, for example, are guaranteed to shrink less than 1 percent). Water repellency, flame retardation, and a variety of aesthetic finishes (glazing, embossing, and others) are among the many treatments given fabrics to improve their serviceability or appearance. Such finishes should be durable enough to last the wear life of the garment.

Checking Workmanship

Quality of construction is equally as important as the quality of the fabric. Good workmanship contributes to the durability of the garment and at the same time enhances its aesthetic appeal.

Cut

Pattern pieces should be cut from the fabric so that they hang grain-perfect on the figure. In most cases this means that the lengthwise threads are perpendicular, and crosswise threads parallel, to the floor. Fabric patterns, such as a stripe or plaid, should be carefully matched along the seam lines and pockets, and the pattern should be balanced at both sides.

Seams and Stitching

Width of the seam allowances is another mark of quality. Skimpy seams usually mean that corners have been cut in other areas of construction as well. Wide seam allowances will lie flat and allow for alterations if necessary. Machine stitching should be straight, with stitches small enough (about twelve to fifteen to the inch) to prevent the seam from splitting open. On fabrics that fray badly, a seam finish more durable than pinking is desirable. Narrow seams on knit constructions should be pliable, and the raw edges should be overcast.

Buttonholes and Fasteners

In women's wear, the better garments usually have tailored or fabric buttonholes. These should be even in width and carefully finished on the side of the facing. In wash dresses and blouses, men's suits and shirts, buttonholes are hand-worked or machine-made. Stitches should be close together and deep enough so they will not pull out. Buttons should be smooth so they will not abrade the edges of the buttonhole and washable if the garment is washable. The quality of snaps, hooks and eyes, zippers, or other fasteners should be examined carefully.

Interfacings and Linings

Interfacings give body and shape retention through such areas as the collar and lapels, cuffs, and centerfront closings. The material used should not be too loosely woven and it should be finished or tacked along the edges to prevent fraying or curling. Linings should be made with a firm weave and be smooth enough to slide easily over other fabrics. Skirt linings are intended to take the strain from the outer fabric and should fit as closely as the outer layer. Linings cut fuller than the skirt merely add bulk or wrinkles.

Hems and Other Detail

A generous hem also allows for alterations and usually hangs better than a narrow one. Hems should be even in width and stitched inconspicuously to the garment. Other details such as reinforcements in the corners of pockets, even top-stitching, facings that lie flat, collars that cover the neckline seam, and edges that roll to conceal the facings are all indexes of careful workmanship in a garment.

Analyzing the Fit

A properly fitted garment will have adequate ease for movement, but it will hang free of wrinkles. It will not restrict or bind the figure, and in general it will be comfortable to wear. If a person has a figure that is difficult to fit, the cost of alterations should be figured into the total cost of the garment.

Making Sound Judgments

The intelligent consumer collects as much information as possible about the article to be purchased in order to make the final choice as objectively as possible. A number of sources provide such information.

Informative labels may state the performance characteristics of the fabric (for instance, crease or stain resistance, Sanforizing, and so on) and give instructions for garment care (machine wash, dry clean, drip dry). We may know from experience what to look for in fabric construction and workmanship, but neither eye nor fingers can tell us much about the quality of the finish or how it will wash. Since manufacturers now are required by law to attach permanent-care labels to all textile apparel products (see Chapter 17), it is a relatively simple matter to estimate the maintenance demands of a given article.

Brand names alone tell the customer very little about the performance that may be expected from a garment. However, they do help to identify a product that, through past experience, has proved to be a satisfactory article. Ranch hands and cowboys, for example, may find that Levis last longer than any other heavy denims or jeans, and it becomes easier to purchase by brand name than to make a judgment about quality when one is not sure whether the unfamiliar product will be as good as one with a known brand name. Manufacturers who sell under brand names or registered trademarks usually make an effort to keep the quality of their products fairly uniform and try to maintain a given standard.

Standards have been established by various groups to describe the minimum expectations desired in a textile or garment. The American Standards Association is a voluntary organization that has attempted to define the minimum performance requirements of textile fabrics for specific end uses, along with the designation of test methods to be used in the evaluation. Adherence to such standards is entirely voluntary, but manufacturers who do comply usually label their products with the test results and provide information relative to proper care and maintenance. The consumer may purchase products bearing the L-22 label (American Standards Performance Requirements for Textile Fabrics)[5] in the knowledge that they will give the service indicated.

Standardization for pattern sizes has also come about through the joint efforts of industry and the Departments of Commerce and Agriculture. Years ago getting a good fit was a serious problem because manufacturers used their own systems of sizing. Research on body measurements has resulted in a set of commercial standards for infants', children's, and girls' wear, boys' apparel, and four different categories of women's sizes (misses', women's, half-sizes, and juniors').[6] Use of the standards is still not mandatory, but many manufacturers, and mail-order companies in particular, have adopted the sizing system enthusiastically.

Advertising is another medium through which the customer can determine the seller's integrity. A seller advertises in order to inform the public about the merchandise and to create an interest in buying it, but the information presented should be accurate. The consumer must assume some responsibility to become educated in order to recognize misleading statements and false claims. Selling gimmicks such as "savings up to one-half," "made to sell for," "valued at twice the cost," or "priced elsewhere" are not accurate guides to true value of an article. The terms *original price*, which refers to the first price at which the garment sold, or *regular price*, meaning the price before the current sale, are more helpful in determining the value of the item being offered although even these could be jacked-up, presale prices. Consumers should be wary of any emotional appeals in advertising that play on the ignorance of less well-educated audiences. Other less obvious but equally misleading claims refer to fiber content and finishes. Since moths do not eat synthetic fibers, a "moth-proofed acrylic" sweater is either falsely or unnecessarily given a useless finish. So, too, less than 5 percent of a status fiber in a blend is an attempt to lure an unsophisticated shopper into thinking that something important has been added. For example, 3 percent silk in a polyester/cotton blend suit is there simply to add the status value of silk. It serves no other useful purpose. Again, it is the consumer's responsibility to check the accuracy of the seller's advertising and refrain from patronizing stores that engage in questionable practices.

Other sources of consumer information about clothing and textiles products include the American Home Economics Association; Consumers Research, Inc.; Consumers Union of the United States; the International Fabricare Institute, Inc.; the National Better Business Bureau; and the National Retail Merchants' Association. Not to be overlooked are the educational materials distributed by reputable commercial concerns, as well as USDA publications and the many state and county extension bulletins available through the local Cooperative Extension office. It pays to remember that the consumer's judgment is no better than the information obtained and used.

---

[5]American Standard L-22, Performance Requirements for Textile Fabrics, American Standards Association, New York, 1960.

[6]*Commercial Body Measurement Standards*, Office of Engineering Standards, Institute of Applied Technology, National Bureau of Standards, Washington, D.C.

CLOTHING MAINTENANCE

Consumer dissatisfaction does not always result from defective or inferior merchandise. The life of a garment depends largely on the care it receives. The proper care of clothing can actually mean considerable savings in time and money.

General Care

A garment will retain its shape longer if it is put on a hanger immediately after wearing and hung in a well-ventilated place to air before storing. Wooden or plastic hangers usually are better designed to conform to the shape of the shoulders than wire hangers from the cleaning plant. The latter sag under heavy garments and sometimes leave crease marks along the shoulders. Closing zippers and buttoning the front opening will help to hold the garment on the hanger and improve shape retention. The day's dust and lint should be removed with a soft-bristled brush. Knitted articles should be stretched out flat to air or hung over a chair back before they are put away in a drawer.

Wear wrinkles usually can be removed from clothing by hanging in a closed bathroom while running a hot shower or tub. This procedure is preferable to pressing with an iron because overpressing may cause fabrics to glaze or shine. Ample time should be allowed for the fabric and seams to dry thoroughly before the clothing is returned to the closet.

Because perspiration causes the leather and stitching in shoes to break down, wear-life will be greatly extended if feet are bathed daily, thoroughly dried, and protected with a clean pair of hose. Resting shoes between wearings will give them a chance to air out and dry completely. Needless to say, shoes should be protected with some type of boot or overshoe in wet weather. Run-down heels also shorten shoe life because they distort the shape and cause a breakdown in other shoe parts.

Renovation Methods

Not all fabrics are washable, and not all garments made from washable fabrics can be laundered successfully because of the possible limitations of trim, construction, or lining. The Care Guide shown in Figure 20.1 was developed by the Consumer Affairs Committee of the American Apparel Manufacturers Association, and it is intended to fill in the brief care instructions found on permanent labels sewn into garments.

Clothing will last longer if the weak spots are strengthened before they break into tears or holes. Garments should be checked after each wearing for needed repairs. Dangling buttons, popped seams, and loose threads or hems should be corrected immediately.

Garments should be checked for rips or needed repairs before laundering, not after, and pockets emptied and turned inside out if possible. Heavily soiled areas should be pretreated, and spots and stains removed. Since many spots are permanently set by the use of the wrong solvent (even plain water can set some stains), a reliable guide to spot and stain removal should be kept in the laundry area. Fresh stains are usually easier to remove than those that have hardened because some deposits form chemical bonds with the fiber that become insoluble after drying.

CONSUMER CARE GUIDE FOR APPAREL

MACHINE WASHABLE

WHEN LABEL READS:	IT MEANS:
Machine wash	Wash, bleach, dry and press by any customary method including commercial laundering and dry cleaning
Home launder only	Same as above but do not use commercial laundering
No Chlorine Bleach	Do not use chlorine bleach. Oxygen bleach may be used
No bleach	Do not use any type of bleach
Cold wash / Cold rinse	Use cold water from tap or cold washing machine setting
Warm wash / Warm rinse	Use warm water or warm washing machine setting
Hot wash	Use hot water or hot washing machine setting
No spin	Remove wash load before final machine spin cycle
Delicate cycle / Gentle cycle	Use appropriate machine setting; otherwise wash by hand
Durable press cycle / Permanent press cycle	Use appropriate machine setting; otherwise use warm wash, cold rinse and short spin cycle
Wash separately	Wash alone or with like colors

NON-MACHINE WASHING

WHEN LABEL READS:	IT MEANS:
Hand wash	Launder only by hand in luke warm (hand comfortable) water. May be bleached. May be drycleaned
Hand wash only	Same as above, but do not dryclean
Hand wash separately	Hand wash alone or with like colors
No bleach	Do not use bleach
Damp wipe	Surface clean with damp cloth or sponge

HOME DRYING

WHEN LABEL READS:	IT MEANS:
Tumble dry	Dry in tumble dryer at specified setting — high, medium, low or no heat
Tumble dry / Remove promptly	Same as above, but in absence of cool-down cycle remove at once when tumbling stops
Drip dry	Hang wet and allow to dry with hand shaping only
Line dry	Hang damp and allow to dry
No wring / No twist	Hang dry, drip dry or dry flat only. Handle to prevent wrinkles and distortion
Dry flat	Lay garment on flat surface
Block to dry	Maintain original size and shape while drying

IRONING OR PRESSING

WHEN LABEL READS:	IT MEANS:
Cool iron	Set iron at lowest setting
Warm iron	Set iron at medium setting
Hot iron	Set iron at hot setting
Do not iron	Do not iron or press with heat
Steam iron	Iron or press with steam
Iron damp	Dampen garment before ironing

MISCELLANEOUS

WHEN LABEL READS:	IT MEANS:
Dryclean only	Garment should be drycleaned only, including self-service
Professionally dry clean only	Do not use self-service drycleaning
No dryclean	Use recommended care instructions. No drycleaning materials to be used.

This care Guide was produced by the Consumer Affairs Committee, American Apparel Manufacturers Association and is based on the Voluntary Guide of the Textile Industry Advisory Committee for Consumer Interests.
The American Apparel Manufacturers Association, Inc.

7/72

Figure 20.1 Consumer care guide for apparel.

If there is any doubt about the nature of a stain or how to remove it, the garment should be taken to a professional cleaner as soon as possible. A cleaner has spotting reagents and techniques the average consumer does not have. Dry cleaning itself may remove many types of soil that cannot be removed by washing. Many washable garments are also dry-cleanable, but not all. Olefin fibers (polyethylene and polypropylene) are degraded by dry-cleaning solvents, and other articles, such as washable leather gloves, lose their washability once they have been dry-cleaned. However, garments shrink less in cleaning than in washing, and colors usually hold up better. The biggest advantage of dry-cleaning, of course, is that the tailoring details are preserved intact.

The consumer may choose to use a self-service coin-machine cleaner, and many people obtain very satisfactory results. In professional cleaning, garments are sorted according to color and fabric type; they are spot cleaned, steamed to remove wrinkles, and pressed to restore shape. Most reliable cleaners also make minor repairs, such as sewing on buttons, replacing trim, or catching a loose hem. Research studies have shown that the two major causes of fabric breakdown are abrasion from the actual wear and the accumulation of dirt and soil. Frequent dry-cleaning extends the wear-life of clothing by removing damaging soil.

The director of Consumer Relations of the International Fabricare Institute suggests that you check the following points when apparel items are returned from dry-cleaning:

There is no odor of dry-cleaning solvent.
Clothes are clean and lint-free.

Entire garment is free from pocket, seam, fastener, and button impressions.
There is no fastener damage.
Spots and stains have been removed, where it was safe to do so.
Colors are bright and true.
Creases are straight and sharp. There are no wrinkles.
Pleats are straight, and hemlines even.
Bows, ornaments, and buttons, if removed in cleaning, are replaced.
Lapels and sleeves are rolled, unless creases were specified.
Collars, shoulders, and necklines are remolded to original fit.
You are notified should problem circumstances have arisen.[7]

If the customer is dissatisfied in any way, the garment should be returned and the cleaner asked to correct any details that may have been overlooked. The customer should never have a soiled article pressed without cleaning, nor should a garment continue to be worn until it becomes excessively soiled. Both practices will set stains and odors and the chances for thorough cleaning later are very slim.

Storage

Seasonal storage of clothing can be damaging unless some precautions are taken. The most important thing is to be sure garments are clean before they are put away for any period of time. Even though man-made fibers do not attract moths and carpet beetles, insects will eat through these

[7]Dorothy S. Lyle, *The Clothes We Wear*, Department of Home Economics, National Education Association, 1966, p. 21.

fibers to get at certain types of soil or food stains. Summer clothes should be washed, left unstarched (starch may attract silverfish), and stored in a box unironed. In damp climates, it is imperative to get adequate air circulation in the closet in order to prevent mildew. This can be accomplished by taking clothes out to air several times during the storage period or by running an electric fan in the closet occasionally to move out dead air.

For storage of winter clothes, any items that do not need washing or cleaning should be aired and brushed thoroughly with collars up, cuffs down, and pockets inside out. All knitwear should be stored flat, but other items may be hung in garment bags. Belts should be removed from their carriers and hung straight to keep the backing from cracking. Paradichlorobenzene crystals or naphthalene balls or flakes are effective in discouraging insects if the storage containers are well sealed. Since their vapors are heavier than air, they should be placed high in the closet or garment bag. Clothes may also be wrapped in heavy paper, sprinkled with a moth repellent, and the paper sealed tightly with masking tape.

Ideally, the storage area should be dry and fairly cool. If temperatures are likely to be high, never use plastic hangers in a closed garment bag with paradichlorobenzene. The plastic is apt to soften and fuse into the fabric. Plastic buttons, plastic containers, even coatings on wire hangers are affected by paradichlorobenzene vapors.

Furs should also be cleaned and stored. Department stores in large cities and local furriers usually have storage vaults with controlled temperature and humidity. If there is not suitable storage space at home, even for regular cloth garments, many dry cleaners will provide seasonal storage for a fee.

CONSUMER SATISFACTION

Over the years, the textiles and clothing industry—fiber producers, fabric makers, garment manufacturers, and retailers—have come to realize that quality control in merchandise is as important to the consumer as price. Many have learned through experience that when they lower their standards, disappointed customers refuse to buy the product.

There is an increasing number of government controls over industry that are designed to guarantee consumer satisfaction. Many people argue, however, that consumers themselves, and not government agencies, are the best judges of what they want. One industry spokesman reasoned:

Acceptance of our products should depend primarily on how well business, education and government do their jobs of communicating with consumers and determining what consumers want and need. That will require much more careful research and interpretation than has been evident in the current emotional binge of consumer protection.[8]

[8]H. W. Close, Chairman of Springs Mills, Inc., and past Chairman of ATMI, speaking at the 1973 Annual Meeting of the American Home Economics Association.

Most reliable firms attempt to establish this kind of communication with their customers, but at the same time many other companies offer the minimum in quality for the biggest price they can get. Even if they go out of business, thousands of consumers are stuck with inferior merchandise before sales are curtailed. Consumers can discourage deceptive business practices either by refusing to buy a garment that does not bear an informative label with the manufacturer's name and address, or returning inferior goods to the place of purchase as soon as the defect is noted.

If the consumer has a justifiable complaint, the majority of retailers and manufacturers seek to generate the goodwill of their customers through a generous refund or replacement policy. Unfortunately, the customer is not always right.

Consumer Expectations

Some consumers expect the impossible. It might be desirable to spend $39.95 for a suit that looks like a million, wears like iron, never needs pressing, and does not soil. But the fact is that our present technology simply does not offer that kind of a product. There are many instances of consumer complaints in which the performance expected from a product was clearly beyond the limits of reasonable usage. One example is the mother who expected the store to replace a pair of jeans she had purchased for her son. The pants were torn when the boy slid down a board and caught them on a protruding nail. The mother honestly thought that jeans should be able to withstand that kind of wear. Another man asked for a refund on a shirt that had worn through at the elbows. The shirt was ten years old.

In order to provide the consumers (as well as manufacturers, retailers, cleaners, and insurance and claims adjusters) with a reasonable estimate of the life expectancies and serviceability of textile products, a set of guidelines was developed under the sponsorship of the National Institute of Drycleaning;[9] the guide now is published by the International Fabricare Institute, which is the successor to the American Institute of Laundering and the National Institute of Drycleaning. Life expectancy rates for specific categories of clothing are given for men's and boys' wear, women's and girls' wear, and children's wear.

In addition, the guidelines state that a textile product shall afford reasonable service in use, and that failure to wear or clean satisfactorily constitutes a justifiable cause for complaint. If care instructions on the label are followed, a garment is expected *not* to

shrink or stretch out of size or shape
become yellow, gray or otherwise discolored or changed physically in appearance
lose or change color, or stain other materials
become stiff, limp or otherwise changed in feel or touch[10]

[9]The guidelines were developed in cooperation with: the Association of Better Business Bureaus, Association of Home Appliance Manufacturers, American Institute of Laundering, National Retail Merchants Association, American Home Economics Association, Menswear Retailers of America, a national insurance adjusting organization, a mail-order firm, a textile licensing company, a fiber producer, and NID's Textile Analysis Advisory Committee. See *International Fair Claims Guide for Consumer Textile Products* (Joliet, Ill.: International Fabricare Institute, Inc., 1973).
[10]*Fair Claims Guide*, p. 4.

The manufacturer or retailer *is not responsible* if a garment fails beyond its life expectancy, or if the damage is due to acts of carelessness or incompetence on the consumer's part.

Fraud by Consumers

Retail stores have considerable evidence that many consumers deliberately set out to deceive or take advantage of the retailer's merchandise return policy. Stores lose a considerable amount of money each year through unreasonable and/or deceptive refund demands. Zabriskie mentions a number of such cases, including the following one:

In the month of June there are a lot of graduation dances and balls. A few young women bought gowns the week before the dance and returned them for credit early the next week claiming they didn't fit. The gowns had make-up, perspiration, and lipstick stains that indicated they had been used and therefore could not be returned.[11]

There are also consumers who shoplift from one store and take the merchandise to another store for a refund. Clearly, as Zabriskie points out, "honest customers pay higher prices to compensate for the activities of the dishonest, shady, and unscrupulous."[12]

Consumers protect their own interests by making informed and intelligent decisions in the marketplace.

SUMMARY

The Informed Consumer

For consumers to make intelligent choices in managing personal and family incomes they must be informed in both the purchase and care of consumer goods. In the case of clothing, effective management includes arranging needs in some order of importance and planning clothing expenditures accordingly. Products must be compared among the wide variety available. Clothing purchases must be made carefully to fulfill needs and desires. Intelligent choices as to where and when to buy help stretch the clothing dollar. Some knowledge of the component parts that clothes are made of—the fibers, fabrics, and finishes—are useful in clothing selection. Proper care after purchase will save money by prolonging the utility and enjoyment of garments.

Consumers have a right to expect value for the money they spend on clothing but they also have a responsibility to learn how to spend this money wisely so as to obtain optimum value from the clothes they buy.

[11]Noel Zabriskie, "Fraud by Consumers," *Journal of Retailing* (Winter 1972–1973), 26.
[12]Ibid., p. 26.

FOR FURTHER READING

Cho, Emily, and Linda Grover. *Looking Terrific: Express Yourself Through the Language of Clothing*. New York: G. P. Putnam's Sons, 1978.

Consumer's Resource Handbook. Ed. Midge Shubow. Published by the White House Office of the Special Assistant for Consumer Affairs, December 1979.

Mauldin, William L., and Marianne S. Beeson, "Reading the Labels on Apparel and Household Textiles," In *The 1973 Yearbook of Agriculture: Handbook for the Home*, pp. 311–316. Washington. D.C.: U.S. Government Printing Office, 1973.

Ryan, Mary Shaw. *Clothing: A Study in Human Behavior*. New York: Holt, Rinehart and Winston, Inc., 1966, pp. 141–188.

Textile Handbook. Washington, D.C.: American Home Economics Association, 1970.

GLOSSARY

absolute advantage the advantage a country has when it can produce certain products more efficiently than another country can

acclimatization unconscious adjustment to extremes of climatic conditions, primarily temperature

accustomization learned responses to extremes of climatic conditions; individual adjustment to the environment

achieved roles those acquired through choice, training, or education

adornment theory the principle that states that the primary purpose of clothing is to make the body beautiful (see decoration theory)

affective based on feelings or emotions

air permiability ability of a material to allow air to pass through it

allergenic reaction individual hypersensitivity to certain chemicals or materials that causes rashes, digestive upsets, or nasal congestion

alternatives variations of universal dress norms that are acceptable within a society

analogous hues colors that lie next to each other on the color wheel

anniversary sale store-wide sale intended to stimulate business during slack periods

annual sale sale of regular merchandise at marked-down prices

anthropology the study of the physical and cultural characteristics of peoples

arbitrary barriers inherent characteristics that prohibit upward social mobility (sex, race, religion)

archaeology the study of the life and culture of ancient peoples

art the branch of learning that studies creative work, such as painting, sculpture, literature, drama, architecture; creative works

artifacts objects made by people; material things

art nouveau an art movement in the late nineteenth and early twentieth centuries; characterized by curvilinear shapes copied from natural objects

ascribed roles those to which an individual is assigned, with no deliberate choice as to membership

atmospheric pressure pressure exerted by the weight of the earth's atmosphere

balance one of the organizing principles of design; that which gives design support and equilibrium

balance of trade the difference between the value of goods exported to other countries and the value of foreign goods imported into a country

bifurcated garments clothing that is divided into two parts; generally used to refer to pants or trousers

body cathexis the satisfaction or dissatisfaction with the body or any of its parts

body image the mental images people have of their own bodies; may be inaccurate

brand name the name given to a product by the producer (see trade name)

burnoose a long, hooded cloak worn in many parts of Northern Africa and the Near East

caftan a floor-length garment with long sleeves, often gathered at the waist with a belt or cord; worn in many parts of North Africa and the Near East

camp an opposition to fashionable tastes; generally refers to art that is so bad it becomes fashionable in an unconventional way; perverted good taste

career apparel specific dress prescribed by a business or corporation; primarily used for identification and to create a corporate image

caste a form of social grouping based on heredity, wealth, or physical characteristics; a social position ascribed at birth

cellulosic fibers fibers built up by nature during the cellular growth of plants

chain stores a group of variety stores or specialty stores that are centrally owned. The United States Department of Agriculture defines chains as those stores that have eleven or more retail outlets.

charge account a form of credit plan offered to customers by merchants

chiton a simple draped garment worn primarily by women in ancient Greece; variety was achieved by arrangement of fabric in pleats and folds

chroma one of the dimensions of color; a term used in the Munsell color system to designate intensity

circulatory system structures of the body that circulate the blood supply, including the heart and blood vessels

classics clothes that are so universally accepted they become part of the normative patterns of dress. They remain popular for long periods and border between fashion and custom.

clearance sale sale of fashion items that have not moved, primarily to get rid of stock

clo unit of measurement. One clo is the amount of

body covering necessary to maintain human comfort under a specified set of conditions.

clothing   all items of apparel *and* adornment used to cover or decorate the body (see dress)

clothing norms   typical or accepted way of dressing in a social group

cognitive   the process of knowing, including perception, memory, judgment, recognition

cognitive dissonance   theory that states that individuals will do many things to achieve consistency in their environment

color   one of the elements of design; a form of light energy; light broken into vibrations of various lengths

command economic system   a system in which decisions on production and distribution of goods are made by a central authority

Common Market   see European Economic Community

comparative advantage   trade in products in which a country has the greatest absolute advantage or the least absolute disadvantage

complementary colors   hues that are opposite on the color wheel

complementary color scheme   one that combines any two hues that are opposite each other

composite garments   clothing that combines features of both tailored and draped garments. Some cutting and sewing is involved, but the clothes do not conform closely to the body.

concepts   words or terms that refer to abstract ideas

conduction   the process of heat transference from a warm object to a cooler one by means of atomic motions transmitted directly through solid material

conformity   behavior adapted to some preexisting norm; acceptance or adherence to the acceptable ways, customs, or dress of a particular social group

Consumer Price Index (CPI)   a measure of certain goods and services over a period of time; an indicator of the general overall cost of living; a measure of the changes in dollar value

convection   the process of heat transference from a warm object to a cooler one by means of air currents

convention   a customary or usual practice

couture   the fashion business, particularly as it applies to women's clothing

couturier   a fashion designer, particularly one who designs women's clothing

crimp   waves or bends in a fiber, which may occur naturally as in wool or be added mechanically to man-made fibers with heat

cultivation   improvements or refinements due to care,

study, and training, which may be due to deliberate instruction or unconscious imitation

culture   the traditional beliefs, values, and ideas of a group of people

custom   a social convention carried on by tradition and enforced by social disapproval

dashiki   a loose-fitting, brightly colored garment copied from African tribal costume

decoration theory   the principle that states that the primary purpose of clothing is to make the body more beautiful and attractive (see adornment theory)

defense mechanisms   denials of reality used unconsciously to relieve unpleasantness; unconscious way of dealing with disturbing elements in life

demographic   descriptive of a group of people

department stores   stores that characteristically carry clothing, household textiles, yard goods, and home furnishings

dhoti   draped, diaper-like pants worn by men in India

diffusion   the spread of culture from one group of people to other groups or societies

discount stores   stores offering mass merchandise at lower than standard retail prices with limited customer services

disposable personal income   the amount of money an individual has after paying taxes; the amount of money a consumer is free to use as desired

distaff   a rod or stick used to hold a bundle of fibers in hand spinning of fibers. Fibers are pulled from the distaff, twisted, and wound onto a spindle.

draped garments   clothing that hangs in loose folds around the body; generally tied with cords or fastened with pins, but not cut and sewn to fit

dress   articles used to cover or decorate the body (see clothing)

eclectic   an art movement in the last part of the nineteenth century; characterized by a great variety of styles, shapes, and forms

economic indicators   a series of statistical economic data that can be used to forecast the level of business activity

emphasis   one of the organizing principles of design; that which focuses attention, points to the most important part, or creates a center of interest

ethnocentrism   the emotional attitude that one's own ethnic group, nation, or culture is superior to all others

etiquette   the forms, manners, and ceremonies established by convention as acceptable or required in social relationships. The word may also mean the rules for such forms, manners, and ceremonies.

European Economic Community (EEC)   an organization of European countries bound together for mutual economic advantages to provide for free movement of goods without tariff barriers among member nations; better known as the Common Market; see p. 432 for member nations

European Free Trade Association (EFTA)   similar in purpose to the European Economic Community; see p. 432 for member nations

evaporation   the dissipation of liquid from a surface by changing to a vapor or gas

explicit values   those that an individual has a conscious awareness of; values that can be expressed verbally

expressiveness of color   individual mental perception of color and emotional feelings that color arouses

extant   still existing; an extant item (garment) is one that is still available to see

extinct   no longer in existence

fads   mini fashions; usually short lived and affecting few people; often confined to a subcultural group

fashion   the popular, accepted, and prevailing style at any given time and place

fashion follower   one who accepts the innovation of fashion leaders and by doing so makes the styles acceptable to the masses

fashion innovation   a departure from socially accepted clothing norms; the creation of new clothing norms

fashion innovator   one who creates new fashions by departing from socially accepted clothing norms

fashion leader   one who is influential in getting others to adopt a new style or replace an old one (not necessarily fashion innovators)

fashion obsolescents   those who continue to wear an item of apparel long after its popularity has waned

fashion therapy   the use of improved appearance in a therapeutic situation

Federal Trade Commission   an agency of the United States government empowered to enact rulings and enforce legislation concerning consumer goods

fiber   the smallest unit of a textile product; a tiny threadlike structure used in combination with others to form a yarn and/or fabric

Flammable Fabrics Act (1953)   Congressional law designed to protect the consumer from unsafe products; under the law manufacturers are prohibited from producing for sale items of apparel that are dangerously flammable

folkways   ways of thinking, behaving, and feeling common to a social group

form   one of the elements of design; the shape or contour of a design

functional   purposeful, necessary; in referring to clothing, that which is needed for a particular purpose and not decorative or frivolous

functional barrier   one that prohibits an individual from achieving the necessary mechanisms for upward social mobility

functionalism   an art movement in the early part of the twentieth century; characterized by basic design without ornamentation; all design was simple and purposeful

funky   that which is out of fashion but becomes accepted as anti-fashion

Fur Products Labeling Act (1951)   Congressional law designed to protect the consumer against the fraudulent use of fur of unknown origin. The act requires (1) the true name of the animal the fur came from, (2) the country of origin, (3) a statement of natural or artificial color, (4) a way of tracing the fur back to its source (manufacturer, distributor, or producer).

General Agreement on Tariffs and Trade (GATT)   an agreement under which the United States government regulates trade and tariffs on imported goods

generalized other   the social group a person refers to as an example for personal identity and ways to behave in social situations

generic names   the names of families of fibers with similar chemical composition; generic names are determined by the Federal Trade Commission

Gross National Product (GNP)   total value of output for goods and services of a country in a given period of time, generally a year

haute couture   French name for high fashion

hennin   high, cone-shaped headdress worn by women in the fifteenth century

high fashion   clothing items at the very beginning of the fashion cycle; worn only by a select few who can afford them

himation   a simple draped outer garment worn primarily by men in ancient Greece, similar in form and function to the Roman toga

history   the study of past events

hue   one of the dimensions of color; the name given to a family of colors; the term used to refer to colors, such as red, yellow, green, blue

identification   unconscious process by which a person forms an image of someone else and then thinks, feels, and acts in a way that resembles this image; a defense mechanism

immodesty theory   the principle that states that the primary purpose of clothing is to call attention to parts of the body that are concealed

imperfect competition   a midpoint between economic systems that feature pure monopoly or pure competition. Various segments of industry operate differently in meeting the market requirements.

implicit values   values that are generally unconscious and are expressed behaviorally

informative labels   those that state the performance expectation of an item and provide information about product characteristics

installment buying   a method of purchase wherein a small down payment is made at the time of purchase and the remaining amount is paid off at regular intervals

instinct   the natural or inherent tendency to act in a certain way

insulation   protective withdrawal from social contacts; a defense mechanism

intensity   one of the dimensions of color; the brightness or dullness of a color

interclass barrier   anything that hinders the interaction of social classes; a deterent to upward social mobility

interdisciplinary   combining information from several branches of learning. The study of clothing is interdisciplinary because it involves material from several fields of study.

interest   the use of variety or contrast in the elements and principles of design

intrinsic restrictions   social barriers due to one's inability to attain the necessary material possessions for upward social mobility

kitsch   art works copied in another medium; a form of anti-fashion

laws   all the rules of conduct established and enforced by local, state, or national authorities

laws of prescription   laws that order, ordain, or direct action; laws that set down or impose rules

laws of proscription   laws that forbid the practice or use of something

lay-away plan   a method of purchasing merchandise wherein the buyer makes a small deposit in cash to hold the goods until the full purchase price is paid

letting-out process   furrier's method of expanding the size of a pelt by cutting it into narrow strips and sewing the strips together

level of consumption   actual consumption of goods

level of living   the actual way that people live as opposed to their standard of living, which represents the way they would like to live

line   (a) one of the elements of design; lines outline contour, connect shapes, and divide space; lines may be straight, curved, zig-zag, vertical, horizontal, and oblique or diagonal. (b) a collection of styles offered to retailers, generally on a seasonal basis

mail order companies   stores that originally sold their merchandise from catalogs by mail. Today many also operate retail stores.

man-made fibers   fibers produced from chemical materials (not natural fibers) or from fibrous materials changed chemically

market economic system   the production and distribution of goods according to the laws of supply and demand

mentifacts   the ideas, ideals, and values of a society

Miller-Tydings Act (1937)   Congressional law designed to allow manufacturers of name-brand products to stipulate the retail price for these products; often inaccurately referred to as "Fair Trade Laws"

mode   a statistical expression meaning the most common form; in the case of clothing, the most common form of dress worn by a given group of people; the greatest frequency of a style

modesty theory   the principle that states that the primary purpose of clothing is to cover the naked body; also called the Mosaic Theory

moisture absorbency   the amount of moisture a fabric will absorb

monochromatic   in color, all values or intensities of the same hue

moral restrictions   social barriers due to one's personal belief in the inappropriateness of obtaining the necessary possessions for upward social mobility; these may be material or nonmaterial

mores   folkways that are considered conducive to the welfare of society and so, through general observation, develop the force of law. Mores often become part of the legal code.

Morrell Land Grant Act (1962)   Congressional law that established a system of state universities (called land grant colleges) by giving each state the necessary land for a college

Munsell Color System   a color system that attempts to standardize the three dimensions of color—hue, value, and intensity

National Income Gross National Product (GNP) minus capital depreciation and indirect business taxes; the *net* value of a nation's output for goods and services in a given year

natural fibers fibers that occur in natural sources, primarily plant and animal life

needle trades all the components of the garment or apparel industry

norms standards of behavior usually followed by a group

operant conditioning behavioral response that is reinforced by a stimulus

order unity, consistency, or harmony between and among the various elements and principles of design

organic restrictions social barriers due to personal physical conditions; deterrents to social mobility

overcompensation reaction to real or imagined problems by overexaggerated means; usually unconscious reaction to compensate for a defect, physical or psychological; a defense mechanism

palla a simple draped outer garment worn primarily by women in ancient Rome; similar in form and function to the Greek himation

pattern grading the process of changing the measurements of a sample or basic pattern into a set of sizes

peer a person of equal status, rank, age, education, or some other identifying characteristic

perception awareness of objects from sensory data such as sight, sound, taste, and touch

Permanent Care Labeling Ruling (1972) ruling of the Federal Trade Commission that requires that all textile apparel products and yard goods have a permanently affixed care label. Items of head, foot, and hand coverings and others approved by the FTC are exempt.

personal income the total income an individual has from all sources prior to payment of personal taxes

pliability that characteristic of a textile fiber that allows it to bend without breaking

Prang Color System a color system using three primary colors—red, yellow, and blue—and three secondary colors—orange, violet, and green

primary colors the basic colors of any color system; the Prang system uses three—red, yellow, blue; the Munsell system uses five—red, yellow, green, blue, purple

projection unconscious act of ascribing to others one's own ideas, impulses, or emotions, usually undesirable ones; a defense mechanism

proportion one of the organizing principles of design; design that deals with the relationship of the parts to the whole

protection theory the principle that states that the primary purpose of clothing is to protect the body from physical and psychological hazards

psychologist a person who studies the behavior of individuals

psychology the study of individual behavior of people and animals

quota a proportional amount allowed; a predetermined amount of goods permitted to be imported from a given country

radiation the process of heat transference from a warm object to a cooler one by means of electromagnetic waves

rationalization the process of devising possible or plausible explanations for behavior usually done without being aware that these are not the real motives; a defense mechanism

reaction formation an unconscious process of concealing real motives by displaying opposite attitudes or actions; a defense mechanism

ready-to-wear (rtw) garments made in factories to standard size measurements

recurring cycles the tendency for clothing items to reappear after a period of time in similar, but slightly altered form

reference group any group that is used by an individual to evaluate attitudes and standards of behavior

regression the process of reverting to earlier, more infantile behavior patterns; a defense mechanism

relative humidity amount of water vapor in the air expressed as a percentage of the maximum amount that can be present at that temperature

repression the process of pushing painful ideas and impulses from the conscious mind to the unconscious; a defense mechanism

revolving credit account a form of charge account with a built-in service charge and planned monthly payments

rhythm one of the organizing principles of design; that which gives design grace and movement through use of repetition of one or more of the elements of design

role position, office, or category in a social situation

Romantic an art movement in the early nineteenth century, characterized by freedom of form and spirit with emphasis on feelings, particularly of the individual artist; almost the opposite (in art) of classicism

sari   a draped garment worn by women in India; formed by the arrangement of a long length of fabric into a wide variety of pleats and folds

sarong   a skirt formed by wrapping a length of fabric around the body, worn by men and women in many South Pacific areas

second-hand clothing stores   stores that sell used clothing; may range from Goodwill thrift shops to those that sell expensive used designer clothing

self-concept   all the personal ideas one has about one's self. It includes personal feelings of worth, ability, aptitude, and value.

sericulture   the commercial cultivation of silk

Seventh Avenue   general reference to the mid-town section of Manhattan where a large part of the garment industry is located

shalivar   with kmeez, a simple pajama-like garment worn in India

Sherman Antitrust Act (1890)   Congressional law designed to protect the market from monopolistic price-fixing

shivering   simultaneous involuntary contractions of small muscle groups that increase heat production by the body

siblings   people born of the same parents; brothers and sisters

social class   a group of people with similar status or prestige in a given society or culture

socialization   the process of adjusting to cooperative group living; adapting and conforming to the needs of one's social group

social mobility   movement up or down the status levels of a society; a change in social class status, either higher or lower

social psychology   the study of individual behavior within groups; the study of the effect of groups on individual behavior

sociofacts   the institutions and divisions that organize a society

sociologist   a person who studies the behaviors and interactions of groups within society

sociology   the study of group behavior

space   one of the elements of design; the background against which forms and shapes are seen

special purchase sales   special price reductions stemming from large lot price reductions at the wholesale level

specialties   clothing norms restricted to particular subgroups

specialty stores   stores that specialize in related categories of merchandise, such as children's wear, women's apparel, home furnishings

spindle   a round, tapered rod used for twisting the fibers, pulled off the distaff, into yarns in hand spinning of fibers into yarns. The yarns are then wound onto the spindle.

standard of living   the way people believe they should live or would like to live. It includes all goods and services that individuals and families consider important and the beliefs and values concerning the use of these goods and services.

standards   minimum performance expectations established by groups or organizations

status   place, position, or rank on a social or economic hierarchy

stereotype   a firmly entrenched idea of a person or group held by many people. The stereotype may be true or false, but it is firmly believed by many regardless of evidence to the contrary.

stratification   the layering of a society into several more or less distinctive categories or classes

style   type of product with specific characteristics that distinguish it from another type of the same product

subculture   a part of society differentiated by common interests and guided by a social system more or less distinctive from the rest of the community

sublimation   the process of expressing unacceptable social impulses in constructive acceptable ways; a defense mechanism

sumptuary laws   legislation passed by governmental authorities that attempt to regulate how consumers may spend their money on consumer goods

sweating   an involuntary, nervous response that speeds up heat loss from the body by evaporation of perspiration from the body surfaces

taboo   social prohibition or restriction that results from convention or tradition

tailored garments   clothing that is cut and sewn to conform to the shape of the body

tapa cloth   nonwoven cloth made from the bark of certain trees, generally mulberry; used for clothing primarily in the island of the South Pacific; also called bark cloth

tariff   a tax placed on goods imported into a country, designed primarily to protect home industries from foreign competition

Textile Fiber Products Identification Act (1958)   Congressional law that requires that all apparel products be labeled with the generic name of all fibers present, by percentages, and in order of predominance by weight of each fiber in the fabric

texture   one of the elements of design; the surface quality of an object

theory   a possible, plausible, and reasonable explanation for observed phenomena

thermoplastic   the property of fibers that causes them to soften and melt at certain temperatures

toga   a simple draped outer garment worn primarily by men in ancient Rome; similar in form and function to the Greek himation

Trade Expansion Act (1962)   Congressional law that gives tariff-cutting powers to the President in an effort to increase foreign trade and strengthen economic and political relations with foreign countries

trade name   the name given to a product by the manufacturer; generally promotional in nature

traditional economic system   the production and exchange of goods with little variety from generation to generation

transvestite   a person who wears the clothing of the opposite sex for abnormal reasons

universal   something that has broad general use. In the case of clothing, it means styles that generally apply to every member of the society—for example, in American society most men wear pants

value   one of the dimensions of color; the lightness or darkness of a color; determined by the amount of light rays that are reflected or absorbed

variety stores   stores that offer a wide variety of relatively low unit-priced merchandise; a mass outlet for lower-priced ready-to-wear

Wheeler-Lea Act (1938)   Congressional law designed to prevent false or misleading advertising

Wool Products Labeling Act (1939)   Congressional law designed to protect the consumer against fraudulent use of wool; all products containing wool must be labeled to show the fiber content by percentages

yang   in Chinese philosophy, the assertive, aggressive masculine force; always used as a complement or contrary force to yin

yarn   a group of fibers twisted together to form a long strand; used in combination with other yarns to form fabric

yin   in Chinese philosophy, the passive female force; always used as a complement or contrary force to yang

NAME INDEX

SUBJECT INDEX

PICTURE CREDITS

Chapter 1

p. 9 French Embassy Press, Collection Louise E. Jefferson;   p. 13 Courtesy American Museum of Natural History;   p. 15 Kendall/Hunt;   p. 17 Oriental Institute, University of Chicago;   p. 19 Emil Schulthess, Black Star;   p. 20, L, Peter Menzel, Stock, Boston, R, French Embassy Press, Collection Louise E. Jefferson;   p. 21, tL, Marburg-Art Reference Bureau, tR, Metropolitan Museum of Art, bR Elizabeth Wilcox;   p. 23, tL, Courtesy of Sony; tR, Black Star, bR, The Frick Collection, New York; p. 25, t, Louise E. Jefferson, b, Owen Franken, Stock, Boston;   p. 27, left to right, far left and left C. Zagourski, from the postcard series "L'Afrique Disparait," photo courtesy J. Racquoi and the Museum of Modern Art, right and far right Louise E. Jefferson, bR, Courtesy the Gillette Company;   p. 28 Schick, Inc.;   p. 29 Lew Merrin from Monkmeyer;   p. 33, t, J. P. Rogot, Stock, Boston, b, Strickler from Monkmeyer

Chapter 2

p. 41, t, Photo Trends, b, Hakim Raquib;   p. 44, t, American Fabrics Magazine, bL, Louise E. Jefferson, bM, Irwin from Monkmeyer, bR, Frank Siteman; p. 45 National Museet, Copenhagen;   p. 46 Cotton, Inc.;   p. 49 Alison Frantz;   p. 54 Wide World

Chapter 3

p. 59 Margaret M. Wheat, from Survival Arts of the Primitive Paiutes, © 1967 by University of Nevada Press;   p. 60 The Irish Linen Guild;   p. 61 Courtesy of the American Museum of Natural History;   p. 62, t&m, Margaret M. Wheat, © 1967 by University of Nevada Press, b, Fur Information and Fashion Guild; p. 64 American Textile Manufacturers Institute; p. 65, b, Smithsonian Institution;   p. 66, t (2), Smithsonian Institution, b, Pfaff American;   p. 67 all L Courtesy Merrimack Valley Textile Museum, tR, Photo Researchers, bR, Whitin Machine Co.;   p. 69, t, Merrimack Valley Textile Museum, m, Draper Division, Rockwell International, b, American Textile

Manufacturers Institute;   p. 71 George Hight photograph, courtesy of the Museum of the American Indian, Heye Foundation;   p. 73 Ilka Hartmann, Jeroboam;   p. 77 (all) Japan Travel Bureau, Inc.;   p. 78, L, Central Office of Information, London, R, Bettmann Archive;   p. 79, t, Cleveland Museum of Art, b, The Metropolitan Museum of Art, the Cloisters Collection, Gift of John D. Rockefeller, Jr., 1937;   p. 80, L, The Metropolitan Museum of Art, Rogers Fund, 1904, R, The Metropolitan Museum of Art, the Bashford Dean Memorial Collection, Gift of Helen Fahnestock Hubbard, 1929, in memory of her father, Harris C. Fahnestock;   p. 81 Monkmeyer

Chapter 4

p. 86, L&R, Monsanto; Mauritius, Black Star; John Lanois, Black Star;   p. 87, L, Tom Hollyman, Photo Researchers, R, Diane Rawson, Photo Researchers; p. 89 Feverlicht from Monkmeyer;   p. 90, t, Moore & Co., bL, Elizabeth Hamlin, Stock, Boston, bR, Lord West Formal Wear;   p. 94 Brown Bros.;   p. 96, tL, Smithsonian Institution, tR, Courtesy Cole of California, bL, Wide World, bR, DuPont;   p. 99 UPI;   p. 100 Owen Franken, Stock, Boston

Chapter 5

p. 112 Ray Ellis, Photo Researchers;   p. 113 James Laver, *Dress*, John Murray Ltd. London.;   p. 114—all Brown Bros.;   p. 115, L, Danskin, R, DuPont; p. 116, L, Genzo Suzino, Tom Stack and Associates, R, Steve McCutcheon, Alaska Pictorial Service, b, George Gerster, Photo Researchers;   p. 117 (2) Levi Strauss;   p. 119 J. C. Allen and Son;   p. 120 Christopher Morrow, Stock, Boston;   p. 121 Fred W. McDarrah;   p. 122, L, I.L.G.W.U., R, American Textile Manufacturers Institute;   p. 123 Bettmann Archive;   p. 124 From the collection of John Murray Ltd., London; Lawrence Langner, *The Importance of Wearing Clothes*, Hastings House, N.Y., 1959; p. 126, L, Hakim Raquib, R, Fred McDarrah; p. 127, L, James Laver, *Dress*, John Murray, Ltd., R, Reproduced by permission of Punch;   p. 129 UPI; p. 130 Louise E. Jefferson;   p. 131, L, Museum of Modern Art, Film Stills Archives, R, Hakim Raquib

Chapter 6

p. 135, t, Mike Mazzachi, Stock, Boston, b, Hart, Schaffner & Marx;   p. 136 Elizabeth Wilcox;   p. 137

James Laver, *Costume Through the Ages*, Thames and Hudson, London, 1963;   p. 138 Rosemary Winckley; p. 139 Frank Siteman;   p. 140, L&R, Hakim Raquib, m, Fred McDarrah;   p. 142 Rick Smolen, Stock, Boston;   p. 148 (both) Levi Strauss; p. 155, L, The Wool Bureau, R, Cotton, Inc.

Chapter 7

p. 160 Tim Carlson, Stock, Boston;   p. 161 S. Hansen, Stock, Boston;   p. 163, L, A. Devaney, Inc., R, Josef Muench;   p. 167 Michigan State University Press;   p. 171, L, Central Office of Information, London, R, Maxwell Coplan;   p. 173 Photo Trends; p. 175, L, Brown Bros., R, Peter Menzel, Stock, Boston;   p. 176, tL, Bill Samaras, bL, Monkmeyer, tR, Frank Siteman;   p. 178 Michigan State University Press;   p. 183 Fred McDarrah

Chapter 8

p. 189, L, James Laver, *Seventeenth and Eighteenth Century Costume*, the Victoria and Albert Museum, R, Reform-Moden-Album, 1904;   p. 190 Cotton, Inc.; p. 191, tL, Optic Nerve, Jeroboam, tR, Courtesy of Kellogg's, b, A. K. Moon, Stock, Boston;   p. 192 t, Allison Lockwood, Courtesy Library of Congress, b, Frederick Bodin, Stock, Boston;   p. 193 Cyldendal, Denmark;   p. 194 Hart, Schaffner & Marx;   p. 197 Wool Bureau;   p. 199, L, Japan Air Lines, R, Frank Siteman;   p. 200, L, Wide World, R, UPI;   p. 201, t, Frank Siteman, bL, Frank Siteman, bR, From *Horseman* Magazine;   p. 202 Joe Clark;   p. 203 Billy the Kid;   p. 210 Frank Siteman

Chapter 9

p. 218 Wide World;   p. 219 Wide World;   p. 220, L, UPI, R, George Gardner, Stock, Boston;   p. 228 Photo Trends;   p. 230 Jerry Keith;   p. 233 Photo Trends;   p. 236, L, Fred McDarrah, R, Wide World;   p. 237, L, UPI, R-2 Wide World;   p. 242 Wide World;   p. 243 Kagan from Monkmeyer; p. 244 UPI

Chapter 10

p. 248 UPI;   p. 251 John Held;   p. 253 Wayne Miller, Magnum;   p. 257 D. Brody, Stock, Boston; p. 260, L, UPI, R, Wide World

Chapter 11

p. 266 Levi Strauss;   p. 272 Lord West Formal
Wear;   p. 273 Saks Fifth Avenue;   p. 274 Wool
Bureau;   p. 277 Sony;   p. 278 Mel Horst;   p. 279
Strickler from Monkmeyer;   p. 281 Rick Smolen,
Stock, Boston

Chapter 12

p. 292, tL, Victor Perard, *Anatomy and Drawing*,
Fearon Pitman Publishing Corporation, R, From "Eye
Movements and Visual Perception" by David Noton and
Lawrence Stark, copyright © 1971 by Scientific
American Inc., all rights reserved;   p. 293, tL,
National Portrait Gallery, London, tR, Collection
Blanche Payne, bL, Rosenberg Palace, Copenhagen,
bR, National Cotton Council;   p. 294, t, The Prado,
Madrid, Marburg-Art Reference Bureau, bL, Museum
of Fine Arts, Boston, bR, The Prado, Madrid; p. 295,
t, Reprinted from *Vogue*, © 1966 by the Conde
Nast, R, Publications, Inc., b, Victor Perard
Anatomy and Drawing, Fearon Pitman Publishing
Corporation;   p. 297 Courtesy the Museum of Fine
Arts, Boston; the Elizabeth Day McCormick
Collection;   p. 299 Hakim Raquib;   p. 301, b,
Munsell Color;   p. 303, t, The Louvre, Paris, b,
Museum of Fine Arts, Boston, the Elizabeth Day
McCormick Collection

Chapter 13

p. 311 Charles Moore, Black Star;   p. 312 Peter
Borsari, Camera 5;   p. 313 (both) Hakim Raquib;
p. 316, L, E. J. Beitler and B. Lockhart, *Design for
You*, John Wiley and Sons, Inc., New York, R, Maitland
Graves;   p. 324 From *Costumes and Styles* by Henny
Harald Hansen. Copyright © 1956 by E. P. Dutton and
Co., Inc., publishers and used with their permission;
p. 325 Reproduced by Courtesy of the Trustees, the
National Gallery, London

Chapter 14

p. 334, L, French Government Tourist Office, R, Cliche
des Musees Nationaux, Paris;   p. 335, L, Bettmann
Archive, R, The Victoria and Albert Museum;
p. 336, L, James Laver, *Costume Through the Ages*,
Thames & Hudson, London, R, James Laver, *Taste and
Fashion*, George G. Harrap, London;   p. 337, t,
Kunsthistorisches Museum, Vienna, b, The
Metropolitan Museum of Art, Harris Brisbane Dick
Fund;   p. 338, L, From the book *Costumes and Styles*

by Henny Harald Hansen. Copyright © 1956 by E. P.
Dutton and Co., Inc., Publishers, and used with their
permission, R, James Laver, *Dress*, John Murray Ltd.,
London;   p. 339, tL, James Laver, bL, Le Corbusier
(Charles-Edouard Jenneret), Armchair with Adjustable
Back, 1929, the Museum of Modern Art, New York,
Gift of Thonet Industries, Inc., bR, Oldenburg, *Soft
Toilet*, Geoffrey Clements from the collection of Mr. and
Mrs. Victor W. Ganz;   p. 340 Pat Hollander Gross,
Stock, Boston;   p. 347 Mike Mazzachi, Stock, Boston

Chapter 15

p. 352, L, NASA, R, UPI;   p. 353, L, Reprinted from
Motorland by courtesy of the California Automobile
Association, copyright owner, R, National Coal
Association;   p. 360 Reprinted from Motorland by
courtesy of the California Automobile Association,
copyright owner;   p. 361 Vincent Maggiora, reprinted
by permission of the San Francisco Chronicle;   p. 364
Clem Albers, reprinted by permission of the San
Francisco Chronicle

Chapter 16

p. 367, L, Naturhistorisches Museum, Vienna, R, Fogg
Art Museum, b, Staatsbibliothek Bildarchiv, Berlin;
p. 368, m, Photo Trends, R, Copyright A.C.L.,
Bruxelles;   p. 375 From the film "The Incredible
Shrinking Man" courtesy Universal Pictures;   p. 389
American Textile Manufacturers Institute

Chapter 17

p. 398, all, American Textile Manufacturers
Institute;   p. 399 American Textile Manufacturers
Institute;   p. 404, L, Brown Bros., R, International
Ladies Garment Workers Union;   p. 405 Photograph
by Streisand, Zuch and Freedman Advertising, New
York;   p. 409, L, Photo courtesy Hughes Aircraft Co.,
Industrial Products Division, R, I.L.G.W.U.;   p. 418
Pat Hollander Gross, Stock, Boston;   p. 421 (both)
J. C. Penney

Chapter 18

p. 439 Photo Trends;   p. 446 Wide World

Chapter 19

p. 469 Singer Co.

Horn/Gurel, The Second Skin, Third Edition

We would like to have your reactions to this third edition of *The Second Skin*. Your evaluation of the book will help us respond to both the interests and needs of readers of future editions. Please fill out the questionnaire, cut out this page, and mail it to us.

College Marketing
Houghton Mifflin Company
One Beacon Street
Boston, MA 02107

What was the title of the course you used the book in? What class level is it?

_____

_____

Have you used parts of the book in other courses? ___ Which chapters? ___

_____ Course title _____ Class level _____

Please give us your overall impression of the book:

	Excellent	Good	Adequate	Poor
1. Writing style/readability	___	___	___	___
2. Explanations of concepts	___	___	___	___
3. Vocabulary	___	___	___	___
4. Illustrations	___	___	___	___
5. Reading level	___	___	___	___

Which chapters or features of the book did you particularly like or dislike?

Why? _____

_____

_____

Which chapters did you find most interesting? _____

Least interesting? _____

Did you have any trouble with the vocabulary? In what way? _____

_____

Did you find the Glossary at the end of the book helpful? _____

Which chapters were required reading in the course? _____

Which chapters did you read on your own? _____

Do you plan to keep the book for future reference? _____

How can we improve the book? _____

_____

_____

_____

We will welcome any other comments you might like to make: